THE BRAHMA SŪTRA

by Radhakrishnan

RECOVERY OF FAITH
EAST AND WEST–SOME REFLECTIONS
THE BHAGAVADGĪTĀ
INDIAN PHILOSOPHY
THE HINDU VIEW OF LIFE
AN IDEALIST VIEW OF LIFE
EAST AND WEST IN RELIGION
RELIGION AND SOCIETY
THE PRINCIPAL UPANIṢADS
(George Allen & Unwin)

EASTERN RELIGIONS AND WESTERN THOUGHT
(Clarendon Press, Oxford)

THE DHAMMADADA
(Oxford University Press)

INDIA AND CHINA
IS THIS PEACE?
GREAT INDIANS
(Hind Kitabs, Bombay)

Edited by Radhakrishnan
MAHATMA GANDHI
HISTORY OF PHILOSOPHY, EASTERN AND WESTERN
Edited by Radhakrishnan and J. H. Muirhead
CONTEMPORARY INDIAN PHILOSOPHY
by A. N. Marlow
RADHAKRISHNAN: AN ANTHOLOGY
(George Allen & Unwin)

Edited by Radhakrishnan and C. A. Moore
A SOURCE BOOK IN INDIAN PHILOSOPHY
(Princeton University Press)

The Brahma Sūtra

THE PHILOSOPHY OF SPIRITUAL LIFE

TRANSLATED WITH AN
INTRODUCTION AND NOTES
BY

S. RADHAKRISHNAN

Ruskin House
GEORGE ALLEN & UNWIN LTD
MUSEUM STREET LONDON

FIRST PUBLISHED IN 1960
SECOND IMPRESSION 1971

ISBN 0 04 294043 5

PRINTED IN GREAT BRITAIN BY
LOWE AND BRYDONE (PRINTERS) LIMITED
LONDON

PREFACE

THIS book is not a product of purely scholarly interests. It has grown out of vital urges and under the pressure of a concrete historical situation. We are in the midst of one of the great crises in human history, groping for a way out of fear, anxiety and darkness, wandering in search of a new pattern in which we can begin life over again. André Malraux makes a prophecy: 'The principal problem of the end of the century will be the religious problem—in a form as unlike any that we now know as Christianity was from the religions of antiquity—but it will not be the problem of Being.' He refers to 'the discovery of what true Hindu thought is'.[1] Hindu thought whether or not we agree with its transcendental claims has survived the storms of the world for over three thousand years. It has seen empires come and go, has watched economic and political systems flourish and fade. It has seen these happen more than once. Recent events have ruffled but not diverted the march of India's history. The culture of India has changed a great deal and yet has remained the same for over three millennia. Fresh springs bubble up, fresh streams cut their own channels through the landscape, but sooner or later each rivulet, each stream merges into one of the great rivers which has been nourishing the Indian soil for centuries.

When we speak of Indian philosophy or Eastern philosophy, we mean the philosophy that has developed in a certain region of the earth. We do not mean that the truth which science or philosophy aims at is of a provincial character. The search for truth may be conditioned, even restricted by the mental attitudes and traditions of different countries, but the aim of philosophy is to reach truth which is universal.[2] One of the chief

[1] *Partisan Review* (Spring 1955), p. 170.

[2] 'By Universal History I understand that which is distinct from the combined history of all countries, which is not a rope of sand, but a continuous development, and is not a burden on the memory, but an illumination of the soul. It moves in a succession to which the nations are subsidiary. Their story will be told, not for their own sake, but in reference and subordination to a higher series, according to the time and degree in which they contribute to the common fortunes of Mankind.'

Lord Acton—A letter to the contributors to the *Cambridge Modern History*, dated March 12, 1898.

features of philosophical thought today is the growing universality of outlook. Even Western thinkers are slowly giving up their provincial outlook and are admitting that thinkers outside their cultural traditions have grappled with the central problems of philosophy and a study of their writings may be helpful to students of philosophy.

In Bunyan's story there is the house of the interpreter which is always kept open. No one understands the mission of the life of the mind in our time who does not wish to have some part in keeping open a house of the interpreter between East and West. Since our ideals and destinies are largely the same, it is essential that mutual acquaintance should grow. To the creative interpreters are confided the hopes of a better world.

The truth which claims to be universal requires to be continually re-created. It cannot be something already possessed that only needs to be re-transmitted. In every generation, it has to be renewed.[1] Otherwise it tends to become dogma which soothes us and induces complacency but does not encourage the supreme personal adventure. Tradition should be a principle not of conservatism but of growth and regeneration. We cannot keep the rays of the sun while we put out the sun itself. Petrified tradition is a disease from which societies seldom recover. By the free use of reason and experience we appropriate truth and keep tradition in a continuous process of evolution. If it is to have a hold on people's minds, it must reckon with the vast reorientation of thought that has taken place. By reintrepreting the past afresh, each generation stamps it with something of its own problems and preoccupations.

Every age emphasises that particular point of view which is most consonant with its own prejudices. Fifty years ago the main issues which dominated schools of philosophy were those connected with religion, faith and doubt, the relation of philosophy and theology. Today new intellectual interests have arisen.[2] Philosophy is no more 'a science of things transcendental' but

[1] Cf. M. Loisy: 'I am of the religion that is in the making and I am quite willing not to belong to the one that is dying.'

[2] See Professor Gilbert Ryle's Introduction to *The Revolution in Philosophy* (1956), p. 4.

has become scientific and secular in its outlook. It has become an arid professionalism made only for the philosophers. 'We know too much and are convinced of too little.' Many people have no kind of contact with any form of religion or its modes of thought. Even in countries where church attendance has increased, there has not been any growth of religious feeling. The majority of people do not see any reason why religion should play any part in their lives. Many of them are not actually atheist; fewer still have qualified by sober reflection to be called agnostic. They have grown up outside any kind of religious organisation and are simply ignorant of the terms and meaning of religion, though they profess a creed which they have adopted from habit or because of the social advantages it brings them or merely for the sake of good form and convenience. For them the creative fire has departed from religion. We cannot say that they adopt a materialist creed and believe that somehow through science and technology mankind can be perfected. Perhaps a few leaders may adopt this creed but the vast majority live from day to day with a hope that does not extend far beyond the immediate future. We live in an age of hectic hurry, of deafening noise where we have no time or inclination for anything beyond the passing hour. True life grows from inside. It is in the inner solitude that a seeker finds his solace; yet our modern life is unwilling to grant us this privilege. Not all of us, however, are defrauded of this right and if there is to be a creative movement some of us at least have to reflect on the hopes and disillusionments of the people. The unrest of the people is due to the thwarted desire for religion.[1] Man is a religious animal. He is prepared to worship anything and many systems compete for his spiritual suffrage, fragmentary faiths, unaesthetic arts, and attractive panaceas. If he cuts himself away from his spiritual dimension, it is an act of perfidy, of alienation from his own nature. We do not realise that religion, if real, implies a complete revolution, a total overcoming of our unregenerate nature, the death of the old man

[1] Dr. C. G. Jung in his *Modern Man in Search of a Soul* (1933) writes of his middle-aged patients: 'Every one of them fell ill because he had lost that which the living religions of every age have given to their followers, and none of them has been really healed who did not regain his religious outlook.'

and the birth of the new.[1] Man's nature is transformed or reformed to a pattern of excellence, because his being is pervaded by the power of truth.

Unfortunately, philosophy today is detached and specialised and is not aware of the peril to the human spirit. It does not seem to realise its responsibility for the time in which it is set. Even those who have a religious allegiance do not seem to feel a religious responsibility.

Plato once remarked that when the modes of music change, the walls of the city are shaken. A change in our philosophy of life is the first symptom of instability that will presently manifest itself in material, political and economic ways leading to the shaking of walls. Though India has impressive achievements to her credit in art and architecture, literature and morals, science and medicine, all these derive their inspiration from philosophy as love of wisdom or the life of spirit. Its aim is to produce not wise Hindus or Christians but wise men. If the spiritual orientation of the country is undermined or disturbed, the nature of the civilisation will change.

The contemporary situation is a challenge to the philosopher of religion. Distances have so shrunk in the modern world that not only people but ideas travel fast. The great religions of the world are interconnected. They face the same dangers and difficulties. That which threatens one will sooner or later endanger another. We have to develop a scheme of life which is at once rational, ethical and spiritual. It will not be wise to look upon ancestral wisdom as infallible. It may be liable to error even as contemporary fashions are. We have to find out what is vital in it. Many centuries ago Cicero said that there is nothing so foolish and so vain which has not been said by some philosopher.

In India the threefold canon of religion, *prasthāna-traya*, consists of the *Upaniṣads*, the *Bhagavadgītā* and the *Brahma Sūtra*. These texts are not only bound up with an historic past but are also a living force in the present. The problems which they raise and attempt to solve are not dissimilar to those which

[1] The answer to Nicodemus's question whether a spiritual rebirth is possible is in *John* iii. 7–8: 'Marvel not that I have said unto thee, ye must be born again. The wind bloweth where it listeth, and thou hearest the sound thereof, but canst not tell whence it cometh, and whither it goeth; so is everyone that is born of the Spirit.'

engage thinkers in other parts of the world. I have written on the *Upaniṣads* and the *Bhagavadgītā* and this study of the *Brahma Sūtra* may be a small contribution to the development of solidarity in thought to which the modern world is committed. While taking note of the traditional interpretations, I have also in mind the problems of our age. It is my endeavour to present a reasoned faith which deals justly with the old Indian tradition and the demands of modern thought. A commentator has ample scope to explain the *Brahma Sūtra* in relation to the religious milieu he represents. His purpose should be not simply to interpret the *Brahma Sūtra* but re-establish it in the minds and hearts of the people and restore the unity of religion and philosophy.

The classics should be not only guardians of the past but heralds of the future. They are dead if they are mechanically and unthinkingly accepted. They are alive if each generation consciously decides to receive them. Any system of thought should satisfy two basic requirements; it should state the truth and interpret it for each new generation. It must move back and forth between these two poles, the eternal and the temporal. Truth is expressed in a human language formed by human thinking. The consciousness of this leads to a continual clarifying and fuller understanding of the truths. The author of the *Brahma Sūtra* deals with the problems raised by his contemporaries with their views on cosmology but these dated answers are not the essentials of its teaching. We may not accept the scientific thought of those days, but the suggestions about the ultimate questions of philosophy and religion which they set forth with philosophic depth and emancipation from the transient preoccupations of the current hour are of value to us even today.

While the *Brahma Sūtra* represents intellectual effort spread over generations, it has also become the starting point of intense reflection. Commentaries and independent treatises have been produced from early times and there does not seem to be any slackening of effort even today.

In this book I have followed principally Śaṁkara's commentary which is accepted generally by others except in those places where doctrinal differences are indicated. In stating the views of the commentators I have omitted the minor details which have no direct bearing on the general interpretation. I have avoided scholastic discussions found in the commentaries since they are not of much contemporary interest.

Since the *Upaniṣads*, the *Bhagavadgītā*, and the *Brahma Sūtra* are said to have unity of purpose and meaning *aikārthya*, I have indicated what, to my mind, is this general purport. My views are based on experience, authority and reflection. The commentator himself is a product of his times. He looks at the past from his own point of view. Just as each individual strives to organise his memory, we have to organise our past. Our picture of the march of centuries determines our attitude and outlook. Though the conditions of modern life have become different and are in some ways better, we cannot say that we are superior to the ancients in spiritual depth or moral strength to grapple with difficulties. It is possible that some may think that my method of treatment is inadequate and imperfect. But whatever the shortcomings may be, it is not, I hope, lacking in great respect for the traditional interpretations.

The Bibliography is by no means exhaustive but I hope it will provide a sufficient guide to the student.

I am indebted to Professor Siddheśvar Bhaṭṭācārya of *Viśva-bhārati* for his kindness in reading the proofs and making many valuable suggestions. Mr. V. Y. Kulkarni of the Sāhitya Akademi, New Delhi, very kindly prepared the Index.

New Delhi, 1959. S. R.

CONTENTS

SCHEME OF TRANSLITERATION

Vowels	a ā i ī u ū ṛ ṝ ḷ e ai o au				
anusvāra	ṁ				
visarga	ḥ				
Consonants					
gutturals	k	kh	g	gh	ṅ
palatals	c	ch	j	jh	ñ
cerebrals	ṭ	ṭh	ḍ	ḍh	ṇ
dentals	t	th	d	dh	n
labials	p	ph	b	bh	m
semi-vowels	y	r	l	v	
sibilants	ś palatal sibilant pronounced like the soft *s* of Russian				
	ṣ cerebral sibilant as in *shun*				
	s as in *sun*				
aspirate	h				

LIST OF ABBREVIATIONS

Bhagavadgītā	B.G.
Brahma Sūtra	B.S.
Bṛhad-āraṇyaka Upaniṣad	B.U.
Chāndogya Upaniṣad	C.U.
Indian Philosophy by Radhakrishnan	I.P.
Kauṣītaki Upaniṣad	K.U.
Mahābhārata	M.B.
Māṇḍūkya Upaniṣad	Mā.U.
Muṇḍaka Upaniṣad	M.U.
The Principal Upaniṣads by Radhakrishnan	P.U.
Rāmānuja	R.
Rāmānuja's commentary on the *Brahma Sūtra*	R.B.
Rāmānuja's commentary on the *Bhagavadgītā*	R.B.G.
Śaṁkara	Ś.
Śaṁkara's commentary on the *Brahma Sūtra*	Ś.B.
Śaṁkara's commentary on the *Bhagavadgītā*	Ś.B.G.
Śvetāśvatara Upaniṣad	Ś.U.
Taittirīya Upaniṣad	T.U.
Upaniṣad	U.
Viṣṇu Purāṇa	V.P.

PART ONE

INTRODUCTION

CHAPTER I

The Brahma Sūtra

The Vedas

THE *Vedas* have remained for centuries the highest religious authority for all sections of the Hindus. There are four *Vedas*, *Ṛg*, *Yajus*, *Sāma* and *Atharvan*. Each of them has four sections —*saṁhitā*,[1] or collection of hymns addressed to the different deities; *Brāhmaṇas*, which describe sacrificial ceremonies and discuss their value; *Āraṇyakas*, forest treatises which dispense with elaborate sacrifices but prescribe meditations on symbols; and the *Upaniṣads*, which deal with the path of knowledge, *jñāna*, rather than with the path of work, *karma*. In early times they were not written down but were handed down from preceptor to pupil. They were literally heard by the pupils and are called *śruti*.[2]

Śruti and Smṛti

The authoritativeness of the *Vedas* in regard to the matters stated in them is independent and direct, just as the light of the sun is the direct means of our knowledge of form and colour; the authoritativeness of personal views, on the other hand, is of an altogether different kind since it depends on the validity of the *śruti* and is mediated by a chain of teachers and tradition.[3]

The *Vedas* are the authoritative utterances of inspired seers claiming contact with transcendental truth. They are the statements of their metaphysical experience. *Smṛti* will have to reckon with the *śruti* and should be consistent with it.

Śruti has no authority in the realm of the perceptible. It is the source of knowledge in matters transcending sense-experience.[4]

[1] *sam*: together; *hita*: put.

[2] *Pāṇini* III. 3. 94.

[3] *vedasya hi nirapekṣam svārthe prāmāṇyam raver iva rūpa-viṣaye; puruṣa-vacasāṁ tu mūlāntarāpekṣaṁ vaktṛ-smṛti-vyavahitaṁ ceti viprakarṣaḥ.* Ś.B. II. 1. 1.

[4] *śrutiś ca no atīndriya-viṣaye vijñānotpattau nimittam:*
Ś. on T.U.; cp. also Ś.B.G. XVIII. 66.
pratyakṣādi-pramāṇānupalabdhe hi viṣaye śruteḥ
prāmaṇyaṁ na pratyakṣādi-viṣaye.

Darśana

A system of thought is called a *darśana*[1] from the root *dṛś*, to see.[2] It is a vision of truth. The *Upaniṣads* which relate these visions or experiences use the language of meditation, *samādhi-bhāṣā*. It is difficult to express the truths of experience through logical propositions, for the most appropriate response to the spiritual experience is silence or poetry. Every utterance is a weak attempt to deal justly with the mystery, the meaning which has been attained. A great deal of passion and ingenuity has been spent on the task of resolving contradictions and reconciling seemingly conflicting statements. The conclusions of the past are brought into agreement with the findings of the present. The scholastic developments are also called *darśanas*.

Āstika and Nāstika

Systems of thought are distinguished into *āstika* and *nāstika*. The former or the orthodox schools are six in number, *Sāṁkhya, Yoga, Vedānta, Mīmāṁsā, Nyāya* and *Vaiśeṣika*. They all accept the authority of the *Vedas*. The *nāstika* or the unorthodox systems do not regard the *Vedas* as infallible. It is said that the *nāstikas* are the deniers of a world beyond the present. Commenting on *Pāṇini*,[3] Patañjali makes out that *āstika* is one who thinks that it exists and *nāṣtika* one who thinks that it does not exist. Jayāditya makes out that an *āstika* is one who believes in the existence of the other world, a *nāstika* is one who does not believe in its existence and a *diṣṭika* is one who believes only in what can be logically demonstrated.[4] Manu holds that he who repudiates Vedic doctrines is a *nāstika*.[5]

[1] *Vaiśeṣika Sūtra* IX. 2. 13.

[2] *Speculari*, from which the word speculation is derived, means looking at something. It is not creation or construction but vision or insight. The Buddhists refer to views as *diṭṭhi*, or Sanskrit *dṛṣṭi* derived from the same root *dṛś*. Haribhadra in his *Ṣaḍ-darśana-samuccaya* (fifth century A.D.) and Mādhava (fourteenth century) in his *Sarva-darśana-saṁgraha* use *darśana* for a system of thought.

[3] IV. 4. 60. *asti-nāsti-diṣṭam matiḥ*. This suggests that the *āstika* is one who believes in the other world, the *nāstika* is one who does not believe in the other world, while the *diṣṭika* is a fatalist.

[4] *para-lokaḥ astīti yasya matir asti sa āstikaḥ; tad-viparīto nāstikaḥ; pramāṇānupātinī yasya matiḥ sa diṣṭikaḥ. Kāśikā* on *Paṇini* IV. 4. 60. Cp. *Śāṇḍilya U.: 'āstikyam nāma vedokta-dharmādharmeṣu viśvāsaḥ.'*

[5] *Veda-nindaka* II. 11.

Mokṣa-śāstra

Every system of philosophy is a *mokṣa-śāstra* and teaches the way to release from *saṁsāra* or bondage to time. The nature of release has been variously conceived, insensibility, dissolution, isolation, life in God. Negatively all these views are agreed that release is from time; positively the accounts differ. They are all united that ignorance, *avidyā*, is the cause of bondage; knowledge, enlightenment, *vidyā*, *jñāna*, lead to release. *Avidyā* is not intellectual ignorance but spiritual blindness.

Mīmāṁsā

We are told that the Scriptures are endless, the knowledge to be derived from them is immense but the time is little and the obstacles are many. So we have to choose the essential Scriptures and study them even as the swan takes in only the milk which is mixed with water.[1]

The task of reconciling the different Vedic texts, indicating their mutual relations, is assigned to a *śāstra* called the *Mīmāṁsā* which means investigation or inquiry. In the orthodox Hindu tradition, *Mīmāṁsā* is divided into two systems, the *Pūrva-mīmāṁsā* by Jaimini which is concerned with the correct interpretation of the Vedic ritual and *Uttara-mīmāṁsā* by Bādarāyaṇa which is called *Brahma-mīmāṁsā* or *Śārīraka-mīmāṁsā* which deals chiefly with the nature of *Brahman*, the status of the world and the individual self. Since it attempts to determine the exact nature of these entities it is also called *nirṇāyaka-śāstra*.

The *Brahma Sūtra* is the exposition of the philosophy of the *Upaniṣads*. It is an attempt to systematise the various strands of the *Upaniṣads* which form the background of the orthodox systems of thought. It is also called *Uttara-mīmāṁsā* or the *mīmāṁsā* or the investigation of the later part of the *Vedas*, as distinguished from the *mīmāṁsā* of the earlier part of the *Vedas* and the *Brāhmaṇas* which deal with ritual or *karma-kāṇḍa*. All the commentators on the *Brahma Sūtra* agree that the *Brahma Sūtra* was intended to be a summary of the teaching of the

[1] *ananta-śāstram bahu veditavyam alpaś ca kālo bahavaś ca vighnāḥ*
yat sāra-bhūtam tad upāsitavyam haṁso yathā kṣīram ivāmbu-miśram.

Upaniṣads. The *Brahma Sūtra* is also called the *Vedānta Sūtra*[1] or *Śārīraka Sūtra*.[2] It takes into account the systems of thought known at that time.

Date and Author

The author of the *Brahma Sūtra* is Bādarāyaṇa.[3] It may be assumed that the *Pūrva-mīmāṁsā*, dealing as it does with ritual, arose at a very early period. Even in the *Brāhmaṇa* literature, we find mention of the word *mīmāṁsā* in connection with the discussions of contested points of ritual. As the *Uttara-mīmāṁsā* deals not with practice but with knowledge, and is concerned with the later parts of Vedic literature, it may have been formulated a little later than the *Pūrva-mīmāṁsā*. There are cross-references to Jaimini and Bādarāyaṇa in the *Pūrva-mīmāṁsā Sūtra* and the *Brahma Sūtra*.[4]

Since B.S. refers to almost all other Indian systems, its date cannot be very early. It was composed about the second century B.C.[5] There have been several attempts to represent the teaching of the *Upaniṣads* in a consistent way and Bādarāyaṇa in his *Sūtra* gives us the results of these attempts. The references to the views of earlier teachers[6] show how the author took into account other efforts at interpretation extending over many generations and summarised them. The ancient teachers quoted

[1] The *Vedānta* philosophy takes its stand on the *Upaniṣads*, the B.G. and the B.S. The *Upaniṣads* are *śruti*, a part of the *Veda*, the B.G. is *smṛti*. It is a part of the M.B. As *smṛti* it supports *śruti*, and clarifies its meaning.

[2] The body is *śarīra*, what resides in it is the *śārīraka*, the self. *Ratna-prabhā*, a commentary on Ś.B., holds that the B.S. is called *Śārīraka* as it deals with the Brahman-hood of the individual soul: *śārīrako jīvas tasya brahmatva-vicāro mīmāṁsā*. Baladeva adopts a different view. *Brahman* is embodied *śarīra* since the whole universe is the body of the Lord.

[3] He is sometimes said to be Vyāsa, literally the arranger. He is said to have arranged the *Vedas* in their present form. Cp. B.G. X. 37. 'of the sages I am Vyāsa'.

[4] According to Śabara, Bādarāyaṇa was respected by Jaimini who quotes him in support of his view of the self-evident character of knowledge. It is generally believed that Bādarāyaṇa was the teacher and Jaimini the pupil.

[5] Jacobi thinks that the B.S. was composed sometime between A.D. 200 and 450. See *Journal of the American Oriental Society* XXXI, p. 29.

[6] Ātreya III. 4. 44.
Āśmarathya I. 2. 29; I. 4. 20.
Auḍulomi I. 4. 21; III. 4. 45; IV. 4. 6.
Kārṣṇājini III. 1. 9.
Kāśakṛtsna I. 4. 22.
Jaimini I. 2. 28, 31; I. 3. 31.
Bādari I. 2. 30.
Bādarāyaṇa I. 3. 26; I. 3. 33.

by Bādarāyaṇa seem to have entertained different views on important points of doctrine. B.S. states the teaching of the *Veda* according to Bādarāyaṇa and defends the interpretation adopted.

Sūtra

The *sūtra* style which aims at clarity and conciseness is adopted in all the philosophical systems as also in works on other subjects like domestic ceremonies, grammar and metres. It tries to avoid unnecessary repetitions. A *sūtra* is so called because it suggests wide meaning.[1] It should be concise, indicative of its purport, (composed) of few letters and words, in every way meaningful. Such are what the wise ones called *sūtras* or aphorisms.[2] In the anxiety for economy of words which is carried to an excess the *sūtras* are not intelligible without a commentary. They are packed with meaning which is inexhaustible. They are like shorthand notes of the teaching of the preceptor to the pupils. The B.S. strings together the *Vedānta* texts like flowers.[3] In determining the purport of a *sūtra*, the commentators adopt the principles formulated in the well-known verse:

> that the beginning, the end, the repetition, the novelty, the objective, the glorifications and the argument—which are the canons for determining the purport.[4]

Contents of the Brahma Sūtra

The B.S. has four chapters or *adhyāyas* and each of them is divided into four *pādas* or parts. Each of these *pādas* is subdivided into *adhikaraṇas* or sections made up of *sūtras* or

[1] Madhva on I. 1. 1. *Sūtra* is a thread, a string. Cp. Latin *sutūra*, English *suture*. *bahvartha-sūcanāt*. *Bhāmatī* I. 1. 1.

[2] *laghūni sūcitārthāni svalpākṣara-padāni ca*
sarvataḥ sāra-bhūtāni sūtrāṇy āhur manīṣiṇaḥ.
Cp. also *alpākṣaram asandigdham sāravat viśvatomukham*
astobham anavadyaṁ ca sūtram sūtra-vido viduḥ.

[3] *vedānta-vākya-kusuma-grathanārthatvāt sūtrāṇām*. Ś.B. I. 1. 2.

[4] *upakramopasaṁhārāv abhyāso 'pūrvatā phalam*
artha-vādopapattī ca liṅgam tātparya-nirṇaye.
Madhva quotes it in his commentary on I. 1. 4. as from *Bṛhat-saṁhitā*. See also Śrīkaṇṭha on I. 1. 4.

aphoristic statements. The number of *sūtras* in each *adhikaraṇa* varies with the nature of the topic dealt therein. Each section according to the commentators deals with a specific point, criticises the views of others and commends its own. The commentary is a reasoned statement of objections, *pūrva-pakṣa*, and answers, *uttara-pakṣa* or *siddhānta*. According to the *Pūrva-mīmāṁsā*, every section or *adhikaraṇa* has five factors: (1) *viṣaya*, subject-matter, (2) *viśaya*, doubt or uncertainty, (3) *pūrva-pakṣa* or the prima facie view, statement of an objection, (4) *siddhānta* or established conclusion or the final truth of an argument, (5) *saṁgati* or connection between the different sections. If an *adhikaraṇa* has more than one *sūtra*, the first is the chief, *mukhya*, and the others are subordinate, *guṇa*, to it. The commentators, in spite of their different philosophical allegiances, do not vary much with regard to the arrangement of the topics or the meaning of the *sūtras* or the reference to the sources or texts intended, the *viṣaya-vākyas*.

The first chapter deals with *samanvaya*. It attempts to offer a coherent interpretation of the different texts of the *Upaniṣads*. We cannot be content with disconnected scraps of knowledge. Our science, our philosophy and our religion must become integral parts of a general pattern of thought. The method of reconciliation requires today to be extended to the living faiths of the world. The second chapter deals with *avirodha* and shows that the interpretation offered in the first chapter is not inconsistent with the writings of other sages and views of other systems. Even when the *sūtras* were formulated, they reckoned with other views and objections from rival schools. Truth would not be sought so industriously if it had no rivals to contend against. The third chapter deals with *sādhanā* and is devoted to an exposition of the means for the realisation of *Brahman*. The fourth deals with *phala* or the fruit of knowledge.

There are slight variations in the readings of the *sūtras* in B.S. Sometimes one *sūtra* is read as two or two as one. Sometimes the last word of a *sūtra* is added to the beginning of the next one. These variations lead to divergent interpretations. Commenting on IV. 3. 7–14, Ś. says, 'Some declare these *sūtras*, which I look upon as setting forth the *siddhānta*, the final view, to state merely the *pūrva-pakṣa* or the opponent's view'. Since the *sūtras* admit of varied interpretations one can honestly admit their validity and still pursue one's own independent line of reflection. The acceptance of the *sūtras* may have a tendency to cripple the discovery of new and fruitful methods of approach but as a matter of fact it has not been so.

We have adopted Ś.'s reading as the standard and noted the divergences from it. His numbering of the *sūtras* is adopted.

CHAPTER 2

The Commentaries

BĀDARĀYAṆA in the B.S. mentions different interpretations of the teaching of the *Upaniṣads*. Āśmarathya[1] adopts the *bhedābheda* relation. The soul is neither different nor non-different from *Brahman* even as the sparks are neither different nor non-different from fire. The relation between the two is not one of absolute identity but of cause and effect. The *bhedābheda* theory has received manifold expression among the commentators of the B.S. Bhartṛ-prapañca, Bhāskara, Yādava-prakāśa, R., Nimbārka, Vijñāna-bhikṣu believe in the reality of the universe as well as its divine origin, in the distinctiveness of individual souls which are treated as centres of divine manifestation, moral freedom and responsibility and faith in a personal God, in the value of knowledge and love, devotion and service as means to the fulfilment of human nature.

Auḍulomi[2] holds that the individual soul is altogether different from *Brahman* up to the time of release. The soul is merged in *Brahman* when it obtains release. This view seems to be based on C.U. VIII. 12. 3; M.U. III. 2. 8. *Bhāmatī* quotes the following from the *Pañcarātra āgama:* 'Up to the moment of reaching emancipation the individual soul and the Highest Self are different. But the released soul is no longer different from the Highest Self since there is no further cause of difference.'

[1] I. 2. 29; I. 4. 20.

[2] I. 4. 21; III. 4. 45; IV. 4. 6.

The difference or non-difference of the two depends on the difference of condition, bondage or release. Auḍulomi's doctrine is known as *satya-bheda-vāda.*

Kāśakṛtsna[1] holds that the individual soul is absolutely non-different from *Brahman.* The individual soul and the Highest Self are one. It is clear that even before Bādarāyaṇa composed the B.S. there were different views about the teaching of the *Upaniṣads.*

There have been many commentaries on the B.S. though only a few have come down to us.[2] Nārāyaṇa Paṇḍit in his *Madhva-vijaya-bhāva-prakāśikā* mentions twenty-one commentators who preceded Madhva, though only three of them are known to us, Ś., Bhāskara and R. Many other commentaries were written after Madhva's time, notable among them being those by Śrīkaṇṭha, Śrīpati, Nimbārka, Vallabha, Vijñāna-bhikṣu and Baladeva. The chief systematic interpretations of the *Vedānta* are the *Advaita, Viśiṣṭādvaita, Dvaita, Bhedābheda* and *Śuddhādvaita* associated with the names of Ś., R., Madhva, Nimbārka and Vallabha. They all follow one or the other of the ancient traditions. Ś. is said to have followed *Varāha-sahodara-vṛtti*, R. *Bodhāyana-vṛtti*, Madhva *Haya-grīva-brahma-vidyā* and Śrīpati *Agastya-vṛtti*. Many of these commentaries are not in the strict sense commentaries but are systematic expositions of varying doctrines.

Even the most original of thinkers do not claim to expound a new system of thought but write commentaries on the three great works, the *Upaniṣads*, the B.G. and the B.S. They use all their ingenuity to discover their views in these works or modify the views expressed in them or even reinterpret the obvious views which they find difficult to maintain. The aim of the commentators is to give a coherent interpretation of the B.S., taking into account the standards and criticisms of their time. They establish the relevancy of the B.S. to their age. Indian thinkers, even when they advance new views, do so in the name of an old tradition. They have a sense of humility and would endorse Hemacandra's statement

[1] I. 4. 22.

[2] Yāmunācārya mentions in his *Siddhi-traya* the names of Taṅka, Bhartṛ-prapañca, Bhartṛ-mitra, Bhartṛ-hari, Brahma-datta, Ś. and Bhāskara.

pramāṇa-siddhānta-viruddham atra
yat kiñcid uktam mati-māndya-doṣāt
mātsaryam utsāryya tad ārya-cittāḥ
prasādam ādhāya viśodhayantu.

May the noble-minded scholars, instead of cherishing ill-will, kindly correct any errors here committed through dullness of intellect in the way of wrong statements and interpretations.

The B.S. is held in such high esteem that anyone setting forth a new system of religious and philosophic thought is at pains to show that his views are consistent with the meaning of the B.S. The views of the different commentators have been accepted by some sections of the people who look upon their teachers as infallible and their teachings above doubt and dispute. When the different systems claim to represent accurately the meaning of the texts, we have to examine them before we accept or reject them.

Bodhāyana was perhaps the first commentator but his work is not now available. The following commentaries on the B.S. will have to be taken note of:—

(1)	Ś.	A.D. 788–820	*Nirviśeṣādvaita*
(2)	Bhāskara	A.D. 1000	*Bhedābheda*
(3)	Yādava Prakāśa	A.D. 1000	*Bhedābheda*
(4)	R.	A.D. 1140	*Viśiṣṭādvaita*
(5)	Madhva	A.D. 1238	*Dvaita*
(6)	Nimbārka	latter half of thirteenth century A.D.	*Dvaitādvaita*
(7)	Śrīkaṇṭha	A.D. 1270	*Śaiva-viśiṣṭādvaita*
(8)	Śrīpati	A.D. 1400	*Bhedābhedātmaka-viśiṣṭādvaita*
(9)	Vallabha	A.D. 1479–1544	*Śuddhādvaita*
(10)	Śuka	A.D. 1550	*Bheda-vāda*
(11)	Vijñāna-bhikṣu	A.D. 1600	*Ātma-brahmaikya-bheda-vāda*
(12)	Baladeva	A.D. 1725	*Acintya-bhedābheda*

On each of these commentaries there are sub-commentaries, glosses, etc.

A. ŚAṀKARA

Śaṁkara

About A.D. 780 Gauḍapāda wrote a commentary on the *Māṇḍūkya U.* called the *Māṇḍūkya-Kārikā*. His disciple Govinda was the teacher of Ś. (A.D. 788–820). Ś. is said to be the incarnation of Śiva on earth.[1] Ś. was a *naiṣṭhika-brahma-cārin* and his life was spent in exposition, discussion and organisation. Four of the *mutts* he established are well known, Dvārakā in the West, Pūri in the East, Badri in the North and Śṛṅgeri in the South. His commentary is well known for its profundity of spirit and subtlety of speculation.[2] Ś. refers to the views of another commentator on the B.S. and his followers are of the view that this other is the *Vṛtti-kāra*.

Advaita Vedānta Literature

Ś.'s *bhāṣya* on the B.S. was followed by a series of studies. Maṇḍana Miśra (A.D. 800), when he became converted to *Advaita Vedānta*, assumed the name of Sureśvara and wrote his famous work *Naiṣkarmya-siddhi*. It is an independent work on Ś.B. Ānandagiri, a disciple of Ś., wrote a commentary on Ś.B. called *Nyāya-nirṇaya* and Govindānanda wrote another commentary called *Ratna-prabhā*. Vācaspati Miśra (A.D. 841) wrote a commentary on Ś.B. called *Bhāmatī*. Amalānanda (thirteenth century) wrote his *Kalpa-taru* on it and Appaya Dīkṣita (sixteenth century) wrote the *Kalpa-taru-parimala* on the *Kalpa-taru*.

Another disciple of Ś., Padmapāda, wrote a commentary on Ś.B. known as *Pañcapādikā*. It deals only with the first four *sūtras*. Prakāśātman (A.D. 1200) wrote a commentary on *Pañca-pādikā* known as *Pañcapādikā-vivaraṇa*. Vidyāraṇya wrote *Vivaraṇa-prameya-saṁgraha* elaborating the ideas of *Pañca-pādikā-vivaraṇa*. His *Jīvan-mukti-viveka* deals with the *Advaita* doctrine of release or *mokṣa* and his *Pañca-daśī* is a popular treatise on *Advaita Vedānta*.

Sarvajñātma-muni's (A.D. 900) *Saṁkṣepa-śārīraka* states the main teachings of Ś.B. Madhusūdana Sarasvatī's *Advaita-siddhi*

[1] *śambhor mūrtiś carati bhuvane śaṁkarācārya-rūpā.*

[2] Vācaspati praises Ś.'s *bhāṣya* as lucid and profound, *prasanna-gambhīra*.

is an important work on *Advaita Vedānta*. His other works include *Vedānta-kalpa-latikā* and *Siddhānta-bindu*. There are many other learned treatises developing the logical side of *Advaita Vedānta*.

Gauḍapāda

Gauḍapāda's *Māṇḍukya Kārikā* may be said to be the first formulation of *Advaita Vedānta*. Ś. in his commentary on *Gauḍapāda Kārikā* gives Gauḍāpada the credit for developing the true meaning of the Mā.U. Gauḍapāda holds that all appearances (*dharma*) are like the vacuous sky (*gaganopama*).[1] There is no such thing as coming into being.[2] He holds the doctrine of *ajāti*.[3] Duality is a distinction imposed on the non-dual (*advaita*) reality by *māyā*. The real does not suffer any change. Whatever has a beginning and an end is unreal.[4] The one is the unborn, the unmoved, not a thing (*avastutva*) and tranquil (*śāntaḥ*). Causality is a false idea. So long as we think of it we suffer birth and rebirth. When that notion ceases there is no *saṁsāra*. All things are produced from a relative point of view (*saṁvṛti*). They are produced only apparently, not in reality. Dependent existence is not real existence. Gauḍapāda says of *Advaita Vedānta* that it is pleasing to all, has no ḍispute with anyone, and is not hostile to anyone.[5]

Reason and Experience

Ś. attempts to build a spiritual view of life on rational foundations. He holds that anyone who adopts any view without full inquiry will miss his aim of beatitude and incur grievous loss.[6]

Ś. tries to show that the *Upaniṣad* passages could be coherently interpreted only on the basis of non-dualism and that any other interpretation of the ideas of the *Upaniṣads* is open to

[1] IV. 98. 99. [2] IV. 2. 4. [3] IV. 19.

[4] Cp. 'How can that which is never in the same state *be* anything', *Cratylus* 439E.

Brahman is *kūṭastha*, immobile, unchanging. *Amara-kośa* says: *eka-rūpa-tayā tu yah kāla-vyāpī sa kūṭasthaḥ*.

[5] *asparśa-yogo vai nāma sarva-sattva-sukho hitaḥ*
avivādo aviruddhaś ca deśitas tam namāmy aham.

[6] *tatra avicārya yat kiñcit pratipadyamāno niḥśreyasāt pratihanyeta, anartham ceyāt.* Ś.B. I. 1. 1.

objections. It is obvious from Ś.'s commentaries on the B.S. and the *Upaniṣads* that he is controverting dualistic interpretations of the teaching of the *Upaniṣads*.[1] Ś. says that he is attempting the commentary to demonstrate the unity of the Self, *ātmaikatva*.

A mere intellectual understanding of reality is not enough. The end of all knowledge is spiritual realisation, *anubhavāvasānam eva vidyā-phalam*.[2] Knowledge and renunciation lead to the experience of self, *svānubhava* or *ātmānubhava*. This is the aim of religion. These experiences are recorded in the *Upaniṣads*. Reason is employed for the discovery of the real purport of the *Upaniṣads*. Truth cannot contradict reason and experience.

Brahman

Brahman, according to Ś., is the cause of the origination, subsistence and dissolution of the world which is extended in names and forms, which consists of many agents and enjoyers:[3] (1) This world must have been produced as the modification of something which is itself unproduced. *Brahman* is the source and if it is produced from something else, we will have *anavasthā* or *regressus ad infinitum*. (2) The world is so orderly that it could not have come forth from a non-intelligent source. *Brahman* is the intelligent source. (3) This *Brahman* is the immediate consciousness (*sākṣin*) which shines as the self and also through the objects of cognition which the self knows. Even when we deny it, we affirm it.

When we look at the created world, *Brahman* is viewed as *Īśvara*. *Brahman*, associated with the principle of *māyā* or creative power, is *Īśvara* who is engaged in creating and maintaining the world. *Brahman* is at once the material cause (*upādāna-kāraṇa*) as well as the efficient cause (*nimitta-kāraṇa*) of the world. There is no difference between cause and effect. Clay is the cause and jugs and jars are the effects. These transformations are appearances of name and shape, *nāma-rūpa*. The

[1] Ś. in commenting on C.U. III. 10. 4 refers to an explanation offered by an *ācārya*, *atroktaḥ parihāraḥ ācāryaiḥ* and Ānanda-giri mentions that the *ācārya* referred to is Draviḍācārya.

[2] *pratyakṣāvagamaṁ cedaṁ phalam, tat-tvam-asīty asaṁsāryātmatva-pratipattau satyām saṁsāryātmatva vyāvṛtteḥ*. Ś.B. I. 4. 14.

[3] Ś.B. I. 1. 2.

world of experience is not the ultimate reality; it is not *pāramārthika*, but only empirically true, *vyavahārika*.

In spiritual experience we feel the identity of subject and object. In the *Śata-ślokī* it is said that we first have the experience of the identity of the Self with *Brahman* and then the experience of the world as *Brahman*.[1] The Supreme *Brahman* which is one with the inmost Self is pure being, awareness and bliss. For Ś. ultimate reality is pure intelligence, *cin-mātra*, devoid of all forms. *Brahman* is devoid of qualities. Whatever qualities are conceivable can only be denied of it: *eko brahma dvitīyo nāsti*. The differences of knower, known and knowledge are imposed on it. When the reality is known, these differences which hide the true nature of reality disappear. Scriptures describe *Brahman* as reality, consciousness and infinity, *satyam, jñānam, anantam brahma*. These are not qualities which belong to *Brahman* but are one with *Brahman*. They constitute the very nature of *Brahman*.

Ś. opens his commentary with the statement of the existence of the pure Self free from any impurity as the ultimate truth. This is affirmed on the authority of the *Upaniṣads*. Our experience is based on an identification of the Self with the body, the senses, etc. This is the beginningless *māyā*. In our waking life we identify the Self with many unreal things but in dreamless sleep, when we are free from phenomenal notions, the nature of our true state as blessedness is partially realised.[2] Ś. argues that the Self is of the nature of pure consciousness and it is permanent and not momentary.

Sureśvara in *Naiṣkarmya Siddhi* says that ignorance of the nature of Self is the cause of all unhappiness.[3] The root cause of all bondage is present in *suṣupti* which leads to dream and waking states. When the knowledge of Self arises it is destroyed.

The Buddhist view that there is no permanent Self cannot account for the feeling of self-identity. The Self cannot be reduced to a series of passing ideas. On such a view it would be impossible to account for the recognition of mental states and

[1] *ādau brahmāham asmīty anubhava udite khalv idaṁ brahma paścāt.*

[2] *suṣuptākhyaṁ tamo'jñānaṁ bījaṁ svapna-prabodhayoḥ svātma-bodha pradagdhaṁ syād bījam dagdham yathābhavam.*

[3] *atas sarvānartha-hetur ātmānavabodha eva.* I. 8. Cp. also IV. 43.

their differences. We cannot say with the Naiyāyika that the self is the inferred object to which cognitions, feelings and volitions belong. The Self is directly and immediately intuited. Otherwise we cannot distinguish between experiences which are our own and those of others. We do not infer the self as the possessor of any experiences but intuit it. The self-revealing character belongs to the Self which is one with knowledge.

The Self is pure consciousness, impersonal, unlimited and infinite. In different ways the Advaitin establishes the supreme reality of a transcendental principle of pure consciousness, which, though always untouched and unattached in its own nature, is yet the underlying principle which can explain all the facts of our experience. Vidyāraṇya in his *Pañca-daśī* states that there is no moment when there is no consciousness whether in our awakened states or dreams or in our dreamless condition. Even in dreamless sleep there is consciousness for later we remember the experience of the dreamless state. The light of consciousness is ultimately real. It is self-luminous. It neither rises nor sets.[1] The Self is pure bliss.

The Status of the World

Brahman is self-luminous, *sva-prakāśa;* it is not the object of any other consciousness. All other things are *dṛśya* or objects of consciousness, while *Brahman* is the *draṣṭā*, the pure consciousness which comprehends all objects.[2] The world of not-self, *anātma-vastu*, derives its meaning from the Self of which it becomes an object. Apart from Self or consciousness the world of objects is non-existent. Only the Self exists for itself, *svārtha*. The world of objects exists for another, *parārtha*. The world does not exist of itself. It is derived from and dependent on *Brahman*

[1] *nodeti nāstamety ekā saṁvid eṣā svayaṁ-prabhā.* I. 7.

[2] Cp. *Dṛg-dṛśya-viveka* I.

rūpam dṛśyam locanam dṛk tad dṛśyam dṛk tu mānasam
dṛśyā dhī-vṛttayas sākṣī dṛg eva na tu dṛśyate.

The form is perceived and the eye is its perceiver. It (the eye) is perceived and the mind is its perceiver. The mind with its modifications is perceived and the witness is verily the perceiver. But the witness is not perceived (by any other). Whatever is cognised is not-self. The body is not the self for it is knowable, like a jar. *deho nātmā dṛśyatvāt ghaṭavat.* Whatever is not-self is an appearance like shell-silver. *brahma-bhinnam sarvam mithyā brahma-bhinnatvāt śukti-rojatavat. Vedānta-paribhāṣā* II.

and so is less real than *Brahman*. The relation of consciousness and its objects is difficult to explain. It cannot be *saṁyoga* or contact or *samavāya* or inherence. Yet consciousness is related to objects. We have to accept the facts as given and describe them and not try to establish them by logic.[1] Ś. suggests that the world is an appearance due to ignorance and so this appearance does not affect the cause in any way, even as a magician is not affected by the illusion he creates for others. That *Brahman* appears to be connected with the three conditions of the world is as illusory as the appearance of a snake in a rope.[2] This is merely to indicate the one-sided dependence of the world on *Brahman*. We cannot say that an illusion is non-existent. Something is perceived though it is interpreted wrongly. The rope which is perceived as snake is contradicted when the perception of snake disappears. But the world does not disappear. When the appearance of the world is said to be *anirvacanīya*, all that is meant is that it is unique. We cannot describe it as existent or non-existent. The world is said to be *sad-asad-vilakṣaṇa* and not non-existent.

The world is *sat* because it exists for a time; it is *asat* for it does not exist for all time. A thing is said to be true only so long as it is not contradicted. Since the world-appearance is found to be non-existing at the rise of right knowledge, it is not true. *Māyā* is neither *sat*, being, nor *asat*, non-being. It is the undefinable cause owing to which this world of distinct individual existences arises.

The world is not of the nature of an illusion, *prātibhāṣika*, which is contradicted by later experiences. The world is not contradicted on the empirical stage. It is *vyavahārika*. Our normal behaviour is based on the world. We cannot be sure that it will not be contradicted at some later stage. What really persists in all experience is being, *sat* and not its forms. This being forms the substratum of all objective forms.[3] Being is the basis, *adhiṣṭhāna*, of all experience.

Reality is one and the world of many is not real. Ś. regards

[1] *durghaṭatvam avidyāyā bhūṣaṇam. Iṣṭa-siddhi* I. 140.

[2] *yathā svayaṁ prasāritayā māyayā māyāvī triṣvapi kāleṣu na saṁspṛśyate avastutvāt . . . māyāmātraṁ hy etat yat paramātmano' 'vasthā-trayātmanāvabhāsanam rajjvā iva sarpādi-bhāveneti*. Ś.B. II. 1. 9.

[3] *ekenaiva sarvānugatena sarvatra sat-pratītiḥ.*

the world as *māyā* which is wrongly translated as illusion. The world is unreal when viewed apart from its basis in the ultimate reality or *Brahman*. When viewed in its relation to *Brahman*, we find that all this is *Brahman*: *sarvam khalv idaṁ brahma*. Ś. sometimes says that the world does not exist in reality and its manifestation disappears when the reality is known. The world appearance is *māyā*.

The question how *māyā* becomes associated with *Brahman* cannot be raised for the association does not begin in time either with reference to the cosmos or with reference to the individual persons. In fact there is no real association for the unchangeable truth is not affected. *Māyā* is not a real entity. It is only wrong knowledge, *avidyā*, that makes the appearance. It lasts so long as *avidyā* lasts. It is dissolved when the truth is known. *Māyā* cannot be said to be either existent or non-existent, *tattvānyatvābhyām anirvacanīyā*. Sometimes it is said that the world is like a dream or an illusory cognition. It exists as it is perceived. It has no other independent existence except the fact of its perception. It has *Brahman* for its basis. The concrete appearances are impositions on this unchanging reality. They are not the effects of *Brahman*, for *Brahman* is not the *upādāna* or the material cause of the world of objects.

There are different views on this matter among the followers of Ś. The author of *Padārtha-nirṇaya* thinks that *Brahman* and *māyā* are jointly the cause of the world, *Brahman* being the unchanging cause and *māyā* the changing cause. Sarvajñāt-ma-muni, in his *Saṁkṣepa-śārīraka*, thinks that *Brahman* is the material cause through the instrumentality of *māyā*. Vācaspati Miśra is of the view that the *māyā* resting in *jīva* as associated with *Brahman* produces the world. Sarvajñātma-muni and his followers think that pure *Brahman* should be regarded as the causal substance, *upādāna*, of the world. Prakāśātman and Mādhava hold that *Brahman* in association with *māyā*, i.e. *Īśvara*, is the cause of the world.

Vācaspati attempts to interpret the relation in a non-dualistic way. *Brahman* is the ultimate truth underlying the world-appearance. The element of change and diversity is due to *māyā*. *Brahman* with *avidyā* is the *upādāna* or the material cause of the world in which the world is grounded and absorbed.[1]

Vācaspati looks upon *Brahman* as the real *vivarta* cause and *māyā* as only *saha-kāri,* an accessory cause. The author of *Siddhānta-muktāvali* is of the opinion that the *māyā-śakti* is the real material cause and not *Brahman* who is beyond cause and effect.[2]

Brahman is the *vivarta* cause and *māyā* is the *pariṇāma* cause. If *māyā* is regarded as the power or *śakti* of *Brahman,* the *śakti* and its transformation cannot be regarded as unreal or false, so long as the possessor of *śakti* is regarded as real and absolute.

The pure Self appears as many individuals and as God through the veil of *māyā.* This self which is consciousness and bliss according to Vidyāraṇya is obscured to us by *māyā* which is described as the power by which is produced the manifold world-appearance. This power, *śakti,* cannot be regarded either as absolutely real or as unreal. It is associated only with a part of *Brahman* and not with the whole of it. Through this association it transforms itself into various elements and their modifications. All objects of the world are the products of *Brahman* and *māyā*. *Māyā* regulates all relations and order of the universe. In association with the intelligence of *Brahman māyā* acts as an intelligent power which is responsible for the orderliness of all qualities of things and their interrelations.[3]

Vidyaraṇya compares the world-appearance to a painting, where the white canvas stands for the pure *Brahman,* the white poster for the inner controller, *antaryāmin,* the dark colour for the dispenser of the crude elements (*sūtrātman*) and the coloration for the dispenser of the concrete elemental world; *virāṭ* and the figures that are manifested thereon are the living beings and other objects of the world. *Brahman* reflected through *māyā* assumes various forms and characters.

Ignorance, *avidyā* or *māyā,* produces the world of appearance. It cannot be said to be existent or non-existent, *sad-asad-anirvacanīyā* and it ceases when *Brahman* is known. It is true that in our ordinary experience we perceive multiplicity and

[1] *avidyā-sahita-brahmopādānaṁ jagat brahmaṇy evāsti tatraiva ca līyate. Bhāmatī* I. 1. 2.

[2] *Siddhānta-leśa,* pp. 12–13.

[3] *śaktir asti aiśvarī kācit sarva-vastu niyāmikā. Pañcadaśī* III. 38.

the Vedic injunctions imply the existence of plurality. The scriptural texts which speak of *Brahman* as the one and only reality have greater validity than those which imply the existence of plurality.

Even according to Ś., the world is not non-existent; it is not absolutely real. *Brahman* with *māyā* or *śakti* as its power is the cause of the world. The world has a relative, empirical existence.

The Individual Self

The *jīva* is the phenomenal self which feels, suffers and is affected by the experiences of the world. The individual self is a phenomenon while the truth is *Brahman*. The world is the play of *Brahman*, his *vilāsa*, his *māyā*. It is the expression of the urge in *Brahman* to become many. But the many are not always aware of the Supreme immanent in them. They believe in their own finiteness and not in the Infinite dwelling in them. Instead of recognising themselves to be one with Ultimate Reality, they identify themselves with the body, the sense-organs, etc. They become agents and enjoyers, accumulate merit and demerit, undergo a series of embodied existences. The Lord as the dispenser of our destiny allots to each soul the form of embodiment earned by its previous actions.

At the end of each of the world periods called *kalpas*, the Lord retracts the whole world; the material world is merged in the non-distinct *prakṛti* while the individual souls free for the time from actual connection with their *upādhis* or adjuncts lie in deep sleep, as it were. But as the consequences of their former deeds are not yet exhausted they re-enter embodied existence when the Lord sends forth a new world.

Perfection and the Way to it

To recognise the highest truth as *Brahman* is to attain release. Meditation, worship, ritual are intended for a lower class of aspirants and *jñāna* or wisdom is the path pursued by the higher class of aspirants who have no desire for earthly prosperity or heavenly joy. The qualifications necessary for a man intending to study the *Vedānta* are:—(1) discriminative knowledge of what is eternal and non-eternal, *nityānitya-vastu-viveka*, (2) disinclination to the enjoyment of the pleasures of this world or the next, *ihāmutra-phala-bhoga-virāga*, (3) attainment of tranquillity, self-restraint, renunciation, patience, deep concentration and faith, *śama-damādi-sādhana-sampat*,[1] and (4) desire for release, *mumukṣutva*. Origen speaks of 'that unspeakable longing with which the mind burns to learn the design of those things which we perceive to have been made by God'. As the eye naturally demands light and colour, as the body desires food and drink, so the soul cherishes a natural desire to know God's truth and free itself from falsehood. This is the passion for liberation. When a person with these qualifications studies the *Upaniṣads*, he will know the identity of self and *Brahman* and be liberated.

Ś. holds that the path of work, *karma*, and the path of wisdom, *jñāna*, are intended for different classes of seekers. The two cannot be pursued together.[2] Ceremonial piety can only lead to new forms of embodied existence. Prosperity is the result of religious duty while knowledge of *Brahman* has release for its result and does not depend on any other observance.[3] The knowledge of the ever-existent *Brahman* does not depend on human activity.[4]

There are two kinds of release, *sadyomukti* or instantaneous release and *krama-mukti* or gradual liberation. The former is the result of *jñāna* or wisdom, the latter of *upāsanā* or worship and prayer. While Ś. is an absolute non-dualist in his metaphysics, he had great faith in *bhakti* or devotion to a personal God. He prays to Viśva-nātha in Kāśī:

yātrā mayā sarva-gatā hatā te, dhyānena cetaḥ-paratā hatā te
stutyānayā vāk-paratā hatā te, kṣantavyam etat trayam eva śambho.

Forgive me, O Śiva, my three great sins. I came on a pilgrimage to Kāśi forgetting that you are omnipresent; in

[1] Ś. asks us to give up any complacency and fight against the fall in moral standards:

yato vinaṣṭir mahatī dharmasyātra prajāyate
māndyam saṁtyajya evātra dākṣyam eva samāśrayet.

[2] *jñāna-karma-samuccayābhāvaḥ.*

[3] *abhyudaya-phalam dharma-jñānam taccānuṣṭhānāpekṣam; niḥśreyasa-phalaṁ tu brahma-jñānam, na cānuṣṭhāṇāntarāpekṣā.* Ś.B. I. 1. 1.

[4] *iha tu bhūtaṁ brahma-jijñāsyaṁ nitya-vṛttatvān na puruṣa-vyāpāra-tantram. Ibid.*

thinking about you, I forget that you are beyond thought; in praying to you I forget that you are beyond words.[1]

He prays to Viṣṇu:

> *satyapi bhedāpagame nātha tavāham na māmakīnas tvam*
> *sāmudro hi taraṅgaḥ kvacana samudro na tāraṅgaḥ*

O Lord, even after realising that there is no real difference between the individual soul and *Brahman* I beg to state that I am yours and not that you are mine. The wave belongs to the ocean and not the ocean to the wave.

Ś. prays to Śāradā-devī:

kaṭākṣe dayārdrām kare jñāna-mudrām kalābhir vinidrām kalāpaiḥ subhadrām
purastrīm vinidrām purastuṅgabhadrām bhaje śāradāmbām ajasram mad-ambām.

I constantly worship my mother, the *śāradāmbā*, the goddess of learning who is soft with compassion in her looks, who has the *jñāna-mudrā* in her hand, who is bright with all the arts, who is blessed with long flowing hair, who is ever watchful, in front of whom flows the Tuṅga-bhadrā.

Ś. is said to have composed a prayer to the *Buddha:*

> *dharā-baddha padmāsanasthāmghriyaṣṭiḥ*
> *niyamyānilam nyasta nāsāgra-dṛṣṭiḥ*
> *ya āste kale yogināṁ cakravartī*
> *sa buddhaḥ prabuddho'stu mac cittavartī.*

While the Absolute is beyond words human nature brings it within the limits of its comprehension by making it into a personal God. Ś. adopts a catholic view with regard to these personal conceptions.

Prayer and worship of the Supreme as *Īśvara* do not lead to final release. The devotee gets into *brahma-loka* where he dwells as a distinct individual enjoying great power and knowledge.

[1] Cp. Francis Thomson's words:

> O world invisible, I view thee;
> O world intangible, I touch thee;
> O world unknowable, I know thee;
> Inapprehensible, I clutch thee.

When he gains knowledge of *Brahman* he obtains final release. Until the final redemption of all takes place, release can take the form of the attainment of the nature of *Īśvara* and not identity with *Brahman*. Ś. makes out that the identity with the Higher Self is not destruction of the soul; there is no more specific cognition or objective knowledge.[1]

B. BHĀSKARA

Bhāskara[2] wrote his commentary on the B.S. which is a criticism of Ś.'s *māyā-vāda*. At the very beginning of his commentary he says that he is writing his work to refute those who express their own opinions, suppressing the real purport of the B.S.[3] He holds that those who adopt the *māyā-vāda* are really Buddhist in their outlook.[4] He is of the view that both difference and non-difference, *bheda* and *abheda*, are real unlike Ś. who argues that only non-difference is real and not difference. The *bhedābheda-vāda* was popular even before Ś. who criticises it. There are references to it in the B.S.[5]

Pramāṇas

Scripture is our guide with regard to the knowledge of supersensible objects. Reason must follow scriptural evidence.[6]

Ultimate Reality

For Bhāskara, *Brahman* is the supreme reality. He is the cause of the universe, material and efficient.[7] *Brahman* has two

[1] *viśeṣa-vijñāna-vināśābhiprāyam etad vināśābhidhānaṁ nātmocchedābhiprāyam.* See P.U., p. 200.

[2] Udayana in his *Nyāya-kusumāñjali* refers to Bhāskara's commentary on the B.S. Bhāskara does not seem to know of R.'s work on the subject. He may be assigned to the ninth century A.D. Some hold that he lived from A.D. 996–1061.

[3] *sūtrābhiprāya-saṁvṛtyā svābhiprāya-prakāśanāt*
vyākhyātaṁ yair idaṁ śāstraṁ vyākhyeyam tan-nivṛttaye.

[4] *vigītam vicchinna-mūlam māhāyānika-bauddha-gāthitam māyā-vādam vyāvarṇayanto lokān vyāmohayanti.* I. 4. 25. [5] I. 4. 20–1. [6] I. 1. 4.

[7] This is the view of the *Pañcarātras* who look upon Vāsudeva as both the material and the efficient cause of the world and so he does not find anything to criticise in their doctrine.

Vāsudeva eva upādāna-kāraṇaṁ jagato nimitta-kāraṇaṁ ceti te manyante... tad etat sarvaṁ śruti-prasiddham eva tasmān nātra nirākaraṇīyam paśyāmaḥ. II. 2. 41.

forms, the causal, *kāraṇa-rūpa*, and the effect, *kārya-rūpa*.[1] It is one as cause and multiple as effect even as gold is one as gold and many as bracelets.[2] The causal form is the original, natural form while the effect form is due to limiting adjuncts, *upādhis*, and so is adventitious, *āgantuka*. But the latter is also real. Ś. argues that when clay is known all objects made of clay are known because they are all modifications, *vikāra*, mere expressions of speech, *vācārambhaṇam*, mere names, *nāmadheyam*, without any real basis.[3] Bhāskara does not agree with this interpretation. Cause and effect cannot be identical. The effect world is the basis of our experience and conduct. The effects are the modifications of the cause itself. Only they come and go, they are transitory whereas the cause is permanent as the ground of all the modifications. The effect is a statement of the cause and so is both identical with the cause and different from it.[4] The difference between what is *svābhāvika* or natural and what is *aupādhika* or adventitious is not a difference between what is real and what is unreal. It is a difference between what is real for ever, *nitya*, and what is real for a time, *anitya*. While Ś. identifies the real with the permanent, Bhāskara holds that a real object need not be permanent.

If it is said that the knowledge of duality is false because the person who hears the dualist texts of the Scriptures is under the influence of *avidyā*, his knowledge of non-duality is also false, since in reading the non-dualist texts of the Scriptures he is under the influence of *avidyā*. The account of *avidyā* as indescribable cannot be accepted for it is the very basis of our world of practical behaviour.[5]

The fact of difference is, for Bhāskara, a matter of direct experience[6] and cannot be dismissed as unreal. That difference and non-difference coexist is a fact of experience. A cow is different from a horse but it is not different from it in so far as it

[1] *tat kāraṇātmanā kāryātmanā dvi-rūpeṇa avasthitam.* I. 1. 4.

[2] *ato bhinnābhinna-svarūpam brahmeti sthitam.* I. 1. 4.

[3] C.U. VI. 1. 1. *Bhāmatī* says that clay alone is real and the objects made of clay do not exist at all. *vācā kevalam ārabhyate vikāra-jātam na tu tattvato'sti yato nāmadheya-mātram etat . . . vastu-śūnyo vikalpa iti.* II. 2. 14.

[4] II. 1. 14.

[5] *yasyāḥ kāryam idam kṛtsnaṁ vyavahārāya kalpate*
nirvaktuṁ sa na śakyeti vacanaṁ vacanārthakam.

[6] *bheda-jñānam api jñānam eva.* II. 1. 14.

is an existent animal. Unity and multiplicity are both real and coexist. If *avidyā* is beginningless and endless there can be no liberation. To say that it is both existent and non-existent involves us in contradiction. A non-existent entity cannot bring bondage. If it is existent, *Brahman* has a second to it.

Sundara-bhaṭṭa, one of the followers of Nimbārka, refers to Bhāskara as the upholder of the *aupādhika-bhedābheda-vāda* while Nimbārka supports *svābhāvika-bhedābheda-vāda*. When *Brahman* manifests himself in the effects, he does not himself become the universe. He remains unchanged in his nature even as a spider remains unchanged though weaving its web out of itself. Creation means the manifestation of *Brahman's* powers by which he produces the world of the enjoyed (*bhogya*) and the enjoyers (*bhoktṛ*). It is the powers of *Brahman* that are modified but he remains unchanged in his own purity, even as the sun sends out his rays and collects them back, without forfeiting his nature.[1]

According to Bhāskara, *Brahman* has a twofold power known as *jīva-pariṇāma*, transformation as the individual soul, and *acetana-pariṇāma* or transformation as matter. The first is the *bhoktṛ-śakti*, the power as the enjoyer, and the second *bhogya-śakti* or the power as the enjoyed. The Absolute puts on a multiplicity of names and forms in *sṛṣṭi* or creation as subjects and objects of experience and withdraws it in the state of *pralaya* or dissolution. *Brahmā* springs from *Brahman's* creative power and is the totality of selves. He is the first-born who manifests himself as a variety of conscious and non-conscious beings according to the moral needs of the individual souls. The universe is grounded in the nature of the Absolute. *Brahman's* immanence in the created effects is not his actual transformation into the effects. It is only his abiding within the universe and in the hearts of men as their inner controller. He is not affected by the defects of the world. The world is the expression of *Brahman*. While *Brahman* is manifested in the world there is also the formless *Brahman* which is transcendent to the world, *niṣ-prapañca*.

In the causal state, *Brahman* and the universe are one; in the effect state, *Brahman* and the universe are different. In the

[1] See II. 1. 27; I. 4. 25.

state of *saṁsāra*, on account of the limiting adjuncts of the body, the sense-organs, etc., the soul is different from *Brahman*. Like the infinite space that is enclosed in jars, the unconditioned *Brahman* on account of the adjuncts exists as the individual soul. In the condition of release when the adjuncts fall away, the soul becomes identical with *Brahman*. In the causal state, *Brahman* is free from all distinctions. He has no internal differences for his powers remain merged in him even as salt in the sea. His qualities like knowledge and the rest are non-different from him even as heat, which is the quality of fire, is non-different from fire.[1]

Brahman is pure being, *sal-lakṣaṇa*, and pure knowledge, *bodha-lakṣaṇa*; yet he is a knower possessing knowledge as his quality. He is omniscient, *sarvajña*, and omnipotent, *sarva-śaktimān*. He has also other qualities, such as freedom from fear, freedom from sin. Though *Brahman* is characterised as *sat*, being, *cit*, consciousness, and *ānanda*, bliss, these do not refer to different entities. They are qualities of *Brahman* which is the substance possessing the qualities. No substance can remain without its qualities and no qualities can remain without their substance.[2] A substance does not become different by reason of its qualities.[3]

The universe has *Brahman* for its essence but *Brahman* has not the universe for his essence. The universe has no existence apart from *Brahman* but *Brahman* is not exhausted by the universe. He has many other aspects beyond the universe. Bhāskara rejects the theory of the four *vyūhas*.

The Individual Soul

The individual soul is knowledge by nature, a knower, an enjoyer and an active agent. It is atomic in size. We have an infinite number of souls. The qualities of the soul are not natural and are due to limiting adjuncts, *upādhis*. They last only so long as the limiting adjuncts last. The qualities of the soul are not natural for then the soul would always continue in *saṁsāra* on account of action and enjoyment. The soul is an agent when it

[1] III. 2. 23.
[2] *na hi guṇa-rahitaṁ dravyam asti, na dravya-rahito guṇaḥ*. III. 2. 23.
[3] *na dharma-dharmi-bhedena svarūpa-bheda iti*. III. 2. 23.

has body, sense-organs, etc.; when these disappear the soul is no longer an agent. The atomicity of the soul is also *aupādhika* or adventitious for *Brahman* is all-pervading by nature and the soul is non-different from *Brahman*.[1] The soul's knowledge and its quality as knower are not *aupādhika* for *Brahman* himself is knowledge and knower. The individual soul is different and non-different from *Brahman* during the state of *saṁsāra;* it is non-different from *Brahman* in the state of release. The non-difference of the soul from *Brahman* is natural, *svābhāvika*, real and lasting; the difference from *Brahman* is *aupādhika*, real but not lasting. Bhāskara criticises Auḍulomi's view that the soul is absolutely different, *atyanta-bhinna*, from *Brahman* during the state of bondage.[2] The *upādhi* or the limiting adjunct cannot make the individual soul absolutely different from *Brahman* even as the spark is not absolutely different from the fire or the ether in the jar is not absolutely different from the universal ether, or as the waves are not absolutely different from the ocean. The soul is only different and non-different, *bhinn-ābhinna*. During the state of mundane existence the individual soul as a part and an effect of *Brahman* is non-different from *Brahman;* at the same time it is different from *Brahman* because of the *upādhi* or the limiting adjunct which separates it from *Brahman*. *Upādhis* are not false or illusory.[3] The *upādhis* are beginningless; they are *buddhi*, the internal organ, and their qualities, attachment based on self-sense. So long as the individual soul is under the influence of *avidyā* and regards itself as absolutely different from *Brahman*, it acts in a selfish spirit, identifying itself with the *upādhis*, body, senses, internal organ, *buddhi*.[4] So long as this relation to *upādhis* exists, the agency of the soul is real.

Brahman is not something to be produced, *utpādya*, but something to be obtained, *āpya*. When the *upādhis* are removed, the soul becomes one with *Brahman*, omniscient, omnipotent and all-pervading. Liberation is not a state of pure consciousness

[1] *jīva-parayoś ca svābhāvikaḥ abhedaḥ aupādhikas tu bhedaḥ; sa tan-nivṛttau nivartate*. IV. 4. 4.

[2] I. 4. 20.

[3] *ṇa caupādhikaṁ kartṛtvam apāramārthikam*. II. 3. 40.

[4] *yāvad ayam ātmā kevalena dvaita-darśanena saṁsarati tāvat-kālabhāvī buddhyādy-upādhi-yogaḥ*. II. 3. 20. Cp. also: *dehādiṣu viparīta-pratipattiḥ brahma-svarūpāpratipattiś ca avidyā*. IV. 1. 1.

but of bliss also, for a state of pure consciousness is not much different from a state of pure unconsciousness.[1] Liberation is not the result of the removal of *avidyā;* it is the attainment of something new. The individual soul becomes absolutely identical with *Brahman.* It is omniscient, omnipotent and one with all souls as God himself.[2]

Nature of Release

Bhāskara does not admit the conception of *jīvan-mukti.* Salvation can be attained only after the destruction of the earthly body. Bhāskara adopts the distinction between *sadyo-mukti* or immediate release and *krama-mukti* or gradual release. If we meditate on the Supreme *Brahman* we become one with it and become free at once. This is immediate release. If we meditate on the *Kārya Brahman* or *Hiraṇya-garbha,* we get to his world and having attained supreme knowledge in that world, we attain to Supreme *Brahman,* along with *Hiraṇya-garbha,* on the dissolution of this world. This is gradual release. When we are in the world of *Hiraṇya-garbha,* we remain distinct from *Brahman* and do not have the power of creating, maintaining and destroying the world. The liberated soul may or may not assume a body as it chooses.[3]

By mere knowledge of texts we cannot attain liberation.[4] When knowledge is combined with work, realisation arises. To attain liberation we must act in the world with knowledge. Mere actions are useless but they become fruitful when they are combined with knowledge.[5] The B.S. is to be studied after the performance of the duties enjoined in the *Pūrva-mīmāṁsā-sūtra.* In this view Bhāskara follows *Upavarṣācārya* whom he calls the founder of the school, *śāstra-saṁpradāya-pravartaka.*[6] Bhāskara adopts *jñāna-karma-samuccaya-vāda,* the co-ordination of knowledge and action.[7] The proper performance of daily

[1] *mukto pāṣāṇa-kalpo 'vatiṣṭhate.* IV. 4. 7.

[2] *muktaḥ kāraṇātmānaṁ prāptaḥ tadvad eva sarvajñaḥ sarva-śaktiḥ.* IV. 4. 7.

[3] IV. 4. 12.

[4] *vākyārtha-jñāna-mātrān na sāṁsārika-nivṛtti-bhāvo' vagamyate.*

[5] *atra hi jñāna-karma-samuccayāt mokṣa-prāptiḥ.*

[6] I. 1. 1; II. 2. 27. Cp. also *ātma-jñānādhikṛtasya karmabhir vinā apavargānupapatter jñānen-'karma samuccīyate.* I. 1. 4.

[7] See C.U. II. 23. 1; B.U. IV. 4. 22; *Īśa U.* 11.
Abhinava-gupta and Ānanda-vardhana adopt this view.

and occasional duties removes the traces of past *karmas*, while knowledge of identity with *Brahman* removes all traces of *avidyā*, passion, attachment, etc. When we desire union with the Highest *Brahman* we reach release; when we desire the objects of this world we are subject to bondage.[1] Knowledge leads to meditation. We have different forms of meditation on *Nir-guṇa Brahman*, the formless *Brahman*, on *Sa-guṇa Brahman* or the manifested *Brahman* and on *pratīkas* or symbols. All these have limited results while meditation on the Highest *Brahman* leads to release.

C. YĀDAVA PRAKĀŚA

Yādava Prakāśa who succeeded Bhāskara made his theory more realistic. Sudarśanabhaṭṭa in his *Śrutaprakāśikā* says that Yādava Prakāśa adopts the views attributed to Āśmarathya in B.S. I. 4. 20 which is said to be one of *bhedābheda*. He accepts *brahma-pariṇāma-vāda* or the theory of the transformation of *Brahman* into the world. The Absolute by its own potential energy *śakti* becomes God and the world of conscious and non-conscious objects, *cit* and *acit*. Yādava Prakāśa postulates both difference and non-difference as the essential relation between *Brahman* and the world. He does not recognise any fundamental distinction between *cit* and *acit*; *acit* is only *cit* in an unmanifested state.[2] While Bhāskara believes that the individual soul is one with *Brahman* and the world of matter, *acit*, is both different and non-different from *Brahman*. Yādava Prakāśa assigns the same status to both individual souls and matter. For him *Brahman* the Absolute is of the nature of pure universal being, *sarvātmakam sad-rūpaṁ brahma*, endowed with three distinct powers as consciousness, matter and God. *Brahman* exists as God or *Īśvara*, and individual souls or *cit* and the world or matter, *acit*. The Absolute is God and the finite centres and not God alone. The Absolute is trinitarian. The finite world is not unreal but an integral expression of the Absolute. Through these powers *Brahman* passes through

[1] *rāgo hi paramātma-viṣayo yaḥ sa mukti-hetuḥ viṣaya-viṣayo yaḥ sa bandha-hetuḥ.*

[2] *yādava-prakāśamate sarvam api cetanam eva; tatra ghaṭādeś caitanyā-nabhivyaktimātram eveti na cid-acid-vibhāgaḥ.* Sudarśanācārya's *Tātparya-dīpikā.*

various phenomenal changes even as one ocean appears in diverse forms as foam and waves.

According to Yādava Prakāśa, the individual is an *aṁśa* or fragment of the Absolute. It is both one with and different from the Absolute. In the state of release the finite self retains its individuality though it is deprived of its finiteness. The Absolute is identical with itself and is not affected by the contingency of the pluralistic world. R. points out that if *Brahman* in its own essence is transformed into the world, such a *Brahman* becomes subject to all the impurities and defects of the world. If it is argued that in one part it is transcendent and has innumerable good qualities and in another suffers impurities, such a being which is impure in one part cannot be called *Īśvara.*

Liberation for Yādava Prakāśa is the realisation of the consciousness of *bhedābheda* or difference-non-difference. It is not the extinction of the finite, but its highest fulfilment. While Bhāskara maintains that the individual soul can attain unity with *Brahman,* Yādava Prakāśa holds that difference and non-difference express two fundamental aspects of the Absolute.

D. RĀMĀNUJA

Viśiṣṭādvaita

R. is the chief exponent of the doctrine of *Viśiṣṭādvaita.* The *viśeṣaṇas* or adjectives are different from the substance which is not a mere assemblage of attributes. The substance is something over and above the attributes and both the substance and the attributes are real, being parts of a whole. The relation between the Supreme Being and the particular beings is that of *viśeṣya-viśeṣaṇa.* Qualified non-dualism is not a correct rendering of *viśiṣṭādvaita.* It is *viśiṣṭasyādvaitam,* the non-dualism of the differenced. It is the unity of the conscious and the non-conscious with and in God whose body they constitute. Perhaps the first commentators on the B.S. were advocates of *Viśiṣṭādvaita* or non-dualism with a distinction. The B.G., for example, mentions the B.S. as supporting its own view.[1] Bādarāyaṇa seems to be a theist more than an absolutist.

[1] *brahma-sūtra-padaiś caiva hetumadbhir viniścitaiḥ.*

Rāmānuja

Rāmānuja (A.D. 1017–1127) became an ascetic after he had lived a married life for some years. The heads of religious centres founded by him are not, however, ascetics. R.'s interpretation of the B.S. is influenced by the *Bhāgavata* doctrines and the *bhakti* cult of the *Ālvārs*. The *Pañcarātra* and the *Pāśupata* systems are mentioned in the M.B.[1] They are referred to in the B.S.[2] They are theistic systems which affirm one Supreme Personal God *Viṣṇu, Śiva* or *Śakti*. While the *Brahman* of the *Upaniṣads* is universal and non-sectarian,[3] the *āgamas* appeal to special classes of worshippers. R. does not draw much on the *Pañcarātra Āgamas* but urges that Bādarāyaṇa does not condemn them.[4] It is clear that the *Bhāgavatas* reached a considerable degree of importance at the time the B.S. was composed.

We find in R.'s system a synthesis of the early *prabandha* literature of the *Ālvārs* and the theistic current of the *Upaniṣads*. R. was greatly influenced by Yāmunācārya though he sometimes differed from his views.

Literature

R.'s chief works are *Gadya-traya*, *Śrī-bhāṣya*, a commentary on the B.S. based on *Bodhāyana-vṛtti*,[5] *Vedārtha-saṁgraha*, *Vedānta-sāra*, *Vedānta-dīpa*, a brief commentary on the B.G., and *Bhagavad-ārādhana-krama*. It is obvious that R.'s doctrine develops an old and established tradition. He mentions several ancient teachers, Taṅka, Dramiḍa, Guha-deva, Kapardin, Bhāruci and quotations from them are to be found in *Śrī-bhāṣya* and *Vedārtha-saṁgraha*. Some of these may have preceded Ś. R.B. was commented on among others by Sudarśana Sūri in his *Śruta-prakāśikā*, by Venkaṭa-nātha (or Vedānta Deśika,

[1] *Śānti-parva:* chapter 350, 63–7.

[2] II. 2.

[3] Some *Upaniṣads* like *Śvetāśvatara*, *Atharva-śikhā*, *Kaivalya*, *Subāla* and others are sectarian.

[4] See R.B. II. 2. 40–3.

[5] *bhagavad-bodhāyana-kṛtām vistīrṇām brahma-sūtra-vṛttim pūrvācāryāḥ saṁcikṣipuḥ. tan-matānusāreṇa sūtrākṣarāṇi vyākhyāyante.* The Vṛtti-kāra of R. is sometimes identified with Upavarṣa whom Ś. mentions in S.B. I. 3. 28; III. 3. 53. Vedānta Deśika in his *Tattva-ṭīkā* says that Upavarṣa is the name of Bodhāyana. *Vṛtti-kārasya bodhayanasyaiva hi upavarṣa iti syān nāma.* See *Proceedings of the Third Oriental Conference*, Madras 1924.

thirteenth century), in his *Tattva-ṭīka*, who also wrote *Tattva-muktā-kalāpa*, *Nyāya-pariśuddhi*, *Para-mata-bhaṅga*, *Śata-dūṣaṇī*, *Saṁkalpa-sūryodaya* and many other works. Two schools of Vaiṣṇavism developed, the *Vaḍa-kalai* under Venkaṭa-nātha and the *Teṅ galai* under Pillai Lokācārya. The latter wrote many works of which the chief are *Tattva-traya*, *Tattva-śekhara* and *Śrī-vacana-bhūṣaṇa*.

R. also quotes Bhāskara and Yādava Prakāśa (II. 1. 15). According to the tradition the latter was R.'s teacher. In his *Vedārtha-saṁgraha* R. mentions not only Bodhāyana but also Taṅka, Dramiḍa, Guha-deva, Kapardin and Bhāruci. Yamunācārya says in his *Siddhi-traya* that Dramiḍācārya commented on the B.S. R. refers to *Dramiḍa-bhāṣya*. He mentions also *Vākya-kāra* (I. 1. 1; I. 3. 14). In one place he also refers to *Bhāṣya-kāra*. It is difficult to establish their identity.

Pañcarātra Āgamas

The *Pañcarātra* doctrines can be traced to the *Puruṣa-sūkta* of the *Ṛg Veda*, where, according to the *Śatapatha Brāhmaṇa*[1] Nārāyaṇa, the great being, performed the *pañca-rātra* sacrifice and attained his purpose. *Nārāyaṇa* is the highest divinity and all other gods, *Brahmā*, *Viṣṇu*, *Śiva* are subordinate to him. Yāmunācārya in his *Āgama-prāmāṇya* argues that the *Pañcarātra āgamas* are as valid as the *Vedas*, since both are derived from the Supreme Person *Nārāyaṇa*.[2] Image worship is an essential feature of the *Pañcarātra* doctrine though it does not find support in the *Vedas*. It was, however, current even in the sixth century B.C. though the orthodox sects were not reconciled to some of their practices. The *Sātvata-saṁhitā* mentions the four *vyūha* manifestations (*vibhava-devatā*). *Ahirbudhnya-saṁhitā* which shows considerable *Tāntric* influence holds that Ultimate Reality is the Beginningless, Endless, Eternal One, devoid of names and forms, beyond all

[1] XIII. 6. 1. Cp. the *Nārāyaṇa Sūkta*
sahasra-śīrṣam devam viśvākṣam viśva-sambhavam
viśvaṁ nārāyaṇaṁ devam akṣaraṁ paramaṁ padam
nārāyaṇam mahājñeyaṁ viśvātmānaṁ parāyaṇam.

[2] Vedānta Deśika, quoting Vyāsa, says:
idam mahopaniṣadaṁ catur-veda-samanvitam
sāṁkhya-yoga kṛtāntena pañcarātrānuśabditam.
Seśvara Mīmāṁsā, p. 19.

speech and mind. He is devoid of all that is evil and the abode of all that is good. He is known by many names, *Param-ātman, Bhagavān, Vāsudeva, Avyakta, Prakṛti, Pradhāna.* He is pure consciousness and yet is regarded as possessing knowledge as a quality. That by which he creates the world is his power, *śakti.*[1] When *Brahman* resolves to split himself into many he is called *Sudarśana.* God's *śakti* exists undifferentiated from him as the moonbeam from the moon. The universe is a manifestation of God's power. With this power of God, *Viṣṇu-śakti,* or *Lakṣmī,* God is always engaged in creative activity.[2]

The Supreme has not only the powers of creation, maintenance and destruction but also favour (*anugraha*) and disfavour (*nigraha*). Though he has no unrealised desires and is utterly independent, he acts like a king just as he wishes in his playful activity.[3]

The *jīvas* enter into God at the dissolution and remain in a potential form in him. They separate out at the time of the new creation. The *jīva* appears as atomic, ignorant and ineffective. He performs actions leading to beneficial and harmful results. He is thus subject to rebirths according to his conduct. Through the grace of God he aims at emancipation. He adopts the adoration of God and service of man as the way to the achievement of perfection. *Prapatti* or *śaraṇā-gati* is complete self-offering to God leaving nothing to oneself.[4] Absolute dependence on God and a sense of utter helplessness of oneself are the marks of *prapatti.* It has for its accompaniment universal charity, friendliness even to one's enemies. The liberated souls enter into God, though they do not become one with him. They have an independent existence in the abode of *Viṣṇu, Vaikuṇṭha.*

Ālvārs

In the *Bhāgavata Purāṇa,*[5] it is said that the devotees of *Viṣṇu* will appear in the South on the banks of *Tāmraparṇī*

[1] *jagat-prakṛti-bhāvo yaḥ sā śaktiḥ parikīrtitā.* III. 2. 57.

[2] *satatam kurvato jagat.* II. 59.

[3] *sarvair ananuyojyaṁ tat svātantryam divyam-iśituḥ*
avāpta-viśva-kāmopi krīḍate rājavad vaśī.
Ahirbudhnya-saṁhitā. XIV. 13.
Cp. *khelati brahmāṇḍe bhagavān.*

[4] See *Ahirbudhnya-saṁhitā.* XXXVII. 27–8.

[5] XI. 5. 38–40.

Kṛtamālā (*Vaigai*), *Payasvinī* (*Pālār*), *Kāverī* and *Mahānadī* (*Periyar*). The reference is to the *Ālvārs*, the ancient *Vaiṣṇava* saints of the South. *Maṇavāḷa mā-muni* says that the earliest of the *Ālvārs* flourished at the time of the Pallavas who came to Kāñcī about the fourth century A.D. Their influence was great about the seventh and the eighth centuries A.D. Their writings in Tamil, about 4,000 hymns, were collected perhaps in R.'s time and are called *Nāl-āyira-divya-prabandham* which is treated by the *Vaiṣṇavas* as of great authority. It gives ecstatic accounts of the emotion of love for God as *Viṣṇu*.

The *Ālvārs* hold that the grace of God is spontaneous and does not depend on the effort or merit of the devotee. Others hold that God's grace depends on the virtuous actions of the devotees. Possibly while God is free to extend his mercy to all, he does so in practice only as a reward to the virtuous. God's mercy is both without cause and with cause.[1] The human soul and the universe are entirely dependent on God.

While the *Ālvārs* were inspired devotees, the *Alagiyas* had in addition to devotion learning and scholarship. Nātha-muni (tenth century) was the first of them. It is said that he was in direct contact with Nammāḷvār or Śaṭhagopa. Nammāḷvar, Nāthamuni, Yāmunācārya otherwise called Āḷavandār belonged to the *pañcarātra* tradition which R. accepted. Yāmunācārya gave philosophical expression to the devotional thoughts of the *Ālvārs* and emphasised the concept of *bhakti*. In his *Siddhi-traya* he argues for the existence of the individual soul independent of God. Release from bondage is attained through devotion to God, according to him. Yāmunācārya invested his disciples with the five *Vaiṣṇava saṁskāras*. He wrote six works, *Stotra-ratna*, *Catuḥ-ślokī*, *Āgama-prāmāṇya* which establishes the authority of the *Pañcarātra Āgamas*, *Siddhi-traya*, *Gītārtha-saṁgraha* and *Mahā-puruṣa-nirṇaya*. He is deeply devoted to the Lord and realises his utter helplessness without his grace.[2] He advocates the doctrine of *prapatti*.

R. was the son of Yāmunācārya's sister Kāntimatī born in

[1] R. in his *Aṣṭādaśa-bheda-nirṇaya* says: *kṛpā svarūpato nirhetukaḥ, rakṣaṇa-samaye cetana-kṛta-sukṛtena sa-hetukā bhūtvā rakṣati*.

[2] *na dharma-niṭṣho'smi, na cātma-vedī, na bhaktimāṁs tvac-caraṇāravinde.*
a-kiñcano nānyagatiś śaraṇye tvat-pāda-mūlam śaraṇaṁ prapadye.
Stotra-ratna, 22.

circa A.D. 1017. He received his training from Yādava Prakāśa who advocated a system of monism.

Ś. and R.

R. takes into account Ś.'s views and develops a theistic interpretation with great feeling, vast learning and brilliant logic. Ś. and R. represent two uninterrupted traditions in Indian thought. To my mind these traditions are not exclusive of each other but complementary. For example, commenting on B.S. I. 3. 19, Ś. explains his view that the individual soul as such cannot claim any reality except in so far as it is identical with *Brahman* but adds, 'there are other thinkers and among them some of us who are of the view that the individual soul as such is real'.[1] Difference on such a vital point did not incline Ś. to exclude its upholders from his own community of Vedāntins. If he had lived to see the later developments of the *Vedānta*, he would not have rejected them.

Pramāṇas

R. admits three *pramāṇas*, Perception, Inference and scriptural testimony.[2] R. writes: 'Scripture, although not dependent on anything else and concerned with objects which are non-perceptible, must, all the same, come to terms with *tarka* (ratiocination), for all the different means of knowledge can in many cases help us to arrive at a decisive conclusion only if they are supported by ratiocination. All means of knowledge equally stand in need of *tarka*: Scripture, however, the authoritative character of which specially depends on expectancy, proximity and compatibility throughout requires to be assisted by *tarka*. In accordance with this, Manu says, he who investigates by means of reasoning only knows religious duty and none other.'[3]

Supreme Reality

For R., there exists One All-embracing Being called *Brahman*, the Highest Self or the Lord. *Īśvara* in his nature is free from

[1] *apare tu vādinaḥ pāramārthikam eva jaivaṁ rūpam iti manyante asmadīyāś ca kecit.*

[2] In R.G.B. he adds intuitive or yogic knowledge. *jñānam, indriya-liṅgāgama-yogajo vastu-niścayaḥ.* XV. 15. Vedānta Deśika includes yogic knowledge under perception.

[3] R.B. II. 1. 4.

all impurities and possesses all the auspicious qualities. He is all-knowing, all-merciful, all-pervading, all-powerful. R. repudiates Ś.'s view that *Brahman* as Ultimate Reality is absolutely unqualified, *nir-viśeṣa*. He argues that we have no means of proving such a reality for all knowledge is of qualified objects. If plurality is false, scriptural texts which point to an absolutely differenceless reality cannot be accepted for Scriptures are based on the assumption of plurality. The texts which refer to *Brahman* as pure being[1] or as transcendent[2] or as truth and knowledge[3] do not indicate that *Brahman* is devoid of qualities but as possessing many auspicious qualities of omniscience, omnipotence, all-pervasiveness and the like. *Brahman* is one in the sense that there is no second cause of the world. *Brahman* being of the essence of knowledge may also be considered to be the possessor of knowledge even as a lamp which is of the nature of light may also be regarded as possessing rays of light.[4]

All knowledge refers to an object. Even in what we call illusion there is an element of reality. When we mistake a conchshell for silver, it is because the conchshell resembles silver in a sense. We do not notice the other qualities on account of our defects in the organs. The knowledge of silver in a conchshell is not unreal but real. It refers to the silver element existing in a conchshell.[5]

Even the dreams which are momentary and appear only to the dreamer are produced by the Lord. R. holds that all cognitions are of the real and dreams and illusions are not an exception to the rule. Things we know are all the result of *trivṛt-karaṇa* and everything contains in it elements of everything else. 'That one thing is called silver and another "shell" has its reason in the relative preponderance of the one or the other element.' In mistaking one for the other, we still cognise what is, not what is not, nor something which neither is nor is not. In dreams we perceive what is real though transient, this being produced for the enjoyment of souls in accordance with

[1] C.U. VI. 2. 1. [2] M.U. I. 1. 5. [3] T.U. II. 1. 1.

[4] *jñāna-svarūpasyaiva tasya jñānāśrayatvam maṇi-dyumaṇi-pradīpādivad ity uktam eva*. I. 1. 1.

[5] Cp. R. *yathārtham sarva-vijñānam iti veda-vidām matam*
śruti-smṛtibhyaḥ sarvasya sarvātmatva-pratītitaḥ.

their merit or demerit. There is no knowledge which has no object. Even in sleep or swoon, we have the direct experience of the self and not the formless experience of pure consciousness. Consciousness is always revealed to a knower or the self. We do not directly experience pure consciousness for all experience is of qualified entities. Even freedom from qualification is a quality. Reality, consciousness, etc., which are said to be *Brahman* indicate characteristics of *Brahman*. Scriptures do not testify to the existence of a characterless reality. *Īśvara* is to be admitted on the authority of scriptural texts. The existence of God cannot be established by perception or inference.

R. does not make any distinction between *Brahman* and *Īśvara*. *Brahman* is *Īśvara* called *Nārāyaṇa* or *Viṣṇu*.[1]

Vedānta Deśika mentions three modified forms of *Vāsudeva*, namely *Saṁkarṣaṇa*, *Pradyumna* and *Aniruddha* who control the individual souls, mind and the external world. These are not three separate entities but are one Lord conceived differently according to his functions.

The Supreme as Antaryāmin

R. takes his stand on the *Antaryāmin Brāhmaṇa*[2] which says that within all elements, all sense-organs, all souls, there dwells an inward ruler, whose body these elements, sense-organs and souls are. *Brahman* comprises within himself all elements of plurality, matter with its various modifications and souls of different classes and degrees. These are real constituents of *Brahman*. *Cit* (soul) and *acit* (matter) are the body of the Lord.[3] They are entirely dependent on and subservient to the Lord who pervades and rules all things, material and immaterial as their inmost self, *antaryāmin*. Their individual existence has been there from all eternity and will never be entirely resolved into *Brahman*. They exist in two different periodically alternating conditions. In *pralaya* state, which occurs at the end of each world-period, when *Brahman* is said to be in a causal condition, *kāraṇāvastha*, distinctions of names and forms disappear. Matter

[1] *vede rāmāyaṇe caiva purāṇe bhārate tathā*
ādāv ante ca madhye ca viṣṇuḥ sarvatra gīyate.
Hari-vaṁśa. III. 323. 94.

[2] B.U. III. 7; see P.U. (1953), pp. 224–30.

[3] *īśvaras-cid-acic-ceti padārtha-tritayam hariḥ.*

is unmanifested, *avyakta*, individual souls are not attached to bodies and their intelligence is in a state of contraction, *saṁkoca*. Even then *Brahman* contains within itself matter and souls in a *bīja* or seed condition. When owing to an act of volition on the part of the Lord *pralaya* is succeeded by *sṛṣṭi* or creation, unmanifested matter becomes gross and evident to the senses and the souls enter into connection with material bodies corresponding to their accumulated merit and demerit and their intelligence undergoes expansion, *vikāsa*. *Brahman* then is in effect condition, *kāryāvastha*. Cause and effect are different names for different conditions or changes, *pariṇāma*.

For R., the world and the souls apart from *Brahman* are not real. The relation between *Brahman* and souls and matter is analogous to that between soul and body or substance and attribute. It is one of non-separation, *apṛthaktva*. The soul and body, substance and attribute are different from one another; yet they are inseparably connected and form a whole. The same is the case with *Brahman* and souls and matter. R. says: 'Everything different from the Highest Self, whether of conscious or non-conscious nature, constitutes its body, while that self alone is the non-conditioned embodied self. For this very reason, competent persons designate this doctrine which has the highest *Brahman* for its subject-matter *śārīraka*, i.e. the doctrine of the embodied self.'[1]

Acit

According to R. there are three kinds of *acit*, *prakṛti* or matter, *kāla* or time and *śuddha-tattva* or pure matter.[2] *Acit* is *prakṛti* or primal matter and its modifications. *Prakṛti* with its three qualities passes through many stages and manifests itself as the phenomenal world, producing happiness or misery in accordance with man's good or bad deeds. The favour or disfavour of *Īśvara* works in accordance with the past conduct of man.

[1] *evaṁ ca sva-vyatirikta-cetanācetana-vastu-jātaṁ sva-śarīram iti sa eva nirupādhikaḥ śārīra ātmā. ata evedam param-brahmādhikṛtya pravṛttaṁ śāstram śārīrakam ity abhiyuktair abhidhīyate.* I. 1. 13. While R. looks upon individual souls and the world of matter as modes, attributes or *Viśeṣaṇas* of God, Nimbārka looks upon them as living parts of the Lord, his powers or *śaktis*.

[2] Nimbārka calls this *aprākṛta*.

Cit

The individual soul is often called *jñāna* or consciousness, since it is as self-revealing as consciousness. It reveals all objects when it comes into contact with them through the senses. It is a knower, an agent, an enjoyer. The Self is a knower, and also possesses the quality of consciousness and knowledge[1] even as light exists both as the light and as the rays emanating from it.[2] Consciousness, though unlimited of itself[3] can contract as well as expand.[4] In an embodied self it is in a contracted state through the influence of its actions. The Self, though pure in itself, becomes associated with ignorance and selfish desires through its contact with matter, *acit*. *Avidyā* or ignorance is lack of knowledge, misunderstanding of characteristics, false knowledge. When the association with matter, *acit*, is cut away, the self becomes freed from *avidyā* and is emancipated. The soul realises itself as forming the body of *Brahman*. The soul is atomic in size but spreads out its knowledge all over the body like the rays of a lamp. It desires things according to its free will and the will of God does not interfere with it. To those who are attached to him he is well disposed and produces in them desires by which they can win him.[5] *Īśvara* exists in us all as the inner controller. He grants good and evil fruits according to our good and evil deeds. His control over us does not deprive us of our freedom.

R. speaks of the souls as being the body of *Īśvara* but Lokācārya argues that as the external material objects exist for the sake of the souls, so the souls exist for God. God is the goal (*śeṣa*) for which the soul exists as the object of his control and support (*śeṣin*).

Yāmunācārya observes that release from the ills of bondage has no meaning or attraction, if the released soul does not survive in its distinctive individuality. The text 'That thou art' is interpreted by R. as expressing oneness without losing the distinctive characters denoted by the two words That and Thou. Whoever cognises and meditates on the Supreme, assisted by

[1] *jñāna-guṇāśraya.*

[2] *maṇi-prabhṛtīnāṁ prabhāśrayatvam iva jñānāśrayatvam api aviruddham.* I. 1. 1.

[3] *svayam aparicchinnam eva jñānam.*

[4] *saṁkoca-vikāsārham.*

[5] II. 3. 40–1.

the grace of the Lord attains at death final emancipation. He passes through the different stages of the path of the gods up to the world of *Brahmā*, there enjoys blissful existence from which there is no return to the world of *saṁsāra*.

Release

The individual for R. lasts for ever and even in release enjoys its individuality. R. criticises the view of release as a refunding into *Brahman* as an earthen vessel is refunded into its own causal substance. This would mean nothing else but complete annihilation, not a worthy end for a human being.[1] For R., *mukti* or release is a state when the individual is freed from *avidyā* and has the intuition of the Supreme. The state of *kaivalya* or realisation of one's own self as the Highest is a lower form of emancipation. Freedom according to Vedānta Deśika is *sāyujya* or sameness of nature with *Īśvara*. The human soul participates in the qualities of *Īśvara* except those of the creation and control of the world and the grant of freedom to other souls. *Mukti* for Vedānta Deśika is servitude to God.

The Way to Release

The way to freedom is through *bhakti*, which according to R. is a species of knowledge, *jñāna-viśeṣa*. Without *bhakti* mere knowledge cannot lead us to freedom. *Bhakti* is supreme self-surrender which one develops when the prescribed duties are performed and true knowledge is obtained from the study of the *śāstras*. *Karma* and *jñāna* help to purify the mind and prepare it for *bhakti*.

According to R., *bhakti* is the means of salvation. *Bhakti* is *upāsanā* or meditation.[2] This *bhakti* is based on knowledge and arises from six essential prerequisites, discrimination (*viveka*), complete disregard for worldly objects (*vimoka*), continued practice (*abhyāsa*), performance of rites (*kriyā*), virtuous conduct like truthfulness and the rest (*kalyāṇa*) and freedom from dejection (*anavasāda*). *Prapatti* or complete surrender to

[1] *ghaṭādivat kāraṇa-prāpter vināśa-rūpatvena mokṣasyāpuruṣārthatvāc ca.*
Cp. *aham artha vināśaś cen mokṣa ity adhyavasyati*
apasarpedasau mokṣa-kathā-prastāva-mātrataḥ.
See R.B. I. 4. 21.

[2] *evaṁ-rūpā dhruvānusmṛtir eva bhakti-śabdenābhidhīyate.*

God is described in the *Śaraṇāgati-gadya.*[1] It elevates all irrespective of caste restrictions.[2] He who adopts *prapatti* does not aim at emancipation. He enjoys servitude to God. Though R. adopted Vedic rituals of initiation and worship, he was catholic in his views and admitted into the *Vaiṣṇava* fold *Jains, Buddhists, Śūdras* and even untouchables.

R. in his work on *Aṣṭā-daśa-rahasyārtha-vivaraṇa* makes out that he who is devoted entirely to God need not follow the ordinary code of duties. The scriptural duties are not binding on him.[3] R. seems to have modified this view in his *bhāṣya.* For R., Vedic ritual alone does not lead to emancipation. Devotion to *Viṣṇu* in the company of *Lakṣmī* is the central feature of his scheme of salvation. Through the concept of *Lakṣmī* who intercedes on behalf of the sinners and persuades *Viṣṇu* to bestow his grace for the good of the devotees, R. develops the concept of *karuṇā.* God has *vātsalya* or filial affection which moves him to remove the sufferings of others.

Later Developments

R.'s *Viśiṣṭādvaita* developed into two schools, *Vaḍa-galai* and *Ten-galai,* associated with Vedānta Deśika and Pillai Lokācārya. They emphasise respectively devotion with personal endeavour or *bhakti* and complete dependence on God or *prapatti.* The former adopts the *markaṭa-nyāya* which holds that the devotee collaborates with God even as a young monkey clings to the back of its mother while the latter adopts the *mārjāra-nyāya,* that God alone is active and carries the surrendering devotee to his goal even as a cat carries a kitten.

Pillai Lokācārya points out that God moves us all to our actions and fulfils our desires according to our karmas. He gives knowledge to the ignorant, power to the weak, mercy to the sufferers and goodness of heart to the wicked. His qualities are for the sake of others, not for himself.

[1] *sarva-dharmāṁś ca saṁtyajya sarva-kāmāṁś ca sākṣarān*
loka-vikrānta-caraṇau śaraṇaṁ te vrajan vibho.

[2] Cp. *Bhāradvāja-saṁhitā.*
brahma-kṣatra-viśaḥ śūdrāḥ striyas cāntara-jātayaḥ
sarva eva prapadyeran sarva-dhātāram acyutam.

[3] *jnāna-niṣṭho virakto vā mad-bhakto hi anapekṣakaḥ*
sa liṅgān āśramān tyaktvā cared avidhi-gocaraḥ, p. 23. Cp. B.G. XVIII. 66.

Many religious leaders have been influenced by the *Viśiṣṭādvaita* doctrines. Nām-deva (A.D. 1269–1295) born in Satara was a devotee of Viṭṭhoba of Pandharpur. He was a tailor by profession and wrote a number of hymns in Marāthi and Hindi. He had four sons and a daughter.

Jñāneśvara (A.D. 1275–1296) was a life-long celibate. He was a personal friend of Nām-deva. He lived for only 21 years. His *Jñāneśvarī* was written in A.D. 1290. According to the Mahārāṣṭra tradition his great-grandfather was a disciple of Gorakhnātha. Though a follower of the *Advaita* of Ś., he encouraged worship of a Personal God. The Personal God is not the phenomenal appearance of the Absolute but is the Absolute itself which has in it the principle of plurality. The world is not the expression of *māyā* but is the outcome of divine love and joy. For Kṛṣṇa and Rādhā, Jñāneśvar substituted Kṛṣṇa in the form of Viṭṭhala and Rukmiṇī.

Rāmānanda (A.D. 1360–1450) was born at Melkote and went to the north and started the Vaiṣṇavite movement of which the chief exponents were Kabīr (A.D. 1440–1518), Nānak (A.D. 1469–1538), Dādu (A.D. 1544–1603), Tulasi-dās (A.D. 1527–1623) and the Mahratta saint Tukārām.

Rāmānanda gave a systematic account of the theory of *avatāras*. The two chief are those of *Rāma* and *Kṛṣṇa*. He had a preference for the worship of *Rāma*,[1] though he mentions *Kṛṣṇa* as a principal object of adoration. In his worship of *Kṛṣṇa* he looked upon *Rukmiṇī* as his *śakti* or energy. Later varieties of *Kṛṣṇa*-worship give this place to *Rādhā*. According to Rāmānanda, anyone can attain release through *bhakti* or devotion. He did not recognise any caste distinctions. He had a number of disciples of whom the famous were Sen, a barber, Dhanā, a Jat, Rai-dās, a Chāmar, Kabīr, a Muslim, and Mīrā, the princess of Jodhpur. Rāmānanda established an ascetic order which had a large membership.

Kabīr, of uncertain parentage, was brought up by a Muslim weaver and became the disciple of Rāmānanda. He condemned the superstitious practices of the people and fostered faith in the unity of God which could be accepted both by the Hindus and the Muslims. He used different names for God, *Rām*, *Allāh* and

[1] *ramante yoginaḥ yasmin sa rāmaḥ.*

others. Though essentially a mystic who, in his state of rapture, rose above the concepts of philosophy and the names of religion, he taught a simple faith in a God of love. He laid stress on the inner purity of life without which fasts, pilgrimages and rites were of no avail. He lived a normal home life, had a son and a daughter. After his death both Hindus and Muslims claimed him. Nothing was found of his body except a heap of flowers, of which each took a share and burned or buried it. Kabīr exercised great influence on Nānak.

Nānak composed *Japji* which is a collection of verses arranged for daily use by the Sikhs for prayer and praise. The *Ādi-granth*[1] of the Sikhs was composed by the fifth guru Arjun in A.D. 1604 and includes Nānak's utterances as well as those of other religious teachers. Many of Kabīr's hymns are included in it. The Supreme, according to Nānak, is *nirguṇa*, devoid of qualities. He is the unrevealed and the unrevealable. The holy men took the place of the *avatāras* or the incarnations of Hinduism. Devotion to the *guru*, service of saints and insistence on the greatness of the name are stressed in Sikhism. Nānak ridiculed superstition, denounced caste distinctions, taught a life of brotherhood. Nānak says:

> There are ignoble amongst the noblest
> And pure amongst the despised
> The former shalt thou avoid
> And be the dust under the foot of the other.

He affirmed equality of sexes. For Nānak woman is *ardh-śarīri* and *mokh-dvārī*. She is the half of a full life and the doorway to liberation.

Tulasi-dās composed his great work *Rāma-carita-mānasa* in A.D. 1574. It is the most popular classic of religion and morals in North India. He took the story from Vālmīki's *Rāmāyaṇa* and *Adhyātma Rāmāyaṇa* and adapted it to his purposes. He thought that his account was faithful to the originals.[2] He lived in Banaras till his death in A.D. 1623. Though he had great faith

[1] See *Occasional Speeches and Writings*. Vol. II (1957), pp. 364–77.

[2] The opening verse of the *Rāma-carita-mānasa* begins with these words: *nānā-purāṇa-nigamāgama-sammatam*.

in devotion, his spiritual leanings were for the non-dualism of Ś. He popularised the worship of *Rāma*.

In his *Vinaya-patrikā* the poet shows his catholicity of outlook by inculcating the worship of the five gods, *Viṣṇu, Śiva, Durgā, Sūrya* and *Gaṇeśa*. All the three paths to spiritual freedom are commended though *bhakti* is the simplest and the easiest.[1]

Madhusūdana Sarasvatī (A.D. 1540–1623) wrote a book called *Advaita-siddhi*, defending non-dualism against its critics; he yet espoused the worship of *Kṛṣṇa*.

E. MADHVA

Madhva

Madhva (A.D. 1197–1273) while still a bachelor became an ascetic of the *Śaṁkara* school. He soon developed a theistic interpretation of the B.S. and identified the Supreme with *Viṣṇu* or *Nārāyaṇa*,[2] who was for Madhva the purport of the *Sūtras, sūtrārthaḥ*. Legend has it that Madhva was an incarnation of *Vāyu* for the purpose of destroying the *Advaita Vedānta*, which is not different from materialism or Buddhism.[3] He was a disciple of Acyuta-prekṣa and received the name of Pūrṇa-prajña at the time of initiation. He is also known as Ānanda-tīrtha.

Works

Madhva is said to have written thirty-seven works of which the chief are the commentaries on some of the principal *Upaniṣads*, the B.G., the B.S., *Aṇu-bhāṣya*, which is a brief

[1] The unfortunate suspicion of women lingers even in our noblest souls. Tulasi-dās makes Sītā insinuate wrong motives to Lakṣmaṇa:

marma bacana sītā jaba holi
hari prerita lakṣmaṇa mati doli.

Rāma-carita-mānasa III.

[2] *nārāyaṇam guṇaiḥ sarvair udīrṇaṁ doṣa-varjitam.*

[3] Nārāyaṇa Paṇḍitācārya, in his *Madhva Vijaya*, a work of the fourteenth century, called the followers of Ś. *pracchana-bauddhāḥ*.

asatpadesan sad-asad-viviktam māyākhyayā saṁvṛtim abhyadattā
brahmāpy akhaṇḍam bala śūnya-sidhyai, pracchanna-bauddhoyam ataḥ prasiddhaḥ. I. 51.

summary of the *Sūtra-bhāṣya, Anu-vyākhyāna, Mahābhārata-tātparya-nirṇaya, Bhāgavata-tātparya-nirṇaya* and *Māyā-vāda-khaṇḍana.*

Madhva's system is called *dvaita* or dualism. It claims ancient authority. The *Padma Purāṇa* mentions that Madhva is connected with the *Brahma-saṁpradāya* even as R. adopts the *Śrī-saṁpradāya.*

By the thirteenth century, in which Madhva lived, Ś.'s non-dualism received great support from its principal exponents like Vācaspati, Prakāśātman, Sureśvara and others. Madhva and his followers, Jaya-tīrtha, Vyāsa-tīrtha and others did their best to repudiate the doctrine of non-dualism and establish the reality of a Personal God, the plurality of the world and the difference between *Brahman* and the self. Jaya-tīrtha's *Nyāya-sudhā, Anu-vyākhyāna* and Vyāsa-tīrtha's *Nyāyāmṛta* are important works which defend Madhva's theistic dualism against Ś.'s non-dualism.

Madhva says that the B.S. was written to repudiate the non-dualistic interpretation. Since the Supreme Being full of auspicious qualities cannot be understood by finite minds, an inquiry starts. The second *sūtra* declares that the Supreme cannot be identified with the individual self as he is the source and support of the world. That *Brahman* is the cause of the world can be understood only by Scripture and scriptural texts can be reconciled only by the recognition of difference or *bheda.*

The Pramāṇas

Madhva says that in writing the *Aṇu-vyākhyāna,* he followed scriptural texts, the *Vedas* and logical reasoning.[1] One can know God not by perception and inference but only by Scripture, the *Vedas.* Scripture, according to Madhva, is *nitya,* eternal, *nir-doṣa,* devoid of defects, *svataḥ-pramāṇa,* self-evident, and *apauruṣeya,* impersonal. The *Vedas* are not produced by any human being. If we do not admit the impersonal origin of the *Vedas,* ethical and religious duties will not have validity. We cannot say that the commands proceed from an omniscient

[1] *ātma-vākyatayā tena śruti-mūlatayā tathā*
yukti-mūlatayā caiva prāmāṇyam trividham mahat. I. 1.

being, for the existence of an omniscient being cannot be known apart from the Scriptures. The impersonal origin of the *Vedas* is valid because we do not know of anyone who has composed and uttered them. The *Vedas* exist in their own nature and have been perceived by God and revealed to the seers, who, at the beginning of each creation, remembered the instructions of their previous birth. Their validity is self-evident. Madhva says in his *Viṣṇu-tattva-vinirṇaya*, 'Neither sense perception nor infeence reveals to us the nature of God. It is only through the *Vedas* that we can know him. Hence it is that they are called *Veda*.'[1] The Scriptures refer to *Nārāyaṇa* as the omniscient creator of all things.

Supreme Reality

The teaching of the Scriptures gains strength by what is known from other *pramāṇas*. Madhva proceeds by way of inference to establish the reality of a Personal God who is omniscient and omnipotent. The world being of the nature of an effect must have an intelligent cause, a maker who is God. He has many qualities. When he is said to be *nir guṇa*, all that is meant is that he is not associated with the qualities and attributes of *prakṛti*. He is *sa guṇa* in that he admits the presence of auspicious spiritual qualities. The Supreme cannot be *avācya* or indescribable. In that case he cannot be the subject-matter of Scriptures. Madhva repudiates the view that though words cannot describe, they may suggest or indicate.[2] *Brahman* is *pari-pūrṇa-guṇa*.[3] Each one of his qualities is boundless.[4] He is the author of the eight acts of creation, preservation, destruction, governance, knowledge, ignorance, bondage and release.[5] He is absolutely free, *sarva-svatantraḥ*. *Viṣṇu* is the all-perfect one. *Brahman* is one in whom there is the fullness of qualities.[6] The acceptance of difference between *Brahman* and

[1] *nendriyāṇi, nānumānam vedā hy evainam vedayanti tasmād āhuḥ vedāḥ, iti pippalāda-śrutiḥ.*

[2] *sarva-śabdāvācyasya lakṣaṇāyukteḥ kenāpi śabdenāvācyasya lakṣaṇāyām api pramāṇam nāsti.*

[3] *brahma-śabdopi hi guṇa-pūrtim eva vadaty ayam. Aṇu-vyākhyāna* I 1. 1.

[4] *pratyekam niravadhikānanta-guṇa-pari-pūrṇatva.*

[5] *sṛṣṭyādy-aṣṭā kartā.*

[6] *bṛhanto hi asmin guṇāḥ.*

the souls does not limit the nature of *Brahman*. *Brahman* is not devoid of all determination or *viśeṣa*. Even the denial of determination is itself a determination which the non-dualists will have to deny. Madhva looks upon Ś.'s system as crypto-Buddhism. There is no difference between the qualityless *Brahman* and the *śūnya* of the Mādhyāmika system.[1] The non-dualists treat it as unspeakable and unknowable, though all knowledge refers to it. Madhva believes in a Personal God endowed with qualities and characters. If all selves were identical then there would be no difference between the emancipated and the unemancipated ones. If all difference is due to ignorance, then God who is free from ignorance will perceive himself as one with all individual selves and experience their sufferings. The world, our experience and bondage are all real. A non-existent universe cannot affect anyone favourably or adversely. Scriptures assert difference between the individual souls and *Brahman*. No one feels that he is omnipotent and omniscient. The text *tat tvam asi* is used with illustrations which affirm the difference between *Brahman* and the souls. When the *Upaniṣad* says that when one is known all is known, the meaning is that the object of knowledge is one, or that one alone is the cause. It does not mean that the other things are false. Were it so, the knowledge of all false things would be derived from the knowledge of the truth.[2] The Scriptures do not declare the falsity of the world.[3]

We cannot say that *Brahman* is one but appears as many because of *upādhis* or limiting conditions. If he is conditioned by *upādhis* he cannot be released from them for his association with the *upādhis* will be permanent. If *upādhis* are the product of ignorance, then ignorance will be of the nature of *Brahman*. If they were different, then we will have dualism of *Brahman* and ignorance. If it is argued that ignorance or *ajñāna* is a quality of *jīva*, we are in a vicious circle. There is no *jīva* without *ajñāna;* there is no *ajñāna* without *jīva*.

[1] Cp.: The state of *samādhi* is void of modifications, of mental activities, of understanding, free from defects, devoid of all, without any distortion.

prabhā-śūnyam manaś-śūnyaṁ buddhi-śūnyaṁ nirāmayam
sarva-śūnyaṁ nirābhāsam samādhis tasya lakṣaṇam.

Uttara-gītā 14.

[2] *na hi satya-jñānena mithyā-jñānam bhavati.*

[3] B.G. XVI. 8–9.

Brahman is the efficient cause of the universe[1] and the giver of salvation.[2] Even in the *Mahā-bhārata-tātparya-nirṇaya* Madhva declares that all those who proclaim the unity of the self with *Brahman* either in bondage or in release are wrong. The world is real with its fivefold difference, viz. that between the self and God, between the selves themselves, between matter and God, between matter and matter and between matter and self.[3] Though the physical world and the individual souls are real they are not independent of the Supreme. They are *para-tantra* while God alone is *sva-tantra*. *Prakṛti*, *puruṣa*, *kāla*, *karma*, *svabhāva* are dependent. Though eternal, these do not exist by their own right but by the will of the Supreme.[4] The Supreme is the only independent real that exists in its own right. All others, finite selves, etc., exist as subordinate to the central Reality of God. There are four categories, God, *prakṛti*, *jīva*, or the individual soul, and matter, *jaḍa*.[5]

The Individual Soul

From *Brahmā* to the grass tip, all belong to the world of living beings, *jīva-rāśi*. The *jīvas* are of three kinds, *deva*, *mānuṣa* and *dānava*.

Karma and Release

The best men attain salvation through knowledge and grace of God; ordinary men pass through cycles of births and rebirths and the worst are damned in hell. The eternally liberated and those cursed in hell are not subject to birth and rebirth. There is no hope for the wicked in hell. Only in Madhva's system do we

[1] In this Madhva agrees with the Pāśupatas: *māheśvarās tu manyante paśupatir īśvaro nimitta-kāraṇam iti*. Ś.B. II. 2. 37.

[2] *vāsudevam anārādhya na mokṣam samavāpnuyāt*. *Viṣṇu Purāṇa* I. 4. 18.

[3] *jagat-pravāhaḥ satyo'yam pañca-bheda-samanvitaḥ.*
jīveśayor bhidā caiva jīva-bhedaḥ parasparam
jaḍeśayor jaḍānāṁ ca jaḍa-jīva-bhedā tathā
pañca-bhedā ime nityāḥ sarvāvasthāsu nityaśaḥ
muktānām ca na hīyante tāratamyaṁ ca sarvadā.
I. 69–71.

[4] *dravyaṁ karma ca kālaś ca svabhāvo jīva eva ca*
yad-anugrahataḥ santi na santi yad-upekṣayā.
Bhāgavata II. 10. 12.

[5] *īśvaraḥ prakṛtir jīvo jaḍam ceti catuṣṭayam*
padārthānāṁ sannidhānāt tatreśo viṣṇur ucyate.

have the doctrine of eternal damnation.[1] *Karma* is to be performed since the *śāstras* require it. *Śāstra* is *aparijñeya* or of transcendental origin and its injunctions are absolutely valid. *Karmas* are to be performed without any desire for fruit. The only desires we may have are for greater knowledge and greater devotion. Without *bhakti* the performance of duties does not help. Even if we commit the worst sin, love of God will save us. God is pleased only with *bhakti* and he alone can save us.

Individual souls are self-luminous in themselves but their intelligence becomes veiled by *avidyā*. When the direct knowledge of God arises, ignorance is dispelled. Bondage is due to attachment and liberation is produced by the direct realisation of God, *aparokṣa-jñānaṁ viṣṇoḥ*. This may be produced in different ways, experience of the sorrows of worldly existence, company of good men, renunciation of the desire for the enjoyment of pleasures in this world or in another, self-control and self-discipline, study, association with good teachers, resignation to God, realisation of the five differences.

Worship is of two kinds, study and meditation, *dhyāna*. The latter is continual thinking of God, leaving all other things aside.[2] *Bhakti* consists of a continual flow of love for the Lord which overcomes all obstacles. When God is pleased we attain salvation.

The state of liberation is of four kinds *sālokya*, *sāmīpya*, *sārūpya* and *sāyujya*. *Sāyujya* is the entrance of the freed souls into the body of God where they share in the enjoyment of God in his own body. Only deities have this kind of liberation. They can at will come out of God and remain separate from him. *Sālokya* is residence in heaven where the freed souls have the satisfaction of the continual sight of God. *Sāmīpya* is continual residence near God as enjoyed by the sages. *Sārūpya* is enjoyed by God's attendants who have outward forms similar to those

[1] Cp. *Mahā-bhārata-tātparya-nirṇaya.*

trividhā jīva-saṁghās tu deva-mānuṣa-dānavāḥ
tatra devāḥ mukti-yogyā mānuṣeṣūttamās tathā
madhyamā mānuṣā ete sṛti-yogyās tadaiva hi
adhamā nirayāyaiva dānavās tu tamo-layāḥ.

[2] *dhyānam ca itara-tiraskāra-pūrvaka-bhagavad-viṣayakākhaṇḍa-smṛtiḥ* *Madhva-siddhānta-sāra*, p. 502.

which God possesses. The freed souls are different from one another.[1]

The doctrine of absolute equality, *parama-sāmya*, is not exclusive of difference. *Jaya-tīrtha* commenting on IV. 4. 17 says that, though the released soul is God's own (*svakīya*), he is a step below him (*avara*) and so is excluded from world-creation, etc. The freed soul comes close to God but does not become one with him. Difference is real and ultimate and does not disappear in the state of release.[2] There is also gradation in the state of release. Even the liberated enjoy bliss through devotion. Madhva believes in *jīvan-mukti*.

Madhva's philosophy had a great influence on Bengal Vaiṣṇavism. Rāmadāsa (A.D. 1608–1682) the adviser of Sivāji followed Madhva's teaching.

F. ŚRĪKAṆṬHA

Śrīkaṇṭha's date is uncertain. He was perhaps a contemporary of R. Some scholars hold that he lived in the thirteenth century and was a contemporary of Meykanda-deva, the author of the Tamil translation of the Sanskrit work *Śiva-jñāna-bodha*. Appaya Dīkṣita suggests that R.'s commentary follows that of Śrīkaṇṭha.[3]

Śrīkaṇṭha introduces his commentary with a statement that he is attempting to clarify the purpose of the B.S., which has been obscured by other teachers.[4] They may be Ś. and Bhāskara whose views are criticised by Śrīkaṇṭha.[5] Appaya Dīkṣita, sixteenth century, wrote a commentary on Śrīkaṇṭha's *bhāṣya* called *Śivārka-maṇi-dīpikā*.

[1] *muktānāṁ ca na hīyante tāratamyaṁ ca sarvadā. Mahā-bhārata-tātparya nirṇaya*, p. 4.

[2] Cp. *Bhāmatī* which quotes a verse from the *pañcarātrikas:*

āmukter bheda eva syāj jīvasya ca parasya ca
muktasya tu na bhedo'sti bheda-hetor abhāvataḥ.

I. 4–21.

[3] *tad-anukṛti-saraṇi.*

[4] *vyāsa-sūtram idaṁ netram viduṣām brahma-darśane*
pūrvācāryaiḥ kaluṣitaṁ śrīkaṇṭhena prasādyate
sarva-vedānta-sārasya saurabhāsvāda-modinām
āryāṇām śiva-niṣṭhānām bhāṣyam etan mahā-nidhiḥ.

[5] See II. 3. 19; II. 3. 42; II. 3. 49.

The Vedas and the Āgamas

Śrīkaṇṭha tried to reconcile the Saivism based on the *Vedas* with that of the *Āgamas*. *Āgama* means texts which have come down to us. Evidently there have been two currents of thought, the *Vedic* and the *Āgamic*, from the beginnings of Indian philosophic speculation. In the Mohenjo-dāro excavations we have a statuette in the form of *Śiva* seated on a bull, surrounded by animals. This is perhaps *Śiva* as *Paśu-pati*. The *Pāśupata* and the *Pañcarātra Āgamas* in which *bhakti* is the criterion of faith are criticised by Bādarāyaṇa in the B.S.[1] But the *Āgamas* themselves claim the support of the *Vedas*.[2] The *Śaiva Siddhānta* system which claims to be based on the *Āgamas* purports to expound the teaching of the *Vedas*.[3] It relates itself to the theistic tendencies of the *Upaniṣads*. It is developed in the thirteenth century by Meykanda-deva and his pupils, Arulnandi and Umāpati.

Whatever may be the origin of the *Āgamas* it is clear that they do not insist on sacrificial religion but support a personal religion in which *Viṣṇu* or *Śiva* or *Śakti* is equated with the Highest Reality. It also has support in the *Upaniṣads*. The *Śaiva-siddhānta* is based on the *Āgamas* and the earliest Tamil exponent of this system is Tiru-mūlar who was followed by later teachers, Māṇikka-vācagar, Appar, Jñāna-sambandhar and Sundarar. Tiru-mūlar holds that the *Vedas* and the *Āgamas* are the creation of the Lord and they are both true. 'The *Veda* with the *Āgama* is the truth; they are the word of the Lord: these revelations of the Lord are to be studied as the general and the special doctrines; on enquiry, they are taken to be different as giving rise to two different sets of conclusions; but to the great ones they are non-different.'[4] Śrīkaṇṭha holds that the *Vedas* and the *Āgamas* are of equal authority; only while the former are studied by men of the three upper castes, the latter may be

[1] II. II. 2.

[2] *veda-sāram idam tantram. Makuṭāgama.*

[3] *siddhānto veda-sāratvāt. Suprabhedāgama.*
vedāntārtham idaṁ jñānaṁ siddhāntaṁ paramaṁ śubham. Makuṭāgama.

[4] *vedamodāgamam meyyā miraivanūl*
odum śirappum poduvu menrullana
nādanurai ivai nādiliraṇḍandam
bhedamadenbar periyorkkabhedame.

studied by all.[1] The Hindu tendency to reconcile different traditions of thought is evident in Śrīkaṇṭha's commentary. He explains his views as conformable to reason and Vedic authority.

Śaivism

From Ś.'s commentary,[2] it may be inferred that Bādarāyaṇa knew about the *Śaiva* system. At any rate, Ś. is acquainted with it. The Jain writer Rāja-śekhara (fourteenth century) calls the *Śaiva* system a *yoga-mata.*[3] He is of the view that the *Naiyāyikas* like Jayanta, Udayana and Bhāsarvajña and the *Vaiśeṣikas* were followers of *Śaivism.* Haribhadra in his *Ṣaḍ-darśana-samuccaya* makes out that the followers of the *Nyāya* and the *Vaiśeṣika* systems adopt the same divinity.[4] The *Śaiva Āgamas* were written in Sanskrit, Prākrit and local dialects according to *Śiva-dharmottara.*[5] They are available in Sanskrit and Dravidian languages like Telugu, Tamil and Kannada. In Mādhava's *sarva-darśana-saṁgraha* we find a treatment of *Nākuliśa-pāśupata,* the *Śaiva* and the *Pratyabhijñā* systems. The *Āgamic Śaivism* is found in South India, the *Pāśupata* system in Gujerat, the *Pratyabhijñā* in Kāṣmīr and other parts of North India, and *Vīra-śaivism* developed by Basava (twelfth century) in Karṇāṭaka.[6] The *Pāśupata* school which dates from the second century B.C. adopts a dualistic view. According to it the Supreme and the individual souls are distinct entities and *prakṛti* is the constituent cause of the world. In the released condition the individual soul shakes off weakness and ignorance and attains boundless knowledge and power of action. In this school release is *sāmīpya* or proximity to God and not identity with God. While Śrīkaṇṭha's system has many

[1] II. 2. 38. [2] II. 2. 35–8.

[3] *atha yoga-matam brūmaḥ, śaivam iti aparābhidam,* p. 8.

[4] *devatā-viṣayo bhedo nāsti naiyāyikaiḥ samam vaiśeṣikānām tattve tu vidyate asau nidarśyate,* p. 266.

[5] *saṁskṛtaiḥ prākṛtair vākyair yaś ca śiṣyānurūpaṭaḥ*
deśa-bhāṣādyupāyaiś ca bodhayet sa guruḥ smṛtaḥ.
Quoted in *Śiva-jñāna-siddhi.*

[6] *Vātulāgama* mentions the different varieties of *Śaivism.*
śaivaṁ catur-vidham proktaṁ samāsāc chṛṇu ṣaṇmukha.
sāmānyam miśrakam caiva śuddhaṁ vīram yathākramam.

points in common with the *Viśiṣṭādvaita* of R. and the *Śaiva Siddhānta*, it has distinctive features of its own.

Supreme Reality and the World

The Supreme is identified with *Śiva* and there is sufficient support for it in the early Scriptures.[1] *Brahman* is *Śiva* who is to be meditated on by all those who seek release.

Ś. treats I. 1. 2 as a statement of the nature of *Brahman*. R. looks upon it as an attempt to reconcile apparently contradictory statements of the *Upaniṣads*. Śrīkaṇṭha argues that God is *inferred* as the primal source and the supreme Lord of the whole of the material and spiritual universe. *Śiva* is possessed of an infinite number of attributes and inconceivable powers. He is free from all defects and faults. He is gracious towards his devotees. *Śiva* is adored by Śrīkaṇṭha as being of the nature of self-substance in his invocation.[2] He is called *Bhava* because he exists everywhere and at all times, *Śarva* because he destroys everything, *Paśu-pati*, the lord of all creatures, *Rudra* because he removes the sorrows of the world, *Śiva* because he is free from all taints and is supremely auspicious.[3] *Śiva* is the cause of the creation, maintenance and dissolution of the world, of the liberation of souls through the cessation of bondage by his grace, and the concealment of the essential nature of the soul thus causing bondage, *janma, sthiti, pralaya, anugraha* and *tirobhāva*. He is also an enjoyer, not of the fruits of *karma* but of his own infinite bliss. He has a celestial non-material body which is free from subjection to *karma*. All these qualities belong to the world of manifestation and do not constitute the essential nature of *Śiva* and so do not limit him. They indicate the nature of *Brahman* but do not disclose his true nature. The manifested world is the *taṭastha-lakṣaṇa* or temporary quality of *Brahman*. When *māyā* transforms itself into the world by the grace of God, God himself, being eternally associated with *māyā*, may in a sense be regarded also as the material cause of the world though he remains outside *māyā* in his transcendence. *Brahman* exists

[1] See R.V. X. 125. 7: *Atharva-Śiras U.* V. 3.

[2] *aum namo'ham-padārthāya lokānāṁ siddhi-hetave*
sac-cid-ānanda-rūpāya śivāya paramātmane.

[3] I. 1. 2; I. 1. 4.

in a transcendent manner apart from the individual souls and the material world. While God is the instrumental and material cause of the world, he is unaffected by the changes of the latter.[1] God is both the transcendent Supreme and the active cause of the world. The various epithets of *Brahman*, being, consciousness and bliss are qualities and not substance of *Brahman*. If *Brahman* were of the nature of consciousness he could not have transformed himself into the material world. For this would mean that *Brahman* was changeable; this would contradict the view of the *Upaniṣads* that *Brahman* was devoid of action, *niṣkriya*. *Brahman* is not pure consciousness but is endowed with omniscience. He does not depend on any external aid for the execution of his power, *anapekṣita-bāhya-karaṇa*. Though *Brahman* is absolutely unchangeable in himself, his energy undergoes transformation in the creation and dissolution of the world. He has within him the energy of consciousness and the energy of materiality.[2]

During the universal dissolution there is nothing, no sun or moon, no day or night, no names and shapes, no sentient and non-sentient objects. Everything is enveloped in darkness and the Lord with all powers withdraws, abides as a cause, absolute, one without a second, self-luminous. When there arises in him the supreme power of knowledge removing the darkness around, he wishes to be many. Then the subtle powers of the sentient and the non-sentient become manifest. The world is said to be both unborn and an effect. It is unborn since it abides as a subtle power of the Lord; it is an effect in the sense that during creation it is manifested in gross forms.[3] The relation between *Brahman* and the universe is analogous to that between the soul and the body, or that between substance and attribute or that between cause and effect. The soul (*śarīrin*) and the body (*śarīra*) are non-different in the sense that the soul cannot exist without the body and vice versa. It is the same with regard to substance, *guṇin* or *viśeṣya*, and attribute, *guṇa* or *viśeṣaṇa*, as well as cause, *kāraṇa*, and effect, *kārya*. *Brahman* cannot exist

1 *jagad-upādāna-nimitta-bhūtasyāpi parameśvarasya niṣkalam niṣkriyam ityādi-śrutibhir nirvikāratvam apy upapadyate.* See II. 2. 36–8.

2 *cid-acit-prapañca-rūpa-śakti-viśiṣṭatvam svābhāvikam eva brahmaṇaḥ.*

3 I. 1. 4. 10.

without the universe which ever exists in him as his power, just as fire cannot exist without heat or a blue lotus without blueness. The universe cannot exist without *Brahman* even as an earthen jar cannot exist without clay. Non-difference means essential and mutual interdependence and not actual identity.[1] Difference means difference of nature.[2] This peculiar relation enables them to form one whole where one cannot exist without the other.

Appaya Dīkṣita says that God himself is not transformed into the form of the world but his *śakti* or energy manifests itself as the world. This *śakti* is of the very being of God. The world is not an illusion. It is not an attribute of God or limb of God where all activities are dependent on the will of God as R. suggests nor is the relation of the world to God of the nature of waves to the sea.

Brahman is the controller of all sentient entities and non-sentient world.[3] He is both knowledge and knower.[4] *Cit* and *acit*, the sentient and the non-sentient, are the powers of the Lord.[5] *Cit-śakti* consists of three factors, knowledge, *jñāna*, volition, *icchā*, and action, *kriyā*. The *acit-śakti* consists of the elements, earth, water, fire, air and ether.[6] These two together consisting of eight forms constitute the body of the Lord, or the attributes of the Lord qualifying him as the body qualifies the soul or as the colour blue qualifies the blue lotus. The Lord has the universe for his form or body, *prapañca-rūpa*. For Śrīkaṇṭha, *Śiva* is both the material and the efficient cause of the universe. He criticises the views of those *Śaiva* sects which look upon the Lord as merely the efficient cause and not the material cause.[7] When *Śiva* is the material cause through his *māyā* or *icchā-śakti*, he is called *Nārāyaṇa* or *Viṣṇu*. He is subordinate to *Śiva* though non-different from him.[8] Subordinate to *Nārāyaṇa* is *Hiraṇya-garbha* or the aggregate of souls of effects.[9]

The Lord is both the efficient and the material cause of the universe which is the result of the transformation of *Brahman*. This transformation does not imply any change or defect in

[1] *prapañca-brahmaṇor ananyatvam nāma vinā-bhāva-rahitatvam*. II. 1. 22.

[2] II. 1. 22. [3] *anena-cid-acin-niyāmakaṁ brahmeti vijñāyate*. I. 1. 2.

[4] II. 3. 29. [5] I. 2. 9. [6] II. 3. 14. [7] II. 2. 35–8.

[8] *yato viṣṇu-śivayor upādāna-nimittayor avasthā-bhedam antareṇa svarūpa-bhedo nāsti*. I. 1. 6. [9] IV. 3. 14.

Brahman. Brahman's pariṇāma or transformation relates only to his *cit-śakti*, the energy of consciousness. This is the material cause which takes on the form of the world. Sometimes *māyā* is said to be the primal matter or *prakṛti*. *Brahman* associated with *māyā*, i.e. subtle consciousness and subtle materiality, is the cause; the same is the effect in its gross manifestation.[1]

Brahman and the universe are non-different but not identical. *Brahman* is qualified by the world, sentient and non-sentient, *cid-acid-prapañca-viśiṣṭa*.

R. and Śrīkaṇṭha adopt the same view of causation. The process is not the changing of one thing into another but the transforming of the same reality from a subtle to a gross condition. The beings sentient and non-sentient are already there in a subtle condition indistinguishable by name and shape. The manifestation of names and shapes marks the transformation of cause into effect. This view is called by Śrīkaṇṭha *viśiṣṭa-śivādvaita-vāda*. *Śiva* is qualified by the sentient and the non-sentient even as the soul is qualified by the body. While for Nimbārka non-difference and difference are on the same level, for Śrīkaṇṭha non-difference is the principal which is qualified by difference. Difference is subordinate to non-difference, even as the body is subordinate to the soul which it qualifies.

Cit-śakti

The sentient and the non-sentient world is the result of the transformation of the *cit-śakti* or the energy of consciousness of the Supreme Lord who is non-different from it. The first manifestation of *cit-śakti* is *Nārāyaṇa* who is the material cause of the world. He is of the form of the universe, *viśvākāra*. *Brahman* himself who is *Śiva* is the efficient cause. *Brahman* and *cit-śakti* are distinguishable aspects and not separate entities. Between *Brahman* and *cit-śakti* there is non-difference. *Brahman* is unchanging and unaffected by the transformation through *cit-śakti*. *Brahman* as different from *cit-śakti* is only the operative cause. *Brahman* as creator is to be viewed as endowed with *cit-śakti*. On account of the relationship to the Lord

[1] *sūkṣma-cid-acid-viśiṣṭaṁ brahma kāraṇam; sthūla-cid-acid-viśiṣṭaṁ tat-kāryam bhavati*. I. 1. 2.

through *cit-śakti*, the world partakes of the three qualities of being, consciousness and bliss of the Supreme. Particular things are a fraction of the existence of *Brahman* and their knowledge and bliss are fragments of the knowledge and bliss of *Brahman*. The identity of *Brahman* and the finite self is not to be taken literally. The relationship is of the nature binding the body and the embodied, the pervaded and the pervader. When the faggot is lit by fire, we speak of it as fire.

Viśiṣṭa-śivādvaita

Śrīkaṇṭha warns us against three possible views: (i) *atyanta-bheda-vāda*, the view that there is an absolute difference between the Lord and the soul as between a jar and a piece of cloth because this conflicts with scriptural texts which deny difference. (ii) *atyantābheda-vāda*, the view that there is absolute non-difference between the Lord and the soul, because this conflicts with scriptural texts which admit difference between the two. (iii) *abhedā-bheda-vāda*, the view that there is both non-difference and difference for this goes against facts of direct experience. Difference and non-difference are mutually contradictory and cannot coexist. Srīkaṇṭha says: 'We are not among those who maintain absolute difference between *Brahman* and the world as between a jar and a cloth, that being opposed to the texts which declare their non-distinctness; and we are not of those who maintain their absolute non-difference; nor do we declare the illusoriness of one of them as in the case of silver and mother-of-pearl,[1] that being opposed to the texts which declare difference between their natural qualities. Nor are we of those who posit both difference and non-difference, that relationship being opposed to fact. We are, however, of those who maintain the non-dualism of the distinct, as exists between body and the embodied, or between a quality and the qualified.'

For R. *Brahman* is a concrete universal, having matter and consciousness always associated with him and controlled by him as the limbs of a person are controlled by the person

[1] *brahma-prapañcayor na vayam atyanta-bheda-vādino ghaṭa-paṭayor iva tad-ananyatva-para-śruti virodhāt. na cātyantābheda-vādinaḥ. na vā śukti-rajatayor ivaikataramithyātva-vādinaḥ, tat svābhāvika-guṇa-bheda-para-śruti-virodhāt. na ca bhedābheda-vādinaḥ, vastu-virodhāt. kiṁ tu śarīra-śarīriṇor iva guṇa-guṇinor iva ca viśiṣṭādvaita-vādinaḥ.*

himself. In his *Śivādvaita-nirṇaya* Appaya Dīkṣiṭa argues against the identification of Śrīkaṇṭha's philosophy with that of R.'s *viśiṣṭādvaita*. He argues that Śrīkaṇṭha's system was essentially a non-dualism, *Advaita*, though he offers the *visiṣṭādvaita* view for the benefit of those who are incapable of comprehending the absolute non-dual *Brahman*. Śrīkaṇṭha does not criticise the *Advaita* doctrine as R. does but expounds the theistic position.

Appaya Dīkṣita commenting on Śrīkaṇṭha's views argues that *Brahman* differs from the sentient (*cetana*) and non-sentient (*acetana*). These are two forms of energy, *cit-śakti* or energy of consciousness which is responsible for conscious beings and *jaḍa-śakti* which transforms itself in the form of the material universe under the instrumentality of *Brahman*. Both these are manifestations of the energy of God. They are the qualities of God and have no existence separate from the nature of God. The soul is an eternal and real substance, a knower, an enjoyer and an active agent, atomic in size. These qualities pertain to the very nature of the soul and endure in bondage as in release. The soul though intelligent is not omniscient. It has limited knowledge and is subject to defects and faults. Though the souls and the Lord are different, they are not absolutely different. The soul is atomic and is not of the nature of pure consciousness. It possesses knowledge as its permanent quality. It is a real part of *Brahman* and not a false appearance due to limitations of causes and conditions. The individual souls are active agents, doing things by themselves. God only helps the realisation of each one's wishes. He cannot be charged with cruelty or partiality.[1]

Even though *Śiva* is all-merciful, he cannot remove the sorrows of all. It is only when by their own deeds the veil of ignorance and impurity is removed that the mercy of God manifests itself in the liberation of the soul. The laws of nature are the manifestation of the grace of God. By our good deeds we earn the mercy of God. By the proper and disinterested performance of duties we purify the mind and help the rise of knowledge. Though *karma* does not directly lead to salvation, it is an indirect means, for it gives rise to knowledge which leads to meditation and meditation leads to salvation.

[1] Appaya Dīkṣita makes God completely responsible. *tathā ca parameśvara-kārita-pūrva-karma-mūla-svecchādhīne yatne, parameśvarādhīnatvam na hīyate.*

Kinds of Meditation

There are various kinds of meditation. Meditation of the Lord in his own nature leads to liberation directly and immediately. The Lord is meditated on as identical with the self of the devotee which helps to remove the *paśutva* or bondage of the soul and leads to the attainment of *Śivatva*. Sarvajñānottara says: 'He who thinks, I am the self, *Śiva*, the supreme self is, indeed, different or he who because of delusion meditates thus does not attain *śivatva*. Give up the thought of difference, "*Śiva* is other than myself", contemplate them always as not-dual, but in the form, what is *Śiva* that is myself.'[1] There is meditation on *Nārāyaṇa* which leads to the attainment of *Nārāyaṇa* and then to that of the Lord *Śiva*.[2]

Release

The grace of the Lord is an essential prerequisite of salvation. While the soul is under the control of the Lord in the state of bondage, it becomes free in the state of release. Liberation is severance of the bondage of worldly existence[3] and attaining to a similarity with *Śiva*. The freed soul becomes omniscient[4] and independent, possessed of all his auspicious qualities and free from all defects.[5] The freed soul becomes similar to the Lord and not identical with him.[6] It is the full development of the soul[7] and not absorption in *Śiva*. It is distinct from the Lord since it is atomic while the Lord is all-pervading. It lacks the power to create, maintain and destroy the universe which only the Lord has. The freed soul shares all the divine pleasures with the Lord.[8] It possesses pure, independent, non-material sense-organs and mind by which it

[1] *aham ātmā śivohy anyaḥ paramātmeti yaḥ smṛtaḥ*
evam yopāsayen mohāt na śivatvam avāpnuyāt
śivo'nyas tv aham evānyaḥ pṛthag-bhāvaṁ vivarjayet.
yaś śivas so'ham eveti hy advayaṁ bhāvayet sadā.
Śiva-ananya-sākṣātkāra-paṭala. 12, 13.

[2] III. 3. 57.
[3] *pāśa-viccheda* and *paśutva-nivṛtti.*
[4] *saṁsāre kiṁcijjñatvam muktau sarvajñatvam iti jñātā eva ātmā.*
[5] IV. 4. 9.
[6] I. 3. 8.
[7] IV. 4. 21.
[8] *pari-pūrṇāhaṁ bhāvaṁ prakaṭam anubhavati.* This egoity is not like the *prākṛta ahaṁ-kāra* which is narrow but embraces the whole world *prapañcāvagāhin.* IV. 4. 17, 18, 19.

enjoys pleasures. It perceives the diversity of the universe.[1] It is united with the Lord in blissful experience and perceives his form. The liberated soul can remain without a body and enjoy all experiences through mind alone or he can at the same time animate or recreate many spiritual bodies which transcend the laws of *prakṛti* and through them enjoy any happiness he wishes to have. He is not subject to the law of *karma;* he has no rebirth but he retains his personality possessing perfect resemblançe with God, *sārūpya*. Salvation is a positive state of supreme and unsurpassed bliss and knowledge. It is not a state of mere unconsciousness. It can be attained only after the death of the earthly body.[2]

For Śrīkaṇṭha there is no *jīvan-mukti*, liberation in this life. All *karmas* which are ripe for producing fruits will continue to give fruits and do so until the present body falls away. Past *karmas* which have begun to take effect have to run their course till the end of this life. In that state we attain knowledge but not liberation. There are two kinds of salvation, immediate and gradual. Those who meditate on the Supreme Lord in his own nature go directly to the Lord and become free at once. Those who meditate on the Lord as sentient and non-sentient or on *Nārāyaṇa* who is the Lord in the form of the material cause of the universe first go to *Nārāyaṇa* and then to *Śiva*.

Śrīkaṇṭha sometimes says that there is no need for the devotees of the non-related, *niranvayopāsakas* to travel by this path of the gods.[3] Some like Appaya Dīkṣita argue that Śrīkaṇṭha was at heart a non-dualist. The expression *niranvaya* is understood by Appaya Dīkṣita as *niṣ-prapañca*. Śrīkaṇṭha seems to admit the existence of *Brahman* without determinations, *Nir-guṇa Brahman*, though his main purpose is to foster faith in and devotion to Personal God, *Sa-guṇa Brahman*. Śrīkaṇṭha asks us to look upon the Lord as master in relation to servants and adopt the path of service, the *dāsa mārga*, but he admits that those who seek release should meditate on the Lord as one with the self and not as standing in the relationship of the embodied to the body.

[1] *vividhaṁ vastu-jātaṁ paśyanti, vimṛśanti cid yasya saḥ*. III. 2. 16.
[2] IV. 28.
[3] *kecin niranvayopāsakānām iha śarīrapāta eva muktir iti arcirādi-gatim aniyatām āhuḥ*. Śrikaṇṭha on IV. 2. 18.

Śaiva Siddhānta

Ś. mentions the name of *Siddhānta-śāstra* composed by *Śiva* himself.[1] He refers to the three categories of *pati*, the lord, *paśu*, the creature, and *pāśa*, the bond. The purpose of creation is to enable the souls to purify and perfect themselves. The *paśu* is in bondage and the *pāśa* can be scotched only by union with *pati*, the Lord. These views were adopted by the *Śaiva Siddhānta* and the *Pāśupata* schools. The *pati* is *Śiva* who is called *Rudra*. Umā-pati who lived in the early half of the fourteenth century says that *Śiva* is the Supreme Being who is neither permanently manifested nor unmanifested, without qualities, without impurities. The *Pāśupata* system deals with five categories, the cause (*kāraṇa*), effect (*kārya*), union with God (*yoga*), rules of conduct (*vidhi*) and end of sorrow (*duhkhānta*). For this system *Paśu-pati*, God is the instrumental cause of the world. The *Naiyāyikas* and the *Vaiśeṣikas* adopt a similar view of God's causality.[2]

Between Śrīkaṇṭha's view and the *Śaiva Siddhānta* there are some differences. The *āṇava mala* or the power which obscures of the *Śaiva Siddhānta* is called *avidyā* by Śrīkaṇṭha. *Śaiva Siddhānta* makes a distinction between *cit-śakti* and *māyā*. Śrīkaṇṭha accepts the *tādātmya* view that the One Reality appears as *guṇin* and *guṇa*, substance and attribute, while the *Śaiva Siddhānta* means by *tādātmya* the close connection of two things which might be regarded as one. The soul is atomic, *aṇu*, for Śrīkaṇṭa while for *Śaiva Siddhānta* it is all-pervading, *vibhu*. Śrīkaṇṭha does not adopt the view attributed to Śaivāgamas that God is only the instrumental cause. For him, as we have seen, he is also the material cause.

For *Śaiva Siddhānta*, the soul is pure consciousness (*cin-mātra*) covered with impurities. It is all-pervading in space and time and goes through the cycle of birth and rebirth. Its nature is both *jñāna* and *kriyā*. It is pure consciousness which appears as distinct on account of the impurities, the *pāśas* with which it is covered. The *malas* or impurities do not affect the purity of

[1] II. 2. 37.

[2] R. mentions *Kāpālikas* and *Kāla-mukhas* as being sects of *Śaivism* which are of an anti-Vedic character (*veda-bāhya*). Ānandagiri's *Śaṁkara-vijaya* mentions the *Kāpālikas* as being outside the pale of the *Vedas*.

the consciousness even as gold is not affected by the dross with which it is associated. The impurities can be removed not by knowledge but by the grace of *Śiva*. The *malas* bind us differently on account of different kinds of *karma*. The obscurations of *mala* differentiate the different souls which are all basically one with *Śiva*. Liberation does not mean transformation. It is only the removal of the impurities, the *malas* on account of which the different individual entities pass through the cycle of *saṁsāra*.

G. NIMBĀRKA

Nimbārka was a Telugu Brahman who was born in Nimba or Nimbapura in the Bellary district but lived in Brindāvana.[1] He was a lifelong celibate, *naiṣṭhika-brahma-cārin*. He seems to be indebted largely to R.'s *bhāṣya* and criticises Śrīkaṇṭha's views. His date may be about the latter half of the thirteenth century.

Literature

Nimbārka's main works are *Vedānta-pārijāta-saurabha*, which is his commentary on the B.S., *Daśa-ślokī* or *Siddhānta-ratna* and *Sa-viśeṣa-nir-viśeṣa śri-Kṛṣṇa-stava-rāja*. He has also written a number of *stotras*. His direct disciple Śrīnivāsa wrote a commentary on Nimbārka's work, called *Vedānta-kaustubha*. Keśava Kāṣmīrin wrote a work on *Vedānta-Kaustubha* called the *Vedānta-Kaustubha-prabhā*.

Bhedābheda-vāda

There are texts which affirm duality between *Brahman* and the individual souls and others which affirm their non-duality. We can reconcile these conflicting texts by adopting the *bhedābheda* or the *dvaitādvaita-vāda* to which we have references in the B.S.

According to Nimbārka there are three equally real and coeternal realities (*tri-tattva*), *Brahman*, *cit* and *acit*. While *Brahman* is the controller, *niyantṛ*, *cit* is the enjoyer, *bhoktṛ*, and *acit* is the enjoyed, *bhogya*. *Acit* or non-sentient reality is of

[1] There is also a view that he was born in Brindāvana on the Yamunā river.

three kinds, (i) *prākṛta* or what is derived from *prakṛti* or primal matter, (ii) *aprākṛta* or what is not derived from *prakṛti* but derived from a non-material substance of which the world of *Brahman* is made and (iii) *kāla* or time. There is a difference of nature between them, *svarūpa-bheda*. Souls and matter, *cit* and *acit*, have a dependent reality, *para-tantra-tattva*.

Nimbārka adopts the view of *svābhāvika-bhedābheda*. Difference and non-difference are both equally real. They coexist but do not contradict each other. The relation between the one and the many is like the sea and its waves[1] or the sun and its rays. *Cit* and *acit*, the souls and the universe, exist in *Brahman* from all eternity and do not become separate from him even when manifested. They retain their specific natures. *Brahman* has a *kāraṇa-rūpa* when he is pure cause without producing any effects, i.e. during the time of universal dissolution. Even in the causal state, he is not absolutely undifferenced or *nir-viśeṣa*, a pure unity or a bare identity. *Brahman* is always *sa-viśeṣa*. *Cit* and *acit* are never absolutely merged in *Brahman*. They retain their individuality and separateness even during salvation and dissolution. God is separated from everything and inseparable from everything. *Brahman* is both transcendent and immanent. *Brahman* is personal, possessed of a celestial body, full of divine beauty and grace. He is *bhakta-vatsala*, a god of love and grace. Nimbārka identifies *Brahman* with *Kṛṣṇa*. For R.'s *Viṣṇu* and *Lakṣmī*, we have in Nimbārka *Kṛṣṇa* and *Rādhā*. *Brahman* assumes earthly forms to help the world.

Brahman is the omniscient, the cause of the origin, sustenance and destruction of the universe. He is all-powerful and all-merciful. While R. insists on the incomparable greatness (*aiśvarya*) of the Lord, Nimbārka lays stress on the sweetness (*mādhurya*). *Brahman* is gracious to his devotees and helps them to have a direct vision of himself.

Scriptural Authority

Brahman, possessed of inconceivable energies, is apprehended through the authority of Scripture. We cannot know the truth

[1] *avibhāgepi samudra-taraṅgayor iva sūrya-tat-prabhayor iva vibhāgas syāt.* II. I. 13.

of things by our own limited powers of perception and inference. We have to rely on Scripture for our knowledge of *Brahman.* Scripture is the record of the experiences of great seers who have attained the power to realise God directly.

Brahman and the World

Brahman's relation to *cit* and *acit* is not one of substance and attribute as is the case with R. but is that of cause and effect. The impure *cit* and *acit* cannot be parts of *Brahman. Brahman* is the material and efficient cause of the universe of souls and matter.[1] The material and efficient causes are ordinarily different from one another. In the case of the jar made of clay, clay is the material cause and the potter is the efficient cause. *Prakṛti* is said to be the cause of all material objects. But according to Nimbārka's follower, Puruṣottama, *prakṛti* is said to be a power or *śakti* of *Brahman.* In his *Vedānta-ratna-manjūṣā,* Puruṣottama observes that creation is the manifestation of the subtle powers of *cit* and *acit* in the form of gross effects. In *pralaya* or dissolution they remain in a subtle state and in *sṛṣṭi* or creation they become manifest. The universe is a real transformation, *pariṇāma,* of *Brahman. Brahman* is greater than the world which is not a complete or exhaustive manifestation of *Brahman. Acit* is *prakṛti* or primal matter. The presence of *cit* and *acit* in *Brahman* does not affect his nature.

Why should the perfect *Brahman,* who can have no motive, no unfulfilled desire create the world? Nimbārka says that he does so in sport, out of the abundance of his joy. Creation does not indicate any insufficiency in *Brahman.* The word *līlā* or sport does not indicate any arbitrariness or irrationality.

Souls and their destiny

Nimbārka believes in an infinite number of souls. Each of them is a distinctive agent, a knower (*jñātṛ*), doer (*kartṛ*) and enjoyer (*bhoktṛ*). The soul is atomic in size and is said to pass out of the body through such small openings as the eye, etc. Though atomic in size, its attribute of knowledge pervades the whole body and is capable of experiencing the various states of

[1] C.U. VI. 2. 3.

the body even as a small lamp can flood a large room with its light.

Nimbārka criticises the doctrine of the all-pervasiveness of the soul. If it were so we would have eternal perception or eternal non-perception. Either it is in connection with all objects when it will have eternal perception or it is not in connection with all objects, when it will have eternal non-perception and there will not be anything outside to bring about any connection. Human individuals undergo experiences in accordance with their past conduct. There are three kinds of destiny for the soul, *svarga* or heaven, *naraka* or hell and *apavarga* or release. The sinners go to hell; the virtuous go to heaven and the knowers go to the world of *Brahman* and are not bound to return any more to *saṁsāra*. They are the released souls. Release is not the annihilation of the individual but is the full development of one's nature, *ātma-svarūpa-lābha*.

One attains freedom by the ceaseless reflection on *Brahman* as the deepest self of the individual soul; not in the sense of absolute identity but in the sense of identity in difference.[1] Freedom is the attainment of the nature of *Brahman, tad-bhāvāpatti* or *brahma-svarūpa-lābha*. As the difference between *Brahman* and the soul is natural and eternal, it persists even in the state of release. In the state of release the individual is not merged in God. When the soul attains its full development, it becomes similar to and not one with the Supreme. The goal is fellowship with the Supreme through the bond of mutual love. The freed soul is both different and non-different from *Brahman*. It is different because its individuality is not lost; it is non-different because it is dependent on and an organic part of *Brahman*. It has the attributes of being, consciousness and bliss and is free from the defects of sin, pain and suffering. It is still atomic in size while *Brahman* is all-pervading. The freed soul has not the power to create, maintain and dissolve the world. Even in the state of release the soul has the power to move about freely and realise its aims. Souls in bondage are attached to material bodies and are subject to rebirth according to their past deeds. The released souls are freed from connection with *karma* and are not liable to be born in the world of *saṁsāra*.

[1] *mumukṣuṇā parama-puruṣaḥ svasya ātmatvena dhyeyaḥ*. IV. 1. 3.

Release is possible only after death. There is no *jīvan-mukti* according to Nimbārka. So long as the material body persists, release is not possible.

The way to salvation is by means of the five *sādhanas*, work, knowledge, devotion and meditation, surrender to God and obedience to the spiritual preceptor. One can undertake the inquiry into *Brahman* only after a study of the Vedic duties leading to different kinds of beneficial results. The function of *karma* is to purify the mind and help the rise of knowledge. Even after the rise of knowledge, the various duties of the different stages of life have to be observed.[1] When we realise that these results of *karma* are different from eternal bliss we attempt to attain *Brahman* through the grace of God. *Brahman* is to be meditated on as *Kṛṣṇa* along with *Rādhā*.[2]

While both R. and Nimbārka hold that the world is real like *Brahman* and is both different and non-different from it, the emphasis is more on non-difference in R. and on both difference and non-difference in Nimbārka.[3]

H. ŚRĪPATI

Śrīpati Paṇḍit, an Andhra Brahmin of Vijayavāda, lived about the latter half of the fourteenth century,[4] and wrote a commentary on the B.S. defending *dvaitādvaita*, unity in duality. He calls his doctrine *viśeṣādvaita dvaitādvaitābhidhāna, bhedābhedātmaka* and is opposed to *Pāśupata* dualism. It is different from

[1] *tasmāt vidyodayāya svāśrama-karmāgnihotrādi-rūpaṁ gṛhasthena, tapojapādīni karmāṇi ūrdhva-retobhir anuṣṭheyāni iti siddham. Vedānta-kaustubha-prabhā.*

[2] This view is to be found not in *Vedānta-pārijāta-saurabha* but in *Daśa-ślokī*.

Jayadeva (twelfth century) described in his *Gīta-govinda* the longing of the human soul for union with the Divine through the love of *Rādhā* and *Kṛṣṇa*. The soul which is divine in its essence longs for union with the Divine from which it is separated by the feeling of individuality and it yearns to return to its original source. Jayadeva had remarkable skill in blending sounds and feelings. Vidyāpati (A.D. 1368–1475) was his follower in poetry though not in religion.

[3] *brahmābhinnopi kṣetrajñaḥ sva-svarūpato bhinna eva.*

[4] Śrīpati refers to Śrīkaṇṭha's *bhāṣya* on B.S. II. 1. 22; III. 2. 8 and is therefore later than Śrikaṇṭha.

pariṇāma-vāda and *vivarta-vāda*. Śrīpati's view combines the *bheda* and the *abheda* views on the analogy of the serpent and its coils or the sun and its rays. There are *advaita* texts like *tat tvam asi* and *dvaita* texts like two birds dwelling on the same tree. If we are not to violate the two sets of texts, we must adopt *dvaitādvaita*. His work is the philosophical basis of *Vīra-śaivism*.[1] Śrīpati's *bhāṣya* is called *Śrīkara-bhāṣya* for Śrīpati wrote it not in his own name but in the name of Śrīkara or Śivakara, for *Śiva* is said to have inspired him to write this work.[2] Śrīpati is a *vīra-śaiva*. *Vīra-śaivas* accept the twenty-eight *Śaiva Āgamas* and the *Śiva-gītā*. Śrīpati does not accept the validity of the Tantric *āgamas* and rites, which R. does.[3] He is also opposed to the Tantric doctrines of *Pāśupatas*.[4]

Unity in Duality

This doctrine of unity in duality has had a long history. It goes back to a period prior to the composition of the B.S. Ś. criticises a similar theory attributed to Bhartṛ-prapañca.[5] According to Professor M. Hiriyanna, Reality for Bhartṛ-prapañca is *bhedābheda* or difference and non-difference. The relation of *Brahman* to the world is analogous to that of snake and its coils or the sun and its radiance. The cause is immanent in the effect. He adopts *pariṇāma* or transformation as against *vivarta* or appearance. *Brahman*, who is one without a second, becomes *Īśvara*, God and the worlds of souls and material objects. The *jīva* or the individual soul is a mode of *Brahman* and not an illusory appearance. Bhartṛ-prapañca adopts *jñāna-karma-samuccaya* or co-ordination of knowledge and work as the means to liberation. This doctrine co-ordinates experience and Scripture. We have *pramāṇa-samuccaya*. Bhāskara and

[1] Cp. *vi-śabdaṁ vā vikalpārthe va-śabdo vahitārthakaḥ*
vikalpa-rahitaṁ śaivam vīra-śaivaṁ pracakṣate.

[2] Baladeva's commentary is called *Govinda-bhāṣya* for he says that it was written at the command of Govinda.
bhāṣyam etad viracitam baladevena dhīmatā
śrī-govinda-nideśena govindākhyām agāt tataḥ.

[3] *paribhāṣā-pradhāna-rāmānuja-śāstraṁ veda-mūlatvābhāvāt avaidikam iti ghaṇṭāghoṣaḥ.* II. 2. 42.

[4] *pāñca-rātrādivat pāśupatyāgamānām nirastatvāt.*

[5] See Ś. on B.U. V. 1. 1.

Yādava Prakāśa, who adopt varieties of this doctrine, are criticised by R.[1]

Śrīpati attacks the materialist (*cārvāka*) view that life is a product of material forces. Life cannot be a product of non-life. Even as a temple has a builder, the world also must have had a builder. Vedic texts declare the reality of *Brahman* as *Śiva*. *Brahman* is different from the world of gross and subtle forms.[2] *Brahman* is identified with *Para-śiva* or *Parama-śiva* who has two forms undivided (*a-dvitīya*) and divided (*dvitīya*). In the latter he has *pradhāna*.[3] *Śiva*, though endowed with the three *guṇas*, is different from the three *guṇas*, or *triguṇātmaka-hetu-bhūta-pradhāna-śakti*, or the threefold creative power. *Śiva* is *nir-guṇa* when, prior to creation, he withdraws all his powers within himself; he is *sa-guṇa* when he expands the powers and is about to create the world.

Śiva is the efficient and material cause of the world. The two are non-different but not one.[4] *Śiva*, through his *cit-śakti*, creates the world.[5] The energy that manifests itself is in *Brahman*. The *ṣaṭ-sthala para-śiva Brahman* is the primal cause of everything.[6] God is indistinguishable from his energies even as the sun cannot be distinguished from his rays. In the original state when there was no world God alone existed, and the world of multiplicity existed in a subtle form wholly indistinguishable from him. When the idea of creation moves him he separates the living beings and makes them different, being associated with different kinds of *karma*. Everything we see in the world is real and has *Śiva* for his substratum.

Criticism of Māyā

Śrīpati criticises the view of the differenceless *Brahman* and the world-appearance. The differenceless *Brahman* can be established only on the authority of Scripture or inference but these are included within the conceptual world of distinctions and cannot take us beyond it to a differenceless *Brahman*. If

[1] R. on B.S. II. I. 15.

[2] *sthūla-sūkṣma-prapañca-vyāvṛtta*.

[3] *śivādhīna-pradhāna-vikāsa-sad-bhāve*.

[4] *abhinna-nimittopādāna-kāraṇatvaṁ na tu eka-kāraṇatvam*.

[5] *bhedābhedātmikā śaktiḥ brahma-niṣṭhā sanātanī*.

[6] *sarva-kāraṇa, vedānta-vedya, pūrva-parāmṛṣṭa-ṣaṭ-sthala-para-śiva-brahmaiva*.

Brahman has *avidyā* as its quality it would cease to be *Brahman*. If *avidyā* belongs to *Brahman*, there ought to be some other entity by whose action *avidyā* is removed. There are many texts which speak of a Personal God. So a differenceless *Brahman* is a wrong assumption. How can a formless *Brahman* be reflected through *māyā* or *avidyā*? If the Personal God, *Īśvara*, is a reflection in *māyā* or *avidyā*, then the destruction of the latter will mean the destruction of God and the individual soul. We must admit that *Brahman* appears in two forms as pure consciousness and as the world. Scriptural texts support *Brahman* with form and without form. The Personal God cannot be mere appearance. An apparent object cannot bestow benefits or be the object of devotion.

There is nothing that can establish the fact of the world-appearance. It exists and fulfils our needs. It is not something which appears without an underlying reality. The world has a substratum. If the appearance is regarded as different from the substratum, we fall into the error of duality. The world has a definite order and system. It is the basis of our knowledge and behaviour. Even dream experiences are real. They are not created by the individual through his personal effort. They are created by God and are not wholly unrelated to the objects of life. They indicate luck or ill-luck in life. Even deep sleep, *suṣupti*, is produced by God when we enter into the network of nerves in the heart. We do not become merged in *Brahman*. When we wake up we remember our past. B.S.[1] repudiates the idea of the non-existence of an external world. The texts that speak of the world as being made up of names and shapes do not lead to the view that *Brahman* alone is real and the world is an appearance. In whatever form the world may appear, it is in reality nothing but *Śiva*.[2]

The manifold world which has come out of *Brahman* is one with him. It cannot be regarded as the body of *Brahman* for the Scriptures declare that in the beginning only pure being existed. The world and *Brahman* are distinct from each other and one cannot be said to be a part of the other. The texts teach

[1] II. 2. 27–8.

[2] *vācārambhaṇa-śrutīnām śivopādānatvāt prapañcasya tad-tādātmya-bodhakatvam vidhīyate, na ca mithyātvam*. I. 1. 1.

both duality and non-duality. The world is different from and identical with *Brahman*. There is no question of the false imposition of the one on the other. Śrīpati repudiates Ś.'s theory of world-appearance and formless *Brahman* as unworthy of acceptance.[1]

Śrīpati takes his stand on the *bhedābheda* texts used also by Bhāskara and R., which state that the relation between God and the world is similar to that between the ocean and the waves. Commenting on I. 4. 22 Śrīpati says that Bādarāyaṇa's view is the *bhedābheda* view of Kāśakṛtsna. The world exists in a subtle form and is developed into gross existence through the power of *Śiva*.[2] He is beyond all worlds and is possessed of all powers. There is nothing impossible for him. The *pradhāna* power is treated as a *bhinna-śakti* while the *cit śakti* is said to be *abhinna-śakti*. *Śiva* remains unaltered in all the three stages of time.[3]

Though God transforms himself into the material world he does not exhaust himself in creation. The greater part of him is transcendent. The individual soul, *jīva*, is beginningless, *anādi*, atomic (*aṇu*), bound down by *māyā* (*māyā-pāśa-baddha*), caught in the whirl of *saṁsāra* (*ghora-apāra-nissāra-saṁsāra-vyāpāra*), subject to the three kinds of passion (*tāpa-traya*) and so subject to birth and death (*nānā-śarīra-praveśa-nirgama*). It is possessed of self-conceit (*abhimāna-visiṣṭa*), leading to attachment and anger (*kāma-krodha*) resulting in happiness and misery (*sukha-duḥkha*). The *jīva* has power of understanding and can act independently. It has the capacity to realise *Brahman*.

Release

When the *jīva* is freed from the fetters of the three *guṇas*, it is freed and becomes one with *Śiva*. Then the *advaita* state prevails. So long as the *jīva* is fettered, he is separate from *Śiva* and the *dvaita* condition is true. The freed soul has no body subject

[1] *smārtān sarva-mata-bhraṣṭān jagan-mithyātva-sādhakān*
gaṇikācāra-sampannān pāṣaṇḍān pari-varjayet. I. 1. 20.

[2] *parcchinna-śakti-viśiṣṭe niravayave jīvātmani sva-manaś-śaktyā vicitra-nānā-vidha-brahmāṇḍa-kalpanām upapannam*.

[3] *kāla-trayepi eka-rūpatayā sthitaḥ*.

to *karma*. The body which he assumes to attain *kailāsa* is non-natural and effulgent like that of *Parameśvara*[1] and is free from causes that make for unhappiness.[2] He is of true resolve, *satya-saṁkalpa* and has no lord over him, *ananyādhipati*. He is as independent as *Śiva* himself, *śivavat svatantraḥ*. The freed souls assume the form of *Śiva* (*śiva-sārūpya*), are omniscient and free from self-conceit (*abhimāna*). They have *Śiva's* own form but still worship him even in the state of release.

Jīva and *Brahman* are different from each other in the state of bondage;[3] in the state of release, the *jīva* is not different from *Brahman*.[4] The intuition of *Brahman*, *brahma-sākṣātkāra*, cannot be had by a study of the *Upaniṣads*. The grace of God and the grace of the *guru* are also needed. By knowledge and devotion we may attain to the supreme state.[5] By *upāsana*, *dhyāna*, *dhāraṇa* and *jñāna* the earthly sheath is cast off and *Śivatva* is reached. Caste distinctions are not insisted on by the *Vīra-śaivas*. Vedic duties are compulsory in all stages of life.[6]

Those who worship *Śiva* go to *Śiva;* those who worship other forms of *Brahman* than *Śiva* go to them.[7] In the interests of devotees God takes all the forms in which we find him.[8] Devotees who meditate on the *mūrta* and *amūrta* forms of *Brahman* realise both these states. Śrīpati points out that on the analogy of *bhramara-kīṭa-nyāya*, by faith, devotion and meditation, the individual soul attains the nature of *Śiva*.[9] The formless *Brahman* can be obtained by means of the worship of personal forms, *sa-guṇopāsanā*. By meditating on *Nīla-kaṇṭha* the supreme three-eyed Lord helped by *Umā*, the saint will

[1] *aprākṛta-jyotir-mayatvena parameśvara-śarīravat.*

[2] *na duḥkha-hetuḥ.*

[3] *svābhāvika-bhinnatvam.*

[4] *tadvad abhinnatvam.*

[5] *jñānaṁ vastu paricchetti dhyānaṁ tat-bhāva-kāraṇam*
tasmāt jīvo bhavet śambhuḥ krimivat kīṭa-cintanāt.

[6] III. 4. 2.

[7] Śrīpati quotes the following *smṛti* text:
śivam bhajanti ye narāḥ śivaṁ vrajanti te narāḥ
śivetaraṁ bhajanti ye sivetaraṁ vrajanti te.

[8] *bhaktānugrahārtham ghṛta-kāṭhinyavad divya-maṅgala-vigraha-dharasya maheśvarasya mūrtāmūrta-prapañca-kalpane apy adoṣaḥ.* I. 1. 2.

[9] *śraddhā-bhakti-dhyāna-yogād avehi' ityādau bhramara-kīṭavat parameś-varopāsanātmaka-dhyāna-jñāna-vaśāt jīvasya śiva-tattva-prāptim upadeśāt.* I. 1. 4.

attain *Śiva*, the origin of created things, who is beyond darkness.[1]

The six positions in the progress of the aspirant aiming at the attainment of freedom from bondage are said to be *ṣaṭ-sthala*.[2] *Ṣaṭ-sthala* is the connecting link between the individual soul and the Supreme Reality. It marks the six stages which signify the acquisition of knowledge which leads to *sāmarasya* or equality with *Brahman*. They are named *bhakti, maheśa, prasāda, prāṇa-liṅga śarana, aikya*. *Śiva* is worshipped as *liṅga*.[3] the symbol which is said to transcend space.

While the worship of *Hari* and *Hara*, *Viṣṇu* and *Śiva* was generally adopted, still in some periods rivalries were pronounced. Haradattācārya's work on *Hari-hara-tāratamyam* is a case in point. The joint worship of *Viṣṇu* and *Śiva* in the form of *Hari-hara* is advised in the well-known Devangere inscription dated A.D. 1224.

I. VALLABHA

Vallabha belongs to the latter part of the fifteenth century.[4] He wrote a commentary on the B.S. called the *Aṇu-bhāṣya*, the small commentary as distinct from the *Bṛhad-bhāṣya*, or the large commentary, which has not come down to us. Like Madhva and Jīva Gosvāmin, Vallabha holds the *Bhāgavata Purāṇa* in high esteem. He wrote a commentary on it called the

[1] *umā-sahāyam parameśvaram prabhuṁ tri-locanaṁ nīla-kaṇṭhaṁ praśāntam*
dhyātvā munir gacchati bhūta-yoniṁ samasta-sākṣiṁ tamasaḥ parastāt.
Kaivalya U. 7.

[2] I. 1. 3.

[3] *līyante yatra bhūtāni nir-gacchanti punaḥ punaḥ.*
tena liṅgam paraṁ vyoma niṣkalaḥ paramaś śivaḥ.

Liṅgam līnam gamayati yat, the unseen background of the universe. Anyone initiated in the *Pāśupata-vrata* wears not only *bhasma* but *liṅga*:

liṅgāṅga-saṅginām caiva punar-janma na vidyate
yeṣā pāśupato yogaḥ paśu-pāśa nivṛttaye
sarva-vedānta-sāroyam atyāśrama iti śrutiḥ.

He who wears the *liṅga* on his body will have no more rebirth. This wearing of the *liṅga* is the *pāśupata yoga* by which we destroy the animal created by bondage. This is the essence of the *Vedānta*, the meaning of *atyāśrama* of the *śruti*.

[4] His dates are given as A.D. 1479–1531 or 1481–1533.

Subodhinī. In his *Aṇu-bhāṣya*, he uses not only the *Upaniṣads*, the B.G. and the B.S., but also the *Bhāgavata*. His commentary is available only up to III. 2. 33 and it was completed by his second son Viṭṭala-nātha. He himself was a follower of Viṣṇu-svāmin (fourteenth century) who is reputed to be the founder of *Viśuddhādvaita*. Viṣṇu-svāmin is said to have written a commentary on the B.S. called *Sarvajña-sūkta*. There is a legend that Viṣṇu-svāmin's successors were Jñāna-deva, Nāma-deva, Tri-locana and Vallabha. Possibly Viṣṇu-svāmin lived about the end of the thirteenth century. He follows Madhva's views except that he advocates the worship of *Rādhā* along with that of *Kṛṣṇa*. In his commentary on the *Bhāgavata Purāṇa* called *Subodhinī*,[1] Vallabha states the view of Viṣṇu-svāmin as propounding a distinction between *Brahman* and the world through the qualities of *sattva, rajas* and *tamas* while he holds that *Brahman* is devoid of qualities.[2] Vallabha's *śuddhādvaita* is distinct from Ś.'s system which he regards as impure on account of its use of the doctrine of *māyā*.

Ultimate Reality

For Vallabha, the Supreme is *Kṛṣṇa*, known as *Brahman* in the *Upaniṣads*, one without a second, being, awareness and bliss, *sac-cid-ānanda*. He is free from all differences, internal or external. There are three forms of *Brahman*: (i) *Para-Brahman, Puruṣottama* or *Kṛṣṇa*, (ii) *Antar-yāmin*, the principle dwelling in the finite souls, (iii) *Akṣara-Brahman*, which is the object of meditation which is regarded as the abode of *Kṛṣṇa*. The *Akṣara* appears as *prakṛti* and *puruṣa* and is the cause of everything. It is higher than *puruṣa* and *prakṛti* and includes innumerable worlds. While *Puruṣottama* is the highest, *Akṣara Brahman* is one expression of it. It appears in four forms: (1) *akṣara*, (2) *kāla* or time, (3) *karman* or action, (4) *svabhāva* or nature. Time is regarded as a form of God. It is supra-sensible and is inferred from the nature of effects, *kāryānumeya*. It is all-pervasive and the cause and support of all things. It is the first cause that disturbs the equilibrium of the *guṇas*.

[1] III. 32. 37.

[2] *te ca sāmpratam̐ viṣṇu-svāmy-anusāriṇaḥ tattva-vādino rāmānujaś ca tamo-rajas-sattvair bhinnā asmat-pratipāditāc ca nairguṇya-vādasya.*

Karma or action is also universal. It manifests itself as different actions in different men.

A third category is *svabhāva*. It is that which produces change.[1] These are eternal principles which are one with God. The souls, the material world and the indwelling spirit are three forms of God and not different from him.[2] The universe consists of these three elements. Inanimate objects have only *sat* or being; consciousness and bliss are absent. The animate creation *jīva* has being and consciousness but not bliss. *Kṛṣṇa*, the Supreme Being, has all the three qualities, being, consciousness and bliss.

God is both agent and non-agent. He cannot be known through the *pramāṇas;* yet is he known when he wills. God is the changeable as well as the unchangeable. He is not *sa-guṇa* or possessed of qualities for the simple reason that the qualities do not stand against him depriving him of his independence. He is the controller of the qualities and so their existence and non-existence depend on him. He is both *sa-guṇa* and *nir-guṇa*.

God has the power to become anything at any time through what is known as his *māyā-śakti*. He is the creator of everything and is the material and efficient cause of the world.[3] God does not create by using *prakṛti* but through his own nature. He is the *samavāya* and the *nimitta-kāraṇa* of the world. Vallabha holds that *Brahman* is the inherent cause or *samavāyī-kāraṇa* since *Brahman* exists everywhere in his tripartite nature as being, consciousness and bliss. *Brahman* manifests his three characters in different proportions in matter, soul and *Brahman*. He is present in his fullness in all objects though he manifests his qualities in different degrees. Multiplicity does not involve any change for it is the one identity that is manifested in varying forms. *Māyā* is the power of *Brahman* and is not different from *Brahman*.[4] The cause, *Brahman*, and the effect, the world, are the same. Though unmanifest and transcendent by creating the world, he becomes manifest and the object of comprehension. The world being a manifestation of *Brahman* is never destroyed

[1] *pariṇāma-hetutvaṁ tal-lakṣaṇam.*

[2] *sa-jātīya-vi-jātīya-sva-gata-dvaita-varjitam sa-jātīyā jīvā, vi-jātīyā jaḍāḥ, sva-gata antar-yāminaḥ; triṣv api bhagavān anusyūtas tri-rūpaś ca bhavatīti. tair nirūpitaṁ dvaitaṁ bhedas tad-varjitam. Tattvārtha-dīpa.*

[3] I. 1. 4.

[4] *māyāyāpi bhagavac-chaktitvena śaktimad-abhinnatvāt.* Puruṣottama's *Prasthāna-ratnākara*, p. 159.

except when the Lord wishes to take it back into himself. The world comes out of the very nature (*svarūpa*) of *Brahman* and not out of *māyā* as Ś. thinks or the body as R. suggests or power or *śakti* as Nimbārka holds. To think that *Brahman* appears as the world through the bondage of *avidyā* is to lower the dignity of God. Vallabha upholds the doctrine of the transformation of the nature of God, *svarūpa-pariṇāma,* though he says that this change does not affect the integrity of *Brahman*. It is *a-vikṛta-pariṇāma*. Vallabha does not argue the point but accepts it on the authority of the Scripture. The nature of *Brahman* can be known only through the testimony of Scripture. In this view Vallabha is in agreement with Bhāskara and R.

Creation

Though God is self-sufficient, he creates the world as his *līlā* or sport. He delights in creation and in withdrawing it within himself. He is related to the world as the spider to its web. Though everything in the world is *Brahman*, different qualities manifest themselves in different objects at the will of the Supreme and are called by different names. On account of ignorance, objects are not seen in their true form but are seen as possessing imaginary attributes. Bondage is the effect of this ignorance, *vyāmohikā-māyā*.

God manifests himself as many through *māyā*. The manifestation is not an error or illusion. It is a real manifestation of God in diverse forms and in partial aspects. Though he is identical with knowledge and bliss he appears as the possessor of them. *Māyā* is not the original cause. It serves to make God manifest himself in the world. It also creates the diversity of the grades of existence as higher and lower. When the multiplicity shuts us away from the reality of God, *māyā* is called *avidyā*. When subject to it, individuals feel that they have a separate existence and thus become subject to bondage. When they are freed from *avidyā*, they become pure intelligence though they have no power to control the affairs of the universe.

Individual Souls

The individual souls come out of *Akṣara Brahman* like sparks from fire. *Brahman* is the support of the *jīva;* all activities of the *jīva* are under the control of *Brahman*. *Brahman* and *jīva* are real, one being the support and the other the supported. The self is one though it appears as many when it becomes associated with diverse kinds of ignorance and limits itself by the objects of knowledge. The notion of the self as doer and enjoyer is due to misconception. If the self were not naturally free, it would not be possible to liberate it by any means. The souls are eternal parts of *Brahman*. Though atomic in size, they pervade the whole body by their intelligence. They are of three classes, *puṣṭi*, *maryāda* and *pravāha*. The first class are the chosen ones who enjoy the grace of God and are ardently devoted to him. The second are devoted to God and worship him through the study of the Scriptures. The last are engrossed in worldly desires and do not think of God.

For the *jīva* to enjoy all blessings along with *Brahman*, it is necessary that it should possess all attributes as *Brahman*. The *jīva* is made in the image of *Brahman*. It is not *ānanda-maya* but when it attains *brahma-knowledge* it enjoys *ānanda*. It does not become *ānanda-maya* for then it would be the creator of worlds like *Brahman*. The Supreme who is *ānanda-maya* gives bliss to the *jīvas* and cannot itself be the *jīva*. There is always a distinction between the giver and the receiver, the attained and the attainer. For the individual to know itself as pure intelligence, *yoga* or knowledge by special vision is essential.

Release and the Way to it

Vallabha holds that the knower of *Brahman* is absorbed in *Akṣara Brahman* and not in *Puruṣottama*. If knowledge is associated with devotion the seeker is absorbed in *Puruṣottama*. There is a still higher stage where the Lord gives to some souls divine bliss. They share the joy of his company, *nitya-līlā*.

Bhakti, of which Vallabha gives a detailed analysis, is the only means to salvation. By it we reach release from birth and rebirth. The state of *bhakti* when we enjoy God with all our senses and mind is better even than release. *Bhakti*, for Vallabha, is *premā* and *sevā*, love and service. Through intense attachment to the Supreme one perceives him in all things, for they are all manifestations of God. *Bhakti* produces *sarvātma-bhāva*.

There are two forms of *bhakti*, *maryāda-bhakti* which is attainable by one's own efforts and *puṣṭi-bhakti* which is attainable by the grace of God alone, without one's own effort. Vallabha adopts the latter position. Those who adopt this way gain release through the grace of the Supreme. They are elected by God whether they have acquired the requisite qualifications or not. This way demands complete surrender to the Supreme. Vallabha does not advocate renunciation or *saṁnyāsa*. Renunciation follows from *bhakti* out of necessity and not out of a sense of duty. The path of knowledge brings its results after many births. The way of *bhakti* is preferable.

Sūr Das (A.D. 1483–1563) was Vallabha's chief disciple and he popularised Vallabha's teaching. Mīrā Bāi (A.D. 1498–1573) in her songs brought out the full implications of the worship of *Rādhā-Kṛṣṇa*. She put herself in the place of *Rādhā* and addressed her songs to *Kṛṣṇa*.

J. ŚUKA

From the quotations in other commentaries we find that Śuka (sixteenth century) is an advocate of *bheda-vāda*. Śuka follows Madhva's teaching on this point. He bases his views on the *Bhāgavata Purāṇa*. He admits differences to be real between the individual soul, *jīva*, and the Lord, *Īśa*, *jīva* and *prakṛti*. The world is real. The B.S. gives us not an unqualified, *nir-viśeṣa Brahman* but a qualified, *sa-viśeṣa Brahman*. While *Para-Brahman* is *nir-guṇa* in so far as he is absolutely free from *sattva*, *rajas* and *tamas*, he is full of auspicious qualities, *ānandādi-sad-guṇas*. He is the source of the creation, maintenance and destruction of the universe.[1] *Brahman* in the form of *Śrī Hari*, *Nārāyaṇa*, *Kṛṣṇa* is to be adored. Śuka believes in *avatāras* which are said to be equal.

The purpose of *jijñāsā* or inquiry is for the attainment of release, *mokṣa-lābha*. The Supreme, out of his grace, grants *mokṣa* or liberation.[2] The released soul is *para-tantra*,

[1] *jagat-janmādi-kāraṇatvaṁ para-brahmaṇo lakṣaṇam bhavatīti prāha janmādyasya iti.*

[2] *bhagavat-prasāda-labdhasya mokṣasya pratyag-ātmana sannihitatvam asti.* IV. 4. 17.

subordinate to *Paramātman*. He enjoys bliss in association with the Supreme Lord.

K. VIJÑĀNA-BHIKṢU

Vijñāna-bhikṣu, a native of Bengal, who lived about the beginning of the seventeenth century, wrote a commentary on the B.S. called *Vijñānāmṛta-bhāṣya*, which develops a theistic *Sāṁkhya*. He attempts to reconcile the *Vedānta* and the *Sāṁkhya* systems. He supports the personal individuality of souls, protests against Ś.'s view and complains that he reduces *Brahman* to the *śūnya* of the Buddhists. He dismisses teachers of non-dualism as *Ku-kalpakas*.[1]

Brahman

Brahman has many qualities, *atyanta-sammiśra-rūpeṇa*. It is *akhaṇḍa*, impartible. *Brahman* is possessed of *śakti*.

There are two forms of the Supreme, *Brahman* and *Īśvara*. *Brahman* is pure consciousness and unchangeable. *Īśvara* possesses energies constituting *prakṛti* and *puruṣa* while *Brahman* is pure consciousness. *Prakṛti* and *puruṣa* have no existence apart from God. Though therefore the world has no permanent reality, it has a relative *vyāvahārika* existence. *Īśvara* is the instrumental and material cause. While in the *Sāṁkhya* system *prakṛti* is associated with *puruṣas* through an inner teleology, according to Vijñāna-bhikṣu, their mutual association is due to the operation of God.[2] *Prakṛti* is the *upādhi* of *Īśvara*. *Brahman* is not directly the material cause of the world; it is only the substratum or the ground cause, *adhiṣṭhāna-kāraṇa*. The relation between the *upādhi* and *prakṛti* is one of the controller and the controlled. Through the instrument of *prakṛti*, God is able to think or will. For in himself God is only pure consciousness. *Prakṛti* acts as the *upādhi* of God with its pure *sattva*. *Kāla* and *adṛṣṭa* are also parts of *prakṛti*.

For Vijñāna-bhikṣu, *Bhagavān* or Absolute God is different

[1] I. 1. 2.

[2] *asmābhis tu prakṛti-puruṣa-saṁyoga īśvareṇa kriyate*. I. 1. 2.

from *Nārāyaṇa* or *Viṣṇu* who are his manifestations even as sons are of the father.[1]

Brahman as God is responsible for the creation, maintenance and destruction of the world. Commenting on I. 1. 2, Vijñānabhikṣu states that the world is real and eternal, *nitya*. While God creates changes, he is not affected by them. *Prakṛti* and *puruṣas* are entities which abide outside God and are coexistent with him. They are moved by God for the production of the universe which is experienced and enjoyed by the *puruṣas* who are ultimately led to liberation beyond bondage. *Puruṣa* and *prakṛti* merge in the end in *Īśvara* by whose will the creative process begins in *prakṛti* at the end of each *pralaya*. *Brahman* as *Īśvara* brings into being *puruṣa* and *prakṛti* which are already potentially existent in God and connects the *prakṛti* with *puruṣa*. God is all-pervasive, the cause of all and the inner controller. The ultimate principle is not *Īśvara* which is the manifestation of pure consciousness in *sattva-maya* body.[2] The Supreme Self does not undergo any change or transformation. He is more real than *puruṣa* or *prakṛti* and its evolutes.

The Individual Soul

The self is devoid of any connection (*asaṅga*). Its association with *prakṛti* is not direct contact. It is the reflection of the pure soul in the conditioning factors which turn it into a *jīva* or the individual. The self is pure consciousness and knowledge of objects is possible through the changes of *antaḥ-karaṇa* and *buddhi*.[3] The *jīvas* are not unreal. While the individual souls and *Brahman* are indistinguishable in character (*avibhāga*), the reality of the individual souls is not denied. They are said to be derived from God as sparks from fire. Though they resemble God in so far as they are of the nature of pure consciousness, they retain their individuality on account of their association with limiting conditions and so they appear as finite and limited, different from *Brahman*.[4] While the *Sāṁkhya* system recognises

[1] Quoting the *Bhāgavata, Kṛṣṇas tu bhagavān svayam*, he explains that *Kṛṣṇa* is a part of God even as the son is part of the father: *atra kṛṣṇo viṣṇuḥ svayam parameśvaras tasya putravat sākṣād aṁśa ity arthaḥ.*

[2] IV. 1. 3. [3] II. 3. 5.

[4] *bhedābhedau vibhāgāvibhāga-rūpau kāla-bhedena aviruddhau anyonyābhāvaś ca jīva-brahmaṇor ātyantika eva.* I. 1. 2.

the individuality and separateness of the souls (*puruṣas*) Vijñāna-bhikṣu maintains that, in spite of their separateness, they are one in essence with *Brahman* and have sprung out of it. When their destiny is fulfilled, they will be merged in *Brahman*. *Brahman* is the final goal of *jīva* but *jīva* is not one with *Brahman*. The ultimate state of realisation is entry into the ultimate being. It is a state of non-difference with it. At the time of release the individuals are not connected with any content of knowledge and are therefore devoid of any consciousness. Even in the state of dissolution, they enter into the great soul even as rivers enter into the ocean. The released soul is an *aṁśa*, not an *aṁśin*. The goal is *sāyujya*, attaining *Brahma-rūpa* and not *aikya* or oneness with *Brahman*. It is the happiness of living near God, *saha-vāsa-bhoga-mātra*. The released soul does not possess the powers of creation, etc., which are the prerogatives of *Īśvara*.[1] To get to the presence of *Brahman* is the highest reward for the devotee. Vijaya-dhvaja, the commentator, writes *mad-darśanam eva sarva-śreyasām phalam iti*.

Vijñāna-bhikṣu holds that the seekers may reach *brahmatva* but they cannot attain *para-brahmatva*. After the completion of enjoyment with *Brahman*,[2] they secure release from rebirth. Those who attain to *kāraṇa-Brahman* have no return. Vijñāna-bhikṣu holds that one can get to *kārya-Brahman* and not to *kāraṇa-Brahman*.

Bhakti as love is the way to the highest realisation.

To know *Brahman*, the aid of the *Sāṁkhya* system is essential.[3] When the seeker realises his nature as pure consciousness and that God is the being from which he has derived his existence, by which he is maintained and to which he will ultimately return, his false attachment to the ego disappears.

[1] Cp. *Bhāgavata* II. 9. 20.

varaṁ varaya bhadraṁ te vareśam mābhivāñchitam
sarva śreyaḥ pariśrāmaḥ puṁsām mad-darśanāvadhiḥ.

[2] *tad-bhoga-samāpty-anantaram.*

[3] Vijñāna-bhikṣu quotes from *Vyāsa-smṛti*: *śuddhātma-tattva-vijñānaṁ sāṁkhyam ity abhidhīyate.*

L. BALADEVA

Baladeva

Baladeva is said to have lived about the beginning of the eighteenth century. He is the author of many works of which the chief are his commentary on the B.S. known as *Govinda-bhāṣya, Siddhānta-ratna, Gītā-bhūṣaṇa,* which is a commentary on the B.G., and *Prameya-ratnāvali*. His views are based on the doctrines of Madhva and the teachings of Caitanya.

The Supreme

Bengal *Vaiṣṇavism* developed by Caitanya (A.D. 1485–1533) is greatly influenced by the teachings of Madhva. Caitanya's doctrine is not pure dualism but what is called *acintya-bhedā-bheda*. It emphasises not only the transcendent majesty (*aiśvarya*) of the Lord, but also his sweetness of motive (*mādhurya-rūpa*). The chanting of the Divine name is exalted.[1] Jīva Gosvāmin, Rūpa Gosvāmin and Baladeva are among the followers of Caitanya. Madhva's influence is found in Baladeva's insistence on the concept of *viśeṣa* and the difference between *Īśvara, jīva* and the world. He also wrote a work called *Kṛṣṇa-caitanyāmṛta* which sets out the essence of Caitanya's teaching. In his commentary on the B.S., Baladeva followed Śuka's commentary on the same work.

Siddhānta-ratna speaks of five *tattvas* or realities which are the same as those admitted by Hari-vyāsa-deva.[2] *Prameya-ratnāvali* lays down nine *prameyas* or propositions: (1) The Lord is the highest reality; (2) He is known from Scripture alone; (3) The universe is real; (4) The difference between the Lord and the individual souls is real; (5) The individual souls are real and are servants of the Lord; (6) The individual souls are different from one another and there are five grades of souls; (7) Release consists in the attainment of the Lord; (8) Worship of the Lord is the cause of release; (9) There are three sources of knowledge, perception, inference and Scripture, the last being the most authoritative and reliable.

[1] Cp. *Ādi-purāṇa* 465.
na nāma-sadṛśaṁ jñānam na nāma-sadṛśaṁ vratam
na nāma-sadṛśaṁ ḍhyānam na nāma-sadṛśaṁ phalam.

[2] *tathā hi īśvara-jīva-prakṛti-kāla-karmāṇi pañca-tattvāni śrūyante.*

Brahman is *Kṛṣṇa, Viṣṇu* or *Hari.* He is the Personal God possessed of infinite auspicious qualities. He is *nir-guṇa* in the sense that he is free from the three *guṇas* of *prakṛti, sa-guṇa* in that he has innumerable auspicious qualities. He is pure consciousness and bliss. He is mighty and majestic and yet sweet and lovely. He has great solicitude for his devotees. He gives his own self to them.[1] His powers and attributes are inconceivable, *acintya*, and mysterious. The Lord is all-pervading, yet atomic. He is of the size of a span, dwelling actually in the heart of his devotees. He is just and impartial and yet shows special grace to his devotees. He is the creator of all and yet is himself unmodified, without any parts and yet possessed of parts, immeasurable and yet measured.[2]

The attributes of the Lord are not different from the Lord; they are nothing except the Lord himself. Even as the coil constitutes the serpent and is not separated from it but is yet the attribute of the serpent, so is it with the attributes of the Lord.[3] Or as the sun is essentially light, yet the substratum of light, so the Lord though essentially of the nature of knowledge, is yet the substratum of the knowledge as well.[4] The Lord is both knowledge and knower, substance and attribute.[5] The Lord has no internal differences.[6] He is not a concrete whole of different attributes, as a tree is a concrete whole of fruits, flowers, roots and leaves. He is one essence throughout and every one of his attributes is identical with him and not a part, separate from him and as such every one of them is full, perfect and unchangeable.[7]

The Lord has three powers, *parā-śakti, aparā-śakti* and *avidyā-śakti*. The first is *Viṣṇu-śakti* or *svarūpa-śakti*, the second *Kṣetrajña* and the third *karma, māyā* or *tamas*.[8] The *parā-śakti* is threefold, *saṁvit* or *jñāna-śakti* or the power of consciousness, *sannidhi* or *bala-śakti* or the power that gives existence and *hlādinī* or *kriyā-śakti*, which is the power that gives bliss. Through the first the Lord who is knowledge knows

[1] *vidyayā parituṣṭo haris svabhaktāya ātmānaṁ dadāti*. III. 4. 1.
[2] II. 1. 27. [3] III. 2. 28. [4] III. 2. 29. [5] III. 2. 30.
[6] III. 2. 28. [7] III. 3. 13.
[8] *viṣṇu-śaktiḥ parā proktā kṣetrajñākhyā tathāparā*
avidyā-karma-saṁjñānyā tṛtīyā śaktir iṣyate.
Prameya-ratnāvali I.

himself and imparts knowledge to the souls. Through the second, the Lord existent by nature gives existence to space, time, matter, souls and *karma*. Through the third, the Lord who is blissful by nature enjoys himself, and gives bliss to others. The *aparā-śakti* and *avidyā-śakti* consist respectively of souls and matter.

The Lord is both the efficient and the material cause of the universe. He is the efficient cause through his *parā-śakti* and is the material cause through his *aparā* and *avidyā śaktis.*[1] When the latter powers are manifested in gross forms, the universe of souls and matter arises. As the operative cause the Lord is unchangeable; as the material cause he is subject to modification or *pariṇāma*. The changes are effected in his powers but he remains unchanged.

God's actions are not in any way determined by motives but they flow spontaneously from his own essential nature through his enjoyment of his own nature as bliss. The world is an effect, the development of *prakṛti* which is also called *māyā* or *avidyā*. It is originally the equilibrium of the three *guṇas* but it is set in motion by a glance of the Lord. The world is real, for God who is reality cannot produce anything which is unreal. During *pralaya* or dissolution souls and matter remain merged in the Lord.

Time is said to be an eternal, non-intelligent substance, a power of the Lord without beginning and end. *Karma* is also an important factor. God is not capricious. He creates the world strictly in accordance with the past deeds of the souls. The three substances, matter, time and *karma* are coeternal with the Lord and subordinate to him. The Lord in the act of creation takes account of them. The Lord is possessed of a celestial non-material form or body,[2] which has the attributes of being, consciousness, bliss and all-pervasiveness. Though the Lord is ordinarily imperceptible to the senses, in absorbed devotion he is perceptible to the senses of the devotee. The devotee sees him with his purified mind even as he sees external objects.[3] The form or body of the Lord is not different from the Lord but is identical with him. It is only as an aid to meditation that the

[1] *tasya nimittatvam upādānatvañcābhidhīyate. tatrādyaṁ parākhyā śaktimad-rūpeṇa, dvitīyam tu tad-anya-śakti-dvayadvāraiva.* I. 4. 26.

[2] II. 1. 31.

[3] III. 2. 24–7.

devotees conceive of his body as distinct from him. When the Lord is said to be formless, it means that he does not possess the form but is the form itself.[1] The Lord has a multitude of forms through which he manifests himself. These are his *avatāras* or incarnations. Though the Lord is not limited by these forms, he is fully manifest in each one of them. Some of the incarnations are partial and some full. In *Kṛṣṇa* we have a full incarnation. Besides this essential form of *Kṛṣṇa*, the Lord has also other energy forms, *vilāsa-rūpa* such as Nārāyaṇa, Vāsudeva, Saṁkarṣaṇa and Aniruddha.[2] Besides the full and partial incarnations, there are certain exalted souls like Nārada and Sanat-Kumāra who are called *āveśāvatāras*. They are not to be worshipped since they do not possess all the attributes of the Lord.[3] The Supreme appears in many places and this is possible on account of his marvellous powers.[4]

The Individual Soul

The individual soul is by nature eternal, i.e. without beginning and without end and self-luminous. It is both knowledge and knower, an enjoyer and an active agent. These qualities belong to the soul in bondage and release. It is not, however, an independent agent like the Lord. In every act, the soul, the body, the different sense-organs, various kinds of energies and the Lord are involved.[5] The soul is not, however, an automaton. Free will on the part of the agent is assured. Even as the acts of the soul in the present life are determined by those in former lives, it can shape its future. God determines the souls in accordance with their nature. Though God is capable of changing the nature of the individuals he does not do so.[6] He leaves it to the free will of the individual. The soul is a part, an effect and a power of the Lord and is both different and non-different from him. It is not a part as a chip cut off from the

[1] III. 2. 14. [2] III. 3. 15. [3] III. 3. 21, 23.

[4] *ekam eva svarūpam acintya-śaktyā yugapat sarvatrāvabhāty eko'pi san; sthānāni bhagavad-āvirbhāvāspadāni tad-vividha-līlāśraya-bhūtāni vividha-bhāvavanto bhaktāś ca.* III. 2. 11.

[5] Cp. B.G. XVIII. 14.

[6] *na ca karma-sāpekṣatvena īśvarasya asvātantram . . . anādi-jīva-svabhāvānusāreṇa hi karma kārayati svabhāvam anyathā-kartuṁ samartho'pi kasyāpi na karoti.* II. 1. 35.

rock is a part of the rock. It is a part in the sense of being subordinate to the Lord, separate from him and yet related to him as the created and the ruled.

In one sense the individual soul and the world are different from *Brahman*; in another sense they are non-different as effects of *Brahman*. The relationship of difference-non-difference is incomprehensible by intellect and is known only through the Scriptures. The union of *Rādhā* and *Kṛṣṇa* symbolises the intimate communion between man and God. The soul is atomic in size and we have a plurality of souls. There are differences among souls owing to their past deeds and aspirations.[1] There are three kinds of souls, the bound, the freed and the ever-free souls. Even the freed souls are different from one another on account of the difference in the quality of their devotion. The world is real. Even dream creations are not false. They are produced through the will of God and disappear through his will in the waking stage.[2]

What is the relation between the Lord and the sentient souls and the non-sentient matter? The latter are the effects of the Lord and so are non-different from him. They are also different because they are ruled and supported by the Lord. The relation of unity of the Lord to the plurality of the world is beyond our grasp. Baladeva recognises difference between the Lord and the soul for it is the basis of all devotion but does not make the difference absolute like Madhva for the effect cannot be absolutely different from the cause. The world and the souls belong to God.[3] Bondage results from turning one's face away from the Lord resulting in the obscuration of one's real nature. Release consists in turning one's face towards the Lord.

Release

The freed soul is different from the Lord in that it is atomic while the Lord is all-pervading and it lacks the power of creation which belongs only to the Lord. The freed soul has a distinctive individuality and is under the control of the Lord. The freed souls are collaborators of the Lord and can assume many forms. The freed soul is in union with the Lord, resides in the same world as the Lord, attains his nature and attributes

[1] II. 3. 42. [2] III. 2. 1–5. [3] *sarvatra tadīyatva-jñānārthaḥ.*

and is in proximity to him.[1] It, however, retains its separate individuality. Baladeva does not admit *jīvan-mukti*.

Bhakti

Bhakti is the sole and direct cause of salvation. *Bhakti* is *premā* or intense love and not *upāsanā* or meditation. According to Baladeva, *dhyāna* or meditation is one form of *bhakti*. When God is worshipped in a limited form, he reveals himself in that same form to the devotee, though he remains as the all-pervasive being. *Bhakti* involves negatively a strong dislike for all objects other than the Lord and positively an intense love of God, *vairāgya* and *premā*. The former is produced by the knowledge of the imperfection and transitoriness of all worldly objects and the knowledge that attachment to them produces endless rebirths while the latter is engendered by the knowledge of the Lord and his attributes of omniscience, omnipotence, loveliness, etc.

Devotion is based on knowledge of the self and the world and of the Lord. *Bhakti* is *jñāna-viśeṣa*. Baladeva distinguishes between two kinds of knowledge, *vijñāna* which is obtained from the study of the Scriptures and *prajñā* or intuitive knowledge or intimate realisation.

The performance of the duties relating to one's own stage of life helps to purify the mind. It is a means to the rise of knowledge and devotion and is not by itself the cause of salvation. When once knowledge and devotion arise, *karma* is no longer necessary even as a horse is necessary for accomplishing a journey but is no longer necessary when the journey is accomplished.[2] Baladeva rejects the theory of *jñāna-karma-samuccaya*. Only *jñāna* or *vidyā* is the cause of salvation. *Vidyā* is devotion preceded by knowledge.[3]

The grace of the Lord is essential. Man cannot reach salvation by his unaided effort. The grace of the Lord is not arbitrary. It depends on the devotion of the souls themselves. The Lord chooses those who are wholeheartedly devoted to him. The grace of the Lord leads to the direct intuition or vision of the Supreme.

[1] IV. 4. 4.
[2] III. 4. 8, 33, 36.
[3] *vidyā-śabdena jñāna-pūrvakā bhaktir ucyate*. III. 3. 48.

CHAPTER 3

Reason and Revelation

Rational Inquiry

EVEN those who feel that religion is an illusion have to investigate religion as a natural phenomenon. It is reason that provokes the religious quest. Man's physical life is not a perfect realisation of an idea. Nor is human life a simple biological process. Man wishes to have a programme of salvation. He wishes to be saved from the dangers of existence, from the snares of life, from the treacherous forces of nature. His ignorance of laws governing natural phenomena, his confused interpretations of nature's striking manifestations impel him to propitiate the forces that govern the universe. As his knowledge increases and he becomes familiar with the regularity and inevitability of natural forces, he understands the conditions under which nature can be controlled and turned to his use. Attention shifts from the natural to the ethical realm. We must love our neighbour and serve him. The ethical emphasis is possible when we recognise the transcendent world of spirit. The conflict in us is indicated by the myth of original sin. We escape from blind servitude to passional experience when we achieve freedom that lies in the inner intuitive vision of the transcendent spirit. There is a subtle interwovenness with the realities of the spiritual world, a kinship between *Ātman* and *Brahman*.

The B.S. opens with the words 'now therefore an enquiry into *Brahman*'. Philosophy as *brahma-jijñāsā* is a consistent effort of reflection. The process of evolution has been at work from the inorganic to the organic, from the organic to the sentient, from the sentient to the rational. A new phase is ahead of us, a life as far above the purely rational as the rational is above the sentient. Through effort and discipline the rational man has to grow to the spiritual man, to the God-man. Ideas manifest themselves in different stages of development and we can understand these stages only in the light of the full development. It is the perfected product that gives us the key to the understanding and interpretation of the imperfect. The full stature of man, his completion as man, is reached when he becomes a God-man. Nature will not do this work for man. He has to struggle and evolve to this higher stage.

Natural Religion

The view of God which we obtain from the employment of reason is what is called in modern theology 'natural religion'. When the B.S. argues in I. 1. 2 that the Supreme is the basis of the whole world process, its origin, maintenance and dissolution, it is adopting the attitude of natural religion. It is essential in this age of science that religious belief should be shown to be reasonable. Plato inscribed the warning above the door of his Academy: 'Nobody untrained in mathematics may cross this my threshold.' In his commentary on the *Māndūkya Kārikā* III, Ś. raises the question whether the non-dualist doctrine can be established only by scriptural evidence or whether it can be proved by reasoning as well. How it is possible to prove the validity of *advaita* by reasoning is shown in the chapter on *Advaita*.[1] Yet reasoning is not all. There is a realm where it has no sway. There are limitations of scientific knowledge. Moral values, wisdom and the life of spirit are beyond it.

The tree of the knowledge of good and evil does not grow from the soil of science. Self-awareness is not a proposition to be proved true or false by scientific tests. Yet it is the ultimate presupposition which is indubitable, according to Ś. and Descartes.

Heracleitus felt that there was a mystery which the human mind cannot comprehend, an incomprehensible and unfathomable element which human thought cannot fully penetrate. Knowledge of that mystery is not derived or derivable from any empirical observation or rational analysis of the facts observed. Socrates was a great advocate of reason but yet a profoundly religious man with mystical feeling. The much abused term existential means that philosophy is not a matter of abstract thinking, but is rooted in the inward soul.

We must get down to the bedrock, the point at which we know our own infinitude, stretching forward and backward in time and upwards to eternity. The meaning of existence, the

[1] *advaitaṁ kim āgama-mātreṇa pratipattavyam āhosvit tarkeṇāpi ity ata āha śakyate tarkenāpi jñātum, tat katham iti advaita-prakaraṇaṁ prārabhyate.*

nature of the spirit of man lies in a realm of mystery and we can live human lives only by a commitment of faith. From that security we must go our way and fulfil our destiny. Philosophy is a school of wisdom and a school of wonder. If it is lacking in wonder, it will be inadequate.

Belief in God is not a scientific conclusion, but it is not inconsistent with the findings of science. In his works Thomas Aquinas tried to demonstrate that the doctrines held to be revealed were also reasonable. If religion is to survive, the schism between the free questioning attitude widely diffused among the educated people all over the world and the insights of religion should be healed.

It is sometimes argued that science examines facts with an open mind, without any preconceived ideas. The scientist uses his reason to interpret the raw material of knowledge provided by the senses. His interpretation may be wrong. The philosopher of religion also accepts the facts, lets reason go wherever the facts lead it. He notes the facts and finds that there must be a spiritual background to life. Even the scientist accepts that the world works rationally and uniformly. This is an act of faith though the scientist calls it a working hypothesis. The Hindu thinkers do not share Barth's utter contempt for nature and reason. In some of his later writings Barth made some concessions to a more humanistic outlook but they have not been integrated with his earlier outlook. Religion for the Hindu thinkers should commend itself to reason even while transcending it. Intuition completes and transforms reason. We cannot make a science of God for God is not an object like other objects of thought.

Modes of Consciousness

Three modes of consciousness are recognised by the *Upaniṣads*, sense perception, logical understanding and intuitive insight. Plotinus, who regards the human individual as a trinity of body, soul and spirit, adopts the same threefold classification, sense perception, discursive thought and spiritual knowledge. Aquinas distinguishes between intellect and reason; only he means by intellect intuitive knowing, and by reason discursive thinking. 'Intellect and reason', he says, 'are not two powers, but distinct as the perfect from the imperfect. . . . The intellect means an intimate penetration of truth; the reason enquiry and discourse.' Near the end of his life Thomas Aquinas laid aside his writing and refused to complete his *Summa* saying that he had seen that which made the writing of books a small and insignificant thing. Spinoza distinguishes imagination, *ratio* or reasoning, *scientia intuitiva* or rational intuition.

F. H. Bradley, who is inclined to follow Kant in his account of logical thought, argues that thought is inadequate to the grasp of reality. The real for him is not the rational and cannot be reduced to an 'unearthly ballet of bloodless categories'. Bradley is clear that we have a different mode of apprehension by which we can acquire a knowledge of the Absolute, a supra-relational experience of which an earnest is found in the immediacy of feeling. The religious experience of God confirms and illuminates man's consciousness of the ultimate as the mystery that permeates everything, embraces everything and completes everything.

Henri Bergson wrote to Jacques Chevalier: 'You are perfectly right in saying that all the philosophy I have expounded since my first *Essay* affirms, against Kant, the possibility of a supra-sensible intuition; taking the word "intelligence" in the very broad meaning given it by Kant, I could call "intellectual" the intuition I speak of. But I should prefer to designate it as "supra-intellectual", because I believed I must restrict the sense of the word "intelligence", and therefore I reserve this name for the set of discursive faculties of the mind, originally destined to think of matter. Intuition *bears toward* spirit'.[1]

Intuitive consciousness is called *pratibhā* or *ārṣa-jñāna* or *parā-saṁvit,* and has the characteristics of immediacy and clarity. It is independent of perception and inference.[2] It is synoptic not analytic, noetic not discursive. It is inarticulate and cannot be readily translated into conceptual terms, though it can become articulate. The two types of knowledge are not incompatible though distinguishable. The seers are those who have seen, heard and handled the word of life. While divine wisdom is eternal and is always possessed by God, intuitive

[1] April 28, 1920. Letters published in *Bergson* by Jacques Chevalier.
[2] See *Yoga Sūtra* III. 84.

consciousness is brought into existence by a mental process. Viśva-nātha in *Bhāṣā-paricchedā*[1] describes *yogic* intuition as twofold, that of *yukta-yogin* who mirrors the eternal light in which the totality of things remains perpetually illumined[2] and that of *yuñjāna-yogin* who requires the aid of reflection, and contemplation for the understanding of eternal wisdom. When mind by gradual training is freed from the influences of the concepts and memory images of the past (*vikalpas*) it merges itself in the object (*dhyeya*) and is absorbed and pervaded by it. The nature of the object is then fully revealed. When we develop *yogic* intuition we have direct knowledge of objects, past and future.[3] I have called it intuition or integral insight. It is different from sense-observation, mathematical and logical reasoning. It comes in a flash as distinct from patient observation or logical analysis. We cannot foresee it or consciously prepare for it. It is creativity. It reveals the central feature of the intuited object. The subject and the object in intuition tend to coalesce. We thus gain an unmediated immediate knowledge and not the mediated, inadequate and always uncertain cognition or idea derived from the sense-perception or logical reasoning. It deals with the reality and not the appearance of the object. It lies at the basis of sense and logical knowledge. The ego disappears. The individual becomes the instrument of the universal lifted above the limitations of the ego. This is the supra-rational divine madness of Plato. It is what Rousseau calls 'sovereign intelligence which sees in a twinkle of an eye the truth of all things in contrast to vain knowledge'. Reason and all other forms of awareness depend on it. Gauss struggling with a mathematical problem reported: 'I succeeded not on account of my painful efforts, but by the grace of God. Like a sudden flash of lightning the riddle happened to be solved. I myself cannot say what was the conducting thread which connected what I previously knew with what made my success possible.'

Spiritual Experience

Man is not saved by metaphysics. Spiritual life involves a change of consciousness. It is a vital process which is more an exertion of the will than a play of the intellect. Wisdom,

[1] 66. [2] *yuktasya sarvadā mānam.* [3] Cp. Ś. on B.S. I. 1. 5.

gnosis, is different from knowledge. It is not a conceptual elaboration of data that reach us through sense-experience. It is the power to recognise absolute values through the spirit in us without the mediation of sense-perception or logical analysis.

Brahma-svarūpa-sākṣātkāra or the realisation of the Supreme is the goal of human existence. What we aim at is not *thinking* but *seeing*.[1] It is a change of being, a rebornness. The sphere of logical thought is exceeded by that of the mind's possible experience of reality, *anubhava* or interior awareness.[2] It is an experience which is a blend of wonder, ecstasy and awe at what is too great to be realised by intellect. It is none of these but something beyond them all and has an element of quite inexpressible strangeness.

Transcendent Being is never given as an object. It is experienced directly in the very failure of discursive reason to reach it. It becomes transparent in illumination.

In early Christian thought, intellect is rated higher than reason. It is capable of intuiting knowledge that is beyond the reach of reason. 'Final and perfect bliss can only consist in the vision of divine being.'[3] Nicholas of Cusa writes: 'It is reason (which is much lower than intellect) that gives names to things in order to distinguish them from one another. This reconciliation of contraries is beyond reason.' Through the power of intellect man can grasp truths which are higher than those accessible to reason. The development of intellect takes place through initiation. 'Self-evidence is the basic fact on which all greatness supports itself. But "proof" is one of the routes by which self-evidence is often obtained.'[4]

Faith is not belief. It arises out of a conflict between doubt and belief. It is an experiencing of that which cannot be known by reason. It does not strive after logical certainty but adores the mystery, which is revealed to the seeker when he enters the inner sanctuary where the bustle of the mind is stilled and truth

[1] The first step in the Buddha's eightfold path is *sammā-dassana*, right seeing. Cp. *Psalm* xxxiv 8: 'O taste and see that the Lord is good.'

[2] Justin Martyr says that 'the aim of platonism is to see God face to face'. *Dialogues* II. 6.

[3] Thomas Aquinas in *Sumna Theologica: ultima et perfectă beatitudo non potest esse nisi in visione divinae essentiae.*

[4] A. N. Whitehead: *Modes of Thought* (1938), p. 66.

shines by its own light. But one cannot stay there all the time and when one leaves it one finds that its light is reflected in the restless world of sense and of thought. We have to think out our faith and use words to communicate our thoughts to others. We begin to expound and argue about it and get back to it continually for refreshment and renewal.

The primary concern of philosophy in India has not been doctrine as change of nature, a total conversion. This was also the view of some philosophers of the West like Pythagoras, Empedocles, Plato, the Stoics, Epicurus, Plotinus, Augustine, Boehme and Schopenhauer. For all these truth is recognised and not created by intellectual activity, though the latter may prepare the mind for intuition. Plato says: 'Suddenly a light, as if from a leaping fire, will be enkindled in the soul.'[1] 'Suddenly there shone from heaven a great light.'[2] Plutarch writes: 'The principle of knowledge that is conceptual, pure and simple, flashes through the soul like lightning and offers itself in a single moment's experience to apprehension and vision.'[3] At a critical point in his life, Socrates gave up the study of physical science in order to seek communion with the spiritual power that informs and governs the universe.[4]

The religious soul is not concerned with arguments for the existence of God. He is alive to God's presence in every manifestation of life, in every impulse implanted by grace in the depths of his heart. Without the succour of the Divine the whole world will instantly crumble into nothingness.[5] Wisdom affirms that there is God and knowledge enquires into his ways, his manifestations, his acts in the great drama of the world which moves through pain and death to the ultimate kingdom of truth and love. Saints do not prove the existence of God for they have apprehended the Divine. They seek to help us to rise in our spiritual stature by forms of worship and service to living creation through whom God works.

Mysticism

Sometimes the word mysticism is used to define spiritual apprehension. It is derived from the Greek word 'I close' and

[1] *Epistle* 7. [2] *Acts* xxii. 6. [3] *De Iside* Ch. 77. [4] See *Phaedo*: 96–7.

[5] Cp. B.G. III. 24 where *Kṛṣṇa* says: 'If I should cease to work these worlds would fall in ruin.'

suggests the shutting of the ears, eyes and lips. This shutting of the senses is the prerequisite of spiritual perception. In order to see in the world of spiritual reality, we must close our eyes to the world in which we ordinarily live. To hear the melodies of the spiritual world we must close our ears to the noise of the world. A seer is one who wraps himself in the mantle of seclusion, closes the avenues of communication with the outside world, not to renounce his powers of sight, hearing and speech but to open the inner eye to spiritual realities, capture the sounds that come from the world above the ordinary one and sing in silence the hymn of praise to the Supreme Being.

We should recognise that there are two strands in mysticism, though some view these as two different types of mysticism. For the *Upaniṣads* they are only two sides. We have the strictly solitary who seeks to liberate his consciousness from the whole burden of materiality, who leads it through zealous purification and inner elevation to beatific reunion with the One Eternal. When once we discover the oneness of our deepest self with the Supreme, we realise our oneness with the whole universe, *sarvam khalv idam brahma*. All this is God. The seer is as one 'who, having looked upon the sun, henceforward sees the sun in all things'.[1] The world becomes the raw material for transfiguration. We do not negate the world but negate what is base and worthless in it. We try to overcome the world and see in it the invisible splendour. Our physical frame, our feeling for the flesh become aids, instruments for the higher life.

While these two phases are organically bound up with each other, in the East as well as in the West, they were sometimes treated as exclusive of each other. Porphyry in his *Life of Plotinus* describes the attitude of the sensitive and receptive spirit who felt ashamed at being clad in a body. It is by a purely personal effort that we can achieve purification and it does not matter if the living reality of the outside world did not exist at all. St Paul and Augustine use the world to rise to the maker of the world. God's divine radiance shines on the world and humanity. 'Hast thou seen thy brother? Then thou hast seen God.' Early Christians had this motto as reported by Clement of

[1] Meister Eckhart.

Alexandria and Tertullian. The spiritual should interpenetrate and renew the life of the world.

Contemplation

The contemplative life is not easy to realise. It is becoming more and more difficult in our age. There is a constant struggle between the biological impulse to adapt to the environment and the human creative impulse. We are inclined to do what others do, think what others think, and not think, feel and act with insight and conviction. We tend to lose ourselves in the anonymity of the human mass, become mere tools of an increasingly efficient social organisation which, the more elaborate and complex it becomes, tends to crush out of existence whatever is human, creative and spiritual in us.[1]

If it is said that the contribution of Greece is primarily science and the arts, that of Rome law and order, Judea, ethics and religion, of China humanism and social peace, it may be remembered that all these are products of the contemplative spirit and creative action. All great works of art and science, literature and philosophy spring from the contemplative spirit.[2] 'Wisdom cometh by the opportunity of leisure.'[3]

Prophetic Religion

Those who have attained wisdom are called *ṛṣis* or seers, the *Buddhas* or the awakened ones, the enlightened. While they identify the ultimate with the ground of all being, their faith is not irrational. Some of the greatest seers of Asia and Europe have also been some of the greatest philosophers. They were outstanding in their clarity, consistency and comprehension.[4]

[1] Cp. M. Jean Cocteau, who in his Oxford address on *Poetry and Invisibility* points out that 'the hectic hurry of our age contributes to the crime of inattentiveness, a crime against the spirit, indeed against the soul'. *London Magazine*, January 1957.

[2] Pushkin, the great Russian poet, writes: 'Until Apollo calls a poet to his sacred sacrifice he is vulgarly silent; his soul is asleep; and among the insignificant children of the world he is perhaps the most trifling. But as soon as the Divine word touches his sensitive ear, the poet's soul rouses as an awakened eagle. He is bored amidst amusements of the world; he is a stranger to the gossips of the mob; he does not bend his proud head to the feet of the popular idol.'

[3] *Ecclesiasticus.*

[4] In *Mysticism and Logic* Bertrand Russell writes: 'The greatest men who have been philosophers have felt the need both of science and mysticism.'

Religion is founded on illumination. It is knowledge revealed to us in our highest consciousness. It is possible that we may have different interpretations of what is revealed but all religions are based on the personal experiences of their founders and prophets. Among the Hebrews there are evident indications of a mystical faith such as the experiences of the great prophets, the visions they saw and the voices they heard. The religions of the Buddha, Jesus and Muhammad were reflections of their experiences.

There is however a tendency to deify the founders of religions. Zarathustra did not claim for himself to be more than a man but he was transfigured by his followers when they came to believe that a superhuman saviour Saoshyant was to be begotten of Zarathustra's seed at the end of time. The Buddha became the enlightened one and his followers felt that he was a superhuman being and expressed their feeling in a set of birth stories. Jesus was identified by his followers with the Messiah who was expected by the Jews to be begotten at the end of time from the seed of David. Other leaders in Jewry both before and after Jesus were identified with the Messiah as Jesus was: for example, Simon Maccabaeus in the second century B.C. and Bar Kokhba in the second century A.D. Muhammad did not claim to be superhuman. He said that he was the latest of the prophets and the last of them that was ever to be. He claimed that he received revelations from God through the Archangel Gabriel and on the night of power he had ascended unto heaven and in the seventh heaven had been admitted into God's presence.

While all these prophets were deified by their followers, orthodox Christians affirm that Jesus is the final self-manifestation of the Divine. Every revealed Scripture is at once both divine self-manifestation and the way in which human beings have received it. There is a reciprocity of inward and outward. Revelation and its reception are inseparably united.[1]

[1] 'The basic error of fundamentalism is that it overlooks the contribution of the receptive side in the revelatory situation and consequently identifies one individual and conditioned form of receiving the divine with the divine itself.' Paul Tillich: *Biblical Religion and the Search for Ultimate Reality* (1955), p. 4. Cp. also 'Revelation is never revelation in general, however universal its claim may be. It is always revelation for someone and for a group in a definite

We are the receptacles of the revelation. Our own form of reception cannot be confused with 'an assumedly undiluted and untransformed revelation' in Professor Paul Tillich's words. 'Wherever the divine is manifest in flesh, it is in a concrete, physical and historical reality.'[1]

Scriptural Testimony

The *Vedānta* adopts six *pramāṇas* of which scriptural testimony is one.[2] In I. 1. 3 the B.S. states that *śāstra* is the source of divine knowledge. The Scriptures register the experiences of seers, they are *āpta-vacana*, the sayings of the inspired men, who have time and again been illuminated by the light of God, *āptena praṇītaṁ vacanam āpta-vacanam.*[3] While the Hindu thinkers accepted the authoritativeness of the *Vedas*, the Buddha did not resort to any authority Vedic or non-Vedic; yet his discourses attained the sanctity of Scripture. The records of the experiences of the great seers who have expressed their sense of the inner meaning of the world through their intense insight and deep imagination are the Scriptures. The word of the *Buddha*, *buddha-vacana*, became the authority for both the *Hīnayāna* and the *Mahāyāna* systems. Even when the Scriptures are traced to divine authorship, it is said that even God is not completely free but has to reckon with the nature of truth.[4] The *Vedas* are received by men. They speak to men in their concrete situations.

The claim to the possession of a special revelation of the Jews, Christians and Muslims is on the same level. It is not necessary for us to close the door to future revelations.

At a time when it has become difficult for the educated person to rest his faith on the infallibility of the Scriptures, or a miraculous revelation in the past, the ultimate basis of religious

environment, under unique circumstances. Therefore, he who receives revelation witnesses to it in terms of his individuality and in terms of the social and spiritual conditions in which the revelation has been manifested to him,' pp. 3–4.

[1] *Biblical Religion and the Search for Ultimate Reality* (1955), p. 5.

[2] *Pratyakṣa* or sense-perception, *anumāna* or inference, *upamāna* or analogy, *śabda* or Scripture, *arthāpatti* or implication, *an-upalabdhi* or negation. See *Vedānta-paribhāṣā.*

[3] *Prameya-kamala-martāṇḍa*, p. 112.

[4] *evam sargāntareṣvapīti, tad-anurodhāt, sarvajño'pi sarva-śaktir api, pūrvāpūrva-sargānusāreṇa vedān viracayan na svatantraḥ. Bhāmatī* I. 1. 3.

trust must be found in personal experience. John Smith, the Cambridge Platonist, says: 'To seek divinity merely in books and writings is to seek the living among the dead; we do but in vain seek God many times in these, where his truth too often is not so much enshrined as entombed. No, seek for God within thine own soul.' Belief in God must grow out of our own consciousness. We require today a spiritual religion which can be developed only by souls of large, spiritual compass and moral power. They alone can inaugurate an age of spiritual vitality and fervour.

Experience and Interpretation

No adequate formulations in logical propositions are possible of experiences which are of an intuitive character. Plato in his Seventh Letter makes out that the knowledge of essential truth cannot be reduced to writing. 'This does not admit of exposition like other branches of knowledge; but, after much discourse about the matter itself and a life lived together, suddenly a light, as it were, is kindled in one soul by a flame that leaps to it from another, and thereafter sustains itself.'[1] St Augustine said: 'I entered, and beheld with the eye of the soul the light that never changes; above the eye of the soul, above my intelligence.' St Angelo of Foligno says: 'I beheld the ineffable fullness of God, but I can relate nothing of it, save that I have seen the fullness of Divine wisdom wherein is all goodness.' St Catherine of Siena observes: '*I now know for certain*, Eternal Truth, that Thou wilt not despise the desire of the petitions I have made unto Thee.' 'If I could only show you a tithe of that Love in which I dwell.' All these are in the presence of an experience which surpasses ordinary levels of feeling, powers of speech and organs of apprehension. These form a great body of witness to humanity's experience of God. All of them agree with the *Upaniṣad* writers that the experience baffles linguistic and logical description. These may vary. Astronomies change but the stars abide. We learn the truth not from books but from a teacher. The true teacher is a live coal from the altar, not an encyclopaedia of what religious books teach. A teacher is a *śikṣā guru*; a preceptor is a *dīkṣā guru*.

[1] 341C.

The spiritual experience cannot be adequately described in words. It is beyond the grasp of empirical thought. It is pure inwardness of which no conceptual description is possible. Through poetry and paradox the seers suggest something of the nature of that which surpasses the bounds of logic. Pure knowledge cannot be transmitted except through symbols. It is covered as by a veil though it becomes transparent to those who desire and know how to look beyond it. No symbol can be taken as final. Scriptural statements reveal the philosophic vision of those in whom the light is kindled. They recognise a profounder reality than that of human life and seek to establish a true harmony between the two.

Scriptures are not infallible in all they say. Truth is eternal in validity and is timeless apart from the texts which may be dated. The truths which are apprehended are timeless though the act of apprehension like all activity is a temporal event. The eternity of the *Vedas*, 'the timelessness of the *dharma*' of the Buddhists, the eternity of the Divine word of the Christians refer not to the texts but to the truths enshrined in them. Experience is never immediate. It is mixed up with interpretation and tradition. Revelation is not found outside some mind. The superhuman wisdom which transcends time is given to us in time. Even though spiritual experience arises with a self-evident certitude, the interpretations we give to it require rational scrutiny.

There is a difference between psychology and philosophy. Our mental states, ideas, impressions and feelings are the subject-matter of psychology but what we think is not a matter of what takes place in our minds. We think of reality, rightly or wrongly. A psychologist may be interested in the private experiences of individuals but a philosopher is investigating what our experiences mean. There is a difference between the vehicle of thought and the meaning of thought. Psychology is a factual enquiry and philosophy is conceptual analysis. F. H. Bradley makes a distinction between images and meanings. Images are facts, neither true nor false, while meanings are capable of being true or false of reality. Philosophy is interested in discussing what images mean and not what they are. Scriptures contain many survivals of crude, imperfect and undeveloped images. These are to be refined and improved in the light of our present knowledge.

Faith and Belief

There is a difference between faith and belief. The two are not necessarily in conflict. An act of faith involves a surrender to the creative intuition which transcends the limited awareness of the intellectual self. Those who live by faith, who had a personal encounter with the Supreme need not abandon the traditional formulations of belief in which they have been reared; for these beliefs were also originally born in the mind of man. To become organic expressions of faith they must be reborn and continually renewed in personal experience. Even when we admit revelation, there must be an answering witness within the soul.

Sometimes these beliefs are more a barrier than an aid to the unfolding of the creative experience. Dogmas and usages tend to stifle the spirit in us. Those who feel the spiritual urge in them sometimes feel the oppressive weight of dogmas. We cannot accept the verbal inspiration of the Scriptures. Indian thought assigns a place to belief in the development of religious experience. *Śravaṇa* or hearing the Scriptures is the first step to spiritual realisation. It is safe to cling to a system of beliefs, lest in seeking reality for oneself, one may miss one's way. But beliefs become moribund when they lack the inward experience which renews their meaning.

Belief should set us on to reflection, *manana*, and contemplation, *nididhyāsana*, which results in *ātma-darśana* or vision of the Self. If we end with beliefs we preserve safety at the cost of life itself. When we rise to the highest experience we abandon the defences.

The orthodox theologians of different religions do not accept experience or immediate knowledge as final.[1] We may have a feeling of certainty but not certainty itself. This experience must be open to reason and not at any rate contrary to it. Even if we have a direct knowledge of God we must establish it on other

[1] Cp. Hermann: 'When the influence of God upon the soul is found solely in an inward experience of the individual, he who seeks in this wise has stepped beyond the pale of Christian piety. He leaves Christ and Christ's Kingdom altogether.' *The Communion of the Christian with God.*

grounds. We cannot be content with stating that the experience is ineffable. The B.S. is an enquiry into the nature of reality revealed by the seers of the *Upaniṣads*. It is its function to interpret the experiences of the seers so as to give a coherent view, to relate their account of reality with the nature of reality given by science and common sense. For nature is of God; its study is his service; its truth is his revelation. The theological doctrines of different religions have been adapting themselves to the intellectual temper of the world, accepting truth from whatsoever source it appeared and discarding erroneous forms of expression.

The authoritative character of the *Vedas* which include the *Upaniṣads* is not inconsistent with philosophy as a criticism of categories. The seers give utterance to their visions of Ultimate Reality. The author of the B.S. systematises them and has referred to oral traditions of their significance.[1]

Today unbelief in the form of certain conviction is yielding to unbelief in the form of doubt. Michael Faraday said: 'In knowledge, that man only is to be condemned and despised who is not in a state of transition.' With sincerity and impartiality we should endeavour to seek solutions of religious questions.

The view that Scriptures of all religions have a claim to our allegiance in so far as their statements are not dated has the support of Indian religious classics. The spiritual community of the future needs for its foundation no geographically limited writings, no groups organised in accordance with ecclesiastical articles and rules. All those who are aware that future salvation does not depend on mechanical or technological development or regulation of economic and social life but solely on the revival of a world of spiritual values which evade empirical analysis but reveal themselves only to faith and hope should band together and work for the world community. In that city which is still out of sight, in that homeland of the spirit, we will understand one another.

Every period of history nurses in its bosom certain unavowed

[1] Professor A. E. Taylor writes: 'What we have a right to demand of the theologian is that the matter upon which his thought works shall be something genuinely *given*, and that in his reflective elaboration of it he shall be true to it. I do not see that we have a right to demand more.' *The Faith of a Moralist*, Vol. II (2nd edition), p. 390.

and unanalysed assumptions which constitute the key to the interpretation of that period. Our generation is aiming at human unity and brotherhood and the establishment of the one and only universal Church. An interpretation of the great Scriptures of the world on the lines outlined here may perhaps provide the basis for such a consummation.

CHAPTER 4

The Nature of Reality

Brahman the Absolute

In spiritual experience, Ultimate Reality impinges on the human spirit. Religion is a living creative power because Ultimate Reality manifests itself to the human spirit. Whether we mean by religion adherence to sect or dogma, an attitude of faith or reverence toward what William James calls the *more* that lies beyond subjectivity, that Platonic pure reason of which Coleridge wrote that it is not 'something which is in us, but something in which we are', it brings us into contact with something out there. The seers have an overpowering conviction of the presence of Spiritual Reality. The experience is a compelling vision or intuitive realisation of the reality of the Supreme.

If religion arises at the point where Ultimate Reality manifests itself to the human spirit, our view of religion will be determined by the view we take of the nature of Ultimate Reality and of the relationship with the human spirit into which it enters. Religion is the self-manifestation of Ultimate Reality in man. The Supreme is completely different from the contingent things of the world. It is the presence behind the phenomena and transcendent to them. The Supreme is non-dual, free from the distinctions of subject and object. The principle of *via negativa* makes out that *Brahman* cannot be the object of rational knowledge. It emphasises the incommensurability of the infinite and the finite. When logical categories are denied of the Supreme Spirit, it only means that it is not an objective existent or a logical category. To use Kantian terminology the reality of spirit is that of freedom rather than that of nature. Spirit exists only in the subject but it is not in the least subjective for the distinction of subject and object as correlatives has meaning only on the logical plane but spirit is reality of another kind, an immeasurably greater and more primal one. Professor R. A. Nicholson in his article on *Sufis*[1] quotes:

In solitude where Being signless dwelt,
And all the universe still dormant lay
In Selfishness, One Being was,
Exempt from 'I' or 'Thou'-ness and apart from all duality.

Subject and object, I and Thou have no place there. We cannot describe the Supreme in personal terms when the non-dual, *advaita* aspect is in view.

Beware! say not, 'He is all-beautiful,
And we His lovers.' Thou art but the glass,
And He the face confronting it, which casts
Its image on the mirror. He alone
Is manifest, and Thou in truth art hid
. . . If steadfastly
Thou canst regard, thou wilt at length perceive
He is the mirror also; He alike
The Treasure and the Casket.

There is nothing else than the Absolute which is the presupposition of all else. The central mystery is that of Being itself. We should not think that emphasis on Being overlooks the fact of becoming. Being as such is free from static or dynamic implications. It is devoid of and is antecedent to any special qualifications. It points to the original fact that there is something and not nothing and to the power of that which resists non-being. We cannot define Being since it is the presupposition of all definition. In it is the coincidence of opposites. It is all and nothing, self and not-self, activity and rest, formlessness and form, the unknown knower in which all things

[1] *Encyclopaedia of Religions and Ethics*. XII. pp. 16–17.

are known, the void from which all fullness flows, ever pouring forth in creation and for ever undiminished in itself.[1]

The primacy of Being is argued on a rational basis. There is the ontological otherness, the otherness of the Transcendent Absolute, source of all existent things, the perfect being from which all existent things derive their being and nature. Apart from this Transcendent Reality existent things neither exist nor persist. The sense of the absolute dependence of all existent things is central to piety. It is this sense that is translated into the argument from the radical contingency of the world to an absolute self-subsistent, non-contingent being as its source. The contemplation of finite things leads to a direct discernment of the Supreme as their absolute source. Ś. says, 'Whenever we deny something unreal, we do so with reference to something real. The unreal snake, for example, is negatived with reference to the real rope. But this is possible only if some entity is left. If everything is denied, then no entity is left, and if no entity is left, the denial of some other entity which we may wish to undertake becomes impossible, i.e. the latter entity becomes real and cannot be negatived.'[2]

We teach *Brahman* without speaking about it, *avacane ca brahma provāca*. Every spoken word narrows down Being. We can say only that Being is itself. Beginningless, absolute *Brahman* is not known by gods or sages. Only the Lord *Nārāyaṇa* knows him.[3] Silence is the only language of worship. Worship is not servile cringing before absolute power but worship or adoration. 'How can he who holds all be brought into a temple? How can he who is the basis of all be confined

[1] Philo observes: 'God is withdrawn from both ends of time, for his life is not Time but Eternity, the archetype of time. And in eternity there is neither past nor future but only present.'

Cp. Dante: 'O Light Eternal who only in Thyself abidest, only Thyself dost comprehend, and, of Thyself comprehended and Thyself comprehending, dost love and smile.'

[2] *kaṁ ciddhi paramārtham ālambya aparamārthaḥ pratiṣiddhyate. yathā rajjvādiṣu sarpādayaḥ. tacca pariśiṣyamāṇe kasmiṁs' cidbhāve'vakalpate. kṛtsna-pratiṣedhetu tu ko'nyo bhāvaḥ pariśiṣyeta. apariśiṣyamāṇe cānyasmin yaḥ itaraḥ pariṣeddhum ārabhyate. tasyaiva paramārthatvāpatteḥ pratiṣedhānupapattiḥ*. S.B. III. 2. 22.

[3] *anādyam taṁ paraṁ brahma na devā na ṛṣayo viduḥ*
ekas tad veda bhagavān dhātā nārāyaṇaḥ prabhuḥ.
Vijñānāmṛta-bhāṣya I. 1. 5.

to a spot? How can there be the circling round of the Infinite? How can there be prostration to him who is our very self?'[1]

There is the other-ness of God felt in the act of worship. He cannot be wholly other for then it would be impossible to know anything about him even on the basis of his own self-revelation. There is an element of non-otherness. The other-ness of God does not exclude the possibility of community of being between God and man. In the act of worship we have a sense of the other-ness of God as well as a sense of wonder that he has bestowed on us a nature akin to his own. It is this kinship that makes communion with him possible.[2] There is an incomprehensible other-ness of God as the source of all, an other-ness which God himself discloses to the soul of man. God is both transcendent to and immanent in the world. He originates, sustains, sets limits to his community of being with the world and transcends it.

When we refer to the Supreme as *Brahman*, as Transcendent Reality, we employ the negative method. The Supreme Principle is conceived in the *Vedas* not only as the substance of the world and of all beings but also as that which transcends them 'by three quarters' existing as the 'Immortal in the heavens'.[3] The *Upaniṣads* hold that the Absolute can be described only as not this, not this, *na iti, na iti*. The *Avadhūta Gītā* says:

advaitam kecid icchanti dvaitam icchanti cāpare
samam tattvam na vindanti dvaitādvaita-vivarjitam

Some prefer non-duality; others prefer duality.
They do not understand the Truth which is the same, free from duality and non-duality.[4]

Asaṅga says:

na san na cāsan na tathā na cānyathā
na jāyate vyeti na cāvahīyate
na vardhate nāpi viśuddhyate punaḥ
viśuddhyate tat paramārtha-lakṣaṇam.

[1] *pūrṇasya āvāhanaṁ kutra, sarvādhārasya ca āsanam*
pradakṣiṇā ca anantasya hi, advayasya kutaḥ natiḥ?

[2] Cp. Augustine: 'What is that which gleams through me and smites my heart without wounding it? I am both a-shudder, and a-glow. A-shudder in so far as I am unlike it; a-glow in so far as I am like it.' *The Confessions* XI. 9. 1.

[3] *Ṛg Veda* X. 90. 3; C.U. III. 12. 6.

[4] I. 36.

It is not existent, nor non-existent; it is not thus, it is not otherwise; it is not born, it does not decay or die or grow, nor does it purify. The ever-pure is the mark of the Ultimate Reality.

Nāgārjuna declares:

> *anirodham, anutpādam, anucchedam, aśāśvatam*
> *anekārtham, anānārtham, anāgamam, anirgamam*
> *na san nāsan na sad-asan na cāpy anubhayātmakam*
> *catuṣkoti-vinirmuktaṁ tattvam mādhyamikā viduḥ.*[1]

Nirvāṇa is described in similar terms:

> *aprahīṇam, asamprāptam, anucchinnam, aśāśvatam*
> *aniruddham, anutpādam etan nirvāṇam ucyate.*

Theologia Germanica says: 'Where this Light is, the man's end and aim is not this or that, I or Thou, or the like, but only the One, who is neither I nor Thou, this nor that, but is above all I and Thou, this and that; and in him all Good is loved as one Good.'

Henry Vaughan writes:

> There is in God (some say)
> A deep but dazzling darkness; as men here
> Say it is late and dusky, because they
> See not all clear;
> O for that night! where I in him
> Might live invisible and dim.[2]

The Ātman

The Supreme Reality is not out there but is one with our deepest self. *Brahman* is *Ātman*, the Universal Spirit. *Tat tvam*

[1] *Mādhyamika-Kārikā.*

[2] Cp. *namostu śūnyatā-garbha sarva-saṁkalpa-varjita*
sarvajña jñāna-sandoha jñāna-mūrte namostu te
saṁbuddhā bodhisattvāś ca(tvattaḥ) pāramitāguṇāḥ
sambhavanti sadā nātha bodhi-citta namostu te.

Hail to thee the birthplace of the void, who art free of all conceits, omniscient one, thou mass of knowledge, knowledge personified, all hail to thee. From you, O Lord, there ever rise into existence Buddhas and Bodhisattvas who possess as their good qualities the great perfections, O the thought of enlightenment, hail to thee.

Prajñopāya-viniścaya-siddhi III. 9 and 11.

asi.[1] The self is an independent entity underlying the conscious personality and the physical frame. The natural man is alienated from the self in him. All that we know and express about the self belongs to the world of change, of time and space but the self is for ever changeless, beyond the world of space, time and cause.

In all the countless months, years and aeons, past and to come, what does not rise or set, that is the one self-luminous consciousness.[2] The *Devi Bhāgavata* says: 'Break of this consciousness is never seen. If it is ever seen, then the seer remains behind embodied as that same consciousness.'[3] *Saṁkṣepa-śārīraka* says: 'This unique undivided selfconsciousness is subject and object at once.'[4] This self is unseizable as an object of thought. 'It is never known but it is the knower.' *avijñātaṁ vijñātṛ*.[5] The self is the point where science and every objective method of approach become inapplicable.[6]

When the *Upaniṣad* thinker says I am *Brahman, aham brahmāsmi*, when the Buddha declares that he is wisdom or enlightenment, when Jesus says, 'I am the Truth', what is the 'I' which is said to be the real and the true? No Western philosopher before Socrates is so interesting as Heracleitus. His 'I sought for myself' expresses the highest consciousness of the problem of philosophy. We cannot seek the 'I' by logical analysis or intellectual observation. A new world is revealed when the soul turns to contemplate itself. Heracleitus says: 'Travel over every road, you cannot discover the frontiers of

[1] The author of the *Imitation* puts into the mouth of Jesus: 'When you think that you are far from me, then, often am I nearest to you.'

[2] *māsābda-yuga-kalpeṣu gatāgamiṣu anekadhā*
nodeti nāstameti eṣā saṁvid ekā svayaṁ-prabhā.
Pañca-daśī I. 7.

[3] *saṁvido vyabhicāras tu naiva dṛṣṭo'sti karhicit*
yadi dṛṣṭaḥ tadā draṣṭā śiṣṭaḥ saṁvid vapuḥ svayam.
III. 32.

[4] *āśrayatva-viṣayatva-bhāginī*
nir-vibhāga-citir eva kevalā.

[5] B.U. III. 4. 2.

[6] Cp. Max Planck: 'Science cannot solve the ultimate mystery of nature. And that is because in the last analysis, we ourselves are part of nature and therefore part of the mystery we are trying to solve. The most penetrating eye cannot see itself any more than a working instrument can work upon itself.' *Where is Science Going?*

the soul—it has so deep a logos.'[1] For conceptual thinking the soul is boundless. Transcendence is the only means of reaching the soul's deeper stratum. The power to transcend is the property of the subject 'I'. It always goes beyond the 'me'. It is greater than the series of empirical selves. In a prayer to *Kṛṣṇa, Brahmā* says: 'We imagine things outside ourselves and look upon our Self as a stranger to us and seek for him outside ourselves. Look at the ignorance of the unenlightened.'[2]

Ś. opens his commentary on the B.S. with a distinction between subject and object, *ātman* and *an-ātman*, with the formulation of the absolute disparity between I and Thou, *asmat* and *yuṣmat*. The pure subject is distinguished from the ego, the psychological or sociological self which is a part of the objective world. The latter is a fragment of nature. In his own depths, in the very core of his existence, the self continues to be himself. This Self, Ś. says, 'the unconditioned, markless, free from the characters of existent and non-existent, is real metaphysically'.[3] 'There are two sights', says Ś. 'One is eternal and unseen viz. the sight of the seer: the other is non-eternal and seen.'[4] 'By his ever-present eternal sight which is his own nature known as the self-shining one, the seer sees the other evanescent sight in the waking state and in dreams, consisting of desires and cognitions.'[5] The perceptible is limited to space and time; the inferrible is also limited but the pure subject is devoid of all limitations and is known immediately though not objectively.[6] If the Self were not immediately manifested the whole world would become blind.[7] Consciousness is the very essence of self as heat is of fire according to Ś.[8] While the content of experience changes, the consciousness does not. Even when there are no objects to be known as in deep sleep, consciousness is present. For its positive manifestation, consciousness like light needs objects but it is never absent.[9]

[1] Fragment 45.

[2] *tvām ātmānam param matvā paramātmānam eva ca.*
ātmā punar bahir mṛgyaḥ aho'jñajanatājñatā.

[3] *tasya nirupādhikasya, aliṅgasya, sad-asādi-viṣayatva-varjitasya ātmanaḥ tattva-bhāvo bhavati.* Ś. on *Kaṭha U.* VI. 13.

[4] *dve dṛṣṭī draṣṭur nityā adṛṣya, anyā'nitya dṛśyeti.* [5] Ś. on B.U. I. 4. 10.

[6] *aparokṣatvāc ca pratyag-ātmā prasiddeḥ.* Ś.: Introduction to Ś.B.

[7] Vācaspati in his *Bhāmatī. jagad-āndhya-prasaṅgāt.* [8] Ś.B. I. 4. 10.

[9] *viṣayābhāvād iyam acetayamānatā, na caitanyābhāvāt.* Ś.B. II. 20. 3.

The *Sāṁkhya* system distinguishes between *puruṣa* and *prakṛti*. Objectivity is foreignness to subjectivity. Object is *avivekin*; it cannot distinguish itself from subjectivity. Rather it is subjectivity that posits the object as the other. Object is *acetana*. It is not self-revealing. It is revealed by something else, the subject.[1] We have to rise to pure subjectivity by gradual stages. Through the subjective realisation of the body as perceived by the senses, of the subject as ego, *ahaṁ-kāra*, as reflective intelligence, *buddhi*, we get to pure subjectivity or *puruṣa*.

For Eckhart, the ground of the soul is the inner citadel in the hidden depths of man's being. It is the uncreated, eternal, pure essence at the centre of man's inmost life. The existentialist philosophers hold that truth is not external and impersonal but is immediate and experienced. It is not so much knowing the truth as being it. Kierkegaard says: 'Truth in its very nature is not the duplication of being in terms of thought. . . . No, in its very being it is the reduplication in me, in you, in him, so that my, your, his life, is striving to attain it . . . is the very being of truth, is a life.'[2]

The Self is experienced as the Absolute Reality in the state of *turīya*. It is raised above the distinction of subject and object.[3] In *suṣupti* or deep sleep, the empirical mind with all its modes is inactive. In *sa-vikalpa samādhi* the mind is concentrated on one object with which it becomes identified. In it we have the consciousness of determinate reality. The consciousness of duality is absent in this state and the self enjoys undifferenced bliss. In both these states the seeds of knowledge and action, *vidyā* and *karma*, are present. In *nir-vikalpa samādhi* we have the intuition of reality transcending all determinations. This is the highest stage, the truth, *Brahman*. 'Desireless, firm, immortal, self-existent, contented with the essence, he is lacking nothing. One fears not death who has known him, the self, serene, ageless, youthful.'[4] Even worship becomes irrelevant when the realisation occurs.

[1] *parataḥ-prakāśa-viṣaya, sāmānya-prasava-dharmin.*

[2] *Training in Christianity*, pp. 201–2.

[3] See P.U., pp. 75ff.

[4] *akāmo dhīro amṛtaḥ svayambhū rasena tṛptena na kutaścanonaḥ*
tam eva vidvān na bibhāya mṛtyor ātmānam dhīram ajaram yuvānam.
Atharva Veda X. 8. 44.

To whom shall I offer my salutation? I am one, free from defects.[1]

Without our participation in the Divine, neither knowledge of God nor love of God is possible. It is the Divine which drives the soul through all levels of reality to Ultimate Reality. To know this Self and make this knowledge effective in human life has been the aim of man, according to the *Vedānta* system.

Īśvara or Personal God

The *Upaniṣads* are not content with a mystery hidden in a cloud of negative phrases. They do not reduce the Absolute deprived of all determinations to a bare abstraction by the ruthless logic of the negative method. The Absolute is a living reality with a creative urge. When this aspect is stressed, the Absolute becomes a Personal God, *Īśvara*.

In religious experience personal encounter is as real as the encounter of subject and object in cognitive experience. We meet a 'Thou' whom we can influence by prayer and worship. While *Brahman* is the trans-personal ground and abyss of everything personal, *Īśvara* is the Personal God. While *Brahman* is the object of *nir-vikalpa samādhi*, *Īśvara* is the object of *sa-vikalpa samādhi*.

In the concept of *Īśvara* the Absolute is brought into closer relationship with the world. There is continuity between the values discerned in God and the values discernible and realisable in human life. God in his perfection is the ultimate source of all values whatsoever which derive from him.

On the human level, person is individuality with self-relatedness and world-relatedness and therefore with rationality, freedom and responsibility.

Brahman and *Īśvara* are not distinct entities but different aspects of the same Reality. *Brahman* is *Īśvara* when viewed as creative power.[2] It is wrong to imagine that the absolutistic doctrine is for the philosophically initiated and the theistic doctrine for others. Even in Ś.'s thought the apprehension of God as personal is a living factor. Theism arises out of the com-

[1] *kasyāpy aho namas-kuryām aham eko nirañjanaḥ. Avadhūta Gīta* I. 3.

[2] *brahmaiva sva-śakti-prakṛtyābhidheyam āśritya lokān sṛṣṭvā niyantṛtvād īśvaraḥ.*

pulsions of the human spirit. It is not a question of higher and lower knowledge. The view that the representation of *Brahman* as *Īśvara* is a concession to the weakness of the human mind as some *Advaitins* hold is not supported by the B.S.[1]

As *Brahman* answers to the content of the *turīya* or the transcendental consciousness, *Īśvara* answers to the *suṣupti* or the consciousness of deep sleep. The principle of objectivity is present in the state of deep sleep. It has the seed of both dream and waking states.[2] The principle of objectivity is called *prakṛti*, the unmanifested, imperceptible all but nothing which receives existence, form and meaning. It is the limit of the downward movement, the lowest form which is all but non-existent. There is nothing in the actual world which is completely devoid of form. *Prakṛti* is the potentiality of all things. The supra-real one and the infra-real matter answer to pure being and pure non-being. The Supreme self-conscious Lord is the wisdom of Solomon which sweetly ordereth all things.

It is said that the Divine Wisdom acts through its opposite *avidyā*, non-wisdom. *Brahman* with *avidyā* is *Brahman* as subject-object which is the basis of the whole world. According to later *Advaita Vedānta*, *Brahman* with *avidyā* is the material cause of the world. The world is grounded in such a *Brahman* and is absorbed in it.[3] *Avidyā* is also regarded as *māyā* and the joint causality of *Brahman* and *māyā* is conceived in a threefold manner. The two are twisted together as two threads into one or that *Brahman* with *māyā* as its power or *śakti* is the cause of the world or *Brahman* being the support of *māyā* is indirectly the cause of the world.

[1] *Kalpa-taru* states that 'the demonstration of *Brahman* as with attributes is out of compassion for those dull-witted persons who have not the capacity to intuit the Supreme *Brahman* without attributes; having thereby directed their minds to the pursuit of the *Brahman* with attributes, *Brahman* devoid of all duality directly manifests itself'.

nirviśeṣaṃ paraṃ brahma sākṣāt kartum anīśvarāḥ
ye mandās te'nukampyante saviśeṣanirūpaṇaiḥ
vaśīkṛte manasy eṣām saguṇa-brahma-śīlanāt.
tad evāvirbhavet sākṣād abhedopādhi-kalpanam.

[2] *suṣuptākhyam tamo-'jñānam bījam svapna-prabodhayoḥ.* Ś. on *Upadeśa-sāhasrī*. Sureśvara in *Naiṣkarmya-siddhi* says: *tasmāt suṣupte ajñānam abhyupagantavyam.*

[3] *avidyā-sahita-brahmopādānaṁ jagat brahmaṇi evāsti tatraiva ca līyate. Bhāmatī* I. 1. 2.

In all creation there is the union of the male and the female. They are two aspects, co-partners of the Supreme Being. The Supreme transcends all opposites but also includes them. Darkness is not the mere negation of light or light of darkness. Each is a necessary condition of the other. The darkness and passivity of the Divine is as real as the light and activity of the Divine. God is father-mother. The inseparable union of being and non-being is the creative mystery. The Supreme is regarded as the Universal Mother, *jagad-ambā*. In one of the hymns attributed to Ś., she is said to have her abode in the form of energy in all things.[1]

The *Ṛg Veda* describes the Supreme as an inconceivable wonder, a sublime unity, a totality from which light shoots forth to generate out of darkness and emptiness a living universe.

The Absolute appears in a double aspect, eternity and time. Though apparently opposed they are one in reality. They are seemingly antagonistic but really complementary aspects of the Absolute. The cosmic process is the interaction between the two principles. It is the supreme *Puruṣa* or God working on *prakṛti* or matter. In the image of *Ardha-nārīśvara* the two opposed but complementary principles are shown as one complete organism. *Rādhā* and *Kṛṣṇa* are said to be one integral whole.[2] We do not have a metaphysical dualism for the principle of non-being is dependent on Being. It is that without which no effort would be possible or necessary. It is a necessary moment in reality for the unfolding of the Supreme. If the world is what it is, it is because of the tension. The world of time and change is ever striving to reach perfection. Non-being which is responsible for the imperfection is a necessary element here; it is the material in which the ideas of God are actualised. Because as Proclus says matter is a 'child of God', it is aiming at transformation into spirit.

[1] *yā devī sarva-bhūteṣu śakti-rūpeṇa saṁsthitā.*

[2] Cp. *Sāma-veda-rahasya*: *anādyo'yam puruṣa eka evāsti, tad evam rūpam dvidhā vidhāya sarvān rasān samāharati: hyayam eva nāyīkārūpaṁ vidhāya samārādhana-tat-paro' bhūtasmāt tām rādhām rasikānandām veda-vido vadanti.*

Kṛṣṇa says, according to *Nārada-pañcarātra*, that his grace is available only to those who meditate on *Rādhā*.

satyaṁ satyaṁ punaḥ satyaṁ satyam eva punaḥ punaḥ
rādhā-nāmnā vinā loke mat-prasādo na vidyate.

God is the infinite mind whose mode of being is at once the consciousness of self and constitutive of what is other than self. For Hegel God realises himself in and through the universe. As the universe proceeds from God it belongs essentially to his own being. When the Divine Subject objectifies itself in this way in the universe, the essential unconditioned freedom of the spirit becomes involved in conditions and limitations which contradict this freedom. Nevertheless it is through this contradiction that the spirit is able to realise itself and return to itself, not now simply as the One but as the One that is in all. In this integration the spirit takes up its opposite into itself and achieves a richer consciousness, a fuller harmony. The goal of attainment is spirit in its completeness.

Judaism, Christianity and Islam look upon Reality as a person and the approach to the Supreme is through prayer and worship. The mystics of these religions, however, look upon the highest goal as union with Reality in which the distinction between subject and object fades away. For them the vision of Reality is a unitive, undifferentiated state of being. So also many Hindu and Buddhist thinkers approach Reality in its super-personal form and their aim is *mokṣa* or *nirvāṇa* which can be attained through the spiritual activity of meditation. But there are large numbers in the Hindu and the Buddhist faiths who look upon the Supreme as a Person and insist on prayer and worship to him. The *Śaiva*, the *Vaiṣṇava* and the *Śākta* cults as well as *Mahāyāna Buddhism* represent the theistic tendency. Though the emphases may be different, all these religions, Judaism, Christianity and Islam as well as Hinduism and Buddhism, admit the vision of Reality as a super-personal state of being and as Personal God. The latter look upon them as two poises of the same Reality. All these religions are aware of personal saviour gods.

Īśvara in the form of *Viṣṇu* is said to be the source, the transcendent God of the created worlds. The waters of life which feed creation are the elementary material aspects, the first tangible emanation of the Divine, which, though beyond form, yet evolves and comprehends all forms. In sculptural representations they are symbolised in the coils of the huge serpent whose dwelling is the cosmic abyss and whose name is *ananta*, endless. God as *Viṣṇu* reclines on this immeasurable body from which temporal existences spring. *Ananta* supports in his expanded hoods both the terrestrial and the celestial spheres. He is the ever-living cosmic ocean from out of which the world and its forms emerge. He rests in the ocean which is perpetually transforming its movement and its colour. He is also called *Śeṣa* or the remainder for he is the abysmal water that has not become transformed into creatures but remains at the bottom of the universe as its primal life-force, the original substance feeding all. Ultimately *Ananta* is identical with *Viṣṇu* himself who, in his human form, is seen recumbent on his coils. *Viṣṇu* and *Ananta* are subject and object, *Īśvara* and *prakṛti*. These are the dual manifestations of a single divine presence which, by and in itself, is beyond the forms it assumes when bringing the world-process into action.

The supreme *Īśvara* is often identified with *Śiva*, and there are symbolic representations of *Śiva* as *Naṭa-rāja*, the King of dancers. *Naṭa-rāja* is the manifestation of the eternal energy in five activities, *pañca-kriyā:* (i) *sṛṣṭi* or pouring forth, creation; (ii) *sthiti* or maintenance; (iii) *saṁhāra* or taking back, destruction; (iv) *tirobhāva* or concealing, veiling, hiding the transcendental reality behind appearances; (v) *anugraha* or favouring, bestowing grace through manifestations that accept devotees. *Naṭa-rāja* is represented as dancing on the dwarfish body of the demon *apasmāra-puruṣa*, forgetfulness, loss of memory, ignorance the destruction of which brings enlightenment which effects release from the bondage of mundane existence. In the figure of *Nāṭa-rāja* we see the contrast between the movement of his limbs and the tranquillity of his face. It symbolises the paradox of time and eternity, of mortal existence and indestructible being.

Sometimes, the Supreme is identified with *Śakti*. This type of worship is not unknown to the West. When the pagan temples were closed, the cult of Virgin Mary replaced that of Virgin Athene.

The act of creation, the relationship between God and man is the revelation of the divine drama of which time and history are the inner content. *Iśvara* is the guide and controller of the world.

Even the *avatāras* or incarnations are identified with the Supreme *Īśvara*. Tulasi Dās, in his *Rāmāyaṇa*, makes *Śiva* tell *Pārvatī:* 'The *Rāma* on whom gods, sages and seers from *Brahmā* downwards meditate in their devotions is not the *Rāma* of history, the son of King Daśaratha, the ruler of Ayodhyā. He is the eternal, the unborn, the one without a second, timeless, formless, stainless.' *bhaktānām anukampārthaṁ devo vigrahavān bhavet.* Out of compassion for the devotees the Supreme assumes a human form.

Jesus of history is represented as the incarnation of the Supreme. He assumed human form for the sake of saving us. St Paul says: 'Our Lord Jesus Christ, though he was rich, yet for your sakes he became poor, that ye through your poverty might be rich.'[1] Irenaeus expresses the view more directly: 'Our Lord Jesus Christ did through his transcendent love become what we are, that we might become what he is.' 'He was made man', said Athanasius, 'that we might be made God.'[2] Jesus asks his disciples to be united with him. 'Abide in me, and I in you.'[3] Even as there is no existence apart from him there is no salvation apart from union with God. Jesus is the forerunner, the first born of many brethren and the first fruits of them that slept.[4]

The different representations of the Supreme as *Viṣṇu, Śiva, Śakti* take into account the traditional beliefs of the different people. They are not cold abstractions but symbolise different ways of communion and fellowship. The spread of Hinduism in India has resulted in the assimilation of the divinities worshipped by the people.

Īśvara is not the ultimate ideal. A Personal God even when theologically sublimated is only a realisation of that which is beyond both being and its opposite non-being. We must leave behind the categories of religious thought and have a direct ascent. In the concept of *Īśvara,* we objectify what is essentially non-objective. We try to naturalise what is beyond nature.

There are many analogies to the conception of *Brahman* and *Īśvara,* Absolute and God in Western religious thought.

To give one example, for Plotinus God is super-being or

[1] II *Corinthians* viii. 9. [2] *De Incarnatione* LV. 4. 3. [3] *John* xv. 4.
[4] *Hebrews* vi. 20; *Romans* viii. 29; I *Corinthians* xv. 20.

nothing, if being is something. In the sphere of the *nous*, the relation of subject and object exists. While the one for Plotinus is the absolute Godhead, the intellectual principle is God.

Brahmā

Brahmā or *Hiraṇya-garbha* is the first-born emanation of the supreme *Īśvara*, who controls the processes of cosmic evolution. *Īśvara* is infinite, has all possibilities in him without limitation. There are inexhaustible ranges of being and value in him which have not yet received realisation. They belong solely to the distinctive being and perfection of God.

Brahmā is created and this world is perishable.[1] Manu says: 'From the Highest *Nārāyaṇa*, there was born the four-faced one.'[2] He says: 'This universe existed in the shape of darkness. . . . The Supreme desiring to create beings of many kinds from his own body, first with a thought created the waters and placed his seed in them. That seed became a golden egg equal to the sun in brilliancy; in that he himself was born as *Brahmā*, the progenitor of the whole world.'[3] *Hiraṇya-garbha* is a manifestation of *Īśvara*. Ś. says that in the *Kaṭha U.*[4] the *mahān ātman* is *Hiraṇya-garbha* and his *buddhi* is the basis of all intellects.[5]

According to R., there are four classes of creatures (godmen, men, animals and plants), and the difference of these classes depends on the individual selves which are attached to various

[1] *yo brahmāṇam vidadhāti pūrvam*. Ś.U. VI. 18.

According to the writings of the Egyptians there was a time when neither heaven nor earth existed, and when nothing had being except the boundless primeval water which was, however, shrouded with thick darkness. At length, the spirit of the primeval water felt the desire for creative activity, and having uttered the word, the world sprang straightway into being in the form which had already been depicted, in the mind of the spirit before he spoke the word which resulted in the creation. The next act of creation was the formation of a germ or egg from which sprang *Ra*, the Sun-God within whose shining form was embodied the almighty power of the divine Spirit. E. A. Wallis Budge: *Egyptian Ideas of the Future Life*, pp. 22–3.

[2] *paro nārāyaṇo devas tasmāj jātas catur-mukhaḥ.*

[3] *tad aṇḍam abhavaddhaimam sahasrāṁśu-sama-prabham*
tasmin jajñe svayam brahmā sarva-loka-pitāmahaḥ.

I. 1. 5, 8–9.

[4] I. 3. 10–11.

[5] *yā prathamajasya hiraṇya-garbhasya buddhis sā sarvāsām buddhīnām paramā pratiṣṭhā*. Ś.B. I. 4. 1.

bodies enabling them to experience the results of their works in the world beginning with *Brahmā* and ending with non-moving objects.[1] By the interaction of subject and object the cosmic process gradually realises the values of spirit in its upward ascent from nothingness to the Kingdom of God or *brahma-loka* under divine inspiration and influence.

The changing historical process is not coextensive with reality. It is a limited manifestation of the Supreme. *Hiraṇya-garbha* is not only the world-soul but also the highest of all beings in the world. 'For as in the series of beings, though having the common attributes of being animated, from man to a blade of grass, a successive diminution of knowledge, power and so on is observed, so in the [ascending] series [extending] from man to *Hiraṇya-garbha*, a gradually increasing manifestation of knowledge, power and so on takes place.'[2]

We cannot say that the Absolute changes into *Īśvara* or *Īśvara* into *Hiraṇya-garbha*. The objection to the *pariṇāma* or change theory is put in several ways. Vācaspati asks: does it change as a whole or in part? If it changes as a whole, how can there be no destruction of old nature; if it changes in part, is the part different from the whole or non-different? If it be different, how can the transformation be of the original reality, for when one thing is changed a different thing is not also changed as that would be an undue extension. Or if it be non-different, how can the transformation be not of the whole?[3]

Viśva-rūpa

The world is a concretisation of the world purpose. It is the *virāt-svarūpa*. The Vedic gods were representations of prominent aspects of nature. *Dyaus*, from *div*, to shine, is the lord of the heavenly light, the source of strength, splendour and knowledge.

[1] *brahmādi-sthāvarāntaṁ catur-vidhaṁ bhūta-jātaṁ tat-tat-karmocita-śarīraṁ tad-ucita-nāma-bhākcākarod ity uktam.* R.B. I. 3. 26.

[2] *yathā hi prāṇitvāviśeṣe'pi manuṣyādi-stamba-paryanteṣu jñānaiśvaryādi pratibandhaḥ pareṇa pareṇa bhūyān bhavan dṛśyate, tathā manuṣyādiṣv eva hiraṇya-garbha-paryanteṣu jñānaiśvaryādy-abhivyaktir api pareṇa pareṇa bhūyasī bhavati.* Ś.B. I. 3. 30.

[3] *tat sarvātmanā vā pariṇamate eka-deśe vā? sarvātmanā pariṇāme kathaṁ na tattva-vyāhatiḥ? eka-deśa-pariṇāme vā sa eka-deśas tato bhinno vā abhinno vā? bhinnaś cet kathaṁ tasya pariṇāmaḥ? na hy anyasmin pariṇama-māne'nyaḥ-pariṇāmati ati-prasaṅgāt abhede vā kathaṁ na sarvātmanā pariṇāmaḥ?*

Varuṇa is the symbol of celestial and regal power and is connected with the idea of *ṛta*, of a cosmic order, of natural and supernatural law. *Mitra* is the god of truth and fidelity. *Sūrya* is the flaming sun from whom nothing is hidden, who destroys every infirmity. In the form of *Savitṛ*, *Sūrya* is the principle of awakening and intellectual animation. *Uṣas* is the dawn, the eternally young, who opens the way for the sun, who gives life, who is the symbol of eternal life. *Indra* is the incarnation of the heroic. He is the god of war, of valour and of victory. *Yama* is the first of the mortals 'who first found the road to the hereafter'.[1] By drinking *Soma*, the symbol of a sacred ecstasy, we become immortal and reach the light.[2]

Vighneśvara is *Ganeśa*, the lord of hosts (*gaṇa*). By his aid we overcome obstacles. He removes all barriers from the path of a devotee. He clears the way by pushing aside whatever lies across the road. He is said to be of the form of an elephant for the elephant forges ahead even through pathless thickets and jungles. It can swim rivers and lakes and with its trunk tears down the branches that block the way and even uproots trees. The print of its feet is the target of all footprints.[3] Where an elephant has trod, other animals can follow. *Gaṇesa's vāhana* or vehicle is the rat which finds and makes its way subtly.

When we come up against the vital elements of nature, when we wash our hands in the waters of a river, when we raise our eyes to the sun, when we prepare ourselves for the joy of eating a slice of bread made of the corn of the earth, we have a sense that nature's elements are the work of God. For the Jews the heavens declare the glory of God. The light is his robe and the clouds his chariot.

The gods who retain their anthropomorphic personifications of the natural forces serve to assist the mind in its attempt to comprehend what is regarded as manifested through them. They are useful symbols which serve as bearers of the divine power or mystery. Our interest in nature has become today an impersonal, technical one, how to master and manipulate it. We have lost our life with nature to our great impoverishment.

In all this analysis we are tearing apart and in a sense

[1] *Ṛg Veda* X. 14. 2.
[2] *Ṛg Veda* VIII. 48. 3.
[3] The doctrine of the Buddha is compared to the footprint of the elephant.

misrepresenting what is presented in a unitary way. *Brahman, Īśvara, Hiraṇya-garbha* and *Virāt-rūpa* are four poises of the one Reality.[1]

CHAPTER 5

The Status of the World

Saṁsāra

The world in Indian thought as in many other systems is said to be a perpetual procession of events where nothing abides. It is a succession of states. The Hindu and the Buddhist systems accept the fact of *saṁsāra*, what Plato calls 'the world of coming into being and passing away'. It is an endless process of becoming and not a state. The universe is not a static one. The actual world is a process whose possibilities are infinite.

Bhartṛhari says: 'We see that life is being wasted every day. Youth is approaching its end, the days that are past do not return. Time devours the world. The goddess of wealth is as unsteady as waves in a river. Life is as fleeting as lightning itself. Therefore, O Lord, save me, seeking refuge in thee, this very instant.'[2] Transiency is the character not only of human life but of the very structure of reality.

[1] See P.U., pp. 701–5.

[2] *āyur naśyati paśyatāṁ prati-dinaṁ yāti kṣayaṁ yauvanam*
pratyāyānti gatāḥ punar na divasāḥ kālo jagad-bhakṣakaḥ
lakṣmīs toya-taraṅga-bhaṅga-capalā vidyuc-calaṁ jīvitam
tasmān māṁ śaraṇāgataṁ śaraṇada. tvam-rakṣa rakṣādhunā.

In the *Phaedrus*, Plato says that 'if man had eyes to see Divine Beauty, pure and clean and unalloyed, not clogged with the pollutions of mortality and all the colours and varieties of human life, his one aim would be to fly away from earth to heaven'.

'Human life! Its duration is momentary, its substance in perpetual flux, its senses dim, its physical organism perishable, its consciousness a vortex, its destiny dark, its repute uncertain—in fact, the material element is a rolling stream, the spiritual element dreams and vapour, life a war and a sojourning in a far country, fame oblivion. What can see us through? One thing and one only—Philosophy; and that means keeping the spirit within us unspoiled and undishonoured, not giving way to pleasure or pain, never acting unthinkingly or deceitfully or insincerely, and never being dependent on the moral support of others. It also means taking what comes contentedly as all part of the process

[*Continued on page 136*

When we speak of the world as *māyā* we refer to the feeling of the vanity of life. 'All this most lovely fabric of things exceeding good', wrote Augustine in the fourth century A.D., 'when its measures are accomplished will pass away; they have their morning and their evening.'[1] The world subject to change, decay and death is not the Ultimate Reality. If the constant is real, the changing is less than real.

Saṁsāra has a pattern

The problem for philosophy is, why is there a world at all and what are we all doing in it? Before we are able to answer these questions, we must know the nature of the world. Even Buddhism which stresses the transiency of life allows the rule of law. Each state is determined by what went before it. The world process has a pattern and a goal. It is marching towards freedom. The path is not smooth or straight. There are blind alleys, relapses. As we shall see, the human individual can shape the future. If we do not have men of sufficient courage, strength and dedication, humanity may lapse into long nights of reaction. Yet, slowly, painfully, but inexorably, it moves on towards an ideal state of happiness, truth, beauty and goodness.

This world is not a wasteland. It is not altogether a world of woe. Human life is not an accident in a blind impersonal process. There is a relation between the self-conscious spirit of man and the reality at the heart of things. Enlightened ideas have a transforming power.

Time and Eternity

Though everything is subject to the law of time, time itself is, in Plato's words, the moving image of eternity. We cannot account for the order and progress we discern in the world, if it is treated as self-sufficient. It is said that this entire triad of worlds would have become blind darkness if the light known as

Continued from page 135]
to which we owe our own being; and, above all, it means facing Death calmly—taking it simply as a dissolution of the atoms of which every living organism is composed. Their perpetual transformation does not hurt the atoms, so why should one mind the whole organism being transformed and dissolved? It is a law of Nature, and Natural Law can never be wrong.' Marcus Aurelius Antoninus, *Meditations* Book II *ad fin.*

[1] *Confessions* XIII. 3. 5.

Word had not been shining in it.[1] If there were no God there would not be anything else.

If we immerse the light in darkness, the world becomes a void, a nothingness, an abyss and a night descends on the depths of the human spirit. The world is not self-sufficient or self-explanatory nor is it meaningless or unintelligible. God is time as well as eternity. Both Nāgārjuna and Ś. admit the factual nature of the pluralistic world. Both of them affirm that it is not ultimate. Its character is indeterminate, *anirvacanīya*, neither real nor unreal.[2]

Māyā

To look upon the temporal process apart from the eternal background is to mistake the nature of the world. The world is not apart from *Brahman*. To look upon the world as self-sufficient is to be caught in *māyā*. The B.G. admits that the world is *anitya*, non-eternal, and *asukha*, painful, but there is the eternal underlying it. There is bitterness at the bottom of every cup, blight in every flower, shadow in every sunshine. To see into the abyss and yet to believe that God is merciful and by his grace man can right his course even when he has strayed is the teaching of the B.G. The temporal is, however, not to be identified with the Eternal.

Eternal Being is non-dual; objectified or known being is dual. Concepts and categories are only a means of apprehending *Dasein* or being in the world, objective existence. The objective universe consists of three things, 'name, form and action'. '*trayaṁ vā idaṁ nāma rūpaṁ karma.*'[3] These three support one another and are really one. To be perceived, to be an object, *dṛśya*, is to forfeit ultimate reality. Time is a fundamental form of the objectification of human existence. The waking and the dream worlds are both unreal in the strict metaphysical sense in that they involve duality and are objective but this is not to reduce a waking experience to a dream state. There is nothing to

[1] *idaṁ andhaṁ tamaḥ kṛstnaṁ jāyeta bhuvana-trayam*
yadi śabdāhvayaṁ jyotirā saṁsāraṁ na dīpyate.

[2] 'Jesus, son of Mary (on whom be peace) said: The world is a bridge; pass over it, but build no house upon it.' This was inscribed by Akbar on the Bulwand Darwaza, the lofty gateway into the palace of Fatehpur Sikri, completed by him A.D. 1571.

[3] B.U. I. 6. 1.

support the view that the entire manifold universe is illusory in character. The tangible objects which we see around us are not the objects of our imagination. The world is distinguished from such self-contradictory entities as the son of a barren woman and dreams and illusions. Ś. takes pains to repudiate the view of mentalism advocated by the *Vijñāna-vādins*. Whatever the outside world depends on, it does not depend on the human mind. Ś. does not favour the modern attempt to dissolve concrete realities like stars and atoms into mathematical equations or mental states. He argues against the subjectivist theory which asserts that everything exists only so far as it is known or is a content of consciousness. The sensation 'blue' is different from the sensation 'red', because the objects given to the sensing consciousness are different. Awareness of something 'blue' and the object 'blue' are not identical.[1] The object of consciousness is not the same as the consciousness of the object and the manner of the existence of the one is not like the manner of the existence of the other. The object 'blue' can exist without requiring that the consciousness of 'blue' should exist. It is just the same whether we are aware of it or not. The object seen is independent of perception.

Even if the world be an illusion, the maker of the illusion is not the individual subject but the divine Lord. *māyāṁ tu prakṛtiṁ viddhi māyinaṁ tu maheśvaram.*[2] The idea of the created world is not our dream but is put into our heads by the Divine Being. If it is imagination that creates the world, it is the cosmic imagination and not any private one. Commenting on II. 4. 20, Ś. clearly makes out that the individual soul is not responsible for the world of objects: 'with regard to the manifold names and forms, such as mountains, rivers, oceans, etc., no soul apart from the Lord possesses the power of evolution; and if any have such power it is dependent on the Highest Lord'.[3] If life is an illusion it is one that lasts endlessly, *anādi, ananta*. It is shared by all human beings, *sarva-loka-pratyakṣa*.[4] It is difficult to draw a distinction between such an illusion and reality.

[1] *artha-jñānayor bhedaḥ.* Ś.B. II. 2. 20. [2] Ś.U. IV. 10.

[3] *na ca giri-nadī-samudrādiṣu nānāvidheṣu nāmarūpeṣv anīśvarasya jīvasya vyākaraṇa-sāmarthyam asti; yeṣv api cāsti sāmarthyaṁ teṣv api parameśvarāyattam eva tat.* [4] Ś.B. I. 1. 1.

Each entity is a mixture of being and non-being. In his finitude the human individual asks the question of the nature of being. He who is infinite does not ask the question of being for he is being completely. A being who does not realise that he is finite cannot ask because he does not go beyond himself. Man cannot avoid asking the question because he belongs to being from which he is separated. He knows that he belongs to it and is now separate from it. What we come across in this world appears to us as real but we soon realise that its reality is only transitory, historical. It was and is no more.

The world is to help human beings realise their destiny. Historical objectification is the path of division which man must tread. He must face his destiny by which he may rediscover his alienation from his self. Our finiteness is the condition of our awareness. Our temporality gives us a chance of knowing the eternal. Our limitation gives us the scope and the opportunity to glimpse the Unlimited. The world is, verily, a passage from existence to reality. The world of becoming is not authentic being, but aspires to be that. 'All things pray except the Supreme', says Proclus.

The world is a different kind of existence, a degraded form when compared to the Supreme Being. Whatever is known is a reflection of the Self in limiting adjuncts. The objective universe is not the subject but is yet derived from it. 'As a spider moves along the thread (it produces), and as from a fire tiny sparks fly in all directions, so from this Self emanate all organs, all worlds, all gods, and all beings. Its secret name (*upaniṣad*) is "the truth of truth" (*satyasya satyam*). The vital force is truth and it is the truth of that (*prāṇā vai satyam, teṣām eṣa satyam*).'[1] The world is actual, existent, but its truth is in the Self. In the Self alone all the world takes its rise, persists and perishes. 'Although one, thou hast penetrated diverse things.'[2] 'The one Lord is hidden in all beings, all-pervading and the Self of all.'[3]

There is not any radical separation between the Supreme

[1] B.U. II. 1. 20. Cf. '[God] giveth to all life and breath, and everything, and he made of one blood every nation of men . . . that they should seek God . . . and find him, though he is not far from each one of us; for in him we live, move, and have our being; as certain even of your own poets have said, for we are also his offspring.' *Acts* xvii. 25–8.

[2] *Taittirīya Āraṇyaka.* III. 14. 3.

[3] Ś.U. VI. 2.

Spirit and the actual world. On the contrary the values of spirit are surprisingly exemplified in the world of existent fact. A realm of subsistent being altogether unrelated to the realm of actual existents is meaningless. Even those who look upon values as belonging to a realm of being which is different from that of actual existents assert that values are realised in actual entities. We speak of beautiful pictures, scenes and persons. Existent objects exemplify subsistent values. Though the world has not absolute reality, it is not to be compared with illusory appearances. The *Advaita Vedānta* emphasises the unity of being, the oneness of the subject. But the object is discrete but not illusory. It is not a bare multiplicity which would be unthinkable. Embodiedness has positive value for the evolution of the soul and every form of life should be respected.[1] The cosmic process is not a meaningless one but aims at the realisation of an ideal. It has selves which are both subjects and objects. Our objective knowledge, though it apprehends an already degraded being, still reveals something of the reality despite its divorce from intimate, inward existence. It is a manifestation or objectification of Spirit, though it may be difficult to account for this fact.

Why should real being suffer the accident of objectification? We may as well ask, why should the world be what it is? Though the world is a manifestation of Spirit, there is no spiritual freedom in it. The final triumph of Spirit would mean the annihilation of the non-authentic objective world, the creation of reality over symbol, the realisation of authentic being. We must realise Spirit, existentially rather than objectively. That is the purpose of human life. Man has Spirit but he must become Spirit, an incarnate Spirit.

Creation

The Sanskrit word *sṛṣṭi* means literally emanation, letting loose. The world is dependent on *Brahman* but this dependence does not take away from the integrity and independence of

[1] A popular verse says that you have acquired this body as the result of great goodness. Cross this ocean of temporal becoming before the body breaks.

mahatā puṇya-paṇyena krīto'yaṃ kāyanaus tathā
pāraṁ duhkhodadhair gantuṁ taraī yāvan na bhidyate.

Cp. also *jantūnāṁ nara-janma durlabham.*

Brahman. The onesided dependence of the world on *Brahman* is sometimes illustrated by the analogy of the rope which gives rise to the appearance of the snake. Though the latter depends on the rope, the rope does not depend on the appearance of the snake. Since the appearance is not factual, it is sometimes imagined that the world is not factual. But Ś. himself explains that the illustrations have only a limited application and are not to be extended to all points.[1] When one thing is compared with another it does not follow that they are similar in all respects. They are similar only in some intended point. Creation of the world out of nothing describes the absolute independence of God as Creator, the absolute dependence of creation and the distance between them.

Even in the instances which Ś. gives, silver which turns out to be mother-of-pearl or a human being who turns out to be a post, there is an object which is misinterpreted. The world is a manifestation, real and unreal, real as *Brahman* and unreal when viewed apart from *Brahman*.

Īśvara is *Brahman* with creative power. He is *Brahman* with the principle of self-manifestation. How is the Eternal Logos related to the contents of the world-process? The classical answer is that the essences or potentialities of the world are eternal in the Divine Mind. Not all of them are manifested in the world. God is absolutely free in respect of creation, with his *māyā-śakti* or power of determination without any impairment of his being. *Īśvara* is not a mere symbol adopted for *upāsanā* or worship. He has two sides, transcendent when he is one with *Brahman*, immanent when he produces the world. As transcendent, *Īśvara* is conceived as devoid of *māyā*, as immanent he is the determiner of *māyā*. He has a double form. As transcendent he is free from *māyā*, other than the world put forth by him, one with *Brahman*, *trīguṇātīta*. He is also the living creative God.

The existence of the world is altogether contingent. It does not flow necessarily from the existence of God. While God can create a world if he wills to do so, he is entirely free with regard to the exercise of his will. There is thus a double contingency with regard to the world. God need not have made a world

[1] *sarva-sārūpye hi dṛṣṭānta-dārṣṭāntika-bhāvoccheda eva syāt*. Ś.B. III. 2. 20.

at all. He need not have made this particular world which he has made.

Why we have this world and not another is something for which we cannot offer an explanation. F. H. Bradley observes: 'That experience should take place in finite centres and should wear the form of finite this-ness is in the end inexplicable.' We have to accept it as the given datum and cannot derive it from the definition of God. The creative thought: 'let me be many' belongs to *Brahman*. It is not simply imagined in him. The energy that manifests itself in *Brahman* is one with and different from *Brahman*.[1] The doctrine of creation out of nothing insists that God is not limited by a pre-existent matter or by any conditions external to himself. God's will is the meaning of the world and it is sovereign over both nature and history. The *Upaniṣads* do not countenance any dualism. They hold that the power which rules the cosmic energies is the determiner of human destiny.

Īśvara, as stated in the previous section, is associated with the principle of objectivity. He is described as the poet, the creator of order out of chaos. The world should become an ordered beauty. Commenting on I. 1. 4, Ś. says that *avyakta* is not to be confused with *pradhāna* or *prakṛti*. It is just the unmanifested *na vyakta*. It is just the subtle cause, the primal state of the existence of the universe. It is dependent on God and is not an absolute reality. If we do not accept such a subtle power abiding in God, God cannot be a creator. He cannot move towards creation. This *avyakta* is *avidyā* or *māyā* depending on God. The individuals lie in it without any self-awakening. The potency of this power is destroyed by knowledge in the case of the emancipated beings. They are therefore not born again.[2]

Bhāmatī says that there are different *avidyās* associated with different selves. When any individual gains wisdom the *avidyā* associated with him is destroyed. The other *avidyās* associated with other individuals remain the same and produce the world. The term *avyakta* relates to *avidyā* in a generic sense. While

[1] *bhedābhedātmikā śaktir brahma-niṣṭhā sanātanī.*

[2] *muktānāṁ ca punar an-utpattiḥ, kutaḥ vidyayā tasyā bīja-śakter dāhāt.* I. 4. 3.

it rests in the individual, it is yet dependent on God who is its agent and object. The support of *avidyā* is *Brahman*. Though the real nature of the selves is *Brahman*, so long as they are surrounded by *avidyā*, they do not realise their true nature.

Hiraṇya-garbha is seeking complete expression in the world. While the world is dependent on *Brahman* and not vice versa, while it is the expression of the creative energy of God, it is the manifestation of *Hiraṇya-garbha*. The *Puruṣa-sūkta* of the *Rg Veda* makes out that in the original act of creation, God has torn himself apart. The act of creation is an act of sacrifice. There is a tearing apart, an aberration and the end of the cosmic process is a return to the Spirit. There is nothing but God and by his will the universe is made ceaselessly. Being good and the giver of all, God gives out himself through countless forms that they may all share his life of infinite bliss. Being perfect he needs nothing for himself but desires recipients of his love. The world is not a completed act, it is still in the process of completion. The world-spirit exists in the human spirit and can attain to a consciousness of itself.

Spirit and matter are aspects of the Uncreated Light from which all creation flows. In creation it is as if the Primordial Light while remaining pure and undivided in itself enters as light into its own divine darkness, as selfhood enters non-self. All forms of evolving life are born and grow of the marriage of the Prime mover and the primal darkness. Nothingness is the veil of Being according to Heidegger. Being conceals itself behind nothingness. Nothingness is most intimately united with Being. It proceeds out of Being and yet conceals it.

The world is an appearance of *Brahman*, a *partial manifestation* of *Īśvara* and an organic manifestation of *Hiraṇya garbha*. These are the conceptions to which we are led by an examination of the given experience. If we are unable to reconcile these different views it does not mean that there is an inner contradiction in the nature of the Supreme but that there is a limit to our powers of comprehension. The emancipated souls understand the fourfold status of reality, the Absolute *Brahman*, God *Īśvara*, world-soul *Hiraṇya-garbha*, and the world *virāt-svarūpa*.

CHAPTER 6

The Individual Self

Duality in human nature

The question of the nature of the self is raised only by human beings. Animals cannot ask this question and redeemed spirits know the self and do not pose the question. The naturalistic world view reduces man to an object utterly insignificant in the vast magnitudes of space-time. Man is not exhausted by body and mind. In the complex of personality there is something which uses both and yet is neither. The waxing years and the waning strength are quite powerless to dim the brightness of spirit. Any change which may spell decay for the body or even for mind may yet be irrelevant for the spirit which is essentially man himself.

The Empirical Self

Buddha and Ś. adopt a view of the self which reminds us of Hume's account. When we look within, we come across an endless procession of thoughts, imaginings, emotions, desires, but not a permanent self. The *Upaniṣads* look upon the individual as a composite of physical and mental traits, *nāma-rūpa*. They both change, the body somewhat more slowly than the mind. We are not aware of the changing for it is continuous and what is constant, relatively speaking, is the name. The permanence of the name produces the illusion of unity. Strictly speaking, man is nothing more than a sequence of physical and mental processes, a chain of events, a series of thoughts, perceptions, emotions and other responses to impressions received from outside. The self is a mental construction. Many of our acts, psychologists say, are automatic, mechanical. Men are, for the most part, machines and many men do not realise that it is possible for them to overcome their automatism. Most of the time we struggle through life completely unaware of what we are doing, responding to external stimuli in an automatic way. We are at the mercy of all chance happenings. If this were all, human mind would be like the animal. But we know that there is a fundamental difference between the two. For example, animal sounds register immediate impulses; human speech gives us more than immediacy. It communicates ideas which transcend immediacy.

Consciousness cannot be defined. It is awareness of thinking, imagining, sensing. There are four states of consciousness according to the *Māṇḍūkya U.*, waking, dream and sleep, and the transcendental consciousness called *turīya*. We generally pass our time awake, dreaming or sleeping but we are not self-aware. We are aware of tables and chairs or in dreams of horses and chariots or we are in sound sleep. In this state, there is consciousness without thought, without any dream or perception. We are rarely aware of our selves standing apart from all that surrounds us, physically or mentally. But the vivid moments of life are those in which man is aware of himself.

The *Sāṁkhya* system argues that all except the pure self, *puruṣa*, is objective, non-self, *prakṛti*. All the divisions of organic and inorganic, mental and non-mental, the intelligent and the non-intelligent are divisions within the object side. This is not materialism for matter itself is invested with a new quality. The human individual belongs to the object side, an element in the perpetual procession we call the universe. There is always and everywhere creative movement and the universe is no exception to it. The difference between material things and living organisms is one of the degree of individuality. Every individual is a composite, a unity in multiplicity. The more individual we are, the deeper is the unity and the larger the complexity. Animals are unities of complex mental elements.[1] The rise of reflective thought at the human level raises new problems.[2] There is a greater unity of behaviour. The possibility

[1] Cp. Walt Whitman, who describes the life of animals thus: 'they are so placid and self-contained, they do not sweat and whine about their condition, they do not lie awake in the dark and weep for their sins, they do not make me sick discussing their duty to God, not one is dissatisfied, not one is demented with the mania of owning things, not one kneels to another, nor to his kind that lived thousands of years ago, not one is respectable or unhappy over the whole earth'.

[2] Cp. St Bernard: 'God who, in his simple substance, is all everywhere equally, nevertheless, in efficacy is in rational creatures in another way than in irrational, and in good rational creatures in another way than in the bad. He is in irrational creatures in such a way as not to be comprehended by them; by all rational creatures, however, He can be comprehended by knowledge; but only by the good is He also comprehended by "love".'

of self-knowledge arises. Human beings are self-conscious and self-directing. They are capable of controlling their conduct by general principles and judgments of value. Their spontaneity becomes transformed into creative freedom.

We philosophise because we are finite and we know that we are finite. We are aware that we are a mixture of being and not-being. The body is that which dissolves itself.[1] It is that which burns itself out.[2] The human self as a centre in the objective series can be analysed into its components, can be regarded as a sum of states or experiences. It knows that it is finite and incomplete, limited by an environment, natural and social. We cannot account for this knowledge of ourselves as finite and imperfect except on the assumption of the infinite and the perfect in us of which we are dimly aware. In his non-being man cannot help but aspire to being. So he cries out for the light from which he has hidden himself. He is not content with the sandy wastes of the human spirit deprived of God. For Sartre, life is absurdity, nothingness and each one has to make of it something meaningful. The sign of hope is that we realise our non-being. It is the eternity in us which makes us aware of time. In our nature the temporal and the eternal meet. We must cease to be mechanical and become conscious. It is then the real 'I' appears. When we wake up we realise our nothingness, our mechanisation, our utter helplessness. Our views and opinions, our tastes and thoughts are not our own. They are borrowed from elsewhere. In some small measure man has governance over himself. Our choices may be conditioned by circumstances over which we have no control. This conditioning may be a limitation on our freedom; yet in some sense we are capable of acting freely.

Jīva and Ātman

The human individual has reason, self-consciousness, freedom. Unlike the rest of nature, he can say 'I'. His self stands against the ego which is a part of nature. He anticipates the death of the ego and runs ahead of himself. The 'I' transcends the 'me' which is subject to moods.

The unseizability of the self has been a commonplace of

[1] *śīryate iti śarīram.* [2] *dahyate iti dehaḥ.*

philosophic thought. Hume in one way and Heidegger in another maintain that the self remains inaccessible to thought. As a centre of action, the self is an activity and an activity cannot be seized.

When philosophers speak of self-knowledge they do not refer to psychological introspection. The Self is pure spirit. The task of human individuals who are weak, finite beings though endowed with a spark of divinity is to work and suffer in an effort to reach a state of perfection. Each individual is a spark from a great flame, a ray of the one Light, differentiated within the body of the Cosmic Spirit. The spark is an encloser of divine potentialities which become manifest through life in the empirical world. At the present stage of its unfoldment it uses on the physical plane a form which includes the mental, emotional and physical bodies. These are collectively called the *persona* or mask, the perishable personality behind which it operates, using it as a tool with which to gather experience for the purposes of the growth of the soul. The text 'That thou art' means that the Divine is all that we are capable of becoming and we must strive on and on till our life becomes an expression of the Divine.

The psychological ego implies the individuation of the Universal Spirit by the non-conscious or material principle. The threefold conception of man as body, mind and spirit implies an important truth, that man is not a mere object, that his spiritual nature is not on the same level as his psychic and corporeal, that his soul and body can participate in a new higher order of spiritual existence. Man can pass from the order of nature to that of freedom, from the region of discord and hostility to that of love and union. Personality is not merely body and mind but Spirit, and Spirit, as we have seen, *is*. It is the primal reality more authentic than anything reflected in the objective world. *Ātman* is the foundation of the ego, the kernel of the personality. It is the Universal Self active in every ego even as it is the universal source of all things. The oneness of the Transcendent or Super-temporal subject is not in conflict with the plurality of empirical selves. The Self in us expresses itself by the power to transcend every objectified form of psychic life. It is, as it were, a divine breath, penetrating existence and endorsing it with the highest dignity, with an inner independence and unity. It is the image and likeness of God in Man. By the impact of the Spirit with the psychophysical organism, there is set up the attempt to realise the idea, the divine purpose concerning the individual. The Spirit hidden in the depths of being is made manifest by a slow conquest achieved in course of time. Man's salvation is dearly bought for he has to gather his soul into his hands and let the Universal manifest through it. Creative action and self-conquest are derived from the Self in us. Each individual attempts to become a real whole, not a sum of parts, an end in itself, not a means to an end. Though it has a material content and foundation, the Self has an autonomous validity which prevents its being converted into a means.

Selfhood involves the possibility of moral failure. The individual is unique and unpredictable. His function lies in his participation in this continually creative act. Freedom vouchsafed to us is like all gifts, a double-edged sword, but that is no reason for ceasing to use it. Life's course is tragic, a progress in which joy is inseparable from suffering. Yet it is enjoined on us to live it. Suffering is the result of alienation from reality and when we get back to it suffering disappears.

As Spirit is opposed to the world of things or of objects or of phenomena, the human individual attempts at becoming a historical reality, one and unique, achieving a unity of originality and value, despite its multiplicity of functions. A unique and indivisible destiny is its essential constituent. The power of free choice is its essential feature. As it is not an objective datum, it fashions and creates itself. Personality is the union of our acts and potentialities, a complex unity of body, mind and spirit. It is the symbol of human integrity, of a constant and unique form created in the midst of incessant flux. It would dissolve itself into nothing as soon as it discarded its limitations and supports, though it would reduce itself to an object if it passively submitted to these limitations. We cannot say that the non-successive is real and the successive is unreal. The whole attempt of creation is to lift up the phenomenon to the level of the subject, to divinise the empirical ego. The self is spirit and body; it includes the super-temporal subject and the temporal experiences. For us in the objective world, the super-temporal has no existence apart from the temporal, though the latter cannot be conceived apart from the former. Time is in us as pure subjects and we are in time as empirical egos. Both are true though neither is true by itself. From the naturalist point of view, man is only a minute part of nature; from the sociological viewpoint he is a small unit of society; from the spiritual point of view, he is real and free. In man is an intersection of several worlds, none of which completely contains his true self. It exists on several planes and is permanently in a process of creative change. It has need of time to realise its potentialities to the full. It always endeavours to resolve contradictions. It will not do if the spirit establishes unity and control within the nature of the ego. It must conquer the world and transform it instead of denying and abandoning it to its fate. It aims above all at the Kingdom of God. Salvation comes only through realising or establishing truth in human relationships, through enabling each individual to realise his personality. The empirical individuals are not really subsistent subjects but are parts of the objective world, abstractions made for practical purposes from the concrete reality of history. Their separate existence and self-control are limited. They are all parts of the objectified universe. God is, however, an existent among existents in no way to be identified with the whole creation though closely concerned with it. His knowledge of the world is perfect and his love for it profound and he works through creation to effect its consummation.

It is incorrect to imagine that the objective process has in it two opposite natures, spiritual and material, of which one must be discarded and the other accepted. These worlds are not separate and hostile. Reality is one with many planes. The material looks upward to the spiritual and finds in it its true meaning. Similarly the spiritual leans to the physical in order to find itself. Every aspect of existence has in it these two in different measures. Eternal *Brahman* is a living God in relation to the temporal world. If existence is a degradation, it is one in which the whole from God to matter shares. The physical world seems to be the first statement of the conditions from which there is a progressive evolution of spirit. One principle acts throughout the cosmic process though it assumes special forms in special regions. It is different in living things and in non-living. In non-living things also we have the distinction of form and matter. Matter is pure potentiality and such a pure potentiality without an actual character or behaviour is just non-existence. So pure matter is never found in itself. It is the lower limit of the range of being. As a concrete existent, it is both being and non-being. Until the purpose of the Spirit in this manifestation is perfectly fulfilled, there is no departure from it. The complete self-finding of Spirit in the cosmic life is the terminus. The Kingdom of God is the fulfilled transfigured life of this world.

Jainism holds that man's nature is dual. It has both material and spiritual content. So man, as he is, is not perfect but he can attain perfection. The soul's true nature is perfection. When it is unencumbered by error, it consists of infinite perception, knowledge and bliss. By this spiritual nature man can control his material nature and when he succeeds in doing it he becomes a *jina* or conqueror, a liberated soul. These souls are of two kinds, those who have attained *nirvāṇa* and those who are still embodied. The latter are called *arhats*. They are the *jīvan-muktas*.

Great religions retain the notion of a state of original innocence in which human beings or at least a couple of them according to the Jews, Christians and Muslims lived in direct communion with God. Supporters of extreme doctrines of transcendence like Karl Barth believe that the distance from the state of innocence is so great that the divine spark in us may be supposed to be completely extinguished and can only be relit by an act of vicarious grace. A world wholly given over to the Devil is the result of pure transcendence. If absolute immanence is accepted, there is no work for man to do. Both these views are unsatisfactory. In human beings as in the world there is both being and non-being. God is both immanent and transcendent. The self comes from God and goes back to him. There are stages in the soul's journey to God.

Philo, Theophilus of Antioch, Clement of Alexandria and Origen hold in the spirit of the *Upaniṣads* and of Plato that God created man in his own image. Man's real being, his spiritual being partakes of the nature of God. But man is also involved in the life of the senses which is alien to his nature.[1] When he tries to mould himself in the pattern of the animal life, he forgets his true nature. A fall is the descent of spirit into matter. It is the condition of earthly existence. The purpose of this existence is to ascend to the light of creative consciousness. To go down into non-entity and to rise again later is the law of growth for every seed of spirit. Spiritual life consists in the process of returning to one's true nature. He must realise what he is, must recover his real nature by destroying the hold of the animal nature. Commenting on Genesis, Origen says: 'The man who was made in God's image is the inner man, the incorporeal, incorruptible, immortal one.'[2] Man loses his likeness to God when he sins.

CHAPTER 7

The Way to Perfection

A. THE WAY OF *KARMA* OR LIFE

The Purpose of Human Life

Everything that lives aims at its own specific perfection. The blade of grass, the flowering tree, the flying bird, the running deer, each one strives to reach the perfection of its nature. While the sub-human species work according to a pre-determined pattern, man, on account of the possession of

[1] Iamblichus writes: 'The soul has a twofold life, a lower and a higher. In sleep that soul is freed from the constraint of the body and enters, as one emancipated, on its divine life of intelligence. Then, as the noble faculty which beholds objects as they are—the objects in the world of intelligence—stirs within, and awakens in its power, who can be surprised that the mind, which contains in itself the principles of all that happens, should, in this its state of liberation, discern the future in those antecedent principles which will make that future what it is to be. The nobler part of the soul is thus limited by abstraction to higher natures, and becomes a participant in the wisdom and foreknowledge of the gods.'

[2] Jean Danielou: *Origen* (1955), p. 295. Cp. Claudefield:

In each human heart is a Christ concealed,
To be helped or hindered, to be hurt or healed.
If from any human soul you lift the veil,
You will find a Christ there without fail.

creative will, has to achieve his fulfilment by his effort and will. Descartes reduced the human self to the status of an object for purposes of scientific understanding. The self was, for him, a counterpart of the body. Spinoza felt that if bodily states were strictly determined, mental states were also subject to a strict determinism. Mind and body became objects of scientific treatment only on the condition of a universal determinism. Freud and Marx adopt a similar objective view of the human self, that it is determined ultimately by unconscious impulses or relations of economic production.

Man is not completely a victim of circumstances. He can say 'no' to life whereas the animal always says 'yes' even when he is in the throes of terror and revulsion. Man can deliberately reject satisfaction at one level for the sake of satisfaction at another, higher level. He can impose discipline on his nature and check the drive of desire. He can create a new nature in which the different elements of his being are harmonised.

Each individual is not one but many, an assemblage of different factors.[1] He must reach unity through inner development. External events impinge on us, emotions are suddenly aroused and become dominant and soon they give way to others which in turn try to govern us. There is a strain in human life which impels us to introduce peace and order into the swarm of impulses, emotions and notions, incongruous and often contradictory. This is a life-time job, perhaps a job for many lives. There is in man the ache for unity, the anguish for beatitude.

Man's quest for perfection consists in organising the things of body, mind and soul into a whole. The activities of the human spirit are interrelated, the artistic and the ethical, the religious

[1] Catullus says :

I hate and I love. You ask how can that be?
I know not but I feel the agony.

Plutarch says: 'Each one of us is made up of ten thousand different and successive states, a scrap heap of units, a mob of individuals.' *Concerning the Delphi*, edited by A. O. Prickard (1918).

Oh, wearisome condition of humanity!
Born under one law, to another bound;
Vainly begot, and yet forbidden vanity;
Created sick, commanded to be sound;
What meaneth Nature by these diverse laws?
Passion and Reason, self-division's cause.

Fulke Greville.

and the rational. Man is a miniature of the universe in which he lives. Man, as he is, is a transitional being, an unfinished experiment. When he is awakened, he is at peace with himself, he thinks and acts in a new way. For this awakening, man has to take another step in his evolution. The Kingdom of Heaven is the highest state attainable by man. So long as our nature is not integrated, our actions are confused and contradictory. In an integrated man, thought, speech and action are of one piece.[1] The M.B. says that there is no thief so dangerous[2] as the hypocrite who says one thing and does another, for his is the sin of the deepest dye. When Jesus attacks the Pharisee, he is attacking the man of pretences who keeps up appearances, who pretends to be good when he is not. The Lord is merciful to the sins of the flesh but wrathful against those of the spirit. We must recognise that evil is in us though such a recognition may wound and shame our pride and presumption. There is only one thing of which we have to be ashamed, i.e. unwillingness to recognise the truth. The lie is the great evil of which the Pharisees are guilty.

Different Ways to Fulfilment

There is an old saying that there are as many ways to God as there are souls on earth. Each person is unique and his way to fulfilment is also unique. It is also true that there is so much in common among human beings that we can distinguish certain broad ways to man's realisation, the *karma-mārga,* the way of work, *bhakti-mārga,* the way of devotion, the *dhyāna-mārga,* the way of meditation. All these lead to *jñāna,* wisdom or enlightenment. All *yoga* is one and includes the different aspects of work, devotion and knowledge.

[1] *manasy ekaṁ vacasy ekam karmaṇy ekaṁ mahātmanām*
manasy anyad vacasy anyad karmaṇy anyad durātmanām.

[2] *yo anyathā santam ātmānam anyathā pratipadyate*
kiṁ tena na kṛtaṁ pāpam caureṇātmāpahāriṇā.

Cp. Plato's description of the just man in his *Republic* IV.

There is a revealing story in Sā-di:

'A righteous man saw in a dream a King in Paradise and a devotee in Hell He enquired: "What is the reason for the exaltation of the former and the degradation of the latter? For I used to think it would be the other way round." A voice came saying: "The King is in Paradise because of his kindness to the poor; and the devotee is in Hell because of his attachment to kings".' *Gulistan* II. 15.

Dharma in a wide sense is used to connote all the means for the achievement of the different ends of life. Samantabhadra says that *dharma* is that which leads people out of the woes of the world and fixes them in the highest bliss.[1]

The Primacy of Ethics

Man is the bridge between nature and spirit. His destiny drives him on to the spirit. Through agonies and ecstasies he has to reach his fulfilment. The programme of duties laid down in *dharma śāstras* is intended to help man to reach his goal. The spiritual goal and the ethical means are bound up with each other and not externally related. The moral law within us is evidence of our citizenship in the world of spirit. Moral discipline makes for spiritual insight. Their relationship is not adventitious. To reach the goal is to perfect the means to it.[2] We cannot bypass the ethical. Almost all the religious classics of India insist on ethical conduct as an indispensable means for spiritual life. Ethics is the basis of spiritual life and its substance. Aśoka's *dharma*, for example, emphasises *śīla* or conduct, not creed or doctrine, worship or ceremony. In his Rock Edict 7, Aśoka says that 'all sects wish [to acquire] self-control and purity of mind'.[3] He calls those without these qualities mean indeed, *nīcāḥ*.

Rock Edict 11 says there is no such gift as *dharma-dāna*. *Dharma* is defined as proper behaviour towards slaves and servants, respect for father and mother, gifts to friends and relatives, to *Brāhmaṇas* and ascetics, non-killing of creatures.

Ś. says that one should undertake enquiry into *Brahman* only

[1] *saṁsāra-duḥkhataḥ sattvān yo dharati uttame sukhe.*

Cf. *Nyāya Sūtra* I. 1. 2. 'Of misery, birth, activity, defect and illusory knowledge, by the destruction of each subsequent one there is the destruction of each earlier one and consequently final release.'

duḥkha-janma-pravṛtti-doṣa-mithyā-jñānānām uttarottarāpāye tad-anantarāpāyād apavargaḥ.

In *Gheraṇḍa Samhita* it is said:

nāsti māyā samam pāśam nāsti yogāt param balam
nāsti jñānāt paro bandhur nāhaṁ —kārat paro ripuḥ.

There is no bond equal to that of *māyā*, there is no strength higher than that of *yoga*, there is no friend higher than knowledge, no enemy greater than self-conceit.

[2] Cp. Ś.B.G. II. 55. *sarvatraiva hi adhyātma-śāstre . . . yāni yatna-sādhyāni sādhanāni lakṣaṇāni ca bhavanti tāni.* See also Ś.B.G. XIV. 25.

[3] In Sanskrit it reads *sarve te samyamaṁ ca bhāva-śuddhiṁ ca icchanti.*

after he acquires self-control, detachment, etc., what he calls *viveka, vairāgya, ṣaṭ-sampatti* and *mumukṣutva.*[1] Moral life is an essential condition for the pursuit of wisdom. Ethical conduct is different from ceremonial piety. The latter is of no use to those who are morally impure.[2] Speaking the truth is much better than performing many sacrifices.[3] There is a popular verse which says that people want the fruits of *dharma* and not *dharma* itself.[4] There is a general insistence on truth in inward nature and not merely conformity in outward conduct.

Freedom of Will

The integration of the individual has to be achieved by a conscious effort. If God had desired to create a world of automata there would have been no evil, no failure, God could have eliminated evil if he had so wished by denying us freedom of choice. Evil is there because we sometimes abuse free will. If the world is a machine, then the human individual has no meaning. Man in so far as he is made in the image of God is a creator. He is not free until he is capable of creative activity. While animals are creatures men are creature-creators. There is no animal delinquency. Evil is not passivity but activity. Without creative freedom man cannot produce either a paradise or a desolation on earth. God permits evil because he does not interfere with human choice.

Man is subjected to different sets of laws. He cannot disobey the law of gravitation. If he is unsupported in mid-air he must fall to the ground like a stone. As a living organism he is subject to various biological laws which he cannot violate. These laws

[1] *tasmāt yathokta-sādhana-sampaty-anantaram brahma-jijñāsā kartavyā.* Ś.B. I. 1. 8.

[2] *ācāra-hīnaṁ na punanti vedāḥ. Vasiṣṭha Dharma-sūtra* VI. 3.

[3] *aśvamedha-sahasrāt tu satyam ekaṁ viśiṣyate.* M.B.

[4] *puṇyasya phalam icchanti puṇyaṁ necchanti mānavāḥ.*

Cp. *yo lubdhaḥ piśunaḥ krūro dāmbhiko viṣayātmikaḥ*
sarva-tīrtheṣvapi snātaḥ pāpo malina eva saḥ.

He who is covetous, hypercritical, cruel, ostentatious and attached to the senses though he bathed in all places of pilgrimage, is still sinful and impure.

nigṛhītendriya-grāmo yatraiva ca vasen naraḥ
tatra tasya kuru-kṣetraṁ naimiṣaṁ puṣkarāṇi ca.

One who controls his senses wherever he stays, that place is for him, Kurukṣetra, Naimiṣāraṇya or Puṣkara.

he shares with the animals but there is a law which he does not share with animals, a law which he can disobey if he so chooses. It is the law of *dharma* or right and wrong. Religion is essentially a passion for righteousness.

The Complaint of World-negation

It is said that for the Hindu all true existence is non-material, unchangeable and eternal and therefore the material, changeable, temporal existence is false. So it is said that the good of man consists not in transforming the world which is a vale of woe but in transcending it. It is not his aim to change the world but turn away from it. If the Hindu adopts an exalted morality, it is not founded on Hindu metaphysics but is inconsistent with it.[1]

The world is not a deceptive façade of something underlying it. It is real though imperfect. Since the Supreme is the basis of the world the world cannot be unreal.[2] *Māyā* has a standing in the world of reality. Ś. says that after filling our sight with wisdom let us see the world as *Brahman*. Such a vision is fruitful, not the vision which looks solely at the tip of the nose.[3]

The world of multiplicity is acknowledged even by those who attempt to explain it away. Heidegger, for example, emphasises the finiteness and contingency of man's condition. Human life is a brief span of existence between original nothingness and death. It is constantly passing away and tends to return to non-being. The threat of nothingness is the source of that fundamental anguish which the existentialists emphasise. Some existentialists like Jaspers and Marcel, following the lead of Kierkegaard, find the counterpoise to the world of nothingness in the reality of God. In Hindu thought, *māyā* is not so much

[1] Albert Schweitzer says: 'World- and life-negation if consistently thought out and developed does not produce ethics but reduces ethics to impotence.' *The Philosophy of Civilisation*, E.T. (1950), p. 288.

Cp. John McKenzie: 'The duties of social life cannot be deduced from the ultimate goal of attainment as the orthodox understand it, nor can they be shown to stand in any vital relation to it.' *Hindu Ethics* (1922), pp. 206–7.

[2] Cp. M.B.

brahma satyam, jagat satyam, satyam caiva prajā-patiḥ.
satyād bhūtāni jātāni satyaṁ bhūta-mayaṁ jagat.

[3] *dṛṣṭim jñāna-mayīm kṛtvā paśyed brahma-mayaṁ jagat.*
sā dṛṣṭiḥ paramodārā na nāsāgrāvalokinī.

a veil as the dress of God. The destiny of the world is to be transformed into the perfect state of the Kingdom of God. The concept of *brahma-loka*, the Kingdom of God, is known to the Vedic seers, the Hebrew prophets and Zarathustra. If we are to share the new existence, we must achieve perfection. We must renounce self-interest and dedicate ourselves to the doing of good. We must work for better conditions for the material and spiritual development of human beings, for civilisation is material and spiritual progress for both the individual and society. The aim is *loka-saṁgraha*, in the words of the B.G.

Man is a social animal. He loves those with whom he lives in close association. Latterly the small social groups have been broken up by the forces of industrialism but new opportunities for larger groups are now available. The whole of society requires to be reconstructed on the principle of social solidarity. Society is approaching what seems to be the final stage of economic evolution. We have passed beyond the hunting and the fishing stages, the pastoral, the agricultural and the industrial stages with their different phases.

Unfortunately, the contemporary world situation where two rival power systems are facing each other is leading to the emergence of a narrowly secular, materialistic, extraverted mass-state. Sensitive people deplore the disintegration, the superficial materialism, the lack of creative vision and the uncontrolled technocracy which are the alarming symptoms of a disease eating at the heart of our modern way of life. Our best attempts are incapable of remedying the disease of which we are all obscurely aware. The crisis which faces us is a spiritual one and what we need is a recovery of spiritual awareness, a new and transforming contact with the inner sources of spiritual inspiration which once animated the soul of our civilisation and produced and maintained its indefeasible unity of consciousness, in other words a healing of the divorce between the outward resources of power which are assuming frightening proportions and the inward resources of the spirit which are decaying or dead. Materialism is the height of unintelligence. The B.G., when it calls upon us to work for a world community, calls us back to the Indwelling Spirit which is in us as in others. Such a faith will help us to bring love where there is hatred, hope where there is despair, light where there is darkness, joy where there is sorrow. We must give if we wish to receive. We shall be able to serve if we are ourselves saved, integrated.

The world is the place where the human individual has to attain his integration, his fulfilment. We are called upon to participate in the life of the world. It is through time that time is conquered.

The transitoriness of earthly possessions is used to emphasise the imperative necessity of the practice of *dharma*. There is a well-known verse which reads: 'Our bodies are not permanent, our prosperity is fleeting; death is always near to us. Therefore one should take to *dharma*.'[1] The goal is a reorientation of human personality, where the self assumes control over cravings and desires. These latter are not to be destroyed but transformed. The kind of life one leads has an importance both for oneself and the world. This world is our home and our lives are dedicated to action. We are not strangers in the world required to develop indifference to it. Each individual appears to be isolated but we soon realise that there is a living substance from which all emerge.

We are called upon to act in a disinterested way, free from egotism. We should not become victims of material interests and vulgar appetites. We should not be preoccupied with our own salvation. The soul is bound so long as it has a sense of mineness; with the absence of the sense of mineness it is liberated.[2] If God is to live in us pride must die in us. For the cultivation of detachment, it is not essential to become a *saṃnyāsin*. It is possible to cultivate *vairāgya* or detachment even as householders.[3]

[1] *anityāni śarīrāṇi, vibhavo naiva śāśvataḥ.*
nityaṁ saṃnihito mṛtyuḥ, kartavyo dharma-saṁgrahaḥ.

Cp. *Hitopadeśa : gṛhīta iva keśeṣu mṛtyunā dharmam ācaret.*

[2] *Paiṅgala U.* IV. 20.

Two words make for bondage and release: freedom from mineness and mineness.

The sense of mineness binds the creature, freedom from mineness produces release.

dve pade bandha-mokṣābhyāṁ nirmameti mameti ca.
mameti badhyate jantuḥ nirmameti vimucyate.

[3] *vane'pi doṣāḥ prabhavanti rāgiṇām gṛheṣu pañcendriya-nigrahas tapaḥ.*
akutsite karmaṇi yaḥ pravartate, nivṛtta-rāgasya gṛhaṁ tapovanam.

Cp., however, what *Kṛṣṇa* says to *Uddhava* in the 11th *skandha* of the *Bhāgavata*: 'A spiritual aspirant should not only give up the company of

There is a popular impression that Hindu ethics requires us to treat the body with contempt. It is well known that the body is regarded as the instrument for righteous living, *dharma-sādhanam*. We are not called upon to fear bodily desires or hate the body. If we adopt fasting and other physical discipline, it does not mean that the fasts and the physical exercises are ends in themselves. The practitioners of *Haṭha yoga* are not the exponents of the best type of sanctity. The body must be disciplined in order that it may serve the ends of righteousness. We must be ready to cast off unnecessary burdens and travel light. Bodily discipline helps us to see the face of God and hear his voice. It helps us to see the needs of people, and undertake fresh acts of service, visit the sick, care for the poor and put an end to injustice wherever we see it.

Ethical Rules

The different virtues of fortitude, justice, love, compassion, self-control are not separate qualities but are the different facets of the personality. Inward awareness, *satya*, and life of compassion, *ahiṁsā*, are the two principal sides of a spiritual life. We must be truthful in our words and deeds. To know the truth we are taken out of the world but only temporarily. We are again brought back to it. The Divine is expressed in nature as an impersonal, non-ethical creative power and as ethical consciousness in human life.

When we realise that the Divine is expressed in us as in others we feel the obligation to help others. Thereby the individual spirit becomes enriched. *Ahiṁsā* is reverence for all life, active devotion to and a sense of union with all that exists. There is no infinite being except being in its infinite manifestations. If we believe in God, we will adopt the principle of *ahiṁsā*. The Qurān says: 'The servants of the merciful are those who meekly walk upon this earth and if the fools speak to them, they say "peace".'[1] Again 'If you forgive and practise forbearance and pardon, verily Allāh is also forgiving and merciful.'[2] The

women but even the company of householders and sit in solitude, free from danger and meditate on me.'

> *strīṇāṁ tat-saṅgināṁ saṅgaṁ tyaktvā dūrata ātmavān*
> *kṣemaṁ vivikta āsīnaś cintayen mām atandritaḥ.*

[1] XXV. 64.

[2] LXIV. 14.

individual is required to treat humanity as his kindred. We must cultivate in our hearts the sentiments of affection and trustfulness. Compassion is the one good that is never exhausted even if the whole world is pursuing it.

The M.B. says that 'nothing is wholly good and nothing is wholly bad. The two, good and evil, pervade the world throughout'.[1] We must be careful before we judge others. The possessions we have are a trust for others. The *Bhāgavata* gives the proper attitude to wealth: 'Living beings have a right only up to what is necessary for satisfying their hunger; he who thinks of acquiring more is a thief and deserves punishment.'[2] This is the basic principle of a socialist order of society. The Creative God is the source of all beings. He is infinite and unfathomable yet we can enter into spiritual relations with him by devoting ourselves to all living beings within the range of our help. In the *Rāmāyaṇa, Rāma* asks *Lakṣmaṇa* 'How shall we seek to please the Divine, who is not within our reach, when we neglect father, mother and teacher who are with us?'[3] When we pierce through the confusions of the world to the strength and certainty of its basis we accept every man as brother and show sympathy, understanding and patience in our dealings with others.

When *ahiṁsā* is said to be the supreme moral law, it is not merely negative abstention from injury to living beings, but positive love for them all. Sympathy and compassion are its expressions. Charity with kind words, knowledge without pride,

[1] *nātyantaṁ guṇavat kiñcit nātyantaṁ doṣavat tathā.*
ubhābhyāṁ guṇa-doṣābhyāṁ vyāptaṁ hi sakalaṁ jagat.

[2] *yāvat bhriyeta jaṭharaṁ tāvat svatvaṁ hi dehinām*
adhikaṁ yo'bhimanyeta sa steno daṇḍam arhati.

Cp. Bhartṛhari:

dānam bhogo nāśas tiśro gatayo bhavanti vittasya
yan na dadāti na bhunkte tasya tṛtīyā gatir bhavati.

Cp. a saying attributed to Muhammad: 'He is not of us who sleeps with his stomach *full* while his neighbour is hungry.'

The prophet Malachi asks:

Have we not all one Father?
Hath not one God created us?
Why do we deal treacherously
Every man against his brother? ii. 10.

[3] *svādhīnaṁ samatikramya mātaraṁ pitaraṁ gurum*
asvādhīnaṁ kathaṁ daivaṁ prakārair abhirādhyate.

II. 30. 33.

courage with forbearance and wealth with renunciation, these four are difficult to attain, but they make for man's progress.[1]

Social Institutions

Whereas the utterances of the founders of religions have a claim on our allegience this is not true of the institutions built round them. These must be flexible enough to be altered to suit progress in human thought. It is said that many pernicious customs pass for religious duties under the influence of ignorant persons of bad character.[2] They are generally adopted out of greed,[3] more often out of inertia.

The main obstacle to social progress in India is conformity. We wish to belong and not be isolated or lonely. Unless we belong to a social whole we feel that we are powerless, insignificant. So we adhere to absurd and degrading customs, because they relate us to others. Whereas the principal demands of truth and love, *satya* and *ahiṁsā*, are absolute, their application depends on the concrete situation. Changes of place, time and circumstance cause changes in *dharma* also. There is one law for men in time of peace and another in time of distress. There is no single law for all time. So *dharma* is known to depend on circumstances. No law has been found which is of help to all. Therefore it is changed for one that seems better and it is again found harmful demanding change. Therefore we see non-unity among customs at all times.[4]

[1] *dānam priya-vāk-sahitam, jñānam agarvam, kṣamānvitam śauryam,*
vittam tyāga-sametam, durlabham etac catur-bhadram.

There is a Christian hymn written by Henry Wotton which ends with the lines:

This man is freed from servile bonds
Of hope to rise, or fear to fall;
Lord of himself, though not of lands
And having nothing, yet hath all.

[2] *mūrkha-duḥśīla-puruṣa-pravartitaḥ*. Medhātithi on *Manu*.

[3] *lobhān mantra-tantrādiṣu pravartate. Ibid.*

[4] *deśa-kāla-nimittānāṁ bhedair dharmo vibhidyate*
anyaḥ dharmaḥ samasthasya viṣamasthasya ca aparaḥ
na hy eva aikāntiko dharmaḥ, dharmo hi āvasthikaḥ smṛtaḥ
na hi sarva-hitaḥ kaścid ācāraḥ sampravartate
tasmād anyaḥ prabhavati, saḥ aparaṁ bādhate punaḥ
ācārāṇām anaikāgryaṁ tasmāt sarvatra lakṣaye.

M.B. *Śāntiparva.*

The Caste System

The vocation of a person is that which manifests his inner nature. It must accord with his temperament.[1] In its origin the caste system represented the division of men into classes according to their capacity and function, *guṇa* and *karma*.[2] Later it became mixed up with heredity. The M.B. says: 'Austerity, learning, birth, these make the *Brāhmaṇa*; he who lacks austerity and learning is a *Brāhmaṇa* by birth alone.'[3] Some of the great leaders of Indian civilisation were of mixed origin. Kṛṣṇa Dvaipāyana Vyāsa was the son of a *Brāhmaṇa* father and a non-Aryan mother. Kṛṣṇa Vāsudeva Vārṣṇeya was the son of a *kṣatriya* prince, Vasudeva, and a non-Aryan princess, Devakī, the sister of Kaṁsa. The system of caste whatever its historical significance has no contemporary value. Today it injures the spirit of humanity and violates human dignity. To offer a cup of water is a sign of friendship, not of defilement. "I consider to be a *Brāhmaṇa* that *Śūdra* who is ever endowed with self-restraint, truthfulness and righteousness. A man becomes a *Brāhmaṇa* by his conduct."[4] If these characteristics be found in a *Śūdra* and if they be not found in a *Brāhmaṇa*, then such a *Śūdra* is not a *Śūdra* and such a *Brāhmaṇa* is not a *Brāhmaṇa*.'[5]

There is a story that when Ś., in spite of his non-dualism, asked an outcaste to clear the way for him, the outcaste who was God

[1] *varaṇīyāḥ svabhāva-guṇa-karmānusāreṇa*
varītum yogyāḥ varṇāḥ-Nirukta.

[2] *ekavarṇam idam pūrvaṁ viśvam āsīd yadhiṣṭhira*
karma-kriyā-bhedena cātur-varṇyaṁ pratiṣṭhitam.

According to the Hebrew Scriptures, Adam, the parent of all mankind, has nothing to do with race, nationality or religion. He is just a human being.

[3] *tapaḥ śrutaṁ ca yoniś cety etad brāhmaṇa-kārakam*
tapaḥ śrutibhyāṁ yo hīno jāti-brāhmaṇa eva saḥ.

Cp. *Manu:* One is born as a *Śūdra*, but through the (performance of) rites he becomes a twice-born. By the study of the *Vedas* he becomes a *vipra* but by the knowledge of *Brahman* he becomes a *Brāhmaṇa*.

janmanā jāyate śūdraḥ saṁskārāt dvija ucyate
vedābhyāsāt bhavet vipro brahma jānāti brāhmaṇaḥ.

[4] *yas tu sūdro dame satye dharme ca satatotthitaḥ*
taṁ brāhmaṇam aham manye vṛttena hi bhaved dvijaḥ.
M.B. *Araṇya parva* 206. 12.

[5] *śūdre caitad bhavel lakṣyaṁ dvije caitan na vidyate*
na vai śūdro bhavec chūdro brāhmaṇo na ca brāhmaṇaḥ.
M.B. *Śānti parva* 182. 8.

himself asked: 'Do you wish my body to leave your body or my spirit to leave your spirit?'[1] If democracy is to be seriously implemented, then caste and untouchability should go.

Women and Family Life

We are not called upon to suppress human desires, reject human pleasures, renounce the world and all its ways and thus freeze the human spirit. The state of the householder is an exalted one. From early times, marriage has been treated as a sacrament and its purpose has been the production of offspring, especially a son. In the *Aitareya Brāhmaṇa*, we read: 'Of what good is dirt, the deer-skin, the unshaven hair, austerities, of what [good are they]? O *Brāhmaṇa*, desire a son. He verily is the blameless source of enjoyment.'[2] Manu says: 'One should direct one's mind to renunciation after discharging the three debts. He who, without discharging [them], practises renunciation goes below.'[3]

In some periods of our history, women were not treated with fairness and dignity. The dominant ideal, however, has been one of perfect equality. When Janaka gives Sītā to Rāma, he asks him to treat her as his companion in all duties.[4]

It would be wrong to hold that Madhva denied *mokṣa* or final release to women, *Śūdras* and fallen *Brāhmaṇas* and non-Hindus. He denied to them one particular method of attaining

[1] *anna-mayād anna-mayam athavā caitanyam eva caitanyāt*
dvija-vara dūrī-kartuṁ vāñchasi kiṁ brūhi gaccha gaccheti.

[2] *kiṁ tu malam, kiṁ ajinam, kimu śmaśrūṇi, kim tapaḥ, putram brāhmaṇa icchadhvam sa vai loko'vadāvadaḥ.*

Professor Berniedale Keith gives the following E.T.

What is the use of dirt, what of the goat-skin.
What of long hair, what of fervour?
Seek a son, O Brāhmin
This is the world's advice.

XXXII. 1. 70. *Harvard Oriental Series*. Vol. 25, p. 300.

Thomas Aquinas in a passage in his *Summa Contra Gentiles* (III. 136) writes: 'Certain men of distorted mind have spoken against the good of sexual moderation. . . . For the union of man and woman is ordained for the good of the species. But this is more divine than the good of the individual. . . . To this may be added the Lord's commandment to our first parents: "Be fruitful and multiply and fill the earth".'

[3] VI. 5.

[4] *iyaṁ sītā mama sutā saha-dharma-carī tava*
pratīccha caināṁ bhadraṁ te pāṇiṁ gṛhīṣva pāṇinām.

release.[1] Other ways were prescribed for them which will lead to the same goal of final release. This exclusion, whatever justification it may have had at the time the commentaries were written, has no excuse today.

In the *Vedas* we find reference to women seers who are *brahma-vādinīs*. They, of course, had a right to *brahma*-knowledge, *brahma-vidyādhikāra*.

Brahma-carya, or chastity of body and mind, is insisted on. It is said in the *Brahma Purāṇa* that a woman who is addressed as mother in speech should be truly looked upon as mother. *Dharma* is a witness to this as also the wise.[2]

Saṃnyāsa—sometimes renunciation of the world is exalted.[3] What is meant is the spirit of renunciation.

Saṃnyāsa is sometimes prescribed as a preparation for service. There are some who take to *saṃnyāsa* when they feel lonely, inadequate and incomplete and in their shock of loneliness and isolation wish to turn back on the world. That, however, is not the proper spirit. We cannot grow as individuals apart from one another.

The order of the *saṃnyāsins* presents itself to the modern world as a scandal. There was a time when it was taken for granted. People's lives were directed beyond the quest of wealth and pleasure, *artha* and *kāma*, and devoted to an invisible God. The true *saṃnyāsins* realise human unity and brotherhood in their souls. Even a *parivrājaka* who abandons the world absolutely has to sustain his life and do the duties that are

[1] *vaidika-brahma-vidyādhikāra.*

Cp. *kirāta-hūṇāndhra-pulinda pukkaśā abhīra kaṅkā yavanāḥ sakādayaḥ*
ye'nye ca pāpā yad-upāsrayāḥ śudyanti tasmai prabhaviṣṇave namaḥ.
Bhāgavata II. 4. 18.

Again: *strī-śūdra-brahma-bandhūnāṁ trayī na śruti-gocarā*
itibhāratam ākhyānaṁ kṛpayā muninā kṛtam.
Ibid. I. 4. 24.

Baladeva, commenting on Jīva-Gosvāmin's *ṣaṭ-sandarbha*, refers to Madhva's doctrine and says that according to it only *Brāhmaṇas* were eligible for *mokṣa*, *bhaktānām viprāṇām eva mokṣaḥ, lakṣmyā jīva-koṭitvam ity evam mata-viśeṣaḥ.* This does not seem to be correct. Madhva confined the pursuit of *Vedic* knowledge to the three upper classes.

[2] *mātar-ity eva śabdena yāṁ ca sambhāṣate naraḥ*
sā mātṛu-tulyā satyena dharma-sākṣī satām api. X. 50.

[3] *Bṛhad-dharma-purāṇa* says:
muhūrtam api saṃnyasya labhate paramāṁ gatim
na saṃnyāsāt paro dharmo vartate mukti-kāraṇam.

allotted to him.[1] The *samnyāsins* work in the world so long as their fellow-men are insensitive and irresponsible and so are unfree. In a sense until all men become free no one is absolutely free.

Beyond Ethics

When one attains the spiritual level, he rises above the ethical, not that he repudiates it but he transcends it. Ś. says 'this is indeed an ornament to us that, when there is the realisation of *Brahman*, there is the destruction of all obligations and the accomplishment of everything that is to be accomplished'.[2]

When we undergo the ethical discipline, there is a change in the inward man which makes us practise good in an effortless, spontaneous way. Freedom from obligation is only for those who have cast off their self-sense. 'I do nothing of myself. The Father that dwelleth in me, he doeth the works.'[3] 'If ye be led of the Spirit, ye are not under the law.'[4] Whoever is born of God cannot sin.[5] When Jesus tells us that our righteousness should be different from that of the Scribes and the Pharisees, he points out that our conduct should be not one of mere conformity to duty with an effort.[6] We must cease to be men of external piety and become men of inner understanding. Then we break the inertia of habit. We become different and act not from expectation of reward or fear of consequences but because the act is good in itself. Jesus says of John the Baptist that he is the highest man born of woman but the least in the Kingdom of Heaven is greater than he.[7] John stands for salvation through moral life. He tells us what to do but we

[1] Cf. Bhāskara: *parivrājakasyāpi saucamāna-snāna-bhikṣāṭanādi karma kāyikaṁ vācikam mānasam tacca aparihāryam dhriyamāṇa-śarīrasya.* III. 4. 20.

[2] *alaṅkāro hy ayam asmākam, yad brahmātmāvagatau satyāṁ sarva-kartavyatā-hāniḥ kṛta-kṛtyatā ceti.* S.B. I. 1. 4. See Ś.B.G. XV. 20.

[3] *John* viii. 28; xiv. 10.

St François De Sales says: 'Tell me, I pray you, Theotimus, if a drop of water, thrown into an ocean of some priceless essence, were alive and could speak and declare its condition, would it not cry out with great joy: "O mortals I live indeed but I live not myself, but this ocean lives in me and my life is hidden in this abyss".'

[4] *Galatians* v. 18. [5] I *John* iii. 9. [6] *Matthew* v. 20.

[7] *Matthew* iii. 2; *Luke* iii. 10–14.

cannot gain release unless we change our nature, become different, are inwardly transformed. John asks us to become better men and Jesus asks us to become new men. There is a stage in which we accept the world, another in which we reject it, a third in which we accept it, gratefully acknowledging its place in the divine scheme.

Those who have full mastery over their natures sometimes do things which may appear wrong to the conventional people. John the Baptist was uneasy when he heard that Jesus and his disciples ate and drank and did not fast. They plucked the ears of corn on the Sabbath day. The *Bhāgavata* says: '*Īśvaras* or masters are sometimes seen to transgress rules of conduct with courage. These are not faults among those with *tejas* or radiance, even as the all-devouring fire is not affected [by the impurities it consumes].[1] He who is lacking in such control [*anīśvarāḥ*] should not even think of imitating such conduct for it can only bring destruction to him even like swallowing poison in imitation of *Śiva*.' Fire may consume a forest or *Śiva* drink poison without any harmful consequences. But ordinary men cannot transgress rules until they have shaken off all selfishness and established control over their nature.

It is easier to fight non-human nature, forests and woods and wild beasts. It is more difficult to fight the passions, the sub-rational elements in human nature. This is a more arduous struggle. We cannot extinguish selfish desire by the mere force of intellect. We have to develop the power of will.[2] The different elements in human nature are divided in a disintegrated man but in an integrated life they are held in harmony. An integrated personality is incapable of doing anything wrong. The ethical man, the economic man and the artistic man are all abstractions obtained by our intellect from the concrete unity of our being. These values are complementary. A great artist may be a great moral force. An ideal personality would be all these, a man of wisdom and holiness, sanity and sanctity.

[1] *tejīyasāṁ na doṣāya vahneḥ sarva-bhujo yathā. Bhāgavata* X. 33. 30.

[2] *Agastya Saṁhitā* says:

> *tapo dadāti saubhāgyam tapo vidyām prayacchati*
> *tapasā durlabhaṁ kiñcin nāsti bhāminī dehinām.*

Tapas gives us welfare, it helps us to attain knowledge.
There is nothing, O Pārvatī, that *tapas* cannot give men.

B. THE WAY OF *BHAKTI* OR DEVOTION[1]

Need for Religious Devotion

It is often said that man is incurably religious. He must have some object or person or cause on which to fix his devotion. The instinct, if we may call it by that name, may become perverted and abused but the need is there. It must be turned to an ideal which is genuine, grounded in truth, an ideal that touches the deepest springs of man's inner life. What a man believes has a determining influence on his character.

There are some thinkers both in the East and the West who feel that man's capacity for integration, for the growth of the individual into a person would be unintelligible unless we have a Divine Personality. McTaggart's notion of a community of personalities living in a kind of spiritual void is not tenable, for the direct apprehension of value which transforms the individual into a person implies an ideal personality who embodies the value apprehended.

It is possible for atheists and agnostics to lead virtuous lives. They may be unaware or unmindful of the divine source of all. Existentialists of the school of Sartre struggle to seek some meaning for human life in a godless universe. If we grant that the world has meaning, it means that it has a purpose. The reality of God does not, however, depend on our views. Our irreligion does not entail the suspension of divine acting.[2]

Bhakti

Bhakti is conscious recognition of and wholehearted response to the source of all goodness, the Divine. It is said 'in this world, not vows, not pilgrimages, not *yoga* practices, not study of Scriptures, not sacrificial rites, not philosophical discourses; only devotion can give us freedom'.[3]

[1] See B.G., pp. 58–66.

[2] Cp. St. Augustine: 'Thou hast always been with me but I have not always been with myself.'

[3] *alaṁ kalau vrataiḥ tīrthaiḥ yogaiḥ śāstraiḥ alam makhaiḥ*
alaṁ jñāna-kathālāpaiḥ bhaktir ekaiva muktidā.

Bhāgavata-Māhātmya.

[*Continued on page 168*

The *Bhāgavata Purāṇa* is treated as the standard work on *bhakti*. 'It is the quintessence of the *Vedānta* philosophy. He who has tasted its nectar-like juice will not be attracted by anything else.'[1] As we have seen, while God is transcendently infinite he is also greatly loving. He takes up human creatures into his range of action if they respond to his call. 'Behold, I stand at the gate and knock. If any man shall hear my voice and open to me the door, I will come in to him, and will sup with him and he with me.' God is the reward of those who wait on him. He helps his devotees to act in this world as partners in his divine work. Our one prayer is that God should increase in us true religion.

Śāṇḍilya Sūtra says *bhakti* is the highest attachment to God, *parānurakti*. In the *Viṣṇu Purāṇa* Prahlāda expresses the wish that he may have that attachment to God that is experienced with regard to sense-objects.[2] One must find one's supreme pleasure in God. Love of man and woman is used to illustrate love of man for God. 'As maid delights in youth and youth in maid, so may my mind rejoice in Thee.'[3] 'When the lovers are together, they are afraid of being separated; when they are not together, they have a painful desire for union.'[4]

Continued from page 167]

Cp. Manu: *tapaḥ pūrvaṁ kṛta-yuge tretāyāṁ yajñam eva ca*
dvāpare dānam ity āhuḥ kalau bhaktir garīyasī.
See *Viṣṇu Purāṇa* VI. 2. 17.

A well-known Sanskrit verse reads:

mīnaḥ snāna-paraḥ phaṇī pavana-bhuk
meṣas tu parṇāśanaḥ
nīraśī khalu pāvakaḥ prati-dinam
śete bile mūṣikaḥ
bhasmoddhūlatatparopi ca kharaḥ
dhyānena yukto bakaḥ
ity evam nahi yānti mokṣa-padavīm
śri-kṛṣṇa-bhaktiṁ vinā.

[1] *sarva-vedānta-sāraṁ hi śrī-bhāgavatam iṣyate*
tad-rasāmṛta-tṛptasya nānyatra syād ratiḥ kvacit. XII. 13. 15.

[2] *yā prītir avivekānāṁ viṣayeṣv anapāyinī*
tvam anu-smarataḥ sā me hṛdayān māpasarpatu.
I. 20. 19: see also B.G. X. 9.

[3] *yuvatīnāṁ yathā yūni yūnāṁ ca yuvatau yathā*
manaḥ abhiramate tadvat manaḥ me ramatāṁ tvayi.

[4] Cp. *Bhakti-mārtaṇḍa* by Gopeśvara:
adṛṣṭe darṣanotkaṇṭhā dṛṣṭe viśleṣa-bhīrutā
nādṛṣṭena na dṛṣṭena bhavatā labhyate sukham.

The clean of heart shall see God. If we sin against the light we will be left in darkness. Devotion implies obedience to the will of the Supreme in all our activities. It brings deliverance from anxiety about the necessities of life. There is a popular verse which says: 'In vain does the devotee worry about food and other necessities of life. Can God who sustains the whole creation ever forget his own devotees?'[1] A devotee is not elated by praise or depressed by censure. In the name of God he does service to the world.[2]

Bhakti and Knowledge

Bhakti opens the way to illumination. R. regards *bhakti* as a kind of knowledge. *Nārada Bhakti Sūtra* says: 'When adored with love God speedily manifests himself and gives his devotees perception.'[3]

Praise of the Devotee

The devotee is praised as the highest of all. 'What speciality is there in being born a member of the highest class? What does it matter even if one possesses learning that includes enquiry into all the systems of thought? In all the three worlds who is there more blessed than the person whose heart is always steeped in devotion to the Supreme Lord?'[4]

The *Bhāgavata Purāṇa* says: 'The devotees are my heart and I am the heart of the devotees. They know no one else than me; I know no one else than them.'[5]

[1] *bhojanācchādane cintāṁ vṛdhā kurvanti vaiṣṇavāḥ*
yo'sau viśvam-bharo devaḥ sa kiṁ dāsānupekṣate.
Cp. *sarvadā sarva-kāleṣu nāsti teṣām amaṅgalam*
yeṣāṁ hṛdistho bhagavān maṅgalāyatanam hariḥ.

[2] *dāsyam aiśvarya-vādena jñātīnām tu karomy aham.* M.B.

[3] *sa kīrtyamānaḥ śīghram evāvirbhavati anubhāvayati ca bhaktān* 80.

[4] *kim janmanā sakala-varṇajanottamena?*
kim vidyayā sakala-śāstra-vicāravatyā?
yasyāsti cetasi sadā parameśa-bhaktiḥ
ko'nyas tatas tri-bhuvane puruṣo'sti dhanyaḥ.
Brahma-saṁhitā.

[5] *sādhavo hṛdayam mahyam sādhūnāṁ hṛdayaṁ tvaham*
mad-anyat te na jānanti nāhaṁ tebhyo manāgapi.
IX. 4. 8.

Liberty of Worship

From early days Hindu tradition has held that truth is a pathless land and cannot be organised. When organised it cripples the individual mind and prevents it from growing. When our minds get incarcerated within the narrow confines of dogma, the spirit of free adventure is checked. Devotion to the Supreme opens our hearts to the new life. Spiritual life is the end. That is why the Hindu permits each individual to worship the aspect of Godhead which appeals to him most. The radiance of reality is mirrored variously according to the mediums in which it is reflected.[1] The different aspects we adore are pointers, not halting places.

Whatever name we may give to the Supreme, it is addressed to the Ultimate Reality. 'I do not mind who he is, *Viṣṇu* or *Śiva*, *Brahmā* or *Indra*, the Sun or the Moon, the blessed *Buddha* or any saint. Whoever he be, that one who is free from the disease of being poisoned by craving and hatred, who is endowed with all noble qualities and is ever ready to act compassionately towards all creatures, to him I bow down always.'[2]

Ś., the great teacher of non-dualism, manifests a spirit of devotion to the different aspects of the Godhead. There are devotional hymns ascribed to him to *Bhavānī*,[3] to *Viṣṇu*,[4] to *Śiva*.[5] Madhusūdana Sarasvatī, a great teacher of *Advaita*, says: 'I know not what truth there is beyond *Kṛṣṇa*.'[6] The Maharastrian saint-poet Eknath identifies *Viṭhoba* of Pandharpur with the *Buddha*.

[1] Lessing in his letter to Rimarius says: 'Each one says what he thinks is the truth, but the truth is with God alone.'

[2] *viṣṇur-vā, tripurāntako bhavatu vā, brahmā, surendro'thavā*
bhānur-vā, śaśa-lakṣaṇo'tha bhagavān buddho'tha siddho'thavā
rāga-dveṣa-viṣārti-moha-rahitaḥ sattvānukampodyato
yaḥ sarvaiḥ saha saṁskṛto guṇa-gaṇais tasmai namaḥ sarvadā.

[3] *gatis tvam gatis tvam tvam ekā bhavānī.*

[4] *avinayam apanaya viṣṇo damaya manaḥ śamaya viṣaya-mṛga-tṛṣṇām.*

[5] *saṁsāra-duḥkha-gahanāj jagadīśa rakṣa.*

[6] *vaṁśī-vibhūṣita-karāt nava-nīradābhāt*
pītāmbarād aruṇa-bimba-phalādharoṣṭhāt
pūrnendu-sundara-mukhād aravinda-netrāt
kṛṣṇāt paraṁ kim api tattvam aham na jāne.

Cp. also his verse where he realises the Absolute *Brahman* in the blue effulgence that sports on the banks of the Yamunā:

dhyānāvasthita tad-gatena manasā yan nirguṇaṁ niṣkriyam
jyotiḥ kiñcana yogino yadi paraṁ paśyanti paśyantu te
asmākan tu tad eva locana-camatkārāya bhūyāc ciram
kālindī-pulinodare kim api yan nīlam maho dhāvati.

Mystics of other religions and some leading thinkers tend to adopt an attitude of respect for other forms of worship than their own. The Word came and dwelt among us, not for the first and last time at Bethlehem but from the moment man was born into the world in the likeness of the divine image and as such distinct from other creatures. As Eternal Wisdom it was and is before all creation in its pure creativeness. For many Christian mystics, Christ is not limited to the historic personality of Jesus. He is the eternal Logos who comes to birth in men whenever they are inwardly united with God.

Justin Martyr in his *Apologia* and *Dialogue with Trypho* presents God as the Primordial Cause of the world, eternal, unchangeable and accessible to reason. Before all creation, from the indefinable Father and Lord of the universe a force emanated called Logos which means Word and Reason. This Logos is the Son generated before all creation, the divine wisdom of Proverbs viii. He spoke through the Prophets and manifested his action also outside Israel.

To justify universal claims for the Logos, Justin argues that those outside the Biblical tradition who have developed spiritual life like Heracleitus, Socrates and his own contemporary Musonius all belong to the Christian fold. If they were called atheists and condemned to death, the Christians also suffered the same fate. Justin says: 'Everything good and beautiful taught by thinkers and poets is ours.' For all that is Christian is due to the working of the Logos. Justin presents Christianity as a philosophical religion which uses Greek ideas, especially the Stoic, in a Biblical garb. Both Clement and Origen were Christian thinkers who wished to express Christian truth through Greek philosophical categories. They believe in the Eternal Logos. They speak about the ultimate oneness of God and man. The deepest self of all rational beings is divine. Every individual attains his fulfilment through unification with the Logos. By imitating Christ the Logos, everyone can obtain the same power as the Logos.

William Law says that the Christ of God is 'the light and life and holiness of every creature that is holy'.[1] He argues: 'Hence it was that so many eminent spirits, partakers of a divine life

[1] *The Spirit of Love.*

have appeared in so many parts of the heathen world. . . . These were the apostles of a Christ within.'[1] 'As many as are led by the Spirit of God, these are the sons of God.' Man in his deepest being is one with God. The goal of life is to enter into the realisation of this hidden unity. Boehme asks 'were we not in the beginning made out of God's substance? Why should we not also abide therein?'[2] William Penn said: 'It is better to be of no Church than to be bitter for any.'[3] Kabīr says that he is 'a child of *Allāh* and *Rām*'. He did not find it necessary to identify himself with any religious faith but was devoted to spiritual realisation.

Religious intolerance does not make for world unity. Religions which aim at the conversion of the whole world to their own doctrines aim at the religion of power which amounts to sacred egoism, to spiritual pride. Reason should teach us to doubt our own infallibility. Unless we do it there is no chance for toleration in the world. If we are convinced of the absolute truth of our revelation and the falsity of others, how can we tolerate those who spread error and lead others astray? It is essential for us to note that while we are convinced of the infallibility of the truth we adopt, others may be equally convinced of the infallibility of their own doctrines. From ancient times, Hinduism adopted a view which would not hurt the religious susceptibilities of others. It enabled the Hindus to welcome the Jews, the Christians, the Parsees and the Muslims.[4]

[1] *The Spirit of Prayer.* [2] *Of the Super-sensual Life.*

[3] Even Karl Barth admits that 'our concepts are not adequate to grasp the treasure of our experience'.

Karl Jaspers says: 'Theology turns the alternative "God or Nothing" into a very different one: "Christ or Nothing" with Christ promptly made synonymous with the doctrine of some Church, and obedience to God equally obedience to that Church and its dogmas.' *Existentialism and Humanism*, E.T. (1952), p. 94. A. N. Whitehead observes: 'It would be impossible to imagine anything more unchristian than Christian theology. Christ probably would not have understood it,' quoted by H. E. Fosdick in his *The Living of These Days* (1956), p. 268. M. Loisy thinks that St Paul was chiefly responsible for imposing an alien mythology on the life and teaching of Jesus. There is a gap between Jesus of the Gospels and the redeemer of St Paul.

[4] 'The result of the honourable place given by the rajas to the Christians, and of their assimilation in social custom to their Hindu neighbours, was that they were accepted as a caste, and often thought of their community in this way. They ranked after the *Brāhmaṇas* and as equals of the *Nāyars*. Many Christians would claim that there was *Brāhmaṇa* convert blood in the community and that for this reason they were superior to *Nāyars*.

'It was in consequence of this position that the St Thomas Christians, so far

The Hindu believes that, varied as all these religions are, behind them all is the same fire. The experience of the fire, though it speaks with many tongues, carries the same message. They all speak of the one realm of spiritual being. Of course, there are characteristic differences among the great religions. They do not all teach the same doctrines of God or of man or of the world or provide the same kind of ritual, myth or norm of behaviour. But these differences are not enough to justify discord and strife. There may be mutual education among religions if they peacefully coexist and there is no doubt that all the religions have helped to produce saints of an exalted character. We should be lacking in charity, even piety, if we denied the high character of sanctity in other religions than our own.[1] Many of the living faiths are passing through self-criticism, are getting infected with secularism and humanism and the loss of the vision of God. Many of the leaders regard themselves as the priests of a new religion. We need not a new religion but a creative vitality in the practice of the old, the recognition that the Kingdom of Heaven lies within man, in his depths, in his integrity, in his inmost truth. God is the potentiality of every man.

Image Worship

There is such a thing as *pratīkopāsanā* or symbol worship. This is an aid to worship.[2] The symbolic is not the imaginary.

as our evidence goes, never attempted to bring their non-Christian neighbours to a knowledge of Christ and so into the Christian Church. The Portuguese Archbishop Menezes did his best to create a sense of evangelistic responsibility among the Indian Christians by preaching to the Hindus whenever he could, and the eighteenth-century Carmelites had a number of baptisms from the heathen every year, so much so that they had to defend their action before the Raja of Travancore, but the Indian Church itself was not aroused to share this work.

'A further consequence of acceptance as a caste was that untouchability was observed by Christians as by Hindus.' L. W. Brown: *The Indian Christians of St Thomas* (1956), p. 173.

[1] 'Those who bow to all the gods, who listen to the doctrine of all the religions, who have faith and who are possessed of tranquil minds, get over all difficulties.'

sarvān devān namasyanti sarva-dharmāṁs ca śṛṇvate
ye śraddhadhānāḥ śāntāś' ca durgāṇy ati-taranti te.

M.B. *Śānti Parva* CX. 18.

[2] Cp. *ajñānāṁ bhāvanārthāya pratimāḥ parikalpitāḥ.*

Slowly we get beyond the symbol to the object symbolised. Until we reach the Highest, we gain rewards great or small, according to our aims and objects.[1] Ś. observes that on account of our imperfections we connect the Omnipresent Lord with limited abodes.[2] 'Image worship is the first, doing *japa* and chanting *mantras* is the middle; meditation or mental worship is superior; reflection on one's own true nature is the highest of all.'[3] Image worship is a means to realisation. When we gain our ends, the means fall away. Lamps are useful so long as we live in darkness, but when the sun arises they cease to be of any help. Kabīr sings: 'There is nothing but water at the holy bathing places; and I know that they are useless, for I have bathed in them. The images are all lifeless, they cannot speak; I know for I have cried aloud to them. The *Purāṇa* and the *Qurān* are mere words; lifting up the curtain, I have seen.'[4]

The Avatāras

The theory of *avatāras* assumes divine concern for human endeavour. God is the light in the soul; our part is to open our being to the Divine Light which is ever shining in us. When the Light in us comes to possess our being we speak of the birth of God in us. The Incarnation is not a special event but a continuous process of self-renewal.[5]

[1] *taṁ yathā yathopāsate tathā tathā phalaṁ bhavati.* See also B.G. IV. 11.

[2] Ś.B. I. 1. 24.

[3] *prathamā pratimā-pūjā japaḥ stotrāṇi madhyamā*
uttamā mānasī pūjā so'ham pūjā uttamottamā.

Even in *Advaita Vedānta* it is accepted as a preparation for pure contemplation.

uttamo brahma-sadbhāvo dhyāna-bhāvas tu madhyamaḥ
stutir japo adhamo bhāvo bahiḥ-pūjā adhamādhamā..

Mahā-nirvāṇa Tantra XIV. 112.

To remain merged in *Brahman* is the highest, meditation is the middle way; prayer to God and repetition of his name are the lowest and external worship is lower than the lowest.

Tantra-sāra says:

prathamā pratimā-pūjā japa-stotrādi madhyamā
uttamā mānasī-pūjā so'ham pūjo'tamo ttamā.

First comes image worship; the middle way is repetition of the name and prayer; good is mental worship; realisation that I am he is the best.

[4] Rabindranath Tagore's E.T.

[5] William Law says that the desire for God 'will lead thee to the birth of Jesus, not in a stable at Bethlehem in Judaea, but to the birth of Jesus in the dark centre of thy own fallen soul'. *The Spirit of Prayer.*

The *avatāras* are born not only to put down evil but to teach us mortals. Great souls appear for the well-being and spiritual enlightenment of creatures.[1] They tell us how to remould our lives so as to serve the purpose of the Divine.[2] Deification is the transfusion of human nature by the Indwelling Spirit of the Divine. *Rāma* says: 'I look upon myself as a man, *Rāma*, the son of Daśaratha. May the Lord [*Brahmā*] tell me who I am, where I belong and whence I come.'[3] *Kṛṣṇa* by the repeated practice of meditation, by uninterrupted concentration for a long period, attaining through intuition of *Brahman* lordship similar to his over the world is seen to reveal that to Arjuna in the *Gītā*.[4] The devotee is slowly transformed into the likeness of the Divine. He becomes what he is called to be. He realises the meaning of his existence. It is said that devotion to the Supreme, experience of the Highest and detachment from other things, all these three occur at the same time.[5]

C. THE WAY OF *DHYĀNA* OR MEDITATION

Yoga System

If we study the history of religions we will note that there is a broad stream of spiritual knowledge which requires us to grow to a higher level of being. It refers to an inner quickening and growth in our nature.[6] The All-pervading Self abides in every heart. Those who turn from him, seeking outside, are inferior

[1] *bhūtānām kṣemāya ca bhavāya ca. Bhāgavata* I. 1. 13.

[2] Jung in his *Psychology and Alchemy* says: 'The call for the Imitatio Christi *ought* to aim at developing and raising one's own inner man, but it is made by superficial believers . . . into an external object of worship, which, precisely through the veneration of its object, prevents the soul from being affected in its depths and transformed into a whole.'

[3] *ātmānam mānuṣam manye rāmam daśarathātmajam*
yo'ham yasya yataś cāham bhagavāṁs tad bravītu me.
VI. 120. 11–12.

[4] *ata eva bhagavataḥ kṛṣṇasyopāsanā-karmaṇy-abhyāsāt cira-nirantaraikāgryāt brahma-sākṣātkāreṇa tadvat jagad-aiśvarya-prāptyām arjunāya tat-prakāśanaṁ gītāsu dṛśyate.* Appaya Dīkṣita: *Śivādvaita-nirṇaya.*

[5] *bhaktiḥ pareśānubhavaḥ viraktiḥ anyatra ca, eṣa trikaḥ, eka-kālaḥ. Bhāgavata.*

[6] Why Mullah, must you ascend the minaret?
God is not deaf, he hears thee here;
For His sake do you call to prayer
Look for Him in thy heart, so says Kabīr.

creatures.[1] 'God is neither in temple nor in mosque', says Kabīr. He would add today: 'neither in Church nor in synagogue'. He is found in the heart of man. God is not doomed to be perpetually overwhelmed by an uncomprehending darkness. Nānak says that we should ascend to the *satya-loka*, the kingdom of truth, the abode of eternal life.

'Lead us from darkness into light' is the prayer of the *Upaniṣads*. We must be awakened out of the sleep of the natural world-view. We must break through the surface in which we live and move. Imprisoned in history we become restricted to the narrow limits of existence. We must be lifted out of this confinement and become aware of our historicity. We must grasp the real which is before all phenomena, before all time and which is equally after all phenomena and all time. Yet it is neither before nor after. It is that which does not become, that which is, real, unhistorical being itself. We cannot think it, enclose it within categories, images and verbal structures. But we know more than we can think and express in historical forms. By discipline of mind we should strive to apprehend the Real. 'True knowledge which is produced by the means of true knowledge and is comparable to its object can neither be brought about by hundreds of injunctions nor be checked by hundreds of prohibitions. For it does not depend on the will of man, but merely on what really and unalterably exists.'[2] A rigorous discipline of mind, heart and will is necessary. Our vision becomes obscure if it is dimmed by vice or weakness. The M.B. says the Supreme is visible only to those who have overcome anger and mastered their senses.[3]

To use Plato's words, we should not be bound to the shadows of the cave but get to see the reality. For this an illuminating revelation, a saving transformation is necessary; an opening of the eyes is essential. We cannot get this experience by detached

[1] *sarvasyaiva janasyāsya viṣṇuḥ abhyantare sthitaḥ*
tam parityajya te yānti bahir viṣṇum narādhamāḥ.

St Augustine says: 'Why do we go forth and run to the heights of the heavens and the lowest parts of the earth, seeking Him who is within us, if we wish to be with Him?'

[2] Ś.B. III. 2. 21.

[3] *svargam dvāram susūkṣmaṁ tam tu paśyanti puruṣā jitakrodhāḥ jitendriyāḥ.* XIV. 27. 84–5.

observation, logical analysis and inference.[1] We must encounter truth as a matter of existential concern, participate in the Ultimate Mystery. It is not an intellectual state but a state of being when we are filled with the Spiritual Presence.

As the *Upaniṣads* declare the state can be gained by *śravaṇa*, hearing, *manana*, reflection, and *nididhyāsana* or concentration.[2] *Dhyāna* is *anavaratānusandhāna*, constant meditation. To learn concentration one should learn to be alone with oneself, without reading or listening to the radio or other pre-occupation. It is to be able to be alone with oneself. It is in moments of meditation that we become self-aware. We do not lose the sense of the eternal in the inevitable distractions of life. We acquire a trust in the foundations of things, a trust that sustains us in the most terrible catastrophes, a firm loyalty to truth in the midst of passions and lures.

The *Yoga* system describes the processes by which our consciousness grows into the life divine by the control of the thinking mind. The cultivation of states of mind and body which permits the full realisation of the ultimate truth requires disciplined effort. The *Yoga Sūtra* says 'that [discipline of mental functioning] practised for long, unintermittently and with *satkāras* [i.e. self-control, austerity, faith, ceremonial piety] is the sure means of realising the truth'.[3]

Boehme in his imaginary dialogue between a disciple and his master in *The Signature of All Things* makes the disciple ask the master what prevents him from apprehending the ultimate truth and the master answers that it is his 'thinking of Self and his willing of Self'. Our confusion of the real Self with the outward selves prevents our awareness of the true Self. Boehme said that

[1] Omar Khayyam in his *Treatise on Metaphysic* says that the *Sufis* are 'those who seek knowledge, not by reflection and speculation (like the theologians and philosophers), but by purifying their soul (the passive and static ego), by correcting their character (the active and dynamic ego), and by freeing the intellect from the obstacles which arise from bodily nature. When this substance is presented, purified, before the Divine Glory, then the [intellectual and principial] models of the [mental and manifested] knowledge will surely be revealed in this other world [of transcendent Reality]'. Frithjof Schuon: *Spiritual Perspectives and Human Facts*, E.T. (1954), p. 73n.

[2] *āgamenānumānena dhyanābhyāsa-rasena ca*
tridhā prakalpayan prajñāṁ labhate yogam uttamam.
Viṣṇu Purāṇa.

[3] *sa tu dīrghakāla-nairantarya-satkāra-sevito dṛḍha-bhūmiḥ*. I. 14.

we could come into a new reality of our being and perceive everything in a new relation 'if we can stand still from self-thinking and self-willing and stop the wheel of imagination and the senses'.[1] The aim of *Yoga* is to help us to discern the being that is at the back of all becoming. It is difficult to reach it, but one should concentrate on that which exists of itself above and continues to be such as it is in itself.

Stages of the Journey

The ascent to union with the Supreme is hard and steep. It is a personal adventure. The categories of metaphysics are verified by states of consciousness. The soul must pass through the period of purgation. We must strip away the merely natural life and wake up to the importance of the spiritual life. The stripping process begins with the withdrawal from the bustle of earthly things. We must become free and unattached. God is the soul's guide on the journey with the purgative, the illuminative and the unitive stages. The soul should realise the nothingness of temporal things and learn to understand that the spiritual world alone is real. With the practice of detachment, spiritual freedom occurs.

Speculation is vision, an intuitive mode of apprehension. It is not irresponsible meandering of the mind. *Yājñavalkya* says that *samādhi* is equanimity.[2] We must steady the mind, concentrate on the truth by which one is intellectually convinced until it culminates in direct experience. By contemplation on a particular form we become one with it.[3] The *Gāyatrī mantra, dhiyo yo naḥ pracodayāt,* inspire our understanding, is

[1] Karl Barth says: 'Men suffer, because bearing within them an invisible world, they find this unobservable inner world met by the tangible, foreign, other, outer world, desperately visible, dislocated, its fragments jostling one another, yet mightily powerful and strangely menacing and hostile.' *Commentary on Romans*, p. 306.

[2] *samādhiḥ samatāvasthā jīvātma-paramātmanoḥ*
brahmaṇy avasthitir yā sā samādhiḥ pratyag-ātmanaḥ.

[3] *mananāt trāyate yastu mantra ity abhidhīyate*
tasmāt mantreṇa tan-mūrtim bhakti-pūrveṇa dhīyatām.
Tantra-sāra-āgama.

Japa is *akṣarāvṛttiḥ* (*Tantra-sāra*, p. 68), repetition of letters. It must be repeated according to rules, *vidhānena mantroccāraṇam. Sabda-kalpa-druma.*

Patañjali makes out that the repetition of the name should be accompanied by reflection on the meaning, *taj-japas tad-artha-bhāvanam.* Y.S. I. 28.

meditated on so that we may see the truth. When the seeker sees the truth he becomes spiritually free. All experience becomes ordered and unified. We do not prove the truth of an idea by merely demonstrating that its author lived centuries ago and was of a saintly disposition. The truth lies in our experience of it when it enters into us. Without the knowledge of one's self, no release is possible even in many ages.[1]

Solitary Meditation

There is an emphasis on a solitary life of meditation in a monastery or a hermitage but this does not mean a turning away from life. B.G.[2] speaks to us of the way in which *dhyāna yoga* should be practised. We do not seek for rewards but aim at transforming our nature. Let a man lift himself by himself.[3] *Vīramitrodaya-paribhāṣā-prakāśa* quotes *Aṅgiraḥ Smṛti* to the effect that excepting efforts for attaining self-knowledge, whatever one does out of his own personal desire is like child's play and unnecessary.[4] We must get into the house of our innermost self, shut the door on everything outer and pray from that inner self.[5] It is said of Muhammad that in his fortieth year he desired solitude. He withdrew to a cave on Mount Hira near Mecca and practised religious austerities.

By undergoing the disciplines of *karma*, *bhakti* and *dhyāna*, the mind gets purified and truth dawns and ineffable peace is experienced. Whatever action we perform is illumined by knowledge and dedicated to the glory of God.

Samādhi when it is *sa-vikalpa* is a state of contact with a Personal Being not evident to the senses, a Person discerned as divine. In *nir-vikalpa samādhi*, the reality is super-personal, the one that changes not, the deepest self in one which is also the

[1] *ātmaika-bodhena vinā ca muktir na siddhyati brahma-śatāntare'pi.*

[2] VI. [3] *uddhared ātmanātmānam.* VI. 5.

[4] *svābhiprāya-kṛtaṁ karma yat-kiñcij jñāna-varjitam*
krīḍā-karmeva bālānāṁ tat-sarvaṁ niṣ-prayojanam.

[5] 'But thou, when thou prayest, enter into thine inner chamber and having shut thy door, pray to thy Father which is in secret and thy Father which seeth in secret shall recompense thee.' *Matthew* vi. 6.

Eternal.[1] The state is one of unalterable bliss, freedom from self-sense, serenity and transcendent peace. Those who attain *samādhi* claim that their experience is far richer and deeper than the most intense satisfaction of this world.

When Ś. says that no amount of temporal activity can take us to the heart of the Eternal, he is emphasising that the distinction between time and eternity is a qualitative one. Our thought must be lifted to another order of being. Time is everlasting but Reality is eternal. Though we may spend all our life doing good deeds, we do not cross from time to eternity. A glimpse of eternity is different from an endless series of finite things. To know the Self we must leap into another dimension. We are then released from the rules of conventional religion. 'The sun of consciousness shines always in the sky of the heart. There is neither rising nor setting of it. How shall I perform the *sandhyā* prescribed in the *śāstras*?'[2]

Dionysius the Areopagite says: 'The simple, absolute and immutable mysteries of Divine Truth are hidden in the super-luminous darkness of that silence which revealeth in secret. For this darkness, though of deepest obscurity, is yet radiantly clear; and though beyond touch and sight, it more than fills our unseeing minds with splendours of transcendent beauty.'

The original meaning of theory is vision. Every philosophy is the exposition and justification of an experience.

By means of the three methods of work, devotion and contemplation (which are not exclusive of each other), we are reborn into the world of spirit. Religion by the use of symbols and metaphors indicates to us the goal of our quest. The festival of Easter, for example, was a pagan one marking the awakening of nature to new life. The Christian Easter refers to the resurrection of Jesus. But even for those who are not disposed to accept the historical evidence, it has a meaning that

[1] Cp. Schweitzer: Rational thinking which is free from assumptions ends in mysticism. . . . All profound world-view is mysticism, the essence of which is just this: 'that out of my unsophisticated and naïve existence in the world there comes, as a result of thought about self and the world, spiritual self-devotion to the mysterious infinite will which is continuously manifested in the universe.' *The Philosophy of Civilisation*, E.T., p. 79.

[2] *cidādityo hṛdākāśe sadā bhāti nirantaram*
udayāstamayo nāsti kathaṁ sandhyām upāsmahe.

we can all be made new. We must become what we are. The Festival of Easter is not a commemoration of a past event but the recognition of a present reality.

The cosmic process has for its goal the Kingdom of free spirits where the son of man becomes the son of God. The first fruits of the new species of spiritual personality are already manifest on earth in the saints and the sages of the different religions who have risen from the disruption of being to its articulation, integration.

In the spirit of the *Vedānta*, the *Buddha* speaks of human fulfilment as the transition from ignorance and craving to enlightenment and compassion. The aim of religion is to release us from the tornness of our life. We must grow from the status of the creature, given to inertia, distractedness, corruption, selfishness to integrality with its unswerving devotion.

The Jews tell us that sin is the isolation of the selfish individual; it is lovelessness. When we turn away from it, our self-alienation, self-estrangement is gone. 'Return ye and make you a new heart and a new spirit.'[1] 'Create me a clean heart, O God, and renew a steadfast spirit within me.'[2] 'A new heart will I give you, and a new spirit will I put within you.'[3] 'Turn me, O Lord, that I may turn.'[4] Religion is a question of turning and renewal. For the Jews, 'The spirit of man is the candle of the Lord.'[5] When the Lord lights the candle, darkness disappears. All the darkness in the world cannot put out the light of the candle.

Speaking of the mystery religions of Greece, Aristotle observes 'The initiated do not learn anything so much as feel certain emotions and are put in a certain frame of mind'. To live one must first die to his old life. Orpheus believed that the soul was 'the son of the starry heaven', that its dwelling in a body was a form of original sin, its earthly life was a source of corruption and its natural aim was to transcend this life. Each human being is a reflection of the celestial light and has his roots below. This view is at the heart of Plato's idealism. Plato tells us in his image of the cave in the *Republic* that we are all prisoners living in shadows. One philosopher shattered his fetters and saw the sun shining of which the fire in the cave was a small reflection.

[1] *Ezekiel* xviii. 30ff. [2] *Psalm* li. 10. [3] *Ezekiel* xxxvi. 26.
[4] *Lamentations* v. 21. [5] *Proverbs* xx. 27.

After having seen the great light, Plato's philosopher does not remain content with his own revelation. He returns to the cave and tells the prisoners shackled there that what they take for reality is only a shadow cast by the light they do not see. The prisoners, not having seen the light, take the shadows to be the only reality and think that the philosopher is insane. Philosophy, for Plato, is the love of wisdom, the fine flower of serenity. Plotinus says: 'Withdraw into yourself and look, and if you do not find yourself beautiful yet, act as does the creator of a statue that is to be made beautiful: he cuts away here, he smoothes there, he makes this line lighter, this other purer, until a lovely face has grown upon his work. So do you also: cut away all that is excessive, straighten all that is crooked, bring light to all that is overcast, labour to make all one glow of beauty and never cease chiselling your statue, until there shall shine out on you from it the godlike splendour of virtue, until you shall see the perfect goodness surely established in the stainless shrine.' He argues that each individual should pass beyond the restlessness of this life, its fragmentariness, its precariousness, its discordance. We have to pass through the depth of the struggle to gain the peace of the One, which is unity, pure and simple.

The inner meaning of crucifixion and resurrection is the story of man's dying to the purely physical and egoistic existence, when he is resurrected into the spiritual awareness of his oneness with the life, love and power of the Supreme. It is the dramatisation of man's deliverance from the tomb of living death in which fear, greed, hate, pride have imprisoned him and his free ascent into the freedom of his divine nature. When we die to the old nature, we are reborn to the new. St Paul said: 'Jesus Christ is in you.'[1] 'Christ in you, the hope of glory.'[2] Christ is the divine self within, waiting to be released and expressed. When the rebirth takes place we become 'partakers of the divine nature'.[3] The author of the Fourth Gospel makes Jesus say, 'I am the Truth'. The religion of truth is based on spiritual inwardness. The descent of the spirit at Jesus' baptism or his temptation in the wilderness must have been the story of his inner experience. In their present form they are externalised. In Christianity we are called upon to follow the

[1] II *Corinthians* xiii. 5. [2] *Colossians* i. 27. [3] II *Peter* i. 4.

example of Jesus. We are to be made like unto him by bringing our natural desires and expectations into subjection to the Universal Purpose. William Law says: 'To have salvation from Christ is nothing else but to be made like unto him; it is to have his humility and meekness, his love of God, his desire of doing God's will.' Jesus asks us to free ourselves from priestly control, and undergo spiritual growth. We must be born again, born of the spirit of Truth. Those who practise the goodness and love illustrated in Jesus' life become sharers in the eternal Kingdom of spirit, a fellowship of redeemed men who live both in time and beyond time. They strive to raise the world to a more stable way and further the time when nation shall not take up sword against nation, neither learn war any more.

A *Sufi* mystic (twelfth century), Ayn al-qudāt at Hamadhāni (d. A.D. 1131) says: 'He who is born from the womb sees only this world; only he who is born out of himself sees the other world.'

Ibn'Arabi (thirteenth century) says: 'I am knowledge, the known and the knower. I am wisdom, the wise man and his wiseness.' (60. 16.)

Both the *Buddha* and Jesus tell us: 'Be of good courage. I have overcome the world.' Renewal, rebirth is the universal aim of all religions. Out of different origins and backgrounds we are reaching out to the one goal.

D. REBIRTH AND PRE-EXISTENCE

Future Life

Belief in some kind of survival is very nearly universal. There is no country or creed in which the great hope of survival has not supported men in the prospect of death and mitigated the grief of bereavement. Even the primitive peoples of whose habits of life we have knowledge assume it as their funerary customs indicate. This universality is often urged as proof in itself of the validity of belief in future life.[1] On a question of truth however, suffrage is not conclusive.[2] But while a strong wish is

[1] Many years ago a questionnaire was sent out by the Society for Psychical Research and it elicited very different views about the fact as well as the desirability of survival. Some believed implicitly and were glad; others were sceptical and were quite satisfied. Apparently men do not seem to think about it unless it be in crises.

[2] Cp. *Gorgias* 472, 474.

not in itself evidence, the consensus of feeling seems to attest a natural instinct. It may not be too much to assume that the instincts of mankind prophesy a fulfilment even as those of the bee and the ant who lay up stores for a winter.[1] Besides, the concurrence of many thinkers in one conclusion is probably the most convincing kind of evidence which is possible on questions of morality and religion. At any rate it is a fact sufficiently impressive to make it worth while to investigate the belief in question.

Unfortunately the consensus of agreement disappears when we examine the nature of survival. Strange and terrifying forms of beliefs, crude and dreary conceptions are found side by side with abstract and exalted notions. The activities of heaven change with our earthly aspirations. The Egyptians looked upon their celestial home as replete with rich wheatfields and harvests produced without labour. The Red Indians dreamed of happy hunting grounds with plenty of game and unending sport. For Isaiah, in the Kingdom of God impotence and infirmities shall be done away, 'the eyes of the blind shall be opened, and the ears of the deaf shall be unstopped, the lame man leap as an hart and the tongue of the dumb sing'. The ancient Teutonic peoples conceived of a Valhalla with endless scope for military exercises and stores of beer to be drunk from the skulls of former enemies. Dante's picture of hell as a pendant to heaven is well known. Dostoievsky makes one of his characters say, 'Why should not eternity be a little bathhouse covered with spiders?' We have believed that the soul lives like a pale shadow craving blood to feed it, that it migrates into innumerable forms of plants and animals, that it repeats indefinitely its main occupations here, that it is tortured in hells for sins, that it sings for ever hymns in heavens. The intellectual demand common to the vivid pictorial forms is to secure for human personality some significance that transcends the world of the senses, to maintain that life is not a formless flux but has a pattern which is not exhausted by this brief span. The dead do not wholly cease to be.

This question of survival has significance only in reference to

[1] Ruysbroek: 'As hunger presupposes bread so does man's longing after God presuppose God.'

human beings. Some materialist thinkers have believed that atoms are absolutely everlasting but they do not speak of them as having future life or immortality because they are not selves.

Survival and Eternal Life

The term 'future life' is ambiguous and means either durational continuance or eternal life, survival after death or immortality. Eternal life differs from life in time, in quality and not quantity. It is a higher state of being which knows nothing of past or future, the divine mode of existence which we may enjoy here and now. Perpetuity which is a form of time is different from eternity which is timelessness. The distinction between rebirth (*punar-janma*) and release (*mokṣa*) is familiar to all systems of Hindu thought. We find it also in some of the philosophies of the West. In Plato, for example, we have these two conceptions. There is the doctrine of the *Symposium*, which is not of a future life but of timeless existence, attainable here and now by an escape from the flux of time. There is the other doctrine of the *Phaedo* involving pre-existence and post-existence which are concepts possessing meaning only with regard to the temporal life of the soul. In the New Testament we have the eschatological teaching with its pictures of the judgment and the Kingdom of God to which the faithful dead shall rise, which are projected into the future in addition to the doctrine of an unseen world which is more real than the present one. According to the latter view, heaven is a subsisting reality, not a remote state. In one passage Jesus substitutes the idea of the present eternal life of individuals for the hope of a general resurrection of the righteous. When Martha says about her brother 'I know that he shall rise again in the resurrection at the last day', Jesus said to her 'I am the resurrection and the life; he that believeth in me, though he die, yet shall he live; and whosoever liveth and believeth in me, shall never die.'[1] He apparently substitutes the conception of a present eternal life which is unaltered by death for a resurrection at some future date, 'the last day'. According to Jesus we can have eternal life while still in the flesh. 'Verily, verily, I say unto you, he that heareth my word, and believeth him who sent me, hath eternal

[1] *John* xi. 23–6.

life, and cometh not into judgment, but hath passed out of death into life.'[1] St Paul affirms that God 'alone hath immortality'.[2] Similarly in the Fourth Gospel, we have the conception of eternal life though the Messianic expectation is not discarded. 'He that believeth in the Son hath eternal life.'[3]

For Philo, time is the moving succession of ever-shifting phenomena while eternity is the motionless duration of unalterable being. In Plotinus we have the distinction of awakening from the body which is not awakening with the body.[4] It is the distinction between the ethical and the spiritual points of view. At the ethical level, we have an infinite progress toward an ideal that is never completely realised. Kant, for example, believed in future life as a postulate of the practical reason. If the holy will is unrealisable here, it can only be realised under the form of an endless progress towards perfection. So ethical consciousness justifies the assumption of infinite time to work out infinite perfection. The spiritual point of view is different. By the identification of the finite self with the divine order, the supreme good is achieved.[5] Thus in the history of thought, future life has been conceived in two ways, either as a prolongation of this earthly life or as a complete change from time to eternity.

When we raise the question of future life, we are concerned with the individual human soul. It is no comfort to know that there is the Divine in man and it is immortal. The Divine, the immutable presence, what the *Advaita Vedānta* calls *sva-prakāśa-caitanya*, the self-luminous consciousness in us may be

[1] *John* v. 24. [2] *Timothy* vi. 16.

[3] *John* iii. 36. Cp. Dr Alexander Nairne: 'This then is the assurance of the Johannine discourse and its concluding prayer: that eternal life is here and now and always and everywhere: that soul or spirit entering the eternal state, gains intercourse, communion, union with the souls it knows: that this is what our affection for one another means and depends upon, and this kind of communion or union cannot be ended by death.' *The Life Eternal, Here and Now*, p. 127.

[4] *Enneads* III. 6. 6.

[5] E. Troeltsch tells us that there is a future life or lives involving a continuous process of moral purification and an ever-increasing identification of the human will with the divine. The end of the ethical process is, however, the identification of the creature with God. 'The actual end would thus be the complete unity of will with the divine will eventually achieved in this further development after death, and a confluence of the finite wills in love, the complete disappearance of the perfected individuals, the yielding up of the personality to the divine life.' Quoted in Braham: *Ourselves and Reality* (1929), p. 173.

insusceptible to change but it does not affect the status of the human self, the *jīvātman*, the complex composite organism which suffers a crisis at death. An unchanging self outside of the succession and supposed to bring connection and unity into otherwise unrelated terms is not the human self in whose survival we are interested. The eternal *ātman*, according to *Advaita Vedānta*, is common to all individuals.[1] Its continuance after the disintegration of the complex of elements which constitute personal existence is not of much interest.

In Plato we have the idea of an indiscerptible soul-substance immortal in its own right. He says in the *Republic*, 'Soul is substance and substance is indestructible'. The soul is what makes us what we are. It is immortal because its very idea and essence is the self-moved and self-moving. Yet we find in Plato the view that the soul is not quite eternal like the divine ideas. It partakes in their nature but it must train itself, by exercising its highest faculties, to think immortal thoughts and identify itself with the eternal world by entering into it. But when Plato speaks of the nature of soul-substance, that it belongs to the invisible world of changeless reality, that it was never born and will never die and that body is part of the unreal world of becoming[2] and not the object of true knowledge, he is reaffirming that the Divine in man is immortal. His proofs in the *Phaedo* from recollection and from the soul's kinship with God prove the eternity of impersonal reason and not of the individual self. For the Neoplatonists the higher soul has life and being in itself and can neither be born nor die and the fate of the lower soul depends on the manner of living. This soul may be lost if it rebels against the higher principle.

Modern psychology is inclined to view the individual as a perpetual becoming, a system of psychological and ethical energies, that is changing as long as it is alive. When William James makes out that the passing thought is the only thinker, he is suggesting by the passing thought the present state of the continuously developing self, which represents in itself all

[1] *Kaṭha U.* II. 16.

[2] 'I cannot persuade Crito, my friends, that I am that Socrates who is now conversing with you, and who methodises each part of the discourse; but he thinks that I am he whom he will shortly behold dead, and asks how he should bury me.'

thoughts and states that went before. The passing thought is a résumé or a sum-total of all its predecessors, the inheritor of the past and the growing point of the future. It takes up in itself the previous moment, makes it its own and gives it up to the next moment of experience.[1] It is the actual self quite distinct from the unchanging self outside of the succession altogether, supposed by its relating activity to bring unity and connection into a series of otherwise unrelated items. The self is constituted by its experience. It is the unity of the conscious experiences of a particular individual centre. It is not a simple atomic unit but a complex living structure, a unity in multiplicity. Each self enjoys a kind of unity and continuity. The states are not detached and the self is not apart from the succession. It is the organised or consolidated unity of all experience. All states occur as belonging to this unity, as elements in a growing self-integrating whole. The unity of self is not a mechanical one. We can destroy a wall and retain the bricks. We cannot destroy a self and retain thoughts and emotions. The self is a different kind of unity where form and content are closely united. The unity of the individual is of a functional rather than of a substantive character. Soul is the name of the composite nature which one knows as oneself and which functions as one person though it passes from life to life or body to body. It is not an abstraction. The conscious self is shaped by all one's experiences; its individuality is the result of the discipline of time.

Immortality has point only if it refers to the human person and his capacity to attain it by consciously realising his unity with the timeless or eternal self. If the world is rational, the final outcome of the age-long organic process must be something better and less ephemeral than man as we know him in ourselves and others—doomed to death. If we are to save the rationality of the universe we must assume that the transition from self-consciousness to God-consciousness is the aim of organic evolution. When the Hindu thinkers, Plato, Aristotle and the

[1] 'Each pulse of cognitive consciousness, each thought dies away and is replaced by another. The other, among the things it knows, knows its own predecessor, and finding it "warm" in the way we have described, greets it, saying: "Thou art mine, and part of the same self with me".' *Principles of Psychology* (1890), Vol. I, p. 339.

Neoplatonists affirm the reality of the Divine in man, they have in mind the possibility of realising the divine quality through the apparatus of mind and body. The presence of the Universal Spirit operates as the ideal to which the organism strives. The simplicity of the human individual, the unity of the human soul are not obvious. They are the ideals we strive for.

We have argued that the process of becoming is not unreal. The human individual is not a false appearance. By means of self-variation the Spirit manifests itself as the universe without at the same time suffering any derogation from its original status. The universe is essentially dynamic and the human individual is the growing point of the future, the agent as well as the offspring of the creative process. His personality is continuously enriched and changed by his experiences and there is no break. The thread in the weaver's loom is not cut; it disappears from our vision. There is an ancient saying that death is natural to embodied beings; it is life that is unnatural.[1]

The conditions which determine the individual unity are organic since every soul known to us is an embodied soul. The Jews, for example, never thought of the soul as distinct from the body or of the body as the prison-house of the soul so far as they escaped Greek influences. Their belief in personal immortality was always belief in the resurrection of dead persons as wholes. It was not an immortality of bare souls. St Paul expresses the faith in which he had been bred thus 'having hope towards God which these also [my Jewish adversaries] themselves look for, that there shall be a Resurrection both of the just and the unjust'.[2] A disembodied state of existence is not admitted. St Paul raises the question 'How are the dead raised? With what manner of body do they come?'[3] Heaven seems to be an organisation which does not undergo decay. 'They shall hunger no more; neither thirst any more; neither shall the sun light on them, nor any heat; for the Lamb which is in the midst of the throne shall feed them and lead them into living fountains of water; and God shall wipe away all tears from their eyes.' 'And there shall be no more death, neither

[1] *maraṇam prakṛtiḥ śarīriṇām vikṛtir jīvanam ucyate budhaiḥ.*
Kavikulacakravartin.

[2] *Acts* xxiv. 15.

[3] I *Corinthians* xv.

sorrow nor crying, neither shall there be any more pain.' It seems to be a simple scheme where we will have life with its goods and not its ills. Those who have tasted sorrow and seen the shadow of death are told that these things will not be. This view admits that every manifestation of life must have its own fit embodiment, its appropriate means of expression. Tertullian takes the extreme position that the soul is nothing if it is not body. Justin considers the doctrine that the soul is taken to heaven at the death of the body to be unchristian.

Rebirth

In this world body is the basis and starting point for the development of life, mind and spirit. Bodiless beings are not known. The assumption of body is called birth and it is essential for the manifestation of the individual on the physical plane. But it cannot be an isolated accident or sudden excursion into physicality without any past or future. In an ordered world, sudden embodiment of conscious life would be meaningless and inconsequential. It would be a violation of the rhythm of nature, an effect without cause, a fragmentary present without a past. Life is a term in a series, a slow development. It cannot be regarded as something which mysteriously appears at or about birth and disappears equally mysteriously at or about death. The individual is constantly changing in his mind as well as in his body. There is, however, unity in so far as each state is a present transformation representative of all those which are past as it will be the producer of all future transformation potentially involved in it. The development of a coherent mind and character is the aim of self-conscious life and it is the reality which the body in its structure and organisation exists to actualise. Though based on the body, the characteristic unity of the self is spiritual, more complete and permanent than any achieved by any individual being. The self of man is not a mere effect of its body or a form of its activity, though it requires the body for its work in this world. It follows that the self existed before it began to animate the body of this life and will exist after it ceases to animate it. Death has no meaning except as a process of life. Death is a condition, not a denial of life. Disintegration of substance and change of form are constant processes of all living beings. One span of life ends to give place to another.

A single life, in many cases, is not enough for achieving perfection. If there are other lives they must be continuous with the present one. God's love being unlimited, the opportunities not made use of in one life will be renewed in other lives till the spirit finds its fulfilment.

If every soul is created at birth, why should it be created sinful? Notable Christian thinkers like Paul, Augustine and Calvin adopt the view of original sin. The soul must at least be born without sin whatever it may make of itself later. It must be born free though it may forge for itself chains later. Some are born from birth deformed and tortured with disease or into circumstances of extreme squalor and misery while others are born into lives of health, ease and happiness. The souls are made to assume bodies with their qualities, capacities and defects made for them and for the use of which they are made responsible, though they are fortuitously connected with them. We are made helpless by what we are and are held accountable for what we shall be, which is largely determined by what we are originally. We start on an unequal level. It offends our logical and ethical sense to assume that a Socrates and a sinner are endowed with different constitutions to strive for eternal life, and if the sinner fails it cannot be a matter for surprise. He made the best of his bad equipment. If the inequalities are to be traced to God, he cannot be freed from the accusations of partiality and favouritism. Again, if every time a baby is born a new soul is created, the universe will be capable of infinite increase.

Though the rise of human souls may be a mystery of faith, the best explanation we can think of is that the physical act provides a body for a soul which awaits rebirth. The soul is not something created at birth. Life here is an episode in a larger life, involving a succession of alternate births and deaths. Individual souls follow their course and their present fortunes depend on the past in an organic and indissoluble manner. Growth is the character of the soul. As a living organism, it is modified by the life it chooses and the way it acts. The forms and properties of matter, plants and animals do not come into existence all of a sudden. The objects of nature develop from stage to stage and, at every stage, nature takes up its past and transforms it into the stuff of its new development. Human nature is not an exception to this rule. It is logical to assume that the soul has developed continuously from almost nothing at the earlier limit of time like a ripple spreading out from a centre. Each soul would appear to be coeval not only with the universe but with time itself. It is this fact that binds him with the physical and organic conditions of the world. From the first the world is equally real with himself. The two, the individual and the world, coexist and subsist together. The individual is placed in an environment which he has chosen, his own natural environment, that which answers to his character. Man is born into the world which he has made.[1] The variety of the world is born of *karma*.[2]

Survival of Death and Personal Immortality

When we think of a person, we think of his body and character, thoughts and feelings which are connected with and conditioned by the body. The belief that we will recognise our friends in another world assumes that personal characteristics are immortal but if by personality we mean the psychophysical organism which was born at a certain date and grew up for a number of years and died at a certain date, it is difficult to say which part of this organism, which is compacted of qualities, physical and mental, inherited and acquired would be preserved, when it is attached to another body or set down in another time and place. Rebirth means that there is change in the physical and even some mental characteristics. Disappearance of body makes a difference to the subtle body as there are psychic elements which have no function except in relation to the body. The persistence of the results of experience is different from the resuscitation of personality.

What is it that survives death, if it is not the body? When Yājñavalkya was asked, 'When the speech of a dead person enters into fire, the breath into air, the eye into the sun, the mind into the moon, the hearing into the quarters, the soul into

[1] *kṛtaṁ lokaṁ puruṣo'bhijāyate. Śatapatha Brāhmaṇa.* VI. 2. 2. 27.

[2] *kármajaṁ loka-vaicitryam. Abhidharma-kośa.* IV.

the ether . . . what then becomes of this person?', he answered 'verily one becomes good by good actions, bad by bad actions'. The lessons learnt at any stage are carried over into the next. Manu says 'The only friend who follows men even after death is *dharma*; for everything else is lost at the same time when the body perishes'.[1] Whatever our character and knowledge in the flesh may be, we arrive with them in the next state.[2] They are the all-commanding things that ultimately matter. Our rank in the scale of being depends on the powers which we exercise and the objects which we contemplate. We become what we love and care about. The knowledge we painfully acquire and the character we develop are carried over to the next life. 'Verily man consists of purpose [*kratu-maya*] and according to the completeness of his understanding when he departs this world, thus he becomes after having passed away.'[3] He will find himself in an environment similar to that to which he is adjusted here. The scribes and the pharisees have their reward for ambition and self-seeking and the craven soul in emptiness of spirit. We must accept our wages, high and noble or petty and shameful, and cast ourselves afresh on the adventure of life. Man grows and flourishes and when at the end of a single life he dies, he leaves behind a seed from which a new plant grows. Man is his own heir, his own ancestor.

Life is not a mechanical recurrence but a significant process. We cannot say that the wheel turns ceaselessly, creating souls whose ideal is to cease to exist. Even in the material world, we have not got mere mechanical recurrence. Rebirth is not an eternal recurrence leading nowhere but a movement from man the animal to man the divine, a unique beginning to a unique end, from wild life in the jungle to a future Kingdom of God. The soul is constantly performing the miracle of self-embodiment which is a means for self-renewal, a growth into light.[4]

[1] B.U. III. 2. 13. *Manu* VIII. 7: see also XI. 51–81.

[2] Cp. *Revelation* xiv. 13. 'They rest from their labours and their works follow them.'

[3] *Śatapatha Brāhmaṇa* X. 6. 3. 1. See also C.U. III. 14. 1.

[4] Lessing asks: 'Why should not every individual man have existed more than once upon this world? Is this hypothesis laughable merely because it is the oldest? . . . Why should I not come back as often as I am capable of acquiring fresh knowledge, fresh expertness?'

The Law of Karma

There is one law for the whole universe for all existence is one existence. There is, however, a persistent variety in existence. The law of *karma* tells us that as in the physical world, in the mental and moral world also there is law. The world is an ordered cosmos. What we sow we will reap. The law of *karma* governs the growth of the human individual. Our acts determine our character which in turn determines our acts. An individual is full of desire.[1] Desire is said to be the agent of action, the impeller of action.[2]

The law of *karma* emphasises the importance of conduct. Man is continually shaping his destiny. The piling up of the past goes on without interruption. Each thought, each action has definitive consequences. 'What a man wills he does; what he does even so he becomes.'[3] 'As a calf finds its mother among a thousand cows, so does the deed previously done follow after the doer.'[4] We can never separate ourselves from our past.[5] We may completely recover from a disease, sincerely repent for a wrong deed but we bear for ever the scar of these events. A well-known verse in the *Garuḍa Purāṇa* tells us that the results of our deeds, good or evil, must be experienced; those that are not experienced do not fade away even in hundreds of millions of ages.[6] The universe is ethically sound. Even as the world would be a logical contradiction without the reign of law, it would be a moral chaos without the moral law. The law of *karma* is not a blind necessity or a mechanical rule but simply the organic nature of life where each successive phase grows inevitably from

[1] *kāma-mayaḥ puruṣaḥ*. B.U. III. 9. 11.

[2] *kāmaḥ kartā kāmaḥ kārayitā.*

[3] B.U. IV. 4–5.

[4] *yathā dhenu-sahasreṣu vatso vindati mātaram*
tathā pūrva-kṛtaṁ karma kartāram anugacchati. M.B. Śānti parva 15. 56.

[5] Cp. Coleridge: 'It may be more possible for heaven and earth to pass away than that a single act, a single thought should be loosened or lost from that living chain of causes with all the links of which the free will, our only absolute self, is coextensive and copresent. And this, perchance, is that dread book of judgment in the mysterious hieroglyphics of which every idle word is recorded.' *Biographia Literaria*, Vol. I. 2nd edition, p. 119. Marcus Aurelius says: 'Of whatever colour are the thoughts you think often, to that colour does your mind grow, for the soul is dyed by its thoughts.' *Meditations* V. 16.

[6] *avaśyam eva bhoktavyaṁ kṛtam karma śubhāśubham*
nābhuktaṁ kṣīyate karma kalpa-koṭi-śatair api.

what has gone before. The law of *karma* intensifies our sense of the tremendous significance of every decision we make for the right or the wrong. Every choice has an influence on our whole moral being not merely for this life but for ever.

Karma and Freedom

If we reduce the spiritual to the animal, free self-determination will be replaced by rigid coercion. The roots of our existence lie in the transcendent sphere. All the time our existence where law or *karma* prevails points and strives beyond itself. If man were a mere object of study in physiology, if he were a mere mind described by psychology, his conduct would be governed by the law of necessity. But man is not just a natural and historical product. He is aware of himself as a free being. He is not altogether self-made. He exists by virtue of something other than himself, something transcendent to his existence. There is in us the Eternal different from the limited chain of causes and effects in the phenomenal world. An objective account of human consciousness is not the whole truth about man. Man is aware of himself not only as an object in the world but as an individual subject, the active source of what he is and does. From this point of view the Transcendence speaks to us from our innermost depths, through our freedom. We must acknowledge the material needs of our existence, otherwise we are not alive; we must admit our relation to the Supreme, otherwise we are not true.

Evil is not disobedience. It is corruption, moral obliquity by which we abuse our creative powers. When the soul of man realises that it is one with the power of Self-existence which manifests the universe, it ceases to be bound by *karma*. Mind, life and body become its apparatus. In man is the seed of all creation. Man is one with the Supreme in his innermost being and the spirit in him is superior to his *karma* but when he mistakes himself for the ego his will is not altogether free. The individual will and personality are bound by many things physical and vital: heredity, past creation of our mental nature and environmental forces, but the soul is greater than its present form.

Karma refers to the limiting force of our equipment and

environment; freedom refers to human plasticity, the variety of possible development opening before a man endowed with a definite character. Spirit is the negation of all inertia. From the point of view of Spirit, there are no good habits and bad habits. All habits are bad. With every habit we form, man's original freedom congeals into bondage. All fixation is a victory of routine over initiative, of inertia over freedom.

Human freedom has to reckon with the necessary law according to which character as modified up to date tends to express itself. If we do not exercise our creative choice, what has been done will rule completely what shall be done. What we have done is past and unalterable. It has entered into us and become a part of us. Character is destiny.[1] If the present state of man is the product of a long past, he can change what he has made. His past which he has built for himself and his present environment may offer obstacles to him but they will all yield in the end to the will in him in proportion to its sincerity and insistence. Life is a constant self-creation.

Karma and Predestination

The law of *karma* has nothing in common with the popular teaching that rewards and punishments are dependent on the arbitrary will of God. If God predestines us for weal or woe regardless of what we do, it is no use bothering about what we do. *Karma* is not predestination. Augustine's teaching that only a small fraction of humanity, the elect, are destined to bliss while the many are 'reprobate', predetermined to everlasting damnation, is contradicted by the law of *karma* which affirms that by doing what is in our power we can dispose the mind to the love of the Eternal and attain salvation. Man's instinctive

[1] Cp. 'Destiny is nothing but what inevitably happens as the good or bad results of our efforts already put forth.'

siddhasya pauruṣeneha phalasya phala-śālinā. *Yogavāśistha.*
subhāśubhārtha-sampattir daiva-śabdena kathyate. *Yogavāśistha.* II. 9. 4.

Destiny is the result of our past efforts, *prāktanam pauruṣam* II. 6. 4. Even as one endeavours, so one achieves. The present can overcome the past (II. 5. 12).

yathā yathā prayatnaḥ syād bhaved āśu phalam tathā
iti pauruṣam evāsti daivam astu tadeva ca. II. 6. 2.

The fools who believe that everything is in the hands of destiny are ruined. *daivāttam iti manyante ye hatās te kubuddhayaḥ* II. 5. 29. The *Rāmāyaṇa* asks us to overcome fate by human efforts: *daivam puruṣakāreṇa nivartayitum arhasi.*

sense of justice is bewildered by the bland relegation of a large part of humanity to everlasting torment. If the law of *karma* is the will of the highest wisdom and God is the sovereign who works the law, then our future may be regarded indifferently as either the fulfilment of the law or a gift of God. If we are rationally-minded we say that the future life is a natural and necessary consequence of the first; if we are theistically-minded, that it is due to the intervention of God who rewards the righteous and punishes the wicked in the manner of an earthly sovereign. If his will is not arbitrary or capricious but wholly reasonable and right, its operations are rational and necessary. God has so ordered the world that if a man lives rightly he will achieve salvation but there is no grace, no free gift of God to enable him to do so. God, of course, is the only source and guarantee. God seeks to draw us, to persuade us but we can resist him. When we resist him, we find ourselves up against punishment. This principle is worked into the moral structure of things. It makes evil in the long run self-defeating.

God is the universal background providing for the multiple manifestation, the actualisation of the different possibilities. Ś. argues that even as rain helps the growth of the different seeds into their own respective plants, so does God serve as the universal concomitant or the unvarying condition in the creation of human beings, while each one's *karma* determines what he grows into.[1] For him the rise of the world is due to moral necessity. The accumulated *karma* of the past requires expiation. The need for moral consummation and continuity brings the world into being.

The Law of Karma and Prayer

If *karma* determines our future, has prayer any use? Can God forgive in answer to prayer? R. says: 'That man who acts with the determination to be wholly on the side of the Supreme Person, the Lord blesses by himself creating in him a taste for such actions only as are a means to attaining him and are extremely good. But he punishes the man who acts with the determination to be wholly against him by creating in him a

[1] Ś.B. II. I. 34.

taste for such actions as stand in the way of attaining him and lead him downward.'[1]

Ethical Value of the Law of Karma

To those discouraged by life's disabilities, the doctrine of *karma* teaches patience and persistent endeavour. When we see the long procession of men either deformed in body or warped in mind, with faint hearts and weak wills, we should not judge them harshly. When man is set alone against the vast background of his destiny, when he finds that he cannot defy his fate and unfaltering despair overtakes him, belief in *karma* steadies his nature. For most of us it may appear that we are playing a part that we have not chosen, in a play which does not interest us. Life to such may seem a dull proceeding and they may pass through it with a certain listlessness. The principle of *karma* tells us that we earned this particular life, indeed we chose it. Our lives are self-begotten and self-born. If what we are is due to what we did, we will be even as we now do. It is open to us to remake our life even as we will have it. The future is not a finished product like the past.

E. SOME OBJECTIONS TO THE HYPOTHESIS OF REBIRTH

Lack of Memory

There is reason for the old belief that between each fresh life, the soul or the ego of the individual drinks of the waters of Lethe. In other words memory of the past is obliterated by the transition from life on another plane to life on earth. The *Bhāgavata Purāṇa* says that death is absolute forgetfulness.[2] If we do not know that we enjoy or suffer in this life on account of our deeds in a previous life, we cannot be said to profit by experience. If we do not know why we suffer, our suffering is not a safeguard against the repetition of our evil deeds.[3] Since

[1] R.B. II. 3. 4.

[2] *mṛtyur atyanta-vismṛtiḥ.*

[3] Professor Pringle Pattison, quoting Leibniz, writes: 'What good, Sir, would it do you to become king of China on condition that you forget what you have been? Would it not be the same as if God, at the moment he destroyed you, were to create a king of China.' *Idea of Immortality*, p. 125.

there is complete discontinuity of consciousness between one life and the next, the reward or punishment cannot in any intelligible sense be experienced by him who has deserved it. If one who has abused his intellectual gifts is reborn as an idiot, how does it help? Our present lives may be continuous with past lives but it does not make any difference so long as we do not remember the fact.

We have no clear ideas about the mechanism of memory, how it inheres and is perpetuated in this life. We do not know how precisely experiences are stored in the organism and by what means they are revived. Psychical dispositions are for James Ward the basis of memory when the cerebral states are shattered. William James makes memory 'a physiological quality given once for all with its organisations which we can never hope to change'. G. F. Stout speaks of psychophysical dispositions. Bergson holds that memories are indestructible psychical entities and as immaterial they have no particular location in space. These memories hang together in associated systems. In *Matter and Memory* Bergson suggests that the true function of the brain is not to enable us to remember things but to forget them. But for this eliminating power of the brain, crowds of recollections which are irrelevant to the purpose in hand would overtake us, making it difficult for us to deal with immediate issues. The brain acts as a kind of sieve allowing only those memories to pass which have relevance to the present situation. Bergson assumes that our experience as it develops itself leaves behind an integral record, complete to the minutest details. When a new situation confronts us and the need for constructive action arises, memory images from the past attach themselves to the present perception, interpreting it. The memories are the acted past and the present consciousness may be active in selecting but the memories themselves are acted, not active. In Freud's view the constituents of the soul are not past actions but present active wishes repressed and more or less actively controlled but producing conflict in their struggle to rise to consciousness and reach fulfilment. Memories are, for him, not pictures hung up in the halls of the mind but active vibrant centres. The unconscious memories keep the unconscious part of our mind alive and occasionally by pressing through the boundary that separates the unconscious from the conscious, bring back varied associations into conscious memory.

In any experience we have two elements. Suppose we cut our finger we have (i) the series of events that produce the pain: the misadventure in handling the knife, the cut, the bleeding, (ii) the sense of pain. The first is in the background while the second holds the centre. Gradually even the second recedes into the background leaving behind not a direct memory as an event but an indirect memory or a tendency to be careful in the handling of knives. If the tendencies persist, it does not matter if the memories lapse. The trained musician plays with a mind free from all recollection of the details of the past labour of learning notes. His fingers remember them and his subconscious mind stores the experience. Reflective knowledge results in an instinctive endowment. Wisdom does not consist in vast stores of knowledge but in the ability to profit by experience. Though we may not have conscious memory there is a persistence of dispositions and tendencies. Though at death we may lose the memory of the detailed knowledge and the skill and the habits, still we start our next life in consequence of having possessed these with more efficient dispositions and a greater power to reacquire the detailed knowledge and insight.[1]

Active memory does not seem to be essential for personal identity. Forgetting may perhaps be essential for making a fresh start. Providence has been more beneficent in bestowing on us the gift of forgetting. We do not deny our existence as an infant or an embryo simply because we do not remember them. Much passes into oblivion even in this life. We cannot identify the infant with the grown-up man if memory of the earlier stage is regarded as essential. Individuality does not depend on memory. Simply because we forget the experiences of our infancy, we do not believe that it is not we who had them. The unconscious processes do not form a part of the conscious ego but belong to the totality of the individual. Simply because the ego is not conscious of them we cannot deny their existence for they reveal themselves in and determine the

[1] See McTaggart: *Some Dogmas of Religion* (1906), pp. 127–37: *The Nature of Existence*, Vol. II (1927), pp. 385–96.

individual's behaviour. If, without a memory of our previous life, we still think that the present life has positive value, absence of memory of previous lives need not be taken as a fatal objection. The hypothesis of rebirth admits that there is a breach of consciousness and yet affirms continuity of self. While memory fades, the modifications remain, the attitude of mind, the habit of judgment, the dispositions of character survive in the new individuality and form its basis.

It is also held that the illumined by the development of psychic powers are able to recollect their past births.[1] Individual cases of memory of past lives are reported.

Inequalities may be due to Heredity

Simply because we are ignorant of the cause of the inequality of human circumstance, we need not postulate previous existences. Inequality is a law of nature which we find in plants and animals also. It is not uncaused, however. The differences in natural endowment can all be traced to heredity. Pre-existence need not be assumed. The nature of any organism is largely determined by that of its biological ancestors. Heredity expresses the large resemblance between parents and children.

Heredity means the transmission of physical form and biological characteristics from a previous life. A lion generates a lion, not a horse or a tiger. Things transmitted are not only physical and biological but psychical also, mental powers and tendencies. If we hold that man's whole nature is derived from his physical birth, that the body and mind of the individual are only a continuation of the body and mind of his ancestors, then the individual has no past being independent of his ancestors, or future independent of his descendants. He prolongs himself in his progeny and there is no rebirth for him. No continued stream of individuality survives the death of the

[1] *Yoga Sūtra* II. 30; *Upaskāra* on *Vaiśeṣika Sūtra* V. 2. 18; VI. 2. 16. Compare also the romantic story of Apollonius of Tyana and the later legendary lives of Pythagoras. See the B.G. IV. 5.

The Buddha, according to Aśvaghoṣa, remembered his past births:

'In recollection all former births passed before his eyes. Born in such a place, of such a name, and downwards to his present birth, so through hundreds, thousands, myriads, all his births and deaths he knew.' *Buddha-carita*. Samuel Beal's E.T.

body. If the parents literally make the child, then we do not require either a prior life or divine agency.

If we posit an element in us which cannot be accounted for by the principle of heredity, a psychic power behind the veil of material process, then it presupposes a past and admits a future evolution other than that of the race mind and physical necessity. Human life manifests itself in a body but is not the product of the body. Its characteristics are determined jointly by those which the self had when it began to animate the organism and by the nature of the organism which it animates. The problem is, how does a certain self become associated with a certain organism when the latter is the product of purely biological causation? The theist argues that God creates a suitable mind whenever an organism is conceived and unites the two. In other words, every birth is a miracle. It is more plausible to think that a pre-existent self becomes associated with a certain organism at the moment when the latter is conceived. In nature this kind of adaptive affinity occurs frequently, in chemical affinity, in the selective affinity of spermatozoa for ova of the same species. Minds and organisms attract each other in the same way. The reincarnating ego is attracted to parents from whom it can inherit a particular set of qualities. The psyche appropriates the body necessary for its realisation. The natural body derived from the parents according to the laws of heredity is taken over by the soul. There are differences also among children of same parents brought up under same conditions and these cannot be accounted for exclusively by heredity.

While the physical heredity (i.e. bodily characteristics) is derived from the parents, social heredity is derived from the family, race, nation and religion; there is psychological heredity which is not derived from the parents or the society. This controls physical and social heredity.

Human and Animal Life

It is argued that the hypothesis of rebirth overlooks the fundamental distinction between human and animal life. There are passages in Hindu texts which declare that persistent ill-doing will cause human souls to be born in animal bodies. Such a view prevailed in the West among the philosophers of the later Platonic school.[1] It is the product of a number of varying tendencies. (i) The view that animals have souls is held by many primitive tribes and when they were accepted in the Hindu fold, their view affected the eschatological speculations of the Hindus. (ii) An obscure sense of the unity of all creation and that the souls of all living things are of like nature helped to foster it. There is something which binds us to all the children of the earth. All forms of life are ultimately identical. (iii) As the hypothesis of rebirth in animal bodies tended to increase the respect for animal life, those who were sympathetically inclined towards it did not discountenance this doctrine. When one considers the wanton destruction and needless suffering we have inflicted on the animal creation, a doctrine which fosters a disinterested love of animals is not to be discouraged. Our general idea is that animals exist to provide food and clothes for men and women. To see and delight in an animal for its own sake involves a high development of charity and selflessness.

These different tendencies found expression in this extravagance of the rebirth hypothesis.

While we must be earnest with the idea of development, we must not pull down the higher or exalt the lower. While we must recognise the identity of principle in the whole universe, we must not abolish the wealth of varieties and stages of progress in which the single principle has found realisation. We must admit our kinship with the lower animals[2] but the difference is also fundamental. Release from rebirth is dependent on knowledge

[1] The religious poem *Katharmoi* of Empedocles speaks of the fall of the soul and the ways by which it may attain the purity which is necessary, if it is to return to its primitive state of blessedness. In the process, it is said, it may go through all kinds of mortal shapes including those of men, animals and plants. In the course of his Purifications, Empedocles states: 'I have already been a youth and a maid, a bush, a bird and a dumb fish of the sea.' Guthrie: *Orpheus and Greek Religion* (1935), p. 175.

[2] Cp. Bradley: 'The frank recognition of a common parentage leaves us still the rulers of our poor relations, but breaks down the barrier which encourages our cruelty, our disregard for their miseries and contempt for their love. And when this moral prejudice is gone, our intellectual prejudice will not long survive. We shall not study the lower animals with the view to make out a case or a claim, but for the pleasure of finding our own souls again in a different form; and for the sake, I may add, of understanding better our own development.' *Principles of Logic*, Vol. II, p. 514.

and conduct of which only human beings are capable and, if once we enter animal life, they become impossible. How can a soul which has once sunk down to an animal life become ethically deserving? When it is said that the human soul suffers the indignity of animal life, the suggestion is figurative, not literal. It means that it is reborn to an irrational existence comparable to animal life, and not that it is actually attached to the body of an animal.[1] Those who so vehemently protest against the rebirth of human souls in animal bodies on the ground that it is incompatible with the organic relation between soul and body must admit that this very organic conception requires us to assume that souls will acquire bodies similar to those which they have abandoned at death.

The Mechanism of Rebirth

In regard to the *modus operandi* of rebirth, different views are held. McTaggart argues that 'souls somehow steer their way back to a suitable rebirth'. 'Each person enters into connection with the body that it is most fitted to be connected with.'[2] As there can be no continuity of life without continuity of organism, a subtle body which carries the impress of its past tendencies[3] is assumed. The gross body (*sthūla śarīra*) is supported by the physical life-force which courses through the whole nervous system and which distinguishes our bodily action from that of an inert mechanical being. It is only the outer instrument. When it disappears the soul is not formless. An individual existence is always conditioned by an organic substratum.

[1] Dr E. B. Tylor writes: 'So it may seem that the original idea of transmigration was the straightforward and reasonable one of human souls being reborn in new human bodies. . . . The beast is the very incarnation of familiar qualities of man; and such names as lion, bear, fox, owl, parrot, viper, worm, when we apply them as epithets to men, condense into a word some leading feature of human life.' *Primitive Culture* (London, 1891), ii. 17. Dr L. A. Waddell writes: 'The pig symbolises the ignorance of stupidity; the cock animal desire or lust; and the snake anger.' *Gazetteer of Sikkim*, ed. by H. H. Risley, p. 267.

[2] *Studies on Hegelian Cosmology*, pp. 45ff.

[3] What departs from the body at death is *manas* (mind), the five senses of knowledge and the five of action, the five subtle elements, life (*prāṇa*) and merit (*puṇya*) and demerit (*pāpa*). C.U. V. 3. 3; V. 9. 1. B.U. IV. 4. 3, 5 and 6; VI. 2. 4 and 15; *Maitri U.* VI. 10; B.G. XV. 7 and 8; *Manu* XII. 16–17; B.S. III. 1. 1–7.

Human life is always attached to some vehicle and we need not assume that the forms of matter with which we are familiar are the only forms that exist in the universe. When the gross body drops, the soul is accompanied by the subtle body, transparent and invisible though material. It is the basis for consciousness and memory. We cannot localise subtle bodies which survive physical death. The subtle body is the reflex image of our personality in all its phases. The *liṅga-śarīra* is the carrier of *karma* and assumes a body which, though different from the present one, is not altogether discontinuous with it. It is sometimes said that when the self leaves the body, it leaves with *vijñāna* which Ś. equates with determinate consciousness due to *vāsanā* and *vidyā, karma* and *pūrva-jñāna.* Ś. admits that the individual, when he passes from one body to another, possesses primary *prāṇa,* senses, and *manas,* also *avidyā, karma* and previous experience. The *jīva* carries with it the subtle elements forming the basis of the body.[1] In the story of Sāvitrī, it is said that *Yama* extracted from the gross body of Satyavān the self which is of the size of a thumb.[2] The subtle body is said to have form. At the point of death, as the servants of a king gather round him when he starts on a voyage, so all the vital functions and faculties of an individual gather around the living soul, when it is about to withdraw from its bodily form.[3] The *ātman* or the Universal Self which is present as *sākṣin* throughout successive experiences is a mere spectator.

History of the Doctrine

Belief in rebirth is widespread in the East and is not unknown in the West. Pythagoras and Plato suggested this theory as an explanation for the inequalities of life. Plato in the famous myth of Er towards the end of his *Republic* shows the disciplinary value of suffering. Virgil, the Mystery religions, the Neo-platonists supported the theory of rebirth. Plotinus says: 'Such things as happen to the good without justice, as punishments,

[1] *dehabījair, bhūtasūkṣmaiḥ sampariṣvaktaḥ.* B.S. III. 1. 1.

[2] *anguṣṭha-mātram puruṣam niścakarṣa yamo balāt.* M.B. Vanaparva 20. 6. 16.

[3] B.U. IV. 3. 28. The process of death and rebirth according to Tibetan Buddhism is given in *The Tibetan Book of the Dead,* ed. by W. Y. Evans-Wentz, third edition (1957).

or poverty, or disease, may be said to take place through offences committed in a former life.'[1]

Caesar reports that the Druids had a belief that 'the soul does not perish, but after death passes from one body to another'. The Cathari taught that the wicked would be reborn in the bodies of animals. Recent anthropological investigations reveal that many African peoples hold the belief in rebirth. Josephus tells us that 'pure and obedient souls obtain a most holy place in Heaven from whence in the revolution of the ages they are sent again into pure bodies.'[2] The general Jewish belief, however, is a resurrection to bodily life on earth. The case of the man born blind is used to suggest belief in pre-existence. If he is not born blind as the result of his own sin it should be due to his conduct in a previous life. Among Christian thinkers Origen believed in the pre-existence of the soul though he held that after death the soul passed into a resurrection body. Jerome believed in pre-existence. Augustine did not deny it, and there was hesitation about the doctrine till the time of Gregory the Great. The Second Council of Constantinople in A.D. 553 issued a *pronunciamiento*: 'Whoever shall support the mythical doctrine of the pre-existence of the soul and the consequent wonderful opinion of its return, let him be anathema.' Thereafter belief in rebirth became a heretical doctrine.

In recent times owing to the spread of the knowledge of the teachings of Eastern religions a few Western thinkers have been attracted to this hypothesis. Schopenhauer admits the usefulness of this doctrine.[3] Sir William Jones, in his letter to Earl Spencer dated September 4, 1787, wrote: 'I am no Hindu; but I hold the doctrine of the Hindus concerning a future state to be incomparably more rational, more pious, and more likely to deter men from vice, than the horrid opinions inculcated by Christians on punishments without end.'[4] For McTaggart, the

[1] T. Taylor: *The Select Works of Plotinus* (1914), p. 229.

[2] *Antiquities* XVIII. 1. 3.

[3] Cp. Wordsworth: 'Our birth is but a sleep and a forgetting.'
Rosetti: 'I have been here before.
But where or how I cannot tell.'

[4] See Arberry: *Asiatic Jones* (1946), p. 37.

Cp. G. Lowes Dickinson: 'If we are to hold, as we must, I believe, if we are to be optimists, that there is some definite goal to be reached by all individuals in a temporal process, then the notion of a series of successive existences, in the

universe is not a person but a society of persons, eternal and perfect, each of whom is in love with one or more of the others. Moreover, it is probable that each human mind, as it really is, is identical with one of these persons. Each one of us is, therefore, eternal in reality and this eternity probably appears *sub specie temporis* as persistence throughout the whole of past and future time. This existence is split up into a sequence of many successive lives each beginning with a birth and ending with a death. Belief in rebirth seems to be the least unsatisfactory of the views held about the future of the human being after death.

F. LIFE ETERNAL

Union with Brahman

Release is life in spiritual consciousness; rebirth is life in becoming. Eternal life is a new life into which we are born by a direct contact with the Divine. It is not a prolongation of the natural life into an indefinitely extended future. Eternity is not endless continuity.

As we have seen any attempt to describe spiritual experience in human language involves the clothing of the truth in imagery borrowed from the thought-forms of time. Even as the Supreme Reality is envisaged in the four forms of the Absolute *Brahman*, Personal *Īśvara*, the world-soul and the world, the liberated has the feeling of oneness with *Brahman*, communion with *Īśvara* and co-operation with the world-soul for the betterment of the world. Ś. says that the highest goal of life is the realisation of *Brahman*.[1] Since the Absolute is indescribable the state of union with the Absolute is also indescribable.[2] The self realises its true nature and its difference from the empirical order. It is

course of which all are gradually purified and made fit for the heaven they are ultimately to attain, would seem to be the one least open to objection. It is also, I think, the one which is gradually popularising itself among those, who, without being students of philosophy, feel an intimate interest in its problems, and are not satisfied with the Christian solution.'

[1] *brahmāvagatir hi puruṣārthaḥ*. Ś.B. I. 1. 1.

[2] Cp. *Sutta Nipāta*: 'He who (like the sun) has gone to rest is comparable to nothing whatsoever. The notions through which his reality can be expressed are simply not to be found. All ideas are nothing as bearing upon him; hence all modes of speech are, with respect to him, unavailing.' 5, 7, 8.

an individual realisation of the Supreme by the individual soul. This is not thinking but seeing, a change of being.[1] According to Ś., this realisation is a modification of the internal organ generated in the mind aided by the impressions produced by hearing, reflection, etc. This, while destroying the ignorance leading to the apprehension of the world as real, roots itself out as well, not being distinct from the universe.[2]

Ś. makes out that the attainment of *mokṣa* is not the destruction of the world but only the displacement of a false view of the world.[3] The world has *Brahman* for its true nature and not vice versa. The cognition of *Brahman* is effected by the dissolution of the view of the reality of names and forms. Otherwise the first released person would have destroyed the world once for all so that at present the whole world would be empty, earth and all other substances having been finally annihilated.[4]

The life of union with *Brahman* is described in different ways. It is said that nothing remains of the individual whether as to name or likeness (*nāma-rūpa*)[5] but only the Universal Reality. He becomes the Self that seems to have been determined or

[1] *na brahma-jñāna-mātram sāṁsārika-nivṛtti-kāraṇam api tu sākṣātkāra-paryantam.* Bhāmatī I. 1. 4.; see also I. 1. 1.

[2] *brahma-sākṣātkāras cāntaḥkaraṇa-vṛtti-bhedaḥ śravaṇa-mananādi-janita-saṁskāra-saciva mano-janmā. sa ca nikhila-prapañca-mahendra-jāla-sākṣātkāram sa-mūlam unmūlayan ātmānam api prapañcatvāviśeṣād unmūlayati.*

[3] *brahma-svabhāvo hi prapañco na prapañca-svabhāvaṁ brahma, tena nāma-rūpa-prapañca-pravilāpanena brahma-tattvāvabodho bhavati.*

[4] *ekena cādimuktena pṛthivyādi-pravilayaḥ kṛta itīdānīm pṛthivyādiśūnyaṁ jagad abhaviṣyat.* Ś.B. III. 2. 21.

[5] For a Buddhist version see *Aṅguttara Nikāya* IV. 1. 8.

'Just as the flowing streams that move towards the sea, on reaching it, are coming home, their name and shape are broken down and one speaks only of the sea, even so of this witness the sixteen parts that move towards the Person, when they reach the Person are coming home, their name and shape are broken down and one speaks only of the Person. As the drop becomes the ocean, so the soul is deified, losing her name and work, but not her essence.' Eckhart Pfeiffer's Edition, p. 314.

Cp. Ruysbroek: 'All men who are exalted above their creatureliness into a contemplative life are with this Divine glory—yea, *are* that glory, and they see and feel and find in themselves by means of this Divine light that they are the same ground as to their uncreated nature. Wherefore contemplative men should rise above reason and distinction and gaze perpetually by the aid of their inborn light, and so they become transformed, and one wills the same light by means of which they see and which they are.' Quoted by Inge: *Christian Mysticism*, p. 189.

particularised but is in fact impartible. Any kind of embodiment or individuality is regarded as a descent from the truth of being, a bondage to ignorance and desire, a self-forgetfulness of spirit. Freedom is absolute identification of the finite with the Infinite. B.U. describes the state of liberation thus: 'As a man when in the embrace of his beloved wife, knows nothing without or within, so the person when in the embrace of the Intelligent Self knows nothing without or within. That, verily, is his form in which his desire is fulfilled, in which the Self is his desire, in which he is without desire, free from any sorrow.'[1] According to the *Praśna U.* the freed individuals lose their specific individualities when they merge themselves in the Supreme Self, even as rivers that flow into the sea lose their names and forms in it. 'As on the destruction of the jar, etc., the ether enclosed in the jar, etc., merges in the *ākāśa* [the vast expanse of ether], even so the individuals merge in the Universal Spirit.'[2]

Communion with the Divine Īśvara

The released soul retains its distinct individuality and becomes a mover at will, *kāma-cārin,* whose will indeed is no

[1] IV. 3. 21.

[2] Gauḍapāda on *Kārikā on Mā. U.* III. 40.

Meister Eckhart says: 'If therefore I am changed into God and He makes me one with Himself, then, by the living God, there is no distinction between us. . . . Some people imagine that they are going to see God, that they are going to see God as if He were standing yonder, and they here, but it is not to be so. God and I: we are one. By knowing God I take Him to myself. By loving God, I penetrate Him.' *Meister Eckhart,* E.T. by R. B. Blakney (1941), pp. 181–2.

St Catherine of Genoa cried: 'My one is God, nor do I recognise any other one except my God himself.'

St John of the Cross likened the soul in search of God to a log of wood which is consumed by fire in which the fire only is operative. 'The soul that is in a state of transformation of love may be said to be, in its ordinary habit, like to the log of wood that is continually assailed by the fire; and the acts of this soul are the flame that arises from the fire of love: the more intense is the fire of union, the more vehemently does its flame issue forth. In the which flame the acts of the will are united and rise upward, being carried away and absorbed in the flame of the Holy Spirit, even as the angel rose upward to God in the flame of the sacrifice of Manue. In this state, therefore, the soul can perform no acts, but it is the Holy Spirit that moves it to perform them; wherefore all its acts are Divine, since it is impelled and moved to them by God. Hence it seems to the soul that whensoever this flame breaks forth, causing it to love with the Divine temper and sweetness, it is granting it eternal life, since it raises it to the operation of God in God.' *The Living Flame of Love,* tr. by E. Allison Peers (1953), pp. 18–19.

longer his own. M.U. says that he attains divine likeness.[1] For R., the distinction between the individual soul and the Universal Self is real and so the two can never become one. Eternal life is love of God. It is essentially restful because the soul rests in God who is sufficient in himself and good unconditionally. Its only desire is to make its love more and more intense and absorbing. There is not with R. any question of the identity of the individual soul with God for such an absorption is not permissible in his philosophy. Love depends on a relation between two persons. The released soul has all the exalted qualities of the Divine except a few special prerogatives such as those of creatorship, etc.

For Madhva life eternal is life in the presence of the Deity. For him difference is fundamental and obtains even in the state of release.

For Ś., liberation is identification with the Self, *sa-ātmaka*; for R. it is direct contact with the Supreme, *sa-yujyatā*; for Madhva it is proximity to the Supreme, *sa-lokatā*.

The author of the B.S. denies to the released souls the right to participate in the cosmic functions of the Lord. Bādarāyaṇa gives us the views of Jaimini and Audulomi. Jaimini holds that the individual in the state of release becomes invested with the highest attributes of *Īśvara* or the Personal God.[2] Release is regarded as the attainment of an unconditioned state where all traces of the manifested world disappear (*prapañcopaśama*). Auḍulomi maintains that the released soul attains the state of pure consciousness. The state of absolute release is oneness of the individual self with the Super-personal Absolute which is the substratum of the world of experience. The unreleased souls look upon it as one of identity with Godhead. All these views are characterised by the negative condition of freedom from rebirth. The state of liberation is one of freedom from the limitative conditions of individual human existence. It is freedom from subjection to time, from birth and death which are marks of time. 'Death, thou shalt die.'

All views agree that eternal life is an absolute fulfilment of what we are, the final affirmation of our progressive self-finding.

[1] III. 1. 3.

[2] IV. 4. 5.

The Self shines forth in its purity.[1] The *Bhāgavata* describes the state of release as the attainment of the individual's natural state by relinquishing its imposed state.[2] The knowledge of God which is equivalent to the direct realisation of Ultimate Reality is the highest human good (*parama-puruṣārtha*). The self as part (*aṁśa*) attains the whole (*aṁśin*). It is brought into personal contact with the Personal God. It is not a question of attaining sameness or identity but attaining similarity. The views affirm the timelessness of our inmost being, an indestructibility without continuance in time, but in the cosmic process, individuation is the method. Until the cosmic process is consummated, the individual centres will continue.

Appaya Dīkṣita in his *Siddhānta-leśa-saṁgraha* writes: 'Liberation being the manifestation of our nature and nothing adventitious, cannot be denied to or withheld from anyone. Universal liberation is more than a possibility; it is a logical necessity. Different souls will require a long or short period of time in proportion to their capacity to get rid of *avidyā* but its final removal is certain. So long as there is a single unrealised soul, *māyā* is not completely destroyed and there can be no absolute realisation for any other soul, however advanced it may be in the path of perfection.'

Appaya Dīkṣita says that as long as the created world lasts, i.e. as long as liberation of all does not happen, the Supreme *Brahman* has the form of *Īśvara*.[3] So from the empirical viewpoint, the fruit of knowledge turns out to be of the form of the attainment of the nature of *Parameśvara* characterised by the possession of desires which come true and so on. The lordship manifested in those who have intuited *Brahman* may be said to be of the nature similar to *Brahman* because of the text 'the stainless one attains absolute equality with the Supreme'.[4]

[1] *svena rūpeṇa abhiniṣpadyate.* C.U. *ātma-svarūpa-lābha* or attaining one's own form is becoming like the Divine for Nimbārka. See *Vedānta-pārijāta-saurabha.* IV. 4. 1–2.

[2] *muktir hitvānyathā-rūpam, svarūpeṇa vyavasthitiḥ.*

[3] *tad eva nirviśeṣam brahma yāvat sarva-mukti saguṇeśvarbhāvam āpadyāvatiṣṭhata iti vyavahāra-dṛṣṭyā satya-kāmatvādi-guṇaka parameśvara-bhāvāpatti-rūpam api bhavati tat phalam. Śivādvaita-nirṇaya* III. 235. 1.

[4] U. III. 1. 3: *brahma-sākṣātkāravatām yad aiśvaryam āvirbhavati tad brahma-sāmya-rūpam iti vaktavyam. nirañjanaḥ paramaṁ sāmyam upaiti. Śivādvaita-nirṇaya.*

Life eternal is not a denial of becoming but a victory over it. The saved souls devote their energies to the spiritualisation of the world, to raising it to its highest levels. They are engaged in the development of the human type into the spiritual. To be free is to live in the integral power of spirit, which does not consist in the repose of a featureless existence indifferent to activity but in the simultaneous possession of a transcendent reality and cosmic activity and existence without which the cosmos will cease to exist. We are in bondage so long as the individual is confined to his superficial mind, ignorant of the spirit in him which is always free master of its world, its manifestation. In *Yajña-varāha-bhagavadgītā* 42, it is said that to the ignorant the world is full of sorrow, to the awakened it is full of bliss even as the world is dark to the blind and is bright to the seeing.[1]

Release (*mukti*) consists not in the shaking off of all bodily life or cosmic existence but in a recovery by the individual conscious being of its spiritual freedom. The spirit in us is the Divine enjoying the possible relations of his oneness in the multiplicity of souls. Individual existence in life is not a thing absolutely apart; it is part of the divine self-manifestation in the universe. The enlightened soul is one with the Divine in himself as well as the Divine in all. An exclusive emphasis on one side of the truth is misleading. The soul that has entered into that complete oneness with the Divine Being must, even as that Divine does, continue to be one with all being. The released souls live in the world though they are no more of the world. Their lives are lit by a steady spiritual flame imparting a new coherence, tranquillity and freedom. They are filled with peace though it is not a peace of the desert. They are vibrant with energy and engaged in meeting the demands of the world. Sudarśanācārya in his *Śruti-sūkti-mālā* gives the following illustration of the contemplation of identity with *Brahman*: '*Padma-nābha* is said to be the Supreme *Brahman* and the Supreme Real, the Supreme Light and the Supreme Lord, since delighting only in contemplation of Thee, he is non-different

[1] *ajñasya duḥkhaugha-mayaṁ jñasyānandamayaṁ jagat*
andhaṁ bhuvanam andhasya prakāśaṁ tu su-cakṣusaḥ.

from Thee, as the magician by the contemplation of Garuḍa is non-different from Garuḍa.[1]

Union with the World-Spirit

These *mukta-puruṣas* or enfranchised souls are those in whose lives the temporal and the eternal interpenetrate. God's light streams not darkly as through a glass but undimmed as through an open window.[2] All the traces of egoism are dissolved and the limitations which condition individuality are extinct in them. They are untouched by the fear of death and untroubled by anxieties concerning the future of their temporal personalities. The divine principle in its eternal being is identical with one's own formless essence, beneath all the conscious and the unconscious qualifications of the personality. It is the non-particular in us, the pure divine non-form, a nameless, shapeless power which sustains the whole personality. The released are not the solitary men cut off from society and severed from the empirical self retreating from the threatening world. Such men of mere negation are sterile and unfruitful. The free souls are full men representing consistent and comprehensive affirmation of the Divine in life. After their enlightenment they get back to the world, love and serve their fellow-men in the light of their blessing. On the plane of spirit, there is an indivisible solidarity of the human race. The free spirits are persons without frontiers. They do not have any barriers of sex, class, race or nation between themselves and the rest of humanity. They are at home with men and women of all religions and no religion. They are the apostolate of the future. The marks of a liberated man are an earthen pot (for drinking water), the roots of trees (for food), coarse cloth, solitude, equanimity towards all.[3]

The life of the liberated has two characteristics. It is free from the egoistic self and its tyrannous desires. It is convinced of the unity with all and so has love for others. The freed man works for the good of others. Though he wants nothing for

[1] *brahmocyate paramasau paramaṁ ca tat-tvaṁ jyotiḥ paraṁ ca parameśvara padma-nābhaḥ.*
tvad-bhāvanaika-rasikas tvad-ananyabhāvān mantrī yathā garuḍa-bhāvanayā garutmān. (42.)

[2] *I Corinthians* xiii. 12.

[3] *kapālam vṛkṣa-mūlāni kucailam asahāyatā*
samatātaiva sarvasmin etad muktasya lakṣaṇam.

himself, he cannot see others immersed in ignorance and suffering. So long as we are seekers of the goal we do unselfish work by conscious effort; when we are free we do it effortlessly.

So long as the cosmic process continues the liberated souls have work to perform. They co-operate with the divine purpose for this world and strive for the redemption of all.[1] According to *Vaiśṇava* philosophy they live in *Vaikuṇṭha* and are unlike human beings in respect of their conditions. They are said to be devoid of bodies and organs of sense.[2]

The appearance of the divine souls in the world gives light to those that live in darkness and in the shadow of death.[3] This is the view of Ś. as indicated by Appaya Dīkṣita. The liberated souls are active wherever a tear falls, wherever an act of injustice or brutality is committed, wherever a heart is seized with despair.[4] In his hymn to the Supreme in the *Bhāgavata*, Prahlāda criticises those performers of penance in the forests who strive for their own salvation indifferent to the sufferings of the erring mortals and he says that he does not desire his own salvation unless these erring people are taken along:

> *prāyeṇa deva munayaḥ sva-vimukti-kāmāḥ*
> *maunaṁ caranti vipine na parārtha-niṣṭhāḥ*
> *naitān vihāya kṛpaṇān vimumukṣa ekaḥ*
> *nānyaṁ tvad asya caraṇaṁ bhramato'nupaśye.*

Life is a continuous drama embracing the beginnings of existence and its end. The light suffers and struggles to overcome the darkness in which evil cloaks itself.

[1] 'For we are labourers *together* with God', fellow-workers with him. I *Corinthians* iii. 9. *Talmud* (*Sabbath*, 10) says:

> 'Any judge who exercises rightful
> judgment even for one hour, of him
> Scriptures say that he becomes, as it were,
> a co-worker with God in the work of Creation.'

In the phrase of Dame Julian of Norwich we are 'partakers in his good deed'. *Revelations of Divine Love.*

[2] *dehendriyāsu-hīnānāṁ vaikuṇṭha-pura-vāsinām. Bhāgavata* VII. 1. 34.

[3] *Luke* i. 79.

[4] Pascal says that Jesus struggles with death until the end of the world. In this boundless Gethsemane which is the life of the universe, he struggles with death, as the personification of all suffering and sorrow.

Jīvan-mukti

Liberation is not a state of existence to follow on physical death but an all-satisfying present experience. It can be had even in life. It is the condition of *Jīvan-mukti*. The fruit of knowledge being present to intuition does not manifest itself at a later time only as the fruits of actions do.[1] Hindu systems of thought describe the state of those who are released while they are in an embodied condition as one of *jīvan-mukti*. They feel that the result of *karmas* which have begun to operate should be exhausted. There is no help for it.[2] But we can escape from those which have not begun to operate, when we gain wisdom.[3]

Eternity is a state of mind, not a place or an environment. Kabīr asks, 'if your bonds be not broken whilst living, what hope of deliverance in death?' Life eternal is not in the future of time. Every moment we stand on the frontier of time. Release is not a state after death but the supreme status of being in which the spirit knows itself to be superior to birth and death, unconditioned by its manifestations, able to assume forms at its pleasure.

It is wrong to think that a *jīvan-mukta* is not wholly perfect, that he is only a *sādhaka* and not a *siddha*. To possess a body does not mean identification with it. *Jīvan-mukti* is not close proximity to final release but it is final release.

A released person continues to have individuality until the whole cosmic process is dissolved or redeemed. Continuance till the dissolution of the primal elements is called immortality.[4]

When ignorance is destroyed by knowledge, it follows that release is obtained forthwith. But the freed soul does not become disembodied. There are passages which declare that only after physical death release is attained. Those who are released in spirit become released in fact after death.[5] Embodiment may continue after the attainment of knowledge

[1] *anubhavārūḍham eva ca vidyā-phalaṁ na kriyā-phalavat kālāntarabhāvīti.* Ś.B. III. 4. 15.

[2] *prārabdha-karmānām bhogād eva kṣayam.*

[3] See B.S. IV. 1. 13–15.

[4] Cp. *ābhūta-samplavaṁ sthānam amṛtatvam hi bhāṣyate.* Quoted in Bhāmatī. I. 1. 1.

[5] Cp. *tasya tāvad eva ciraṁ yāvan na vimokṣye atha sampatsye.* C.U. VI. 14. 2. Again: *vimuktaś ca vimucyate. tasyābhidhyānād yojanāt tattva-bhāvāt bhūyaś cānte viśva-māyā-nivṛttiḥ.*

and therefore release. It is the liberated people that teach us the truth. Ś. says: 'It should not be disputed whether the knower of *Brahman* is embodied for a time or is not embodied. How can one's own intimate experience of the knowledge of *Brahman* existing together with embodiment be denied by another?'[1]

Those who hold that all embodiment is the effect of ignorance contend that full release is possible only after death. They assume that embodiment is a sign of ignorance and *karma*. If ignorance persists release is not gained. We are adepts and not perfected men. Bondage and release cannot coexist.

Release relates to the frame of mind. It does not depend on embodiment or non-embodiment. Even after physical death, the released soul may assume individual form to work for the world. That is why it is sometimes said that the released soul becomes one with *Īśvara*, the creative dynamic side of *Brahman*. Even as *Īśvara* controls his manifestation and is not bound by it, the released soul controls his individuality and is not bound by it as a limitation. Even as *Īśvara* expresses himself in various forms to help suffering humanity, the released souls may assume forms to help the unregenerate. The individual soul becomes identical with *Īśvara* and when the world process is redeemed, he along with *Brahmā* or the World-spirit lapses into the Absolute-God, *Brahman-Īśvara*.[2]

Salvation is possible for all and till that consummation is attained, the individual souls work in the world with a feeling of identity with God. While possessing wisdom they may act in the world. This action may take many forms. A popular verse reads '*Kṛṣṇa* was an enjoyer, *Śuka* was a renouncer, *Janaka* and *Rāma* were kings, *Vasiṣṭha* was a performer of ceremonies. These five kinds of knowers are to be regarded as equals.'[3] To each is the way ordained by his nature. The way of the householder is suited for some, that of the houseless wanderer for others. We have to renounce not the things of the world but the desires of the heart. 'Whether one is interested in renunciation or

[1] *naivātra vivaditavyaṁ brahma-vidaḥ kiñcit kālaṁ śarīram dhriyate na dhriyata iti. Kathaṁ hy ekasya sva-hṛdaya-pratyayam brahma-vedanam deha-dhāranaṁ cāpareṇa pratikṣeptum śakyate.* Ś.B. I. 4. 15.

[2] See Appayya Dīkṣita: *Siddhānta-leśa-saṁgraha* 3. 2351–3. 2355.

[3] *kṛṣṇo bhogī śukas tyāgī nṛpau janaka-rāghavau*
vasiṣṭhaḥ karma-kartā ca pañcaite jñāninaḥ samāḥ.

enjoyment, in company or in solitude, he whose mind delights in the Supreme, he, verily, rejoices', says a verse attributed to Ś.[1] He looks upon all creation as equal.[2] He is detached but not isolated from the world; if isolated, he is isolated only in spirit.

Yoga-Vāsiṣṭha tells us how a liberated soul should act in the world. 'Steady in the state of fullness which shines when all desires are given up and peaceful in the state of freedom in life, behave in this world, O *Rāghava*. Inwardly free from all desires, dispassionate and detached, but outwardly active in all affairs, behave in this world, O *Rāghava*. Outwardly full of zeal in action but free from any zeal at heart, active in appearance but inwardly peaceful, behave in this world, O *Rāghava*. Free from egoism, with mind detached as in sleep, pure like the sky, ever untainted, behave in this world, O *Rāghava*. Conducting yourself nobly and with tenderness, conforming to the forms of society but inwardly renouncing all, behave in this world, O *Rāghava*. Unattached at heart but outwardly acting as if with attachment, inwardly cool but outwardly fervent, behave in this world, O *Rāghava*.'[3] The *jīvan-mukta* wears his life like a light garment.

Hindu thought points out that what binds is not action but the spirit in which it is done. It is the desire for or aversion from the results that bind the individual soul. But so long as the

[1] *yoga-rato vā bhoga-rato vā saṅga-rato vā saṅga-vihīnaḥ*
yasya brahmaṇi ramate cittam, nandati, nandati, nandaty eva.

[2] *samatā sarva-bhūteṣu etan muktasya lakṣaṇam.*

[3] *pūrṇo dṛṣṭim avaṣṭabhya dhyeya-tyāga-vilāsinīm*
jīvan-mukta-tayā svastho loke vihara rāghava
antaḥ saṁtyakta-sarvāśo vītarāgo vivāsanaḥ
bahiḥ sarva-samācāro loke vihara rāghava
bahiḥ kṛtrima-saṁrambho hṛdi saṁrambha-varjitaḥ
kartā bahir akartāntaḥ loke vihara rāghava
tyaktāhaṁkṛtir āsuptamatir ākāśa-śobhanaḥ
agṛhīta-kalaṅkāṅko loke vihara rāghava
udāra-peśalācāraḥ sarvācārānuvṛttimān
antaḥ sarva-parityāgī loke vihara rāghava.
antar nairāsyam ādāya bahir āśonmukhe hitaḥ
bahis tapto'ntarāśīto loke vihara rāghava.

William Law quotes: 'Do but suppose a man to know himself, that he comes into this world on no other errand but to arise out of the vanity of time. . . . Do but suppose him to govern his inward thought and outward action by this view of himself and then to him every day has lost all its evil; prosperity and adversity have no difference because he receives them and uses them in the same spirit.' *The Works of William Law* (1749), Vol. VII, p. 1, reprinted in 1893.

action is performed in a selfless spirit, without desire for fruit, it is one with the creative activity of God. Without action, the world would cease to exist. We hear of many cases of liberated individuals who are engaged in the work of the world. They live as universal men with no private attachments or personal feelings. When the realised soul returns to the plane of conduct, his action will neither add to nor detract from the value of his realisation. Action itself will be of a different kind. It has no selfish motives behind it but is a manifestation of spiritual peace.

The individual who is enlightened by knowledge does not renounce all activity. He acts to sustain his body and social relationships. He is incapable of selfish action as his egoism is burnt out. He is free from selfish desire, *a-kāma*. He who has attained truth which is its own fruition acts selflessly and with full freedom.[1]

Sarva-mukti

Whatever pathway we take, the end is the transformation of the individual and, as a result, the transformation of all human relationships. Individuals cannot be fully transformed in separation from each other. The word *sarva-mukti* means the liberation of all. In a deeply spiritual sense there can be no other salvation. *Brahma-loka* or the Kingdom of God implies corporate salvation.[2] We are all wayfarers towards the Divine Kingdom and so cannot rest until the goal is reached.

In the *Yoga* system the sage is likened to one standing on the

[1] Cp. 'That is right action which does not make for bondage; that is right knowledge which makes for liberation.'

tat karma yan na bandhāya
sā vidyā yā vimuktaye.

Eckhart says: 'It is permissible to take life's blessings with both hands provided thou dost know thyself prepared in the opposite event to leave them just as glądly.'

[2] *Siddhānta-muktāvali* quotes a verse: 'Men who duly observe the rites, who perform worship at the junctions of time [morning, noon and evening], their sins removed go to the world of *Brahmā* which is free from harm [literally disease].'

sandhyām upāsate ye tu satataṁ saṁśitavratāḥ
vidhūta-pāpāḥ te yānti brahma-lokam anāmayam.

Augustine observes: 'How could the city of God have a beginning or be developed or fulfil its destiny if the life of the saints were not a social life?'

hilltop and looking down on the suffering multitude below.[1] This infinite compassion impels him to build for himself a new body and mind and teach the saving wisdom to the world.[2] In *Mahāyāna Buddhism, Avalokiteśvara,* the future *Buddha* looks downwards on all less elevated beings helping and expecting them to rise. So long as there are unreleased souls, the released souls will have work in the temporal order. The conception of the solidarity of mankind tells us that the saved souls and the sinning are bound to one another. The former work on the latter by persuasion and love until they are transformed and reborn into spiritual souls alive with the life that grows more and more into life eternal. In the saved souls there is a never completely resolved strain of temporality which makes them members of the cosmic order. If the last vestige of succession and contingency is removed time will have disappeared with it.

The world is a whole where everything is necessary to all the rest. If anyone finds his end in himself he suffers defeat.[3] So long as the cosmic plan is not fulfilled work will continue, in a spiritual selfless way by the saints, in a material selfish way by others. When the consummation of the world is reached, it lapses back into the Absolute.

Two conditions are essential for final salvation, (i) inward perfection attained by intuition of self, (ii) outer perfection possible only with the liberation of all. The liberated souls which obtain the first condition continue to work for the second. So long as the cosmic process continues, life is not a resting but a going on. It goes on never pausing, always restless, always straining forward for something that has not been but should be.

[1] *prajñā-prasādam āruhya aśocyaḥ śocato janān*
bhūmiṣṭhan iva śailasthaḥ sarvam prājno'nupaśyati.
Yoga-bhāṣya I. 47.

[2] *ādividvān nirmāṇacittam adhisthāya kāruṇyād bhagavān*
paramarṣir āsuraye jigñāsamānāya tantraṁ provāca.
Yoga-bhāṣya I. 25.

Kapila is said to have taught Āsuri out of compassion.

[3] Cp. 'Strike me out of the Book of Life or forgive my people their trespass', said Moses to God. Origen believed that God's infinite love would finally prevail over all evil and even Satan and his fallen angels would be ultimately redeemed. Such a view of universal restoration questions the justice of eternal damnation. It is impossible for any believer in God to assume that countless human souls could be for all time beyond the possibility of redemption, beyond the reach of God's love. It means the ultimacy of evil and the defeat of God's purpose.

Till the end is achieved the temporal process has a meaning and a value as the stage of soul-formation and growth. The world is not an adequate expression of reality and cannot therefore share the eternity which is characteristic of reality. It can only be an unending succession of transitory states. True individuality of human self is to be found in the achievement of the unity of the world.

In that cosmic harmony which is the destiny of the historical process, each individual has his distinct place, has an eternal value, *dharma*, form or idea. Distinction does not any more mean opposition since all individuals strive for the same end and are inspired by the same ideal. They all know even as they are known. They all have a sense of communion with the Cosmic Spirit and devote their lives to its purpose. Each particular individual expresses the universal in its own way.[1]

The world-redemption (*sarva-mukti*) is not to be confused with cosmic millennia or earthly paradises. It is not a gradual accumulation of material comforts through the ages. It deals with values of spirit which may be gained sometimes through convulsions of nature and history. The question of universal salvation is not to be confused with the realisation of finite purposes in time. The chances of time, its fulfilments and frustrations, have little to do with the new mode of living which is independent of time. This view is not bound up with the inevitability of progress as that term is understood by us. Inner desolation and outward wealth may well go together. But the possibility of a spiritual life for the whole race is indicated by the theory of the indwelling of God. We may well cherish the hope that the ascent of the soul to God achieved by several individuals during the course of human history may be an earnest of what humanity will one day attain. The Kingdom of God, a society of saved souls, is the cosmic destiny. It is one expression of the Absolute but not the Absolute itself. It is a manifestation of one of its possibilities. The Absolute, however,

[1] 'They see themselves in others. For all things are transparent and there is nothing dark or resisting but everyone is manifest to everyone internally and all things are manifest, for light is manifest to light. For everyone has all things in himself and again sees in another all things, so that all things are everywhere and all is all and each is all and the splendour is infinite.' *Enneads* V. 8. 4.

is not limited by its manifestation in such a divine society. The peace, the bliss and the oneness of the Absolute are not constituted by or limited to the perfection of this cosmic process.

It may be said that it is an utterly futile business for the Creative Spirit to have brought individual souls into existence, spent infinite pains on their education only to get them disintegrated at the end. Is all this difficult process of soul-making to end in their breaking up again? Personality, love and service should not be allowed to disappear in some infinite sea of undifferentiated being. Let us understand the implications of such a demand. Unless we regard imperfection as an end in itself, a state may arise when there is nothing for human minds to know or human wills to do. When the self-disclosure of personalities is accomplished, when the integral revelation of the world possibility is achieved, a simple continuance of such a state becomes a useless luxury. As Lotze argues, souls will exist as long as their existence has meaning for the universe. When this world order ends, the creative freedom of the Absolute may find expression in forms of which we have no knowledge today; other possibilities may be realised in other frameworks.

While R.'s account of the independent existence of the liberated souls represents the cosmic destiny, S.'s view of the final identification of the liberated with the Supreme represents the state of the released, when the cosmic destiny is fulfilled. So long as the cosmic plan is in process of fulfilment, we have a dynamic fellowship of liberated spirits working for it, in co-operative union with God; when it reaches its fulfilment, there is unity of substance.

There is support for the doctrine of the kingdom of spirit or *brahma-loka* in the *Upaniṣads*. A passage in the M.U. declares that 'those who have their intellects firmly rooted in the principles of the *Vedānta*, and purified themselves by methods of renunciation, go to the world of *Brahmā* with whom they attain to final dissolution at the time of the great end'.[1] The B.U. says that the knowers of *Brahman* go to the world of heaven (*svargam lokam*).[2] Even *Advaita Vedānta* is not incon-

[1] Cp. B.G. II. 12: 'Nor at any time verily was I not, not thou nor these princes of men; nor verily shall we cease to be hereafter.'

[2] IV. 4. 8.

sistent with this view. It believes in the multiplicity of empirical selves.

According to the doctrine that the whole universe including other finite selves is a creation of one's mind, the release of that one ego will mean the release of all. But this *eka-jīva-vāda* is not sustainable. The consciousness of the ego arises and gets strengthened by its clash with other egos. When anyone is released, does *avidyā* continue to exist or not? If the answer is negative, it means that all souls are released; if it is in the affirmative, what is the relation of the released soul to the *ajñāna* which still binds others? His position is one of identity, not with *Brahman* but with *Īśvara*. If he is not aware of the existence of *avidyā* at all, then he is in a condition where there are no bound souls. Either the release of all is a fact or his awareness is a delusion. Though some later Advaitins adopt the theory of *eka-jīva*, Ś. is opposed to it. If all the different souls are only one *jīva*, then when for the first time any soul attains liberation, bondage should have terminated for all which is not the case.[1] From the empirical standpoint a plurality of individuals is assumed by Ś. and many of his followers. On this view, salvation does not involve the destruction of the world. It implies the disappearance of a false view of the world.

Ś. admits that the world appearance persists for the *Jīvan-mukta* or the *Sthita-prajña* of the B.G. The *Jīvan-mukta*, though he realises *mokṣa* or *brahma-bhāva*, still lives in the world. The appearance of multiplicity is not superseded. It is with him as with a patient suffering from *timira* that, though he knows there is only one moon, he sees two. Only it does not deceive the freed soul even as the mirage does not tempt one who has detected its unreal character.

Freedom consists in the attainment of a universality of spirit or *sarvātma-bhāva*. Embodiment continues after the rise of saving knowledge. Though the spirit is released, the body persists. While the individual has attained inner harmony and freedom, the world manifestation still persists and engages his energies. Full freedom demands the transfiguration of the world as well. Ś.'s view of the *Jīvan-mukta* condition makes out that inner perfection and work in the finite universe can go together.

[1] III. 2. 21.

This view is not to be confused with *krama-mukti* or gradual release which is the aim of those who are devoted to *Kārya-Brahmā* or *Hiraṇya-garbha*. Ś. is discussing not gradual release but release consequent on *brahma-jñāna* which is attainable here and now; and for even such released souls, persistence of individuality is held not only as possible by Ś. but necessary in the interests of what is called world maintenance. In other words, the world will persist as long as there are souls subject to bondage. It terminates only when all are released, i.e. absolute salvation is possible with world-redemption.

There are Advaitins who argue that each soul is an individual existence trying to get away from its own self-deceiving. They insist on the necessity for individual salvation and this has little to do with the destiny of the cosmos or other souls. Such a view is more in accordance with the *Sāṁkhya* theory of a plurality of spirits (*puruṣa*) for in it each spirit is a separate eternal entity which falls into subjection to *prakṛti* (nature) and pursues its separate cycle of cosmic existence and works for its separate release. The *Sāṁkhya* theory affirms a dualism between spirit and nature and we cannot be certain that the free spirit that has once fallen into subjection by the disturbance of the equilibrium will not again fall into subjection by a repetition of the disturbance. According to the *Advaita Vedānta,* in each soul separately the one spirit has assumed the form of individual being. If it gets rid of the deception it may be saved, but the continuance of the self-deception in myriads of other souls will make for the time process. If the spirit is eternally free in itself and is also bound in the cosmos, it is not enough for a few souls to release themselves from time to time out of this deception.

PART TWO

TEXT, TRANSLATION AND NOTES

Section 1 (1)

THE DESIRE TO KNOW *BRAHMAN*

I. 1. 1. The object of the study is indicated in this section.
athāto brahma-jijñāsā.
Now therefore the desire to know Brahman (the Ultimate Reality).
atha: Now. It may also mean 'then' signifying immediate succession. *ānantaryārthaḥ.* Ś. and R.
ataḥ: therefore; *brahma:* Ultimate Reality.
jijñāsā: desire to know, to enquire into, to examine and test.

The *viṣaya-vākya* or the text referred to is the passage in B.U. 'Verily, it is the Self that should be seen, heard of, reflected on and meditated upon.'[1] Cp. also T.U. 'Seek to know *Brahman*'.

The word *atha* indicates that the desire to know *Brahman* arises subsequent to the fulfilment of certain conditions, according to Ś. The antecedent condition for the rise of the desire to know cannot be the study of the *Vedas* for that is necessary for the knowledge of both *Brahman* and *dharma*. It cannot be the performance of religious duty, for one can have the desire to know *Brahman* by a study of the literature of the *Vedānta*. Religious duty has temporal prosperity for its goal while knowledge of *Brahman* leads to eternal bliss. The latter is not dependent on human activity while the fruit of *dharma* is dependent on it. The knowledge of *Brahman* results immediately in realisation. *brahma-vit brahmaiva bhavati.* The desire to know *Brahman* has for its antecedent conditions the possession of the qualities of discrimination of things eternal and non-eternal, non-attachment to the enjoyment of fruit here or hereafter, possession in abundance of the qualities of calmness, equanimity and other such means, and desire for release.[2] When we know that the Self alone is eternal and all others non-eternal and contemplate the impermanence, impurity and painful character of the world, non-attachment arises.[3] Then follow *śama*, calmness, *dama*, control, *titikṣā*, indifference to objects, *uparati*, turning away from them and *śraddhā*, faith in the truth. The word *atha* indicates that the desire to know *Brahman* arises subsequent to the fulfilment of these conditions.

While the result of the performance of religious duty may lead to

[1] II. 4. 5. P.U., p. 197.

[2] *nityānitya-vastu-vivekaḥ, ihāmutrārtha-bhoga-virāgaḥ, śama-damādi-sādhana-sampat, mumukṣutvam . . . atha śabdena yathokta-sādhana-sampaty-ānantaryam upadiśyate.*

[3] *nityaḥ pratyag-ātmā; anityaḥ dehendriya-viṣayādayaḥ . . . asmin saṁsāra-maṇḍale anityāśuci-duḥkhātmakam prasaṁkhyānam upāvartate . . . virāgo abhogātmikopekṣābuddhiḥ. Bhāmatī.*

earthly prosperity, even residence in heaven, knowledge of *Brahman* leads to liberation from bondage. The two cannot be regarded as complementary to each other. Ś. does not accept *jñāna-karma-samuccaya-vāda*.

Sureśvara holds that *karma* is an indirect means to liberation since it purifies the soul and helps the acquisition of knowledge. Ritual is a means of liberation though it is not as effective as knowledge.[1]

Bhāskara is of the view that the enquiry regarding *Brahman* must be preceded by a study of the *Pūrva Mīmāṁsā*. One has a right to know *Brahman* and obtain release only after one has discharged his three debts to the ancestors, to the seers, and to the gods. In other words only those who are self-controlled are eligible to undertake an enquiry into *Brahman*. Bhāskara holds that we enquire into the nature of religious duty and of *Brahman* since works and knowledge both play an important part in the achievement of salvation. He adopts the doctrine of *jñāna-karma-samuccaya* or a combination of knowledge and works.

R. interprets *atha* to denote temporal succession to the study of the *karma-kāṇḍa* of the *Vedas*.[2] When we reach the knowledge that the result of mere works is limited and non-permanent we get the desire for final release. A systematic study of religious duty is the necessary antecedent of the enquiry into *Brahman*. The conditions which Ś. lays down as essential for the enquiry into *Brahman* presuppose an understanding of the nature of duty.

Madhva and his followers make out that the use of *atha* is for the sake of auspiciousness.[3] He suggests that the study of the *Vedānta* has to be undertaken after the attainment of certain preliminary qualifications and the acquisition of certain spiritual and moral qualities.[4] Those who have devotion are eligible for the enquiry into the nature of *Brahman*. Madhva takes *atha* to indicate the beginning of a subject. The word *ataḥ* means that the knowledge of *Brahman* leads to release and so the enquiry into *Brahman* is justified. Madhva interprets it to mean 'through the grace or kindness of the Lord *Viṣṇu*'. The reason for the enquiry into the nature of *Brahman* is the grace of the Lord. By a proper knowledge of him, we can obtain favours. According to Madhva there are three stages of fitness for the study of the *Vedānta*. A studious person devoted to the Lord is the lowest: one endowed with the six moral qualifications is the next higher; the highest is he who is solely attached to the Lord and detached from the world which he knows to be transitory. The desire

[1] *Sambandha-vārttika* 1133–1134.

[2] *karma-vicārānantaraṁ tata eva brahma-vicāraḥ kartavyaḥ.*

[3] *maṅgalārthaḥ*. Cp. Jaya-tīrtha: *kartavyam eva kāryārambhe maṅgalācaraṇam kṛtam ca bhagavatā sūtra-kāreṇa niveśitaṁ ca granthādau. Nyāya-sudhā.*

[4] *adhikārāntaryārthaś ca.*

to know starts us on the path of enquiry, *mīmāṁsā*.[1] Madhva looks upon *jijñāsā* not as desire to know but as *vicāra* or enquiry to determine the nature of *Brahman* and his qualities. The distinction of the knowledge of the eternal and the non-eternal, *nityānitya-vastu-viveka* cannot be a prerequisite for it is the ultimate goal. Wherever there is doubt we have to use our reason to resolve the doubt.[2]

For Śrīkaṇṭha an enquiry into *Brahman* can begin only after a study of the nature of *dharma*.[3] When the mind is purified by the performance of Vedic duties one becomes entitled to enquire into the nature of *Brahman*. While Ś. speaks of the inner values and qualities as qualifying one for the enquiry into *Brahman*, Śrīkaṇṭha insists on the discipline of sacrificial duties as essential for such an enquiry. Appaya Dīkṣita reconciles the two by arguing that the performance of Vedic duties without any desire for fruit leads to the acquisition of the moral qualities insisted on by Ś. and so qualifies those possessing them for *brahma*-knowledge.

Śrīkaṇṭha adopts the view that a knowledge of religious duties is a necessary antecedent to the enquiry into *Brahman* for the two stand in the relation of *ārādhana*, worship, and *ārādhya*, the worshipped, *sādhana*, means, and *sādhya*, end. Works purify the mind and help the growth of the knowledge of *Brahman*.

Nimbārka says that one who has read the *Veda*, whose mind is assailed by doubts about the results of actions, who has studied the *Pūrva Mīmāṁsā* in order to remove such doubts and has a proper knowledge of *karma* and its fruits should try to acquire a knowledge of *Brahman*. The two *mīmāṁsās* form one whole.[4] The study of the B.S. must be preceded by the study of the *Pūrva Mīmāṁsā*.

Nimbārka holds that the *karma* and *jñāna-kāṇḍas* form a whole.

Vallabha holds that both the *mīmāṁsās*, *pūrva* and *uttara*, deal with one topic, God, who possesses innumerable divine qualities including *kriyā* or sacrifice and *jñāna* or knowledge. The two *mīmāṁsās* deal with the two qualities. He also holds that the word *atha* is used to signify the auspicious. He makes out that it denotes the commencement of a new topic. The performance of duty should precede knowledge of *Brahman*. Knowledge of *Brahman* does not result in the cessation of activity. Even *jīvan-muktas* perform all *karmas*.

Śrīpati makes *atha* mean 'afterwards' or 'then'. When the desire to learn is there, there is *adhikāra* or fitness. It is attained after the seeker frees himself from the three kinds of wordly sins, *mala-traya*, arising from mind, speech and body. He also suggests that it is after

[1] In his *Gītā-tātparya*, Madhva says that *mīmāṁsā* is of three kinds, *brahma-mīmāṁsā*, *daiva-mīmāṁsā* and *karma-mīmāṁsā* and all the three should be studied.

[2] *sandigdham sa-prayojanaṁ ca vicāram arhati*. Jñānottama on *Naiṣkarmya-siddhi* I. 29.

[3] *dharma-vicārānantaram*.

[4] *vakṣyati ca karma-brahma-mīmāṁsayor aikaśāstryam*.

obtaining initiation, *dīkṣānantaram*, that one can enquire into the nature of *Brahman*. Śrīpati gives a long passage about the preliminaries for the study of *Brahman*.[1]

Vijnāna-bhikṣu says that *atha* indicates authority[2] and auspiciousness.[3] The realisation of *Brahman* is the goal.

Baladeva argues that the word *atha* means immediate sequence but contends that the mere knowledge of *karma-mīmāṁsā* or the acquisition of the qualifications laid down by Ś. does not give us the desire to enquire into the nature of *Brahman*. We need, in addition to all these, association with saintly people.

All except Ś. seem to agree that a previous study of *Pūrva Mīmāṁsā* is necessary before *Uttara Mīmāṁsā* is taken up and the two form one whole.

The knowledge of *Brahman* is not a matter of faith but the result of enquiry. Science comes by observation, not by authority. If religion is to be scientific it must be found through reasoned processes rather than by revelations from external authorities. If we use authority we do not use reason but memory as Leonardo da Vinci observes. Philosophy wishes to understand; religion is content to experience. Insistence on a logical approach to religious problems has been a persistent feature of the Indian tradition.[4]

Brahma-jijñāsā is *brahmaṇaḥ jijñāsā*, discussion about *Brahman*. This discussion goes on till the realisation of *Brahman* is attained. *Jijñāsā* is the desire to know. The knowledge culminating in realisation is the object of the desire expressed by the suffix *san*. The realisation of *Brahman* is the end of man, since it destroys all evils, *avidyā*, etc., all the seeds of rebirth. Therefore, *Brahman* is what is to be desired to be known.[5]

Philosophy is not mere logical analysis or epistemological enquiry. It is the love of wisdom. The urge to metaphysical inquiry is a natural one. It arises from the human situation. It is a natural propensity of the human mind to seek the presuppositions of thought and experience. The ultimate question is about the nature of being, what is meant by saying that something is.

The objection is raised that an enquiry is unnecessary if *Brahman* is

[1] *nigamāgama-ubhaya-vedānta-pratipādita-bhakti-kriyā-jñāna-kāṇḍa-traya-vihita-sthūla-sūkṣma-cid-acit-prapañca-prakāśaka-ṣaṭsthala-para-śiva-sākṣāt-kāra-kāraṇa-bahu-janma-kṛta-śivārpita-yajana-yājana-tapodhyānādy-aneka-puṇya-pūrva-phalaka-śarīra-traya-gata-mala-traya-dhvamṣaka-kāruṇya-kalyāṇa-kaivalya-vibhūti-traya-pra-dāyaka-aṣṭāvaraṇa-pañcācāra-sadguru-karuṇā-kaṭākṣa-labdha-śakti-pātādy-avacchinna-para-para-śiveṣṭa-liṅga-dhāraṇātmaka-pāśupata-dīkṣānantaryam iti.*

[2] *adhikāra-vācaka.*

[3] *maṅgala-rūpa.*

[4] Cp. 'I seek to know the self mentioned in the *Upaniṣads*'. *tam tv aupaniṣadaṁ puruṣaṁ pṛcchāmi.*

[5] *jñātum icchā jijñāsā. avagati-paryantam jñānam san-vācyāyā icchayāḥ karma . . . brahmāvagatir hi puruṣārthaḥ. niḥśeṣa-saṁsāra-bījāvidyāy-ādy anartha-nibarhaṇāt, tasmāt brahma jijñāsitavyam.* Ś.

known (*a-sandigdha*) and futile (*a-prayojana*) if it is not known. If *Brahman* is pure and absolute intelligence, it is open only to direct intuition and is not a proper object for enquiry and discussion. Desire to know can only be with reference to an object which is not definitely known,[1] so that by reasoning and discussion we can reach a definite conclusion. Ś. says that *Brahman* is known for *Brahman* is one's own self, *ayam ātmā brahma*. No one thinks that he does not exist. Each one cognises the existence of himself.[2] Yet an enquiry into the nature of *Brahman* is essential since there are conflicting views about its nature. *Brahman* is often confused with the body, the sense-organs, mind or intelligence. It is said to be the doer or the enjoyer. These definitions are due to a confusion between object and subject, thou and I.[3] We superpose the qualities of the object on the subject and the subject on the object through non-discrimination, *a-viveka*, and so we mix up the true and the untrue.

We find in experience such expressions as 'I am this', 'this is mine'.[4] The Ultimate Reality which is the pure Self, the inward subjectivity, is made into an object, a substance in empirical usage and this is the result of *āropa*, *avidyā*, *bhrānti*, *ajñāna*, which are synonymous terms.

Vācaspati argues that the Self is known through indubitable, non-erroneous and immediate experience.[5] Whatever experiences we pass through, the Self is constant and unchanging. 'That which is constant in whatever is variable, that is different from the latter even as a string [is different] from the flowers [strung on it].'[6] The Self is distinct from the body, the sense-organs, the mind, the intellect and all objects. The Self which is of the nature of intelligence is the subject; the non-intelligent intellect, sense-organs, body and the objects are the objects of cognition.[7]

The consciousness of 'I' is the consciousness of the Self limited by the adjuncts of body, sense-organs, intellect, etc. It is the consciousness of the *jīva*, the individual self. The *pratyag-ātman* is in reality non-object since it is self-luminous, *svayam-prakāśa*. It becomes the object of the idea of the ego in so far as it is conditioned by the adjuncts of internal organ, senses, intellect, subtle and gross bodies. The empirical ego or agent is different from the Self present in all.[8]

[1] *jñātum icchā hi sandigdha-viṣaye nirṇayāya bhavati. Bhāmatī.*

[2] *sarvo hy ātmāstitvaṁ pratyeti na na aham asmi'iti.*

[3] Ś. opens his commentary with the words: *yuṣmad-asmat-pratyaya-gocarayo viṣaya-viṣayinos tamaḥ-prakāśavad viruddha-svabhāvayor itaretarabhāvānupapattau siddhāyām.*

[4] *satyānṛte mithunīkṛtya, 'aham idam' 'mamedam' iti naisargiko'yam loka-vyavahāraḥ.* Ś.B.

[5] *a-sandigdha, a-viparyaya, aparokṣānubhava.*

[6] *yeṣu vyāvartamāneṣu yad anuvartate tat tebhyo bhinnam, yathā kusumebhyaḥ sūtram. Bhāmatī.*

[7] *cit-svabhāva ātmā viṣayī, jaḍa-svabhāvā buddhīndriya-dehaviṣayā viṣayāḥ.*

[8] *ahaṁ-pratyaya-viṣaya-kartṛ-vyatirekena, tat sākṣī sarva-bhūtasthaḥ sama ekaḥ kūṭastha nityaḥ puruṣaḥ . . . sarvasyātmā.* Ś.B. I. 1. 4.

The Self is a non-object, *aviṣaya*, of empirical knowledge but it is the object of the notion of 'I' and of immediate realisation.[1] It is of the nature of light which is self-luminous, one, immutable, eternal, without parts.[2] The Self is immediately perceived. If it were not manifested, nothing else can be manifested. The whole world would cease to be manifest and become blind.[3]

Vācaspati makes out that when the inner self is made into an object, it becomes determinate, limited, and this limitation is apparent, not real.[4] The Pure Universal Self appears in the concept of the individual soul *jīva*, as agent and enjoyer. For the *Ātman* which is indifferent there cannot occur the capacity to act or to enjoy.[5] The body, the organs, etc., cannot act and enjoy without the aid of intelligence, *caitanya*. So the Self whose nature is intelligence linked with the body and the organs acquires the capacity to act and enjoy. It is these adjuncts that make for the differences among souls.

The discrimination between the Self and the not-self, *ātmānātma-vastu-viveka*, is essential for salvation. Life in *saṁsāra* is traceable to the non-experience of the true nature of Self and will end with the recognition of the Self.[6] Ś. observes that the superposition, wise men hold, is *avidyā*, ignorance, and as distinct from that the determination of the nature of reality is *vidyā* or knowledge.[7] 'Superposition is the cognition as something of what is not that.'[8] The superimposition of the not-self on the inner Self is the cause of ignorance but this ignorance does not affect the Supreme even to the smallest extent, *aṇumātreṇāpi*. The whole empirical universe with its distinctions of valid knowledge and means thereof and the sacred teachings relating to prescription, prohibition and release, *śāstrāṇi, vidhi-pratiṣedha-mokṣaparāṇi*, is the result of *avidyā* or ignorance or non-discrimination between the Self and the non-self.

Vidyā or knowledge referred to is the removal of *avidyā* or ignorance. It is the final cognition which is of the same type as what is removed by it, though it is of a higher degree in so far as it requires

[1] *asmat-pratyaya-viṣayatvāt, aparokṣatvāc ca pratyag-ātmā prasiddheḥ.* Ś.

[2] *tad ayaṁ prakāśa eva svayaṁ prakāśa ekaḥ, kūṭastho nityo nir-aṁśaḥ pratyag-ātmā. . . . Bhāmatī.*

[3] See M.U. II. 2. 11.

[4] *tathāpi anirvacanīyānādy-avidyā-parikalpita-buddhi-manaḥ-sūkṣma-sthūla-śarīrendriyāvacchedaka-bhedena anavacchinno'pi vastuto 'vacchinna iva abhinno'pi bhinna iva, akartāpi karteva abhoktāpi bhokteva aviṣayo'pi asmat-pratyaya-viṣaya iva jīva-bhāvam āpannaḥ avabhāsate.*

[5] *na ca udāsīnasya tasya kriyā-śaktir bhoga-śaktir vāsambhavati.*

[6] *saṁsāraś ca ātma-yāthātmyānanubhava-nimitta ātma-yāthātmya-jñānena nivartanīyaḥ. Bhāmatī.*

[7] *tam etam evaṁ-lakṣaṇam adhyāsam paṇḍitā avidyeti manyante, tad-vivekena ca vastu-svarūpāvadhāraṇam vidyām āhuḥ. Avidyā* is unillumined knowledge, limited to empirical perception and discursive thinking.

[8] *adhyāso nāma atasmin tad-buddhiḥ.* Ś.

nothing else for its own removal. The final cognition removes the obscuration of the Self which is knowledge caused by *avidyā*. That cognition is spoken of as knowledge only figuratively. Self is knowledge. The final cognition helps to reveal it and is knowledge only secondarily. So long as the self is a knower it is an agent in respect of knowledge. Without knowership there can be no activity of the means of valid knowledge.[1] All knowledge belongs to the world of experience. When it is knowledge itself, it ceases to have cognition.

The tendency to objectivisation of the pure subject is wrong but it does not follow that the objective universe is an apparition or illusion. For the Scriptures declare that 'all this is *Brahman*'. Later *sūtras* repudiate any suggestion of treating the world as non-existent or dreamlike. The world is, according to Ś., *sarvaloka-pratyakṣa, sarvānubhava-siddha*.[2]

Even when the texts declare that the real is one and secondless, they do not contradict the empirical reality of the world we perceive. They only say that the reality of the world is not of an ultimate or absolute character.[3] It is however beginningless[4] and so is its cause, non-discrimination between the Self and the not-self.

Even when Ś. says that *Brahman* appears as the world even as nacre appears as silver or as a single moon appears as having a second,[5] he means that the manifestation is terminable.[6] The world is subject to changes.

Even as the nacre is more real than the silver, so the Absolute is more real than its manifestation. The manifestation is not devoid of reality for it is the combination of the real and the non-real, *satyānṛta-mithunam*.

The world of *saṁsāra* is beginningless, *anādi*, and endless, *ananta*. It has everlastingness, *pravāhānāditva*, and not eternity which is *svarūpānāditva*.

Ś. mentions that all the *Vedāntas* are set forth for the removal of the cause of evil and the attainment of the knowledge of the oneness of the Self.[7] The goal is the attainment of knowledge which is not to be confused with mere repetition of names or performance of rites.[8] It is not mere intellectual knowledge but intuitive realisation.

Brahman, derived from the root *bṛh*, to grow, become great, means

[1] *na ca pramātṛtvam antareṇa pramāṇa-pravṛttir asti.* Ś.

[2] *evam ayam anādir ananto naisargiko'dhyāso mithyā-pratyaya-rūpaḥ kartṛtva-bhoktṛtva-pravartakaḥ, sarvaloka-pratyakṣaḥ.*

[3] *na hi āgama-jñānam sāṁvyavahārikam pratyakṣasya prāmāṇyam upahanti yena kāraṇābhāvān na bhavet, api tu tāttvikam. Bhāmatī.*

[4] *svābhāvikaḥ, anādir ayam vyavahāraḥ. Bhāmatī.*

[5] *śuktikā hi rajatavad avabhāsate, ekaś candraḥ sa-dvitīyavad iti.*

[6] *avasannaḥ avamato vā bhāsaḥ avabhāsaḥ. Bhāmatī.*

[7] *asyānartha-hetoḥ prahāṇāya ātmaikatva-vidyā-pratipattaye sarve vedāntā ārabhyante.* Ś.

[8] *pratipattiḥ prāptiḥ, tasyai, na tu japa-mātrāya, nāpi karmasu pravṛttaye.*

the Being of unlimited greatness, supreme perfection.[1] Ś. derives *Brahman* from the root *bṛhati*, to exceed *atiśayana*. It means eternity, purity, intelligence. Its main features are being, consciousness, infinity and freedom. While these are the primary qualities, *svarūpa-lakṣaṇa*, there are the qualities of omnipotence, omnipresence, omniscience. These have a meaning when *Brahman* is looked at from the cosmic point of view. They are the *taṭastha-lakṣaṇa*.

For R., *Brahman* is *Nārāyaṇa*. He is free from imperfections, comprises within himself all auspicious qualities[2] and enjoys originating, preserving, re-absorbing, providing and ruling the universe. The Highest Reality is determinate and the world which is the manifestation of his power is real.

Madhva holds that those who suffer from bondage wish to be released from it and so desire the knowledge of *Brahman*. Bondage is real.[3] Even Ś. holds that bondage, though unreal, is terminable. *Brahman* for Madhva is *Viṣṇu*, the one Supreme God who bears all the names of the deities. He quotes R.V. in support of his view.[4] God has a multiplicity of attributes. The *Upaniṣad* asserts that the knowledge of the *Vedānta* is essential for release.[5]

The main emphasis of this *sūtra* is that a candidate for spiritual knowledge and life should be morally pure. His conduct should be upright. The quarrel of many thinking men is not so much with the foundations of faith but with the degradation in practice by its votaries. Though philosophy as *brahma-jijñāsā* is a consistent effort of reflection it is not possible with indulgence in ways of life which show lack of restraint. A life dedicated to the pursuit of wisdom must be an ethical life. Etienne Gilson says: 'Wisdom is the prize, not only of a quest, but also of a conquest. We all have to win it the hard way.'[6]

[1] *samasta-kalyāṇa-guṇātmakam.*

[2] *paraṁ brahma sa-viśeṣaṁ tad-vibhūti-bhūtaṁ jagad api pāramārthikam eva.*

[3] *mithyātvam api bandhasya naiva muktir apekṣate. Aṇu-vyākhyāna.*

[4] *yo devānāṁ nāmadhā eka eva, taṁ sampraśnaṁ bhuvanā yānty anyā* X. 82. 3.

[5] *vedāntārtha-vijñānaṁ mokṣa-hetuḥ.* See M.U. III. 26. P.U., pp. 690–1.

Nārāyaṇa Pandit's *Nyāya-candrikā* sums up the substance of this section thus:

atha-śabdenādhikāram ata ity amunā phalam
brahma-śabdena viṣayaṁ sūcayāmāsa sūtra-kṛt.

[6] *History of Philosophy and Philosophical Education* (1948), p. 46.

Section 2 (2)

GOD THE WORLD-GROUND

I. 1. 2. The second section defines *Brahman* as the source from which the world proceeds, by which it is maintained and ended.

janmādy asya yataḥ.
(*Ultimate Reality is that*) *from which origin, etc.* (*i.e. subsistence and destruction*) *of this* (*would proceed*).
janmādi: origin, etc. Etcetera means subsistence, *sthiti*, and destruction, *bhaṅga*. To these three Madhva adds *niyati* (control), *jñāna* (enlightenment), *āvṛti* (ignorance), *bandha* (bondage) and *mokṣa* (release).[1] Śrīkaṇṭha extends *ādi*, etc., to cover '*janma-sthiti-pralaya tirobhāvānugraha-rūpaṁ kṛtyam*'; *asya:* of this; *yataḥ:* from which.

The relevant text is the *Taittirīya Upaniṣad* passage 'That from which these beings are born, that by which when born they live, that into which when departing they enter. That, seek to know. That is *Brahman*'.[2]

Our age has been greatly influenced by the emergence of the scientific world-view. We cannot believe unless our beliefs are consistent with the world we know and live in. Science is one of the languages in which God can be described. There is a general impression that the spirit of science is opposed to a spiritual view of the world and supports materialism. Astronomy is said to present us with a mindless universe which is governed by impersonal, automatic forces. Darwinism tells us that man is an animal. Freud and the Behaviourists explain away the soul. Marxism accounts for history on the basis of economic forces. This is sometimes said to be the scientific view of the universe. We may use the scientific instruments and know more about the nature of the world but what sees through them is the human eye and the achievements of science are the outcome of the human mind. Science describes facts and interprets them but these interpretations have varied from time to time. The B.S. gives us an explanation which is still relevant to the scientific facts. The Oxford group of scientists who founded the Royal Society of England were religious-minded. Its first Secretary, who was also its first historian, Sprat, rose to be a Bishop. They were keen to make people religious-minded without making them intolerant. The assumption of philosophy is that this universe makes sense. This faith is not unwarranted. The world has a pattern. Philosophers seek to find it. Plato's Idea of the Good or Marx's economic development of history is a principle of explanation. Bergson finds in the

[1] See V.S. III. 2. 5.
[2] III. 1. P.U. 553. Cp. an Orphic saying quoted by Plato that God holds 'the beginning, middle and end of all existence'.

world an *élan*, Samuel Alexander the *nisus*, General Smuts the holistic tendency and A. N. Whitehead the Creative Advance of Nature.

This *sūtra* gives us what is called natural theology.[1] We build up a theory of ultimate being from empirically observable facts. The next *sūtra* takes us to authoritative sources. From the nature of the world, we infer the existence of One Supreme, Personal, Self-subsistent Mind to whose creative and ruling activities the world owes its existence, nature, coherence and consummation. The earlier stages of the cosmic process are adapted to the later ones. The temporal world taken as a whole suggests a cosmic meaning and admits of a consistent interpretation.

While science may explain *how* things happen, it does not tell us *why* they happen. From a study of the universe with its ordered growth and plan which cannot be conceived by the mind,[2] we infer the reality of an omniscient and omnipotent cause.[3] Udayana's *Kusumāñjali* attempts to prove the existence of God by logical reasoning.

Ś. in his commentary brings together the cosmological and the teleological arguments. Every effect has a cause.[4] We cannot trace the world with its order and design to 'non-sentient *pradhāna*, or atoms or non-being, or a being subject to rebirth, to its own nature or to a human creator'.[5] It cannot be traced to the world-soul or *Hiraṇya-garbha* for he is subject to the changes of the world.[6] The universe has its roots in being, *san-mūla*, has its basis in being, *sad-āśraya*, and is established in being, *sat-pratiṣṭha*. This being transcends all distinctions of subject and object and yet when we speak of *Brahman*, we have to use empirical forms. When viewed as the creator and governor of the universe *Brahman* is said to be the personal God, *Īśvara*. *Brahman* and *Īśvara* are both valid forms of reality. Only *Īśvara* or God is the cause of the world.

[1] By his bequest of 1887 Lord Gifford founded his well-known lectureship in the four Scottish Universities for the promotion and diffusion of natural theology 'treated as a strictly natural science like astronomy or chemistry without reference to or reliance upon any supposed special, exceptional or so-called miraculous revelation. . . '. St Thomas Aquinas tells us of 'an ascent, by the natural light of reason, through created things to the knowledge of God' and on the other hand of 'a descent, by the mode of revelation, of divine truth which exceeds the human intellect, yet not as demonstrated to our sight but as a communication delivered for our belief'. *Summa Contra Gentiles*, Vol. IV. Chap. I. There are some like Karl Barth who feel that rational thinking is not relevant to the religious faith.

[2] *acintya-racanā*. Ś.

[3] *sarvajñāt sarvaśakteḥ kāraṇād bhavati*. Ś.

[4] *yat kāryam tat sa-kartṛkam*.

[5] *pradhānād acetanāt, aṇubhyo vā, abhāvād vā, saṁsāriṇo vā, utpadyādi sambhāvayitum śakyam na ca svabhāvataḥ. etad evānumānaṁ saṁsāri-vyatirikteśvarāstitvādi-sādhanam manyante īśvara-kāraṇa-vādinaḥ*. Ś.

[6] Cp. *kecit tu hiraṇya-garbhaṁ saṁsāriṇam . . . jagad-hetum ācakṣate*. Ānandagiri.

When we work from the cosmic end, we get to the Supreme as the Lord who presides over the world, who experiences all.[1] *Brahman*, the pure spirit beyond the subject-object distinction, and *Īśvara*, the subject confronting the non-subject or object, are the two forms of one Reality.[2]

Brahman has two kinds of qualities, essential, *svarūpa-lakṣaṇa*, and accidental, *taṭastha-lakṣaṇa*. The definition of *Brahman* as creator is of the latter type since it is only in association with *māyā* that *Brahman* can be said to be the cause of production, etc., of the world.[3]

Among the *Advaitins*, many acute differences arose with regard to the causality of *Brahman*. Sureśvara and his follower Sarvajña in his *Saṁkṣepa-śārīraka* argue that *Brahman* alone is the cause of the world. Padmapāda contends that *Brahman* and *māyā* together constitute the cause. Prakāśānanda following Maṇḍana Miśra believes that *māyā* alone is the cause of the world.

R. emphasises the creative aspect and makes it the highest reality. B.S. is not intended to give us a knowledge of *Brahman* without differences (*nirviśeṣa-brahma*). He quotes a verse from the *Viṣṇu Purāṇa* which reads: 'From *Viṣṇu* the world has sprung, in him it exists: he is the cause of the subsistence and dissolution of this world and the world is he.'[4] In the first *sūtra* we reach the conclusion that we should enter on an enquiry into the nature of *Brahman* and the second *sūtra* gives a description of that *Brahman* and not of something else. R. says that the knowledge of *Brahman* may be gained on the ground of its characteristic marks such as its being the cause of the origination, etc., of the world, free from all evil, omniscient, all-powerful and so on.[5]

Madhva believes that the characteristics mentioned belong to the nature of *Brahman*. Creativity is an essential defining quality of *Brahman*. If a crow sits on a house, its association with the house is an accidental feature. *Brahman* has infinite qualities and their possession forms *Brahman's* defining character.[6] The *sūtra* differentiates God from souls and inanimate objects.[7]

[1] *sarvānubhūḥ*. B.U. II. 5. 19.

[2] *dvi-rūpam hi brahmāvagamyate, nāma-rūpa-vikāra-bhedopādhi-viśiṣṭam, tad-viparītaṁ sarvopādhi-varjitam*. Ś.

[3] *Pañcapādikā-vivaraṇa* by Prakāśātman, pp. 222–3.

[4] *viṣṇoḥ sakāśād udbhūtam, jagat tatraiva samsthitam*
sthiti-samyama-kartāsau jagato'sya, jagac ca saḥ. I. I. 35.

[5] *ataḥ sakala-jagaj-janmādi-kāraṇam, niravadyam, sarvajñam satya-saṁkalpaṁ sarva-śakti brahma lakṣaṇataḥ pratipattuṁ śakyata iti siddham*.

[6] *ananta-guṇa-sattvam eva brahmaṇo lakṣaṇam. Nyāya-sudhā*, p. 107.

[7] Madhva quotes in his *Aṇu-bhāṣya* a verse from *Skanda Purāṇa*
utpatti-sthiti-saṁhāra-niyatir jñānam āvṛtiḥ
bandha-mokṣaṁ ca puruṣād yasmāt sa harir eka-rāt.

Jaya-tīrtha refers to another interpretation of the *sūtra*:
janma-ādyasya hiraṇya-garbhasya yatas tad brahma.

Is the universe the result of an accident? Is the cosmic process where matter prepares the way for life and life for mind and mind for intelligence a long chain of accidents?[1] Look at the many favourable conditions that had to be provided for the advent of life and the preparations that had to be made in living conditions for the advent of mind. If we have an understanding of the gradual evolution of intelligence, we will be struck by the vast creative plan of the universe, its marvellous structure. The spectacle of life emerging from primal matter at some distant point of time and space and developing into God-men gives us a sense of mystery. If we wish to explain, the higher can account for the lower and not *vice versa*. To think that the mindless generates mind is as absurd as to think that a monkey given a typewriter and sufficient time would produce the plays of Kālidāsa or Shakespeare. Professor Planck writes: 'I regard matter as derivative from consciousness.' Mind can account for matter but matter cannot account for mind. So the highest reality can account for the whole creation. God is the illuminating, unifying interpretative principle.[2]

C. D. Broad tells us that there has been only one plausible argument for supporting religious belief by science. It is the existence of laws which govern the events of the world. *A priori* it is not self-evident or even plausible that there should be such laws but science tells us that they exist. The belief that nature is ruled by laws is the content of what Einstein called 'cosmic religion'. These laws give testimony of God's presence in the universe.

In this *sūtra* we exclude the appeal to religious experience and take into account facts which are firmly established and universally acknowledged. The world tells its own story and offers its own suggestions.

The most significant quality of early Greek religion, as we find in the Homeric view of life, is its acceptance of nature. The miraculous, in the sense of transcending the natural order, does not play an important role. Even if Homeric gods interfere in mortal affairs, they do so, not by changing the natural course of events, but by participating in it. Mr Otto observes of the Greeks, 'the divine is not

[1] Plato commented on his times as follows: 'They say that fire and water and earth and air all exist by nature and chance. . . . The elements are severally moved by chance and some inherent force, according to affinities amongst them, of hot and cold, or of dry with moist, etc. After this fashion and in this manner the whole heaven has been created as well as animals and plants. . . . Not by the action of mind, as they say, or of any god, but as I was saying, by chance alone.'

[2] Cp. Plotinus who says, concerning the seer, that his art is 'to read the written characters of Nature which reveal order and law'. *Enneads*, E.T. III. 1. 6.

Paracelsus looks upon Nature as a collection of books which are entire and perfect 'because God himself wrote, made and bound them and has hung them from the chains of his library'.

superimposed as a sovereign power over natural events; it is revealed in the forms of the natural, as their very essence and being. If we look more closely at the occasions when these divine interventions take place, we find that they always come at the critical moment when human powers suddenly converge, as if charged by electric current, on some insight, some resolution, some deed. These decisive turns which, as every attentive observer knows, are regularly experienced in an active life, the Greeks regarded as manifestations of the gods'.[1] The Olympian gods, though they were symbols, represented genuine aspects of human experience. The early Greeks apprehended divinity under different names in all forms of heightened experience. Plato and his successors could not believe in the physical reality of the Homeric gods and held that in moments of intellectual insight the human personality was irradiated with influences from another dimension of being.

A distinction was drawn between nature and super-nature. Plato looked upon material things as merely shadows of the divine ideas. The Jews and the Christians believed that the world was governed by an omnipotent deity who could be trusted to punish the wicked and help the weak and the oppressed. 'The heavens declare the glory of God; and the firmament sheweth *his* handywork.'[2] 'I the Lord, the first, and with the last; I am he.' 'I am Alpha and Omega, the beginning and the end, the first and the last.'[3] God is defined as that 'which is, which was, and that which is to come'. 'To God belong the East and the West; whithersoever you turn, there is the Face of God.'[4] 'We indeed created man; and we know what his soul whispers within him, and we are nearer to him than the jugular vein.'[5]

This view repudiates the familiar pessimistic doctrine that the world of history is as indifferent to us as the physical world, that it has no concern with the moral aspirations of men. Such a view represents the mood of many people who have seen two wars in one generation, disconsolate, despairing, strident, sick of the world, but incapable of love. They look upon the world as a ferment of fear, envy, hatred and horror. When we think of our encounters with disease and death, we are inclined to believe that we are in the hands of chance, that there is no providence which guides, corrects and leads us onward. There is no rational process of the world, no dialectic of reality, no moral duty to follow it. We live in a world of universal caprice. The era of fire from the sky may begin any day for Machiavelli seems to have penetrated deeply into human nature when he said: 'Men get discontented with the good.' Belief in God is possible only if we draw a veil over the agony and suffering of the world. The atheist argues that there is no God. If he is benevolent, evil is unthinkable. We cannot make God responsible only for the good and the creatures

[1] Walter F. Otto: *The Homeric Gods: The Spiritual Significance of Greek Religion*, E.T. (1954). [2] *Psalm* xix. 1. [3] *Revelation* xxii. 13; see also i. 8.
[4] Quran II. 109. [5] *Ibid.* I. 15.

responsible for evil. Such a God who takes the credit for the good and shirks the responsibility for evil is not what we mean by God. Stendhal says: 'The only excuse for God is that he does not exist.'

This *sūtra* asks us to take a more universal and dispassionate view. The world moves: we cannot turn it backward or hold it where it is. Nothing in it stands still. It either grows or degenerates. This applies to every item in the universe from the atom to the stars. The world is not perpetual repetition. It is a perfecting process making towards perfection. It will change and, if we are wise, it will change for the better and the forces of the world will back us. The future is open. When we face disaster, we begin to doubt and despair. Goethe once wrote: 'A man who is unable to despair has no need to be alive.' We are afraid that mankind will destroy itself. There is no inevitability about it. It will yet become a family. For the laws of nature and God co-operate with one another and the darkness we now are in is a herald not of death but of the dawn of a new era.

The first *sūtra* refers to *Brahman;* the second *sūtra* refers to the same *Brahman* in another aspect. The first is Absolute Being, awareness and freedom; the second is the creative side of the Absolute. It is also evident that the world is not a transformation of *Īśvara* in the sense that *Īśvara* is obliged to express or manifest himself in this universe. When we limit our attention to the world which is one expression of the Creative *Īśvara*, we get the concept of *Hiraṇya-garbha*. This last becomes. Whatever becomes is neither pure being nor pure non-being.

Section 3 (3)

SOURCE OF SCRIPTURE

I. 1. 3. This section affirms that *Brahman* is the source of the *Veda*.

śāstra-yonitvāt.

From its being the source of Scripture

or

From Scripture being the source (*of its knowledge*).

śāstra: the *Veda* and the other sacred books.

yonitvāt: from being the source or cause.

Ś. gives two interpretations: (i) *śāstra-yoni*, the cause of the Scripture; (ii) that of which Scripture is the cause or source of revelation or *pramāṇa*. The first interpretation means that *Brahman* is the cause of the revelation of the *Vedas*. No one but an omniscient being could be their source. The second interpretation means that only the *Vedas* can prove to us that *Brahman* is the cause of the production, etc., of the world.[1]

[1] *śāstrād eva pramāṇā jagato janmādi-kāraṇaṁ brahma adhigamyate.* Ś.

Īśvara's causality of the world is confirmed in this *sūtra*. The relevant text is: 'As from a lighted fire laid with damp fuel, various [clouds of] smoke issue forth, even so, my dear, the *Ṛg Veda*, the *Yajur Veda*, the *Sāma Veda*, *Atharvāṅgirasa*, history, ancient lore, sciences, *upaniṣads*, verses, aphorisms, explanations and commentaries. From this, indeed, are all these breathed forth.'[1] *Īśvara* is the source of the *śāstra*, *śāstrasya yoniḥ*.

The Supreme *Īśvara* is the source of the *Veda*, etc. He breathes forth all knowledge effortlessly, on the analogy of play, like human breathing.[2] The Supreme is omniscient; his knowledge extends to all things. The *Veda* is said to be *apauruṣeya*, independent of human origin. The *Pūrva Mīmāṁsā* teaches the transmission of the eternal *Veda* through a succession of teachers and pupils, who are not its authors. Even those who hold that *Īśvara* creates the *Vedas* admit that the Creator, though omniscient and omnipotent, creates the *Vedas* in accordance with what they were in earlier creations and has not freedom in regard to it.[3] Even as the world is beginningless so are the *Vedas*. On this both the followers of *Pūrva Mīmāṁsā* and *Vedānta* agree, though they use it for different purposes.[4] The authors of the *Vedas* are only the seers of truth and not makers of it. The defects, if any, of the authors, do not affect the truth of the *Vedas*.[5] To say that the *Vedas* are produced by God by his deliberate desire would be to accept the views of the *Nyāya* and the *Vaiśeṣika* systems. The view of the eternity of the *Vedas* is then abandoned. If the *Vedas* had come out of *Brahman* like the breath of a man, the production of the *Vedas* would be involuntary as all breathing is. It will not show the omniscience of God. If he produces the *Vedas* in the same order in which they existed in the previous *kalpa*, then *Brahman* is subject to some necessities and is not independent.

The *sūtra* may also be constructed to mean that the Scripture is the source of the knowledge of *Brahman*. *śāstram yoniḥ kāraṇam pramāṇam*. Scripture is the means of right knowledge through which we understand the nature of *Brahman*. If I. 1. 2 suggests mere inferential knowledge[6] of *Brahman*, this suggests scriptural knowledge of *Brahman*.

Reason as the regulator of human life must have a source which transcends it though it must conform to it. Even a thousand *upaniṣads* cannot negative what is established by experience. The texts cannot be opposed to experience. 'A thousand Scriptures,

[1] B.U. II. 4. 10; P.U., p. 199.

[2] *līlā-nyāyena puruṣa-niḥśvāsavat*. Ś.

[3] *sarvajñopi sarva-śaktir api pūrva-pūrva-sargānusāreṇa vedān viracayan na svatantraḥ*.

[4] *puruṣāsvātantrya-mātram cāpauruṣeyatvam rocayante jaiminīyā api, tac cāsmākam api samānam anyatrābhiniveśāt. Bhāmatī*.

[5] See, however, *Vaiśeṣika Sūtra* VI. 1. 1. *buddhi-pūrvā vākya-kṛtir vede*.

[6] B.U. II. 4. 10; P.U., p. 199.

verily, can not convert a pot into a cloth',[1] says Vācaspati. Ś. says that the source of knowledge is knowledge itself. 'The origin of a body of Scripture possessing the quality of omniscience cannot be sought elsewhere but in omniscience itself.' Scripture is not a written text. It is eternal truth interpreted with the help of the doctrine of *samanvaya*.

Śāstra for Ś. includes the four *Vedas*, the epics, the *purāṇas* and other branches of learning, *vidyāsthāna*. *Bhāmatī* says: 'The *Vedas* are his breath, his glance the five elements, the movable and immovable [universe] is his smile and his sleep is the final deluge.'[2]

Objects require proofs to establish their reality but proofs like perception and inference are different modes of knowledge based on consciousness. Consciousness is the revealer, the proof of all things. It does not require any proof to prove it.[3]

Reason and experience are two different approaches in man's quest for God. Both are responses of the human soul to God's self-disclosure, through nature and history and spiritual experience. They reveal life's transcendental meaning. Reason reveals to us God as a matter of speculation; in experience it ceases to be an object of speculation but becomes a present reality. The method of natural sciences is not the only instrument by which it is possible to discover truth. Spiritual experience offers a valid proof for the existence of God.

In spiritual experience which is registered in the *Śāstras* we have a sense of power, of release from bondage. It is not a subjective impression but cognition of an object. Spiritual experience has this in common with perceptual experience that in both there is the recognition of something given. It is an experimental knowledge of the things of God.[4] The knowledge of *Brahman* culminates in experience and has an existent object for its content.[5] The knowledge of the true nature

[1] *na hi āgamāḥ sahasram api ghaṭaṁ paṭayitum īśate*. I. 1. 1.

[2] *niḥśvasitam asya vedā, vīkṣitam etasya pañca-bhūtāni, smitam etasya carācaram, asya ca suptam mahā-pralayaḥ*.

[3] *ātmānubhavam āśritya pratyakṣādi prasiddhyati, anubhūteḥ svataḥ-siddheḥ kā'pekṣā, ātma-siddhaye?*

[4] 'You will discover a sense that will perceive the Divine.' Proverbs ii. 5. We have a sense of sight for perceiving non-corporeal things, of hearing voices that make no sound with air, tasting the bread that gives life (John vi. 51 ff.); the sense of smell that made Paul say that he was 'the good odour of Christ' (II Corinthians ii. 15); a sense of touch which John used when he handled the '*word of life*' (I John i. 1). See also John i. 14; Hebrews vi. 5; Romans vii. 22.

[5] Ś.B. I. 1. 2. Cp. Nietzsche who describes the role of intuition or inspiration. In the state of creative inspiration, he writes: 'One becomes nothing but a medium for super-mighty influences. That which happens can only be termed revelation; that is to say, that suddenly, with unutterable certainty and delicacy, something becomes visible and audible and shakes and rends one to the depth of one's being. One hears, one does not seek; one takes, one does not ask who it is that gives; like lightning a thought flashes out of necessity,

of a thing is not dependent on human intellection. It depends on the thing itself.[1] The knowledge of *Brahman* depends on the thing itself because its content is an existent thing.[2] It is not an object of the senses.[3] By nature the senses have objects as their content and do not have *Brahman* as their content.[4] *Brahman* is not perceived by the senses. It is inferred from the world or learnt from the texts or experienced by the individual.

The problem of communication is difficult. We cannot make the experience intelligible to others, cannot adequately express it through the limitations of language. Kabīr says: 'That which you see is not; and for that which is you have no words.' Again: 'It cannot be told by the words of the mouth; it cannot be written on paper. It is like a dumb person who tastes a sweet thing—how shall it be explained?'[5]

The old days when the Scriptures were accepted on trust that God was their author are no more. There is a new approach today. We do not accept scriptural documents as books apart from other books, unquestionable in their accuracy and advice. The view that they are the inerrant word of God does not carry conviction. Disturbed by the attacks of modern knowledge and criticism, some people resort to what is called fundamentalism, a forthright assertion of complete verbal inspiration coupled with a total rejection of all that modern knowledge has contributed to a real understanding of the Scriptures.

There is another view of the *Veda* as *āpta-vacana* or sayings of the wise, those who had attained to a realisation of *Brahman*, *brahma-prāpti*. This view is supported by Ś. who makes out that the *Śruti* or Scripture is *pratyakṣa*[6] or records of the direct experiences of the seers, which are of a self-certifying character. 'How can one', Ś. asks,

complete in form. It is a rapture . . . a state of being entirely outside oneself. Everything happens in the highest degree involuntarily, as in a storm of feeling, freedom, of power, of divinity.'

[1] *na vastu-yāthātmya-jñānam puruṣa-buddyapekṣam . . . vastu-tantram eva tat.* Ś.B.

[2] *brahma-jñānam api vastu-tantram eva, bhūta-vastu-viṣayatvāt. Ibid.*

[3] *indriyāviṣayatvena.* See also Ś.B. I. 1. 4.

na ca pariniṣṭhita-vastu-svarūpatve'pi pratyakṣādi-viṣayatvam brahmaṇaḥ.

William Law said: 'Away, then, with the fictions and workings of discursive reason, either for or against Christianity! They are only the wanton spirit of the mind, whilst ignorant of God and insensible of its own nature and condition. . . . For neither God, nor heaven, nor hell, nor the devil, nor the flesh, can be any other way knowable in you or by you, but by their own existence and manifestation in you. And any pretended knowledge of any of those things, beyond and without this self-evident sensibility of their birth within you, is only such knowledge of them as the blind man hath of the light that has never entered into him.'

[4] *svabhāvato viṣaya-viṣayānīndriyāni, na ca brahma-viṣayāṇi.* Ś.B. See also *Kaṭha U.* II. 1. 1; P.U., p. 630.

[5] Rabindranath Tagore: *Kabīr's Poems*, pp. 95, 121.

[6] I. 3. 28; III. 2. 24.

'contest the truth of another possessing knowledge of *Brahman*, vouched for as it is by his heart's conviction?'[1] The experience is intimate, ineffable, incommunicable. It is an act of pure apprehension when our whole being is welded into one, an act of impassioned intuition which excludes all conceptual activities. 'Whereas I was blind, I now see.' The self alone is witness to it.[2] The experience of *Brahman* cannot be adequately expressed in words. This is true even of ordinary immediate experiences of given objects. Vācaspati says: 'the distinctive attributes of various things cannot, indeed, be declared, though experienced. The difference in the sweetness of the sugar-cane, milk and jaggery cannot, verily, be given expression to, even by the Goddess of Learning.'[3] The experiences which we cannot know from perception or inference are described in the *Vedas*; hence their authoritativeness.[4] Even those who look upon *Brahman* as personal God admit that his nature is inconceivable except through the *Vedas*.[5]

Mere inferential knowledge will not do for the realisation of *Brahman*. It is to be used as an aid for the interpretation of the *Vedānta* texts. This is admitted by the Vedic Scripture.[6]

R. repudiates the idea of inferring the existence of an omniscient and omnipotent God from the nature of the world. He holds that the reality of God cannot be known through any means of proof such as perception and inference. He is known only through scriptural evidence.

Madhva also believes that inference by itself cannot prove that *Brahman* is the cause of the production, etc., of the world.

[1] Ś.B. IV. 1. 15.

[2] *ātma-sākṣikam anutpannam*. Ś. on B.U. IV. 4. 8.

Bergson says that religion represents 'the crystallisation of what mysticism has poured, while hot, into the soul of man. Through religion all men get a little of what a few privileged souls possessed in full'. *The Two Sources of Morality and Religion*, E.T. (1935), p. 227.

Francis Rous (seventeenth century) says: 'The soul has two eyes—one human reason, the other far excelling that, a divine and spiritual light. By it the soul doth see spiritual things as truly as the corporal eye doth corporal things.' *The Threefold Life* III. 31.

[3] *na hi te te asādhāraṇa-dharmā anubhūyamānā api śakyā vaktum; na khalv ikṣu-kṣīra-guḍādīnām madhura-rasa-bhedāḥ śakyāḥ sarasvatyāpy ākhyātum.* I. 1. 3.

[4] Sāyaṇa in his introduction to the *Ṛg Veda* quotes a verse:

pratyakṣeṇānumityā vā yas tūpāyo na dṛśyate
enaṁ vidanti vedena tasmād vedasya vedatā.

[5] Cp. *Skanda purāṇa:*

nendriyaiḥ nānumānaiś ca na tarkaiḥ śakyate vibhum
jñātuṁ nārāyaṇaṁ devaṁ veda-vedyaṁ sanātanam.

II. 7. 19. 14.

[6] *śrutyaiva ca sahāyatvena tarkasyāpy abhyupetatvāt.* Ś.B. I. 1. 2. See B.U. II. 4. 5; C.U. VI. 14. 2.

Śrīpati holds that the *Vedas* were created by *Śiva* and the texts were intended for the glorification of *Śiva*. This is against the *Pūrva Mīmāṁsā* view that the *Vedas* are eternal and uncreated. The nature of *Brahman* can be understood not through discussion but through the testimony of the *Vedas*.

Vallabha combines the second and the third *sūtrās* in one. He believes that we can know only on the evidence of the Scriptures that *Brahman* is the cause of the world.

A rationalist takes the high *a priori* road and attempts to deduce the universe from a few fixed principles. The inadequacy of rational knowledge is accepted by all knowers of God.[1] There are religious leaders both in the East and in the West who demand a complete sacrifice of the intellect. If they say that empirical science can give no knowledge of God or that our thoughts of God cannot be adequate to the Divine Reality but fall inevitably into contradictions or that mere thinking is not a substitute for experience, they are not unreasonable. But highest experience is not irrational. Faith seeks understanding.[2] The God one infers is an idea and does not give religious apprehension. It is direct experience that is registered in the Scriptures. Faith is not blind acquiescence in external authority. 'The wise man after studying the Scriptures and becoming devoted to wisdom and knowledge throws away the Scriptures even as one throws away the straw after collecting the grain.'[3] 'When one knows the truth there is no need for the *Vedas*.'[4]

There are those who have neither experience nor rational knowledge of God. They have neither sight nor proof. They have faith in the Scriptures. In faith we believe with our hearts while in science we believe with our minds. But the word faith has another meaning. It is not merely acceptance of authority without proof or experience. It is the response of the whole man, which includes assent of intellect and energy of will. Men of faith are men of power who have assimilated the truth and made it into a creative principle. God becomes the light and life from which they act, the strange power

[1] 'The wisdom of this world is foolishness with God.' I Corinthians iii. 19; see also ii. 14.

[2] Cp. St Anselm: *Fides quaerens intellectum.* 'O Lord, I do not dare to search into thy depths, for my understanding is in no wise equal thereto. Yet I *do* yearn to understand something of thy truth which my heart believes. Not indeed that I seek to understand in order that I may believe, but I believe in order that I may understand.' (*Credo ut intelligam.*)

St Thomas Aquinas states the rationality of the beliefs he holds. Vidyāraṇya says that reasoning in accord with experience is useful, not mere reasoning. *svānubhūty anusāreṇa tarkyatām mā kutarkyatām. Pañcadaśī* VI. 30.

[3] *grantham abhyasya medhāvī jñāna-vijñāna-tat-paraḥ*
palālam iva dhānyārthī tyajet grantham aśeṣataḥ.

Uttara Gītā 20.

[4] *vedair nāsti prayojanam. Ibid.* 22.

beside which our own power is weakness. God is the name we give to that interior principle which exceeds us while forming the very centre of our being.

The second and third *sūtras* demonstrate the intimate connection and continuity of reason and intuition.

The greatest of the mystics are particularly sensitive to the rational aspect of existence. They rise to the mystical elevation not only through intuition but through the strictly logical sequence of rational thought. The seers of the *Upaniṣads* and the *Buddha,* Plato and Plotinus point to the validity of mystical experience on grounds of logical thought. In these days when many regard themselves as the elect of God, as the chosen instruments of the Holy Spirit, and possess a sublime confidence in their own infallibility, it is essential to emphasise the continuity of reason and intuition and the predominantly rational character of religious insight. As the experience has a cognitive quality about it, the judgments based on it should be subjected to logical analysis. Logical scrutiny is the one safeguard against mere caprice. If the tradition is to be preserved we need men who illustrate it in their own experience. When the Princess in the story cried out in despair as to what would happen to the Vedic tradition,[1] Kumārila Bhaṭṭa reassured her that there was no need for fear as the great teacher was alive.[2]

Section 4 (4)

HARMONY OF TEXTS

I. 1. 4. This section declares that *Brahman* is the meaning of all scriptural passages. Their differences are only apparent and are capable of reconciliation. The many passages have one purport.

tat tu samanvayāt

But that is the result of the harmony (of the different scriptural statements).

tat: that; *tu:* but.

samanvayāt being the result of the harmony of the different texts.

The word *tu*, but, according to Ś., excludes the *prima facie* view.[3] The objection is raised that the Scriptures which are said to be the source of our knowledge of *Brahman* speak of *Brahman* in different ways. We must get the connected meaning of the different texts of the *Upaniṣads.*[4]

[1] *kiṁ karomi kva gacchāmi vedān ka uddhariṣyati.*

[2] *mā vibheṣi varārohe bhaṭṭācaryo'sti bhūtale.*

[3] *tu śabdaḥ pūrva-pakṣa-vyāvṁtyarthaḥ.* Ś.

[4] *evam eva samanvito hy aupaniṣadaḥ pada-samudāyaḥ.* R.

Even as there are order and harmony in the universe so in knowledge. Though the mystery of *Brahman* is, strictly speaking, incommunicable, it would be hidden and mute without some form of knowledge. When words come up fresh and breathless from the embrace of Reality they carry power and authority.[1] Language is, at best, an instrument and all instruments are subject to imperfection.

Ś. starts his discussion on this *sūtra* by stating the objection that the *Vedas* deal with ritual and the *Vedānta* passages are not intended for ritual.[2] We cannot have an injunction with regard to a thing already existing,[3] and so the *Vedas* dealing as they do with ritual cannot be the source of the knowledge of *Brahman*. If it is said that the *Vedas* enjoin us to contemplate, we have to note that contemplation, which depends on the establishment of differences of the contemplated, contemplator, contemplation cannot occur in the case of *Brahman* which is devoid of all differences and is to be known only through the *Vedānta*.[4] Though Vedic statements are generally treated as authoritative in relation to injunctions, the authoritativeness of the means of valid knowledge consists in their generating knowledge which is uncontradicted, not already understood and indubitable.[5] Though the generation of this kind of knowledge is known by the nature of presumptive implication from the nature of the effect, yet in the generation of this knowledge, it is not dependent on any other means of valid knowledge. The *Vedas* give us not only injunctions with regard to ritual but also *Brahma*-knowledge.[6] The authority for *Brahman* is the sacred teaching.[7]

[1] Cp. Max Picard: 'The perfect silence is heard in the perfect word.' Wittgenstein says: 'There is, indeed, the inexpressible. This *shows* itself: it is the mystical.' *Tractatus Logico-Philosophicus* (1922).

[2] *āmnāyasya kriyārthatvād ānarthakyam atadarthānām. Pūrva Mīmāṁsā* I. 2. 1. Cp. also: *tad bhūtānāṁ kriyārthena samāmnāyaḥ.* 'The [words] denoting those existent things are to be connected with [passages] whose purport is ritual.' *Purva Mīmāṁsā* I. 1. 25. *dṛṣṭo hi tasyārthaḥ karmāvabodhanaṁ nāma.* 'Its purport is indeed seen to be what is called the teaching of ritual.' Śābara on *Pūrva Mīmāṁsā* I. 1. 1. Again: *codaneti kriyāyāḥ pravartakaṁ vacanam.* 'An injunction is a statement which prompts to action.' Śābara on *Pūrva Mīmāṁsā* I. 1. 2.

Cp. also: *pravṛttir vā nivṛttir vā nityena kṛtakena vā*
puṁsām yenopadiśyeta tacchāstram abhidhīyate.

'Participation in activity or abstention from it in respect of the obligatory or the occasional, that by which these are taught to men is called sacred teaching.' Quoted in *Bhāmatī* I. 1. 4.

[3] *na ca pariniṣṭhite vastu-svarūpe vidhiḥ sambhavati, kriyā-viṣayatvād vidheḥ.*

[4] *upāsyopāsakopasānādi-bheda-siddhyadhīnopāsanā na nirasta-samasta-bheda-prapañce vedānta-vedye brahmaṇi sambhavati. Bhāmatī.*

[5] *abādhitānadhigatāsandigdha-bodha-janakatvam hi pramāṇatvam pramāṇānām. Bhāmatī.*

[6] *īdṛg-bodha-janakatvaṁ ca kārye vidhīnām. Bhāmatī.*

[7] *tasmāt siddham brahmaṇaḥ śāstra-pramāṇatvam.* Ś.

Another objection is raised. Though the *Veda* is the means of gaining a right knowledge of *Brahman*, yet it suggests *Brahman* only as the object of certain injunctions even as the sacrificial post, the *āhavanīya* fire, etc., though they are supra-mundane, are intimated by the sacred teaching (only) as subsidiary to an injunction.[1] Even if it is said that there is a distinction between the fruit of the knowledge of *Brahman* and the fruit of the knowledge of religious duty, a mere statement of the truth of *Brahman* is not enough to give us the knowledge of *Brahman*. That is why one is asked to seek the Self, desire to know the Self. So the objector holds that *Brahman* should be acknowledged to have sacred teaching as authority only as the content of an injunction of realisation.[2]

It is said in reply that there is a difference in nature between ritual and *Brahman*, in respect of their knowledge and fruit.[3] The fruits of actions, meritorious or simple, are happiness and misery. There are gradations of happiness, rising in degrees of excellence from the world of men to that of *Brahmā*. Similarly there are degrees of misery from the world of men down to the hell known as *avīci*. All that is both produced and destructible.[4] The fruit of the knowledge of the Self is, however, final, unembodied, unsurpassable and being naturally established is eternal and unproduced. This eternal reality is not the fruit of an injunction whose content is contemplation. The state of final release which is non-embodiment is distinct from the fruit of ritual to be observed. It is eternal.[5]

In eloquent phrases, Ś. describes the state of *mokṣa*. 'This is absolute, immutably eternal, all-pervasive like the ether, devoid of all modifications, eternally contented, without parts, self-luminous by nature, which merit and demerit together with their fruit do not approach, not the three times [past, present and future]. This is the non-embodiment called final release.'[6] If this is the nature of final release, it is not something to be accomplished, or done. As soon as

[1] *yady api śāstra-prāmāṇakam brahma: tathāpi pratipatti-viṣayatāyaiva śāstreṇa brahma samarpyate, yathā yūpāhavanīyādīny-alaukikāny api vidhi-śeṣatayā śāstreṇa samarpyante tadvat.* Ś.

[2] *tasmāt pratipatti-vidhi-viṣayatāyaiva śāstra-pramāṇakam brahmā-bhyupagantavyam.* Ś.

[3] *karma-brahma-vidyā-phalayor vailakṣaṇyāt.* Ś.

[4] *puṇyāpuṇya-karmaṇoḥ phale sukha-duḥkhe, tatra manuṣya-lokam ārabhya ā-brahma-lokāt sukhasya tāratamyam adhikādhikotkarṣaḥ evam manuṣya-lokam ārabhya duḥkha-tāratamyamācavīci-lokāt, tasya tasya sarvaṁ kāryam ca vināśi ca. ātyantikaṁ tv aśariratvam, anatiśayam svabhāvasiddhatayā nityam akāryam ātma-jñānasya phalam. Bhāmatī.*

[5] Cp. *ata evānuṣṭheya-karma-phala-vilakṣaṇam mokṣākhyam aśarīratvam nityam iti siddham.* Ś.

[6] *idaṁ tu pāramārthikam kūṭastha-nityaṁ, vyomavat sarva-vyāpi, sarva-vikriyā-rahitam, nitya-tṛptam, nir-avayavam, svayam-jyotiḥ-svabhāvam, yatra dharmādharmau saha kāryeṇa kālatrayaṁ ca nopāvartate, tad etad aśarīratvam mokṣākhyam.*

knowledge arises, ignorance disappears.[1] Ś. affirms that the knowledge of *Brahman* is not dependent on human activity.[2] It is not something to be attained: it is by nature attained by all.[3] It is not to be understood by anyone either through the ritual part of the *Veda* or logical reasoning.[4]

If the aims of the two *śāstras*, *Dharma-mīmāṁsā* and *Brahma-mīmāṁsā* were not different, there would have been no justification for two separate *śāstras*. Their very distinction makes out that the knowledge of *Brahman* is enjoined for the purpose of final release even as sacrifices are enjoined for the purpose of obtaining the heavenly world and the like.

There is no opposition between the two *śāstras*. Madhva argues that the Scriptures declare *Viṣṇu* to be *Brahman*, the ultimate cause of the world and not *Śiva*.

Bertrand Russell admits that great thinkers are sometimes led by mysticism (I. 1. 3) and sometimes by science (I. 1. 2) to the problems of philosophy. 'But', he observes, 'the greatest men who have been philosophers have felt the need *both* of science and of mysticism; the attempt to harmonise the two was what made their life, and what always must, for all the arduous uncertainty, make philosophy, to some minds, a greater thing than either science or religion.'[5] Science and religion require to be reconciled.

Today the *samanvaya* or harmonisation has to be extended to the living faiths of mankind. Religion concerns man as man and not man as Jew or Christian, Hindu or Buddhist, Sikh or Muslim. As the author of the B.S. tried to reconcile the different doctrines prevalent in his time, we have to take into account the present state of our knowledge and evolve a coherent picture.[6] Beliefs retain their vigour for a long time after their roots have withered or their sources have silted up. We must express our beliefs in the context and shape of the real questions and search of modern men. The way in which faith has hitherto expressed itself, the categories which it has evolved, the very nature of the world and the hope towards which faith directs its attention have lost their meaning and reality for the

[1] *vidyodaya evāvidyā-nivṛttiḥ. Brahmasiddhi*, p. 32.
[2] *na puruṣa-vyāpāra-tantrā brahma vidyā.* [3] *nityāpta-svarūpatvāt.* Ś.
[4] *vidhi-kāṇḍe tarka-samaye vā kenacid adhigataḥ.* Ś.
[5] *Mysticism and Logic* (1918).
[6] Origen writes to his former pupil Gregory the Wonder-worker: 'I should like to see you use all the resources of your mind on Christianity and make that your ultimate object. I hope that to that end you will take from Greek philosophy everything capable of serving as an introduction to Christianity and from geometry and astronomy all ideas useful in expounding the Holy Scriptures; so that what philosophers say of geometry, music, grammar, rhetoric and astronomy—that they assist philosophy—we too may be able to say of philosophy itself in relation to Christianity.' Epistle Gregory I, quoted in *Origen* by Jean Danielou (1955), p. 16.

modern world. Our society is shaken to its foundations. The conventional call on the part of religions to believe in God, work for his glory and purpose has become open to question. Philosophy is not a mere intellectual pursuit labelling and classifying the contents of thought but the creation of a new awareness of oneself and the world. *Samanvaya* or reconciliation is the need of our age. The global, all-comprehensive changes which are taking place represent something new in the structure of human society, though they are not deviations from the normal course of history. The world community which we envisage can be sustained only by a community of ideals. We have to look beyond the political and economic arrangements to ultimate spiritual issues. We have to fashion a new type of man who uses the instruments he has devised with a renewed awareness that he is capable of greater things than mastery of nature.

Unfortunately rivalries among religions are retarding the growth of an international community, the fellowship of man. If we accept the view that the Scriptures of the world are the records of the experiences of the great seers who have expressed their sense of the inner meaning of the world through their intense insight and deep imagination, we will not adopt an attitude of dogmatic exclusiveness. Symmachus in his controversy with St Ambrose said: 'It is impossible that so great a mystery should be approached by one road only.' Nicholas of Cusa, echoing the words of the prophet Muhammad, observes: 'God is sought in various ways and called by various names in the various religions . . . he has sent various prophets and teachers in various ages to the various peoples.' The view is in agreement with the concept of universal revelation that has the support of Justin, Clement and Origen. The Logos or the Word of God inspired all that is true and good in the religious thinking of men. The seeds of Logos, *Logos Spermatikos*, were scattered in all mankind. Justin proclaims: 'All who have lived according to the Logos are Christians, even if they are generally accounted as atheists, like Socrates and Heracleitus among the Greeks.'[1] Clement of Alexandria looked upon Greek philosophy as 'a preparation for Christ'; 'a schoolmaster to lead us to Christ'.[2] He brought about the marriage between Platonism and Christianity. The early Fathers enriched Christian mysteries by using the ideas of Socrates and Plato. They expressed Christianity in terms familiar to the people trained in Greek thought. Augustine's views are well known. 'The salvation brought by the Christian religion has never been unavailable for any who was worthy of it.' 'What is now called the Christian religion always existed in antiquity and was never absent from the beginning of the human race until Christ appeared in the flesh. At this time, the true religion which was already there, began to be called Christianity.'[3] It is now admitted that in the course of its development

[1] *Apology* I. 46. [2] *Stromata* IV. 28, 32. [3] *Retractions* I. 13.

Christianity has drawn upon Greek metaphysics and mystery religions. The religion of the New Testament according to St Paul is 'debtor both to Greeks and barbarians'.[1] Now that the religious environment has been world-wide and the living faiths are encountering one another the idea of fellowship among religions is gaining ground and a reconciliation or *samanvaya* is taking place.

The great sages are symbols of the Spirit in which they are one. While we have to communicate our faith through words and symbols, forms and creeds in accordance with the accidents of our race, nation or training, we use them to help us to realise the presence of the Spirit in us. If we strive with a sincere intent and a whole heart, we get not to a new faith but to the heart of all faith.

The first four *sūtras* are said to be the essence of the teaching of the B.S.

Section 5 (5-11)

INADEQUACY OF NATURALISM

I. 1. 5. Section 5 (5–11) suggests by various arguments that the cause of the world is conscious reality and cannot be identified with the non-conscious *pradhāna* or matter as the *Sāṁkhya* system holds.

īkṣater nāśabdam.

Because of seeing (*matter which is*) *not founded on the Scripture is not* (*the cause*).

īkṣateḥ: on account of seeing; *na:* not; *aśabdam:* not founded on Scripture.

The primary matter, *pradhāna,* is sometimes said to be the root cause of the world. From the principle that every effect has a cause, to avoid infinite regress, we affirm a primary cause which itself is uncaused. 'That in which the world, divested of name and shape, resides, some call *prakṛti,* others *māyā,* others atoms.'[2] *Devī Māhātmya* says: 'You are the power of *Viṣṇu,* endless valour. You are the source of the universe, the primal *māyā*. By you all this is enchanted [confused]. When you are gracious you are the cause of final emancipation.'[3]

The *Sāṁkhya* thinkers argue that the non-intelligent matter *pradhāna* consisting of the three strands of *sattva, rajas* and *tamas* is the cause of the world. This view is devoid of scriptural evidence.

[1] *Romans* i. 14.

[2] *nāmarūpa-vinirmuktam yasmin saṁtiṣṭhate jagat.*
tam āhuḥ prakṛtim kecin māyām vanye pare tv aṇūn.
Quoted from *Bṛhad-Vāsiṣṭha* in the *Pātanjala-bhāṣya-Vārttika.*

[3] *tvam vaiṣṇavī śaktir ananta-vīryā viśvasya bījam paramāsi māyā sammohitaṁ devi samastam etat tvaṁ vai prasannā bhuvi mukti-hetuḥ.*

Pradhāna cannot be the cause, for the quality of seeing, thinking is ascribed to the cause in the Scripture. The passage says *tad aikṣata bahu syām prajāyeyeti.*[1] 'It saw, [thought], may I be many, may I grow forth.' Thought is prior to all creation.[2]

The *Sāṁkhya* thinkers may say that thought is a quality of the *sattva* (goodness) quality of the *pradhāna.* It is said that when the three *guṇas* are in equipoise in the state of *pradhāna* knowledge which is a quality of goodness is not possible. There can be no knowledge without a witnessing principle of consciousness.[3] If it is said that *pradhāna* possesses the quality of knowledge owing to the witnessing principle, the Lord, then it would be more reasonable to assume that the all-knowing *Brahman* itself is the cause of the world.

This *sūtra* is used to suggest that the Ultimate Reality is not *nirguṇa-Brahman,* but *saguṇa,* Personal God. R. develops his view that the universe of sentient and non-sentient beings constitutes the body of the Lord. According to Śaivites, *Śakti* and *Śiva* are both *Brahman* and through their harmony they ensoul the world.[4] According to Śrīkaṇṭha, *Śiva* qualified by *Śakti, śakti-viśiṣṭa-śiva,* is *Brahman.*

Baladeva gives a different interpretation: 'Since [*Brahman* is] seen [i.e. mentioned by the Scripture] [he is] not inexpressible.'

Vijñāna-bhikṣu points out that *Brahman* must be a person since it is said that he perceives or desires. Perception or desire cannot be attributed to unconscious *prakṛti.* Vijñāna-bhikṣu questions Ś.'s assertion that the purport of the *sūtra* is that *prakṛti* is not the cause of the world since the idea of *prakṛti* is un-Vedic. He quotes from the *Upaniṣads* many passages where *prakṛti* is spoken of as the cause of the world, as the energy of God, for example, in the Ś.U. Even though the magician may withhold his magic, the magic power is in him.[5]

It is clear that the Sūtrakāra does not hold that the world is due to *avidyā.* He takes the problem of the creation of the world seriously and urges that the world is the product not of *pradhāna* of the *Sāṁkhya* system but of *Brahman* possessed of intelligence. There is no suggestion here of the unreality of the world.

Ś. holds that *Brahman's* power is *māyā,* that it exists and functions only as residing in *Brahman,* that, though thus informed, it is transcended by *Brahman.* The effect is *Brahman* functioning through *māyā* and is not non-existent. The world is unreal apart from *Brahman* but is real as founded in *Brahman.*[6]

[1] C.U. VI. 2. 3; P.U., p. 449; see also *Aitareya Āraṇyaka* II. 4. 1. 2. *Praśna U.* VI. 3.

[2] *sarveṣv api sṛṣṭi-prakaraṇeṣvīkṣā-pūrvikaiva sṛṣṭiḥ pratīyate.* R.

[3] *nāsākṣikā sattva-vṛttir jānāti nābhidhīyate, na cācetanasya pradhānasya sākṣitvam asti.* Ś.

[4] *śaktiḥ śivaś ca sac-chabda-prakṛti-pratyayoditau*
tau brahma-sāmarasyena samasta-jagad-ātmakau.

[5] *māyāyā vyāpāra-nivṛttir evāvagamyate na nāśaḥ.*

[6] *brahma-vyatirekeṇa kārya-jātasyābhāva iti gamyate.* Ś.

I. 1. 6. *gauṇaś cen nātma śabdāt*

On account of the word self (used for the cause), (the meaning of the word 'seeing') is not secondary (figurative).
gauṇaḥ: secondary, figurative; *cen:* if; *na:* not; *ātma-śabdāt:* on account of the word 'self'.

If it is argued that the word 'seeing' is used in a secondary or figurative sense in some passages 'That fire thought; that water thought',[1] and it may be so treated here, the answer is that the word 'self' is actually employed. It is the self that sees or thinks and there is no need to look upon seeing as figurative. In the passages 'fire thought' or 'water thought' what thinks is the self acting through them.[2]

Baladeva gives a different interpretation. If it be said that the creator of the world is *gauṇa* (i.e. *saguṇa Brahman* associated with the qualities of *prakṛti* possessing the *sattva guṇa*), the *sūtra* says it cannot be on account of the term 'self'. This term 'self' can apply only to the *nirguṇa-Brahman*, free from the qualities of *prakṛti*.

I. 1. 7. *tan-niṣṭhasya mokṣopadeśāt*

Because release is taught of him who takes his stand on (is devoted to) that (Brahman).
tan-niṣṭhasya: of him who concentrates on that Self (or *Brahman*).
mokṣopadeśāt: because of the instruction of release.

If it be said that the term 'self' may be used in regard to *pradhāna*, figuratively, that the real (*sat*) meant in the *Upaniṣad*[3] is the non-intelligent matter, it is said in reply that release is possible only with concentration on Self which is intelligence. The whole teaching in the *Upaniṣad* is clear that release is possible for one who is devoted to the Real as self, *tat satyam, sa ātmā.*

Devotion to the non-intelligent principle is the cause of all suffering; it cannot lead to release. Even those who advocate the view of *pradhāna* as the cause of the world do not maintain that he who is devoted to *pradhāna* attains release.[4]

Baladeva argues that salvation is promised to him who relies on *nirguṇa-Brahman.*

I. 1. 8. *heyatvāvacanāc ca*

And because there is no statement that it has to be discarded.
heyatva: the quality of being discarded; *avacanāt:* because there is no statement; *ca:* and.

The word *sat* has not been used to indicate *pradhāna* even as a first step to the knowledge that the real is *Brahman*. In such a case

[1] C.U. VI. 2. 3, 4; P.U., p. 449. *tat teja aikṣata. tā āpa aikṣanta.*
[2] C.U. VI. 3. 2.
[3] C.U. VI. 2ff.
[4] *pradhāna-kāraṇa-vādinopi hi pradhāna-niṣṭhasya mokṣam nābhyupagacchanti.* R.

there would have been instruction to discard the provisional definition of *Brahman* as *pradhāna*. There are no statements that this view has to be discarded.

What is called *arundhatī-nyāya* is adopted here. If we are to point out the small star Arundhatī, we first direct attention to a big star near it and say 'that is Arundhatī' though it is really not so. Later on, we withdraw the first direction and point to the real Arundhatī. It is possible in the same way that the teacher may direct the pupil through the non-self, *pradhāna*, to the self but in that case there would have been a statement that the self is not of the nature of *pradhāna* but there is no such statement.

Ca for Bhāskara means contradiction of the original proposition.

Nimbārka says [*pradhāna*] cannot be denoted by the terms Existent, Self, etc., for there is no [scriptural] statement of its having to be discarded. *Pradhāna* cannot serve the purpose of salvation. Scripture does not give any other purpose for Scripture does not teach anything which does not fulfil a purpose.

Baladeva says that if *saguṇa-Brahman* were the Creator of the world, Scripture would have said that he was inferior and fit to be discarded.

In some versions there is, at this point, another *sūtra*, *pratijñāvirodhāt*. R. and Nimbārka have it as a separate *sūtra* while Ś., Bhāskara, Vallabha and Baladeva do not mention it.

On account of the contradiction of the initial statement.
pratijñā: initial statement, definite thesis.
virodhāt: on account of the contradiction.

The initial statement is that through the knowledge of the one reality, all things are to be known.[1] From the knowledge of *pradhāna*, we cannot know all things for conscious beings cannot be the effects of non-conscious principle. There would thus arise a contradiction of the view that through the knowledge of one, there would be the knowledge of all.

I. 1. 9. *svāpyayāt*

On account (of the individual soul) entering the self.
sva: the Self, *ātman*.
apyayāt: on account of entering.

Pradhāna cannot be the Self for it is said 'When a person sleeps, as it is called, then he has reached pure being. He has gone to his own, *svam apīto bhavati*. Therefore, we say, he sleeps for he has gone to his own.'[2] Here the Real is said to be the Self. It cannot be the *pradhāna*.

If we say that the word 'own' denotes *pradhāna* we will have the absurd position that an intelligent entity is being resolved into a

[1] C.U. VI. 1.
[2] C.U. VI. 8. 1; P.U., p. 456.

non-intelligent one.[1] There is also the other passage that in the state of dreamless sleep the Self is absorbed in the Self.[2] It cannot be absorbed in the non-conscious *pradhāna*.

R. quotes the *Vṛttikāra* to the effect: 'Then he becomes united with the Real—this is proved by [all creatures] entering into it and coming back out of it.'

Baladeva reads the *sūtra* differently, *svāpyāt*, and interprets it differently. '[The Creator is not the Personal God] because "he [the Creator] merges into himself" and *saguṇa-Brahman* merges into something other than himself.'

I. 1. 10. *gati-sāmānyāt*

On account of the uniformity of teaching (Brahman is to be treated as the cause).

gati: teaching, primary meaning, *pravṛtti*. R. apprehension. *avagati*, Niṁbārka.

sāmānyāt: on account of uniformity.

The *Vedānta* texts are agreed in teaching that the cause of the world is the intelligent *Brahman*.[3] There is no disagreement on this point.

R. says that the import of the scriptural texts is uniform, that *Brahman* alone is the cause and not any other.

Madhva holds that there is *tāratamya* among the nine different kinds of devotees.[4] Śuka is of a different view. For him those who practise *bhakti* in the nine forms mentioned in the *Bhāgavata* are on a level.[5]

Nimbārka points out that as a conscious cause is indicated by all the scriptural texts, a non-conscious cause is not acceptable.

Baladeva says that Scriptures uniformly teach *nirguṇa-Brahman* and not *saguṇa-Brahman*.

I. 1. 11. *śrutatvāc ca*

And because it is stated in the śruti (that the all-knowing Brahman *is the cause of the world).*

śrutatvāt: because it is stated in the *śruti*, i.e. Vedic Scripture; *ca:* and.

The reference is to the Ś.U.[6] where the All-knowing Lord is said to be the cause.

Ś. gives a number of passages where the Supreme is described in

[1] *pradhānam ātmīyatvāt sva-śabodenocyeta, evam api cetano 'cetanam apyetīti. viruddham āpadyeta.* Ś.

[2] B.U. IV. 3. 21.

[3] *samānaiva hi sarveṣu vedānteṣu cetana-kāraṇāvagatiḥ.* Ś.

[4] *mokṣāhkye laye tāratamyaṁ devānām api dṛśyate. Mahābhārata-tātparya-nirṇaya.* I.

[5] *tasmād anyatamāpi navānām api bhaktīnām mokṣa-rūpa-phalasya samānatvāt.*

[6] VI. 9.

negative terms and others where he is said to be all-knowing, etc. He suggests that this dual description of *Brahman* is relative to our states of knowledge and ignorance.[1]

R. affirms that the *Brahman* which forms the object of enquiry possesses attributes such as thinking and so on in their real literal sense. On the theory that *Brahman* is nothing but distinctionless intelligence, even the witnessing function of consciousness would be unreal.

There are passages which describe *Brahman* as devoid of determinations and others which describe *Brahman* as endowed with all auspicious qualities. They indicate that from the cosmic end *Brahman* is viewed as *Īśvara* and in himself as absolute being devoid of all determinations. The *Upaniṣads* do not suggest any status of inferiority to one or the other. The *Sūtrakāra* in I. 1. 10 makes out that the teaching of the texts is uniform.

This whole section is viewed by Madhva not as repudiating the *Sāṁkhya* view of *pradhāna* but as critical of the *Advaita* view of the indescribability of *Brahman* as being beyond the scope of Vedic utterances. *na cāśabdatvam itara-siddham.* The witnessing character of the Supreme is inconsistent with the Absolute without determinations. *Brahman* is described in the Scriptures for they enjoin that *Brahman* should be perceived. If *Brahman* cannot be grasped and described by any of the *pramāṇas*, there would not be any proof of its existence.

Though R. follows Ś. in his interpretation of this section, he says that *this section* does not support the non-dualistic theory of *Brahman* without determination.[2]

While this section (5–11) is viewed by the other commentators as dealing with the question whether *Brahman* or *pradhāna* is the creator of the world, Baladeva discusses in this section the question whether *nirguṇa-Brahman* or *saguṇa-Brahman* is the creator of the world.

Section 6 (12–19)

THE SUPREME AS BLISS

It is now established that the cause of the world is an intelligent principle and cannot be identified with the non-intelligent *pradhāna* of the *Sāṁkhya* system. From this section onwards to the end of the chapter, we find a discussion of certain terms used in the *Upaniṣads*,

[1] *evam sahasraśo vidyāvidyā-viṣaya-bhedena brahmaṇo dvi-rūpatām darśayanti vedānta-vākyāni.*

[2] *ata eva, nirviśeṣa-cinmātra-brahma-vādino'pi sūtrakāreṇābhiḥ śrutibhir nirastā veditavyāḥ. pāramārthika-mukhyekṣaṇādi-guṇa-yogi jijñāsyam brahmeti vyavasthāpanāt; nirviśeṣavāde hi sākṣitvam apy apāramārthikam.* R.

whether they refer to the Supreme Lord, the individual soul or unintelligent matter. The first topic considered is the meaning of *ānanda* or bliss in relation to the Supreme Reality.[1]

I. 1. 12. *ānandamayo'bhyāsāt*

(*Brahman is*) *a being full of bliss, because of repetition.*
ānandamayaḥ: full of bliss; *abhyāsāt:* because of repetition.

The text considered in this *sūtra* is the second chapter of the T.U. (1–5) where we have a progressive definition of the nature of self as consisting of *anna*, food, *prāṇa*, life, *manas*, mind, *vijñāna*, understanding. Then it is said 'different from and within that which consists of understanding is the self consisting of bliss'.[2] If it be said that the Self consisting of bliss is a secondary and not the principal self, that it is the empirical self subject to rebirth,[3] as it forms a link in a series of selves, since it is said to have joy and so forth for its limbs and as it is embodied, the reply is given that it is the Highest Self on account of frequent repetition in the *Upaniṣads*. Though it is a link in a series of selves, it is the innermost self of all. For the purpose of logical exposition and easy comprehension, we are led on from one stage to another till we reach the Highest. This accounts for the attribution of limbs and body to it. It is not said of *ānanda* that there is another self inside it, as it was said of matter, life, mind and understanding.[4] The objector quotes the text, *brahma puccham pratiṣṭhā:*[5] *Brahman*, the lower part is the foundation. If *Brahman* is the foundation, *ānanda* cannot be *Brahman*. When it is said that *Brahman* is the *puccha*, it is meant that it is the foundation of all, *sarvādhāra*, and not that it is merely a limb (*avayava*) of *ānanda*. The self consisting of bliss is the Supreme Self.[6]

Ś. gives a twofold explanation of the *ānanda-mayādhikaraṇa*.

R. says that the self of bliss is other than the individual soul, it is *Brahman* itself.[7] He argues that the self consisting of knowledge is the

[1] Ś. holds that the enquiry is continued to explain the distinction between *nir-viśeṣa Brahman*, or the Absolute without determinations, and *sa-viśeṣa Brahman*, or the Absolute with determinations. George Thibaut writes 'But that such an investigation is actually carried on in the remaining portion of the first *Adhyāya*, appears neither from the wording of the *Sūtras* nor even from Ś.'s own treatment of the Vedic texts referred to in the *Sūtras*'. Introduction to Vol. I of the *Vedānta Sūtras with the Commentary of Ś.* (1890), pp. xxxii–xxxiii.

[2] *tasmād vā etasmād vijñāna-mayāt anyo'ntara ātmā ānanda-mayaḥ*. II. 5. P.U., p. 546.

[3] *saṁsāry evānanda-maya-ātmā*. The individual self does not become *ānanda-maya* for then it would be the creator of the worlds like the Supreme. The Supreme who is *ānanda-maya* gives bliss to the individuals and cannot itself be an individual. There is always a distinction between the giver and the receiver, the attained and the attainer.

[4] See Ś.B. I. 1. 19.

[5] T.U., II. 5; P.U., pp. 546–7.

[6] *para eva ātmā*. Ś.

[7] *ato vijñāna-mayāj jīvād anya eva paramātmā*. R.

individual self, while the self consisting of bliss is the Highest Self.[1] When *Brahman* is said to be the support, it means that *Brahman* has no support outside itself. *Brahman* is rooted in itself.

For Śrīkaṇṭha, the self of bliss is the *parā-śakti*, otherwise called *param-ākāśa* of which *Brahman* is the support. The Sūtrakāra refers to *Brahman* itself as the self of bliss since there is no fundamental difference between *parā-śakti* which is the attribute or *dharma* of *Brahman* and that which possesses the *dharma*. The *dharmin* is referred to on account of its essential non-difference from *dharma*.

For Nimbārka, that which consists of bliss is the Supreme Self alone and not the individual soul.

I. 1. 13. *vikāra-śabdānneti cen na prācuryāt*

If it is said (*that anandamaya*) *does not* (*denote the highest Self*) *since it is a word denoting modification, it is not so on account of abundance.*
vikāra-śabdāt: because of the word denoting modification.
na iti cet: if it is held that it does not (refer to the Highest Self).
na: not so; *prācuryāt:* on account of abundance.

If the word '*mayaṭ*' is taken to mean 'made of', a product or a modification, then it cannot apply to the Highest Self which is not a product or a modification. It is stated in reply that the word *mayaṭ* need not always mean *vikāra* or modification, it may also mean *prācurya*[2] or abundance. *Brahman* abounds in bliss and this bliss is immeasurable.[3]

Śuka says that it is the Supreme Self only that is primarily contemplated and there is not a suggestion of non-difference between the individual soul and the Supreme Self.[4]

I. 1. 14. *taddhetu vyapadeśāc ca*

And because (*Brahman*) *is declared to be the cause of it* (*the bliss*).
tat: of it (bliss); *hetu* (cause); *vyapadeśāt:* because (*Brahman*) is declared; *ca:* and.

The Self which causes bliss[5] must itself abound in bliss, even as one who gives wealth to others must himself possess abundant wealth.

According to Śrīkaṇṭha, the self of bliss is *cit-śakti*, the energy of consciousness, while the *Brahman* spoken of as the tail or the support is the Supreme *Brahman*.

[1] See B.U. III. 7. 22; P.U., p. 229.
[2] *Pāṇini* V. 4. 21.
[3] T.U. II. 8.
[4] *tasmāt iha śārīratvasya param-ātmany eva paryavasānāt na jīveśvara-abheda-prasakti-gandho'pi iti niścīyate.* See Jaya-tīrtha's *Nyāya-sudhā* I. 1. 25.
[5] *eṣa hy evānandayati.* T.U. II. 7.

I. 1. 15. *māntra-varṇikam eva ca gīyate*

And because the same (Brahman) which is described in the mantra is sung (in the Brāhmana).
māntra-varṇikam: what is described in the *mantra; eva:* the same; *ca:* and (hence); *gīyate:* is sung.

Ānandamaya is *Brahman* because the *Mantra* and the *Brāhmaṇa* portions of the T.U.[1] agree in referring to the same *Brahman.*

I. 1. 16. *netaro'nupapatteḥ*

(Ānandamaya is) not the other, because of inappropriateness.
na: not; *itara:* the other; *anupapatteḥ:* because of inappropriateness.

The individual soul is not capable of the activities of creation, etc. Ś. says that it is impossible for the individual soul or any being other than the Highest Self, to brood over himself before sending forth whatever there is. To think about things to be created and to create the things in such a way as to be non-different from himself are possible only for the Highest Self.[2]

The Sanskrit word for creation is derived from *sṛj,* to emit, to discharge. Creation is an outflow from the Divine. It is not creation out of nothing.

R. explains that the higher self is not *Brahman* without determinations but the all-knowing, blissful *Brahman.* The clause 'from which speech returns along with mind' means that mind and speech are not means for the knowledge of *Brahman.*[3]

Śrīkaṇṭha makes out that *Hiraṇya-garbha,* world-soul, is not the cause of the world, on account of inappropriateness. He begins a new section here consisting of *sūtras* 17–20, to deal with the question whether the Supreme *Iśvara* is the cause of the world or someone else, viz. *Hiraṇya-garbha. Prajā-pati* in the context is equivalent to *paśu-pati.*

I. 1. 17. *bheda-vyapadeśāc ca*

And on account of the declaration of difference (between the two).
bheda: difference; *vyapadeśāt:* on account of the declaration; *ca:* and.

The individual soul and the Self of bliss are represented as different in the *Upaniṣad.*[4] 'That, verily, is the essence of existence. For truly on getting the essence, one becomes blissful.' He who attains cannot be that which is attained.[5]

[1] II. 1 and 5.

[2] *tatra prāk-charīrādyutpatter abhidhyānaṁ sṛjyamānānāṁ vikārāṇām sraṣṭur avyatirekas sarva-vikāra-sṛṣṭiś ca na parasmād ātmano'nyatropapadyate.* Ś.

[3] *vāṅ-manasayos tatrāpramāṇatām vadet.* R.

[4] T.U. II. 7; P.U., pp. 548–9.

[5] *na hi labdhaiva labdhavyo bhavati.* Ś.

Ś. suggests that this and the previous *sūtra* relate to the difference between the Highest Self and the individual self, for in his view the two are the same. The difference between the individual soul and the Absolute Self cannot be regarded as fictitious according to this *sūtra*, though Ś. holds that there is no difference in reality between the individual soul and *Brahman*.

R. refers to another passage in the T.U. (II. 5) and holds that the difference between the individual soul and the Self of bliss is real.

Śrīkaṇṭha says that the *sūtra* states the difference between *Hiraṇya-garbha* and the Supreme Lord.

1. 1. 18. *kāmāc ca nānumānāpekṣā*

And on account of desire, there is no dependence on inference.
kāmāt: on account of desire; *ca:* and; *na:* not; *anumānāpekṣā:* dependence on inference.

The desire 'to become many and to create' makes out that the non-intelligent *pradhāna* cannot be the cause of the world or be one with the Self of bliss for it is incapable of volition. Thought (I. 1. 5) and desire in this *sūtra* suggest that the inference made by the *Sāṁkhya* that *pradhāna* is the root cause of the world is wrong. Will is possible for a conscious being or for the Self of bliss and not for matter, *pradhāna*.

R. and Nimbārka argue that if the individual soul is admitted to be the cause, it must depend on a material cause, *pradhāna*, as a potter depends on clay, etc. But the Supreme Self has no need to depend on any factor outside himself.

Śrīkaṇṭha points out that though *Hiraṇya-garbha* is said to have created the world, it does not stand to reason for it is the Lord himself who is said to have created the world in the form of *Hiraṇya-garbha*.

I. 1. 19. *asminn asya ca tad yogaṁ śāsti*

Besides, in this the union of this with that (Scripture) teaches.
asmin: in this; *asya:* of this; *ca:* and; *tad-yogam:* union with that; *śāsti:* teaches.

Scripture teaches the union or *yoga* of the individual soul with the Self of bliss. When the individual soul attains knowledge, it is united with the Self of bliss, i.e. in the state of release, the two are united. This is possible only if we understand by the Self of bliss, the Highest Self and not either *pradhāna* or the individual soul.[1]

Ś. gives another interpretation of these *sūtras* (12–19). We cannot hold that the affix *mayaṭ* means product or modification with reference to food, life, mind and understanding and means something different, 'abundance' when we come to *ānanda*. The words belong

[1] *tac ca param-ātma-parigrahe ghaṭate, na pradhāna-parigrahe jīva-parigrahe vā; tasmād ānanda-mayaḥ param-ātmeti siddham.* Ś.

to one series and it would be wrong to suggest that only the last word of the series refers to *Brahman*. If *ānanda-maya* denotes *Brahman*, even *anna-maya* should denote it.[1] If it is argued that for other members, there is an inward self, while no such inner self is mentioned for *ānanda-maya*, limbs are attributed to it and *Brahman* is said to be its lower part or support. It is not *ānanda-maya* that is *Brahman* but its support is *Brahman*.[2] *Puccha* is to be taken as support or resting place. B.U. says: 'Only on a particle of this bliss [of *Brahman*] all other creatures live.'[3]

If, in spite of this, we still hold that *ānanda-maya* self is *Brahman*, Ś. urges that it refers to the determinate *Brahman* and not the *Brahman* without determinations.[4] *Ānanda* is the quality of *Brahman* qut not *ānanda-maya*. So the affix *mayaṭ* does not mean abundance but product or modification.[5] Ś., after telling us that the *ānanda-maya-ātmā* or the Self of bliss is the Highest Self,[6] rejects this view and holds that *Brahman* as the foundation is the indeterminate *Brahman* and *ānanda-maya-ātmā* is only the determinate *Brahman*.

The first explanation that *Brahman* is *ānanda-maya*, full of bliss, is accepted by Ś., R., Keśava-Kāṣmīrin, Vallabha and others. Since this interpretation goes against the unqualified character of *Brahman*, Ś. offers a strained explanation that *ānanda-maya* is a vesture of *Brahman*.

The Sūtrakāra evidently means that *Brahman* is full of bliss.

While the indeterminate *Brahman* cannot be spoken of by words or concepts, when we attempt to describe it we state it to be characterised by bliss and the whole creation is an expression of this bliss or joy. The controversy raised by Ś. relates to the relative superiority of *Brahman* and *Īśvara*, Absolute and God, but the two are co-ordinate though logical and not temporal priority may be given to the indeterminate *Brahman* for *Brahman* must be before it can create.

Bhāskara interprets *tad-yogam* as union with the Lord, i.e. salvation.

Śrīkaṇṭha says that the Lord himself creates the world in the form of *Hiraṇya-garbha*. The latter is the soul of this world.

Baladeva interprets *tad-yogam* as union with fearlessness.

[1] *anna-mayādīnām api tarhi brahmatva-prasaṅgaḥ*. Ś.

[2] *pratiṣṭhā, parāyaṇam eka-nīḍam*. Ś.

[3] IV. 3. 32.

[4] *sa-viśeṣam brahmābhyupagantavyam*. Ś.

[5] *tasmād anna-mayādiṣv ivānanda-maye'pi vikārārtha eva mayaḍ vijñeyo na prācuryārthaḥ*. Ś.

[6] *para evātmā ānanda-mayo bhavitum arhati, tasmād ānanda-mayaḥ param-ātmā iti sthitam*. Ś.B. I. 1. 12; I. 1. 19.

Section 7 (20 and 21)

THE GOLDEN PERSON IN THE SUN AND THE EYE

I. 1. 20 *antas tad-dharmopadeśāt*

The person within (appearing within the sun and the eye is the highest God) because his qualities are mentioned.
antaḥ: within; *tad-dharma-upadeśāt:* because his qualities are mentioned.

This section purports to show that the Golden Person seen within the sun and the Person seen within the eye[1] do not refer to any individual soul of eminence but to the Supreme *Brahman*. While the *Upaniṣads* stress the relativity of all logical knowledge, they yet use this knowledge through symbol and similitude to approximate to the absolute truth, though without ever being able to attain it. The Ultimate can be approached only asymptotically. It can be apprehended in a sort of penumbral manner by way of what Nicholas of Gusa, a distinguished thinker of the fifteenth century, calls conjecture. In Nicholas's view, conjecture does not mean a guess at the truth or a hypothesis but actual though necessarily inadequate truth. This view bears some resemblance to the Thomistic doctrine of Analogy. The *Upaniṣads* use this method. The sun which not only illumines but warms is the best image of the Divine used by the ancient Indians, the Iranians and others.

The passages referred to are C.U. I. 6ff. and I. 7. 5. The objector argues that the person described as possessing form and features, a golden beard, etc., cannot be *Brahman* without determinations. He is not all-pervading and his powers are limited. To this, Ś. answers that only the qualities of God are mentioned in regard to him. The person in the sun is called *ut* and is said to be free from all sins. Freedom from sins is a feature of God and not any individual soul, however eminent. The Person in the eye is declared to be *Ṛk, Sāman*, etc., and is the cause of them all. When it is said that those who sing unto him become wealthy (C.U I. 7. 6), the reference can only be to the Supreme. Ś. says that the Golden Person represents the determinate *Brahman* who is the object of meditation. God by his power can assume any form for the sake of bestowing grace on his devotees.[2]

R. agrees with the view that the Supreme by his mere will can take any shape, human, divine or otherwise so as to render it suitable for the apprehension of the devotee and then satisfy him.[3]

Śrīkaṇṭha identifies the golden person within the sun with *Śiva*

[1] C.U. I. 6.

[2] *parameśvarasyāpīcchā-vaśān māyā-mayaṁ rūpaṁ sādhakānugrahārtham.* Ś.

[3] *tad idaṁ svābhāvikam eva rūpaṁ upāsakānugraheṇa tat pratipatyānuguṇākāram, deva-manuṣyādi-saṁsthānaṁ karoti: svecchāyaiva paramakāruṇiko bhagavān.*

and accounts for the mention of two eyes only and not the third by saying that the third eye is ordinarily closed.

I. 1. 21. *bheda-vyapadeśāc cānyaḥ*

On account of the declaration of difference, there is another (different from the individual souls residing in the sun, etc.).

bheda: difference; *vyapadeśāt:* on account of declaration; *ca:* and; *anyaḥ:* another.

The passage considered is B.U. III. 7. 9 which declares that the Self which resides and rules from within is different from the individual soul and the body of the sun or of any other being. The Supreme is the inward principle of all beings.[1]

Section 8 (22)

ĀKĀŚA (SPACE) AS *BRAHMAN*

I. 1. 22. *ākāśas tallingāt*

Ākāśa (is Brahman) since the characteristic marks (of Brahman) are mentioned.

ākāśaḥ: space; *tat:* that; *lingāt:* on account of characteristic marks.

The passage considered here is C.U. I. 9. 1, which holds that all beings originate from *ākāśa*, space. This refers to the highest *Brahman. Ākāśa* is equated with *ānanda* in T.U. II. 7; see also C.U. VIII. 14. 1. As all the prominent characteristics of *Brahman* are mentioned in regard to *ākāśa*, it cannot refer to the element *ākāśa*, but only to *Brahman*. Besides, the synonyms used for *ākāśa*, *vyoman*, *kha*, are used for *Brahman. Ākāśa* is that which shines everywhere.[2]

The word *ākāśa* is translated by ether, space, though both these are inadequate equivalents.

Section 9 (23)

LIFE AS *BRAHMAN*

I. 1. 23. *ata eva prāṇaḥ*

For the same reason, life (is Brahman).

ataḥ: hence, for the same reason; *eva:* also; *prāṇaḥ:* life, vital breath.

The question arises whether in the passages (C.U. I. 10. 9; I. 11. 4 and 5) *prāṇa* or life refers to the vital principle or *Brahman*. The

[1] P.U., pp. 226–7.

[2] *āsamantāt kāśata iti ākāśaḥ*. See Śrīnivāsa's *Vedānta-kaustubha*.

same argument of the presence of characteristic marks is used here to make out that *prāṇa* does not mean the life principle (or the fivefold vital breath) but the Supreme *Brahman*.

R. states that life is not present in all things; for example, it is not present in stones, wood, etc.: *Brahman* is called life because he bestows the breath of life on all beings.[1]

Section 10 (24–27)

LIGHT AS *BRAHMAN*

In these *sūtras*, the light mentioned in C.U. III. 13. 7 is established to be not the physical light but the highest *Brahman*.

I. 1. 24. *jyotiś caraṇābhidhānāt*

(The word) light (indicates Brahman) on account of the mention of feet.
jyotiḥ: light; *caraṇa:* feet, *pāda; abhidhānāt:* on account of the mention.

The passage considered is C.U. III. 13. 7. To what does 'light' refer? The objector says that it refers to physical light. Ordinarily light and darkness are opposed to each other and so light must mean the physical light. The word 'shines' refers to sun and similar sources of light. It cannot refer to *Brahman* which is devoid of colour. Since a physical boundary is mentioned for light it cannot mean *Brahman* which is the self of all and has no boundary. If it is suggested that the light mentioned is the original, invisible first principle of light, it cannot be made an object of devotion or used to dispel darkness. The attributes 'beyond heaven' or 'on this side of heaven' cannot apply to *Brahman* which has no sides or supports. This light beyond the heaven cannot be identified with *Brahman* as it is said to be the same as the light within the body,[2] which is physical in character. Meditation on this light is said to make one celebrated and beautiful. But meditation on *Brahman* gives us not these precarious goods but final release. No special characteristic marks of *Brahman* are given here. The previous section of the *Upaniṣad* (C.U. III. 12) deals with *gāyatrī* alone and not with *Brahman*.

To all these objections, the reply is made that the word 'light' refers to *Brahman* since in the preceding passage (C.U. III. 12. 6)[3] *Brahman* is spoken of as having four feet. One foot of it covers all beings: three feet of it are the immortal in heaven. This immortal in heaven cannot be the ordinary light.

The one topic discussed in this section of the *Upaniṣad* as also

[1] *ataḥ prāṇayati sarvāṇi bhūtānīti kṛtvā paraṁ brahmaiva prāṇa-śabdenābhidhīyate.*
[2] *antaḥ puruṣe jyotiḥ.*
[3] *pādo'sya sarvā bhūtāni, tripād asyāmṛtaṁ divi.*

the preceding and the succeeding is *Brahman*. As the general topic considered is *Brahman*, it is futile to argue that the words 'light', 'to shine', apply to physical light only and exclude reference to *Brahman*. They refer to *Brahman* in so far as it is characterised by the physical shining light which is its effect.[1] In several passages (B.U. IV. 3. 5 and *Taittirīya Saṁhitā* I. 6. 3. 6) whatever illuminates something else is spoken of as light and so *Brahman* which gives light to the entire world may be called light.[2] To the objection that the omnipresent *Brahman* cannot be viewed as being bounded by heaven, Ś. says that it is not contrary to reason for it serves the purpose of devout meditation.[3] So Scripture speaks of different kinds of devout meditation as specially connected with certain localities. For the same reason it is possible to attribute to *Brahman* a multiplicity of abodes. Even the fire in the body may be regarded as a symbol or outward appearance of *Brahman*. For Ś. meditation on the Highest *Brahman* as the Universal Self results in final release; worship of other symbolic representations of *Brahman* result in various rewards. *Brahman* is the light of lights, *jyotiṣāṁ jyotiḥ*.[4]

I. 1. 25. *chando'bhidhānān neti cen na, tathā ceto'rpaṇanigadāt tathā hi darśanam*

If it be said that (Brahman is) not (mentioned) since the metre is mentioned, (the reply is) not so because the fixing of the mind (on Brahman by means of the metre) is declared. This also is seen (elsewhere).
chandaḥ: metre; *abhidhānāt:* being mentioned; *na:* not; *iti:* so; *cet:* if; *na:* no; *tathā:* so; *cetaḥ:* mind; *arpaṇa:* fixing; *nigadāt:* on account of being declared; *tathā:* this; *hi:* also; *darśanam:* being seen.

R. reads *nigamāt* for *nigadāt*. *Nigama* is a sacred precept or direction or instruction.

If it be objected that the passage considered in the previous *sūtra* refers to the *gāyatrī* metre and not to *Brahman*, it is said in reply that the metre is to be used for fixing the mind on *Brahman*. Light, metre, etc., are used as means for the meditation on *Brahman*.

Ś. quotes the *Vṛttikāra* as holding that the *gāyatrī* directly denotes *Brahman*, on account of the fact that the *gāyatrī* and *Brahman* have both four feet or quarters. Even on this view, only *Brahman* is spoken of in this *sūtra*.

Baladeva means by *darśanam* consistency. For him *tathā hi darśanam* means: 'for by such an explanation alone the above passage gives a consistent meaning'.

[1] See also *Taittirīya Brāhmaṇa* (III. 12. 9. 7): 'That by which the sun shines [first] and illumines others' "*yena sūryas tapati tejaseddha*".'

[2] *brahmaṇopi caitanya-rūpasya samasta-jagad-avabhāsa-hetutvād upapanno jyotiś-śabdaḥ.* Ś.B.U. IV. 4. 16.

[3] *sarva-gatasyāpi brahmaṇa upāsanārthaḥ pradeśa-viśeṣa-parigraho na virudhyate.*

[4] B.U. IV. 4. 16.

I. 1. 26. *bhūtādi-pāda-vyapadeśopapatteś caivam*

Thus also (Brahman is the topic) for the indication that the beings, etc., are the feet is reasonable.
bhūtādi: beings, etc.; *pāda:* feet; *vyapadeśa:* indication; *upapatteḥ:* because of reasonableness; *ca:* and; *evam:* thus.

The passage considered is that 'all the beings are one foot [or quarter] of it'. *Ṛg Veda* (X. 90) mentions this verse with reference to *Brahman*. See also B.G. (X. 42).

I. 1. 27. *upadeśa-bhedānneti cen nobhayasminn apy avirodhāt*

If it be said that (Brahman cannot be recognised as the same in the two passages,) on account of the difference in teaching, (we reply that) it is not so because there is nothing contrary (to such recognition) in both cases.
upadeśa: teaching; *bhedāt:* on account of difference; *na:* not; *iti:* so; *cet:* if; *na:* not; *ubhayasmin:* in both cases; *api:* even; *avirodhāt:* without contradiction.

The objection states that the two passages are actually contradictory. The passages are: 'Three feet of it are what is immortal in heaven', *tripādasyā'mṛtaṁ divi:* (C.U. III. 12. 6); the other is 'that light shines above this heaven', *atha yad ataḥ paro divo jyotir dīpyate*' (C.U. III. 13. 7). In one, heaven is designated as the abode, in the other as the boundary. There is thus a difference between the two. In spite of it they both refer to *Brahman*. Ś. gives an analogy for argument. 'Just as in ordinary language a falcon, although in contact with the top of a tree, is not only said to be on the tree, but also above the tree, even so *Brahman* though being in heaven is referred to here as being beyond heaven also.'[1] Another explanation is also offered. A falcon, though not in contact with the top of a tree, is said to be above the top of the tree and also on the top of the tree.[2]

Section 11 (28–31)

LIFE AS *BRAHMAN* (contd.)

I. 1. 28. *prāṇas tathānugamāt*

Life (is Brahman) on account of (intelligible) connection.
praṇāḥ: life; *tathā:* in that way; *anugamāt:* on account of (intelligible) connection.

A connected consideration of the passages referring to life or

[1] *yathā loke vṛkṣāgreṇa sambaddho'pi śyena ubhayathopadiśyamāno dṛśyate. vṛkṣāgre śyeno vṛkṣāgrātparataḥ śyena iti ca.* Ś.

[2] *yathā loke vṛkṣāgreṇāsambaddho'pi śyena ubhayathopadiśyamāno dṛśyate; vṛkṣāgre śyeno vṛkṣāgrātparataś śyena iti ca.*

prāṇa (K.U. 111. 1, 2, 8),[1] requires us to look upon *prāṇa* as *Brahman*. It cannot be treated as breath or modification of air or the individual soul or the self of some divinity. The different passages can be construed as a whole only if they are viewed as referring to *Brahman* and not to vital air.[2]

I. 1. 29. *na vaktur ātmopadeśād iti ced adhyātma-sambandha-bhūmā hy asmin*

If it be said that (Brahman is) not (indicated) because the speaker refers to himself, (we reply that it is not so) for here (in this Chapter) references to the inner self are numerous.

na: not; *vaktuḥ:* of the speaker; *atmopadeśāt:* because of reference to himself; *iti:* so; *cet:* if; *adhyātma:* inner self; *sambandha:* references (relationships); *bhūmā:* numerous; *hy:* because; *asmin:* in this.

The objection considers Indra's statement 'Know me only'[3] and later on 'I am *prāṇa*, the intelligent self'.[4] Of *Brahman*, it is said, 'It is without speech, without mind'.[5] Indra praises himself by listing a number of his qualities. *Prāṇa* cannot denote *Brahman.*

I. 1. 30. *śāstra-dṛṣṭyā tūpadeśo vāmadeva-vat*

But the teaching (of Indra that he is one with Brahman) (is justifiable) through the insight of Scripture as in the case of Vāmadeva.

śāstra-dṛṣṭyā: through the insight of Scripture; *tu:* but; *upadeśāḥ:* teaching; *vāmadeva-vat:* like Vāmadeva.

The individual self Indra, perceives through the intuition of transcendental truth that his self is identical with the Supreme Self and so instructs Pratardana about the Highest Self through the words 'Know me only'.

By a similar intuition, the sage Vāmadeva attained the knowledge expressed in the words: 'I was Manu and Sūrya.'

Intuitive insight is defined in Govindānanda's *Ratna-prabhā* as the self-evident intuition rendered possible through the knowledge acquired in previous existences.[6] Compare the famous statement, *brahmavid brahmaiva bhavati.* The knower of *Brahman* becomes *Brahman.*[7] The individual in a supreme effort stretches towards the indefinable and adorable and in that condition he is lost and absorbed.

R., in accordance with his doctrine, makes out that the object of meditation is the Highest Self of which his own individual person is the body. The sage Vāmadeva perceiving that *Brahman* is the inner

[1] P.U., pp. 774ff.

[2] *sarvam etat parasmin brahmaṇyāśrīyamāṇe anugantuṁ śakyate na mukhye prāṇe.* Ś.

[3] *mām eva vijānīhi.*

[4] *praṇośmi prajnātmā.*

[5] *avāg amanā.* B.U. III. 8. 8.

[6] Cp. *janmāntara-kṛta-śravaṇādinā asmin janmani svatas-siddhaṁ darśanam ārṣam.*

[7] Cp. *ya evaṁ veda aham brahmāsmi.* B.U. I. 4. 10.

self of all, that all things constitute his body and that the meaning of words denoting a body extends up to the principle embodied, denotes with the word 'I' the Highest *Brahman* to which he himself stands in the relation of a body and then predicates of this 'I', Manu, Sūrya and other beings.[1]

I. 1. 31. *jīva-mukhya-prāṇa-liṅgān neti cen nopāsāt traividhyād āśritatvād iha tad-yogāt*

If it is said that (Brahman) is not (meant) because the characteristic marks of the individual soul and the chief breath (are mentioned), (we say) no, because (on this interpretation) three types of devotion (would result); because (our view) is accepted elsewhere; and because (characteristic marks of Brahman) are connected (with the passage under discussion).

jīva: individual soul; *mukhya-prāṇa:* chief breath; *liṅgāt:* on account of characteristic marks; *na:* not; *iti:* so; *cet:* if; *upāsāt:* on account of meditation; *traividhyāt:* on account of threefoldness; *āśritatvāt:* because of acceptance; *iha:* here; *tad-yogāt:* because of its connection with that.

The passage refers to a single type of meditation and so cannot be treated as suggesting different objects of meditation. It says 'Know me only' and then 'I am life, the intelligent self, meditate on me as life, as immortality' and concludes 'And that life, indeed, is that intelligent self, blessed, imperishable, immortal'. As the beginning and the conclusion are seen to be similar, the whole passage must be taken as referring to one and the same type of meditation. Again, we have passages where life is treated as equivalent to *Brahman*. Besides, the characteristic marks of *Brahman* are assigned to life.

The *Vṛttikāra* gives a different interpretation, that the section aims at enjoining three kinds of meditation on *Brahman* as life, as intelligent self and in itself. So *Brahman* is the topic of this section, whether in its own nature or in the form of its two adjuncts of the individual soul and life.

Bhāskara omits '*āśritatvād iha tad-yogāt*'.

R. argues that the threefold view of *Brahman* is quite appropriate: (i) meditation on *Brahman* in his own nature as the cause of the world, (ii) meditation on *Brahman* with the totality of the enjoying souls as his body, (iii) meditation on *Brahman* with the objects and means of enjoyment for his body.[2]

Śrīkaṇṭha follows R. in holding that the three kinds of meditation on the Lord are (1) *svarūpeṇa*, in his own nature, (2) *bhoktṛ-śarīreṇa*,

[1] *yathā vāmadevaḥ parasya brahmaṇaḥ sarvāntarātmatvaṁ sarvasya taccharīratvaṁ śarīravācināṁ śabdānām śarīriṇi paryavasānaṁ paśyann aham iti svātma-śarīrakaṁ paraṁ brahma nirdiśya tat sāmānādhikaraṇyena manu-sūryādīny vyapadiśati.* R.

[2] *nikhila-kāraṇa-bhūtasya brahmaṇaḥ svarūpeṇānusandhānam, bhoktṛ-varga-śarīrakatvānusandhānam, bhogya-bhogopakaraṇa-śarīrakatvānusandhānam.*

as having the totality of enjoying souls for his body, (3) *bhogya-rūpeṇa,* as having the objects and means of enjoyment for his body.

In this first part of the first chapter of the B.S. we get an indication of the governing principle that gives life to the great structure of Hinduism. Regarded from the outside, it may have the appearance of a confused mass of conflicting ideas, a congeries of contradictory elements, a complex of varied forces. There is, however, an identity, not mechanical but organic. To understand it we must live in the Hindu life-stream. Then we can know its full meaning and complete reality and feel the forces which pulsate through the whole body.

We should not get imprisoned in our ideas as intellectuals do or in our flesh as sensualists do. Enlightenment comes only with self-surrender and we do not surrender ourselves so long as we cling to our ideas. When reason leads us to experience, we know the meaning of life. This experience is variedly interpreted but the interpretations are no substitute for the experience.

Section 1 (1–8)

MIND AS *BRAHMAN*

Certain other passages which are not clear about their reference to *Brahman* are taken into consideration in this part. The eight *sūtras* of this first section show that the being which consists of mind, whose body is breath, etc., mentioned in C.U. III. 14, is not the individual soul but the Highest *Brahman*.

I. 2. 1. *sarvatra prasiddhopadeśāt*

(*That which consists of mind is Brahman*) *because of the teaching of what is well known everywhere.*

sarvatra: everywhere; *prasiddha:* well known; *upadeśāt:* because of the teaching.

The passage considered is C.U. III. 14. The doubt arises whether what is pointed out as the object of meditation by means of attributes such as 'consisting of mind', etc., is the individual soul or the Highest *Brahman*. For it is the individual soul that is connected with mind, etc., and not *Brahman* 'who is unborn, without breath and without mind, pure'.[1] Since we are asked to meditate with a calm mind, the object of meditation need not be *Brahman*. The other descriptions, 'He to whom all works, all desires belong', 'He is my self within the heart, smaller than a grain of rice, smaller than a grain of barley', apply to the individual soul. The object of meditation indicated by the qualities of 'consisting of mind', etc., is the individual soul.

The objection is answered by the *sūtra* which says that all the *Vedānta* passages speak of the cause of the world.

R. says that the text which declares *Brahman* to be without mind and breath is meant to deny that the thought of *Brahman* does not depend on a mind and that its life does not depend on breath.[2]

I. 2. 2. *vivakṣita-guṇopapatteś ca*

And because qualities desired to be expressed are appropriate (*in Brahman*).

vivakṣita: desired or intended to be stated;[3] *guṇa:* qualities; *upapatteḥ:* because appropriate; *ca:* and.

The qualities useful in meditation belong to *Brahman* alone. He is *satya-saṁkalpa*, having true purpose. This applies to the Highest Self which has unimpeded power to create, maintain and dissolve the

[1] M.U. II. 1. 2; P.U., p. 680.

[2] *mana-āyattaṁ jñānam prāṇāyattaṁ sthitaṁ ca brahmaṇo niśedhati.*

[3] *vaktum iṣṭaṁ vivakṣitam.*

world.[1] Similarly in C.U. (VIII. 7. 1) the Self is said to be 'free from sin'. It is omnipresent like *ākāśa*, space. See also Ś.U. IV. 3; B.G. XIII. 13.

I. 2. 3. *anupapattes tu na śārīraḥ*

But, as (the qualities desired to be expressed) do not belong (to the individual soul, the self denoted by mano-maya, etc.), is not the embodied one.
an-upapatteḥ: not belonging to; *tu:* but; *na:* not; *śārīraḥ:* embodied one.

The qualities of 'consisting of mind' and so on are applicable only to *Brahman* and not the individual soul. It is true that God resides in the body but he is outside as well and is all-pervading. See C.U. III. 14. 3. The individual soul resides in the body alone since he experiences the effects of his action in the form of pleasure and pain through the body. The attributes of 'having true resolves', etc., are appropriate only to the Highest Lord and not the individual soul.

Śrīkaṇṭha begins a new section (3–8) here, which considers whether the passage in the *Mahā-Nārāyaṇa U.* (XI. 3) refers to *Nārāyaṇa* or *Śiva*. Śrīkaṇṭha concludes that it refers to *Śiva* and not to *Nārāyaṇa.*

I. 2. 4. *karma-kartṛ-vyapadeśāc ca*

And because activity and agent are (separately) mentioned.
karma: activity; *kartṛ:* agent; *vyapadeśāt:* being mentioned; *ca:* and.

The passage considered here is C.U. III. 14. 4. 'Into him, I shall enter, on departing hence.' Here the object of meditation is declared to be different from the meditator who is the individual soul. One and the same thing cannot be both subject and object. The embodied soul cannot possess the qualities mentioned in the *Upaniṣad. Brahman* which possesses these qualities cannot be the embodied self.

R. puts it clearly. 'The soul which obtains is the person meditating and the Highest *Brahman* that is to be obtained is the object of meditation. *Brahman,* therefore, is something different from the attaining soul.'[2]

Śrīkaṇṭha suggests that the Supreme Self is *Śiva* and not *Nārāyaṇa* as he is the object to be worshipped and *Nārāyaṇa* is the worshipper.

I. 2. 5. *śabda-viśeṣāt*

On account of the difference of words.
śabda: word; *viśeṣāt:* on account of difference.

[1] *satya-saṁkalpatvaṁ hi sṛṣṭi-sthiti-saṁhṛtiṣv apratibaddha-śaktitvāt param-ātmano'vakalpate.* Ś.

[2] *prāpta jīva upāsakaḥ, prāpyaṁ paraṁ brahmopāsyam iti prāptir anyad evedam iti vijñāyate.*

The passage considered is in the *Śatapatha Brāhmaṇa*.

'Like a grain of rice or a grain of barley or a millet seed or the kernel of a millet seed thus that golden person is in the self.'[1] Here *Brahman* indicated by the word person in the nominative is distinct from the individual soul indicated by the locative. The two are different as they are denoted by different words.

Śrīkaṇṭha argues on scriptural authority that the Supreme Being *Śiva* is other and higher than *Nārāyaṇa, nārāyaṇāt param brahma*.

Nimbārka refers to C.U. III. 14. 3 and 4.

I. 2. 6. *smṛteś ca*

And on account of smṛti.

smṛteḥ: on account of *smṛti; ca:* and.

The passage considered is B.G. XVIII. 6. 1.

Ś. points out that the difference is not to be taken as real and that it is due to limiting adjuncts. Space or *ākāśa*, though in reality unlimited, appears limited owing to certain adjuncts such as jars and other vessels. When we grasp the truth that there is only one Universal Self, there is an end to the whole practical view of the world with its distinctions of bondage, release and the like.[2]

R. finds it easy to explain these *sūtras*. He says that the Highest Self is free from all evil and is not subject to the effects of works as the individual soul is. The difference is maintained between the individual soul who is the meditating subject and the Highest Self which is the object of meditation.[3]

For Śrīkaṇṭha *Nārāyaṇa* is the worshipper, different from *Śiva*.

I. 2. 7. *arbhakaukastvāt tad-vyapadeśāc ca neti cen na, nicāyyatvād evam vyomavac ca*

If it be said that (Brahman is) not (referred) because of the smallness of the abode and is so designated (we reply that it is) not so because (Brahman) is to be meditated thus; and (this is to be understood) like space.

arbhakaukastvāt: because of the abode being small; *tat:* that; *vyapadeśāt:* being (so) designated; *ca:* and; *na:* not; *iti:* so; *cet:* if; *na:* not; *nicāyyatvāt:* being meditated; *evam:* thus; *vyomavat:* like, *ākāśa*.

For the purposes of meditation, the omnipresent *Brahman* may be said to occupy a limited space. Although present everywhere, Ś. says, the Lord is pleased when meditated upon as limited in, for example,

[1] *yathā vrīhir vā yavo vā śyāmāko vā śyāmāka-taṇḍulo vaivam ayam antar-ātman puruṣo hiraṇmayaḥ*. X. 6. 3. 2.

[2] *yathā ghaṭa-karakādy-upādhivaśāt aparicchinnam api nabhaḥ paricchinnavad avabhāsate, tad-vat gṛhītetv ātmaikatve bandha-mokṣādi-sarva-vyavahāra-pari-samāptir eva syāt.*

[3] *śārirakam upāsakam param-ātmānaṁ copāsyaṁ smṛtir darśayati.*

connection with the eye of a needle. The Lord of the entire universe may be said to be the Lord of *Ayodhyā*, so the Supreme Self abiding everywhere may very well be denoted as abiding within the heart.[1] We worship the Supreme through an image, *yathā sālagrāme hariḥ.* Ś. For Ś. the limitations are not real. So we cannot say that if *Brahman* has its abode in the heart and these heart-abodes are different in different bodies, it is affected by the imperfections of the different bodies.

For R., the Supreme Lord is designated to occupy a small abode only for purposes of meditation.[2]

Baladeva remarks that the Lord may dwell in the heart of man because he is possessed of inconceivable powers.

I. 2. 8. *saṁbhoga-prāptir iti cen na, vaiśeṣyāt*

If it be said that (because the individual soul and the Universal Self are one) there may arise experience (of pleasure and pain for the Universal Self also) it is not so since there is difference in nature (of the two).
saṁbhoga: experience; *prāptiḥ:* attainment; *iti:* so; *cet:* if; *na:* not; *vaiśeṣyāt:* on account of difference.

The embodied self acts and enjoys, acquires merit and demerit and is affected by pleasure and pain and so on; the Universal Self is of a different nature; it is free from all evil, etc. On account of the difference between the two the experiences of the individual soul do not affect the Supreme Self. See M.U. III. 1. 1. The individual soul undergoes pleasure and pain because it is subject to *karma*, whereas the Lord is not subject to it. It is not living in the body but subjection to *karma* that involves a soul in the experiences of pleasure and pain.

Bhāskara holds that simply because the Lord abides in the heart, it does not follow that he shares its experiences. Coexistence and consequent interrelationship do not imply the sharing of the same attributes. The ether, for example, though in connection with a burning place, does not burn itself.

R. means by *vaiśeṣyāt*, on account of the difference of the cause of enjoyment, *hetu-vaiśeṣyāt.*

Nimbārka means by *vaiśeṣyāt*, on account of the difference of nature between the individual soul and *Brahman.*

[1] *sarvagato'pīśvaras tatropāsyamānaḥ prasīdati.*
[2] *ata upāsanārtham evālpatva-vyapadeśaḥ.*

Section 2 (9–10)

THE SUPREME SELF AS THE EATER OF THE WORLD

I. 2. 9. *attā carācara-grahaṇāt*

The eater (is the Highest Self) on account of the taking in of (whatever is) movable and immovable.
attā: eater; *carācara:* movable and immovable; *grahaṇāt:* on account of taking in.

The passage considered is *Kaṭha U.* I. 2. 25, where the *Brāhmaṇas* and the *Kṣatriyas* are treated as food and death itself as a sauce.[1] The doubt arises whether the eater is fire (*agni*) or the individual soul or the Highest Self. B.U. I. 4. 6 suggests fire and M.U. (III. 1. 1) says that the Supreme Self looks on without eating. Against these objections, the *sūtra* affirms that the Supreme Self is the eater for he consumes or absorbs in himself the movable and the immovable worlds.[2] The *Brāhmaṇas* and the *Kṣatriyas* are mentioned as representatives of the whole world. When the *Upaniṣad* says that the Self does not eat but looks on, it means that the Self is not subject to actions.

Grahaṇa may mean understanding or taking in or eating. *Brahman* is the eater because the movable and the immovable worlds are understood here as the food or because the two worlds are taken in.

I. 2. 10. *prakaraṇāc ca*

And on account of the topic under discussion.
prakaraṇāt: on account of the context; *ca:* and.

The general topic discussed in the *Kaṭha U.* I. 2. 18, 22–23 is the Highest Self and so we should take it as the topic in that context.

Section 3 (11–12)

THE SUPREME AND THE INDIVIDUAL SELVES IN THE CAVE

I. 2. 11. *guhāṁ praviṣṭāvātmānau hi tad-darśanāt*

The two who have entered into the cave are the selves (the individual soul and the Supreme Self) because that is seen.
guhām: into the cave; *praviṣṭau:* who have entered; *ātmānau:* the (two) selves; *hi:* because; *tat:* that; *darśanāt:* is seen.

The passage considered is *Kaṭha U.* I. 3. 1. Are the two selves

[1] P.U., p. 621.
[2] *sarva-vedānteṣu sṛṣṭi-sthiti-saṁhāra-kāraṇatvena brahmaṇaḥ prasiddhatvāt.* Ś.

intelligence (*buddhi*) and the individual soul (*jīva*) or are they the individual soul and the Highest Self? Both alternatives seem to be possible. The opponent says that the reference is to the individual soul and intelligence: (i) For the cave is a small and special place and the Infinite Self cannot enter it. (ii) The statement that they enter the world of good deeds obviously refers to the individual soul and intelligence for they are subject to the law of *karma* and not the Highest Self (B.U. IV. 4. 23). (iii) Again, the analogy of shade and light applies to the individual soul and intelligence, for the former is intelligent and the latter *buddhi* is treated as non-intelligent, *jaḍa*.

The answer is given to these points: (i) As the two beings are said to be of the same nature, *ātmānau*, the reference should be to the individual self and the Supreme Self and not to the individual soul and *buddhi*. (ii) If a special local position is assigned to the Omnipresent Self, it is for the purpose of meditation. See *Kaṭha U.* I. 2. 12; T.U. II. 1. (iii) The attribute of existing in the sphere of good works, no doubt, belongs to the individual soul only and not to *Brahman*, though it may apply to *Brahman* in a figurative way, even as a group of men is described as having an umbrella though only one of them has it. (iv) The individual soul and the Supreme Self are correctly described as being disparate in nature. They are not the same.

I. 2. 12. *viśeṣaṇāc ca*

And on account of the distinctive qualities (mentioned).

viśeṣaṇāt: on account of distinctive qualities; *ca:* and.

Kaṭha U. (I. 3. 3 and 9) speaks of the body as the chariot and the individual soul as the charioteer making his journey from the world of becoming, *saṁsāra*, to final release. Another passage (I. 3. 9)[1] speaks of the Highest Self as the abode of *Viṣṇu*. The individual soul is said to be the meditator and the Supreme Self the object of meditation. The two who have entered the cave have distinctive qualities.

The passage from the M.U. (III. 1. 1 and 2) which refers to two birds, one eating the fruit, the other abstaining from eating but looking on, refers to the individual soul and the Supreme Self.

Ś. quotes *Paiṅgi-rahasya Brāhmaṇa* which discredits the two interpretations of (i) the individual soul and *buddhi*, and (ii) the individual soul and the Supreme Self and holds that the being which eats the fruit is the internal organ by means of which a man dreams and the being which merely looks on without eating is the individual soul, who is really not the enjoyer but the Supreme *Brahman*. The dualism exists only within the sphere of experience.

R. refers to *Kaṭha U.* 1. 20 and says that the question raised by Naciketas relates to the problem of release. When a man qualified for release dies and is released from bondage, a doubt arises as to his existence or non-existence. Philosophers are not agreed about the

[1] See P.U., pp. 624–5.

nature of release. Some hold that the Self is constituted by consciousness only and release consists in the total destruction of this essential nature of the Self. Others define release as the passing away of ignorance, *avidyā*. It is sometimes said that the Self is itself non-conscious like a stone but possesses in the state of bondage certain distinctive qualities as knowledge and so on. Release consists in a total removal of these qualities, the Self remaining in a state of pure isolation.[1] R. declares that release consists in the intuition of the Highest Self which is the natural state of the individual souls and which follows on the destruction of ignorance, *avidyā*, i.e. the influence of the beginningless chain of works.[2]

Section 4 (13–17)

THE PERSON WITHIN THE EYE IS *BRAHMAN*

I. 2. 13. *antara upapatteḥ*

The Person within (the eye is Brahman) on account of appropriateness.
antaraḥ: the Person within; *upapatteh:* on account of appropriateness.

The passage considered is C.U. IV. 15. 1. The point is raised that it may refer to the image of some person standing before the eye, or the individual soul who sees the forms of objects through the eye, or the sun, the deity of the sense of sight which causes the eye to see (B.U. V. 5. 2). It cannot refer to God.

The *sūtra* says that the Person in the eye is the Highest God for immortality and fearlessness are mentioned as his characteristics. The eye is described as his abode. The other features mentioned in C.U. IV. 15. 2 apply only to God.

I. 2. 14. *sthānādi-vyapadeśāc ca*

And on account of the statement of place and other things.
sthānādi: place and other things; *vyāpadeśāt:* on account of the statement; *ca:* and.

The objection is raised that the omnipresent *Brahman* cannot be confined to the eye. The answer is that it is not the only locality that is assigned to the Lord. Earth and so on are mentioned as his residence (B.U. III. 7. 3). Not only place but name and form are attributed to *Brahman* (C.U. I. 6. 7. 6). *Brahman*, though devoid of qualities, is spoken of as possessing qualities for purposes of

[1] *kecid vitti-mātrasy ātmanaḥ svarūpocchitti-lakṣaṇam mokṣam ācakṣate. anye vitti-mātrasyaiva sato'vidyāstamayam. apare pāṣāṇakalpasyātmano jñānādy-aśeṣa-vaiśeṣika-guṇoccheda-lakṣaṇam kaivalya-rūpam.*

[2] *jīvasyānādi-karma-rūpāvidyā-tirohita-svarūpasyāvidyoccheda pūrvaka-svābhāvika-paramātmānubhavam eva mokṣam ācakṣate.*

meditation. To assign a definite locality is not contrary to reason, since it serves the purpose of meditation.

R. mentions that the Highest is directly intuited by those who practise *yoga* or concentration of mind.[1]

I. 2. 15. *sukha-viśiṣṭābhidhānād eva ca*

On account also of the mention only of what is characterised by pleasure.
sukha: pleasure; *viśiṣṭa:* characterised by; *abhidhānāt:* on account of mention; *eva:* only; *ca:* and.

Brahman which is spoken of as being characterised by pleasure at the beginning of the section (C.U. IV. 10. 4) is also referred to in the present passage.[2]

R. here has another *sūtra* which is not found in Ś., Bhāskara and Baladeva. Niṁbārka and Śrīkaṇṭha have it.
ata eva ca sa brahma: Also for that very reason, that is *Brahman.*
ataḥ: for that reason; *eva:* alone; *ca:* and or also; *sa:* that; *brahma:* *Brahman.*
ākāśa which is denoted by *kha* is also *Brahman.* C.U. IV. 10. 5.

I. 2. 16. *śrutopaniṣatkagatyabhidānāc ca*

Also on account of the mention of the path of him who has heard the Upaniṣads.
śruta upaniṣatka gati: the path of one who has heard the *Upaniṣads*; *abhidhānāt:* on account of the mention; *ca:* also.

The passage considered is *Praśna U.* I. 10 which describes the path of the gods, *deva-yāna.* See also C.U. IV. 15. 5; B.G. VIII. 24. From all these it follows that the person in the eye is no other than *Brahman.*
śrutopaniṣatka is one by whom the *Upaniṣad* has been directly heard from a teacher. *Vedānta-Kaustubha.*

I. 2. 17. *anavasthiter asambhavāc ca netaraḥ*

(*The Person in the eye is*) *no other* (*than the Highest Self*) *because of the non-permanence* (*of others*) *and on account of the impossibility.*
anavasthiteḥ: because of non-permanence; *asaṁbhavāt:* because of impossibility; *ca:* and; *na:* not; *itaraḥ:* other.

To the objection raised that the Person in the eye is either the reflection of someone standing before the eye, or the individual soul or the self of some deity, the answer is given that all these are non-permanent. Since immortality, fearlessness are ascribed to the Person in the eye, it can only be *Brahman.*

Śrīkaṇṭha takes this as a separate section dealing with the question whether the Person of the size of a thumb (*Māhānārāyaṇa*

[1] *sākṣātkāra-vyapadeśo'pi yogibhir dṛśyamānatvād upapadyate.*
[2] P.U., p. 413.

U. X. 6. 3) is the Lord or someone else and concludes that he is the Lord and not any other on account of the non-permanence of others and the impossibility of any other view.

Section 5 (18–20)

THE INDWELLING SPIRIT

I. 2. 18. *antaryāmy adhidaivādiṣu tad-dharma-vyapadeśāt*

The Indwelling Spirit of gods and others (is the Self) for his (characteristic) marks are mentioned.

antaryāmi: inner controller, indwelling spirit; *adhidaivādiṣu:* in gods and others; *tat:* his; *dharma:* defining or characteristic marks; *vyapadeśāt:* on account of mentioning.

R., Nimbārka read this *sūtra* in a slightly different way, *antaryāmy adhi-daivādhi-lokādiṣu*: The indwelling spirit of gods, the worlds and others.

The passage in question is B.U. III. 7. 1. Who lives inside and controls all? Is he the self of some deity, or a *yogin* who has acquired extraordinary powers or the Highest Self or some other being? The answer is given that it is the Highest Self for his qualities are mentioned. The universal rulership implied in the statement that, dwelling within, it rules the entire aggregate of created beings, inclusive of the gods is an appropriate attribute of the Highest Self, since omnipotence depends on the Omnipotent Ruler being the cause of all things. The qualities of selfhood and immortality belong to the Highest Self. He is declared to be different from the deities of the earth, etc. The objection that the Highest Self cannot be a ruler for he has no organs of action is untenable because organs of action may be ascribed to him since those whom he rules possess organs of action. If it is argued that the admission of an internal ruler in addition to the individual self will force us to assume again another and yet another ruler, *ad infinitum*, the answer is that there is no ruler other than the Highest Self. So the internal ruler is the Highest Self.

Vācaspati suggests that the Highest Self is not different from the individual self.[1]

R. quotes Ś.U. (III. 19) 'he sees without eye, hears without ear'[2] and comments: what terms such as 'seeing' and 'hearing' really denote is not knowledge in so far as it is produced by the eye and the ear, but the intuitive presentation of colour and sound. In the

[1] *na cānavasthā, hi niyantrantaraṁ tena niyamyate kiṁ tu yo jīvo niyantā ālokasiddhaḥ, sa paramātmaivopādhyavaccheda-kalpita-bhedaḥ. Bhāmatī.*

[2] P.U. 729–30.

case of the individual soul whose intellectual nature is obscured by *Karman*, such intuitive knowledge arises only through the mediation of the sense-organs; in the case of the Highest Self, on the other hand, it springs from its own nature.[1]

I. 2. 19. *na ca smārtamatad-dharmābhilāpāt*

And (the Indwelling Spirit) is not that which is assumed by the smṛti (the Sāṁkhya system) on account of the mention of characteristics not belonging to it (the pradhāna).
na: not; *ca:* and; *smārtam:* assumed by the *smṛti; atat:* not belonging to it; *dharma:* characteristics; *abhilāpāt:* on account of mention.

R. and Srīkaṇṭha add to this *sūtra* at the end *śārīraś ca,* which is found at the beginning of the next *sūtra* in Ś. and Niṁbārka.

I. 2. 20. *śārīraścobhaye'pi hi bhedenainam adhīyate*

And the embodied soul (is not the Indwelling Spirit) for in both also it is taught as different.
śārīraḥ: the embodied self; *ca:* and; *ubhaye:* in both; *api:* also; *hi:* for; *bhedena:* as different; *enam:* this; *adhīyate:* taught.

To the suggestion that the Indwelling Spirit is the embodied Self, the *sūtra* says that it cannot be, for both the rescensions, the *Kāṇva* and the *Mādhyandina* describe the individual soul as different from the Indwelling Spirit. See B.U. III. 7. 22.[2] The *Kāṇvas* read 'He who dwells in knowledge'; the *Mādhyandinas* 'He who dwells in the self'. Both refer to the individual soul and declare it to be different from the Indwelling Spirit.

Ś. believes that the declaration of the difference between the embodied soul and the Indwelling Spirit has its reason in the limiting adjunct consisting of the organs of action presented by ignorance, and is not absolutely true. For the Self within is one only; two internal selves are not possible. But owing to its limiting adjunct the one Self is practically treated as if it were two, just as we make a distinction between the space in the jar and the universal space.[3]

R. uses this to establish the difference between the individual soul and the Indwelling Spirit, the Supreme free from all evil.[4] The two

[1] *na ca darśana-śravaṇādi-śabdāś cakṣurādi-karaṇajanmano jñānasya vācakā api tu rūpādi-sākṣātkārasya. sa ca rūpādi-sākṣātkāraḥ karma-tirohita-svābhāvika-jñānasya jīvasya cakṣurādi-karaṇa-janmā, parasya tu svata eva.* R.

[2] *avidyāpraty-upasthāpita-kārya-karaṇopādhi-nimitto' yaṁ śārīrāntaryāmiṇor bheda-vyapadeśo na pāramārthikaḥ eko hi pratyag-ātmā bhavati, na dvau pratyag-ātmānau sambhavataḥ. ekasyaiva tu bheda-vyavahāra-upādhi-kṛtaḥ, yathā ghaṭākāśo mahākāśa iti.*

[3] P.U., p. 229.

[4] *ato antaryāmī pratyag-ātmano vilakṣaṇo'pahatapāpmā paramātmā nārāyaṇa iti siddham.*

are different because the individual soul is the abode and the Indwelling Spirit is the one who abides therein.

Section 6 (21–23)

THE INVISIBLE AS *BRAHMAN*

I. 2. 21. *adṛśyatvādiguṇako dharmokteḥ*

That which possesses the qualities of invisibility and others (is Brahman) on account of the mention of the characteristics (peculiar to it).

adṛśyatvādi: invisibility and others; *guṇakaḥ:* one who possesses the qualities; *dharmokteḥ:* on account of the mention of the characteristics.

The passage considered is M.U. I. 1. 5–6. Is *bhūta-yoni*, the source of all existences, the *pradhāna*, the embodied soul, or *Brahman*? The opponent contends that the passage in the M.U. (I. 1. 7): 'As a spider sends forth and draws in [its thread], as herbs grow on the earth, as the hair [grows] on the head and the body of a living person, so from the imperishable arises here the universe' suggests that the world is produced by the non-intelligent *pradhāna* even though it may be guided by the intelligent *puruṣa*. The qualities mentioned belong to the *pradhāna* and the others like 'knowing all' 'perceiving all' may refer to that which is higher than the *pradhāna*. Again, if the word *yoni*, source, is taken as the efficient cause, then the embodied soul is the efficient cause.

The *sūtra* refutes this view. The imperishable source is spoken of as omniscient and the source of created things (I. 1. 7 and 9). In II. 1. 2, also, the same idea is under discussion. The *Upaniṣad* distinguishes between higher knowledge, *parā-vidyā*, and lower knowledge, *aparā-vidyā*, the first leading to bliss and the second to worldly prosperity. Ceremonial observances lead to worldly prosperity; knowledge of *Brahman* leads to eternal life. The reference here is to the latter. If *Brahman* is known, everything else becomes known (I. 1. 3). The knowledge of *pradhāna* or the embodied soul does not produce knowledge of everything else. So the reference in the passage is to *Brahman* and not to *pradhāna* or the embodied soul.[1]

I. 2. 22. *viśeṣaṇa-bheda-vyapadeśābhyāṁ ca netarau*

The two others (the individual soul and pradhāna) are not (the source of all beings) on account of the mention of distinctive qualities and difference.

viśeṣaṇa: distinctive qualities; *bheda:* difference; *vyapadeśābhyām:* on account of the mention (of the two); *ca:* and; *na:* not; *itarau:* the two others.

[1] *adṛśyatvādi-guṇako bhūta-yoniḥ parameśvara eva.* Ś.

Bhūta-yoni, the source of all, is neither the *pradhāna* nor the individual soul, for the mention of attributes 'all-pervading' (M.U. I. 1. 6, II. 1. 2) and of difference 'higher than the high, imperishable' (II. 1. 2) rules out these. Ś. makes out that the Imperishable is the unmanifested entity which represents the seminal potentiality of all names and forms, contains the subtle parts of the material elements, abides in the Lord, forms limiting adjunct and being itself no effect is high when compared to other effects. 'Higher than the high, Imperishable' expresses a difference between the Imperishable and what is higher than that and so the reference is to the Highest Self.[1]

R. quotes Parāśara to the effect that 'the cause of attaining him is knowledge and work and knowledge is twofold according as it is based on sacred tradition or arises from discrimination'.[2] The *aparā-vidyā* or lower knowledge mentioned in the M.U. refers to the knowledge of the *Ṛg Veda* up to the *dharma-śāstrās*. This prepares for the intuition of *Brahman*.[3] The higher kind of knowledge is called *upāsanā*, has the character of devout meditation and consists in direct intuition of *Brahman*.[4]

R. develops his own view of the relation of God to the world in his commentary on this *sūtra*. The qualities of omniscience, etc., enable the Highest *Brahman* to create and from the indestructible Highest *Brahman*, the effect (*kārya*) *Brahman* arises, distinguished by name and form and comprising all enjoying subjects and objects of enjoyment. The Highest Self constitutes the Self of all things and has all things for its body, for its outward form, and emits all things from itself.[5] The term *akṣara*, imperishable, may be explained etymologically as either that which pervades (*aśnute*) or that which does not pass away (*a-kṣarati*). In either sense it applies to the Highest Self. It pervades all effects; it does not pass away or decay.

I. 2. 23. *rūpopanyāsāc ca*

Also, on account of the description of (his) form.

rūpa: form; *upanyāsāt:* on account of the description; *ca:* also.

In M.U. II. 1. 3–4, there is a description of the form which can

[1] *akṣaram, avyākṛtam, nāma-rūpa-bīja-śakti-rūpam, bhūta-sūkṣmam, īśvarāśrayam, tasyaivopādhi-bhūtam sarvasmād vikārāt paro, yo' vikāraḥ, tasmāt parataḥ para iti bhedena vyapadeśan param-ātmānam iha vivakṣitaṁ darśayati.*

[2] *tat-prāpti-hetur jñānaṁ ca karma coktam mahāmune āgamotthaṁ vivekāc ca dvidhā jñānaṁ tathocyate.*

[3] *brahma-sākṣātkāra-hetu-bhūtaṁ parokṣa-jñānam.*

[4] *upāsanākhyaṁ brahma-sākṣātkāra-lakṣaṇaṁ bhakti-rūpāpannaṁ jñānam.*

[5] *sarvajñāt satya-saṁkalpāt parasmād brahmaṇo'kṣarād etad kāryākāram brahma nāma-rūpa-vibhaktam bhoktṛ-bhogya-rūpam ca jāyate . . . svarūpa-guṇaiḥ saha sarva-bhūtāntarātmatayā viśva-śarīratvena viśva-rūpatvam, tasmād viśva-sṛṣṭiṁ ca.*

belong to God alone and not to the individual soul or *pradhāna*. *Pradhāna* cannot be the self of all and the individual is of limited power.

Ś. mentions an alternative view that the inner self of creation is *Hiraṇya-garbha* or *Prajā-pati* and not the Highest Self. R.V. (X. 1. 21. 1) says: '*Hiraṇya-garbha* arose in the beginning; he was the one born lord of things existing. He established the earth and the sky.' He may be called the inner self of all beings. M.U. (II. 1. 4–9) describes the creation, the inner self of which is not the Highest Self but *Hiraṇya-garbha*, who is the *sūtrātman* of the later *Vedānta*, the breath of life in everything.

If the *sūtra* refers to M.U. (II. 1. 10), then the Highest Self is described.

Baladeva has a *sūtra* here, *prakaraṇāt*. This is not found in other commentaries. It means 'on account of the context'.

Section 7 (24–32)

VAIŚVĀNARA IS *BRAHMAN*

I. 2. 24. *vaiśvānaraḥ sādhāraṇa-śabda-viśeṣāt*

Vaiśvānara is (the Highest Self) on account of the distinction (qualifying) common words.

vaiśvānaraḥ: Vaiśvānara; sādhāraṇa: common; *śabda:* word; *viśeṣāt:* on account of the distinction.

The passage considered is C.U. V. 11. 18. The question is raised whether the word *Vaiśvānara* refers to the fire in the body, or the element fire or the deity fire. Does the word self mean the individual soul or the Highest Self? The *sūtra* says that though the words *Vaiśvānara* and Self have various meanings, on account of the distinction mentioned, the terms refer to the Highest Self.[1] *Vaiśvānara* is the self of the worlds and is described as having head, eyes, etc., for the purposes of meditation. As the cause of all, God possesses within him all the stages of all the effects and so the description of the several worlds and beings as the limbs of God is adequate. The statement regarding the result of meditation on *Vaiśvānara*, viz. 'he eats the food in all worlds, beings and self' has meaning only with reference to God. So also the passage in C.U. V. 24. 3. The general topic of discussion is also *Brahman*. So *Vaiśvānara* refers to *Brahman*.

[1] *yady apy etāvubhāvapy ātma-vaiśvānara-śabdau sādhāraṇa-śabdau vaiśvānara-śabdas tu trayāṇāṁ sādhāraṇaḥ, ātma-śabdaś ca dvayoḥ tathāpi viśeṣo dṛśyate. yena parameśvara-paratvaṁ tayor avagamyate.*

I. 2. 25. *smaryamāṇam anumānaṁ syād iti*

Because that which is stated in the smṛti is an inference.

smaryamāṇam: that which is stated in the *smṛti; anumānaṁ:* inference; *syād:* may be; *iti:* because.

The reference is to the passage in the *Viṣṇu Purāṇa*. 'He whose mouth is fire, whose head the heavenly world, whose navel the ether, whose feet the earth, whose eye the sun, whose ears the regions, reverence to him, the self of the world.'[1] From the shape described in the *smṛti* passage we infer a *śruti* text on which the *smṛti* rests and that is the *Chāndogya* passage mentioned in the previous *sūtra*. Even if the *smṛti* passage is taken as a eulogy, it must have a *śruti* text for its basis.

I. 2. 26. *śabdādibhyo'ntaḥ-pratiṣṭhānācca neti cen na, tathā dṛṣṭyupadeśād asambhavād puruṣam api cainam adhīyate*

If it be said that (Vaiśvānara is the fire in the body and) not (the Highest Self) on account of the words, etc., and on account of his abiding within (which is the characteristic of the fire residing in the body), (we say) not so, because of the teaching of the vision (of the Lord) thus, on account of impossibility and because also they speak of him as the Person.

śabdādibhyaḥ: on account of word, etc.; *antaḥ:* within; *pratiṣṭhānāt:* on account of abiding; *ca:* and; *na:* not; *iti:* so; *cet:* if; *na:* not; *tathā:* in that way, thus; *dṛṣṭi:* vision; *upadeśāt:* because of the teaching; *asambhavāt:* because of the impossibility; *puruṣam:* person; *api:* also; *ca:* and; *enam:* him; *adhīyate:* is taught or studied.

For *puruṣam* we read in some versions '*puruṣa-vidhaṁ*'. *puruṣa-vidham* is *puruṣākāram*. The form of *puruṣa* or person cannot be assigned to the fire in the body; so the reference is only to the Supreme Self.

Vaiśvānara, it is objected, is the fire within the body because of several passages (*Śatapatha Brāhmaṇa* X. 6. 1. 11; C.U. V. 18. 2). Again, the Scripture speaks of *Vaiśvānara* as abiding within. So he is not the Highest Self. The reply quotes passages where we are advised to look upon *Vaiśvānara* as the symbol of *Brahman*. The attributes mentioned apply to the Highest Self and not to the fire in the body. Again, we are taught by the Vājaseneyins to look upon *Vaiśvānara* not as residing within man but as a person.

I. 2. 27. *ata eva na devatā bhūtaṁ ca*

For the same reason (the Vaiśvānara) is neither the deity (of fire) nor the element (of fire).

ataḥ: therefore; *eva:* also; *na:* not; *devatā:* deity; *bhūtam:* element; *ca:* and.

[1] *yasyāgnir āsyam dyaur mūrdhā khaṁ nābhiś caraṇau kṣitiḥ*
sūryaś cakṣur diśaḥ śrotram tasmai lokātmane namaḥ.

See also M.B.: Śānti Parva 47: 65. M.U. II. 1. 4.

It has been shown that *Vaiśvānara* does not apply to the fire in the body; here it is said that it cannot be the deity fire or the element fire. We cannot call heaven, etc., as the head of either of these. So *Vaiśvānara* is the Highest Self.

I. 2. 28. *sākṣād apy avirodhaṁ jaiminiḥ*

(There is) no contradiction, says Jaimini, even if (the Highest Self is taken as the object of worship as Vaiśvānara) directly.
sākṣāt: directly; *api:* even; *avirodham:* no contradiction; *jaiminiḥ:* Jaimini.

Even if we worship *Vaiśvānara,* not as a symbol but as God himself, there is no contradiction. Ś. explains the term *Vaiśvānara* in three ways: (i) the Self of all things including the soul; (ii) the cause of all modifications; (iii) the ruler whose subjects are the souls.[1] It means the Highest Self.

I. 2. 29. *abhivyakter ity āśmarathyaḥ*

On account of manifestation (thinks) Āśmarathya.
abhivyakteḥ: on account of manifestation; *iti:* so; *āśmarathyaḥ:* *Āśmarathya.*

If the objection is raised that according to the Scripture, the Supreme is measured by a span (C.U. V. 18. 1), this *sūtra* answers that the Supreme though he transcends all measurements manifests himself for the benefit of his devotees in limited forms.

R. and Śrīkaṇṭha take *abhivyakti* to mean definiteness. For helping the thoughts of the devotees, the Lord assumes definite forms.

I. 2. 30. *anusmṛter bādariḥ*

On account of remembrance (thinks) Bādari.
anusmṛteḥ: on account of remembrance; *bādariḥ: Bādari.*

The Highest Self is said to be measured by a span since he is remembered by means of the mind located in the heart which is of the measure of a span. Or the Highest Self though not really measured by a span is to be remembered (meditated upon) as being of the measure of a span.[2]

I. 2. 31. *sampatter iti jaiminiḥ tathā hi darśayati*

According to Jaimini, (God is said to be a span in length) on account of imaginative identification; the same (Scripture) shows.
sampatteḥ: on account of imaginative identification; *jaiminiḥ: Jaemini; tathā hi:* the same; *darśayati:* shows.

[1] *viśvaś cāyaṁ naraś ca viśvāvaraḥ; viśveṣām vāyam naraḥ, viśve vā narā asyeti viśvānaraḥ param-ātmā sarvātmakatvāt.*

[2] *prādeśa-mātra-hṛdaya-pratiṣṭhitena vāyam manasānusmaryate, tena prādeśamātra ity ucyate.*

The account of *Vaiśvānara* in the *Śatapatha Brāhmaṇa* (X. 6. 1. 11) and in the C.U. (V. 11–18) is the same in essentials. Both the passages use the expression 'measured by a span'. So Jaimini says that it is appropriate to call the Highest Self *pradeśa-mātra* and the Scripture declares him to be so imagined for the purpose of meditation.

Baladeva takes *sampatti* to mean mysterious power. For him the Supreme is said to be of the measure of a span on account of his mysterious power.

I. 2. 32. *āmananti cainam asmin*

Moreover they (*the* Jābālas) *speak* (*of the Highest Self*) *in that* (*the space between the forehead and the chin*).

āmananti: (they) speak; *ca:* and, moreover; *enam:* him; *asmin:* in that.

The text considered is *Jābāla U.* I. The statement which ascribes to the Highest Self the measure of a span is appropriate. The Highest is called *abhi-vimāna*[1] for the inward self of all; he is directly measured or known by all sentient beings or the word may be explained as 'he who is near everywhere—as the inward self—and who at the same time is measureless'; or else it may denote the Highest Lord as he, who, as the cause of the world, measures it out, i.e. creates it. By all this it is proved that *Vaiśvānara* is the Highest Lord.[2]

[1] *abhi vimīyate ity abhi-vimānaḥ. abhigataś ca vimānaś ca abhi-vimānaḥ: abhi-vimimīte sarvam ity abhi-vimānaḥ.*

[2] See P.U., p. 895.

Section 1 (1–7)

BRAHMAN IS THE SUPPORT OF HEAVEN, EARTH, ETC.

I. 3. 1. *dyubhvādyāyatanaṁ sva-śabdāt*

The support of the heaven, the earth and the rest (is Brahman) because of the word 'own'.

dyu: heaven; *bhū:* earth; *ādi:* and the rest; *āyatanam:* support, abode; *sva-śabdāt:* because of the word 'own'.

The passage considered is M.U. II. 2. 5 which speaks of the being 'in whom the sky, the earth and the inter-space are woven as also the mind along with all the vital breaths'. This is said to be the bridge to immortality. The point is raised that this being is different from *Brahman* which is said to be without end and without any other bank. B.U. II. 4. 12. It may be *pradhāna* or air (B.U. III. 7. 2) or the individual soul. The use of the word *ātman*, self, denotes *Brahman* and not unintelligent matter or the individual soul. *Ātman* is said to be *sat* or reality in C.U. VI. 8. 4. This is the implication of other passages in M.U. (II. 1. 10; II. 2. 11). Ś. in his comment on this *sūtra* argues that the world and *Brahman* should not be regarded as separate from each other. The Self is not to be regarded as many or as qualified by this world of manifold effects.[1] It is to be known as one homogeneous substance. The word 'bridge' does not mean that there is another bank. It holds together or lends support, from the root *si*, to bind. It means only that the knowledge of Self is the means for attaining immortality.

I. 3. 2. *muktopasṛpya-vyapadeśāt*

And because it is mentioned as that to be attained by the released.

mukta: the released; *upasṛpya:* to be attained; *vyapadeśāt:* because it is mentioned.

R. and Niṁbārka add '*ca*' at the end of the *sūtra*.

The goal of the released is *Brahman*. See M.U. II. 2. 8; III. 2. 8; see also B.U. IV. 4. 7; IV. 4. 21.

R. holds that those freed from *saṁsāra* attain to *Brahman* for the state of *saṁsāra* consists in the possession of name and form, which is due to the connection with non-conscious matter, such connection springing from good and evil works. The Person therefore who is the abode of heaven, earth, etc., and whom the text declares to be the aim to be achieved by those who, having freed themselves from good and evil, and hence from all contact with matter, attain supreme

[1] *yat sarvam avidyāropitaṁ tat sarvaṁ paramārthato brahma na tu yad brahma tat sarvam ity arthaḥ. Bhāmatī.*

oneness with the Highest *Brahman*, can be none other than the Highest *Brahman* itself.[1]

I. 3. 3. *nānumānam atacchabdāt*

Not that which is inferred on account of there being no text to indicate it.
na: not; *anumānam:* what is inferred; *atac-chabdāt:* on account of there being no text to indicate it.

R. and Śrīkaṇṭha take this and the next *sūtra* as one.

Pradhāna is arrived at by inference. We argue that every effect must have a cause and that cause another and so on until we reach an uncaused first cause. As the effects are non-conscious the cause is inferred to be non-conscious since the cause and the effect are assumed to be of similar nature. This is the reasoning adopted by the *Sāṁkhya* system to establish the reality of *pradhāna*.

We cannot infer that the support of heaven, earth, etc., is *pradhāna* or air since there is no word to suggest it; on the other hand, words like omniscient, etc. (M.U. I. 1. 9), indicate that the support is an intelligent being.

I. 3. 4. *prāṇabhṛc ca*

(not) the bearer of the vital breaths (the individual soul) too.
prāṇa-bhṛt: the bearer of the vital breaths; *ca:* and.

Some readers omit '*ca*' at the end.

Though the individual soul is intelligent, it is not omniscient and all-pervading. The individual soul may be taken as the instrumental cause of the world since its unseen store of merit and demerit requires the world for enjoying the fruits. It cannot, on any account, be called the material cause of the world. The individual soul is not the support of heaven, earth and the rest for the reason that there are no texts to indicate it.

I. 3. 5. *bhedavyapadeśāc ca*

And on account of the declaration of difference.
bheda: difference; *vyapadeśāt:* on account of the declaration; *ca:* and.

In the text, 'Know him alone as the Self'[2] (M.U. II. 2. 5), a distinction is made between the knower and the known. The individual soul seeking release is the knower and the Highest Self is the object of knowledge. The latter is the abode of heaven, earth, etc.

[1] *saṁsāra-bandhād vimuktā eva hi vidhūta-puṇya-pāpā nirañjanā nāma rūpābhyām vimuktāś ca. puṇya-pāpa-nibandhano'citsaṁsarga-prayukta-nāma-rūpabhāktvam eva hi saṁsāraḥ. ato vidhūta-puṇya-pāpair nirañjanaiḥ prakṛti-saṁsarga-rahitaḥ pareṇa brahmaṇā param-sāmyam-āpannaiḥ prāpyataya nirdiṣṭo dyu-pṛthivyādy-āyatana-bhūtaḥ puruṣaḥ param brahmaiva.*

[2] *tam evaikaṁ jānatha ātmānam.*

R. considers here M.U. III. 1. 2 and refers to the distinction between the bewildered and grieving individual soul and the detached Supreme Self, both dwelling on the same tree.

I. 3. 6. *prakaraṇāt*

On account of the context.

The whole chapter in M.U. discusses the nature of the Highest Self. It must also be the topic here.

I. 3. 7. *sthity-adanābhyāṁ ca*

And on account of (the two conditions) abiding and eating.
sthity-adanābhyām: on account of abiding and eating; *ca:* and; *sthiti:* abiding; *adana:* eating.
Another reading *sthityodanābhyām sthiti* and *odana*. See Śrīnivāsa's *Vedānta Kaustubha.*

The passage considered is M.U. I. 1. 3. There are two birds, one who eats and the other who looks on. The former is the individual soul; the latter is the Supreme Self. The bridge to immortality, the soul of all, the support of heaven and the rest is the Supreme Self.

Even if the two birds are taken to mean *buddhi* or understanding and the individual soul devoid of *upādhis* or adjuncts, as the *Paiṅgi U.* suggests, the individual soul limited by the adjuncts is not the Highest Self and the latter alone is the support of heaven, etc.

Ś. points out that the distinction between the individual soul and *Brahman* is no more real than that between the ether within a jar and the universal ether.

Section 2 (8–9)

BHŪMAN IS *BRAHMAN*

I. 3. 8. *bhūmā sam-prasādād adhyupadeśāt*

The Bhūman is Brahman since the instruction (about it) is additional to the state of serenity (deep sleep).
bhūmā: Bhūman; saṁ-prasādāt: to the state of serenity; *adhi:* additional to; *upadeśāt:* on account of the instruction.

The passage considered is C.U. VII. 23 and 24. Sanat-kumāra tells Nārada that *Bhūman* is that where one sees nothing else, hears nothing else and understands nothing else. The doubt arises whether it is the life-principle, *prāṇa*, or the Highest Self. The objector makes out that *Bhūman* is *prāṇa* for after a series of questions about what is greater and greater still, *prāṇa* is affirmed to be the greatest of all and *Bhūman* is said to be *prāṇa*. He who knows the *prāṇa* is said to be an *ati-vādin* (VII. 15. 4). Even the statement that he sees nothing else, hears nothing else applies to a condition in which all the senses become merged in *prāṇa* (see *Praśna U.* IV. 2) and only the *prāṇa* keeps awake. The immortality of *Bhūman* can apply to *prāṇa* (C.U. VII. 24. 1, K.U. III. 2). *Prāṇa* is also treated as the self of all (C.U. VII. 15. 1). It is spoken of as the nave of the wheel in which all the spokes of the things in the world are fixed.

The answer to this is that *Bhūman* can represent the Highest Self. *Saṁ-prasāda*[1] is serenity and refers to the state of deep sleep as it is mentioned along with the states of waking and dream (B.U. IV. 3. 15). It belongs to the *prāṇa* and *Bhūman* is described as subsequent to *prāṇa* and so must refer to an entity different from it. What is said about *Bhūman* is different from what is said about *prāṇa*. The statement regarding the *ati-vādin* is made not only with regard to the man who has the knowledge of *prāṇa* but also later with regard to one who has the knowledge of truth. Sanat-Kumāra leads his pupil Nārada by a series of steps beyond *prāṇa* to *Bhūman*. *Prāṇa* is a product since it is said to spring from the Self (C.U. VII. 26. 1). *Bhūman* is said to reside in his own glory (C.U. VII. 24. 1). The same topic is continued to the end of the chapter with the sole change of the word Self (*ātman*) for *Brahman*. So *Bhūman* is the Highest Self.

I. 3. 9. *dharmopapatteś ca*

And on account of the appropriateness of the attributes.
dharma: attributes; *upapatteḥ:* on account of appropriateness; *ca:* and.

The attributes assigned to the Highest Self and *Bhūman* agree (see C.U. VII. 24. 1; B.U. IV. 5. 15). The serenity of deep sleep applies to *Brahman* or *Bhūman* and not to *prāṇa* for it is said to be great and not little (C.U. VII. 23. 1); see also B.U. IV. 3. 32. The absence of the activities of seeing, etc., in the state of deep sleep (*Praśna U.* IV. 2) indicates the non-attachedness of the self. The qualities of immortality, truth, omnipresence, self-existence and being the self of all apply to the Highest Self and *Bhūman*.

Section 3 (10–12)

THE IMPERISHABLE IN WHICH SPACE IS WOVEN IS *BRAHMAN*

I. 3. 10. *akṣaram ambarāntadhṛteḥ*

The Imperishable (is Brahman) on account of its supporting (all things) up to space.
akṣaram: the imperishable; *ambara:* sky or space; *anta:* end; *dhṛteḥ:* because it supports.

[1] *sam-prasīdaty asminn iti sam-prasādaḥ.*

The passage considered is B.U. III. 8, 7 and 8. Does *akṣara* refer to the syllable or the Highest Self? The objector mentions the collection of fourteen *sūtras* which *Pāṇini* is reported to have received from Śaṁkara, *akṣara-samāmnāya*. C.U. (II. 23. 4) mentions the syllable *Aum* as the symbol of *Brahman*, the Self of all and worthy to be meditated upon.

If it is suggested that the *ambara* may be the *pradhāna*, R. says that the support of that *pradhāna* cannot itself be the *pradhāna*.

The conclusion is that while all things find their support in *ākāśa*, *ākāśa* itself is supported by *Akṣara*. It can only be the *Brahman*. *Akṣara* is that which is not perishable (*na kṣaram*), which is all-pervading (*aśnute*) and so can refer to *Brahman* only. *Aum* is used as a symbol for *Brahman* for purposes of meditation. It is also called *praṇava*. *prakarṣeṇa nūyate anena iti praṇavaḥ*. It is called *praṇava* because it is the best *stotra*.[1]

Atharva-Śikha U. (I. 17) says: 'It is called *praṇava* because it is effective in restraining the senses and directing them to the Supreme Self.[2] *Brahman* as the support of *ākāśa* is *Brahman* as *Īśvara*.

Śrīkaṇṭha suggests that there is a difference between the support and what is supported. The former is *Brahman* and the latter is *cit-śakti*. *Ākāśa* is referred to as being woven as warp and woof in *Akṣara* in B.U. III. 8. 11.

I. 3. 11. *sā ca praśāsanāt*

And this (*supporting*) (*belongs to the Highest Lord only*) *on account of command.*

sā: this; *ca:* and; *praśāsanāt:* on account of command.

If it is argued that the cause which supports all effects called the Imperishable is *pradhāna* and not *Brahman*, the answer is that it is the work of God alone and not non-conscious *pradhāna* (see B.U. III. 8. 9), for non-conscious causes such as clay and the like are not capable of command[3] with reference to their effects such as jars, etc.[4]

R. says that the supreme command through which all things in the universe are held apart cannot possibly belong to the individual soul in the state of either bondage or release.[5] It belongs to the Supreme Person. Śrīnivāsa accepts this position.

[1] Bhoja's *Yoga-sūtra-vṛtti*.

[2] *prāṇān sarvān paramātmanaṁ praṇāmayati iti etasmāt praṇavaḥ.*

[3] *prakṛṣṭam śāsanaṁ:* unrestricted commanding.

[4] *praśāsanaṁ ca pārameśvaraṁ karma nācetanasya pradhānasya praśāsanaṁ sambhavati. na hy acetanānāṁ ghaṭādi-kāraṇānām mṛdādīnām ghaṭādi-viṣayaṁ praśāsanaṁ asti.* Ś.

[5] *na cedṛśam sva-śāsanādhīna-sarva-vastu-vidharaṇam baddha-muktobhay-āvasthasyāpi pratyag-ātmanaḥ sambhavati. ataḥ puruṣottama eva praśāsitṛ akṣaram.* R.

I. 3. 12. *anyabhāvavyāvṛtteś ca*

And on account of the exclusion of a different nature.
anya: different; *bhāva:* nature; *vyāvṛtteḥ:* on account of exclusion; *ca:* and.

Other alternatives are excluded. The Imperishable cannot be the *pradhāna* for the *Akṣara* is said to be seeing, hearing and perceiving, which *pradhāna* is not capable of (B.U. III. 8. 11). When it is said that there is no other seer but the Imperishable, no other hearer, etc., individual souls are excluded. Even the limiting adjuncts are excluded for the Imperishable is said to be 'without eyes, without ears, without speech, without mind' (B.U. III. 8. 8). The Imperishable is *Brahman.*

Section 4 (13)

THE SYLLABLE *AUM*

I. 3. 13. *īkṣati-karma-vyapadeśāt saḥ*

On account of the mention as the object of seeing, he (is the Highest Self).
īkśati: seeing; *karma:* action; *vyapadeśāt:* on account of mention; *saḥ:* he.

Ś. thinks that the passage (*Praśna U.* V. 2) refers to *Brahman* without determinations and not *Brahman* with determinations. The objector contends that as the reward promised is a limited one confined to *brahma-loka,* it is not a worthy reward for one who knows the Highest Self. It is said that he will reach the Highest, *para-puruṣa,* but this has reference only to the physical body. *Hiraṇya-garbha* is the vital principle in all creatures.[1] To all this Ś. answers that the object of meditation is the object of sight. Though it is possible that an object of meditation may be unreal, the object of sight must be real and existing. The Highest Self is the object of meditation and perfected sight or intuition.[2] The object of meditation is not the *jīva-ghana* (*Praśna U.* V. 5) but that which transcends it, as the use of the words *para* and *puruṣa* indicate. When *jīva-ghana* is itself said to be transcendent, it is only in the sense that it transcends the sense-organs and their objects. Or if *jīva-ghana* is taken as referring to the *brahma-loka* presided over by *Brahmā* or *Hiraṇya-garbha* the cosmic Person[3] including in him all the *jīvas,* the man who meditates on the *Aum* with its three elements does not stop there but goes further along in attaining the vision of the Highest Self which exceeds the *jīva-ghana* and yet dwells in them all. Scripture also holds that the Highest Person is *Brahman.* From the

[1] *piṇḍaḥ sthūlo dehaḥ, prāṇaḥ sūtrātmā.* Ānandagiri.
[2] *samyag-darśana-viṣayī-bhūta.* Ś.
[3] *Pāṇini:* IV. 3. 77, *mūrttaṁ ghanaḥ.*

worship of the determinate, we pass to the meditation of the Indeterminate. In other words, one attains to freedom by degrees along with *Brahmā*.[1]

R. holds that meditation and seeing have the same sense as seeing is the result of devout meditation.[2] The doubt considered by R. is whether the Highest Person mentioned in the text is *Hiraṇya-garbha* or the Lord of all. The objection is raised that it refers to *Brahmā* or *Hiraṇya-garbha*,[3] as he who meditates on *Aum* as having one *mātrā* obtains the world of men; he who meditates on it as having two *mātrās*, obtains the world of the atmosphere and so those who meditate on it as having three syllables reach the world of *Brahmā*, who is constituted by the aggregate of the individual souls. This collective soul is higher than the many souls which are associated with the body and the sense-organs. R. answers that the Highest Person is referred to and not *Brahmā*. For the text says that the object of seeing is the Highest Self (C.U. IV. 15. 1). *Brahmā* is himself *jīva-ghana* for he is created (Ś.U. VI. 18) and his world is perishable.

While for Ś. the question relates to *Brahman* or *Īśvara*, for R. it relates to *Īśvara* or *Brahmā*. Ś. says that the reference is to *Brahman* without determinations. R. holds that the reference is to the Highest Person *Īśvara* and not *Brahmā, Hiraṇya-garbha*.

Section 5 (14–21)

ĀKĀŚA WITHIN THE HEART OF *BRAHMAN*

I. 3. 14. *dahara uttarebhyaḥ*

The small (space) (is Brahman) on account of what follows.

dahara: small; *uttarebhyaḥ:* on account of what follows.

In the *Adhikaraṇa-ratna-mālā*, the *sūtras* 14–21 are divided into two sections comprising 14–18 and 19–21. Both these discuss the question whether *ākāśa* within the lotus of the heart is the element *ākāśa* or the individual soul or *Brahman*.

The passage considered is C.U. VIII. 1. The doubt arises whether 'small' here refers to the element *ākāśa* or the individual soul or *Brahman*. It may mean the element (*bhūtākāśa*). Though it is all-pervading, it is spoken of as small since it is located in the heart. Though there is one *ākāśa*, it may be conceived as two, one inside

[1] *tri-mātreṇauṁkāreṇālambanena paramātmānam abhidhyāyataḥ; phalam brahma-loka-prāptiḥ, krameṇa ca samyag-darśanotpattir iti. krama-mukty abhiprāyam etad bhaviṣyati.* Ś.

[2] *atra dhyātīkṣati-śabdāv eka-viṣayau, dhyāna-phalatvād īkṣaṇasya.* R.

[3] *jīva-samaṣṭi-rūpo'ṇḍāthipatiś catur-mukhaḥ.* R.

and the other outside, for the purpose of meditation and it is possible to compare them (C.U. VIII. 1. 3). *Brahma-pura* is the city in the form of the body and the Lord of the city is the individual soul. The soul dwells in the heart which is the seat of mind. It is spoken of as small since it is compared to the point of a goad. (Ś.U. V. 8.) *Dahara* may also mean the quality of something else residing within the small *ākāśa* in the heart and in no case can it apply to *Brahman* who is not connected with body.

Ś. answers these points. *Dahara* does not refer to the element *ākāśa*, for the teacher asks us to search and understand that which is in the heart and it cannot be the element *ākāśa*. The space within is said to be as large as the space without. It is free from sin, etc. These qualities cannot apply to the element *ākāśa*.

If the reference is to the individual soul, it cannot be said to be all-pervading like *ākāśa*. *Brahma-pura* need not mean the city in which the individual soul resides; it means the city of *Brahman*. (*Praśna U.* V. 5; see also B.U. II. 5. 18.) This body is not only the abode of *Brahman*,[1] but is useful for its realisation. Even if *brahma-pura* is the city of the individual soul, we are told that *Brahman* resides in the body in close proximity with the devotee even as the image of *Viṣṇu* is said to be accessible in the *sālagrāma* stone.[2] When we find that the results of the knowledge of the *dahara* are imperishable as compared with the perishable nature of the results of works, it is clear that *dahara* refers to the Highest Self and not to the individual soul. (C.U. VIII. 1. 6.)

Śrīkaṇṭha holds that the passage stating that what is within *daharākāśa* is to be sought (C.U. VIII. 1. 1) suggests that the seat is *cit-śakti* and what is seated is *Brahman*.

I. 3. 15. *gati-śabdābhyāṁ tathā hi dṛṣṭaṁ liṅgaṁ ca*

(*The small is Brahman*) *on account of the movement and of the word for thus it is seen* (*elsewhere*) *and there is reason for inference as well.*

gati-śabdābhyām: on account of the movement and of the word, *tathā hi:* for thus; *dṛṣṭam:* it is seen; *liṅgam:* reason for inference; *ca:* too.

The reference is to C.U. VIII. 3. 2, where it is said that all creatures here go day after day into the *Brahma*-world. Here the word 'creatures' is used for the individual souls and *Brahma*-world for the small one. Again, in C.U. VI. 8. 1, it is said that during sleep the individual soul becomes one with pure being. *Brahma-loka* is *Brahman* and not the world of the god *Brahmā*. The term 'world of

[1] *upalabdher adhiṣṭhānam brahmaṇa deha iṣyate tenāsādhāraṇatvena deho brahma-puram bhavet. Bhāmatī.*

[2] *athavā jīva-pura evāsmin brahma sannihitam upadekṣyate, yathā sālagrāme viṣṇus sannihitaḥ iti tadvat.* Ś.

Brahmā' in apposition with the word which refers to the small one is an inferential mark that the small one is *Brahman*.

I. 3. 16. *dhṛteś ca mahimno'syāsminn upalabdheḥ*

(The small is Brahman) because of support also and because his greatness is observed in him.

dhṛteḥ: because of support; *ca:* and; *mahimnaḥ:* greatness; *asya:* his (the Supreme Self's); *asmin:* in him; *upalabdheḥ:* because it is found or observed.

C.U. (VIII. 4. 1) declares that the Highest Self is the bridge, support and boundary which keeps the worlds apart. The greatness of the *dahara* or the small is indicated in B.U. III. 8. 9. See also IV. 4. 22. *Dahara* is the Highest Self.

R., Śrīkaṇṭha and Baladeva adopt the same view; they interpret the words differently; *asya:* of the Lord; *asmin:* in the small space. The *sūtra* reads: Because supporting the worlds is a greatness of him (the Lord) is observed in it (the small space).

I. 3. 17. *prasiddheś ca*

And because it is well known (that dahara is the Highest Self).

prasiddheḥ: because it is well-known; *ca:* and.

When it is said that *ākāśa* alone manifests names and forms (C.U. VIII. 14), that 'all these beings spring forth from *ākāśa*' (C.U. I. 9. 1), *ākāśa* cannot mean the element but only the Highest Self.

Śrīkaṇṭha refers to passages in the *Mahā U.* and *Kaivalya U.*, where the Supreme Lord is said to be the object worshipped as abiding in the small lotus (of the heart).

I. 3. 18. *itara-parāmarśāt sa iti cen nāsambhavāt*

If it is said that on account of reference to the other (the individual soul), he is (the dahara), (we say) no for it is impossible.

itara: other; *parāmarśāt:* on account of reference; *sa:* he (is the small); *iti:* thus; *cen:* if; *na:* no; *asaṁbhavāt:* for it is impossible.

In the previous *sūtras*, reference to the element of *ākāśa* is rejected. In this and the following *sūtras*, reference to the individual soul is considered.

The objector takes up C.U. VIII. 3. 4 and argues that *saṁ-prasāda* applies to the individual soul. Ś. answers that the individual soul qualified by the adjuncts of *buddhi*, etc., cannot be compared with the unlimited *ākāśa*. Again, qualities such as freedom from sin cannot apply to a being who is limited by adjuncts.

R. points out that the individual soul cannot be the *dahara* as the qualities attributed to it such as freedom from sin, etc., can apply only to the Supreme Lord.

I. 3. 19. *uttarāc ced āvirbhūta-svarūpas tu*

If it be said (that dahara is the individual soul) on account of subsequent (statements), (we say) (but the subsequent passage refers to the individual soul only in so far as) its real nature has become manifest.

uttarāt: on account of what is subsequent; *cet:* if; *āvirbhūta:* become manifest; *svarūpaḥ:* one's real nature; *tu:* but.

The objector takes up the dialogue, which comes after the *dahara-vidyā* between Indra and Virocana on the one hand and Prajā-pati on the other. (C.U. VIII. 7. 1 ff.) Prajā-pati, while declaring that he is teaching the truth of the Self which is free from sin, old age, death, etc., speaks only of the individual soul, the person seen in the eye, the dream and sleep conditions of the individual soul and it is the individual soul which rises in the form of *saṁ-prasāda* from the body, meets the Highest Light and appears in its own form.

Ś. points out that Prajā-pati is not speaking of the individual soul qualified by the conditions of waking, dream and sleep but the self which has manifested its real nature, after rising beyond the consciousness of body into realisation of its oneness with *Brahman.* According to Ś. the individual soul whose nature has become manifest is no longer the individual soul. It is this freed individual (M.U. III. 2. 9) that is referred to by Prajā-pati.

If it be objected that if the true nature of the individual soul is *Brahman,* all this discussion about its activities, its rise from the body becomes meaningless, Ś. argues that just as a crystal which is white and transparent is not discerned to be separate from the adjunct of real or blue colour, the individual soul which is pure consciousness or light appears to be of the nature of the *upādhis* or the adjuncts of body, sense and mind and to be endowed with the activities of hearing, seeing, etc., on account of the lack of discrimination. The moment discrimination arises, when the crystal appears as white and transparent, the individual soul appears in its original form of the Self. The embodied or the disembodied condition of the soul is the result of the absence or presence of discriminative knowledge;[1] notwithstanding the possession of body, the soul is without the body if it has the knowledge that it is one with *Brahman.* If it has no such knowledge it remains an individual soul bound up with the *upādhis.* Prajā-pati gradually leads us on to the true nature of the individual soul as nothing but the Highest Self. According to Ś. the author of the *sūtras* disproves the erroneous doctrine of the duality of the Highest Self and the individual soul. He distinguishes the Highest Self from the individual soul but does not distinguish the individual soul from the Highest Self.[2] The latter as the support

[1] *vivekāvivekāmātreṇaivātmano'śarīratvaṁ sa-śarīratvaṁ ca.* Ś. See B.G. XIII. 31; *Kaṭha U.* I. 2. 22.

[2] *paramātmano jīvād anyatvaṁ draḍhayati, jīvasya tu na parasmād anyatvaṁ pratipipādayiṣati.*

is different from the things imagined to exist but the imagined things cannot exist apart from the support on account of which they are imagined. The rope exists by itself and is different from the serpent but the serpent which is imaginary cannot exist apart from the rope.

Ś. also refers to some who belong to his own school of thought who hold that the individual soul as such is real.[1]

For Bhāskara the statement of Prajā-pati does not refer to the individual soul as such but to the soul which has attained the form of the Supreme Self.

R. holds that Prajā-pati's teaching and the statement about *dahara* have different topics. What refers to the *dahara* does not apply to the individual soul even when it has freed itself from bondage and become free from sin.

Nimbārka argues that the Highest Self having his real nature ever manifest is the small one but not the individual soul who has his real nature manifest, not always but only during release.

I. 3. 20. *anyārthaś ca parāmarśaḥ*

And the reference to the individual soul has a different meaning.
anya: other; *arthaḥ:* meaning; *ca:* and; *parāmarśaḥ:* reference.

The reference to the individual soul in regard to *saṁ-prasāda* means that when the soul is tired of the activities of waking and dream and becomes desirous of resting, it goes beyond the consciousness of gross and subtle bodies, in deep sleep. It then reaches the highest light or *Brahman* and so appears in its own real nature. Here the reference to the individual soul is to make us aware of its real nature.

Nimbārka holds that the reference to the individual soul is for showing that the Supreme Self is the cause of the manifestation of the real nature of the individual soul.

I. 3. 21. *alpa-śruter iti cet tad uktam*

If it be said that (*ākāśa cannot mean the Highest Self*) *on account of its being mentioned by the śruti as small, we say that*) *that* (*point*) *has already been considered.*
alpa: small; *śruteḥ:* on account of mention by *śruti; iti:* thus; *cet:* if; *tat:* that; *uktam:* (has been) said.

In I. 2. 7, it has already been said that the Supreme, though all-pervading, is capable of being meditated upon, as dwelling in the small heart. It has also been said that the *ākāśa* within the heart is as large as the *ākāśa* without.

[1] *apare tu vādinaḥ pāramārthikam eva jaivaṁ rūpam iti manyante. asmadīyāś ca kecit.* Ś.

Section 6 (22–23)

UNIVERSAL LIGHT AS *BRAHMAN*

I. 3. 22. *anu-kṛtes tasya ca*

And on account of acting (shining) after and (of the word) his.
anu-kṛteḥ: on account of acting after; *tasya:* his; *ca:* and.

While Ś. treats the two *sūtras* 22 and 23 as a new section R. holds that they do not start a new topic but furnish additional arguments for the conclusion reached in the preceding *sūtras*.

The passage considered is *Kaṭha U.* II. 2. 15. 'Everything shines only after that shining light. His shining illumines all this world.' (See also M.U. II. 2. 11.) The doubt is raised whether this being is a luminous body or the Highest Self. The answer is that it is the Highest Self for C.U. (III. 14. 2) says that his form is light, *bhā-rūpaḥ*. Luminosity being the common nature of all, there is no need for one to shine first and the others to follow. Imitation does not depend on similarity. Iron is different from fire and dust is different from wind; yet a red-hot iron ball burns things like the fire and the dust on the ground blows after the blowing wind.

The word 'his' refers to the source of the light of the sun, moon. B.U. (IV. 4. 16) says of him that he is the light of lights (*jyotiṣāṁ jyotiḥ*). Obviously this does not refer to the physical light.

Ś. suggests that we may take it not merely as the cause of the light of the sun, moon, etc., but as the cause of all this, *sarvam idam*. (See M.U. II. 2. 5; B.U. IV. 2. 4, IV. 3. 6.)

R. takes *anu-kṛti* to mean imitation and quotes M.U. III. 1. 3. The individual soul in Prajā-pati's teaching is the imitator and *Brahman* which is imitated is the *dahara*.[1] Niṁbārka follows this interpretation.

I. 3. 23. *api ca smaryate*

And the same is declared in the smṛti.
api: also (the same); *ca:* and; *smaryate:* is declared in *smṛti*.
ca is omitted by R. and Baladeva.

The reference here is to B.G. XV. 6, 12. 'That splendour of the sun that illumines this whole world, that which is in the moon, that which is in the fire, that splendour, know as mine.'

R. mentions B.G. XIV. 2. 'Having resorted to this wisdom and become of like nature to me, they are not born at the time of creation; nor are they disturbed at the time of dissolution.' Niṁbārka accepts this interpretation. Śrīnivasa says: *Smṛti* declares the equality of the individual soul, freed from all bondage, in B.G. XIV. 2. So it is established that the *daharākāśa* is none but the Supreme Self.

[1] *ato'nukartā prajā-pati-vākye nirdiṣṭo'nu-kāryam brahma daharākāśaḥ*. R.

K*

Section 7 (24–25)

THE PERSON OF THE SIZE OF A THUMB IS *BRAHMAN*

I. 3. 24. *śabdād eva pramitaḥ*

On account of the text itself, what is measured (*by a thumb*) (*is the Highest Self*).

śabdāt: on account of the text; *eva:* itself; *pramitaḥ:* is measured.

The passage considered is *Kaṭha U.* II. 1. 12–13. 'The person of the size of a thumb resides in the middle of the body. After knowing him who is the lord of the past, and the future, one does not shrink (from him). This, verily, is that.' 'The person of the size of a thumb resides in the middle of the body, like a flame without smoke. He is the lord of the past and the future. He is the same today and the same tomorrow. This, verily, is that.'[1]

The objector contends that the person referred to is the individual soul and not the Highest Self who cannot be measured. The soul limited by adjuncts, *saṁsāri-jīva*, may be taken as being measured by a thumb. In the M.B., Yama is said to have dragged out forcibly by his noose the thumb-sized person from out of the body of Satyavān.

The person can be the Highest Self alone for none else can control the past and the future. The words 'this is that' are an answer to the question by Naciketas who is asking about *Brahman*. The person is the Highest God and not the individual soul.

I. 3. 25. *hṛdyapekṣayā tu manuṣyādhikāratvāt*

In the reference to the heart, however, (*the Supreme is said to be of the size of a thumb*) *because men have a right* (*to the study of the Veda*).

hṛdi: in the heart; *apekṣayā:* with reference to; *tu:* however; *manuṣya:* man; *adhikāratvāt:* because of a right.

But how can a measure be attributed to the Omnipresent Self? The *sūtra* answers this doubt. To the objection that the size of the heart varies in different classes of beings and so the measure of the size of a thumb cannot apply to all, the *sūtra* says it applies to men only. The Scripture, though propounded without any distinction, does in reality entitle men only to act according to its precepts for they alone can act (according to the precepts); they alone are desirous (of the results of actions), they are not excluded by prohibitions and are subject to the precepts about *upanayana* ceremony, etc.[2] Animals, gods and seers are excluded. Gods cannot perform sacrifices for they involve offerings to the gods. Seers cannot perform sacrifices, as the ancestral seers are involved in the performance of

[1] P.U., pp. 634–5.

[2] *śāstraṁ hy aviśeṣa-pravṛttam api manuṣyānevādhikaroti śaktatvād arthitvād aparyudastatvād upanayanādi-śāstrāc ceti.* Ś.

the sacrifices. Again, those who desire release do not care for the perishable fruits of sacrifices. The third and the fourth reasons give the right only to the three higher castes and *upanayana* is prescribed as indispensable for the study of the *Veda*.[1] As the human body has a fixed size the heart also has a fixed size. The Scripture says that 'the person of the size of a thumb is the inner self, etc.': *Kaṭha U.* II. 3. 17.[2]

R. argues that men are qualified for devout meditation. In so far as the Highest Self abides in the heart of the devotee—which heart is of the measure of a thumb—it may itself be viewed as having the measure of a thumb.[3]

Śrīnivāsa gives alternative explanations. The Lord is said to be one who makes three strides (*tri-vikrama*) in reference to the three worlds. If he can be said to be of three strides why not 'of the size of a thumb'. Again, the Lord manifests himself to be of the size of a thumb to please his devotees. *Apekṣayā* is treated as a reference to the worshipper's wishes.

Though Ś. admits that Scriptures are of universal application, and are to be followed by all, some restrictions were imposed on certain sections of the people.

Section 8 (26–33)

GODS ARE CAPABLE OF THE KNOWLEDGE OF *BRAHMAN*

In this section the question whether the gods are capable of the knowledge is answered in the affirmative but incidentally other problems are raised such as the relation of the different species of beings to the words denoting them.

I. 3. 26. *tad-upary api bādarāyaṇaḥ sambhavāt*

Also beings above them (men) (are qualified for the study of the Vedas), as Bādarāyaṇa holds, on account of possibility.

tad: them; *upari:* above; *api:* also; *bādarāyaṇaḥ:* as Bādarāyaṇa holds; *sambhavāt:* on account of possibility.

Gods may have the desire for formal release caused by the reflection that all effects, objects and powers are non-permanent. Just as men are led to seek for salvation as the earthly rewards do not yield permanent fruits, so also gods who realise the transitoriness of even heavenly enjoyments are led to worship the Supreme Lord. It may be argued that gods cannot practise meditation since they do not have physical bodies and the God they meditate on should have a form.[4]

[1] See *Pūrva Mīmāṁsā Sūtra* VI. 1.

[2] P.U., pp. 647–8.

[3] *paramātmana upāsanārtham upāsaka-hṛdaye vartamānatvād upāsaka hṛdayasyāṅguṣṭha-pramāṇatvāt tad-apekṣayedam aṅguṣṭha-pramitatvam upapadyate.* R.

[4] *na hi nirviśeṣa-devatā-dhiyam adhirohati.* R.

Gods are known to possess bodies, from the accounts of them we read in the epics and the *purāṇas*, from paintings and images. In their case there is no need for the *upanayana* ceremony since the *Vedas* are open to them. We know that they accept discipleship. Indra lived as a disciple of Prajā-pati for 101 years (C.U. VIII. 11. 3). Bhṛgu approached his father Varuṇa to teach him the knowledge of *Brahman* (T.U. III. 1). Gods and sages may be incapable of action such as a sacrifice (see *Pūrva Mīmāṁsā Sūtra* VI. 1. 5) as there are no other gods whom they have to please or other sages to whose families they would belong. So far as the knowledge of *Brahman* is concerned no action need be performed. So far as the size of the Person is concerned, it may be measured by the thumb of a god, even as it is measured in the case of men by the thumb of a man.

B.U. I. 4. 10 says: '*Brahman*, indeed, was this, in the beginning. It knew itself only as "I am *Brahman*". Therefore it became all. Whoever among the gods becomes awakened to this, he, indeed, becomes that. It is the same in the case of seers, the same in the case of men.'

R. says that wish and capacity exist in the case of gods[1] as they also are liable to suffering, arising from the assaults hard to be endured, of the different kinds of pain and as they also know that supreme enjoyment is to be found in the Highest *Brahman*, which is untouched even by the shadow of imperfection and is full of auspicious qualities of the highest perfection.

I. 3. 27. *virodhaḥ karmaṇīti cen nānekapratipatter darśanāt*

If it be said (*that possession of bodies would result in*) *a contradiction to* (*sacrificial*) *works,* (*we say that*) *it is not so because it is observed that* (*gods*) *assume many forms.*

virodhaḥ: contradiction; *karmaṇi:* in action; *iti:* thus; *cet:* if; *na:* not; *aneka:* many; *pratipatteḥ:* assumption; *darśanāt:* because it is observed.

The difficulty is mentioned that, if gods have bodies, they may be expected to be present like priests on the occasion of a sacrifice. How can God Indra be present at many sacrifices, if they are performed at the same time? In answer, it is stated that one and the same deity can assume various forms at the same time. B.U. (III. 9. 1–2) indicates that one and the same divine Self may at the same time appear in many forms. It is mentioned in the M.B. (XII. 110–62) that a *yogin*, who has acquired supernatural powers, can assume many forms, have many experiences and take them all back into himself.[2]

[1] *arthitva-sāmarthyayoḥ sambhavāt.*

[2] *ātmanāṁ vai sahasrāṇi bahūni bharatarṣabha*
kuryād yogī balam prāpya taiś ca sarvair mahīm caret
prāpnuyād viṣayān kaiścit kaiścid ugram tapaś caret
saṁkṣipec ca punas tāni sūryo raśmigaṇān iva.

Another explanation is also possible. Just as a *Brāhmaṇa* who cannot be fed by different people at the same time can nevertheless be saluted by them all at the same time, a deity can without leaving his place be the common object of reverence of several persons who may at the same time give their offerings to him. The embodiedness of gods is in no way a hindrance to their sacrificial activity.

Nimbārka answers the objection that embodiedness of the deity will result in a contradiction with regard to work by 'the observation of the assumption' simultaneously of many bodies by one and the same deity. Śrīnivāsa takes a different view. 'Because of the observation of many worships.' Just as one and the same teacher is found to be saluted simultaneously by many worshippers, so different performers of sacrifices may give their offerings to one and the same corporal deity who abides in his own place.

I. 3. 28. *śabda iti cen nātaḥ prabhavāt pratyakṣānumānābhyām*

If it be said that (a contradiction will result in regard to) word, (we say) that it is not so because perception and inference show the origination of everything from this (the word).

śabda: word; *iti:* so; *cet:* if; *na:* not; *ataḥ:* from this; *prabhavāt:* on account of origination; *pratyakṣānumānābhyām:* from perception and inference.

The problem of the relation in which the different species of beings stand to the words which denote them is taken up for consideration here. Ś. opposes the views of Upavarṣa, the *Mīmāṁsaka* according to whom the word is nothing but the aggregate of the letters which constitute it as well as the view of the grammarians who teach that over and above the aggregate of the letters, there exists a supersensuous entity called *sphoṭa,* which is the direct cause of the apprehension of the meaning of a word.

In this *sūtra,* the objection is considered whether the authoritativeness of the *Veda* is not contradicted by the attribution of bodies to divinities. The possession of body subjects them to the changes of birth and death, so the eternal connection of the eternal word with a non-eternal thing is inconceivable.[1] The *sūtra* answers it by saying that the world with the gods and other beings originates from the *Veda*. But this is not consistent with I. 1. 2 which holds that *Brahman* is the origin of all things and, again, the word or name comes into existence after the object which is given the word or the name. As the objects are transitory even the words or names are transitory and so cannot be self-valid and eternal. In reply it is said that the words are connected with the *jāti,* or the class which is eternal, and not with the individuals which may be infinite in number and transitory. Words connote some permanent meanings on account of whose presence in individual objects, the names are extended to them. It is in this sense

[1] See *Pūrva Mīmāṁsā Sūtra* I. 1. 5.

that the individuals are said to originate from words and not in the sense that the word is, like *Brahman*, the material cause of the universe.

The evidence for the view that the universe arises on account of the efficient cause of the word lies in perception and inference. Perception means *śruti*; for its validity it is not dependent on anything else; inference is *smṛti*.[1] Ś quotes texts from *śruti* and *smṛti*, *Ṛg Veda* IX. 6. 2; B.U. I. 2. 4; M.B. XII. 233. 24 and 25; *Manu* I. 21. Just as we make jars after conceiving the meaning of the word jar, the Creator first conceives the words and then corresponding to them creates the universe.[2]

The question is raised about the nature of the word which causes the universe. The grammarians contend that it is the *sphoṭa* which arises in the mind: after the word is uttered and on account of it, the meaning of the word becomes known. The *sphoṭa* is the eternal entity and not the letters which perish as soon as they are uttered.[3] Gods, etc., cannot arise from the perishable words but only from the imperishable *sphoṭa*. Upavarṣa, the *Mīmāṁsaka*, opposes this view and argues that there is no separate perception of the *sphoṭa* over and above the perception of the letters. The letters are not short-lived because they are recognised to be the same. They are not different on different occasions. The object of cognition is not *sphoṭa*, an additional something which is suddenly perceived after the accumulation of the successive impressions of the letters. The letters of a word which succeed each other in a certain order give all the meaning they have to our intelligence in one single act of cognition. There is no need for the assumption of a *sphoṭa*. Whether the word is of the nature of letters or class or *sphoṭa*, the theory that the gods originate from the eternal words remains unaffected.

R. quotes *Manu*, *Viṣṇu Purāṇa* and others. Cp. 'In the beginning there was sent forth by the Creator, divine speech beginningless and endless—in the form of the *Veda* and from it originated all creatures'.

Nimbārka quotes *Taittirīya Brāhmaṇa* (II. 6. 2. 3), 'He evolved name and form by means of the *Veda*'. Śrīnivāsa also states the objection and answer. The objection says that the gods who possess bodies which are non-eternal must themselves be non-eternal whereas the Vedic words which denote the gods are eternal. How can

[1] *pratyakṣaṁ hi śrutiḥ prāmāṇyaṁ praty anapekṣatvāt; anumānam smṛtiḥ prāmāṇyaṁ prati sāpekṣatvāt.* Ś. *śrutiṁ paśyanti munayaḥ smaranti ca tathā smṛtim.*

[2] *api ca cikīrṣitam artham anutiṣṭhan tasya vācakam śabdam pūrvam smṛtvā paścāt tam artham anutiṣṭhatīti sarveṣāṁ naḥ pratyakṣam etat. tathā prajā-pater api sraṣṭuḥ sṛṣṭeḥ pūrvam vaidikāś śabdā manasi prādurbabhūvuḥ; paścāt tad-anugatān arthān sasarjeti gamyate. tathā ca śrutiḥ : sa bhūr iti vyāharat sa bhūmim asṛjata. Taittirīya Brāhmaṇa* II. 2. 4. 2.

[3] *anādi-nidhanā hy eṣā vāg utsṛṣṭā svayambhuvā*
ādau veda-mayī divyā yataḥ sarvā prasūtayaḥ.

there be an eternal connection between the non-eternal gods and the eternal Vedic words? The answer states that the individual gods are non-eternal but this does not show that the Vedic words are meaningless for they denote not the individual (*vyakti*) but the type (*ākṛti*). While the individual is non-eternal, the type is eternal. The non-eternal individuals are created at the beginning of each creation in accordance with the eternal types which are indicated by the eternal Vedic words.

I. 3. 29. *ata eva ca nityatvam*

And for this very reason, the eternity (of the Vedas follows).
ataḥ: therefore, for this reason; *eva:* very or same; *ca:* and; *nityatvam:* eternity.

The *Veda* is the eternal source of the universe. *Ṛg Veda* (X. 71. 3) tells us that the eternal speech dwelling in the sages was found out by those who performed the sacrifice. See also M.B. which says: 'Formerly the great sages, with the permission of the Self-born, obtained through their penance the *Vedas* together with the epics, which had been hidden at the close of the cosmic period.'[1]

The Vedic *mantras* or hymns are said to be composed by different seers like Viśvāmitra and so on. It may be argued that the Vedic *mantras* are non-eternal as their authors are non-eternal. But the seers are not really the authors or composers of the hymns which are eternal. They only utter or reveal the Vedic *mantras* and these revealers change from age to age.

I. 3. 30. *samāna-nāma-rūpatvāc cāvṛttāv apy avirodho darśanāt smṛteś ca*

And on account of the similarity of name and form (there is) no contradiction (to the eternity of the word of the Veda) even with regard to the recurrence (of the world), (as is clear) from what is perceived (śruti) and the smṛti.
samāna-nāma-rūpatvāt: on account of the similarity of name and form; *ca:* and; *āvṛttau:* recurrence (repetition of cycles of births and deaths); *api:* even; *avirodhaḥ:* absence of contradiction; *darśanāt:* from what is perceived; *smṛteḥ:* from the *smṛti; ca:* and.

The eternity of the *Vedas* is not affected even though there are new creations with new *Indras* and other gods because the names and forms of each new creation are the same as those of the preceding world. In spite of periodical creations and dissolutions, *saṁsāra* is beginningless and endless. Even as a man who has awakened from sleep goes on with his affairs even as he did before he went to sleep, so also creations and dissolutions do not disturb the continuity. See K.U. III. 3.

[1] *yugānte'ntarhitān vedān setihāsān maharṣayaḥ*
lebhire tapasā pūrvam anujñātās svayambhuvā.

If the objection is raised that the dissolution or *mahāpralaya* is like death and not sleep and if continuity is kept up, it is because all men do not sleep at the same time, so that those who are awake remind others of their previous lives, the answer is that gods do not suffer from the defects which afflict men; the gods remember the past even after dissolution. Besides, the world is nothing but the results of the actions of beings done in the previous creation. It provides opportunities for experiencing the pleasures and pains consequent on past conduct. By our present actions we prepare for future creation. So the world moves on perpetually from desires to actions, from actions to their results and from the results to desires. There remains always a potentiality of the world to become actual through the same names and forms, same desires and actions in spite of apparent dissolution. The new creation is not an effect without a cause. See *Ṛg Veda* X. 190–3.

Vāk is sometimes described as subtle, eternal, imperishable and incomprehensible to the senses.[1] Those who meditate on *Vāk* overcome death.[2] *Taittirīya-Brāhmaṇa* II. 8. 8 says:

> Whom the Sages, the Makers of Hymns, the Wise Ones,
> And the Gods also, sought with austerity and with Effort:
> Her, the Divine Speech, with this Offering we pray;
> May She vouchsafe Welfare unto the World.[3]

In Proverbs viii. and Job xxviii. Wisdom is said to have its origin in God and also its place beside God. Wisdom is represented as a pre-existent divine associate of God in his creative activity. She was before the foundation of the world. 'Whoso findeth me [i.e. wisdom] findeth life and shall obtain favour of the Lord. But he that sinneth against me [i.e. wisdom] wrongeth his own soul: all they that hate me love death.'[4] St John's Prologue begins: 'In the beginning was the Word; the Word was with God.' The Word marks the transition from eternity to history.

I. 3. 31. *madhvādiṣv asambhavād anadhikāram jaiminiḥ*

On account of the impossibility (*of the gods having a right to the knowledge of*) *the honey and the rest they* (*the gods*) *are not qualified,* (so) *Jaimini* (*thinks*).

madhvādiṣu: in *madhu* (honey), knowledge and others; *asambhavāt:*

[1] *yāṁ sūkṣmāṁ nityāṁ atīndriyāṁ vācam ṛṣayaḥ sākṣātkṛta-dharmāṇo mantradṛśaḥ paśyanti.* Puṇyarāja on *Vākyapadīya* I. 6.

[2] *te mṛtyum ati-vartante ye vai vācam upāsate.*

[3] *yām ṛṣayo mantrakṛto manīṣiṇaḥ*
anvaicchan devās tapasā śrameṇa
tāṁ devīṁ vācaṁ haviṣā yajāmahe
sā no dadhātu sukṛtasya loke.

[4] *Proverbs* viii. 35–6.

on account of impossibility; *anadhikāram:* no fitness or qualification; *jaiminiḥ:* Jaimini (thinks).

In C.U. III, it is said the sun is the honey of gods, the sky is the bee-hive, the Vedic hymns the trees, the sacrifices are the flowers and the offerings of *soma*, milk, etc., are the honey itself. Led by Agni, Indra and others, the gods live on this honey. It is possible for men to meditate on the sun and not for gods. They cannot at once be the meditators and the objects of meditation. Again, certain divinities like Fire, Wind, Sun, Directions are each declared to be a foot (*pāda*) of *Brahman* and as such are recommended to be the objects of meditation for men; it is not possible for gods to meditate on themselves. (C.U. III. 18. 2; III. 19. 1; IV. 3. 1.) Similarly the right and the left ears are to be meditated on as Gautama and Bhāradvāja respectively (B.U. II. 2. 4). It is not possible that these sages should meditate on themselves. So Jaimini holds that deities and sages are incapable of acquiring the knowledge of *Brahman*.

I. 3. 32. *jyotiṣi bhāvāc ca*

And because (*the words denoting the deities*) *are used in the sense* (*or sphere*) *of light.*

jyotiṣi: in the sphere of light; *bhāvāt:* because used; *ca:* and.

Agni, Āditya belong to the sphere of light. How can these be endowed with a bodily form or intelligence or choice? Since they are not personal beings, they are not capable of or qualified for the knowledge of *Brahman*. Other sources of knowledge which give personality to these luminous beings are not acceptable; so the objector contends that *devas* and similar beings are not qualified for the knowledge of *Brahman*.

R. Nimbārka hold that the objection is that as the gods meditate on the light of lights, *Brahman* (B.U. IV. 4. 16), they are not entitled to the honey meditation and the rest.

I. 3. 33. *bhāvaṁ tu bādarāyaṇo'sti hi*

But Bādarāyaṇa (*maintains*) *the existence* (*of qualification for Brahma-knowledge on the part of the deities*) *for there is certainly* (*evidence to show this*).

bhāvam: existence; *tu:* but; *bādarāyaṇaḥ:* Bādarāyaṇa; *asti:* is; *hi:* certainly.

The objection stated in the two previous *sūtras* is repudiated here. Though the qualification of the gods for *madhu-vidyā*, etc., may not be admitted, for the gods themselves are involved in them, the qualification for the pure knowledge of *Brahman* need not be denied to them.[1] Scripture says that the gods are qualified for *Brahma-*

[1] *yady api madhv-ādi-vidyāsu devatādi-vyāmiśrāsu asambhavo' dhikārasya, tathāpi asti hi śuddhāyām brahma-vidyāyām sambhavaḥ.* Ś.

knowledge. B.U. I. 4. 10; C.U. VII. 7. 2. Words like *Āditya*, though they refer to light, convey the idea of certain divine persons endowed with intelligence and pre-eminent power. By their power they reside within the light and assume any form they like. The Vedic injunctions presuppose certain characteristic shapes of the several divinities. The status of divinity is a stage leading to final emancipation.

Bhāskara thinks that there is scriptural evidence that the gods are entitled to the honey meditation and the rest.

Nimbārka holds that the gods are entitled not only to the knowledge of *Brahman* in general but also to the meditations in which they themselves are implicated.

Section 9 (34–38)

THE DISQUALIFICATION OF *ŚŪDRAS* FOR *BRAHMA*-KNOWLEDGE

I. 3. 34. *śugasya tad-anādara-śravaṇāt tad ādravaṇāt sūcyate hi*

The grief which he (Jānaśruti) felt on hearing the disrespectful words (about himself) made him run (toward Raikva) for that alone is indicated.

śuk: grief; *asya:* his; *tad-anādara-śravaṇāt:* on hearing the disrespectful words; *tad:* that; *ādravaṇāt:* because of running; *sūcyate:* indicated; *hi:* alone.

The objector urges that the *Śūdras* have a right to *Brahma*-knowledge for they desire that knowledge and are capable of it. There is no scriptural prohibition as we have in the matter of offering sacrifices. 'Therefore the *Śūdra* is unfit for sacrificing' (*Taittirīya Saṁhitā* VII. 1. 1. 6). The reason which disqualifies the *Śūdras* for sacrifices is their being without the sacred fires but that is no disqualification for knowledge. In C.U. (IV. 2. 3)[1] *saṁvarga-vidyā*, which is a part of *Brahma*-knowledge, is admitted for Jānaśruti. *Śūdras* like Vidura are spoken of as possessing *Brahma*-knowledge.

The answer is given that the *Śūdra* who is not competent for the *upanayana* ceremony cannot study the *Vedas* and is therefore disqualified for *Brahma*-knowledge. The word '*Śūdra*' does not refer to caste. It may refer to the grief of Jānaśruti and not to Jānaśruti himself. Whether Jānaśruti came to grief or grief fell on him or whether he rushed to Raikva on account of grief, the word '*śūdra*', refers to one of these three things and not to caste.[2]

[1] P.U., pp. 401ff.

[2] *śucā gurum abhidudrāveti śūdraḥ. śucam abhidudrāveti śūdraḥ. śucā abhidudruva iti śūdraḥ. haṁsa-vākyād ātmano'nādaraṁ śrutvā jānaśruteḥ śugutpannety etad eva kathaṁ gamyate yenāsau śūdra-śabdena sūcyate, tatrāha spṛśyate ceti. Ānandagiri.*

R. says that Jānaśruti, when taunted by a flamingo for his lack of *Brahma*-knowledge, was overtaken by grief and resorted to Raikva who had *Brahma*-knowledge. When Raikva addresses Jānaśruti as '*śūdra*', he refers to Jānaśruti's sorrow and not to his being a member of the fourth caste. The word *śūdra* etymologically considered means he who grieves or sorrows (*śocati*).

Śrīnivāsa, in his *Vedānta Kaustubha*, in stating the objection mentions that Vidura and others as well as women like Sulabhā, are found to possess *Brahma*-knowledge. Sulabhā carried on a highly learned discussion with Janaka, according to the M.B. (XII. 321).

As we will see, Ś. makes out that Sūta, Vidura and others, though born *Śūdras*, on account of the merit acquired in their previous lives, have obtained *Brahma*-knowledge. The author of *Parimala* argues that, though the *Śūdras* may not have a right to Vedic study, by listening to the Epics and the *Purāṇas*, on account of the strength of their merit previously acquired, they attain to a knowledge of *Brahman*. Thus knowledge of *Brahman* is open to all. The ways to it may be different for different people. All human beings by virtue of their humanity are entitled to *Brahma*-knowledge and salvation.

I. 3. 35. *kṣatriyatvagateś cottaratra caitrarathena liṅgāt*

(*Jānaśruti was not a śūdra because his kṣatriyahood is known from the inferential sign* (*supplied by his having mentioned*) *later on with Caitraratha* (*who was a kṣatriya*).

R. and Śrīkaṇṭha divide this into two *sūtras*: (i) *kṣatriyatvā gateś ca*; (ii) *uttaratra-liṅgāt*.

Bhāskara reads *kṣatriyatvā-gateś ca*; others as *kṣatriyatva-avagateś ca*.

kṣatriyatvagateḥ: nature of a *kṣatriya* being known; *ca*: and; *uttaratra*: later on; *caitrarathena*: with Caitraratha; *liṅgāt*: because of the inferential sign.

As Jānaśruti and Caitraratha are mentioned together we gather that Jānaśruti was also a *kṣatriya*. (C.U. IV. 3. 5.)

I. 3. 36. *saṁskāra-parāmarśāt tad-abhāvābhilāpāc ca*

On account of the mention of the ceremonies (*purificatory in the case of the three twice-born castes*) *and the absence of mention of them* (*in the case of the fourth caste*).

saṁskāras: ceremonies; *parāmarśāt*: on account of mention; *tad*: its; *abhāva*: absence; *abhilāpāt*: on account of mention; *ca*: and.

In *Śatapatha Brāhmaṇa* (XI. 5. 3. 13); C.U. (VII. 1. 1); *Praśna U.* (I. 1), *saṁskāras* like *upanayana*, initiation, are mentioned for the three twice-born castes, which are not for the fourth caste. See *Manu* X. 4; X. 126.

I. 3. 37. *tad abhāva-nirdhāraṇe ca pravṛtteḥ*

And because of (Gautama's) proceeding (to initiate Jābāla) on the ascertainment of the absence of that (viz. his śūdrahood).

tad-abhāva-nirdhāraṇe: on the ascertainment of the absence of that; *ca:* and; *pravṛtteḥ:* because of proceeding.

C.U. (IV. 4.5) tells us that Gautama was satisfied that Jābāla, who did not know his *gotra* or family name, was not a *śūdra* because he possessed the quality of speaking the truth and initiated him. Gautama said: 'A non-*Brāhmaṇa* cannot speak thus.'[1]

It is obvious from the *Chāndogya* episode that character and not birth was the test of Brahminhood. Jābāla was given initiation because he did not deviate from truth.

I. 3. 38. *śravaṇādhyayanārtha-pratiṣedhāt smṛteś ca*

And because (the Śūdra) is forbidden by smṛti from hearing and study (of the Vedas) and (understanding their) meaning.

śravaṇa: hearing; *adhyayana:* study; *artha:* meaning; *pratiṣedhāt:* because (it is) forbidden; *smṛteḥ:* by the *smṛti; ca:* and.

R. and Nimbārka state *smṛteś ca* as a separate *sūtra,* while Ś., Bhāskara and Baladeva treat the text given as one *sūtra.*

See *Gautama Dharma-śāstra* (XII. 4, 5, 6; X. 1); *Manu* (IV. 80). Obviously uneasy about these prohibitions, Ś. observes that Vidura, and Dharmavyādha had *Brahma*-knowledge as the result of deeds in their previous births and the fruit of knowledge, that is release, is inevitable.[2] Gaining knowledge through Vedic study is forbidden but gaining knowledge through other means is encouraged.

R. argues that on the theory of *Advaita* which holds that the sole Reality is *Brahman* of pure indeterminate intelligence and that bondage is ended by the mere cognition of the nature of Reality, restrictions imposed on the *Śūdras* cannot be justified. Even a *Śūdra* can free himself from the bondage as soon as the knowledge of the true nature of things has arisen in his mind through a statement resting on the traditional lore of men knowing the *Veda.* The knowers of truth will teach all for they are not bound by injunctions and prohibitions.[3] On this view the *Śūdras* have a perfect right to the knowledge of *Brahman.*[4] After attacking the *Advaita* doctrine, R. concludes that the way to release is by means of devout meditation. Such meditation by which we attain the grace of the Supreme can be

[1] *naitad a-brāhmaṇo vivaktum arhati.*

[2] *pūrva-kṛta-saṁskāra-vaśād vidura-dharmavyādhaprabhṛtīnām jñānotpattis teṣāṁ na śakyate phala-prāptiḥ pratibaddhum. jñānasyaikāntika-phalatvāt.* Ś.

[3] *śūdrasyāpi vedavit-sampradāyāvagata-vākyād vastu-yāthātmya-jñānena jagad-bhrama-nivṛttir api bhaviṣyati.* R.

[4] *śūdrādīnām eva brahma-vidyādhikāraḥ su-śobhanaḥ.*

learned from Scripture only. This is open only to those who are purified by such ceremonies as *upanayana*.[1]

The different methods of gaining salvation, meditation, devotion which lead to *Brahma*-knowledge are open to all. The restrictions with regard to *Vedic* study cannot be defended. If we take our stand on the potential divinity of all human beings, whatever be their caste or class, race or religion, sex or occupation, the methods for gaining release should be open to all.

Section 10 (39)

LIFE PRINCIPLE IN WHICH EVERYTHING TREMBLES IS *BRAHMAN*

I. 3. 39. *kampanāt*

On account of trembling (of the world, the life-principle is Brahman).

kampanāt: on account of trembling.

The discussion of the right for *Brahma*-knowledge was a digression. We get back to the meaning of the *Vedānta* texts. *Kaṭha U.* (II. 3. 2)[2] speaks of the whole world as trembling in life. The doubt is raised whether this life-principle cannot be air. In the context, it can only be *Brahman*. The passage makes out that *Brahman* constitutes the abode of the whole world. *Brahman* is the life of life (B.U. IV. 4. 18). *Kaṭha U.* (II. 2. 5) says that there is another on which the two life-breaths (*prāṇa* and *apāna*) depend.[3] *Brahman* is the cause of the great fear for it is said that the whole world carries on its many functions for fear of *Brahman* (T.U. II. 8. 1). Again, knowledge of air can give us a relative reward and not life eternal. See Ś.U. VI. 15.

R. and Nimbārka do not take it as a new section but only resume discussion of section 7, about the person measured as of the size of a thumb.

Baladeva begins a new section and discusses the question whether *vajra*, the thunderbolt, is *Brahman* or not.

[1] *yasya tu mokṣa-sādhanatayā vedānta-vākyair vihitaṁ jñānam upāsana-rūpaṁ tac ca para-brahma-bhūta-parama-puruṣa-prīṇanam tac ca śāstraika-samadhigamyam. upāsanā-śāstram copanayanādi-saṁskāra-saṁskṛtādhīta-svādhyāyajanitaṁ jñānaṁ viveka-vimokādi-sādhanānugṛhītam eva svopāyatayā svīkaroti.* R.

[2] P.U., p. 642.

[3] P.U., pp. 637–8.

Section 11 (40)

THE LIGHT IS *BRAHMAN*

I. 3. 40. *jyotir darśanāt*

The light (is Brahman) because it is seen (in the scriptural passage).
jyotiḥ: light; *darśanāt:* because it is seen.

The passage considered is C.U. VIII. 12. 3. 'That serene one when he rises up from this body and reaches the highest light appears in his own form. Such a one is the Supreme Person.'[1] Does this light refer to the physical sun which dispels darkness or *Brahman*? It is *Brahman* because the topic of discussion from VIII. 7. 1 onwards is the Self which is free from sin and is said to be the object of enquiry. VIII. 12. 1 speaks of freedom from body which is possible only in *Brahman*. To the objection that the Scripture (C.U. VIII. 6. 5) speaks of a man to be released as going to the sun, the release referred to in it is not the ultimate release which has nothing to do with going or departing. The light is spoken of as the 'highest light' and the 'highest Person'. This view is adopted by Ś., Bhāskara and Śrīkaṇṭha.

R. thinks that this section continues the preceding and makes out that the passage about the *anguṣṭha-mātra-puruṣa* which speaks of a primary light can only be *Brahman*.

Nimbārka adopts this view and says that the measured person is the Supreme Being.

Baladeva argues that the *Vajra* or thunderbolt is the Lord because in a preceding passage he is called light.

Section 12 (41)

ĀKĀŚA IS *BRAHMAN*

I. 3. 41. *ākāśo'rthāntaratvādi-vyapadeśāt*

Space (is Brahman) since it is mentioned as something different in meaning and so on.
ākāśaḥ: space or ether; *arthāntaratv-ādi:* being different in meaning and so on; *vyapadeśāt:* since it is mentioned.

The passage considered is C.U. VIII. 14. 1.[2] *Ākāśa* is said to be the cause of the manifestation of names and forms. These are contained in the immortal *Brahman*, the Self. The doubt is raised whether the *ākāśa* cannot be the elemental ether. The answer is given that it is *Brahman*. It contains within it names and forms. It is only *Brahman* that is different from names and forms. Elemental ether belongs to the world of created things, having names and forms, and is not

[1] P.U., p. 509.

[2] See P.U., p. 511.

different from them. For the manifestation of names and forms, the creative power of *Brahman* is ultimately responsible.[1] See C.U. VI. 3. 2. The words '*Brahman*, immortal, Self' all refer to Reality. This *sūtra* supports further what was said in I. 1. 22.

Nimbārka says that *Brahman* is something different even from the freed souls. Śrīnivāsa raises the question whether the reference here is to elemental ether, or the soul freed from the bondage of mundane existence, or the Supreme Self. It applies to the source of all manifestations. The freed soul, it will be pointed out later, cannot cause creation, etc., of the world.

Section 13 (42–43)

HE WHO CONSISTS OF KNOWLEDGE IS *BRAHMAN*

I. 3. 42. *suṣupty-utkrāntyor bhedena*

(*On account of the mention of the Highest Self*) *as different* (*from the individual soul*) *in the states of sleep and departure from the body*).
suṣupti-utkrāntyoḥ: in the states of sleep and departure.
bhedena: because of difference.

While Ś. takes these two *sūtras* (42 and 43) as beginning a new topic, R. takes the three *sūtras* 41–3 as one section, dealing with the question whether the ether in the C.U. passage (VIII. 14) refers to *Brahman* or the individual soul in the state of release. The latter doubt arises from the fact that the released soul is the theme of the passage immediately preceding. 'Shaking off evil as a horse his hairs, shaking off the body as the moon frees itself from the mouth of Rāhu, I, a perfected soul, obtain the uncreated *Brahma*-world, yea, I obtain it.' Does not this passage show that the released soul and *Brahman* are identical?

The objection is raised that the B.U. passage IV. 3. 7 refers to the embodied soul, that it describes how, in the state of deep sleep, being not conscious of anything, it is held embraced by the all-knowing Highest Self (IV. 3. 21). So also with reference to departure, it is said that 'the self in the body mounted by the self of intelligence moves creaking'. The *sūtra* says that the Highest Self is mentioned as different from the embodied soul in the states of deep sleep and departure from the body. There is nothing to be gained by describing the nature of the embodied self which is already well known. Both the beginning and the end of the chapter deal with one topic, viz. the Highest Self. The reference to the conditions of sleep and

[1] *na ca brahmaṇo'nyan nāmarūpābhyām arthāntaraṁ sambhavati. sarvasya vikāra-jātasya nāma-rūpābhyām eva vyākṛtatvāt. nāma-rūpayor api nirvahaṇaṁ niraṅkuśam na brahmaṇo'nyatra sambhavati.* Ś.

departure is used to note the difference of the Highest Self from such conditions. See B.U. IV. 3. 14–16 and 22.

I. 3. 43. *patyādi śabdebhyaḥ*

On account of the words, lord and others.

paty-ādi: Lord and others; *śabdebhyaḥ:* on account of words.

B.U. IV. 4. 22 uses words like *adhipatiḥ, vaśi, īśānaḥ* the great Lord, the Controller, the Protector of all. These cannot refer to the embodied soul. The quality of being neither great by good deeds nor small by evil deeds is not ascribable to any except God. The *sūtra* refers to the non-transmigrating supreme Lord.[1]

R. states that we have here declarations of general unity, that all conscious and non-conscious beings are effects of *Brahman* and have *Brahman* for their inner self.[2]

[1] *asaṁsārī parameśvaraḥ.*

[2] *aikyopadeśas tu sarvasya cid-acid-ātmakasya brahma-kāryatvena tad-ātmakatvam.* R.

Section 1 (1–7)

THE UNMANIFESTED DENOTES THE BODY

I. 4. 1. *ānumānikam apy ekeṣām iti cen na śarīra-rūpaka-vinyasta-gṛhīter darśayati ca*

If it be said that what is derived by inference (*pradhāna*) *too* (*is the avyakta, the unmanifested*) *according to some,* (*we say that*) *it is not so, because* (*the term*) *of understanding what is referred in the simile of the body and* (*the text*) *shows* (*this*).

ānumānikam: what is derived by inference; *api:* too, even; *ekeṣām:* of some; *iti cet:* if it be said; *na:* not; *śarīra:* body; *rūpaka:* simile; *vinyasta:* referred, contained; *gṛhīteḥ:* because of understanding; *darśayati:* shows.

This section discusses the *Kaṭha U.* passage (I. 3. 10 and 11)[1] where the terms *mahat,* the great, *avyakta,* unmanifested, are used in the *Sāṁkhya* sense, where *avyakta* is a synonym for *pradhāna.* Ś., after an elaborate review of the topics mentioned in the *Kaṭha U.*, argues that the term *avyakta* has not the special meaning given to it by the *Sāṁkhya* system but denotes the subtle body, the *sūkṣma śarīra,* as also the gross body which is viewed as an effect of the subtle one.

We have already seen that *Brahman* is the cause of the origin, maintenance and dissolution of the world (I. 1. 2), that *pradhāna* is not the cause (I. 1. 5, 10). But as there are some texts which seem to favour the view that *pradhāna* is the cause, we have to show that *Brahman* is the cause and not *pradhāna.*[2]

The passage under discussion comes after another passage where the simile of the chariot is used (I. 3. 3–4). In both the passages, the senses, the mind and the understanding are mentioned. By *buddhi* we may mean the human understanding and by *mahān-ātman* the understanding of *Brahmā* or *Hiraṇya-garbha* for it is his *buddhi* that can be truly considered to be the support of all the *buddhis* of beings. In the passage it is only the body which can be identified with *avyakta.* The whole section shows that the embodied soul is bound to body, mind, senses, etc., while it is, for Ś., in reality nothing but the Supreme Self. The simile of the chariot shows that our final destiny is the abode of *Viṣṇu* (*Kaṭha U.* I. 3. 12). By the practice of *Yoga* we reach it. In all this, there is no place for the hypothesis of *pradhāna.*[3]

R. argues that *avyakta* does not denote *pradhāna* independent of *Brahman* but denotes the body represented as a chariot in the simile

[1] See P.U., p. 625.

[2] *kāsu cicchākhāsu pradhāna-samarpaṇābhāsānāṁ śabdānām śrūyamāṇatvāt. ataḥ pradhānasya kāraṇatvaṁ veda-siddham eva mahadbhiḥ. paramarṣibhiḥ kapila-prabhṛtibhiḥ parigṛhītam iti prasajyate.* Ś.

[3] *nāsty atra para-parikalpitasya pradhānasyāvakāśaḥ.*

of the body.[1] R. also points out the differences between the *sāṁkhya* view and the *Upaniṣad* arrangement.

I. 4. 2. *sūkṣmaṁ tu tad arhatvāt*

(The word avyakta means), however, the subtle body for this is the appropriate (meaning) of that (word).
sūkṣmam: (the subtle body); *tu:* however; *tad:* that; *arhatvāt:* because it is appropriate.

If it is said that the gross physical body (*sthūla śarīra*) is *vyakta*, manifested, and not *avyakta*, the *sūtra* says that *avyakta* means the subtle body which consists of the subtle parts of the elements and it applies to its effect of the gross physical body. It is not uncommon to use the name of the effect for the cause. See *Ṛg Veda* (X. 46. 4; B.U. I. 4) where the present manifest world is referred to by the former non-manifest condition.

R. interprets appropriateness in a different way. The unmanifested matter alone, when it assumes the form of the effect (body) is fit to undertake activities furthering the purposes of man like the chariot.[2]

I. 4. 3. *tad-adhīnatvād arthavat*

On account of dependence on him, it has a meaning.
tad-adhīnatvāt: on account of dependence on him; *arthavat:* has a meaning.

To the question whether the non-manifest condition of the world may not be called *pradhāna*, the answer is given that the previous condition of the world is not an independent cause but is dependent on the Highest God. The potential primordial power of the Highest God is called by Ś. *avidyā, māyā, avyakta, ākāśa* and *akṣara*. It is known as *ākāśa* because of its unlimited extent, *akṣara* because it does not cease to exist until there is knowledge, *māyā* on account of its wonderful power, *avyakta* because being the power of *Brahman*, it is neither different nor non-different from *Brahman*. See B.U. VII. 8. 11; M.U. II. 12; Ś.U. IV. 10.

Sometimes it is said that the word *avyakta* means the subtle body only, since the bondage and release of the soul are possible on account of this. The soul is in *saṁsāra* when the desires bind the subtle body; when they cease to do so, the subtle body is destroyed and release attained. The answer is given that even as the word chariot refers to both gross and subtle bodies, *avyakta* also refers to both. Even if it is taken as referring to the subtle body, it is clear that the *Kaṭha U.* passage has no reference to *pradhāna*.

Bhāskara holds that the subtle body is designated as subtle in

[1] *nāvyakta-śabdenābrahmātmakam pradhānam ihābhidhīyate . . . śarīrākhya-rūpaka-vinyastasyāvyakta-śabdena gṛhīteḥ.* Ś.

[2] *puruṣārtha-sādhana-pravṛtty-arhatvāt.* R.

reference to the gross body and it is rightly called unmanifest. Bondage and release have meaning in so far as they are dependent on the subtle body.

R. makes out that matter in its subtle states is meaningful and serves human ends only in so far as it is dependent on the Supreme Self. *Avyakta* and its effects constitute the body of the Lord who constitutes their self.

For Śrīkaṇṭha the soul, the body and the rest have a meaning as dependent on the Lord.

Śrīnivāsa makes out that the *Sāṁkhya pradhāna* cannot give rise to effects and so for producing effects it is dependent on *Brahman*.

I. 4. 4. *jñeyatvāvacanāc ca*

Also because there is no mention of its being an object to the known.
jñeyatva: an object to be cognised; *a-vacanāt:* there being no mention; *ca:* and, also.

Whereas for the *Sāṁkhya* system, knowledge of *pradhāna* as distinct from *puruṣa* is said to be essential for achieving the liberation of the soul, in the *Kaṭha U.* passages *avyakta* is not mentioned as an object of knowledge or meditation. The word '*avyakta*' is used incidentally for body after the passage of the chariot, to indicate the nature of the highest abode of *Viṣṇu*.

I. 4. 5. *vadatīti cen na prājño hi prakaraṇāt*

And if it be said that (pradhāna as the object of knowledge) is mentioned (in the śruti), (we say that) it is not so for the intelligent self (is meant) on account of the general subject-matter.
vadati: says, is mentioned; *iti cet:* if it be said; *na:* not; *prājñaḥ:* intelligent self; *hi:* for; *prakaraṇāt:* from the context.

Kaṭha U. speaks of that 'which is without sound, without touch and without form, undecaying, without taste, eternal, without smell, without beginning, without end, beyond the great, abiding, by discerning that one is freed from the mouth of death'. This description cannot apply to *pradhāna*. It applies to the Highest Intelligent Self. The Person is said to be the goal for there is nothing beyond him. We can have a vision of him by the practice of self-control, etc. Even on the *Sāṁkhya* theory, liberation is not possible by a mere knowledge of *pradhāna*. It is possible only by a knowledge of *puruṣa* as distinct from *pradhāna*. In the *Vedānta* texts, these qualities are possible only with regard to the Highest Self.

I. 4. 6. *trayāṇām eva caivam upanyāsaḥ praśnaś ca*

And thus there are statement and question about three (things) alone.
trayāṇām: of three; *eva:* only; *ca:* and; *evam:* thus; *upanyāsaḥ:* statement; *praśnaḥ:* question; *ca:* and.

The three questions in the *Kaṭha U.* I relate, according to Ś., to the fire sacrifices, the individual soul and the Highest Self. There is no separate question and answer in regard to *pradhāna*. So it cannot be said to be either the object of knowledge or indicated by the word '*avyakta*'.

Ś. here urges his theory of the unity of the individual soul and the Highest Self. The denial of birth and death in the case of the individual soul suggests the non-difference of the soul and *Brahman*. *Kaṭha U.* II. 1. 4 suggests that the Self which perceives both dream states and working states is clearly the intelligent Self, *Prājña*. Again II. 1. 10 censures those who find a difference between what is here and what is there.

I. 4. 7. *mahadvac ca*

And like the word 'great'.
mahat-vat: like the word *mahat; ca:* and.
The word *mahat* does not refer to *pradhāna*.

The *Sāṁkhya* uses the word *mahat* in the sense of *sattā* or *buddhi* since it it the first product of *pradhāna*, and enables one to achieve both prosperity and freedom. The *Vedic* meaning of *avyakta* is *puruṣa* or *ātman*, knowing whom there is an end to all sorrow,[1] and not *pradhāna*. See *Kaṭha U.* I. 2. 22; Ś.U. III. 8.

Section 2 (8–10)

AJĀ (SHE-GOAT) OF RED, WHITE AND BLACK COLOURS IS NOT *PRADHĀNA*

I. 4. 8. *camasavad aviśeṣāt*

As in the case of the bowl (the ajā, the unborn, is not pradhāna) because of the absence of special characteristics.
camasa-vat: like the bowl; *aviśeṣāt:* because of the absence of special characteristics.

The advocates of the *pradhāna* theory quote Ś.U. IV. 5[2] and argue that *ajā*, she-goat of red, white and black colours which produces manifold offspring, similar in form (to herself) refers to *pradhāna* which has the three qualities of *sattva* (white), *rajas* (red) and *tamas* (black). On account of attachment to *prakṛti*, some souls are deluded and pass through *saṁsāra;* others on account of discrimination and non-attachment attain release.

The *Sūtrakāra* answers that there is no special reason why *ajā*

[1] *avyakta-śabdo'pi na vaidike prayoge pradhānam abhidhātum arhati.* Ś. *ātmā mahān ity ātmā. śabda-prayogāt. Ratnaprabhā.*

[2] See P.U., p. 732.

should be treated as equivalent to *pradhāna*. There are no special features which justify us in giving the meaning of *pradhāna* and not any other. In B.U. II. 2. 3 there is the passage: 'There is a bowl with its mouth below and bottom up.' This by itself does not tell us what bowl it is but the next passage provides the sense that the bowl refers to the head. So also the meaning of the word '*ajā*' has to be understood from some other passage.

R. quotes *Cūlikā U.* (3–7) which teaches that the Supreme Person is the self of *prakṛti*, *Garbha U.* (3), Ś.U. I. 8–10; V. 9–10; VI. 16 and B.G. XIII. 19–21; XIV. 5; IX. 7, 8, 10. From all these texts, R. concludes that *ajā* is not *prakṛti*. The *prakṛti* indicated is *brahmātmikā*.

Nimbārka suggests that the unborn one, *ajā*, must have *Brahman* for its soul. It is dependent on *Brahman*.

I. 4. 9. *jyotir-upakramā tu tathā hy adhīyata eke*

(Ajā), however, (means the three elements) beginning with light; for some read (their text) in that manner.

jyotiḥ: light; *upakramā:* beginning with; *tu:* however; *tathā:* in that manner; *hi:* for; *adhīyate:* study; *eke:* some.

C.U. VI. 4. 1[1] refers to the colours red, white and black as those of the three elements of fire, water and earth. Others have arisen from the highest God. We need not give up these primary meanings and adopt secondary meanings of the three *guṇas* of *prakṛti*. Ś.U. 1. 3 describes the power of the Supreme as the cause of the universe. Other passages 4, 5, 10, 11 indicate the causality of the Supreme Self. So the *ajā* passage cannot suggest a different view in that context. The divine power is said to possess the three colours of the three elements of fire, water and earth.

Ś. means by *ajā*, the unborn, unproduced *māyā*.

R. refers to the passages which refer to *Brahman* as the light of lights. (B.U. IV. 4. 16; C.U. III. 13. 7.) He quotes the *Mahānārāyaṇa U.* which instructs us about the aggregate of things other than *Brahman* and yet originating from *Brahman*. So *ajā* is a creature of *Brahman* and has its self in *Brahman* and this is the meaning of the Ś.U. passages also.

I. 4. 10. *kalpanopadeśāc ca madhvādivad avirodhaḥ*

And on account of the mention of the image, as in the case of honey and others, there is no contradiction.

kalpanā-upadeśāt: on account of the mention of the image; *ca:* and; *madhu-ādi-vat:* as in the case of honey and others; *a-virodhaḥ:* no contradiction.

Ś. asks, if *ajā* is taken to mean the three elements of the C.U.

[1] See P.U., p. 451.

(VI. 4. 1), how can the three elements be conceived as having the form of the she-goat or be thought of as unproduced, since they are the products of *māyā?* This *sūtra* gives the answer. Even as the sun is imagined as honey or the speech as cow or the heavenly world as fire (C.U. III. 1; B.U. V. 8; VI. 2. 9), even so, *prakṛti* which consists of the water and the earth, is imagined as the she-goat. It is imagining only, *kalpanā*. It is not literally unborn but only figuratively. It represents *prakṛti*, the source of all things, even as the sun which is not really honey is represented as such. It therefore stands to reason that *ajā* means fire, water and earth taken together. This view is followed by Bhāskara.

R. takes *kalpanā* as formation as in the passage, the Creator made sun and moon, '*yathā sūryā-candramasau dhātā yathā-pūrvam akalpayat*'. *Mahā-nārāyaṇa U.* V. 7. The world is unborn (*ajā*) in the causal condition and in the effect condition it divides itself into names and forms, into fire, water and earth, appearing as red, white and black. Between these two conditions there is no contradiction. *Ajā* is to be taken as denoting the causal state of the three elements.

R. criticises the view that *prakṛti* is to be imagined as the she-goat. While *ajā* for Ś. is the power of the Lord from which the world springs, it is for R. the primary causal matter from which the world is fashioned.

Nimbārka agrees with R. and holds that no contradiction is involved in taking one and the same substratum of qualities as unborn and having at the same time *Brahman* for its material cause. The unborn has *Brahman* for its self.

Section 3 (11–13)

THE FIVE GROUPS OF FIVE ARE NOT THE TWENTY-FIVE PRINCIPLES OF THE *SĀṀKHYA*

I. 4. 11. *na saṁkhyopasaṁgrahād api nānābhāvād atirekāc ca*

Not even on account of the mention of the number (*can it be said that pradhāna has scriptural authority*) *on account of diversity* (*of the categories*) *and on account of excess* (*over the number of the categories*).

na: not; *saṁkhyā:* number; *upasaṁgrahāt:* on account of the mention; *api:* even; *nānābhāvāt:* on account of many differences; *atirekāt:* due to excess; *ca:* and.

B.U. IV. 4. 17 mentions 'that in which the five groups of five and space are established' is the Self, the Immortal. The five groups of five make twenty-five and this is the number of the principles mentioned in the *Sāṁkhya Kārikā* (3). *Prakṛti* or *pradhāna* is not an effect. *Mahat* or *buddhi*, understanding, *ahaṁ-kāra* or the self-sense, the five *tanmātras* or subtle elements are the seven effects of *prakṛti* but are causes too of the sixteen which are effects only, viz. the five gross elements and the eleven organs (*indriyas*). *Puruṣa* or the self is neither effect nor cause. As the same number twenty-five is found in the *Upaniṣad* passage and the *Sāṁkhya Kārikā*, it is urged that *pradhāna* has the authority of *śruti*.

The *sūtra* refutes this suggestion for each one of the twenty-five principles of the *Sāṁkhya* is different from the others. The *Sāṁkhya* principles cannot be classed into five groups of five principles, there being no common quality among the members of any group. Again the word 'five, five' (*pañca, pañca*) need not be taken as indicating twenty-five for where it is possible to indicate the number directly as twenty-five it is not correct to say that it has been indicated indirectly as five groups of five. Besides, the second word *pañca* is not independent but is a part of the compound *pañca-jana* as in the passage *pañcānāṁ tvā pañca-janānām* (*Taittirīya Saṁhitā* I. 6. 2. 2). So we cannot say that the word *pañca* is repeated twice. *Pañca-jana* indicates five distinct persons and not groups. *Jana* does not mean any principle or category. The phrase *pañca pañca-jana* cannot refer to the *Sāṁkhya* principles for the Self and space, *ātman* and *ākāśa*, are stated independently while they are included in the *Sāṁkhya* twenty-five principles. We cannot arbitrarily interpret the expression *pañca pañca-jana* as referring to the principles of the *Sāṁkhya*. It may refer to any other group of twenty-five things. The *Sāṁkhya* advocate asks about the interpretation of *pañca-jana*. According to *Pāṇini* (II. 1. 50), words indicating direction or number are compounded with other words and then mean only a name of something or person. The word '*pañca-janāḥ*' indicates not number five, but a particular class of beings. It suggests that beings known as *pañca-jana* are five in number as the beings known as *saptarṣi* are seven in number.

I. 4. 12. *prāṇādayo vākya-śeṣāt*

The life-principle and others (are the pañca-janāḥ) on account of the complementary passage.

prāṇādayaḥ: life-principle and others; *vākya-śeṣāt:* from the complementary sentence (which follows).

The next passage (B.U. IV. 4. 18) reads: 'They who know the life of life, the eye of the eye, the ear of the ear and the mind of the mind, they have realised the ancient primordial *Brahman*.' The word *pañca-jana* refers to the life-principle and other beings.

It has also been taken to mean: (i) the five beings of gods, fathers, *gandharvas*, *asuras* and *rākṣasas* or (ii) the four castes of *Brāhmaṇas*, *Kṣatriyas*, *Vaiśyas*, *Śūdras* with the *Niṣadas* added to them. Whatever be the interpretation, it has obviously no connection with the *Sāṁkhya* categories.

I. 4. 13. *jyotiṣaikeṣām asaty anne*

When food is not present (i.e. not mentioned) in the case of some (the Kāṇvas) (number five is completed) by light.
jyotiṣā: by light; *ekeṣām:* of some; *asati:* when not present; *anne:* food.

In the *Kāṇva* rescension of the B.U. there is no mention of the being of food while the *Mādhyandina* mentions it. For the former, the fifth number is light which is mentioned in the preceding passage IV. 4. 16.

Section 4 (14–15)

NO CONFLICT IN PASSAGES REGARDING *BRAHMAN'S* CAUSALITY

I. 4. 14. *kāraṇatvena cākāśādiṣu yathā-vyapadiṣṭokteḥ*

And on account of (Brahman) as described being declared to be the cause of space and the rest.
kāraṇatvena: as cause; *ca:* and; *ākāśa-ādiṣu:* of *ākāśa* and others *yathā:* as; *vyapadiṣṭokteḥ:* declared as described.

According to Ś., the objection raised relates to apparently conflicting passages which deal with creation. The order of creation varies from passage to passage in B.U. I. 4. 7; C.U. VI. 2. 1–3; T.U. II. 1; *Praśna U.* VI. 4. The *sūtra* makes out that though there may be contradictions in the order of creation, there is no such contradiction regarding the Creator. He is described in all passages as omniscient, lord of all, the inner soul of everything and as the one and only cause without a second.[1] See T.U. II. and 6; C.U. VI. 2. 1–3; *Aitareya U.* I. 1.

R. and Nimbārka also make out that the intention of the *sūtra* is to affirm that the Highest Person alone, endowed with the attributes of omniscience, omnipotence and the rest is the cause of the universe.

Śrīkaṇṭha does not begin a new section here but continues the consideration of the five-five people (B.U. IV. 4. 17). These refer to the life-principle and the rest and not to the *Sāṁkhya pradhāna.*

I. 4. 15. *samākarṣāt*

On account of the connection
samākarṣāt: on account of connecting or linking up.

There are passages which tell us that 'all this, verily, was in the beginning non-being' (*asat*) (T.U. II. 1). This does not mean absolute non-existence. If *sat* indicates the being of *Brahman* with all the

[1] *yathā-bhūto hy ekasmin vedānte sarvajñas sarveśvaras sarvātmaiko'dvitīyaḥ kāraṇatvena vyapadiṣṭaḥ.*

manifest names and forms, *asat* indicates the being of *Brahman* without names and forms. It indicates the condition of the world prior to its manifestation. The same interpretation should be given to C.U. III. 19. 1; B.U. I. 4. 7. The evolution of the world, C.U. (VI. 3. 2) tells us, takes place under the supervision of the Omniscient Ruler.[1] If we read the passage about non-being in its context, we will see that the previous passage speaks of the Self consisting of bliss (*T.U.* II. 7). Ś. and Bhāskara treat this section as dealing with the general question of the concordance of all texts with regard to *Brahman*. This is evident from the way Ś. comments on this section at the very beginning.[2]

Nimbārka uses this *sūtra* for the refutation of the *Sāṁkhya* view of *pradhāna*.[3]

Section 5 (16–18)

BRAHMAN'S CAUSALITY

I. 4. 16. *jagadvācitvāt*

Because of the denoting of the world.

jagat: world; *vācitvāt:* because (it is) denoted.

The text considered is K.U. IV. 19. 'He, verily, who is the maker of these persons, he of whom all this is the work (*karma*), he alone is to be known.' What is the object of knowledge? Is it the individual soul, or the chief vital breath or the Highest Self?

Arguments for the chief vital breath, *mukhya-prāṇa*, are set forth. It is the support of all activity or work. In a complementary passage (IV. 20), the word '*prāṇa*' occurs. *Prāṇa* is said to be the creator of the persons in the sun, moon, etc. See also B.U. III. 9. 9.

There are also arguments in support of the view that the object of knowledge is the individual soul. The work of the soul will mean its deeds of merit and demerit. The soul may be considered to be the cause of the persons in the sun, etc., inasmuch as the sun, the moon are said to be the sources of pleasure and pain to be experienced by the soul. Besides, we find in a later passage a characteristic mark of the individual soul. Ajātaśatru failed to awaken a sleeping man by merely shouting at him. He roused him from his sleep when he pushed him with a stick. It shows that the individual soul is different from the life-principle. There is another characteristic mark given in IV. 20. The individual soul and the selves in the sun and the moon are helping each other. The individual soul as the support of *prāṇa* is itself called *prāṇa*.

[1] *sādhyakṣām eva jagato vyākriyāṁ darśayati.*

[2] *tatra idam aparam āśaṅkate: na janmādi-kāraṇatvaṁ brahmaṇo brahma-viṣayaṁ vā gati-sāmānyaṁ vedānta-vākyānāṁ pratipattuṁ śakyam.*

[3] *na pradhāna-śaṅkā-gandho'pīti bhāvaḥ.*

Both these suggestions are refuted by the *sūtra*. Bālāki begins his conversation with Ajātaśatru with the offer: 'Let me declare *Brahman* to you.' The maker of all these individual souls cannot be a soul lower than *Brahman* for then the introductory offer would be meaningless. Only the Highest Lord is capable of being the maker of all those mentioned for he alone is truly independent. The word *karma* does not indicate movement, or merit or demerit accruing from it. So it cannot refer to *prāṇa* or the individual soul. It cannot denote persons in the sun for *puruṣa* is masculine and is used in genitive plural and *karma* is neuter and is used in the singular number. *Karma* cannot refer to the activity of producing the persons on the result of that activity for both these are included in the agent without whom they would not exist. The passage 'he of whom all this is the work' means that the entire world and the person in the sun, etc., are only a part of this world which is nothing but the work of God. The passage sets forth the maker of the world in a twofold way, as the creator of a special part of the world and as the creator of the whole remaining world.

R. opposes the view which holds that the person to whom the work belongs is the enjoying soul, the ruler of *prakṛti*. For work, meritorious or the contrary, belongs to the individual soul only. The generally accepted meaning of *karma* is good and evil actions. The origination of this world is caused by the various actions of the individual souls. The explanation given by Ajātaśatru to Bālāki, who has been unable to say where the soul goes at the time of deep sleep, that all the speech and other organs become one in *prāṇa* in deep sleep clearly refers to the individual soul which alone passes through the states of dream, deep sleep and waking. This view is controverted by R. who makes out that the work is the world and the Supreme Person is the sole cause of the world. Though the origination of the world has for its condition the deeds of the individual souls, yet those souls do not independently originate the means for their own retributive experience but experience only what the Lord has created to that end in agreement with their works.[1]

I. 4. 17. *jīva-mukhya-prāṇa-liṅgān neti cet tad vyākhyātam*

If it be said that this is not so on account of the characteristic marks of the individual soul and the chief vital breath, (*we reply that*) *that has been already explained.*

jīva: individual soul; *mukhya:* chief; *prāṇa:* vital breath; *liṅgāt:* due to characteristic marks; *na:* not; *iti cet:* if it be said; *tad:* that; *vyākhyātam:* (is) already explained.

Bhāskara reads this *sūtra* and the next as one section.

[1] *jagad-utpatter jīva-karma-nibandhanatve'pi na jīvaḥ sva-bhogya-bhogopakaraṇādeḥ svayam utpādakaḥ. api tu sva-karmānuguṇyeneśvara-sṛṣṭaṁ sarvam bhuṅkte.* R.

If it be said that the characteristic marks of the individual soul and the chief vital breath are given in the passage, Ś. observes that when a text is ascertained, as referring to *Brahman* by a comprehensive consideration of the opening and the concluding clauses, all characteristic marks which point to other topics must be so interpreted as to fall in with the principal topic. In the text under consideration, at the outset it is said: 'Let me declare *Brahman* to you.' In the middle, the clause 'of whom this is the work' refers to the Highest Person who is the cause of the whole world. At the end again, we hear of a reward which relates itself only with meditations on *Brahman* by *śraiṣṭhyam:* eminence, *svārājyam:* independence, *ādhipatyam:* supremacy. All other topics must be interpreted so as to conform to this main topic of *Brahman.*

Again, the refutation has already been made in I. 1. 31; only the creation of the world was not there referred to *Brahman.* The word *prāṇa* is used with reference to *Brahman* in C.U. VI. 8. 2. Ś. adds that whatever characteristic marks we may have about the individual soul, we shall be justified in considering them as indicative of *Brahman,* since the *jīva* is identical with *Brahman.*[1]

I. 4. 18. *anyārthaṁ tu jaiminiḥ praśna-vyākhyānābhyām api caivam eke*

But Jaimini *thinks that (the reference to the individual soul) has another purport, on account of the question and the explanations and so some others too (read the text).*

anyārtham: another purport; *tu:* but; *Jaiminiḥ:* Jaimini; *praśna-vyākhyānābhyām:* on account of the question and the explanation; *api:* also; *ca:* and; *evam:* so; *eke:* some others.

Even assuming that there is a reference to the individual soul, it is only to indicate the knowledge of *Brahman.* This is clear from the nature of the question and the explanatory answer given in this connection. When Ajātaśatru asked as to where the person was asleep and whence he came back to the waking state, the reply given is that during dreamless sleep a person becomes one with this *prāṇa* (*Brahman*) alone; and that it is from this Self alone that the *prāṇas* depart to their abode; and from *prāṇa* depart the gods and from gods the beings (K.U. IV. 19 and 20). It is the *Vedānta* view that during sleep the soul becomes one with *Brahman* and it is from *Brahman* that the world and the *prāṇa* proceed. That in which the sleeping soul becomes devoid of cognition of the waking life and enjoys tranquillity is *Brahman* itself which is the object fit to be known. Again, in B.U. II. 1. 16 and 17 it is said that the soul as distinct from the Highest Self lies in the *ākāśa* within the heart. C.U. VIII. 1. 1 says that this small *ākāśa* is nothing but the Highest Self. It is the

[1] *brahma-viṣayatvād abhedābhiprāyeṇa yojayitavyam.* Ś.

source of all as the empirical selves are said to spring from it. B.U. II. 1. 20. All these lead to the conclusion that the Self exists beyond both *prāṇa*, life-principle, and *jīva* or the individual soul. This view that the section deals with the general agreement of all texts with regard to *Brahman* is supported by Bhāskara.

R., while adopting the same view as Ś., directs his attack on the *Sāṁkhya* theory of *pradhāna.*

Śrīkaṇṭha holds that this section deals with the difference between the individual soul and *Brahman.*[1]

Section 6 (19–22)

THE SELF TO BE SEEN, HEARD, ETC., IS THE HIGHEST SELF ON ACCOUNT OF THE CONNECTION OF TEXTS

I. 4. 19 *vākyānvayāt*

On account of the connection of sentences (the Self to be seen, heard, etc., is the Highest Self).

vākya: sentence; *anvayāt:* on account of the connected meaning.

The passage considered is B.U. IV. 5. 6. 'Verily, the Self is to be seen, to be heard, to be reflected on, to be meditated upon; when, verily, the Self is seen, heard, reflected on and known, then all this is known.' The doubt arises whether the Self to be seen, heard, etc., is the individual soul or the Highest Self.

The opponent contends that the reference is to the individual self: (i) because the objects of enjoyment, husband, wife, wealth, etc., can only have in view the enjoying soul and so the self which is the object of sight and so on can only be the individual soul; (ii) the sentence 'how should one know the knower?' can denote only the agent, the individual soul and so the declaration that through the cognition of the Self, everything becomes known must be taken to mean that the world of the objects of enjoyment is known through its relation to the individual enjoying soul.

The answer is given that the reference is to the Highest Self on account of the meaning and mutual connection of passages. Maitreyī wishes to know that by which she can become immortal and this can be reached only by the knowledge of the Highest Self. In subsequent passages it is said: 'Brāhmaṇahood deserts him who knows Brāhmaṇahood in anything else than the Self' and so on. It means that all these have no independent existence apart from the Self. The next passage that 'everything is the Self' tells us that the entire aggregate of existing things is non-different from the Self. The similes of drum and so on confirm this view. Yājñavalkya urges that

[1] *punar api jīvāt parameśvarasya anya-bhāvam upapādayati.* I. 4. 16.

the Highest Self is the cause of the world of names and forms and works. He leads us to the same conclusion that the Self is the centre of the whole world with the objects, the senses and the mind, that it has neither inside nor outside, that it is altogether a mass of knowledge.

R. thinks that this *sūtra* is an answer to the suggestion that the *Sāṁkhya puruṣa* or soul is meant by the text. According to the *Sāṁkhya* system, immortality is obtained through the cognition of the true nature of the soul viewed as free from all erroneous imputation to itself of the attributes of non-conscious matter. The world originates from the soul in its quality as the ruler of *prakṛti*.

R. answers this objection by stating that the Self which Yājñavalkya speaks of as the proper object of knowledge leading to immortality is the Highest Self. See Ś.U. III. 8. The knowledge of the true nature of the individual soul which obtains immortality, and which is a mere manifestation of the power of the Supreme Person, is useful for the cognition of the Supreme Person who brings about release and is not by itself instrumental for such release. The causal power with regard to the entire world can belong to the Supreme Person only. Again, everything cannot be known through the cognition of one individual soul only. It is possible only through the knowledge of the Highest Self which is the self of all. All search for dear objects as husband, wife, etc., should be given up and only the Self should be sought. It is the Highest Self alone that makes objects dear. R. quotes *Viṣṇu Purāṇa* to the effect: 'The same object which gave us delight later on becomes a source of grief. What was the cause of wrath later tends to peace. Hence there is nothing that is in itself of the nature either of pleasure or of pain.'[1]

I. 4. 20. *pratijñā-siddher liṅgam āśmarathyaḥ*

(*The reference to the individual soul as the object to be seen, heard, etc.*), *indicates the proof of the statement;* (*so thinks*) *Āśmarathya.*

pratijñā: statement; *siddheḥ:* of proof; *liṅgam:* indicatory sign; *āśmarathyaḥ:* Āśmarathya.

If the individual soul were different from the Highest Self, then the knowledge of the latter will not involve the knowledge of the former and thus the statement that through the knowledge of one thing everything will be known would not be fulfilled. If the implications of this statement are to be realised, then the individual soul and the Highest Self are non-different.

R. argues that if the individual soul were not identical with *Brahman* as its effect, then the knowledge of the soul—being something distinct from *Brahman*—would not follow from the knowledge

[1] *tad eva prītaye bhūtvā punar duḥkhāya jāyate*
tad eva kopāya yataḥ prasādāya ca jāyate
tasmād duḥkhātmakaṁ nāsti na ca kiñcit sukhātmakam.
II. 6. 46–7.

of the Highest Self. He quotes texts declaring the oneness of *Brahman* previous to creation (*Aitareya Āraṇyaka* V. II. 4. 1. 1) as well as those which make out that the souls spring from and merge in *Brahman* (M.U. II. 1. 1). The souls are one with *Brahman* in so far as they are its effects.

Śrīpati quotes B.U. II. 4. 6; C.U. VI. 1. 4 and holds that 'if one is known all is known' is according to the *nyāya* of *dadhi-kṣīra,* curds resulting from milk. When the cause is known the effects are known. Āśmarathya considers both the doctrines of *a-samyukta-bheda-vāda* which differentiates between the individual soul and *Brahman* as between a jar and a cloth and the doctrine of *aṅgāṅgivat-samyukta-bheda,* which connects the soul with *Brahman* as closely as a body is connected with its members.

Śrīnivāsa points out that since the individual soul is reckoned among the effects of *Brahman* there is a difference between effect and cause. Thus the texts declaring duality are correct. But since the effect is non-different from the cause, being born from it, non-difference between the two is equally a fact. So between the individual soul and *Brahman* there is a natural relation of difference and non-difference. So it is possible for words denoting effects to denote the causes as well as in the case of the pot and the clay. So through the knowledge of one, the knowledge of all is established.

Āśmarathya holds that the soul stands to *Brahman* in the *bhedā-bheda* relation. It is neither absolutely different nor non-different from *Brahman,* as sparks are neither different nor non-different from fire.

I. 4. 21. *utkramiṣyata evaṁ bhāvād ity auḍulomiḥ*

(*The identification of the individual soul with the Highest Self is possible*) *because the soul when it will rise* (*to depart from the body*) *is such* (*i.e. one with the Highest Self*)*;* (*so thinks*) *Auḍulomi.*

utkramiṣyataḥ: of one who rises up (to depart); *evam:* so; *bhāvāt:* because of being; *iti:* thus; *auḍulomiḥ:* Auḍulomi.

C.U. VIII. 12. 6 says: 'That serene one when he rises up from this body and reaches the highest light appears in his own form.' M.U. III. 2. 8 reads: 'Just as the flowing rivers disappear in the ocean casting off name and shape, even so the knower, freed from name and shape, attains to the divine person, higher than the high.' So Auḍulomi thinks that the reference to the individual soul as non-different from the Highest Self is appropriate. It is in view of the future condition that is acquired by the individual soul that it is described as non-different from the Highest Self.

Auḍulomi teaches that the soul is altogether different from *Brahman* up to the time of its final release when it is merged in *Brahman.*

Vācaspati quotes a verse from the *Pañcarātrikas* which states that difference is real until release when it becomes extinct.[1] While Ś. and Bhāskara mean by *bhāva* identity with the Supreme Self, *paramātmaikyopapatti*, R. and Śrīkaṇṭha mean by it the state of the Supreme Self, *paramātma-bhāva*. Śrīpati interprets the *sūtra* thus: *utkramiṣyataḥ, svām vidyopādhiṁ tyajataḥ, jīvasya ghatākāśa mahākāśavat, brahma-bhinnatvāt sarvadā brahma-bhinnatayā jīvopakramaṇam.* When the erroneous knowledge of *jīva* is removed, *jīva* realises its identity with *Brahman*.

Śrīnivāsa develops Nimbārka's theory of difference-non-difference. Auḍulomi suggests difference between the individual soul and *Brahman* in the state of bondage and non-difference in the state of release. This difference-non-difference is admitted by Auḍulomi, according to Śrīnivāsa, for the benefit of the dull-witted. But strictly even during the state of bondage the individual soul which is atomic in size and possesses very little knowledge, though different from *Brahman* who is all-pervasive, is yet non-different from him since it has no separate existence and activity, even as a leaf is non-different from the tree, a ray from the lamp, an attribute from its substratum and the sense-organs from the vital principle. Even so, though, in release, it is non-different from him, it having no separate existence and activity, it is also different from him. See C.U. VIII. 3. 4.

According to Baladeva, the released soul becomes dear to all.

I. 4. 22. *avasthiter iti kāśakṛtsnaḥ*

(*The identification of the individual soul with the Highest Self is possible*) *because* (*the Highest Self*) *exists* (*in the condition of the individual soul*), (*so thinks*) *Kāśakṛtsna.*

avasthiteḥ: because of existence; *iti:* thus; *kāśakṛtsnaḥ:* Kaśakṛtsna.

Ś. points out that Āśmarathya believes in the non-difference of the individual soul from the Highest Self but he does so to establish the possibility of the knowledge of all things as a result of the knowledge of the Highest Self. His belief in non-difference is relative and not absolute for he views the Highest Self and the individual soul as cause and effect. Audulomi admits the difference between the two in the state of bondage and identity in the state of release. Kāśakṛtsna interprets *tat tvam asi*, that thou art, in a proper way. The individual soul is described as non-different from the Highest Self for it is the Highest Self that lives in the form of the soul.[2]

Kāśakṛtsna holds that the soul is absolutely non-different from

[1] *āmukter bheda eva syāj jīvasya ca parasya ca*
muktasya tu na bhedo'sti bheda-hetor abhāvataḥ.
Bhāmatī I. 4. 21.

See also C.U. VIII. 12. 3; B.G. XIV. 2.

[2] *asyaiva paramātmano'nenāpi vijñānātmabhāvenāvasthānād upapannam idam abhedābhidhānam iti, kāśakṛtsna ācāryo manyate.*

Brahman, which somehow presents itself as the individual soul. The individual soul abides in the Supreme. The term *avasthita* suggests the abiding of one thing in another rather than identity. But Ś. believes in absolute identity. The individual soul and the Highest Self differ only in name.[1] Ś. agrees with Kāśakṛtsna that the Highest Self itself appears as the individual soul. The eternally unchanging Self which is one mass of knowledge does not perish. By means of true knowledge there is effected its dissociation from the elements and the sense-organs which are the product of *avidyā*. When the connection is severed, specific cognition which depended on it no longer takes place. We cannot therefore insist on the distinction of the individual and the Highest Self.

Ś. and Bhāskara interpret the word *avasthiteḥ* as meaning 'because of *Brahman's* abiding as the individual soul', *vijnānātma-bhāvena.*

R. objects to the view that the soul, when departing, becomes one with *Brahman*. If the soul is not *Brahman* previous to its departure, is it due to its essential nature or limiting adjuncts? If the former, it can never become *Brahman* for then its essential nature will be violated. If it becomes *Brahman*, it perishes utterly. If the difference before departure is due to limiting adjuncts, it is *Brahman* even before departure and there is no point in saying that it becomes *Brahman* only when it departs. The adjuncts cannot introduce differences into *Brahman* which is without parts and incapable of difference. The difference resides altogether in the adjuncts and so the soul is *Brahman* even before departure from the body. If the difference due to the adjuncts is not real, then what is it that becomes *Brahman* on the departure of the soul? If it is said that *Brahman's* true nature is obscured by *avidyā* or ignorance, *Brahman* whose true nature is eternal, free, self-luminous intelligence cannot possibly be hidden by *avidyā*. When light belongs to the essential nature of a thing, there cannot be any obscuration of it. If there is obscuration, it means that the thing is completely destroyed. So *Brahman's* essential nature being manifest at all times, there is no point in speaking of *becoming Brahman* at the time of departure.

R. interprets Kāśakṛtsna's view as meaning that *Brahman* abides as itself within the individual soul which thus constitutes *Brahman's* body.[2] See C.U. VI. 3. 2. 1; B.U. III. 7. 22. All the texts can be understood if we accept Kāśakṛtsna's view.

Nimbārka takes this section to be connected with the refutation of the *Sāṁkhya* doctrine.

[1] *eko hy ayam ātmā nāma-mātra-bhedena bahudhābhidhīyata iti.* Ś.

[2] *sva-śarīra-bhūte jīvātmanyātmatayāvasthite jīva-śabdena brahma pratipādanam iti kāśakṛtsna ācāryo manyate sma.*

Section 7 (23–27)

BRAHMAN IS THE MATERIAL AND THE EFFICIENT CAUSE OF THE WORLD

I. 4. 23. *prakṛtiś ca pratijñā-dṛṣṭāntānuparodhāt*

(*Brahman is*) *the material cause also, for this view does not conflict with the* (*initial*) *statement and illustration.*

prakṛtiḥ: material cause;[1] *ca:* and; *pratijñā:* (initial) statement; *dṛṣṭānta:* illustration; *anuparodhāt:* because of non-contradiction.

The opponent holds that *Brahman* is the efficient cause of the world only and not the material cause. See *Praśna U.* VI. 3 and 4. *Brahman* first reflects before creating. Like kings of different places, he is the lord of the world and so possesses only efficient power. Besides, the world is non-conscious, impure and consists of parts and so its cause also should be of the same nature. But *Brahman* 'is without parts, without activity, tranquil, irreproachable, without blemish' (Ś.U. VI. 19). So *Brahman* is not the material cause. Something different from *Brahman*, the *prādhāna* of the *Sāṁkhyas* is the material cause and *Brahman* is only the efficient cause.

The answer to this objection is that it is the material cause also for C.U. VI. 1. 3 says that to know the Self is to know everything else. This is possible only with regard to the material cause for the effect is not different from the material cause. We cannot say that of the efficient cause. The illustrations given apply only to the material cause. 'As by one clod of clay all that is made of clay becomes known . . . by one nugget of gold all that is made of gold becomes known.' (C.U. VI. 1. 4–8.) M.U. I. 1. 7 speaks of herbs growing on the earth. B.U. IV. 5. 8ff. gives illustrations of drum, conch, etc. All these prove that *Brahman* is the material cause of the world. T.U. III. 1 speaks of that from which, *yataḥ*, these beings are born. This indicates the material cause of the beings.

While in the case of clay or gold, efficient causes like potters and goldsmiths are needed for turning clay or gold into vessels or ornaments, no other efficient cause of the world is possible than *Brahman*. If there were, the statement and the illustrations would become false. The knowledge of everything else would not follow from the knowledge of one thing. So *Brahman* alone is both the efficient and the material cause of the world.

R. holds that the *pūrva-pakṣa* here is *śeśvara Sāṁkhya* or theistic *Sāṁkhya* which holds that the Lord creates this world only in so far as he guides *prakṛti*, which is the material cause. Ś.U. IV. 9. 10; B.G. IX. 10. In ordinary experience the material and the efficient causes are different. We also know that the production of effects

[1] *jani kartuḥ prakṛtiḥ.* Patañjali I. 4. 30.

requires invariably several instrumental agencies. So it is urged that *Brahman* is only the operative, not the material cause of the world, while the material cause is the *pradhāna* guided by *Brahman*.

R. answers this objection by using the same texts. With reference to the difficulty caused by texts like those of *Cūlika U*. which declare *prakṛti* to be eternal and the material cause of the world, R. answers that *prakṛti* in such passages denotes *Brahman* in its causal phase when names and forms are not yet distinguished for there is not any principle independent of *Brahman*. The Highest *Brahman*, having the whole aggregate of non-conscious and conscious beings for its body, is the self of all. Sometimes, however, names and forms are not evolved, not distinguished in *Brahman*; at other times they are evolved, are distinct. In the latter state, *Brahman* is called an effect and manifold; in the former it is called one, without a second, the cause.[1] As for the passage that the unevolved originates and passes away, it means that *Brahman* having non-conscious matter for its body, the state which consists of the three *guṇas* and is denoted by the form *avyakta*, unmanifested, is something effected. In total dissolution non-conscious matter having *Brahman* for its self, continues to exist in a highly subtle condition. This highly subtle matter stands to *Brahman* in the relation of a mode (*prakāra*). As for the contention that, in ordinary experience, one and the same principle cannot be both the operative and the material cause and that effects cannot be brought about by one agency, this applies to ordinary forces and not to the Supreme.[2]

R.'s view is adopted by Nimbārka and Śrīnivāsa.

I. 4. 24. *abhidhyopadesāc ca*

And because of the statement of volition (on the part of the Self).

abhidhya: volition; *upadeśāt:* because of statement; *ca:* and.

There are passages like, 'He wished, may I be many', '*sokāmayata, bahusyām prajāyeyeti*', or He reflected 'May I be many', '*tad aikṣata, bahusyām prajāyeyeti*', which show that the Self is an agent of independent activity, which is preceded by the Self's reflection. So the Self is the efficient cause. It is also the material cause, since the words 'May I be many' indicate that the reflective desire of multiplying itself has the inward Self for its object. (C.U. VI. 2. 3; T.U. II. 6.)

[1] *sarva-cid-acid-vastu-śarīratayā sarvadā sarvātma-bhūtam param brahma kadācid vibhakta-nāma-rūpam, kadācic cāvibhakta-nāma-rūpam 'yadā vibhakta-nāma-rūpam tadā tad eva bahutvena kāryatvena cocyate, yadā vibhakta-nāma-rūpam tad-aikam-advitīyaṁ kāraṇam iti ca.*

[2] *sakaletara vilakṣaṇasya parasya brahmaṇaḥ sarvaśakteḥ sarvajñasy aikasyaiva sarvam upapadyate.* R.

I. 4. 25. *sākṣāc cobhayāmnāyāt*

And because of the direct mention of both in the sacred text.
sākṣat: direct; *ca:* and; *ubhaya:* both; *āmnāyāt:* because (of mention in) the sacred text.

Brahman is stated in the *śruti* as the material cause of the world, as that from which the world comes into being and in which it is reabsorbed. See C.U. I. 9. 1. The effects cannot be absorbed by anything else than their material cause. 'Both' refers to the origin and the dissolution of the world. This view is supported by Ś. and Bhāskara.

R. and Niṁbārka quote *Taittirīya Brāhmaṇa* II. 8. 9. 7. '*Brahman* was the wood, *Brahman* the tree from which they shaped the heaven and the earth; you wise ones, I tell you, it stood on *Brahman*, supporting the worlds.'

I. 4. 26. *ātmakṛteḥ pariṇāmāt*

(Brahman is the material cause) on account of action referring to itself. (This is possible) owing to transformation.
ātma-kṛteḥ: on account of action concerning itself; *pariṇāmāt:* because of transformation.

T.U. II. 7. '*tad ātmānaṁ svayam akuruta*' makes out that 'that *Ātman* (Self) transformed itself into its own self'. Even as clay is changed into its effects, the Self got itself transformed into the things of the world. The word 'itself' excludes the possibility of any other cause.

Bhāskara criticises Ś.'s theory of *adhyāsa* by which everything is destructible. Bhāskara says that Ś. is adopting a *mahāyāna* view.[1]

Pariṇāmāt is taken by R. and Śrīkaṇṭha as a separate *sūtra*. It means that *Brahman* became *sat* and *tyat* (T.U. II. 6), the visible things of the earth like water and light and the invisible beings of air and *ākāśa* or the defined and the undefined things. *Brahman* has become the whole world of effects. R. holds that *Brahman* has for its body the entire universe with all its conscious and non-conscious beings and constitutes the Self of the universe. These beings abide in a subtle condition and become one with the Supreme Self in so far as they cannot be designated as something separate from him. When this *Brahman* resolves to become many, it invests itself with a body consisting of all conscious and non-conscious beings in their gross manifest state which admits of distinctions of name and form and thereupon transforms itself into the form of the world. When *Brahman* undergoes change into the form of this world, all changes exclusively belong to non-conscious matter, which is a mode of *Brahman*, and all imperfections and sufferings to the individual

[1] *mahāyānika-bauddha-gāthitam māyāvādam vyāvarṇayanto lokān vyāmohayanti.*

souls which also are modes of *Brahman*. *Brahman* himself is *nirdoṣa, nirvikāra,* free from all imperfection and change.

I. 4. 27. *yoniś ca hi gīyate*

And because (Brahman) is celebrated as the source.

yoniḥ: origin; *ca:* and; *hi:* because; *gīyate:* is sung.

Brahman is described as the source of all beings, *bhūta-yoni* (M.U. I. 1. 6); *brahma-yoni* (III. 1. 3). 'Source' generally means the material cause. See M.U. I. 1. 7 where the spider is said to be the cause of the threads which he sends forth and draws in.

Brahman is the material cause of the world even as the rope is the basis of the appearance of snake.[1] This does not mean that the world is as illusory as the snake. It is only the dependence of the world on *Brahman* that is brought out. It is also implied that the integrity of *Brahman* is not affected by the changes of the world, even as the rope is not affected by the changes in the apparent snake. The illustrations used are unfortunate, in that they suggest that the world is also an illusion even as the appearance of snake is. There are *Advaita Vedāntins* who hold such a view.

Nimbārka takes this section as directly connected with the refutation of the *Sāṁkhya* view.

Section 8 (28)

THE EXPLANATION OF ALL

I. 4. 28. *etena sarve vyākhyātāḥ vyākhyātāḥ*

Hereby all (the doctrines opposed to the Vedānta view) are explained, explained.

etena: by this; *sarve:* all; *vyākhyātāḥ:* are explained.

The repetition of 'explained' is to mark the end of the chapter. The *Sāṁkhya* doctrine of *pradhāna* has been refuted. It is taken up for special notice as it stands near to the *Vedānta* doctrine, admits the non-difference of cause and effect and is also accepted by some of the authors of the *dharma-sūtras* like Devala and others. The atomic and other views are not founded on scriptural authority and are contradicted by several *Vedic* passages.

The *Sāṁkhya* system, unlike many others, is anxious to prove that its views are warranted by scriptural authority. So the *Sūtrakāra* attempted a refutation of the *Sāṁkhya* theory of *pradhāna* as the only cause of the world.

[1] *iyaṁ copādāna-pariṇāmādi-bhāṣā na vikārābhiprāyena api tu yathā sarvasyopādānaṁ rajjuḥ evaṁ brahma jagad-upādānaṁ draṣṭavyam. Bhāmatī.*

Section 1 (1–2)

REPUDIATION OF *SMṚTI* OPPOSED TO *ŚRUTI*

II. 1. 1. *smṛty-anavakāśa-doṣa-prasaṅga iti cen nānyasmṛty-anavakāśa-doṣa-prasaṅgāt*

If it be said that there will result the defect of not allowing room for certain smṛtis (we say) not so, because there will result the defect of not allowing room for some other smṛtis.

smṛti: smṛti texts; *an:* not; *avakāśa:* room; *doṣa:* defect; *prasaṅgaḥ:* result, occasion; *iti:* that; *cet:* if; *na:* not; *anya:* other; *smṛti: smṛti* texts; *an:* not; *avakāśa:* room; *doṣa:* defect; *prasaṅgāt:* on account of the result.

In the first chapter dealing with the concordance or harmony of texts, it is established that the omniscient Lord of all is the material and efficient cause of the universe. He is the Self of all. The *Sāṁkhya* view that *pradhāna* is the cause of the universe is shown to be lacking in scriptural authority. In the second chapter known as *avirodha*, non-contradiction, the first part is devoted to show that there is no contradiction between the conclusions of the first chapter and the statements of certain *smṛtis*; the second part shows that opinions about *pradhāna* and others are based on defective reasoning, the third and fourth parts show that the *śruti* passages do not contradict one another when they deal with cosmology, individual soul and the sense-organs.

The opponent argues Kapila's *Sāṁkhya-smṛti* and the views of his followers, Āsuri and Pañcaśikha, urge that the cause of the universe is the independent non-conscious *pradhāna*. These are not like *Manu smṛti* concerned with the duties and rules of life, sacraments, etc. They claim to impart the knowledge of liberation. How are we to interpret them so as not to contradict the *śruti* passages?

It is no answer to say that, in the first chapter, with the aid of the *śruti* passages, we have shown that the omniscient *Brahman* alone is the cause of the universe. It is true that where *smṛtis* conflict, those which follow the *śruti* are to be accepted and those which conflict with *śruti* are to be disregarded. This is in accordance with the *Pūrva Mīmāṁsā Sūtra* (I. 3. 3).

Kapila-smṛti has not got a *śruti* supporting it but is in conflict with the existing *smṛtis* and so it should be rejected. Kapila's own intuitive experience cannot be said to be the authority for his *smṛti*, for his experience of the transcendental reality is itself the result of religious practices based on the *śruti* injunctions. Again, the word Kapila in the Ś.U. need not necessarily mean the author of the *smṛti*. He may be the Kapila who burnt the sons of Sagara. Manu who is mentioned with respect in *Taittirīya Sāṁhitā* (II. 2. 10. 2) criticises the views of

Kapila and commends the person who has realised the Self in all things (XII. 91). M.B. also gives again the *Sāṁkhya-yoga* view (I. 2. 360. 1–3). See *Iśa U.* 7. The doctrine of Kapila is in conflict with the *Veda* and *Manu-smṛti* which follows the *Veda*.

The opponent continues, while it is possible for men of great ability to interpret the *śruti* texts by means of their intellect, ordinary people look to the *smṛtis* and the *Purāṇās* for a proper interpretation of them. They have great regard for sages like Kapila. Ś.U. (V. 2) looks upon Kapila as the first among created beings, one who was well instructed. How can his *smṛti* be set aside?

If there are certain *smṛtis* which do not support *Brahman's* causality of the world, there are others which support it. In M.B. (*Śānti-parva* 334, 29) it is said that the *pradhāna* which consists of the three *guṇas* comes into being and is absorbed in the indeterminate Person who alone is the Self and the knower of all that is created.[1] See also B.G. VII. 6.

II. 1. 2. *itareṣāṁ cānupalabdheḥ*

And on account of the non-perception of others.

itareṣām: of others; *ca:* and; *anupalabdheḥ:* on account of non-perception.

A *smṛti* is accepted when it refers to things in our experience or mentioned in the *śruti*. *Kapila-smṛti*, on the other hand, refers to things like *mahat*, the great, *ahaṁ-kāra*; the self sense of which we have no experience; nor are they mentioned in the *śruti*. If it is said that *Kaṭha U.* (I. 3. 11) mentions *mahat* the great and *avyakta* the unmanifested, in I. 4. 1, it has been explained that these refer to the intellect and body of *Hiraṇya-garbha* and not the great and *pradhāna* of the *Sāṁkhya*. If *Kapila-smṛti* cannot be trusted in the treatment of the effects, it follows that it cannot be trusted in the treatment of the cause also, i.e. *pradhāna*.[2]

Nimbārka says that if persons like Manu do not perceive that the *Veda* is concerned with *pradhāna*, the *smṛti* which is opposed to the *Veda* is unacceptable.

Baladeva holds that on account of the non-perception in Scripture of many other doctrines found in the *Sāṁkhya* system such as the doctrine that the souls are pure consciousness and all-pervading, the *śruti* has to be accepted.

[1] *avyaktaṁ puruṣe brahman niṣkriye sampralīyate.*
Āpastamba Dharma Sūtra I. 8. 23, 2.

[2] *kārya-smṛter a-prāmāṇyāt kāraṇa-smṛter apy a-prāmāṇyam yuktam ity abhiprāyaḥ.* Ś.

REFUTATION OF THE *YOGA* DOCTRINE

II. 1. 3. *etena yogaḥ pratyuktaḥ*

Thereby the Yoga (smṛti) is refuted.

etena: by this; *yogaḥ:* the *Yoga smṛti; pratyuktaḥ:* is refuted.

The *Yoga* philosophy maintains that *pradhāna* is the independent cause of the universe and the great one and self-sense are its effects. This view is refuted already. The *Yoga* system with its eightfold discipline is not opposed to the *Vedas*. It is a way to the realisation of the Self. B.U. II. 4. 5; *Kaṭha U.* II. 6, 11, 18; Ś.U. II. 8, VI. 13 uphold the *Yoga* doctrine. So one is likely to think that the *Yoga* system may be relied upon, as it is in partial agreement with the *Veda*. Ś.U. III. 8 tells us that *Sāṁkhya* knowledge of *Yoga* discipline is not enough. What we need is knowledge of the Self. We accept the systems of *Sāṁkhya* and *Yoga* in so far as they are in conformity with the *śruti* and reject them when they contradict *śruti*. *Taittirīya Brāhmaṇa* says: 'No one who does not know the *Veda* knows the Highest Self.'[1] See also B.U. III. 9. 26. These observations apply also to other *smṛtis*.

Section 3 (4–11)

BRAHMAN'S NATURE IS NOT VIOLATED BY HIS CAUSALITY OF THE WORLD

II. 1. 4. *na vilakṣaṇatvād asya tathātvaṁ ca śabdāt*

(Brahman can) not (be the cause of the world) on account of difference of nature of this (the world) and its being such (i.e. different from Brahman) (is known) from Scripture.

na: not; *vilakṣaṇatvāt:* on account of difference of nature; *asya:* of this; *tathātvam:* its being like this; *ca:* and; *śabdāt:* from Scripture.

This *śutra* states the opponent's viewpoint. Reasoning is also possible as a means of knowledge in the case of *Brahman*. If there are conflicting passages of *śruti*, their reconciliation is possible through reasoning. Again, the knowledge of *Brahman* through reasoning is said to culminate in an intuition of *Brahman* which dispels all ignorance and causes release.[2] It is thus superior to *śruti*. B.U. (II. 4. 5) says that the Self is to be heard, to be thought, etc. If we apply our reason to the question of *Brahman's* causality of the world,

[1] *nāvedavin manute taṁ bṛhantam.* III. 2. 1. 9; III. 2. 9. 7.

[2] *anubhavāvasānaṁ ca, brahma-vijñānam avidyāyā nivartakam mokṣa sādhanam.* Ś. *brahma-sākṣātkārasya moksopāyatayā prādhānyāt tatra śabdād api parokṣagocarād aparokṣārthàsādharmya-gocaras tarko' ntaraṅgam iti tasyaiva balavatvam ity arthaḥ.* Ānandagiri.

we find that there is a difference of nature between *Brahman* the cause and the world the effect. *Brahman* is conscious and pure; the world is unconscious and impure. Cause and effect cannot be different in nature. Gold ornaments are made of gold and not of earth; earthen vessels are made of earth and not of gold. So this world which is non-conscious and comprises pleasure, pain and infatuation (*sukha-duḥkha-mohānvitam*) is impure and its cause cannot be the pure *Brahman*. The world is not conscious for it is an instrument of the conscious soul. If the universe were itself conscious, it cannot be of use to the conscious soul even as one lamp cannot be of use to another. If it is said that the world too may be conscious and the apparent absence of consciousness is due to a modification of consciousness itself as may appear in the condition of sleep and swoon and it is not necessary for the things of the world to be utterly unconscious to be useful to the soul as instruments of action and the relation between souls and objects may be one of superior to subordinate, this position, however, which minimises the distinction between the conscious *Brahman* and the non-conscious world will not explain away the difference in nature between the two which the *śruti* asserts. T.U. (II. 6) speaks of *Brahman* as manifesting itself in two forms, intelligent and non-intelligent (*vijñānaṁ cāvijñānaṁ ca*). If it is said that there are passages in the *śruti* such as the earth spoke, fire thought, the *prāṇas* quarrelled (*Śatapatha Brāhmaṇa* VI. 1. 3, 2 and 4; C.U. VI. 2. 3–4; B.U. VI. 1. 7, I. 3. 2), this objection is answered in the next *sūtra* by the *Pūrva-pakṣin*.

R. uses the same arguments but adds another objection that things of different essential characters stand to each other in the relation of cause and effect. From man who is a conscious being, there arise nails, teeth and hair which are non-conscious things. The sentient scorpion springs from the non-sentient dung and the non-sentient threads spring from the sentient spider. R. answers this objection by saying that in these instances the relation of cause and effect rests only on the non-sentient elements.[1]

Śrīnivāsa, following R., answers the objection of the *pūrva-pakṣin* that it is possible to imagine that there is consciousness in stones, wood and the rest, though it is not manifest, by saying that it is unreasonable to take what is known by direct perception to be incorrect on the ground of mere imagination.

Baladeva gives an absolutely different interpretation. He makes this *sūtra* a separate section and gives it a new meaning. '[The idea] is not [unauthoritative like the *Sāṁkhya* and the rest] on account of its difference [from them] its being so is known from the text.' The *Veda* is non-human in origin unlike the *Sāṁkhya* and therefore it is authoritative.

[1] *yatas tatrāpy acetanāṁśa eva kārya-kāraṇa-bhāvaḥ.*

II. 1. 5. *abhimāni-vyapadeśas tu viśeṣānugatibhyām*

But the reference is to the presiding deities on account of the distinctive nature and relatedness.

abhimāni-vyapadeśaḥ: reference to presiding deities; *tu:* but; *viśeṣa-anugatibhyām:* on account of distinctive nature and relatedness.

When it is said that 'the earth spoke', 'the fire thought', etc., the reference is not to the elements but to the deities which control them. See K.U. II. 14; C.U. VI. 3. 2; *Aitareya U.* I. 2. 4. So the objection holds that the world being different in nature, *Brahman* cannot be its material cause. In agreement with *smṛti* confirmed by reasoning, the *pūrva-pakṣin* holds that *pradhāna* is the universal material cause.

Baladeva thinks that the *sūtra* states not the objection but the correct conclusion. If it be said that we cannot reconcile the sayings of the *Veda* as the Earth spoke and the Fire willed, the answer is that in these passages the reference is to the presiding deities.

II. 1. 6. *dṛśyate tu*

But (it) is seen.

dṛśyate: is seen; *tu:* but.

Here the objection stated in *sūtras* II. 1. 4 and 5 is refuted. That the world cannot proceed from *Brahman* because the two are different in nature cannot be accepted. For non-intelligent hairs and nails proceed from intelligent beings like men and scorpions and other sentient beings spring from cow-dung. Even if we say that they come out of the bodies and not souls, the difference in nature still remains between the cause and the effect for it is the non-intelligent body which is the abode of the intelligent soul, though neither the cow-dung nor the hair and the nails are the abodes of it. It is due to the presence of the soul that the body undergoes changes of colour, form, etc., before it manifests as the hair and the nails, or the cow-dung changes into the body of the scorpion. If there were complete identity between the two, there would be no distinction of cause and effect. If a partial identity is allowed, say between the element of earth in the body of the scorpion and the cow-dung, a similar identity in nature can be established between the world and *Brahman*, viz. the fact of existence itself, *sattā-lakṣaṇa*.

What exactly is the meaning of the difference in nature between *Brahman* and the world? (i) Does the opponent mean the non-occurrence in the world of the entire characteristics of *Brahman* or (ii) the non-occurrence of a few characteristics or (iii) the non-occurrence of the characteristic of intelligence. If the first alternative is taken, there can be no causal relation at all. For unless there is some difference between the two, there can be no causal connection. The second alternative is not acceptable for the quality of existence is present in the world. The third is incapable of proof. So this entire complex of things has *Brahman* for its material cause. Scripture supports this view.

Scripture is the way to prove the reality of *Brahman*. For being devoid of form and other sensible qualities *Brahman* is not the object of perception. It cannot be an object of inference or comparison because there is no perceivable sign or similarity in it. So it is to be known through the Vedic teaching. See *Kaṭha U*. 1. 2. 9; *Ṛg Veda* X. 130. 6.

If it is said that reasoning is useful for attaining the knowledge of the Scripture, it is reasoning which comes after the hearing of *śruti* and is favourable to it. It is reasoning which is subservient to *anubhava* or spiritual experience.[1] Reasoning applied to *śruti* helps us to understand the *śruti* better. For example, we learn that the Self is not connected with the waking or dream conditions as they are exclusive of each other. Since during sleep the individual soul becomes one with the Universal Self without the consciousness of the world, the individual soul is in reality the Universal Self. Since the world has arisen out of *Brahman* and the effect is not different from the cause, the world cannot be different from *Brahman*. T.U. II. 6 can be explained by those who believe in an intelligent cause of the world which is manifold and unmanifested in the two parts of the world *cetana and acetana*. The *Sāṁkhya* system which believes that the non-intelligent *pradhāna* is the cause would not be able to make any sense of the *śruti* passage. The cause of the world is an intelligent being, in spite of its being different from its effect.

R., Nimbārka and Śrīnivāsa hold that the objection that the universe on account of its difference from *Brahman* cannot have *Brahman* for its material cause is not valid for 'it is seen' that nails, hair, etc., arise from a person from whom they are different.

Baladeva adopts the same interpretation but looks upon this *sūtra* as a separate section.

II. 1. 7. *asad iti cen na pratiṣedha-mātratvāt*

If it be said that (in that case the effect is) non-existent, (we reply) that it is not so because it is a mere negation (without an object which is to be negated).

asat: non-existent; *iti cet:* if it is said; *na:* not; *pratiṣedha-mātratvāt:* because it is a mere negation.

The *Vedāntin* maintains the view that the effect exists in the cause already. The objection is raised that this view is violated, because the impure world which is the effect cannot exist in pure *Brahman*. The effect must be treated as non-existing before its actual origination. The answer is given in the *sūtra*. If you negate the existence of the effect before its actual origination, you are negating something which

[1] *śruty anugṛhīta eva hy atra tarko'nubhavāṅgatvenāśrīyate*. Ś.

does not exist.[1] If the negation has for its object the existence of the effect previous to its origination, then prior to its coming into being the effect does exist in the form of its cause and so it cannot be negated. Even after coming into being the effect does not exist independently, apart from the cause. So either in the past or in the present, the effect by itself is non-existent without the cause. As it is always one or the other form of the cause it cannot be negated. The world with all its qualities does not exist without the cause, *Brahman*, either now or before the beginning of the effect. So it cannot be said that the effect was non-existent before its actual beginning. See B.U. II. 4. 6.

For R., the objection considered is that since *Brahman*, the cause, differs from the world, the effect, they are two separate things and so the effect does not exist in the cause. This means that the world originates from what has no existence. R. says that, while cause and effect are not of the same nature, the effect is not altogether different and separate from the cause. *Brahman* the cause modifies itself so as to assume the form of a world differing from it in character. There is difference of characteristics but as in the case of gold and golden bracelets there is oneness of substance.[2]

II. 1. 8. *apītau tadvat prasaṅgād asamanjasam*

Because at the time of the dissolution, (Brahman will be) of the same nature (as the world) (the doctrine of the causality of Brahman) is inadequate.

apītau: in dissolution; *tadvat:* of the same nature; *prasaṅgāt:* because of an occasion; *asamañjasam:* inadequate or unsatisfactory.

Another objection is raised to the causality of *Brahman*. At the time of the dissolution, when the effect becomes one with the cause, *Brahman* will be polluted by the qualities of grossness, absence of intelligence, limitation, impurity, etc. Besides, as all distinctions will be resolved into a state of non-distinction, there would be no special causes left at the time of a new beginning of the world and so the new world could not arise with its distinction of enjoying souls, objects of enjoyment and so forth. If, however, we assume the origin of a new world even after the annihilation of all works of the enjoying souls which enter into the state of non-difference from the Highest *Brahman*, then even the released souls may be subject to rebirth in the world. If, to avoid these difficulties, it is held that the world remains separate from *Brahman* even during the period of the dissolution, the view that the effect is non-different from the cause is violated.

[1] *pratiṣedhaṁ hīdam nāsya pratiṣedhasya pratiṣedhyam asti.*

[2] *kāraṇa-bhūtam brahmaivasvasmād vilakṣaṇa-jagad-ākāreṇa pariṇamata iti . . . kṛmi-mākṣikayor api hi sati ca vailakṣaṇye kuṇḍala-hiraṇyayor iva dravyaikyaṁ asty eva.* R.

R. takes this *sūtra* to mean that the relation of embodied being and body cannot subsist between *Brahman* and the world and if it did subsist, all the imperfections of the world would cling to *Brahman* also. If we accept the doctrine of the oneness of substance of cause and effect, then the imperfections of the effect will affect the cause. We cannot say that *Brahman* in its causal as well as in its effected state has all conscious and non-conscious beings for its body and as imperfections inhere in the body only, they do not affect *Brahman* in its causal or effected state. If there is a causal relation between *Brahman* and his body, then the imperfections of the latter would affect the former. It is also objected that the conscious and non-conscious beings cannot constitute the body of *Brahman*. Embodiedness is the result of *karma* and the Highest Self is free from it. He is not capable of enjoyment through sense-organs and has no life dependent on breath. So *Brahman* cannot have a body constituted by conscious souls and unconscious objects. If it is said that the body of a being is constituted by that, the nature, subsistence and activity of which depend on the will of that being and so a body may be ascribed to the Lord in so far as the essential nature, subsistence and activity of all depend on him, it is not correct, for the nature of a body does not depend on the will of the intelligent soul joined to it. An injured body does not obey the will of its possessor. The persistence of a dead body does not depend on the soul that tenanted it. Intelligent souls control the movements of puppets and the like but we do not say that the latter constitute the bodies of the former. Again, the nature of an eternal intelligent soul does not depend on the will of the Lord. We cannot say that the body of a being is constituted by that which is exclusively ruled and supported by that being and stands to it in an exclusive subservient relation (*śeṣa*) for this definition would include actions also. Several texts declare that the Lord is without a body.

II. 1. 9. *na tu dṛṣṭānta-bhāvāt*

But not so for there are (*parallel*) *instances.*

na: not; *tu:* but; *dṛṣṭānta-bhāvāt:* because there are instances.

The *Vedānta* view is not inadequate for there are instances of effects which do not affect by their qualities the causes into which they are reabsorbed. Things made of clay are of different shapes and sizes but these latter do not affect the clay into which they may be reduced. So also with gold ornaments which do not affect the gold into which they are reabsorbed by their qualities. Similarly with regard to earth and the organic beings which spring from it. The opponent cannot quote any instance to the contrary. Reabsorption is impossible if the effect retains its particular qualities. In spite of the non-difference of cause and effect, the effect has its self in the cause but not the cause in the effect. See II. 1. 14. Again, the identity of cause and effect holds good not only in the period of dissolution but at all times. See B.U. II. 4. 6; C.U. VII. 25. 2; M.U. II. 2. 11. Ś. argues that the effect and its qualities are mere appearances due to ignorance and so do not affect the cause in any way either during dissolution or subsistence of the world in *Brahman*,[1] even as a magician is not affected by the illusions he creates for others or a person is not affected by the illusions of his dream. The Self who is the eternal witness of the three states of the world is not affected by any one of them, since each is exclusive of the other two.[2]

The other objection about the rebirth of the liberated souls is set aside on the ground that rebirth after dissolution is possible only to those who are subject to ignorance which persists both in sleep and dissolution. See C.U. VI. 9. 2–3. The liberated souls are not born again because their ignorance is wiped out by the knowledge of the Real. As for the plea that the world remains distinct from *Brahman* in dissolution, we cannot accept such a dualist position.

R. argues that *Brahman* has all conscious and non-conscious beings for its body and constitutes the self of that body. *Brahman* is connected with two states, a causal and an effected one, the essential characteristics of which are expansion and contraction. These apply not to *Brahman* but to conscious and non-conscious beings. The imperfections of the body do not affect *Brahman* and the good qualities belonging to the self do not extend to the body, even as youth, childhood and old age which are attributes of embodied beings such as gods or men belong to the body only, not to the embodied self; while knowledge, pleasure and so on belong to the conscious self only, not to the body.[3]

As for the objection that the world comprising matter and souls, either in its subtle or gross condition, cannot stand to *Brahman* in the relation of a body, it is based on faulty reasoning. There are many texts which declare that the entire world stands to *Brahman* in the relation of a body. See the *Antaryāmin Brāhmaṇa* of B.U., *Subāla U.*, etc. Again, the word 'body' is not like the word 'jar' used in one sense. The opponent's definitions are erroneous. The view that body is 'that which is the cause of the enjoyment of the fruits of action' does not apply to earth and the like, nor does it apply to the bodily forms which the Lord or the released souls assume for these embodi-

[1] *kāryasya tad dharmāṇāṁ cāvidyādhyāropitatvān na taiḥ kāraṇaṁ saṁsṛjyata iti apītāv api sa samānaḥ.* Ś.

[2] *avasthā-traya-sākṣy eko'vyabhicāryavasthā-trayeṇa vyabhicāriṇā na śaṁspṛśyate.* Ś.

[3] *cid-acid-vastu-śarīratayā tad-ātma-bhūtasya parasya brahmaṇaḥ saṁkoca-vikāsātmaka-kārya-kāraṇa-bhāvāvasthādvayānvayepi na kaścid virodhaḥ. yataḥ saṁkoca-vikāsau para-brahma-śarīra-bhūta-cid-acid-vastu-gatau. śarīra-gatās tu doṣānātmani prasajyante. ātma-gataś ca guṇā na śarīre yathā deva-manuṣyādīnāṁ sa-śarīrāṇāṁ kṣetra-jñānāṁ śarīra-gatā bālatva-yuvatva-sthaviratvādayo nātmani sambadhyante. ātma-gatāś ca jñāna-sukhādayo na śarīre.* R.

ments do not subserve the fruition of the results of actions. These bodily forms of the Lord are not the combinations of earth and the other elements. The other definition that the body is 'that, the life of which depends on the vital breath with its five modifications' is too narrow since it does not apply to plants. Though vitality is present in plants, it does not take five modifications. We cannot say that the body is the abode of sense-organs or the cause of pleasure and pain. It does not apply to the bodies of stone or wood which are bestowed on *Ahalyā* and other persons in accordance with their deeds. The correct definition of body is this. Any substance which a conscious soul is capable of completely controlling and supporting for its own purposes and which stands to the soul in an entirely subordinate relation, is the body of that soul.[1] In the case of an injured body the power of control is obstructed; in the case of a dead body the body begins to decay the moment the soul departs from it and we speak of it as a body because it is a part of the aggregate of matter which previously constituted a body. In this sense all conscious and non-conscious beings together constitute the body of the Supreme Person for they are completely controlled and supported by him for his own ends and are entirely subordinate to him.[2] When the texts deny a body to him, they deny to him a body due to *karman*. They actually declare that the universe is his body.

II. 1. 10. *sva-pakṣa doṣāc ca*

And because the defects (alleged to be in the Vedānta view by the Saṁkhya are found) in his own view also.

sva: one's own; *pakṣa:* side; *doṣāt:* due to defects; *ca:* and.

The objections against the *Vedānta* view dealt with already apply to the *Sāṁkhya* view of *pradhāna* as the cause of the world. The world with form and sound is different in nature from *pradhāna* which does not possess form and other qualities. The objection that the effect was non-existent before origination is common to both the *Vedānta* and the *Sāṁkhya* which accept *sat-kārya-vāda*. Again, in *Sāṁkhya* also, the effect becomes one with the cause in dissolution and so will pollute the cause. Again, as the reasons which are responsible for the joys and sorrows of different persons are destroyed in dissolution, there is no reason why a new creation should arise. If there can be a new creation without any cause, the rebirth of the released is also possible. If it is said that some distinctions remain unabsorbed even in dissolution, these distinctions are not the effects of *pradhāna*; for otherwise they would not have been non-distinct

[1] *ato yasya cetanasya yad dravyaṁ sarvātmanā svārthe niyantuṁ dhārayituṁ ca śakyaṁ tac-cheṣataika-svarūpaṁ ca, tat tasya śarīram iti śarīra-lakṣaṇam āstheyam.*

[2] *ataḥ sarvam parama-puruṣeṇa sarvātmanā svārthe niyāmyaṁ dhāryaṁ tac cheṣataika-svarūpam iti sarvaṁ cetanācetanaṁ tasya śarīram.*

from *pradhāna*. So far as the *Vedānta* is concerned, these objections have been answered.

R. makes out that the *Sāṁkhya* theory cannot account for the origination of the world. It holds that owing to the *puruṣā's* approximation to *prakṛti*, the attributes of the latter are fictitiously superimposed on the *puruṣa* which consists of pure intelligence free from all change and on this depends the origination of the empirical world. What is the nature of approximation? Does it imply change in *prakṛti* or change in *puruṣa*? Not the latter for *puruṣa* is incapable of change; not the former for changes in *prakṛti* are supposed to be the effects of superimposition and cannot therefore be the cause. If approximation means the mere existence of *prakṛti*, then even the released soul would be liable to that superimposition. The *Sāṁkhya* is unable to give a rational account of the origination of the world.

II. 1. 11. *tarkāpratiṣṭhānād apy anyathānumeyam iti ced evam apy avimokṣaprasaṅgaḥ*

If it be said that, notwithstanding the ill-foundedness of reasoning, it is to be inferred otherwise, (we say) that, in that way, too, there will be the result of non-release.

tarka: reasoning; *apratiṣṭhānāt:* because of ill-foundedness; *api:* notwithstanding; *anyathā:* otherwise; *anumeyam:* be inferred; *iti cet:* if so; *evam:* in that way; *api:* too, even; *avimokṣa:* non-release; *prasaṅgaḥ:* result, consequence.

Ś. states the *pūrva-pakṣa* thus: Mere reasoning cannot be depended upon in matters which must be understood in the light of *śruti*. Reasoning rests on individual opinion. The arguments of some clever men are refuted by others. On account of the diversity of men's opinions, it is impossible to accept mere reasoning as a sure guide. Even men of outstanding intellectual eminence as Kapila, Kaṇāda and others are seen to contradict one another. If it be said that all reasoning is not unsound, even this assumption is based on reasoning. If some arguments are devoid of foundation, it does not follow that others are also devoid of foundation. If all reasoning were unfounded, the whole course of practical life would come to an end. Men act on the assumption that in the past, the present and the future nature is uniform. When there is a conflict among different interpretations of *śruti* it is reasoning that enables us to fix the correct meaning of words and sentences. Manu asks us to determine what is *dharma* by means of reasoning (XII. 105–6). We require reasoning to detect and avoid fallacies. Because the argument of the *pūrva-pakṣa* is fallacious, it does not follow that the *siddhānta* is also fallacious.

To all this the *sūtra* replies. Though reasoning may hold good in certain cases, with regard to ultimate questions on the nature of Reality and release, reason is not of use if it is not backed by *śruti*. *Brahman* is not an object of perception or inference. It has neither form to be seen nor sound to be heard nor any sign from which it can be inferred. Again, release is the result of the right kind of knowledge which is constant and uniform. We do not have different views about it. It is similar to the knowledge of fire that it is hot.[1] A mere inference may take different forms and may leave us in doubt about the nature of the object. It need not be universal and constant like the perception of heat in fire. The *Sāṁkhya* views based on reasoning are not accepted by all. The knowledge of the *Veda* being self-evident and eternally the same is incapable of being challenged by any logician. Release cannot be attained by any other means than the right kind of knowledge imparted to us by the *Upaniṣads*. So by reasoning which is faithful to *śruti*, it is proved that the intelligent *Brahman* is both the efficient and the material cause of the universe.

R. and Śrīkaṇṭha break this *sūtra* into two, *tarkāpratiṣṭhānād api* and *anyathā . . . prasaṅgaḥ*.

R. points out that the theories based on human reasoning are liable to be upset or modified by those more skilled in reasoning. With regard to transcendental issues, Scripture alone is authoritative and reasoning is to be applied only in support of Scripture.

Nimbārka reads for *vimokṣa*, *anirmokṣa*.

Section 4 (12)

REFUTATION OF OTHER THEORIES

II. 1. 12. *etena śiṣṭāparigrahā api vyākhyātāḥ*

By this those (theories) also which are not accepted by competent authorities are explained (i.e. refuted).

etena: by this; *śiṣṭāḥ:* competent authorities; *aparigrahāḥ:* not accepted; *api:* also; *vyākhyātāḥ:* are explained.

As the *Sāṁkhya* which is closest to the *Vedānta* in view of its acceptance of *sat-kārya-vāda*, identity of cause and effect, and the independent existence of the Self, its powerful support by reasoning and approval by competent persons, if disproved, the other theories like atomism, etc., which are less reasonable may be taken as being disproved.

R. points out that the atomists disagree in many ways about the nature of the atoms, whether they are fundamentally void or non-void, whether they have a merely cognitional or objective existence, whether they are momentary or permanent, definite or indefinite, real or unreal, etc. This disagreement proves that these theories are ill-founded.

[1] *samyaj-jñānam eka-rūpaṁ vastu-tantratvāt. eka-rūpeṇa hy avasthito yo'rthas sa paramārtho loke tad viṣayaṁ jñānaṁ samyaj-jñānam ity ucyate yathāgnir uṣṇa iti.*

R. and Śrīnivāsa mean by *śiṣṭāḥ*: the remaining ones. While Ś., Bhāskara and Śrīkaṇṭha explain the compound as *śiṣṭaiḥ aparigrahāḥ*, R., Nimbārka, Śrīnivāsa and Baladeva explain it as *śiṣṭās ca aparigrahāś ca.*

Section 5 (13)

BRAHMAN AND THE ENJOYING SOUL AND THE OBJECTS OF ENJOYMENT

II. 1. 13. *bhoktrāpatter avibhāgaś cet syāl lokavat*

If it be said that there will be no distinction (between the individual souls and their objects of enjoyment) on account of the enjoyer being reduced to the condition (of the objects) (we say that the distinction may exist as is seen) in ordinary experience.

bhoktṛ: enjoyer; *āpatteḥ:* on account of being reduced to the condition (of objects); *avibhāgaḥ:* no distinction; *cet:* if; *syāt:* may be; *lokavat:* as in ordinary experience.

If the world were non-different from *Brahman*, then the distinction of enjoyers and the objects of enjoyment would be nullified. So the doctrine of *Brahman's* causality should be given up since it negates the well-established distinction between enjoyers who are intelligent embodied souls and the objects of enjoyment. To this the reply is made that the distinction may exist as ordinary experience furnishes us with analogous examples. Waves, foam, bubbles and other modifications of the sea, though they are not different from sea-water exist sometimes in a state of mutual separation and sometimes in conjunction. Because they are non-different from the sea-water it does not follow that they pass over into each other. So also the enjoyers and the objects of enjoyment do not pass over into each other, though they are not different from the Highest *Brahman*.

According to Ś., though the enjoyer is not really an effect of *Brahman* but is the unmodified creator himself, in so far as he enters into the effect (T.U. II. 6) it passes into a state of distinction on account of the effect, acting as a limiting adjunct, even as the universal *ākāśa* is divided by its contact with jars and other limiting adjuncts.[1]

R. criticises Ś.'s interpretation of the *sūtra* given above and puts the objection differently. The theory of an embodied *Brahman* being the universal cause does not allow of a distinction in nature between the Lord and the individual soul. Besides, *Brahman* becomes the abode of all the imperfections attaching to the world as a lump of clay or gold shares the imperfections of the things fashioned

[1] Cp. *saty api bhedāpagame nātha tavāhaṁ na māmakī nas tvam*
sāmudro hi taraṅgaḥ kvacana samudro'sti tāraṅgaḥ.

out of it. To this objection the answer is, if a soul experiences pleasures and pains, it is not due to its being joined to a body but to its *karman* in the form of good and evil deeds. The body is originated by *karman*. (See C.U. VII. 26. 2; VIII. 2. 1; 12. 3.) He who is freed from bondage is not touched by evil, even if he has a body. The Highest Self has a body of conscious and non-conscious beings but is not connected with *karman* and is therefore free from evil. We also see in ordinary life that a ruler may reward or punish those who observe or transgress the rules but he does not, simply because he has a body, himself experience the pleasures and pains due to the observance or transgressions of any of his commands. Again, *Brahman* does not undergo changes like clay or gold for he is said to be free from all change and imperfection.

In support of his reading of the *sūtra* and interpretation, R. quotes *Dramiḍa-bhāṣya.*

Section 6 (14–20)

NON-DIFFERENCE OF THE EFFECT FROM THE CAUSE

II. 1. 14. *tad ananyatvam ārambhaṇa-śabdādibhyaḥ*

The non-difference of them (*cause and effect*) (*results*) *from words like beginning and others.*

tad: that; *an-anyatvam:* non-difference; *ārambhaṇa-śabdādibhyaḥ:* words like beginning and others.

In the previous *sūtra,* the distinction between enjoyers and the objects of enjoyment was acknowledged from the empirical standpoint. Here it is said that the effect, world, is non-different from the cause, *Brahman.* C.U. VI. 1. 4 says: 'Just as, my dear, by one clod of clay all that is made of clay becomes known, the modification being only a name arising from speech, while the truth is that it is just clay. . .' Ś. says these modifications or effects are names only, exist through or originate from speech only, while in reality there exists no such thing as a modification.[1] In so far as they are names they are untrue; in so far as they are clay they are true. The entire body of effects has no existence apart from *Brahman.*[2] Ś. does not affirm the absolute oneness of *Brahman* and the world but only denies their difference.[3] The world does not exist apart from *Brahman.* Therefore to know *Brahman* is to know everything else.

It may be said that *Brahman* has in it elements of manifoldness. As the tree has many branches, *Brahman* possesses many powers.

[1] *vācaiva kevalam asti . . . na tu vastu-vṛttena vikāraḥ kaścid asti.*

[2] *brahma-vyatirekeṇa kārya-jātasyābhāva iti gamyate.* Ś.

[3] Cp. *na khalu ananyatvam iti abhedaṁ brūmaḥ, kiṁ tu bhedaṁ vyāsedhāmaḥ. Bhāmatī.*

Unity and manifoldness are both true. A tree considered in itself is one; it is many when viewed as having branches. The sea is one and yet manifold as having waves and foam. Unity is used for achieving release and multiplicity for work in the world. Ś. answers this view by saying that the Highest Reality is one according to the Vedic texts. The independent existence of the world and the individuals is denied in many texts. If both unity and multiplicity are real, then he who is engrossed with the manifold world cannot be regarded as ignorant. A text like 'He goes from death to death, who sees in it, as it were, diversity' (B.U. IV. 4. 19) will be unmeaning. If unity and multiplicity are both true, bondage cannot be the result of multiplicity nor release the result of the perception of unity. How can the knowledge of unity remove the knowledge of manifoldness if both are true.[1]

Another objection is raised: If absolute unity is the truth, then the ordinary means of right knowledge, perception, etc., become invalid, since the absence of manifoldness deprives them of their objects. The idea of a man, for example, becomes invalid, when the true idea of the post has presented itself. Again, texts embodying injunctions and prohibitions lose their meaning if the world does not exist. The entire body of doctrine which refers to final release will collapse. The answer to these objections is that so long as the knowledge of *Brahman* by the self has not arisen the entire complex of phenomenal existence is taken as true, even as the phantoms of a dream are taken as true until the sleeper wakes. Until awakening the ordinary course of secular and religious activity goes on undisturbed.

Another objection is raised: How can passages of the *Vedānta* which belong to the phenomenal world produce a knowledge of the identity of the soul with *Brahman*? It is said, in reply, that death occurs sometimes as the result of the mere suspicion that a venomous snake has bitten. Even when the dream is over, knowledge of the dream persists in waking life. Events in the dream, though unreal, are said to be indications of actual future events in life. See C.U. V. 2. 8. *Aitareya Āraṇyaka* III. 2. 4. 7. The Vedic statements have a purpose whereas the knowledge of the unity of the Self has nothing else above it. Vedic knowledge removes ignorance and is therefore useful.

Another objection is raised that the illustrations of clay, etc., suggest that *Brahman* too is capable of modifications. The answer is that *Brahman* is incapable of modifications. Modification is only appearance. The illustrations are used to show that *Brahman* alone is real.

Another objection is that if *Brahman* alone is real, there is no room for the distinction of a God who rules and the world and the souls

[1] *ubhaya-satyatāyāṁ hi katham ekatva-jñānena nānātva-jñānam apanudyata iti.*

ruled by him. The world is neither one with nor different from *Brahman*. It is said to be indescribable, *māyā*, the product of *śakti* or *prakṛti* of the omniscient God.[1] For the liberated soul there is no distinction of ruler and ruled. C.U. VII. 24. 1. The entire phenomenal world does not exist for him who has realised the Self.[2] From the viewpoint of the Highest Reality, there is non-difference of cause and effect. With reference to the phenomenal world which is considered to be real from the practical point of view, *Brahman* is said to be the ocean and the world is the waves. The transformation (*pariṇāma*) is accepted by the *Sūtrakāra* in so far as there is insistence on devotion to Personal God. It is only then that the world is treated as real and God is said to be omniscient, omnipotent and omnipresent.[3]

Bhāskara criticises Ś.'s view and insists on the reality of difference.

In his commentary on the *sūtra*, R. considers the views of the *Vaiśeṣika* system and Ś. He criticises the doctrine of *avidyā* or ignorance. If the soul in its essential form and not fictitiously imagined form is the abode of *avidyā*, this means that *Brahman* is the abode of *avidyā*. If it is said that the soul as different from *Brahman* and fictitiously imagined in it, is the abode of *avidyā*, this would mean that the non-conscious (*jaḍa*) is the abode of *avidyā*. If it be maintained that the abode of *avidyā* is the soul in its essential nature, as qualified by the fictitiously imagined aspect, the soul which has an absolutely homogenous nature cannot be qualified apart from *avidyā*. Again, if by release is understood the destruction of *avidyā*, when one soul attains release and *avidyā* is destroyed, all souls should be released. But it is not so. If we say that there is a separate *avidyā* for each soul, this implies distinction of souls. Is this distinction real or a product of *avidyā*? It cannot be the former, because the soul is pure, non-differenced intelligence: if the latter, does *avidyā* belong to *Brahman* or the souls? Not to *Brahman*. If to souls, we are arguing in a circle. *Avidyās* are established on the basis of the distinction of souls and the distinctions are established on account of *avidyās*. If it is urged that these defects do not touch *avidyā* which is itself unreal, in that case it would cling even to the released souls and the Highest *Brahman*. When the *avidyā* of a soul passes away on the rise of true knowledge, does the soul perish or not perish? If it perishes, release means the destruction of the essential nature of the soul; if it does not, then the soul continues to exist different from *Brahman*.

[1] *sarvajñasyeśvarasyātma-bhūte ivāvidyā-kalpite nāma-rūpe tattvānyatvābhyām anirvacanīye saṁsāra-prapañca-bīja-bhūte sarvajñasyeśvarasya māyā-śaktiḥ prakṛtir iti ca śruti-smṛtyor abhilapyete.*

[2] *evaṁ paramārthāvasthāyāṁ sarva-vyavahārābhāvaṁ vadanti vedāntāḥ.* Ś.

[3] *sūtrakāro'pi paramārthābhiprāyeṇa tad ananyatvam ity āha. vyavahārābhiprāyeṇa tu syāl lokavad iti mahā-samudrādiṣṭhānīyatām brahmaṇaḥ kathayati. apratyākhyāyaiva kārya-prapañcaṁ pariṇāma-prakriyāṁ cāśrayati saguṇopāsaneṣūpayokṣyata iti.*

R. criticises the distinction of *māyā* and *avidyā*. *Brahman* cannot be the abode of *māyā*. R. says that none but a person who is not in his right mind would take pleasure in an unreal play, carried on by means of implements unreal and known by him to be unreal.

R. takes the *sūtra* to be an answer to Kaṇāda's view that the effect constitutes a substance different from the cause. The subtle and gross conditions of the conscious and non-conscious beings which constitute the body of *Brahman* are the cause and effect. He interprets the phrase *vācārambhaṇa* as follows: *vācā*, on account of speech; *ārambhaṇa:* what is touched or taken; *ā-rabh*, *ā-labh*, *ālambhaḥ*, *sparśa-hiṁsayoḥ*. For the bringing about of activity, 'fetch water in the jar', the clay must enter into contact with the effect, *vikāra*, i.e. a particular make or configuration and a special name, a *nāmadheya*.

R. and Nimbārka look upon the relation of *Brahman* and the universe as one of soul-body relationship.

Śrīkaṇṭha, after R., adopts the *Viśiṣṭādvaita* view: 'What has been set out already as to *Śiva* alone, without a second—the Self qualified by the universe both conscious and non-conscious, becoming both cause and effect, that constitutes the doctrine of the qualified non-dualism of *Śiva*.'[1]

Śrīkaṇṭha explains *vācārambhana* in two ways: That which is the beginning, i.e. the cause, of speech, i.e. of speech and of practical activity. So the text means that an effect *vikāra* is a name, *nāmadheya*, which is the cause of speech and practical activity. Another explanation is that which has speech for its beginning. So the text means that an effect, *vikāra*, is just the object of such expressions as 'this is a jar', i.e. a special condition which the clay has assumed for practical purposes. It is not a separate entity from the clay.

II. 1. 15. *bhāve copalabdheḥ*

And because of the perception (*of the effect*) *on the existence* (*of the cause*).

bhāve: on existence; *ca:* and; *upalabdheḥ:* because of perception.

The effect cannot be independent and different from the material cause. We can have a jar only when the clay exists. If it be said that fire and smoke continue to be two different things, though smoke is seen only where the fire exists, it is not correct for smoke may be observed in a jar in which it is collected even after the fire is extinguished. The jar makes us aware of the material cause while smoke does not make us conscious of fire.

The *sūtra* may be read as *bhāvāc ca upalabdheḥ*. The non-difference of effect from cause is a fact of perception. A cloth is nothing but threads crossing each other, which we perceive. It is these perceived

[1] *yad uktaṁ pūrvatra cid-acid-prapañca-viśiṣṭaḥ śiva evādvitīyaḥ kāryaṁ kāraṇaṁ ca bhavati iti viśiṣṭa-śivādvaitam.*

facts which enable us to infer that the smallest parts of things are ultimately nothing but the three elements of fire, water and earth, represented by the three colours of red, white and black. C.U. VI. 4. These are connected with air, air with *ākāśa* and *ākāśa* with *Brahman*. All means of proof lead back to *Brahman* as the cause of the world, and not *pradhāna*.

For R., the effect denotes nothing else than the causal substance which has passed over into a different condition. Gold which is the cause is perceived when the ear-ring is present. The fact that we do not recognise fire in smoke does not disprove this view. Fire is the operative cause of smoke and smoke originates from damp fuel joined with fire.

II. 1. 16. *sattvāccāparasya*

And on account of the existence of what is posterior.
sattvāt: on account of existence; *ca:* and; *aparasya:* of what is posterior or afterwards.

That which is posterior in time, i.e. the effect, is declared in the Scripture to have its being in the cause, prior to its actual beginning. 'Being only was this in the beginning.' C.U. VI. 2. 1; *Aitareya Āraṇyaka* II. 4. 1. 1. We cannot produce oil from sand. The effect is non-different from the cause.

Some read *avarasya* for *aparasya*.

II. 1. 17. *asad-vyapadeśān neti cen na dharmāntareṇa vākya-śeṣāt.*

If it be said that on account of the mention of what is non-existent, (*the effect is*) *not* (*existent prior to creation*) (*we say*) *not so because with reference to complementary passage* (*the mention of non-existence means*) *another quality* (*only*).
asat: non-existence; *vyapadeśāt:* on account of mention; *na:* not; *iti cet:* if so; *na:* not so; *dharmāntareṇa:* due to another quality; *vākya-śeṣāt:* on account of the complementary passage.

The objection is raised in regard to certain scriptural texts which declare 'In the beginning this was that only which is not'. (C.U. III. 19. 1.) 'Non-existent, indeed, this was in the beginning.' (T.U. II. 7.) So being cannot be ascribed to the effect before its production. The reply is given that non-existence does not mean absolute non-existence but only a different quality or state in which name and shape are not manifested. In reference to this condition the effect is called non-existent though it existed as one with the cause. Later passages make out that absolute non-existence was not meant.

R. Niṁbārka take this, along with the next *sūtra*, as one. Ś., Bhāskara and Baladeva adopt the reading given here.

II. 1. 18. *yukteḥ śabdāntarāc ca*

From reasoning and from other Vedic text.

yukteḥ: from reasoning; *śabdāntarāt:* from another Vedic text; *ca:* and.

That the effect exists before its origination and is non-different from the cause can be ascertained from reasoning and Scriptures. Experience teaches us that if we wish to produce curd, earthen jars or gold ornaments, we employ milk, clay and gold; we do not employ clay for curds or milk for making jars. If the effect were non-existent in the cause, all this should be possible. Besides, all the effects being non-existent in the cause, anything might come out of anything else. If it is argued that there exists in each cause power to produce a special effect, *atiśaya,* milk for curd and clay for jars, then we assume something prior to the effect which later becomes the effect. If the specific power is considered to be non-existent before its appearance, then the objection is valid that anything may come out of anything else. Is this specific power non-existent before its appearance or is it different from both cause and effect? The specific power view does not help us. If it is said that the cause and the effect do not appear different because they are held together by the connection known as *samavāya* and not because they are identical with each other, then we ask whether *samavāya* is connected with the terms between which it exists or is independent of them entirely. If the former, then to explain one connection of *samavāya* we have to postulate a second connection and to explain that another and so on *ad infinitum.* If the latter, the cause and the effect will fall apart from each other and be totally unconnected. The relation of *samavāya* is unnecessary as experience tells us that cause and effect are identical. If the relation between the cause and the effect is regarded as that which exists between the parts and the whole and if the two are said to be held together by *samavāya,* the question arises whether the whole resides in all the parts simultaneously or only in some parts successively. If the former the whole may not be perceptible at all. The other side of a jar may not be in contact with the eyes. If the latter, we may infer the knowledge of the whole from the perception of a part. The knowledge of a part of the sword we hold in the hand makes us aware of the whole, though we have no perceptual knowledge of the whole on account of its being hidden in the sheath. The hidden parts of the sword are different from those of the sheath. Thus we introduce a new series of parts between the original parts and the whole or between the cause and the effect. To pervade the second series of parts, a third will have to be devised and so on *ad infinitum.* In short, the effect will be further and further removed from the cause. The effect as a whole cannot be said to reside in each of the parts simultaneously, for in that case, it would be more than one whole. One man cannot reside in two places at the same time. It is possible only when there are two men. The whole cannot reside in each one of the parts simultaneously in the manner in which one *sāmānya* or *jāti* of cow is said to reside in each of the cows simultaneously. For as every cow manifests the *sāmānya* or general character, every part of the cause might manifest the whole of the effect. This is not invariably experienced. Besides, if the whole were to reside fully in each part, one may as well have the milk of the cow from her horns. Again, if the effect be non-existent before its origination, there would be no notion of origination itself because origination implies a reference to the particular effect and the substratum in which it takes place. Unless the existence of the jar is assumed before it is produced, in the form of its cause, clay, the sentence 'the jar is produced' will have no meaning. If it is argued that origination is the connection of the effect with the existence of the cause, we ask, how can something which has not yet obtained existence enter into connection with something else? Connection is possible of two existing things only, and not one existing and one non-existent thing or of two non-existing things. Only existing things can be spoken of as having limitations. Absolute non-existence or what is altogether featureless cannot be spoken of as 'being prior to' origination. To say that the son of a barren woman was king before Pūrṇavarman is absurd. For the son of a barren woman is not only non-existent but is an unreality and so no temporal limitation can be set to him. Even so, at no time will the absolute non-existence of the effect, viz. a jar, be a reality, whatever may be the efforts of the potter. If the non-existent can never become existent, the *asat-kārya-vādin* may ask, what is the purpose of the operative causes, the potter, etc. If the effect exists in the cause and is non-different from it, where is the need of the potter to bring out a jar into existence. As the potter puts forth effort, one must assume the non-existence of the effect prior to its origination. To this the answer is that the operative agents arrange the cause in the form of the effect. Even the form is not absolutely new. A mere change in form does not transform one thing into an altogether different thing. People may be seen in different moods and yet they are recognised as the same. If it is argued that they are recognised as the same persons because their conditions are not separated by death, the case of the jar is different because the clay is as good as destroyed. Ś. says that the analogy is not correct. Milk continues to exist in a different form when we say that it has become curd. Even when the continued existence of the cause is not perceivable, when the seed is not seen to exist in the tree, we have to notice the earlier stages of the tree such as the sprouts, to know that they are the later stages of the seed. It is the seed which becomes visible in the form of the sprout, with the accumulation of particles of matter. It becomes invisible, not non-existent, when the sprouts change into something else. Incidentally Ś. says we have refuted the Buddhist theory of momentary existence for we have proved the eternal continued existence of cause. On the *asat-kārya-vāda* the operative agents have no purpose to serve. For it non-existence cannot be the object of any activity as the sky cannot be modified in any way by weapons. Nor can the cause clay which is said to be *samavāyi* and existent be the object of the activity of the operative agent, for if the effect which is non-existent is to arise from a cause which is different in nature, then anything may arise from anything else. If it is said that the effect is nothing but the specific power of the cause, then *sat-kārya-vāda* is accepted. The text C.U. VI. 2. 1 is quoted: 'In the beginning this was Being alone, one without a second.' This repudiates the suggestion of the non-existent as the source on the ground that the existent cannot come out of the non-existent. The effect exists prior to its origination in the form of the cause and is identical with it and so is it that everything else becomes known when *Brahman*, the cause, is known. C.U. VI. 1. 3.[1]

Śrīnivāsa, following Nimbārka, argues that names and forms, knowable by means of the evidence of direct perception and the rest are real, because they are perceived. An agent makes a jar out of a lump of clay that is existent. Here like the lump of clay, the existence of the jar is also known from perception. The activity of the agent is not useless since it helps manifestation. What was unmanifest before is made manifest. The origin of a non-existent effect is not tenable since we do not see a barley sprout from fire.

II. 1. 19. *paṭavac ca*

And like a piece of cloth.
paṭavat: like a piece of cloth; *ca:* and.

Even as a rolled piece of cloth is not different from what it is when it is spread out, so is the effect not different from the cause. What is not manifest in the cause becomes manifest in the effect. The length and breadth of the rolled piece of cloth which were not manifest when the cloth was rolled up become manifest when it is spread out. Similarly a piece of cloth which was not manifest in the threads becomes manifest owing to the operative agents such as the shuttle, the loom and the weaver.

R. says even as threads joined in a special cross-arrangement are called a piece of cloth, thus acquiring a new name, a new form and new functions, so is it with *Brahman* also.

Śrīnivāsa holds that the universe remains existent, indeed, prior to creation, though not known to be a universe, having its name and form unmanifest but is clearly known as the universe at the time of creation when its name and form are manifest.

II. 1. 20. *yathā ca prāṇādi*

And as in the case of vital breaths.
yathā: just as; *ca:* and; *prāṇādi:* vital breath and others.

[1] I.P., Vol. II, pp. 528ff.

The different *prāṇas*, ascending, descending, may be held up from functioning by holding our breath. In that case they remain in their causes only keeping the body alive. When they manifest as separate from one another, they not only keep the body alive but perform other functions such as binding and stretching the limbs. Then the movement which was not manifest in the cause becomes so in the effect. The world being an effect of *Brahman*, is not different from it. So if *Brahman* is known, everything else becomes known. (C.U. VI. 1. 3.)

R. says that as the one air, according as it undergoes in the body different modifications, acquires new names, new characteristics, new functions, being then called *prāṇa*, *apāna*, etc., even so the one *Brahman* becomes the world, with its manifold moving and non-moving beings.

Section 7 (21–23)

GOD AND THE PROBLEM OF EVIL

II. 1. 21. *itara-vyapadeśāddhitākaraṇādi-doṣa-prasaktiḥ*

On account of the mention of another (the individual soul as non-different from Brahman) there would attach (to Brahman) faults like not doing what is beneficial to others and the like.

itara: another; *vyapadeśāt:* on account of mention; *hita:* what is of benefit; *akaraṇādi:* not doing and the like; *doṣa:* fault; *prasaktiḥ:* would follow.

The scriptural passages convey the non-difference of the individual soul and *Brahman*. From this it follows that the power of creation also belongs to the individual soul. This soul being an independent agent might be expected to produce only what is beneficial to itself and not things of a contrary nature, such as birth, death, old age, disease. No free person will build a prison for himself and take up his abode in it.[1] Again, how can the pure self look upon this unclean body as part of itself? It would free itself from the painful results of its former actions and enjoy only the pleasant results. When it remembers that it created this manifold world, it would like to withdraw it. Apparently it cannot withdraw even its own body. So a doubt arises whether the world has been created by an intelligent cause.

R. says that if the soul is *Brahman*, then certain imperfections attach to *Brahman*. If *Brahman* is omniscient and omnipotent, why does he create a world full of pain? No rational independent person

[1] *svatantraḥ kartā san hitamevātmanaḥ saumanasyakaraṁ kuryāt nāhitaṁ janma-maraṇa-jarā-rogādyanekānartha-jālam. na hi kaścid aparatantro bandhanāgāram ātmanaḥ kṛtvā'nupraviśati.* Ś.

endeavours to produce what is clearly non-beneficial to himself.[1] If it is argued that the texts declaring difference are due to limiting adjuncts and those which declare non-difference mean eventual non-difference, the question arises whether *Brahman* knows or does not know the soul which is non-different from it. If it does not, *Brahman's* omniscience is compromised; if it does, then *Brahman* is conscious of the suffering of the soul which is non-different from *Brahman* and therefore itself suffers. It follows that *Brahman* does not create what is beneficial to itself and creates what is non-beneficial to itself. If it is said that the difference between *Brahman* and the soul arises on account of *avidyā* on the part of both, then the old difficulties about the locus of *avidyā* arise. So *Brahman's* causality of the world seems to be untenable.

Baladeva carries this section to *sūtra* 33. He takes the whole section as concerned with showing that *Brahman* and not the individual soul is the cause of the world. He takes this *sūtra* as stating the correct conclusion and not the *prima facie* view. He reads it as follows: 'There will be the consequences of faults like not doing what is beneficial and the rest from the designation of another (i.e. if the individual soul be designated as the creator of the world).' The individual soul would not have created a world full of miseries. So *Brahman* and not the individual soul must be the creator.

II. 1. 22. *adhikaṁ tu bheda-nirdeśāt*

(But Brahman) is something more (than the individual soul) on account of the indication of difference.

adhikam: something more than or additional to; *tu:* but; *bheda:* difference; *nirdeśāt:* on account of indication.

The word 'but' suggests that the objection stated in the previous *sūtra* is refuted. *Brahman,* the creative principle, is different from the embodied self. The *jīva* cannot create himself or destroy himself. The faults such as doing what is not beneficial and the like do not attach to *Brahman*. There is nothing beneficial to be done by it or non-beneficial to be avoided by it. There is nothing which *Brahman* cannot know or do. The individual soul, being different in nature, may have the defects mentioned. For a declaration of difference between *Brahman* and the individual soul, see B.U. II. 4. 5; IV. 3. 35. VI. 8. 1; C.U. VIII. 7. 1. In all these passages actions such as seeing, seeking and meditating point to the individual soul as the subject and the Supreme Self as the object. If it is said that there are passages which declare non-difference between the individual soul and the Supreme Self, Ś. points out that the difference is real, so long as the knowledge does not arise. In the condition of ignorance, *Brahman* which is the object of enquiry and search is different from

[1] *na cedṛśe svānarthe svādhīno buddhimān pravartate.* R.

the individual soul. The individual soul is a creature and not the creator. The defects therefore do not belong to *Brahman.*

R. gives a number of texts in support of the difference between *Brahman* and the individual soul: B.U. III. 7. 22, IV. 3. 21, IV. 3. 35; Ś.U. I. 6, 9, IV. 6, 9, VI. 13, 16.

II. 1. 23. *aśmādivac ca tad anupapattiḥ*

And like stones and the rest, these (defects) cannot be conceived.

aśmādivat: like stones and the rest; *ca:* and; *tad:* that; *anupapattiḥ:* cannot be conceived.

We find a great variety among stones, some of them valuable like diamonds, others not. The same piece of ground yields different trees like sandal and cucumber which have different leaves, flowers, fruits, fragrance and juice. The same food assumes different forms. In the same *Brahman* we may have various distinctions. But *Brahman,* however, is not affected by the defects of the individual soul and the world. Ś., in view of his own position, says that the distinctions have their origin in speech only and are like phantoms of a dreaming person.

R. makes out that even as it is impossible for non-conscious objects like stones and the rest to be identical with *Brahman,* so the individual soul cannot be one with *Brahman.*

Śrīkaṇṭha gives the same interpretation.

Śrīnivāsa argues that even as a ray of the diamond is non-different from its substratum, the diamond, and yet is different from it, the embodied soul is by nature different from *Brahman* though it is at the same time non-different from him as having him for its soul. The soul is subject to *saṁsāra,* while *Brahman* is not. So faults like not doing what is beneficial and the rest do not apply to *Brahman.*

Section 8 (24–25)

BRAHMAN'S INDEPENDENCE OF MATERIAL AND INSTRUMENTS OF ACTION

II. 1. 24. *upasaṁhāra-darśanān neti cen na kṣīravadd hi*

If it be said that on account of the observation of the collection (of instruments for the production of something) (Brahman) is not (the creator of the world) (we say) not so for (he acts alone) like milk.

upasaṁhāra: collection; *darśanāt:* on account of observation; *na:* not; *iti cet:* if it be said; *na:* not so; *kṣīravat:* like milk; *hi:* for.

The objection states that we notice in ordinary life that potters, weavers, etc., before they produce jars or cloth, provide themselves with various implements, clay, wheels, string, etc., and *Brahman* cannot be the cause of the world since there are no instruments for him to work with. The answer is given that causation is possible as the result of the peculiar constitution of the causal substance like milk. Even as milk and water turn into curds and ice respectively without any extraneous help, so is it with *Brahman*. If it is said that milk in order to turn into curds requires an extraneous agent, heat, the answer is given that milk by itself undergoes a certain amount of definite change and this is only speeded up by heat. *Brahman* does not require any extraneous help. See Ś.U. VI. 8. *Brahman*, though one only, is, owing to its manifold powers, able to transform itself into manifold effects like milk.[1]

Baladeva gives a different interpretation. The soul's power of action is like the cow's power of producing milk. Although the soul is an agent and can as such bring works to completion, yet it is not an independent agent but has to depend on the Lord for its activities even as a cow cannot by herself produce milk but has to depend on the life energy.

II. 1. 25. *devādivad api loke*

And (the case of Brahman is) like that of gods and other beings in ordinary experience.

devādivat: like gods and others; *api:* also; *loke:* in ordinary experience.

If it be said that non-conscious beings like milk may change of themselves without extraneous means into curds, etc., *Brahman* being intelligent, like the potter, cannot be conceived to create without other external means. The answer is that gods and sages are reported in the *śāstras* to have the ability to produce palaces and chariots by the sheer force of their will. So *Brahman* may create the world without any extraneous means. *Brahman* is free to create without depending on any means.

Baladeva says that the Lord, though invisible, is the creator of the world even as gods, though invisible, are seen to work in the world, i.e. produce rain and so forth.

Section 9 (26–29)

BRAHMAN'S INTEGRITY IS UNAFFECTED BY THE WORLD

II. 1. 26. *kṛtsna-prasaktir niravayavatva-śabda-kopo vā*

(If Brahman be the material cause of the world) there will result either

[1] *ekasyāpi brahmaṇo vicitra-śakti-yogāt kṣīrādivad vicitraḥ pariṇāma upapadyate.* Ś.

(the change of) the entire (Brahman) or the violation of the texts (declaring Brahman) to be without parts.

kṛtsna: entire; *prasaktiḥ:* will result; *niravayavatva:* being without parts; *śabda:* texts; *kopaḥ:* violation; *vā:* or.

The objection is raised that if the whole of *Brahman* is transformed into the world, then *Brahman* would cease to exist and there is no point in asking us to see *Brahman* or in saying that *Brahman* is unborn. If, on the other hand, we hold that a part of *Brahman* is transformed, then we assume that *Brahman* is capable of being divided into parts. This would be a direct violation of the texts which declare that *Brahman* is partless, etc. See B.U. II. 4. 12, III. 8. 8; III. 9. 26, M.U. II. 1. 2; Ś.U. VI. 19.

Ś. uses these objections to support his view that the world is only an appearance (*vivarta*) of *Brahman* and not a transformation (*pariṇāma*).

In *Bṛhan-nāradīya-purāṇa* it is said that by means of *yoga* we perceive the identity of God with his *māyā* and thus attain release from it. *Māyā* is not unreal, not real, not both. It creates the sense of diversity in the Supreme Being.

> *māyino māyayā bhedam paśyanti paramātmani*
> *tasmān māyām tyajed yogān mumukṣur vipra-sattamāḥ.*
> *nāsad-rūpā nasad rūpā māyā vai nobhayātmikā*
> *anirvācyāhritā jñeyā bheda-buddhi pradāyinī.*
>
> 31: 69–70.

Viṣṇu-dharma adopts the difference—non-difference (*bhedābheda*) view:

> *advaitaṁ paramārtho hi dvaitaṁ tad bheda ucyate*
> *ubhayaṁ brahmaṇo rūpaṁ dvaitādvaita-vibhedataḥ.*
>
> 96. 225.

R. states the objection in a different way. If the entire *Brahman* enters into the effected state, its conscious part dividing itself into the individual souls and the non-conscious part into ether, air and so on, this violates the texts which declare that *Brahman* in the causal state is devoid of parts. If it is without parts, it cannot become many. It is not possible that there should persist a part not entering into the effected state.

Śrīnivāsa argues that if *Brahman* is without parts, then the entire *Brahman* will become the effect and there will not remain a transcendent *Brahman* beyond *saṁsāra* to be approached by the liberated. To attribute divisions to *Brahman* will be opposed to the Scripture.

Baladeva reads *vyakopa* for *kopa* and thinks that the *sūtra* is the statement not of *pūrva-pakṣa* but of *siddhānta*. If the individual soul be the creator, since it is without parts, its entire being is present in every act. This is not the case. While lifting a blade of grass, one's whole nature is not functioning. Or else we must conclude that the individual soul possesses parts and this again is opposed to scriptural authority. So the individual soul is not the creator.

II. 1. 27. *śrutes tu śabda-mūlatvāt*

But (it is not so) on account of Vedic testimony since (Brahman's causality) has its ground in Scripture.
śruteḥ: on account of *śruti* or *Vedic* testimony; *tu:* but; *śabda-mūlatvāt:* because *śruti* is the ground.

The entire *Brahman* does not undergo transformation as *śruti* declares that *Brahman*, the source of the world, exists apart from the world. C.U. III. 12. 6; VI. 3. 2. If *Brahman* were completely transformed it would have been perceptible as the world is, which is not so.

If it is held that it is difficult to understand how *Brahman* is partless and yet does not undergo transformation as a whole, Ś. says that *śruti* is the only source of our knowledge of *Brahman*. Even with regard to ordinary things such as gems, herbs, spells which have varying effects on different occasions, we cannot understand them unaided by instruction. Much less can reasoning tell us about the unthinkable. Ś. quotes a text which says: 'Do not apply reasoning to what is unthinkable; the mark of the unthinkable is that it is above all natural causes.'[1]

Ś. states the objection again. *Brahman* is either partless or is transformed partially. If it is partless, it is transformed as a whole or not at all. If it is only partially transformed, then it consists of parts. Ś. overcomes the difficulties by his view that *Brahman* ever remains the same in reality. It does not undergo any change, though it is the ground of the multiplicity of name and form in the phenomenal world. These distinctions are the products of ignorance and arise from speech alone.[2]

The negative descriptions of *Brahman* are intended to draw our attention to the non-phenomenal character of *Brahman*.

For R., creation is merely the visible and the tangible manifestation of what existed previously in *Brahman* in a subtle and imperceptible condition. He also cites the support of Scripture for *Brahman* cannot be proved or disproved by means of generalisations from experience.[3] For R., Scripture tells us that the Supreme possesses various powers.

[1] *acintyāḥ khalu ye bhāvā na tāṁs tarkeṇa yojayet*
prakṛtibhyaḥ paraṁ yac ca tad acintyasya lakṣaṇam.

Ānandagiri observes: *prakṛtibhya iti, pratyakṣa-dṛṣṭa-padārtha-svabhāvebhyo yat param vilakṣaṇam ācāryādy-upadeśa-gamyam tad acintyam ity arthaḥ.*

[2] *avidyā-kalpitena ca nāma-rūpa-lakṣaṇena rūpa-bhedena vyākṛtāvyākṛtātmakena tattvānyatvābhyām anirvacanīyena, brahma-pariṇāmādi-sarva-vyavahārāspadatvam pratipadyate. pāramārthikena ca rūpeṇa sarva-vyavahārātītam apariṇatam avatiṣṭhate.*

[3] *na sāmānyato dṛṣṭam sādhanaṁ dūṣaṇaṁ vārhati brahma.*

For Nimbārka, it is Scripture that declares that *Brahman* creates the world and yet remains untransformed. For Śrīnivāsa, transformation means nothing but projection of powers and this is also declared by Scripture.

II. 1. 28. *ātmani caivam vicitrāś ca hi*

For thus it is even within the Self and wondrous.
ātmani: within the self; *ca:* and; *evam:* thus; *vicitrāḥ:* wondrous; *ca:* and; *hi:* even.

B.U. IV. 3. 10 speaks of chariots, horses and roads which the dreamer creates in the state of dream. Gods and magicians create elephants, etc., without losing their own unity of being. So there may exist a manifold creation in *Brahman* without impairing his real nature and unity.

R. says that in the soul, the attributes of the non-conscious objects are not found for there are manifold powers in different objects. A conscious soul differs from non-conscious objects and does not possess their qualities. The non-conscious objects like fire, water and the rest do not share each other's qualities. So *Brahman* who is different from both the conscious and the non-conscious objects does not possess their attributes but has numerous others not found in them. This view is followed by Śrīkaṇṭha.

Baladeva uses this *sūtra* to indicate that the Lord is possessed of mysterious powers.

II. 1. 29. *sva-pakṣa-doṣāc ca*

And because there is fault in the (*opponent's*) *own view.*
sva: own; *pakṣa:* side, *doṣāt:* because of the faults; *ca:* and.

The *Sāṁkhya* theory of *pradhāna* is considered. Does it change into the world wholly or partially? If the former there will be no *pradhāna*; if the latter, the view that it is partless must be given up. If we say that the three *guṇas* are the parts of *pradhāna*, it does not improve the position. For creation is the combination of all the three *guṇas*. It cannot be said that one or two of them evolve and not all. Again, the *guṇas* are partless and so no one part can evolve. Besides, if *pradhāna* possesses various powers, it is saying what the *Vedānta* says and nothing special.

The atomists' case is taken up.[1] If the partless atoms combine and occupy the same space, they become one atom; if the atom is conceived as coming into contact with another in some of its parts, then the atomists give up their view that the atom is partless.

[1] Comparing ancient and modern atomic theories Sir Charles Sherrington says: 'The atom of today is no untested *a priori* speculative dogma. It is unrelated, except by misnomer, to its namesake of antiquity.' 'The speculations of Democritus and Leucippus cannot be put beside [the modern] scheme. They were relatively to it essays in fancy.' *Man on his Nature* (1946), pp. 365, 301.

Baladeva points out that the objection whether *Brahman* creates with his entire nature or part of it only applies equally to the view that the individual soul is the creator. While we can overcome the objection, the opponent cannot.

Section 10 (30–31)

THE MANIFOLD POWERS OF *BRAHMAN*

II. 1. 30. *sarvopetā ca tad-darśanāt*

And (Brahman) is endowed with all (powers) because that is seen from Scripture.

sarva: all; *upetā:* endowed with; *ca:* and; *tad-darśanāt:* because that is seen.

This manifold world of effects is possible for *Brahman*, though one only, is endowed with various powers as we see from the scriptural texts. See C.U. III. 14. 4, VIII. 7. 1; B.U. III. 8. 9; M.U. I. 1. 9.

R. cites Ś.U. VI. 8; C.U. III. 14. 2, VIII. 1. 5.

II. 1. 31. *vikaraṇatvān neti cet tad uktam*

If it be said that (Brahman cannot be the cause) on account of the absence of the organs, (we say that) this has been explained (already).

vikaraṇatvāt: on account of the absence of the organs; *na:* not; *iti cet:* if it be said; *tad:* that; *uktam:* has been stated or explained.

When it is described only in negative terms, how can *Brahman* be endowed with powers? Besides, how can it produce the world when it is said to be 'without eyes, ears, speech or mind'? B.U. III. 8. 9. The *sūtra* says that the answer has been given. See I. 2. 18–20; II. 1. 4. We cannot understand the nature of *Brahman* by mere reasoning. We have to rely on Scripture. Ś.U. III. 19 says: 'Without foot or hand, yet swift and grasping, he sees without eye, he hears without ear.' Ś. adds that *Brahman* is conceived as being endowed with powers when we assume in its nature an element of plurality which is the product of *avidyā*.

R. thinks that the refutation of this objection is to be found in II. 1. 27, 28.

Section 11 (32–33)

THE WORLD OF GOD'S *LĪLĀ*

II. 1. 32. *na prayojanavattvāt*

(Creation is) not (possible for Brahman) on account of having a motive.

na: not; *prayojanavattvāt:* on account of having a motive; another reading is *prayojanatvāt*.

The objection is raised that no one acts in the world without a motive. God cannot have a motive or a need for creating the universe for he is all-sufficient. Without a motive there can be no activity and the Supreme cannot have a motive. So God's creation of the world cannot be accepted.

R. says that all activities are undertaken with the motive of doing something beneficial to themselves or to others. All the wishes of *Brahman* are eternally fulfilled. He does not attain through the creation of the world any object not attained before. If, however, he concerns himself with others, it can only be to help them. No merciful divinity would create a world so full as ours is of evils of all kinds—birth, old age, death, hell and so on. If he created at all, pity would move him to create a world altogether happy.[1] So *Brahman* cannot be the cause of the world.

Nimbārka also states the objection that God has no need to create the world as he has his desires eternally fulfilled.

II. 1. 33. *lokavat tu līlā kaivalyam*

But, as in ordinary life, creation is mere sport (to Brahman).

lokavat: as in ordinary life; *tu:* but; *līlā:* sport; *kaivalyam:* merely.

But indicates the refutation of the objection set forth in the previous *sūtra*. Men in high position, who have no unfulfilled desires, indulge in sport. Ś. uses the example of breathing which goes on without reference to any extraneous purpose, merely following the law of its own nature. So also creation proceeds from the nature of the Supreme without reference to any purpose.[2] We cannot question why God's nature is what it is.[3] We have to accept it. Even though we may detect some subtle motives for sportful action among men, we cannot attribute any to the Supreme. We cannot say that he does not act or acts like a senseless person. He is omniscient. The passages relating to creation do not refer to the Absolute Transcendent Being.[4] But so far as the divine Creator is concerned it is his nature.

Baladeva makes out that *līlā* or sport is the overflow of the joy within. As in ordinary life, a man full of cheerfulness on awakening from sound sleep dances about without any motive or need but simply from the fullness of spirit, so is the case with the creation of the world by God.

[1] *na hi parasya brahmaṇaḥ svabhāvata evāv āpta-samasta-kāmasya jagat-sargeṇa kiñcana prayojanam anavāptam avāpyate. nāpi parārthaḥ; āpta-samasta-kāmasya parārthatā hi parānugraheṇa bhavati. na cedṛśa-garbha-janma-jarā-maraṇa-narakādi-nānā-vidhānanta-duḥkha-bahulam jagat karuṇāvān sṛjati. pratyuta sukhaikatānam eva sṛjej jagat karuṇayā sṛjan.* See also R.B. II. 2. 3.

[2] *evam īśvarasyāpy anapekṣya kiñcit prayojanāntaraṁ svabhāvād eva kevalaṁ līlā-rūpāpravṛttir bhaviṣyati.* Ś.

[3] *na ca svabhāvaḥ paryanuyoktum śakyate.* Ś.

[4] *na ceyam paramārtha-viṣayā sṛṣṭi-śrutiḥ.* Ś.

In many systems of religious thought, self-sufficiency is regarded as an attribute of deity. If God is constrained by an inner necessity to create, he depends on others. The unmoved perfection is for Aristotle the cause of all motion but it is only its final cause. The bliss which God unchangingly enjoys in his never-ending self-contemplation is the good after which all existences aspire. Aristotle tells us that the Timeless Incorporeal One is not only the logical ground but the dynamic source of the temporal universe. He says in his *Metaphysics*[1]: 'it is not necessary that everything that is possible should exist in actuality' and 'it is possible for that which has a potency not to realise it'. Why does something exist rather than nothing? The answer is that the Absolute is also fecundity. Its joy overflows into existence. This spontaneous outflow is symbolised by the theory of *līlā*.

Section 12 (34–36)

THE PROBLEM OF SUFFERING AND EVIL

II. 1. 34. *vaiṣamya-nairghṛṇye na sāpekṣatvāt tathā hi darśayati*

Inequality and cruelty cannot (be attributed to Brahman) for (his activity) has regard to (the works of souls); besides the same (Scripture) shows.

vaiṣamya-nairghṛṇye: inequality (of dispensation) and cruelty; *na:* not; *sāpekṣatvāt:* on account of regard to; *tathā:* the same; *hi:* also; *darśayati:* shows.

There are inequalities among the souls; some are happy and others unhappy. Does it mean that the Divine has also the qualities of passion and malice? As there is so much pain in the world, are we to treat him as cruel also? For these reasons *Brahman* cannot be the cause of the world. The objections are not valid. The inequalities of creation are due to the merit and demerit of the creatures. They are not a fault for which the Lord is to blame. An analogy is given. As Parjanya, the giver of rain, is the common cause of the production of rice, barley and other plants, and the differences are due to the potentialities of the seeds themselves, even so God is the common cause of the creation while the differences are due to the merit and demerit of the individual souls. There are many scriptural texts in support of this view. B.U. III. 2. 13 says: 'One becomes good by good acts, bad by bad actions.' See also K.U. III. 8; B.G. IV. 11.

R. quotes *Viṣṇu Purāṇa* I. 4. 51–2 to the effect that the Lord is the operative cause only in the creation of new beings; the material cause is constituted by the potentialities of the beings to be created.

[1] II. 1003a2 and XI. 1071b13.

II. 1. 35. *na karmāvibhāgād iti cen nānāditvāt*

If it be said that this is not (possible) on account of the non-distinction of works (before the first creation we say that it) is not so for (saṁsāra) is without beginning.

na: not; *karma:* works; *avibhāgāt:* on account of non-distinction; *iti cet:* if it be said; *na:* not so; *anāditvāt:* on account of beginninglessness.

Many passages in the *Upaniṣads* tell us that 'In the beginning there was Being only, one without a second'. There was no *karma* which had to be taken into account before creation. The first creation at least should have been free from inequalities. The answer is given in the *sūtra*. The world is without beginning. Work and inequality are like seed and sprout. They are caused as well as causes.

Bhāskara reads the first part of this *sūtra* differently: *asmād vibhāgād iti cen nānāditvāt.*

R. and Nimbārka take this and the next *sūtra* as one. R. says though the individual souls and their deeds form a perpetual stream, without a beginning, non-distinction is reasonable for, prior to creation, the substance of the souls abides in a very subtle condition, without names and shapes, and thus is incapable of being designated as something apart from *Brahman* though in reality they constitute *Brahman's* body only. If we do not admit that the distinctions in creation are due to *karma* it would follow that the souls are requited for what they have not done and not requited for what they have done.

II. 1. 36. *upapadyate cāpy upalabhyate ca*

(The beginninglessness of saṁsārā) is ascertained (by reason) and is observed (in Scripture).

upapadyate: is ascertained; *ca:* and; *api:* also; *upalabhyate:* is found.

If the world had a beginning, it would follow that it came into being without a cause, then it would be possible for the released souls to return to *saṁsāra*. There would then be no justification for inequalities. That the Lord cannot be the cause of inequality has already been established. *Avidyā* cannot be the cause as it is of a uniform nature; without *karma* no one can come into existence; without coming into existence *karma* cannot be formed. So we must accept that the world is without a beginning. Scripture also affirms it. See C.U. VI. 3. 2; *Ṛg Veda* X. 190. 3; B.G. XV. 3.

R. quotes other texts, *Kaṭha U.* I. 2. 18; B.U. I. 4. 7; B.G. XIII. 19, and concludes 'As *Brahman* thus differs in nature from everything else, possesses all powers, has no other motive than sport and arranges the diversity of the creation in accordance with the different *karmas* of the individual souls, *Brahman* alone can be the universal cause'.[1]

[1] *ataḥ sarva-vilakṣaṇatvāt sarva-śaktitvāl līlaika-prayojanatvāt kṣetrajña-karmānuguṇyena vicitra-sṛṣṭi-yogād brahmaiva jagad-kāraṇam.* R.

Baladeva holds that the grace of the Lord is not partial. It is shown by the Lord to his devotees. The grace is not arbitrary but depends on the devotion of the souls themselves. It is also observed in Scripture.

Section 13 (37)

BRAHMAN HAS ALL THE QUALITIES FOR THE CREATION OF THE WORLD

II. 1. 37. *sarva-dharmopapatteś ca*

And because all the qualities (for the creation of the world) are present (in Brahman).

sarva: all; *dharma:* qualities; *upapatteḥ:* on account of presence or availability; *ca:* and.

The qualities of *Brahman,* omniscience and so on, are such as to enable *Brahman* to create the world.

Baladeva suggests that the Lord is possessed of paradoxical and mysterious powers and it is possible for the Lord to have not only the attributes of perfect justice and impartiality but also the quality of showing special favour to his devotees.

Section 1 (1–10)

CONSIDERATION OF THE *SĀṀKHYA* THEORY

II. 2. 1. *racanānupapatteś ca nānumānam*

Because the orderly management of the world is not possible (*on that hypothesis*), *that which is inferred* (*by the Sāṁkhya, viz. the pradhāna*) *cannot be* (*the cause of the world*).

racanā: orderly arrangement; *anupapatteḥ:* because (it is) impossible; *ca:* and; *na:* not; *anumānam:* that which is inferred.

The second part of the second chapter is devoted to the refutation of the more important philosophical views in regard to the cause of the world which are opposed to the *Vedānta* position. In the first section of this part the *Sāṁkhya* view, which has already been briefly considered, is taken up. It is shown that a non-intelligent first cause such as the *pradhāna* cannot account for the creation and orderly arrangement of the world. Here Ś. says that we refute the *Sāṁkhya* theory by independent arguments and not by reference to the Vedic texts.[1]

The different phases of the cosmic process, its evolution from the primal nothingness, a matter still unformed but capable of receiving all forms gave rise to elements. These advanced to higher forms; organisms appeared and man attained to reason. These phases constitute the history of the generation of the universe and suggest the realisation of a plan. Religion has to fight today not heresy but materialism.

The *Sāṁkhya* argues that as vessels made of clay have clay alone as their cause, even so the external and internal world of effects, whether house, body or mind, endowed as it is with the characteristics of pleasure, pain or infatuation must have for its cause a being which possesses these characteristics. These qualities together form the *pradhāna*. Like clay it is non-conscious. It evolves spontaneously into various modifications for the sake of fulfilling the purposes of the soul, viz. the enjoyment of worldly pleasures and release. There are other reasons also which lead us to infer that *pradhāna* is the cause of the world. See *Sāṁkhya Kārikā* 15.

The answer to this objection is next given. A non-conscious object like stone cannot serve any purpose, unless it is guided by an intelligent being. Palaces and pleasure gardens do not come into existence of their own accord. How can this world with its wonderful variety and arrangement be created by an unconscious principle? Vessels are made out of clay only if a potter is there; so also *pradhāna* can evolve only under the guidance of an intelligent being. This is in

[1] *iha tu vākya-nirapekṣas svatantras tad-yukti-pratiṣedhaḥ kriyata ity eṣa viśeṣaḥ.*

conformity with *śruti* which declares that there is an intelligent cause of the world.

Ca: and, indicates other reasons for not accepting *pradhāna* as the cause. The external and internal objects of the world are not of the nature of pleasure, pain and infatuation, but they occasion these feelings in the individual according to their mental condition. If the followers of the *Sāṁkhya* from their limited observation tell us that some distinct and limited things like roots, sprouts, etc., are the results of the conjunction of several things and therefore all objects of the world are effects of conjunctions of several things, we can also say to them that the three constituent qualities of *pradhāna, sattva, rajas* and *tamas* arise on account of previous conjunctions of several things, for they also limit one another and are distinct and separate.

R. and Śrīkaṇṭha combine this and the next *sūtra* into one.

II. 2. 2. *pravṛtteś ca*

On account of the tendency to activity.

pravṛtteḥ: because of the tendency to activity; *ca:* and.

Even according to the *Sāṁkhya*, the original disturbance of the three *guṇas* from the condition of equipoise which is essential for creative manifestation cannot be due to the unintelligent *pradhāna*. Clay does not change into pots without the help of a potter nor does a chariot move without a horse. So *pradhāna* cannot be the cause of the world unless there is an ultimate intelligent principle.

It may be argued that we do not see the principle of intelligence or its activity. Only the existence of the intelligent principle and not its activity can be inferred from the actions which take place in a living body which is dissimilar in nature to inanimate objects like chariots.

The intelligent principle is found only when there exists a body and no intelligent principle is found when there is no physical body. So the materialists (*lokāyatikas*) argue that intelligence is a mere attribute of the body. Activity belongs only to what is non-intelligent. Ś. replies that though activity is observed in non-intelligent things, it is due to an intelligent principle. Even the materialists admit that activity is present in a living body and not in a corpse, in a chariot drawn by a horse and not a mere chariot. Intelligence therefore possesses the power to move. If it is said that, according to the *Vedānta*, pure consciousness is incapable of activity and incapable of making others active, Ś. says that a thing may be devoid of volition and yet capable of moving other things. A magnet may not move itself but moves a piece of iron. The Supreme Being can move the universe, himself remaining unmoved. If it is said that there is one *Brahman* and nothing else and therefore there can be no motion at all, Ś. answers by saying that, as the entire world of names and forms is the work of *māyā* or *avidyā*, God too is conceived as connected with it as the substratum on which the appearance rests. So there is scope for activity if the ultimate cause is conceived to be *Brahman*, and not when it is taken to be non-intelligent *pradhāna*.

R. says that the *Sāṁkhya* assumes three *guṇas* and not one ultimate cause. If it is said that creation is accomplished, as the three *guṇas* are unlimited, then R. says, if they are unlimited and therefore omnipresent, then no inequality can result and so no effects can originate. To explain the origination of results, it is necessary to assume limitation of the *guṇas*.

II. 2. 3. *payo'mbuvac cet tatrāpi*

If it be said that (pradhāna may be active) like water and milk (we say that) then too (the activity is due to an intelligent principle).

payaḥ: milk; *ambu:* water; *vat:* like; *cet:* if it be said; *tatra:* then; *api:* even.

If it be said that if milk flows naturally for the nourishment of the calf and water flows for the benefit of mankind, even so *pradhāna* may transform itself into the world for enabling men to achieve the highest end of life, Ś. replies that, as in the case of chariots, the non-intelligent milk and water must be assumed to be guided by intelligence. Besides, it is the intelligent cow loving her calf that makes the milk to flow and the flow is aided by the sucking of the calf. The flow of the water depends on the level of the ground. In a general way it is dependent on the intelligent principle of *Brahman* which is present everywhere. See B.U. III. 7. 4; III. 8. 9. There is no contradiction between this and II. 1. 24 where it was shown from ordinary experience that the effect may take place in itself, independent of any external, instrumental cause. This does not conflict with the view based on Scripture, that all effects depend on the Lord.

R. uses the illustrations in a different way. Milk when turning into curds undergoes, of itself, many changes. It does not depend on anything else. Similarly, water discharged from the clouds spontaneously proceeds to transform itself into various saps and juices of different plants. So also *pradhāna* whose essential nature is change, may, without being guided by another agent, abide in equipoise between two creations and then, when the time for creation arises, may modify itself into various effects due to the loss of equilibrium on the part of the *guṇas*. See *Sāṁkhya Kārikā* I. 16.

R. says that even in these instances of milk and water, activity is not possible without the presence of an intelligent principle.

Śrīnivāsa adds that the cow gives milk even when the calf is dead because she remembers the calf or because she loves her master and wishes to be of benefit to him.

II. 2. 4. *vyatirekānavasthiteś cānapekṣatvāt*

And because there is nothing different, (pradhāna is not the cause) on account of non-dependence.

vyatireka: different, separate, other; *anavasthiteḥ:* because of non-existence; *ca:* and; *anapekṣatvāt:* on account of non-dependence.

Since, according to the *Sāṁkhya, pradhāna* is the three *guṇas* in equilibrium and there is no other principle which can make it active or inactive, it is impossible to know why it should sometimes transform itself into the effects of *mahat*, etc., and at other times not. *Puruṣa* is indifferent and so cannot cause action or cessation from activity. God, on the other hand, as a principle of intelligence, can act or not as he chooses.

R. says that *pradhāna* guided by the Lord explains the alternating states of creation and dissolution which are to carry out God's purposes. *Pradhāna* which is not guided by an intelligent principle cannot account for them.

Śrīnivāsa gives an alternative explanation. *Pradhāna* cannot be the cause because there is no object to be instigated and there is no instigator other than *pradhāna*. If the works of souls stimulate *pradhāna* to creation, then works will be the cause of the world and not *pradhāna*. Besides, how can works stimulate *pradhāna?* The works bear fruits according to the wishes of the Lord. It cannot be said that *pradhāna* acts through the proximity to *puruṣa* for this proximity being eternal, its activity should also be eternal. See II. 2. 7.

II. 2. 5. *anyatrābhāvāc ca na tṛṇādivat*

Nor (*does pradhāna modify itself spontaneously*) *like grass, etc.* (*which turn into milk*) *for* (*milk*) *does not exist elsewhere* (*than in the cow*).

anyatra: elsewhere; *abhāvāt:* because of absence; *ca:* and; *na:* not; *tṛṇa-ādi-vat:* like grass and other things.

Grass is transformed into milk without any other cause. If there were any other cause, men would employ it to produce as much milk as they liked. It is a natural process. We may expect the same in *pradhāna*. The answer is that some other cause is responsible for changing grass into milk. It is only grass that is eaten by a cow that changes into milk and not grass that is not eaten or eaten by an ox. An event need not be said to be natural simply because men cannot accomplish it. Things not brought about by men are brought about by divine activity. Even men feed the cows with plenty of grass, if they need more milk. So we cannot admit the spontaneous modification of *pradhāna*.

II. 2. 6. *abhyupagame 'py arthābhāvāt*

Even if there be the admission (*of the spontaneous activity of pradhāna still it cannot be the cause*) *on account of the absence of a purpose.*

abhyupagame: admitting; *api:* even; *artha:* purpose; *abhāvāt:* on account of absence.

If *pradhāna* is said to be active spontaneously, it means that it is not in need of any other principle, that it acts independently of any purpose. But the *Sāṁkhya* holds that the *pradhāna* becomes active for fulfilling the purpose of man. What is the purpose? It cannot be to provide appropriate pleasures and pains to the *puruṣa*, for the *puruṣa* is eternally unchanging and cannot undergo modifications of increase or decrease in his nature. If pleasure and pain are the only motives for the activity of *pradhāna*, then there would be no release. The purpose cannot be to achieve the liberation of *puruṣa* for *puruṣa* is in the state of liberation even before the activity of *pradhāna*. If the motive is not to provide with the pleasures and pains of life, there would be no empirical life at all. If it is said that both the pleasures and pains and liberation are the purposes, we find that neither is possible. Liberation is not possible for the objects produced by *pradhāna* are infinite and there would be no occasion at all for final release. Satisfaction of human purposes cannot be attributed to *pradhāna* for it is not intelligent. We cannot attribute desire to *puruṣa* which is pure and passionless. If, to avoid all these difficulties, we say that *pradhāna* acts on account of its inherent power to produce and the power of *puruṣa* to look on, *saṁsāra* will be permanent and there will be no liberation at all. We cannot therefore maintain that *pradhāna* enters on its activity for the purposes of the soul.

In R.'s commentary, this *sūtra* is No. 8. He quotes *Sāṁkhya Kārikā* I. 2. 1, that the purpose of *pradhāna* is fruition and final release on the part of the soul. But both these are impossible. As the soul consists of pure intelligence, is inactive, changeless and spotless and is eternally emancipated, it is not capable of either fruition or consciousness of *prakṛti* or release which is separation from *prakṛti*. If nearness to *prakṛti* makes the soul capable of fruition, i.e. of being conscious of pleasure and pain which are special modifications of *prakṛti*, it follows that as *prakṛti* is ever near, the soul will never accomplish emancipation.

II. 2. 7. *puruṣāśmavad iti cet tathāpi*

If it be said that (*the puruṣa moves the pradhāna as a lame*) *man* (*may lead a blind man*) *or as the magnet* (*may attract the iron*), *thus also* (*the difficulty remains*).

puruṣa: person; *aśmavat:* like magnet; *iti cet:* if it be said; *tathā:* thus; *api:* also.

Even if it be said that like a lame man devoid of the power of motion but possessing the power of sight makes the blind man who is able to move but not to see and move of his own or, like a magnet, not moving itself moves the iron, so the soul moves the *pradhāna*, we say that this doctrine is not free from difficulties. First of all, the position that *pradhāna* moves of itself is abandoned. Again, how can the indifferent *puruṣa* move the *pradhāna*? A lame man makes a blind man move by means of words and the like but the *puruṣa* is devoid of action and qualities. We cannot say that *pradhāna* moves by mere proximity as the magnet moves the iron. As this proximity is permanent, so movements should also be treated as permanent. The proximity of the magnet to iron is not permanent but depends on a certain activity and adjustment of the magnet in a certain position. So the analogies of the lame man and the magnet do not apply. *Pradhāna* is non-intelligent and *puruṣa* is indifferent and there is no third principle and so there can be no connection between the two. If the soul sees and *pradhāna* is capable of being seen, then capacities which are permanent imply the impossibility of final release. For Ś, the Highest Self endowed with *māyā* is superior to the *puruṣa* of the *Sāṁkhya*.

For R., this is the fifth *sūtra.*

II. 2. 8. *aṅgitvānupapatteś ca*

And because the relation of principal (and subordinate) is impossible (pradhāna cannot be active).
aṅgitva: the relation of principal; *anupapatteḥ:* on account of impossibility; *ca:* and.

Pradhāna cannot be active as the three *guṇas, sattva, rajas* and *tamas* abide in themselves in a state of equipoise without standing to one another in the relation of principal and subordinate. For activity the equipoise should be disturbed. There is no external principle to stir up the *guṇas.*

For R. this is *sūtra* 6. He says that in the *pralaya* state there is no relation of superiority and subordination among the *guṇas* and so the world cannot originate. If it be said that there is a certain inequality even in the state of *pralaya*, then creation would be eternal.

II. 2. 9. *anyathānumitau ca jña-śakti-viyogāt*

And if there be an inference in another way, (pradhāna cannot still be the cause) on account (of pradhāna) being devoid of the power of being a knower.
anyathā: in another way; *anumitau:* if inferred; *ca:* and; *jña-śakti:* the power of being a knower; *viyogāt:* being devoid of.

We may infer the nature of the *guṇas* from that of their effects and say that *guṇas* are of an unsteady nature and so enter into a relation of mutual inequality even while they are in a state of equipoise. Even then the objection holds that a non-intelligent *pradhāna* cannot account for the orderly arrangement of the world. If the *Sāṁkhya* attributes intelligence to *pradhāna*, then it admits our position that there is one intelligent cause of the multiform world. *Pradhāna* would then be equivalent to *Brahman.*[1] Even if the *guṇas* are capable

[1] *cetanam ekam aneka-prapañcasya jagata upādānam iti brahma-vāda-prasaṅgāt.* Ś.

of undergoing inequality in spite of their equipoise, there must be an adequate cause for it; or else if they were an operative cause, being a non-changing circumstance, the world always would be *saṁsāra* and there would be no scope for release.

In R., this is *sūtra* 7.

II. 2. 10. *vipratiṣedhāc cāsamañjasam*

And on account of contradictions, (the Sāṁkhya doctrine) is unsatisfactory.

vipratiṣedhāt: on account of contradictions; *ca:* and; *asamañjasam:* is not satisfactory.

Ś. points out that the *Sāṁkhya* mentions seven senses and sometimes eleven. In some places it teaches that the subtle elements of material things proceed from the great principle, *mahat,* at others from the self-sense or *ahaṁ-kāra*. Sometimes it speaks of three internal organs, and sometimes of one only. Besides, it contradicts Scripture which declares that the Lord is the cause of the world.

The *Sāṁkhya* brings a countercharge that the *Vedānta* does not make a distinction between the suffering souls and the objects which cause suffering since it believes that *Brahman* is the self of everything and the cause of the whole world. If the causes of suffering and the sufferer constitute one self, it follows that final release is impossible. If they are assumed to constitute separate classes, then the possibility of release is not excluded. Ś. replies that the distinction of the two classes is in the phenomenal world only. The distinction between the two, the suffering soul and the cause of suffering, is the product of *avidyā*.

R. criticises the *Sāṁkhya* view. The eternally non-active, unchanging *puruṣa* cannot become witness, an enjoying and cognising agent. It cannot be subject to error resting on superposition for these are of the nature of change. Mere proximity to *prakṛti* cannot bring about changes. The *Sāṁkhya* teaches that *prakṛti*, when seen by any soul in her true nature, retires from that soul (*Sāṁkhya Kārikā* 59, 61). But as the soul is eternally released and above all change, it does not see *prakṛti*; nor does it attribute to itself her qualities. *Prakṛti* cannot see herself as she is non-intelligent; she cannot impute to herself the soul's seeing of itself as her seeing of herself. R. says that these difficulties are to be found in the theory of an eternally unchanging *Brahman* which, being conscious of *avidyā*, experiences unreal bondage and release. He feels that the *Advaita* doctrine is more irrational than the *Sāṁkhya* which admits a plurality of souls.

Section 2 (11–17)

CONSIDERATION OF THE *VAIŚEṢIKA* THEORY

II. 2. 11. *mahad-dīrghavad vā hrasva-parimaṇḍalābhyām*

Or (*the world may originate from Brahman*) *as the great and the long* (*originate*) *from the short and the spherical.*

mahat-dīrgha-vat: as having dimensions of the great and the long; *vā:* or; *hrasva-parimaṇḍalābhyām:* from what is short and spherical.

The *Vaiśeṣika* argues that the qualities which inhere in the substance constituting the cause reappear in the substance constituting the effect. From white threads white cloth is produced. If the intelligent *Brahman* is the cause of the world, intelligence must be present in the effect also. But this is not the case. So the intelligent *Brahman* cannot be the cause of the world. The answer is given in the *sūtra*. According to the *Vaiśeṣika*, from spherical atoms binary compounds are produced which are minute and short and ternary compounds which are big and long but not anything spherical; again from binary compounds which are minute and short, ternary compounds, etc., are produced which are big and long and not minute and short. So a non-intelligent world may spring from intelligent *Brahman*. If it is argued that the binary and ternary compounds are endowed with qualities opposed in nature to those of the causes, so that qualities of the causes being overpowered do not appear in the effects, it is said that non-intelligence is not a quality opposed in nature to intelligence but its very negation. So there is nothing to prevent *Brahman* from reproducing its quality of intelligence in the world. The reply is given to this objection. The two cases are parallel. If the qualities of sphericity and so on existing in the cause do not produce corresponding effects, it is the same with intelligence. Endowment with other qualities does not modify the power of originating effects which belongs to sphericity. For it is admitted that the substance produced remains for a moment devoid of qualities and only after that, other qualities begin to exist. The origin of other forms is due to other causes. See *Vaiśeṣika Sūtra* VII. 1. 9, 10, 17. So if sphericity, etc., do not produce like effects, it is due to their own nature. If it is the nature of sphericity, etc., not to produce like effects, it may be the nature of *Brahman* to produce an unlike effect, the non-intelligent world. Besides, there is also the observed fact that, from conjunction (*saṁyoga*) there originate substances belonging to a class different from that to which conjunction itself belongs. The doctrine that effects should belong to the same class as the causes from which they spring is too wide. See also II. 1. 6.

Bhāskara adopts this interpretation.

R. and Nimbārka hold that this *sūtra* refutes the theory of atoms constituting the universal cause. If the atoms consist of parts, there will result an infinite regress; if they are without parts, they cannot account for the production of other evolutes. The atomic view is untenable.

II. 2. 12. *ubhayathāpi na karmātas tad-abhāvaḥ*

Even in both ways activity is not possible (on the part of the atoms); hence the absence of that (the creation of the world).
ubhayathāpi: even in both ways; *na:* not; *karma:* activity; *ataḥ:* hence; *tat-abhāvaḥ:* absence of that.

Ś. states the atomic theory and then criticises it. The conjunction which takes place between the separate atoms at the time of creation is due to some action like the one required to bring about the conjunction of threads into a piece of cloth. The action implies effort on the part of the soul or the impact of one thing like wind against another tree. The effort of the soul is possible only when the mind is joined with the soul and there is impact only after the creation of products like wind, etc. But neither is possible in the state of dissolution for then there is neither the physical body nor any evolved product or thing except in its atomic condition. Creation out of atoms is inexplicable. If it is said that the principle of *adṛṣṭa*, the unseen accumulation of merits and demerits causes the original motion of the atoms, where does it reside, in the soul or in the atoms? As a non-intelligent principle, it cannot be the cause of action. Nor can it be guided by the soul for, according to the *Vaiśeṣika*, the soul is not intelligent. Even if it is said to reside in the soul, there will be no connection between the principle and the atom. If the unseen principle in the soul is said to be connected with the atoms indirectly, there will be perpetual activity and perpetual creation and therefore no dissolution at all. In the absence of any definite cause of action, there will be no activity in the atoms and so no creation. Even dissolution will be impossible in the absence of any visible cause for the separation of atoms.

R. asks whether *adṛṣṭa* resides in atoms or souls and rejects both views.

II. 2. 13. *samavāyābhyupagamāc ca sāmyād anavasthiteḥ*

And because of the admission of the relation of inherence, and on account of infinite regress (arising therefrom) because of sameness (there will be neither creation nor dissolution).
samavāya: the relation of inherence; *abhyupagamāt:* on account of admission; *ca:* and; *sāmyāt:* owing to sameness; *anavasthiteḥ:* on account of infinite regress.

The relation of *samavāya* cannot account for the creation and dissolution of the world. A binary which inheres in two atoms is different from them and the relation of inherence which is equally different from two atoms must be inherent in them on account of a second relation of *samavāya* and so on *ad infinitum*. If *samavāya* is said to be eternally present in the things seen here and before us, *saṁyoga* also may be said to be eternally connected with things which are joined together and need not depend on a further connection, *samavāya*. Both of them are different from the terms they relate.

II. 2. 14. *nityam eva ca bhāvāt*

And there will be permanent (activity or non-activity of atoms) alone on account of existence.
nityam: permanent; *eva:* alone; *ca:* and; *bhāvāt:* on account of existence.

The atoms may be essentially active or non-active or both or neither. If active, there will be no dissolution; if non-active there would be no creation. Their being both is impossible because of mutual contradiction. If they were neither, their activity or non-activity would depend on an operative cause. Such causes as *adṛṣṭa* being in permanent proximity to the atoms, permanent activity would result. If they are not operative causes, permanent non-activity will result. So the atomist view is untenable.

R. says that if the *samavāya* relation is eternal, that to which the relation belongs is also eternal and so the world is eternal. Śrīkaṇṭha and Baladeva accept this position.

II. 2. 15. *rūpādimattvāc ca viparyayo darśanāt*

And on account (of the atoms) having colour and so on, the opposite conclusion (will follow) because it is observed (in daily experience).
rūpādimattvāt: on account of possessing colour and so on; *ca:* and; *viparyayaḥ:* an opposite conclusion; *darśanāt:* because it is observed.

The *Vaiśeṣika* assumes that when substances are broken up into parts, a limit is reached beyond which the process of breaking up cannot be continued. The atoms are the limit. They belong to four different classes, are eternal, possess the qualities of colour, etc. These are the originating principles from out of which this material world of colour, form, etc., is made.

If atoms have colour, etc., then they are gross and non-permanent. We find from daily experience that things possessing colour, etc., are, compared to their causes, gross and non-permanent. A piece of cloth is gross when compared to the threads of which it is made and non-permanent; so the threads are gross compared to the filaments of which they are made. So the atoms possessing colour must be gross and non-eternal compared to their causes. So *Vaiśeṣika Sūtra* (IV. 1. 1) that 'that which exists without having a cause is eternal' does not apply to the atoms. Secondly, the reason which the *Vaiśeṣika* gives for the permanence of the atoms, that if, as causes, they are not permanent, there is no point in referring to the non-eternity of effects (*Vaiśeṣika Sūtra* IV. 1. 4) is not satisfactory. The eternal cause may be *Brahman*. Again, a word need not always imply the existence of the thing implied by the word. The object must be established as existing by other means of knowledge. If ignorance or non-perception of the cause is assigned as the reason for believing that the atoms are eternal, this is too wide for we may believe even binary compounds to be eternal for they produce perceptible effects and are themselves produced by non-perceived atoms. If it is said that non-perception in IV. 1. 5 means that the atoms cannot be destroyed either by the destruction of the cause or by disintegration and therefore they are to be regarded as eternal, we reply that this reasoning applies only to things that come into being as the result of the combination of several substances. Then the things perish when the substances become separate from each other or are themselves destroyed, but the view of the *Vedānta* is that the destruction of the effect is possible only by a modification in its condition as solid ghee is destroyed when it is reduced to a liquid condition. So atoms may not be destroyed or disintegrated but may be transformed into a prior non-atomic condition, which is the condition of the being of *Brahman*.

II. 2. 16. *ubhayathā ca doṣāt*

And on account of defect in both ways.
ubhayathā: both ways; *ca:* and; *doṣāt:* owing to defect.

Earth has the qualities of smell, taste, colour and touch and is gross. Water has colour, taste and touch and is fine; fire has colour and touch and is finer still; air is finest of all, having the quality of touch only. Do the atoms constituting the four elements possess a larger or smaller number of qualities than their elements? If we say that some atoms possess more numerous qualities, then their size will be increased and they will cease to be atoms. If to save the equality of atoms, we say that there is no difference in the number of their qualities, they must have one quality only, then we will not perceive touch in fire or colour and touch in water or taste, colour and touch in earth, since the qualities of effects have for their antecedents the qualities of their causes. If all atoms are assumed to have all the four qualities we should perceive what we do not actually perceive, smell and taste in air. For all these reasons the atomic doctrine is unacceptable.

This is *sūtra* 15 in R. and Śrīkaṇṭha.

R. says that there is defect in both ways, i.e. either if the atoms be possessed of colour, etc, or if they be not. On the first view, they cannot be eternal; on the second, their effects cannot be possessed of colour and the rest.

II. 2. 17. *aparigrahāc cātyantam anapekṣā*

And because of non-acceptance there must be an absolute disregard (of the atomic theory).

aparigrahāt: on account of non-acceptance; *ca:* and; *atyantam:* complete or absolute; *anapekṣā:* disregard.

Some competent persons accept the *Sāṁkhya* but not the *Vaiśeṣika*. While the *Vaiśeṣika* holds that there are six categories it makes substance the principal one on which the other five are dependent. If these are dependent, then they may be different forms and conditions of one and the same substance. But this is to give up the *Vaiśeṣika* point of view. It cannot be said that substance and quality are separate for in a white blanket, a red cow or a blue lotus, the qualities of white, red and blue reside only in some substances. If it is said that substance and qualities stand in the relation of one not being able to exist without the other (*ayutasiddhi*), then they must be either non-separate in place, non-separate in time or non-separate in character and none of these alternatives agrees with the *Vaiśeṣika* principles. Again, the distinction between *saṁyoga* or conjunction of things which can exist separately and *samavāya* or inherence or connection of things which are incapable of separate existence is futile since the cause which exists before the effect cannot be said to be incapable of separate existence. If it is argued that it is the effect which is inherent in the cause, the quality cannot exist independently and apart, say from a piece of cloth. How can the quality which has not come into existence be related to the cause at all? Nor can it be said that the effect comes into existence first and is then related with the cause for this would mean that the effect exists prior to its coming into existence and is capable of separate existence. The relation between the two is conjunction and not inherence. Again, there is no proof to show that *saṁyoga* and *samavāya* are themselves actual entities beyond the things in which they exist as relations. Simply because things have names of their own and produce distinct cognitions in us, it does not follow that they are actual entities. Things have an original nature of their own before they acquire a new nature on account of their being related with other things. *Saṁyoga* and *samavāya* have no nature of their own apart from what accrues to them from the relatedness of the things. Atoms cannot enter into *saṁyoga* with each other and *saṁyoga* of the soul with the atoms cannot be the cause of the motion of the latter and *saṁyoga* of the soul and *manas* cannot be the cause of cognitions for these have no parts. If we are asked to assume *samavāya* because otherwise the relation of that which abides and the abode is not possible we will be guilty of mutual dependence. The *Vaiśeṣika* doctrine cannot be sustained.

Section 3 (18–27)

CONSIDERATION OF THE *SARVĀSTIVĀDA*

II. 2. 18. *samudāya ubhaya-hetu-ke'pi tad-aprāptiḥ*

Even (if we assume) collections due to two causes, it is not established.
samudāyaḥ: collection; *ubhayahetuke:* due to two causes; *api:* even; *tad-aprāptiḥ:* there is non-establishment of that.

Ś. refers to the different developments of Buddhism and mentions three, the *Sautrāntika* and the *Vaibhāṣika* which believe in the reality of every object, *sarvāstivāda*; and the *Vijñānavāda* which opines that thought alone is real. For the nihilists everything is void or unreal; they adopt *Śūnyavāda*.

The *Vaibhāṣikas* maintain the reality of external objects which are directly perceivable. The *Sautrāntikas* hold that external objects are inferable through cognition and are not directly perceived. The *Vijñānavādins* maintain the reality of cognitions alone without any substratum. All these are of the view that the objects admitted by them are momentary. The view of *Śūnyavāda* is that everything is void. In this *sūtra,* realism is taken up for consideration. The realists assume that the external world of elements, sense-organs and qualities and the internal world are both real. The external world arises out of four kinds of atoms, earth, water, fire and air. The inward world consists of five groups or *skandhas*: *rūpa* (sensation), *vijñāna* (knowledge), *vedanā* (feeling), *saṁjñā* (verbal knowledge) and *saṁskāra* (dispositions). Neither the atoms nor the *skandhas* can achieve the groupings as assumed by the realists. They are non-intelligent. If they are assumed to be active of their own nature, they will be always active and there will be no scope for release. The activity of the mind which is said to be the cause of the collections is not possible without the accomplishment of the groupings, i.e. without the presence of the body. The theory does not allow the existence of any other permanent and intelligent being such as the soul which enjoys and the Lord who governs. A series of cognitions of one's own self cannot be the cause. If the series is different in character from the several momentary cognitions of which it is made, then this is to admit a permanent self. If the series is momentary, it cannot be active and bring into being the external and the internal worlds.

R. asks how on the doctrine of momentariness, the aggregates the theory postulates can ever come into being. If we are referred to the doctrine of dependent origination, *pratītya-samutpāda,* it does not solve the difficulty. For, though ignorance may lead to desire and so on as they say and in the end to ignorance once again, this does not explain the origination of the aggregates about which there is ignorance. To take the shell for silver may be an act of ignorance.

But how about the aggregate which is known as the shell and what is the substratum of ignorance in this case? Ignorance does not account for that. Again, everything being momentary, the subject who experiences the silver in the shell passes away with that experience. If desire and aversion result from ignorance, they occur not to a subject that was ignorance but to a different subject. We are thus left with the anomalous consequence of one man's ignorance causing another's suffering.

Śrīnivāsa says that the view is faulty since it rejects *Brahman*, admits the collections of atoms, unseen and unheard, but a cause for their collection is impossible.

II. 2. 19. *itaretara-pratyayatvād iti cen notpattimātra-nimittatvāt*

If it be said that (groupings of atoms and skandhas are possible) on account of mutual causality (of avidyā and the rest), (we say) they are the cause only of origin (and not of groupings).

itaretara: mutual; *pratyayatvāt:* on account of causality; *iti cet:* if it be said; *na:* not so; *utpatti:* origin; *mātra:* only; *nimittatvāt:* because of being the cause.

R. reads *pratyayatvād upapannam.* . . . If it be said that it is to be explained through mutual causality. . . .

Nimbārka follows this reading.

Bhāskara reads . . . *pratyayamanyatvāt.*

The objection is raised that, even though there is no permanent ruling principle, the world of *saṁsāra* is made possible because of the causal force of the series beginning with *avidyā* and ending with death and return to life. The answer to this is given that that causality accounts for the origination of the different members and not for their groupings, external and internal. The series of *avidyā*, etc., are themselves dependent on groupings and so cannot account for them. Even if we assume that the two *avidyā* and the rest and the groupings of the atoms and the *skandhas* arise simultaneously, it may be asked whether the successive groupings are like or unlike each other. In the former case they will be unable to change; in the latter they will change, irrespective of their good or bad actions. Again, if even the souls are momentary, how can they wait till the formation of the objects of enjoyment? Release and enjoyment become impossible.

II. 2. 20. *uttarotpāde ca pūrva-nirodhāt*

Because on the origination of the subsequent (moment) the preceding one ceases to be (therefore there can be no causal relation between avidyā and the rest).

uttara: subsequent; *utpāde:* as it arises; *ca:* and; *pūrva:* preceding; *nirodhāt:* on account of ceasing to be.

Between two momentary things, there cannot be any relation for the first has ceased to be, when the second comes to exist. If we say that every consequent has in it the essence of the antecedent, we deny the doctrine of universal momentariness. If origin and destruction are the earlier and the later stages of one and the same thing, then the thing is assumed to exist for three moments of time.

II. 2. 21. *asati pratijñoparodho yaugapadyam anyathā*

When (the cause) is absent, (if the effect is present) there results the contradiction of the admitted principle or else simultaneity (of cause and effect).

asati: when absent; *pratijñā:* an admitted principle; *uparodhaḥ:* contradiction; *yaugapadyam:* simultaneity; *anyathā:* otherwise.

If it be said that there may be an effect, even when there is no cause, the main principle of the school that the mind and its states arise on account of the four causes, material cause (*ālambana*), impression (*samanantara*), sense (*adhipati*) and auxiliary cause (*sahakāri*) will have to be given up. If no cause is required, anything may come into being at any time. If it is said that the antecedent continues to exist until the consequent is produced, we accept the simultaneous existence of cause and effect and reject the theory of universal momentariness.

Baladeva interprets the phrase *pratijñoparodhaḥ* as the contradiction of the initial proposition that the world originates from the *skandhas*.

II. 2. 22. *pratisaṁkhyā'pratisaṁkhyā-nirodhāprāptir avicchedāt*

Since there is no discontinuity in the series, there is the non-establishment of the voluntary and the involuntary destruction.

pratisaṁkhyā: voluntary; *apratisaṁkhyā:* non-voluntary; *nirodha:* destruction; *aprāptiḥ:* non-establishment; *avicchedāt:* on account of non-discontinuity.

The Buddhists maintain that universal destruction goes on constantly. They hold that whatever forms an object of knowledge and is different from the triad is produced and momentary.[1] The triad are non-substantial and merely negative in character, *abhāva-mātra*. Destruction dependent on a voluntary act of the mind is when one by an act of will smashes a jar; destruction not so dependent is that which is due to the material decay of things. The third is *ākāśa* which means the absence of anything occupying space which will be taken up later. Destruction, dependent on voluntary or involuntary acts, is impossible for it must refer to the series of things as a whole or to the things themselves. The series cannot be destroyed for its members are connected together as cause and effect in an unbroken manner. The things cannot be destroyed for in the various states or conditions of a thing, there remains something by which the

[1] *buddhi-bodhyam trayād anyat saṁskṛtaṁ kṣaṇikaṁ ca.*

thing itself is recognised either by perception or by inference. So there is no kind of destruction possible.

Bhāskara reads *asambhavaḥ* for *avicchedāt.*

II. 2. 23. *ubhayathā ca doṣāt*

And on account of defectiveness both ways.

ubhayathā: both ways; *ca:* and; *doṣāt:* on account of defectiveness.

If destruction of *avidyā*, etc., results from perfect knowledge and the adoption of the ethical path, we must give up the view that destruction takes place without any cause. If *avidyā*, etc., are destroyed of their own accord, what is the use of the ethical path and the knowledge that everything is momentary, painful and void?

R. makes out that both origination from nothing and passing away into nothing are impossible. If the effect originates from nothing, it will itself be of the nature of nothing; but the world is not seen to be of the nature of nothingness. Again, if that which exists undergoes destruction, it would follow that after one moment the entire world would pass away into nothingness. On both the views, origination and destruction cannot take place as described by the Buddhists.

Śrīkaṇṭha follows R. Bhāskara does not mention this *sūtra.*

II. 2. 24. *ākāśe cāviśeṣāt*

In the case of ākāśa also, there being no difference (it cannot be treated as a nonentity).

ākāśe: in the case of *ākāśa; ca:* also; *aviśeṣāt:* on account of non-difference.

Scripture says that *ākāśa* is an entity, a real thing. T.U. II. 1. It is inferred from the quality of sound as earth and the other elements are inferred from smell, etc. The Buddhists claim that *ākāśa* is the support of air. So it must be an entity. Again, we cannot say that *ākāśa* like the two kinds of destruction is a nonentity and at the same time eternal. That which is non-existent can be neither eternal nor non-eternal.

R. says that when we say 'here a hawk flies, there a vulture', we are conscious of *ākāśa* as marking the different places of the flight of the different birds. It cannot be regarded as a nonentity. For R., non-existence, *abhāva*, is a special state of something actually existing. Even if *ākāśa* were admitted to be of the nature of *abhāva*, it would not be a futile nonentity, *na nirupākhyatvam.*

II. 2. 25. *anusmṛteś ca*

And on account of remembrance.

anusmṛteḥ: on account of remembrance; *ca:* and.

If we believe in the doctrine of universal momentariness, then the experiencing subject will also be momentary and the act of remembrance becomes inexplicable. The subject cognising a thing and the subject remembering it should be the same. The moments of cognition and recognition, perception and remembrance should belong to the same person and so he cannot be regarded as momentary. If it be said that belief in one and the same experiencing subject arises from the similarity of two or more cognitions of the self, the recognition of similarity implies a person who is permanent enough to discern the similarity of different cognitions. To argue that the knowledge of similarity is a new cognition independent of prior cognitions occupying the different moments or of a permanent experiencing subject, etc., does not help, for when we say this is similar to that, this and that as well as similarity between them are expressed in one act of judgement. If similarity were a distinct cognition unconnected with things which are similar, then similarity has no reference to this or that. It is an admitted fact. Whatever may be said with regard to objects, there can be no doubt with reference to the conscious subject. He is distinctly aware that he is the same subject who remembers today what he apprehended yesterday.

R. means by *anusmṛti*, recognition.[1] He points out that not only recognition but inference which presupposes the ascertainment and remembrance of general propositions would become inexplicable. He would not even be able to prove the assertion that things are momentary for the subject perishes the very moment he states the proposition to be proved and another subject will be unable to complete what has been begun by another and about which he himself does not know anything.

Śrīnivāsa says that if a permanent soul were not acknowledged, there would be no practical activities at all.

II. 2. 26. *nāsato'dṛṣṭatvāt*

(*Entity does*) *not* (*arise*) *from non-existence since it is not observed.*
na: not; *asataḥ:* from non-existence; *adṛṣṭatvāt:* since it is not seen (observed).

Those who hold that the effect does not arise without the destruction of the cause, maintain that existent things spring from non-existent ones. This view is refuted by the *sūtra*. If things spring from non-existence, there is no point in the assumption of special causes. Non-existence is the same in all cases. Sprouts could not come from seeds but from the horns of hares, which we do not observe. If it is said that there are different kinds of non-existence with special features, then they cease to be non-existent and become entities. Non-existence as such cannot possess causal efficiency. Again, if existence came from non-existence all effects would be affected by non-existence whereas they are positive entities distinguished by

[1] *anusmaraṇaṁ pūrvānubhūta-vastu-viṣayaṁ jñānaṁ pratyabhijñānam ity arthaḥ.* R.

special characteristics. When a seed becomes a sprout the cause is those permanent particles of the seed which are not destroyed (even when the seed undergoes decomposition). This doctrine of entity springing from non-entity, is inconsistent with their own view that all material aggregates spring from the atoms and mental aggregates from the *skandhas*.

R. considers here the *Sautrāntika* view that to be an object of cognition means nothing more than to be the cause of the origination of cognition. So even a thing that has perished may have imparted its form to the cognition and on the basis of that form the object is inferred. The manifold character of cognitions is derived from the manifold character of real things. The *sūtra* makes out that the special forms of cognitions cannot be the forms of things that have perished. For it is not observed that when a substrate of attributes perishes, its attributes pass over into another thing. The manifoldness of cognitions can result from the manifoldness of things only on the condition of the persistence of the thing at the time of cognition.

Śrīkaṇṭha begins a new section here. This *sūtra* and the next deal with the refutation of the *Sautrāntika* view that an object is inferred from the impressions left on our mind by it. But a momentary and therefore non-existent entity cannot produce any impression.

III. 2. 27. *udāsīnānām api caivaṁ siddhiḥ*

And thus there will be accomplishment on the part of the indifferent as well.

udāsīnānām: of indifferent (inactive) persons; *api:* even; *ca:* and; *evam:* thus; *siddhiḥ:* accomplishment.

If the doctrine that entity arises from non-entity is accepted, then non-existence can be achieved without any effort. Anyone can attain release.

R. says that as all effects are accomplished without a cause, even perfectly inert men will accomplish all the ends to be reached in this and in the next life, including final release.

Since there is never any attainment of knowledge or release by one who is inactive, this doctrine is false.

Section 4 (28–32)

CONSIDERATION OF *VIJÑĀNA-VĀDA*

II. 2. 28. *nābhāva upalabdheḥ*

The non-existence (of external objects) cannot be maintained on account of perception.

na: not; *abhāvaḥ:* non-existence; *upalabdheḥ:* on account of perception.

In this *sūtra*, the view that ideas are the only reality is considered. According to *Vijñāna-vāda* the process whose constituting members are the act of knowledge, the object of knowledge and the result of knowledge is altogether an internal one. Even if things exist in the outside world, we can have experience of them through mental processes. External objects cannot be apprehended for they are either atoms or their groupings. Atoms are imperceptible and so are their groupings which cannot be different from the atoms which enter them. The differences of cognitions of pillar, wall or jar are mental in character. The forms of the objects of knowledge are determined by ideas and not the reality of the external world. As our knowledge of objects in the form of ideas and of the objects themselves, is simultaneously presented, they must be one and the same. If they were different, we may be conscious of one and not of another. So *Vijñāna-vāda* argues that the world of external things is not real. This view is confirmed by the similarity of our perceptions of waking life and experiences of our dreams and illusions. Our perceptions of objects are only simple ideas. The variety of ideas can be accounted for by *saṁskāras* or impressions of past ideas. The ideas and impressions succeed each other as necessarily as the seed and the sprout. Even the *Vedānta* admits that in dreams, when there are no external objects, knowledge arises on account of prior mental impressions.

To all this the reply is made in this *sūtra*. Our perceptions point out to us external things like pillars and walls. We are aware in perception, not of perception but of the object of perception. *Vijñāna-vāda* admits it when it says that the internal object of cognition appears like something external. If we have no experience of the external world, how can we say that it seems like something external? We apprehend things through means of knowledge. If there are no external objects, how can the ideas have the form of objects? If they have the form of objects it does not mean that objects have become reduced to forms. Objects are apprehended as external and distinct from ideas. Between the idea and the object there is not identity but only causal connection. We have knowledge of different attributes black and white as also of different objects. Again, if the ideas occupy different moments of time and vanish immediately after they have been felt in consciousness, we cannot say of them that they are either the knower or the known. If the idea does not last even for two consecutive moments, then there cannot be talk about ideas being different from each other, about anything being momentary and void, between individuals and classes, between existence and non-existence due to *avidyā* and about bondage and release.

The *Vijñāna-vāda* argues that while an idea illumines by itself as a lamp, the external objects do not and so we become conscious of the idea and not of the external world. The obvious fact is that ideas make us aware of external things. We cannot say that one idea depends on another and so on for it is the self who cognises the ideas and yet the self and the cognitions are of a different nature. They are related to each other as the knower and the known or as subject and object. The witnessing self exists by himself and cannot be doubted. This witnessing self of the *Advaita Vedānta* is one, permanent, and self-illuminating while the ideas of the *Vijñāna-vāda* are transitory and many and therefore require for their manifestation an intelligent principle beyond them.

Incidentally, this *sūtra* repudiates the interpretation of the *māyā* doctrine which holds that all objects are illusory or non-existent. It maintains the reality of external objects and says that cognitions arise from the contact of sense-organs with particular objects. The external object is other than the cognition of it.

There are texts which look upon the world as self-contradictory and therefore non-existent. See, for example, the following verse from the *Teja-bindūpaniṣad*.

vandhyā-kumāra bhītiś ced asti kiñcana
śaśa-śṛiṅgeṇa nāgendro mṛtaś cej jagad asti tat.

If you are afraid of the barren woman's son, if a serpent is killed when hit by the horns of a hare, then the world exists.

II. 2. 29. *vaidharmyāc ca na svapnādivat*

And on account of difference in nature, (ideas of the waking life) are not like those in a dream, etc.

vaidharmyāt: on account of difference in nature; *ca:* and; *na:* not; *svapnādivat:* like dream, etc.

If it is argued that ideas in the waking life arise as those in a dream, without the stimulus of external objects, the *sūtra* states that the two kinds of ideas are different in nature. Whereas the dream-states are negated in waking life, waking experiences continue to exist without being negated. What we experience in dream is due to memory, while what we experience in waking life is immediate apprehension. The difference between remembered and perceived experience is marked by the presence and absence of objects. Therefore waking life is different from dream.

Even Ś. admits that the things that we apprehend in the waking state are not negated in any state.[1] It will not be correct to argue that the *Sūtrakāra* is here establishing the phenomenal reality of the world, *vyāvahārika-satyatva*, for the Buddhists do not deny it.[2] The *sūtra* denies the subjective idealism of the *Vijñāna-vāda* and affirms the extra-mental reality of the world of waking experience.

[1] *naivaṁ jāgaritopalabdhaṁ vastu stambādikaṁ kasyāñcid apy avasthāyāṁ bādhyate.* Ś.

[2] *dve satye sam-upāśritya buddhānāṁ dharmadeśanā*
loke saṁvṛti-satyaṁ ca satyaṁ ca paramārthataḥ.
Nāgārjuna: *Mādhyāmaka Kārikā* XXIV. 492.

Bhāskara says that those who follow the Bauddha system are *māyā-vādins* who are rejected by the *Sūtrakāra*.[1]

II. 2. 30. *na bhāvo'nupalabdheḥ*

The existence of (impressions) is not (possible) on account of non-perception.

na: not; *bhāvaḥ:* existence; *an-upalabdheḥ:* on account of non-perception.

Vijñāna-vāda attempts to account for the variety of ideas by the variety of mental impressions without any reference to external objects. Without the perception of external objects, the existence of mental impressions is impossible. For the variety of mental impressions is caused by the variety of the objects perceived. How can various impressions arise if no external things are perceived? The positive and the negative method of argument[2] is in favour of the reality of external objects. Cognitions arise when there are external objects; they do not arise when there are no external objects. Even in the absence of impressions, we believe in the existence of the external world. Again, the impressions require a substratum in which they reside. Such a substratum cannot be cognised by any means of knowledge.

R. argues that we do not perceive mere cognitions devoid of corresponding objects. We nowhere perceive cognitions not inherent in a cognising subject and not referring to objects.[3] Even dream cognitions are not devoid of objective content.

II. 2. 31. *kṣaṇikatvāc ca*

And on account of (the ālaya-vijñāna) being momentary, (it cannot be the substratum of mental impressions).

kṣaṇikatvāt: on account of being momentary; *ca:* and.

If *pravṛtti-vijñāna* or the cognitions having the form of external things cannot be the substratum of impressions, even *ālaya vijñāna* cannot be the substratum for it is also momentary in character. Facts of memory, recognition, etc., imply a being which continues to exist and is therefore connected with the past, the present and the future.

As for the *Śūnya-vāda*, Ś. contends that complete denial of everything is not possible except on the recognition of some truth which cannot be denied.

R., Bhāskara and Śrīkaṇṭha do not mention this *sūtra*.

[1] *ye tu bauddha-matāvalambino māyā-vādinas tepy anena nyāyena sūtrakāreṇaiva nirastā veditavyāḥ.*

[2] *anvaya* and *vyatireka.*

[3] *na hy akartṛkasyākarmakasya vā jñānasya kvacid upalabdhiḥ.*

II. 2. 32. *sarvathānupapatteś ca*

And on account of being defective in all ways.
sarvathā: in all ways; *anupapatteḥ:* on account of being defective; *ca:* and.

The different doctrines of the reality of external objects, or of ideas and general nothingness contradict one another. The Buddhist doctrine cannot be accepted.

Bhāskara does not have this *sūtra.*

R. takes this *sūtra* as a separate section dealing with the refutation of the *Śūnya-vāda* that nothing whatever is real.

Modern existentialism is reminiscent of some forms of *Advaita Vedāntā* and Buddhism that the quest for reality is prompted by the perception of the misery and vanity of existence. The world we know is various, mutable. Its events lapse into non-entity at the very moment of their birth. The world is *saṁsāra,* a perpetual flux of states and relations of things, an evershifting phantasmagoria of thoughts and perceptions devoid of any substance. The objects of empirical knowledge are unstable, contingent, for ever breaking down logically into new relations to other things, which, when scrutinised, prove equally relative and elusive. The glory of this imperfect world is that it puts us on the track of apprehending the Real Being which underlies and informs this unstable world. It also helps us to become emotionally detached from the triumphs and tragedies of life.

Section 5 (33–36)

CONSIDERATION OF *JAINISM*

II. 2. 33. *naikasminn asambhavāt*

(*The Jaina doctrine*) *cannot* (*be accepted*) *on account of the impossibility* (*of contradictory attributes*) *in one thing.*
na: not; *ekasmin:* in one thing; *asambhavāt:* on account of impossibility.

Ś. summarises the *Jaina* view according to which there are seven entities, *jīva* (soul), *ajīva* (non-soul), *āsrava*[1] (issuing forward), *saṁvara* (restraint), *nirjara*[2] (destruction), *bandha* (bondage) and *mokṣa* (release). Soul and non-soul refer to the enjoying souls and the objects of enjoyment. *Āsrava* is the forward movement of the senses towards their objects; *saṁvara* is the restraint of the activity of the senses; *nirjara* is self-mortification by which sin is destroyed; *bandha* or bondage consists of works and *mokṣa* or release is the ascent of the soul to the highest regions after bondage has ceased. These are

[1] *āśravati iti āśrava.*

[2] *nirjarayati iti nirjara.*

brought under the two categories of the soul and the non-soul. Sometimes five *asti-kāyas* or existing bodies are mentioned, viz. soul, *jīva;* body, *pudgala;* merit, *dharma;* demerit, *adharma;* space, *ākāśa*. The reasoning known as *sapta-bhaṅgi-naya* is applied to all these. Maybe it is; maybe it is not; maybe it is and is not; maybe it is indescribable; maybe it is and is indescribable; maybe it is not and it is indescribable; maybe it is and is not and is indescribable.[1]

The *sūtra* says that this reasoning is untenable since contradictory attributes cannot belong to one and the same thing. A cognition of indefinite nature cannot be a source of knowledge. If indefiniteness belongs to all things, knowledge and the means of knowledge, knowing subject and the objects of knowledge, the *Jain* teachers do not teach us anything definite or certain. Again, to call the *asti-kāyas* indescribable and yet to describe them is to contradict oneself. If heaven is nothing definite in regard to its existence or duration, how can one aim at it? As for the doctrine of atoms or *pudgalas*, it has already been refuted in considering the *Vaiśeṣika* theory.

The *Jaina* doctrine of *anekānta-vāda* describes the complexity of objects. The different qualities possessed by an object are not contradictory to one another.

II. 2. 34. *evam cātmākārtsnyam*

And likewise (there results) the non-pervasiveness of the soul.
evam: thus; *ca:* and; *ātmā:* the soul; *akārtsnyam:* non-pervasiveness.

For the *Jainas*, the soul has the same size as the body. Being limited in extent, it is non-eternal, *anitya*. If it enters a large body like that of an elephant, it cannot occupy the whole of it; in a small body like that of an ant, it will not have sufficient space. The same difficulties are felt if we consider the different stages of one person, his childhood, youth and old age. If it is argued that the soul consists of an infinite number of parts, which are capable of being compressed or expanded, then if the infinite particles occupy different places, they cannot be contained in a small body; if they occupy the same place, the size of the soul will always be very small. Again, where the soul has a limited extent, why should we assume that the particles are infinite in number?

II. 2. 35. *na ca paryāyād apy avirodho vikārādibhyaḥ*

Nor also is there non-contradiction (if particles join or fall away from the soul) by modification, on account of change and the rest.
na: not; *ca:* and; *paryāyāt:* by modification; *api:* also; *avirodhaḥ:* non-contradiction; *vikārādibhyaḥ:* on account of change, etc.

If the *Jainas* say that the particles join or fall away when the soul

[1] *syād asti, syān nāsti, syād avaktavya, syād asti ca nāsti ca, syād asti cāvyaktavyaś ca, syān nāsti cāvaktavyaś ca, syād asti ca nāsti cāvaktavyaś ca.*

enters into a large or a small body, the *sūtra* points out that this view implies that the soul is capable of undergoing change and is therefore non-permanent. This is inconsistent with the *Jaina* view of release of the soul, the ascent of the soul when its bonds are sundered; which is likened to the rise of the gourd to the surface of the water, when it is freed from the encumbering mud. The particles cannot be of the nature of self, since they have origin and destruction. We cannot say that one of these particles is permanent, for we do not know which it is. Nor do we know where they come from or go, when they join or fall away from the soul. On the *Jaina* view both the particles and the soul are indefinite.

If it is argued that the soul may be considered to be permanent in spite of its changes, even as a stream of water is said to be permanent in spite of the changing water, it is said in reply that if the stream is not real, we get the theory of the void; if the stream is real, then the soul becomes of a changing nature.

II. 2. 36. *antyāvasthiteś cobhaya-nityatvād aviśeṣaḥ*

And on account of the permanence of the final (size of the soul) and because of the permanency of the two (earlier sizes) there is non-distinction of the size.

antya-avasthiteḥ: on account of the permanency of the final; *ca:* and; *ubhaya-nityatvāt:* because of the permanence of the two (earlier sizes); *aviśeṣaḥ:* there is non-distinction (of size).

Since the *Jainas* hold that the final state of the soul is permanent, it follows that the two earlier, initial and intervening ones also are permanent, otherwise there would be three different conditions of one and the same soul. This means that the different bodies of the soul have one and the same size and it is not required to enter into larger and smaller bodies.

Or we may say that the dimensions of the soul being the same in its three conditions, the soul is either small or large and cannot vary according to the size of the body. So the *Jaina* view cannot be accepted.

R. argues that the final size of the soul, i.e. its size in the state of release is enduring since the soul thereafter does not pass into another body. This size being permanent belongs to it previously also. Therefore there is no difference in size and the soul cannot have the size of its temporary bodies.

Śrīnivāsa is of the same view. The soul has a permanent and constant size in a gross body as well as in a subtle body, in the state of bondage as well as in that of release. So the doctrine that the soul is of the size of the body is untenable.

Baladeva gives a different interpretation: 'On account of the non-distinction of the final state [of release from that of bondage], both being permanent.' According to the *Jaina* view there is no difference between the state of release and that of bondage for the former, is a constant progress upward or remaining in the *alokākāśa*. Movement whether in the world or upward is a characteristic of bondage. No one can possibly feel happy in the state of constant motion or standing still in a place without any support. So there is no difference between release and bondage on this view.

Section 6 (37–41)

CONSIDERATION OF THE VIEW THAT GOD IS ONLY THE EFFICIENT CAUSE

II. 2. 37. *patyur asāmañjasyāt*

(*The doctrine*) *of the Lord* (*as only the efficient cause of the world*) (*is untenable*) *on account of inadequacy.*

In I. 4. 23–4, it is shown that God is both the material and the efficient cause of the world. The view that God is merely the efficient and not the material cause of the world is here considered. Some forms of *Sāṁkhya* and *Yoga* look upon God as the efficient cause different from *puruṣa* and *pradhāna*. The *Māheśvaras* hold that *Paśupati, Śiva*, is the efficient cause. There are other systems which hold that God is only the efficient cause of the world.

If the Lord assigns to different people different positions according to his liking, he will be like any one of us, subject to hatred, passion and so on. If we say that these positions high, intermediate and low, are determined by the merit and demerit of living beings, this leads to mutual dependence. To suggest that this mutual dependence is beginningless does not solve the problem. If imperfection leads to activity[1] as the *Nyāya Sūtra* (I. 1. 18) states, then even God who is active is imperfect. The *Yoga* view is that God is a special kind of soul (*puruṣa-viśeṣa*). In that case he must be devoid of all activity.

R. mentions the different schools of *Śaivism* here and argues that the Scripture refers to *Nārāyaṇa* as the universal creator. He quotes *Mahopaniṣad*. 'Alone, indeed, there was *Nārāyaṇa*, not *Brahmā*, not *Iśāna*, he being alone did not rejoice.'[2]

Both R. and Nimbārka insert a negative particle 'not'. The doctrine is *not* acceptable, on account of inconsistency.

Śrīkaṇṭha refers here only to those *Śaivas* who look upon the Lord as the efficient cause only, while *māyā* is the material cause and *Śakti* is the instrument. Ś. and Bhāskara consider under this *sūtra* not only the *Pāśupata* doctrine, but the *Sāṁkhya-Yoga* as well as other views which maintain that the Lord is the efficient cause only and not the material cause of the world.

[1] *pravartanā lakṣaṇā doṣāḥ.*

[2] *tathaiko ha vai nārāyaṇa āsīn na brahmā neśānaḥ. . . . sa ekākī na ramate.*

II. 2. 38. *sambandhānupapatteś ca*

And on account of the impossibility of the relation.
sambandha: relation; *an-upapatteḥ:* on account of being impossible; *ca:* and.

A Lord distinct from *pradhāna* and the souls cannot be their ruler unless he is related to them. This relation cannot be *saṁyoga* or conjunction for all the three are of infinite extent and devoid of parts. It cannot be *samavāya* or inherence for it is impossible to say which is the abode and which is the abiding thing. We cannot assume any other connection which can be inferred from the world as effect for we have yet to decide whether the world is an effect. This difficulty does not apply to the *Vedānta* which assumes the connection to be one of identity, *tādātmya.* While the *Vedānta* accepts *śruti* from its self-evidence, others, i.e. those who derive the authoritativeness of the *Vedas* from their divine authorship, suffer from the defect that the authoritativeness of the *Vedas* is derived from the omniscience of the Lord and the omniscience of the Lord is derived from the authority of the *Vedas.*

This *sūtra* is not found in R., Bhāskara and Śrīkaṇṭha.

II. 2. 39. *adhiṣṭhānānupapatteś ca*

And on account of the impossibility of a support (*or substratum*) (*the Lord cannot be the maker*).
adhiṣṭhāna: support; *anupapatteḥ:* on account of being impossible; *ca:* and.

The Lord cannot produce action in the *pradhāna* as the potter does in the clay, for *pradhāna,* which is devoid of colour and other qualities, is not an object of perception. It is therefore different in nature from clay, etc., and so it cannot be looked upon as the object of the Lord's action.

R. says that those who do not accept the authority of the *Vedas* establish the Lord's rulership over the material cause from observation. We cannot prove that the Lord is the ruler of *pradhāna* even as the potter is the ruler of clay. Again, the power of ruling material causes is possible only for embodied beings but the Lord is without a body. If it is said that the Lord has a body, the difficulties mentioned in I. 1. 3 apply.

Nimbārka says that *Paśupati* is not the cause of the world as he cannot have an eternal body, since it is opposed to what is observed, or a non-eternal one, since it arises later. All non-eternal objects arise later as effects and *Paśupati,* the Lord, is prior to everything.

According to Śrīkaṇṭha, the study of the *Āgamas* is open to all castes, while the study of the *Vedas* is permitted only to the three upper castes.

II. 2. 40. *karaṇavaccen na bhogādibhyaḥ*

If it be said that as in the case of sense-organs (we say) no on account of enjoyment and the rest.

karaṇavat: as in the case of sense-organs; *cet:* if it be said; *na:* not; *bhogādibhyaḥ:* on account of enjoyment and the rest.

If it be said that the Lord rules the *pradhāna* in the same way as the soul rules the sense-organs which are devoid of colour and are therefore not objects of perception, the *sūtra* says that the analogy is misleading. We know that the organs are ruled by the soul from the fact that they experience pleasure, pain, etc., but we do not observe that the Lord experiences pleasure, pain, etc., caused by the *pradhāna*.

The two *sūtras* 39 and 40 may be explained in a different way. Experience shows that kings who rule countries are not without a material abode, a body. So we may attribute to the Lord some kind of abode to serve as the substratum of the organs.

In reply, it is said that we cannot ascribe such a body to the Lord, for all bodies are later than creation. So the Lord is devoid of a support and so cannot act. If, on the other hand, we ascribe a body to him, he becomes like any of us, an ordinary transmigrating soul undergoing pleasure and pain.[1]

Nimbārka says that it is not possible to suppose that the Lord has sense-organs and the body like the individual soul, for then the Lord will have enjoyment and the rest.

II. 2. 41. *antavattvam asarvajñatā vā*

(On this view there will result) finitude or non-omniscience.

antavattvam: finitude, liability to end; *asarvajñatā:* non-omniscience; *vā:* or.

While Ś. and Bhāskara take the particle *vā* in the sense of 'or', R. and Nimbārka take it in the sense of *and.*

If the omniscient God knows the duration, extent and number of himself, *pradhāna* and the souls, then like all measured things they are of finite duration only, like jars and the like. When all the souls get released, *saṁsāra* ends. That means that *pradhāna* which under the guidance of the Lord had modified and manifested itself, for the good of the souls, also will end and there will be nothing for the Lord to rule. If, on the other hand, we say that God does not know the measure, the extent, etc., then he is lacking in omniscience. So the doctrine that God is only the efficient cause of the world is untenable.

R. says that if the Lord is under the influence of *adṛṣṭa*, he, like the individual soul, is subject to creation, dissolution, etc., and that he is not omniscient. Besides, though there are features in the *Pāśupata* system acceptable to the *Veda*, it rests on an assumption contrary to the *Veda*, viz. of the difference of the general instrumental and

[1] *sa-śarīratve hi sati saṁsārivad bhogādi-prasaṅgād īśvarasyāpy anīśvaratvam prasajyeta.* Ś.

material causes, and implies an erroneous interchange of higher and lower entities.

Nimbārka follows R.'s interpretation.

In the M.B. the *pāśupata* and *pāñcarātra* doctrines are distinguished from the Vedic religion: 'listen, O saintly king, the *Sāṁkhya*, the *Yoga*, the *Pāñcarātra*, the *Vedas*, the *Pāśupatas* are types of knowledge propounding different views.'[1]

The *Tantras* claim to be of Vedic origin and are based on the Yoga system. They are Hindu and Buddhist, cast in the form of dialogues between *Śiva* and *Parvatī* or the Buddhas and their Saktis. They deal with the nature of the cosmos, its evolution and dissolution, rules regarding human behaviour, different forms of worship and spiritual training, etc.

Section 7 (42–45)

CONSIDERATION OF THE *BHĀGAVATA* VIEW

II. 2. 42. *utpatty asambhavāt*

On account of the impossibility of origination

utpatti: origination; *asambhavāt:* on account of impossibility.

The *Bhāgavata* view admits that God is both the efficient and the material cause. It holds that *Vāsudeva* is the highest reality and is of the nature of pure knowledge. He assumes four forms, *Vāsudeva, Saṅkarṣaṇa, Pradyumna* and *Aniruddha*.[2] These answer to the Highest Self, the individual soul, the mind and the self-sense. *Vāsudeva* is the ultimate causal essence and the three others are the effects. Ś. does not object to the theory that *Vāsudeva* is the Highest Self, higher than the undeveloped, and the self of all, that he appears in manifold forms (C.U. VII. 26. 2) and that by devotion and meditation we reach the Highest Being. Only Ś. objects to the doctrine of origination of *Saṅkarṣaṇa* from *Vāsudeva*. If such were the case, the individual soul would be non-permanent and there is no possibility of release.

[1] *sāṁkhyaṁ yogaḥ pāncarātraṁ vedāḥ pāśupataṁ tathā*
jñānāny etāni rājarṣe viddhi nānāmatāni vai.
XII. 349. 64.

[2] In the M.B. *Aśvamedha Parva*, Yudhiṣṭhira asks Bhīṣma:
kathaṁ tvam arcanīyo'si mūrtayaḥ kīdṛśāś ca te
vaikhānasāh kathaṁ brūyaḥ kathaṁ vā pāncarātrikāḥ
and Bhīṣma replies:
viṣṇuṁ ca puruṣaṁ satyam acyutaṁ ca yudhiṣṭhira
aniruddhaṁ ca māṁ prāhuḥ vaikhānasa-vido janāḥ
anyetv evaṁ vijānanti māṁ rājan pāñcarātrikāḥ
vāsudevaṁ ca rājendra samkarṣaṇam athāpi vā
pradyumnaṁ cāniruddhaṁ ca catur-mūrtiṁ pracakṣate.

N*

Bhāskara agrees with Ś. that this section deals with the *Pāñcarātra* doctrine and not with the *Śakta* view as suggested by Madhva and Nimbārka. He, however, defends the *Pāñcarātra* doctrine and argues against S.'s view. He holds that the *Pāñcarātra* doctrine is not against Scripture.

R. holds that the origination of the individual soul is contrary to Scripture. *Kaṭha U*. II. 18. This is, for R., the *prima facie* view.

Nimbārka and Śrīnivāsa refer to the view of the *Śāktas* that *Śakti* alone is the producer of the world and refute it. The origin of the world from *Śakti* without *puruṣa* is impossible. There is a different explanation also. The origin of the world is impossible for it is eternal. As the world is not something produced, *Śakti* cannot be its cause. If the authority of the Scripture is quoted, then we find that, according to Scripture, the cause of the world is *Brahman*. The causality of *Śakti* is without any basis.

II. 2. 43. *na ca kartuḥ karaṅam*

Nor is the instrument (produced) from the agent.
na: not; *ca:* and; *kartuḥ:* from the agent or doer; *karaṇam:* instrument.

We do not observe that the instrument of doing anything springs forth by itself from the doer. Devadatta may use an axe but the axe does not come out of Devadatta. The *Bhāgavatas* hold that from the individual soul termed *Saṅkarṣaṇa* arises its instrument, viz. the internal organ termed *Pradyumna*, and from this another instrument called *ahaṁ-kāra* or self-sense.

R. points out that the view that the internal organ originates from the individual soul is opposed to the text that 'from him there is produced breath, mind and all sense-organs'. M.U. II. 1. 3. The authoritativeness of the *Bhāgavata* view cannot be admitted. The two *sūtras* for R. constitute the *pūrva-pakṣa*.

Nimbārka and Śrīnivāsa refer to the *Śakti* doctrine. If it is said that the world is something produced and the Creator helps *Śakti*, the *sūtra* answers that no sense-organ is possible on the part of the Creator, since there is no sense-organ prior to creation. Without a sense-organ, it is not possible for the Creator to be a helper, nor is it established that the world is something produced.

II. 2. 44. *vijñānādibhāve vā tad apratiṣedhaḥ*

Or if (Vāsudeva, etc., are taken as) possessing knowledge and other (qualities), there will be no exclusion (of the defect of non-origination).

If we take *Saṅkarṣaṇa*, etc., not as individual soul, mind, but as lords possessing knowledge, power, glory, etc., even then the objection holds. If the four individual lords have the same attributes, there is no need to have more than one. To admit four lords contradicts their own position that the one supreme essence is *Vāsudeva*.

If it be said that the four forms possessing the same attributes spring from the one Higher Reality, the objection of non-origination holds. *Saṅkarṣaṇa* cannot be produced from *Vāsudeva,* nor *Pradyumna* from *Saṅkarṣaṇa* nor *Aniruddha* from *Pradyumna.* Since they all possess the same attributes, there is no superiority of one to the other. The relation of cause and effect requires some superiority of the cause over the effect. The *Bhāgavata* view holds that they are all forms of *Vāsudeva* without any special distinctions. The forms of *Vāsudeva* need not be confined to four as the whole world from *Brahman* down to a blade of grass is a manifestation of the Supreme Being.[1]

R. says that 'or' in the *sūtra* refutes the view set forth in the two previous *sūtras. Apratiṣedhaḥ* is taken to mean that there is no contradiction (to the *Bhāgavata* doctrine). The doctrine teaches not an inadmissible origination but that the Highest *Brahman* called *Vāsudeva* from compassion abides in a fourfold form so as to render himself accessible to the devotees.[2] *Saṅkarṣaṇa, Pradyumna, Aniruddha* are thus mere bodily forms which the Highest *Brahman* voluntarily assumes. Scripture declares 'not born, he is born in many ways'[3] and it is this birth consisting in the voluntary assumption of bodily form, due to tenderness towards its devotees, which the *Bhāgavata* system teaches.

Nimbārka and Śrīnivāsa argue that the doctrine of *Śakti* is set aside through the admission of *Brahman.* What is possessed of all attributes is the Highest Deity. (II. 1. 29.)

Śrīkaṇṭha takes this *sūtra* as representing the *prime facie* view. It is not contended that there is the origin of the individual soul, etc., but only that *Saṅkarṣaṇa,* etc., assume the forms of the individual soul.

Baladeva argues that if the *Śāktas* hold that the Lord has a non-material body composed of knowledge and so on, then we have no objection, since this view is identical with our own doctrine.

II. 2. 45. *vipratiṣedhāc ca*

And on account of contradiction.

vipratiṣedhāt: on account of contradiction; *ca:* and.

There are several contradictions in the *Bhāgavata* view. Sometimes these four are mentioned as qualities, sometimes as bearers of the qualities. The *Vedas* are sometimes criticised.[4]

Śāṇḍilya's criticism is only to eulogise, says R., the *Bhāgavata* view.

[1] *brahmādi stamba-paryantasya samastasyaiva jagato bhagavad-vyūhatvā-vagamāt.* Ś.

[2] *vāsudevākhyam param brahmaivāśrita-vatsalam svāśrita-samāśrayaṇī-yatvāya svecchayā caturdhāvatiṣṭhata iti hi tat prakriyā.* R.

[3] *ajāyamāno bahudhā vijāyate. Taittirīya Āraṇyaka* III. 12.

[4] *caturṣu vedeṣu evaṁ śreyo'labdhvā śāṇḍilya idam śāstram adhītavān.*

The criticism is on a par with Nārada's words (C.U. VII. 2) that one knows only the texts but should know the knowledge of the Self. He quotes a verse which says that 'the wise Lord Hari, impelled by kindness for those devoted to him, extracted the essential meaning of all *Vedānta* texts and summed it up in an easy form'.[1]

R. affirms that the *sūtras* do not reject all the doctrines of the *Sāṁkhya, Yoga, Pāñcarātra* and the *Pāśupata* systems. We reject only their weak points and accept whatever is valid in them though the teachings of the *Jainas* and the *Buddhists* are rejected entirely.

While Ś. rejects the *Bhāgavata* view in the same way in which he rejects the other theories, R. points out that the *Bhāgavata* view is consistent with Scripture and is approved by the *Sūtrakāra*.

This *sūtra* is not found in Bhāskara.

Nimbārka refutes the causality of *Śakti* and accepts the supremacy of *Brahman*.

Śrīkaṇṭha stresses the opposition of the *Pāñcarātra* doctrine to Scripture.

The *Bhāgavata* doctrine stresses the importance of devotion and praise of God. Ś. in his commentary on *Viṣṇu-sahasra-nāma* observes that adoration in the form of praise is superior to other forms of worship, since it involves no injury to any living being, does not depend on men or material and is independent of place, time or procedure.[2]

[1] *vedānteṣu yathā sāraṁ saṁgṛhya bhagavān hariḥ*
bhaktānukampayā vidvān saṁcikṣepa yathā sukham.

[2] *asya stuti-lakṣaṇasya arcanasya ādhikye kiṁ kāranam? ucyate: hiṁsād puruṣāntara dravyāntara desa-kālādi-niyamānapekṣatvam ādhikye kāranam.*

Section 1 (1–7)

ĀKĀŚA IS AN EFFECT

II. 3. 1. *na viyad aśruteḥ*

Ākāśa is not created on account of non-mention in the Scripture.
na: not; *viyat: ākāśa,* space or ether; *aśruteḥ:* on account of non-mention in the Scripture.

The third part of the second chapter considers whether the forms of existence which constitute the world are created or not, whether they are coeternal with *Brahman* or issue from it to be resolved into it at stated intervals.

The *prima facie* view is that *ākāśa* is not created since there is no scriptural statement to that effect. In C.U. VI. 2. 3, fire, water and earth are mentioned as produced and not *ākāśa.*

II. 3. 2 *asti tu*

But there is.
asti: there is; *tu:* but.

The answer to the objection is stated here. There are scriptural passages which mention the origination of *ākāśa.* T.U. II. 1 says: 'from that Self sprang *ākāśa*'. There is apparently a conflict between the two texts, one which mentions fire as the first created product, the other which mentions *ākāśa* as the first created product.

II. 3. 3. *gauṇy asambhavāt*

It is used in a secondary sense, on account of impossibility.
gauṇī: in a secondary sense; *asambhavāt:* on account of impossibility.

The text dealing with the origination of *ākāśa* is not to be taken literally but only secondarily because the creation of *ākāśa* is impossible since it has no parts. *Ākāśa* is all-pervading and so can be inferred to be eternal and without origin. Ś. here refers to the *Vaiśeṣika* view that whatever is originated springs from inherent, non-inherent or operative causes. We cannot conceive of such causes for *ākāśa.* Those elements like fire which have an origin exist in different conditions at an earlier and later period. No such divisions can be conceived for *ākāśa.*

R. quotes another text which declares that air and *ākāśa* are eternal. *vāyuś cāntarikṣam caitad amṛtam.* B.U. II. 3. 3; *Śatapatha Brāhmaṇa* XIV. 5. 3. 4. The text about the origination of *ākāsa* can only be metaphorical.

II. 3. 4. *śabdāc ca*

And on account of the text.
śabdāt: on account of the word, the text; *ca:* and.

The opponent may quote a number of scriptural texts. We have already mentioned B.U. II. 3. 3. Omnipresence and eternity are attributed to *ākāśa*. *ākāśavat sarvagataś ca nityaḥ*. Again, as the *ākāśa* is infinite, so the Self is to be known as infinite: *sa yathānanto-'yam ākāsaḥ evam ananta ātmā veditavyaḥ*. Again, '*Brahman* has *ākāśa* for its body': *ākāśa śarīraṁ brahma, ākāśa atmā*.

R. and Nimbārka take *sūtras* 3 and 4 as one.

The question relates to the origination of *ākāśa*. The *prima facie* view is that it is not, since the origination is mentioned in some texts, not in others. So where the word origination, *sambhūtaḥ*, occurs, it should be taken in a secondary sense. It is to be taken literally with reference to fire and so on and figuratively with reference to *ākāśa*. This is on the analogy of the word *Brahman* which in M.U. I. 1. 8 and 9 is used literally in one case and figuratively in the other as referring to *prakṛti*. The analogy is not complete because the word *sambhūtaḥ* is used once, while *Brahman* is used twice.

R. treats the difference as immaterial since a figurative sense may be understood in addition to the literal sense even when a word is carried on just as much as when it is repeated.[1]

II. 3. 5. *syācchaikasya brahma-śabdavat*

The one word may be (*taken in its primary as well as secondary senses*) *like the word Brahman.*

syāt: may be, is possible; *ca:* and; *ekasya:* of one word; (*sambhūta-śabda*); *brahma-śabdavat:* like the word *Brahman.*

The objection that one and the same word, sprang, cannot be used in its primary sense with regard to fire and in a secondary sense with regard to *ākāśa* is answered here. The word '*Brahman*' is used (T.U. III. 2–6) in the primary sense with regard to bliss and in the secondary sense with regard to food. It is said *tapo brahma*, austerity, is the means of knowing *Brahman* which is the object of knowledge. The word is used for both austerity and the object of knowledge.

R. quotes M.U. II. 1 for the twofold use of *Brahman* (8 and 9).

II. 3. 6. *pratijñāhānir avyatirekāc chabdebhyaḥ*

(*There is*) *non-abandonment of the initial statement on account of non-distinction* (*of the world from Brahman*) *according to scriptural texts.*

pratijñā: initial statement; *ahāniḥ:* non-abandonment; *avyatirekāt:* on account of non-distinction; *ca:* and; *śabdebhyaḥ:* from the scriptural texts.

The statements in C.U. VI. 1. 3; B.U. IV. 5. 6; M.U. I. 1. 3 that by the knowledge of one thing, everything is known are not contradicted because the entire aggregate of things is non-different from *Brahman.* So *ākāśa* will also be one of the effects of *Brahman;* otherwise it could

[1] *anuṣaṅgeca śravaṇāvṛttāv iva.*

not be known when *Brahman* becomes known. There are also texts which declare that all this is *Brahman* and *ākāśa* is included in the world. So *ākāśa* is a created product. The C.U. text in which *ākāśa* is not mentioned is to be interpreted in relation to the *Taittirīya* passage. *Ākāśa* and air are first created and then fire. There is no contradiction between the different scriptural passages.

R. and Śrīkaṇṭha break this *sūtra* into two, *śabdebhyaḥ* being the second.

II. 3. 7. *yāvad vikāraṁ tu vibhāgo lokavat*

But as far as there is effect, there is division as in ordinary life.
yāvat: as far as there is; *vikāram:* effect, modification; *tu:* but; *vibhāgaḥ:* division; *lokavat:* as in the world, in ordinary life.

'But' refutes the view that *ākāśa* is not created. The creation of *ākāśa* is not impossible. Whatever is divided is an effect; whatever is not an effect is not divided as the Self. *Ākāśa* is divided from earth and so on and it is therefore an effect. It cannot be said that the Self also is divided from *ākāśa* and so on, for the Self is self-established while *ākāśa* and others are to be established by other means of knowledge. An adventitious thing may be refuted but not that which is the essential nature of him who refutes. The Self is therefore not an effect. Ś. points out that *Brahman* existed before *ākāśa* was produced. Besides, *ākāśa* is non-eternal because it is the substratum of a non-eternal quality like sound. Statements regarding the eternity of *ākāśa* are to be taken in a relative sense. *Ākāśa* is an effect of *Brahman*. Whatever is an effect has an origin.

Ākāśa has *Brahman* for its material cause.

Section 2 (8)

AIR SPRINGS FROM *ĀKĀŚA*

II. 3. 8. *etena mātariśvā vyākhyātaḥ*

etena: by this; *mātariśvā:* air; *vyākhyātaḥ:* is explained.

Objections to the origination of air are considered. In the chapter of the C.U. which treats of the origination of things, air is not mentioned. A different opinion that it sprang from *ākāśa* is mentioned in the T.U. So the opponent argues that the passage which refers to the origination of air should be taken in a secondary sense for, as in the case of *ākāśa* the literal sense cannot be adopted. Besides, there is a passage which denies that air ever rests. B.U. I. 5. 22. There are passages which declare air to be eternal. The *sūtra* contends that air is a product for it is conformable to the general tendency of Scripture. Whatever is capable of division is an effect. The denial of its ever setting refers to lower knowledge, *aparā vidyā*.

Section 3 (9)

BRAHMAN IS NOT A PRODUCT

II. 3. 9. *asambhavas tu sato'nupapatteḥ*

But there is no origin of that which is on account of the impossibility (of such an origin).
asambhavaḥ: no origin; *tu:* but; *sataḥ:* of that which is, i.e. *Brahman*; *anupapatteḥ:* on account of impossibility.

The *pūrva-pakṣa* says that *Brahman* does originate in view of statements like 'non-existent was this in the beginning'. *asad vā idam agra āsīt.* The *sūtra* asserts the non-origination of that which is, on account of the impossibility of its being originated. *Brahman* is the only thing which is unborn. *Brahman* whose self is being cannot be suspected to have sprung from anything else. *Brahman* which is mere being cannot spring from mere being as there is a certain superiority on the part of the cause in the relation of cause and effect. Particulars spring from what is general and not vice versa. Nor can *Brahman* spring from that which is not. See C.U. VI. 2. 2. Ś.U. VI. 9 denies that *Brahman* has any progenitor. The fundamental cause of all effects, which is not itself an effect, is *Brahman.* Śrīkaṇṭha agrees with this view of Ś.

For R., the *sūtra* teaches the origination of everything else except *Brahman,* the latter alone being non-originated. Śrīkaṇṭha seems to agree with this interpretation. 'Hence non-origination applies to *Brahman* alone; origination applies to all else, on account of failure otherwise of the promise that everything will be known.'[1]

Nimbārka agrees with Ś. Bhāskara criticises Ś.'s interpretations.

Section 4 (10)

FIRE SPRINGS FROM AIR

II. 3. 10. *tejo'tas tathā hy āha*

Fire springs from this (air) (for) thus (the text) verily says.
tejaḥ: fire; *ataḥ:* from this; *tathā:* thus; *hi:* verily; *āha:* says.

The opponent mentions C.U. VI. 2. 3 where fire is said to have for its source *Brahman* and the T.U. II. 1, where the source of fire is said to be air and argues that *Brahman* is the source of fire for everything without exception is born from *Brahman* (M.U. II. 1. 3; see also C.U. III. 14. 1; T.U. II. 6). The *sūtra* says that fire springs from

[1] *tataḥ brahmaṇa evāsambhavo'nutpattiḥ, tad-anyasya sarvasya sarva-vijnāna-pratijñānupapatteḥ sambhava utpattir iti.*

Brahman through intermediate links. Though all things are traced to *Brahman* they are not the immediate effects of *Brahman*.

Ś., Bhāskara and Baladeva take this as the correct conclusion. Nimbārka takes this as stating the *prima facie* view.

Section 5 (11)

WATER SPRINGS FROM FIRE

II. 3. 11. *āpaḥ*

Water (*springs from fire*).

The *sūtra* explains the order of creation, *sṛṣṭi-krama*. See C.U. VI. 2. 3; T.U. II. 1.

While this is the *prima facie* view for Nimbārka, it is the correct conclusion or *siddhānta* for Ś., Bhāskara and Baladeva.

There is a *sūtra* which is not mentioned by Ś., Bhāskara and Baladeva. 'The Earth originates from water.' *pṛthivī*.

Section 6 (12)

FROM WATER EARTH

II. 3. 12. *pṛthivyadhikāra-rūpa-śabdāntarebhyaḥ*

The earth (*is meant by the word anna, food*) *on account of the subject-matter, colour and other scriptural texts.*

pṛthivī: earth; *adhikāra-rūpa-śabdāntarebhyaḥ:* on account of the subject-matter, colour and other scriptural texts.

C.U. VI. 2. 4 says that water sent forth food. Does *anna* mean objects fit to be used as food like rice, barley and the like or cooked food or earth? The opponent claims that *anna* should mean food and not earth. The *sūtra* contends that the word occurs in the treatment of the elements fire, air, water and so the reference is to the element earth. In a complementary passage the black colour is said to be the colour of *anna*. Earth has black colour while eatable things are not necessarily black. Even though earth may have different colours, its predominant colour is black. Many scriptural texts support the view of *anna* as earth. See T.U. II. 1; B.U. I. 2. 2. Therefore *anna* denotes earth.

R. quotes M.U. I. 1. 9.

Nimbārka adopts the same interpretation though he regards it as the *prima facie* view.

Section 7 (13)

BRAHMAN IS THE CREATIVE PRINCIPLE

II. 3. 13. *tad-abhidhyānād eva tu tal liṅgāt saḥ*

But he (Brahman is the creative principle abiding within the elements) on account of his desire only and indicatory mark.
tad-abhidhyānāt: because of his desire; *eva:* only; *tu:* but; *tat-liṅgāt:* on account of his indicatory mark; *saḥ:* he.

Brahman is described in some texts as the creator of everything. There are other passages where certain elements are said to produce certain effects. If the opponent points to this conflict, the *sūtra* maintains that the Supreme residing within these elements produces these effects and so there is no contradiction. See B.U. III. 7. 3; C.U. VI. 2. 3–4. The elements become causes only through the will of the Supreme who resides in them.

Nimbārka states that the correct conclusion is indicated in this *sūtra*. Independent creatorship belongs only to the Supreme Self and not to anything else.

Section 8 (14)

THE REABSORPTION OF THE ELEMENTS INTO *BRAHMAN*

II. 3. 14. *viparyayeṇa tu kramo'ta upapadyate ca*

The order (in which the elements are resolved into Brahman) is the reverse of that (i.e. the order in which they are created) and this is proved.
viparyayeṇa: in the reverse order; *tu:* indeed; *kramaḥ:* order; *ataḥ:* from that (the order of creation); *upapadyate:* is proved; *ca:* and.

If the opponent says that the retractation of the elements is not in any definite order, the *sūtra* says that it is the reverse of the order of creation. This is seen in ordinary life. He who ascends a stair, has to descend it by taking the steps in the reverse order. Each effect passes back into its immediately antecedent cause, until the last cause is resolved into *Brahman*.

R. does not look upon this *sūtra* as concerned with the order of dissolution. He continues the topic of the order of evolution. He mentions texts which designate the vital breath and the rest as rising directly from *Brahman*, in opposition to the real order of evolution, viz. *prakṛti*, *mahat* and so on. These texts are explicable only on the view that everything arises directly from *Brahman*.

Śrīkaṇṭha begins a new section here and reads *pāram-paryeṇa* in place of *viparyayeṇa*. He deals with the question of the origin of sense-organs, mind and the like.

Baladeva follows R.'s interpretation, though he takes this *sūtra* as constituting a separate section.

Section 9 (15)

THE ORDER OF THE CREATION AND ABSORPTION OF ELEMENTAL SUBSTANCES IS NOT AFFECTED BY THE CREATION AND ABSORPTION OF SENSE-ORGANS, MIND AND THE LIKE

II. 3. 15. *antarā vijñānamanasī krameṇa tal-liṅgād iti cen nāviśeṣāt.*

If it be said that in between (Brahman and the elements) intellect and mind (are mentioned and so their creation and absorption are to be placed somewhere) in the order on account of the inferential indications (in the texts) to that effect, (we say) not so, on account of the non-difference (of the intellect and the mind from the elements).

antarā: in between; *vijñāna-manasī:* intellect and mind; *krameṇa:* in the order; *tat-liṅgāt:* owing to inferential indications of that; *iti cet:* if it be said; *na:* not so; *aviśeṣāt:* on account of non-difference.

In *Kaṭha U.* I. 3. 3–4 and M.U. II. 1. 3, mind, intellect and senses are mentioned as arising from the Self and so there is a variation from the previously stated order of creation and reabsorption. The *sūtra* denies this on the ground that the organs themselves are non-different from the elements. See C.U. VI. 6. 5. If the organs are sometimes mentioned separately from them, it is only in the same way as the mendicant *Brāhmaṇas* (*parivrājakas*) are mentioned separately from the *Brāhmaṇas*. Besides the M.U. gives an enunciation of the organs and the elements and not the order of their creation. So the origination of the organs does not constitute a break in the order of the origination of the elements.

Section 10 (16)

BIRTH AND DEATH REFER TO THE BODY ONLY AND FIGURATIVELY TO THE SOUL CONNECTED WITH THE BODY

II. 3. 16. *carācaravyapāśrayas tu syāt tad-vyapadeśo bhāktās tad-bhāva-bhāvitvāt*

But the mention of that (viz. the birth and death of the individual soul) is with regard to (the bodies) of moving and non-moving beings; it is secondary (figurative) if applied to the soul, on account of (the forms) depending on the existence of that (the body).

carācaravyapāśrayaḥ: depending on the bodies of moving and non-moving beings; *tu:* but; *syāt:* may be; *tat-vyapadeśaḥ:* the mention of that; *bhāktaḥ:* secondary, figurative; *tat-bhāva-bhāvitvāt:* on account of those forms depending on the existence of that (the body).

In ordinary usage we say that Devadatta is born or Devadatta is dead, and certain ceremonies are also prescribed at the birth and death of people. The *sūtra* refutes such a doubt and says that the soul has neither birth nor death. These belong not to the soul but to the body with which the soul is connected. Birth and death do not belong to the soul but indicate only the connection and disconnection with the body. See C.U. VI. 11. 3; B.U. IV. 3. 8.

R. gives two interpretations resulting from two readings *bhākta* and *abhākta.* (i) The reference to moving and non-moving beings is figurative, secondary because of their being permeated by *Brahman.* All the words denoting moving and non-moving beings really denote *Brahman* since all objects are modes of *Brahman.* (ii) The forms denoting moving and non-moving beings are primary with regard to *Brahman* since the denotative power of all forms depends on the being of *Brahman.*

Nimbārka follows Ś.

Śrīkaṇṭha follows R.'s second interpretation. Baladeva, on the whole, follows R.

Section 11 (17)

THE ETERNITY OF THE INDIVIDUAL SOUL

II. 3. 17. *nātmāśṛuter nityatvāc ca tābhyaḥ*

The soul is not (originated) on account of the statement of śruti and also the eternity resulting therefrom.

na: not (originated, produced); *ātmā:* the individual soul; *aśruteḥ:* since it is not mentioned in the Scriptures; *nityatvāt:* on account of being eternal; *ca:* and; *tābhyaḥ:* from them.

If it is urged that at the beginning there was only one *Brahman* without a second and some scriptural passages mention that living souls are like sparks produced from a fire and are therefore produced from *Brahman* (B.U. II. 1. 20; M.U. II. 1. 1), it is said in answer that the individual soul is not a product for there are no scriptural statements to that effect and it is said to be eternal, i.e. not-produced; see C.U. VI. 11. 3, VI. 3. 2, VI. 8. 7; B.U. IV. 4. 25; *Kaṭha U.* I. 2. 18; T.U. II. 6. We cannot argue that the soul is divided and therefore is a product for it only appears divided on account of limiting adjuncts. The passages which speak of the soul's production, etc., relate to the soul's connection with the limiting adjuncts.

According to R., the individual soul is, no doubt, an effect of *Brahman* but has existed in *Brahman* from all eternity as an individual being and a mode, *prakāra,* of *Brahman.* It is true that the material elements also subsist in *Brahman* but there is a difference. The material elements exist in a subtle condition prior to creation and do not possess the qualities which render them objects of ordinary experience. They are said to originate when they pass into a gross condition at the time of creation. The souls, on the other hand, possess at all times the same essential qualities. They are cognising agents. Only at the time of the new creation they connect themselves with bodies and their intelligence undergoes a certain expansion or development, *vikāsa*, as distinct from the contracted state (*saṅkoca*) in which they were prior to creation. The change is not one of essential nature, *svarūpānyathābhāva*.

R., Śrīkaṇṭha and Baladeva read *śruteḥ* instead of *aśruteḥ* but give the same interpretation.

Section 12 (18)

THE SOUL AS INTELLIGENCE

III. 3. 18. *jñyo'ta eva*

(*The soul is*) *intelligence, for this very reason.*

jñaḥ: intelligence; *ata eva:* for this very reason.

There are different views about the nature of the soul, whether its intelligence is adventitious or natural to it. The opponent argues that as the soul does not remain intelligent in the states of sleep, swoon, and as we say when we wake up from sleep that we are not conscious of anything, it is clear that intelligence is intermittent and so adventitious only. The answer to this objection is stated by Ś. Intelligence is not a product. *Brahman* is of the nature of intelligence and appears as the individual soul owing to its contact with the limiting adjuncts. See B.U. III. 9. 28. 7, IV. 3. 11, IV. 3. 14. IV. 5. 13; C.U. VIII. 12. 4; T.U. II. 1. While the soul's essential nature is intelligence the senses serve the purpose of determining the special object of each sense such as smell and so on. See C.U. VIII. 12. 4. Even in sleep persons have intelligence. For if intelligence were non-existent in sleep, the individual could not say that he did not know anything in deep sleep. The absence of objects is mistaken for the absence of intelligence even as the light pervading space is not apparent owing to the absence of things to be illuminated and not to the absence of its own nature. The view of the *Vaiśeṣika* and others that the soul is itself non-intelligent and intelligence is adventitious is wrong.

R. explains *jñaḥ* by *jñāṭr*, the knower, and uses the *sūtra* against the *Sāṁkhya* and the *Advaita Vedānta*. He maintains that the soul is not pure intelligence but a knowing agent. *Jñaḥ* is *jñātṛ* and not *jñānam*. R. is opposed both to the *Vaiśeṣika* which holds that the soul is of a non-conscious nature and to the *Advaita Vedānta* which holds that the soul is pure consciousness.

Nimbārka follows R.

Section 13 (19–32)

THE SIZE OF THE SOUL

II. 3. 19. *utkrānti-gaty-āgatīnām*

(The soul is not infinite in size on account of the scriptural declarations of) passing out, going and returning.
utkrānti-gati-āgatīnām: passing out, going and returning.

The question taken up for consideration is the size of the soul, whether it is atomic or medium-sized or of infinite size. There are passages which declare the soul to be of atomic size. The opponent maintains that its passing out and returning will be possible only if it is of limited size. See B.U. IV. 4. 6; K.U. III. 3, I. and 2. Movement is impossible in the case of an all-pervading being. If it is of limited size, it can only be of the atomic size since the position that it is of the same size as the body has already been refuted.

II. 3. 20. *svātmanā cottarayoḥ*

And on account of the latter (*going and returning*) *being connected with their soul* (*the soul is of atomic size*).
svātmanā: (being connected directly) with their soul; *ca:* and; *uttarayoḥ:* the latter two.

So far as passing out is concerned, it may be said that the soul passes out when it ceases to be the ruler of the body, when the results of its former actions are exhausted. A ruler of the village may be said to go out when he ceases to be the ruler. But the other two activities are not possible in the case of a being who does not move. Going and returning are activities abiding in the agent. Some texts mention the parts of the body from which the soul starts in passing out. B.U. IV. 3. 11; IV. 4. 2; IV. 4. 1. So the soul is the size of the atom.

II. 3. 21. *nāṇuratacchruter iti cen netarādhikārāt*

If it be said that (*the soul is*) *not atomic, as the Scriptures state it to be otherwise* (*i.e. all-pervading*) (*we say*) *not so on account of the other one* (*the Highest Self*) *being the subject-matter* (*of those texts*).
na: not; *aṇuḥ:* atomic; *atat-śruteḥ:* since the Scriptures (state it) to be otherwise; *iti cet:* if it be said; *na:* not so; *itarādhikārāt:* owing to another principle being the subject-matter.

If it be said that there are scriptural passages which hold that the soul is all-pervading (B.U. IV. 4. 22; T.U. II. 1), the opponent argues that these refer to the Highest Self and not to the individual soul.

R. mentions B.U. IV. 4. 13 as referring to *pratibuddha ātmā* and not to the individual soul.

II. 3. 22. *svaśabdonmānābhyāṁ ca*

And also on account of direct statements and infinitesimal measure (the soul is atomic).
svaśabda-unmānābhyām: on account of direct statements (of the texts) and infinitesimal measure; *ca:* and.

M.U. III. 19 refers to the atomic self, *aṇur ātmā*. From passages (Ś.U. V. 8 and 9) that 'this living self is to be known as a part of the hundredth part of the point of a hair divided a hundredfold' the self seems to be of the size of the point of a goad. It is clear that the soul is of atomic size. *unmāna* is *uddhṛtya mānam*, a measure which is distinct from all gross measures. It means an intensely minute measure according to Śrīnivāsa.

II. 3. 23. *avirodhaś candanavat*

(There is) no contradiction as in the case of the sandal-paste.
avirodhaḥ: no contradiction; *candanavat:* like the sandal-paste.

If the objection is raised that if the soul is assumed to be of the atomic size and so to occupy only one point of the body, how can one feel any sensation over the whole body as one does when he is bathing in a river or feels hot over the whole body in summer, the answer is given by way of an example. Though sandal-paste is applied only to a particular part of the body, it gives an agreeable sensation extending over the whole body. The soul may occupy only one part of the body and yet experience pleasure and pain extending over the whole body. See also B.G. XIII. 33.

II. 3. 24. *avasthiti-vaiśeṣyād iti cen nābhyupagamād dhṛdi hi*

If it be said (that the two cases are not parallel) on account of the special position (of the sandal-paste), (we say that it is) not so on account of the admission (in the Scriptures of a special seat for the soul, viz.) in the heart alone.
avasthiti-vaiśeṣyāt: on account of the special position; *iti cet:* if it be said; *na:* not so; *abhyupagamāt:* on account of the admission; *hṛdi:* in the heart; *hi:* alone.

A possible objection to the atomic size of the soul is mentioned. It is true that the sandal-paste occupies a particular part of the body and yet gladdens the whole body, but we do not know that the soul occupies a particular place. To this the answer is given that the soul, according to some texts, is said to reside within the heart (B.U. IV. 3. 7). So it is atomic in size.

II. 3. 25. *guṇād vā lokavat*

Or on account of its quality (intelligence) as in the world.
guṇāt: on account of quality; *vā:* or; *lokavat:* as in the world.

In the world we find that a light placed in one corner illumines the whole room. So also the soul, though atomic and so occupying a particular portion of the body, may, because of the quality of intelligence, pervade the whole body and experience pleasure and pain throughout the body.

Sandal-paste consists of parts and by the diffusion of its imperceptible particles may refresh the entire body but the soul as atomic does not possess any parts. A quality cannot extend beyond that in which it inheres and abide elsewhere. The whiteness of a cloth does not extend beyond the cloth. We cannot say that the soul is like the light diffused from a lamp for the light itself is admitted to be a substance. The reply to this objection is given in the next *sūtra*.

R. and others read *ālokavat.*

II. 3. 26. *vyatireko gandhavat*

The extending beyond is as in the case of smell.
vyatirekaḥ: extending beyond the object; *gandhavat:* like smell.

Even as the smell extends beyond the substance which gives it off, so the quality of intelligence extends beyond the soul which is atomic.

R. points out that just as smell which is a quality of earth is distinct from earth, so is knowledge different from the knowing subject.

II. 3. 27. *tathā ca darśayati*

Thus also (the Scripture) declares or shows.
tathā: thus; *ca:* also; *darśayati:* shows or declares.

Scripture declares that the atomic soul pervades the whole body on account of the quality of intelligence. See K.U. IV. 20; B.U. I. 4. 7.

R. and Nimbārka treat the *sūtra* as part of the previous one.

II. 3. 28. *pṛthag upadeśāt*

On account of the separate teaching (about soul and intelligence).
pṛthak: separate; *upadeśāt:* on account of teaching.

There are passages (B.U. II. 1. 17) which declare soul and intelligence to be separate. See also K.U. III. 6.

According to Ś., *sūtras* 19–28 state the *pūrva-pakṣa* or the *prima facie* view that the soul is atomic while the *siddhānta* is stated in the next *sūtra*. It is not usual to state the *prima facie* view at such length.

R. mentions B.U. IV. 3. 30, III. 7. 22; T.U. II. 5. 1.

According to R., *sūtra* 19 states the *siddhānta* that the soul is of minute size. *Sūtras* 20–25 confirm this view and repudiate objections raised against it. *Sūtras* 26–29 consider the question already raised in *sūtra* 18 about the relation of *jñātṛ*, the knower, to *jñāna*, knowledge.

Baladeva considers the objection that intelligence is not a permanent attribute of the soul and holds that it is, since there is a separate statement in Scripture to that effect.

II. 3. 29. *tad-guṇa-sāratvāt tu tad vyapadeśaḥ prājñavat*

But that declaration (as atomic) is on account of its having for its essence the qualities of that (i.e. the buddhi) even as the Intelligent Self (which is all-pervading is said to be atomic).

tad-guṇa-sāratvāt: on account of its having for its essence the qualities of that; *tu:* but; *tat:* that; *vyapadeśaḥ:* declaration (as to atomic size); *prājñavat:* like the Intelligent Self.

For Ś., this *sūtra* discusses the size of the self. Ś. argues that atomicity essentially belongs to *buddhi* or understanding and is wrongly referred to the Self which is the Highest *Brahman.* As *Brahman* is all-pervading, the soul also is all-pervading. See B.U. IV. 4. 22. If the soul were of atomic size, it could not experience sensations extending over the whole body. It cannot be said that this is possible owing to the soul's connection with the sense of touch (the skin) for then, when we tread on a thorn we should experience pain over the whole body and not merely in the sole of the foot, which is not so. The quality of an atom cannot diffuse itself beyond the confines of the atom. The light emitted from a lamp is not a quality but a different kind of substance. Again, if the intelligence of the soul pervades the whole body, the soul cannot be atomic. Intelligence constitutes the essential nature of the soul, even as heat and light constitute the nature of fire. It has already been shown that the soul is not of the same size as the body: II. 2. 34. It can only be all-pervading. Its atomic nature is due to its association with mind, etc., in the empirical world. When Ś.U. V. 9 states that the soul is atomic and again that it is infinite, its infinity is primary or real and its atomicity is metaphorical. See also Ś.U. V. 8 and M.U. III. 1. 9. All statements about the soul's abiding in the heart or passing out depend on the limiting adjuncts. See K.U. III. 6, *Praśna U.* VI. 3. 4; C.U. III. 14. 2 and 3.

According to R., this *sūtra* belongs to the *jñānādhikaraṇa,* the section dealing with the self as knower. The self may be referred to as knowledge also, for knowledge is the self's essential characteristic. *Brahman* is described as *jñānam* in the text, *satyam, jñānam, anantam, brahma.*

Śrīkaṇṭha and Baladeva agree with R.'s view.

II. 3. 30. *yāvad ātma-bhāvitvāc ca na doṣas tad darśanāt*

There is no fault (for the connection of the soul with the intelligence lasts) as long as the soul exists, because this is observed (in the Scripture).

yāvat: so long as; *ātma-bhāvitvāt:* the soul exists; *ca:* and; *na doṣaḥ:* there is no fault; *tat-darśanāt:* because it is seen.

If the objection is raised that the conjunction of the soul and the intellect which are different entities is bound to end sometime and then the soul will cease to exist altogether or at any rate cease to be an individual, *saṁsārin,* the reply is given that the conjunction will last as long as the soul continues to be an individual and its ignorance is not destroyed by the realisation of knowledge. This is evident from the Scriptures. See B.U. IV. 37.

R. and Śrīkaṇṭha hold that because it is seen that all cows are hornless and so on and are called cows since they possess the generic character of cowness, knowledge is an attribute which is met with wherever a self is, there is no objection to the self being designated by that attribute. While Ś. holds that the soul may be called *aṇu* or atomic, since it is connected with the *buddhi* or intellect in the *saṁsāra* condition, R. holds that the soul may be called *vijñāna* or knowledge because the latter constitutes its essential quality as long as it exists.

II. 3. 31. *puṁstvādivat tv asya sato'bhivyakti-yogāt*

As in the case of virility and so on, verily, on account of the manifestation being possible only on its existing potentially.

puṁstvādivat: as in the case of virility, etc.; *tu:* verily; *asya:* its (of the connection with the intellect); *sataḥ:* existing; *abhivyakti-yogāt:* on account of the manifestation being possible.

If the objection is raised that in *suṣupti*, or deep sleep, there is no connection with the intellect (see C.U. VI. 8. 1) and so it is wrong to say that the connection lasts as long as the individualised state exists, the answer is given in this *sūtra* that even in the state of deep sleep the connection exists in a potential form. Were it not so, it could not have become manifest in the awakened state. See B.U. VI. 8. 2 and 3. Virility becomes manifest in youth because it exists in a potential condition in the child.

R. holds that consciousness is always there; only in waking state and dream, it relates itself to object. *jñātṛtvam eva jīvātmanaḥ svarūpam.* To be a knower, subject is the essential character of the self. When it is said that the released self has no consciousness, *saṁjñā* (B.U. II. 4. 12), it only means that it has no consciousness of birth, death and so on, which, in the state of *saṁsāra*, is caused by the connection of the self with the elements.

Bhāskara agrees with Ś. in holding that the soul's connection with intellect exists potentially in the state of deep sleep, etc., and is manifested in the state of waking.

II. 3. 32. *nityopalabdhyanupalabdhiprasaṅgo'nyatara-niyamovānyathā*

Otherwise (i.e. if no intellect existed) there would result either constant perception or (constant) non-perception or else the limitation of the power of either of the two (of the soul or the senses).

nityopalabdhi: constant perception; *anupalabdhi:* (constant) non-perception; *prasaṅgaḥ:* there would result; *anyatara-niyamaḥ:* limitation of the power of either of the two; *vā:* or else; *anyathā:* otherwise.

If the internal organ (*antaḥ-karaṇa*) of which the intellect is a mode is not accepted, then as the senses are always in contact with their objects, there would result the perception of everything as the requisites of the soul, the senses and objects are present. If this is denied, then there can be no knowledge and nothing would ever be known. The opponent will have to accept the limitation of either the soul or the senses. The self is changeless. The power of the senses which is not impeded either in the previous moment or in the subsequent moment cannot be limited in the middle. We have therefore to accept an internal organ through whose connection and disconnection, perception and non-perception result. We find texts which say: 'I am absent-minded. I did not hear it.' B.U. I. 5. 3. So there is an internal organ of which intellect is a mode and it is the connection of the self with this that causes individuation in *saṁsāra*.

R. criticises the view that the self is omnipresent and mere knowledge, for then consciousness and non-consciousness would take place together permanently everywhere or else there would be definite permanent restriction either to permanent consciousness or non-consciousness. This would mean that there would be everywhere and at all times simultaneous consciousness or non-consciousness. If, on the other hand, it were the cause of consciousness only there would never and nowhere be unconsciousness; if it were the cause of non-consciousness there would never and nowhere be consciousness of anything. R. holds that the self abides within bodies only and consciousness takes place there only and nowhere else.

R. criticises the *Vaiśeṣika* view of the self also.

Nimbārka states that on the view of an all-pervasive soul the perception and non-perception, the knowledge and the release of the soul must all become eternal. The soul will be either eternally bound or eternally free; thus there must be a restriction with regard to the one or the other.

Śrīnivāsa following Nimbārka holds that the individual soul is possessed of the attribute of being a knower, is knowledge by nature and atomic in size.

Ś. views *sūtras* 19–28 as the statement of the *pūrva-pakṣa* that the individual soul is atomic in size and holds *sūtra* 29 as the statement of the *siddhānta* that the individual soul is all-pervading but is spoken of as atomic in some scriptural passages because the qualities of the internal organ which is atomic constitute the essence of the individual soul as long as the latter is implicated in *saṁsāra*. R. contends that the *sūtra* 19 states the *siddhānta* view that the soul is of minute size, *sūtras* 20–25 confirm this position and refute objections to it. According to him, *sūtras* 26–29 consider the relation of the soul as knowing agent to knowledge.

Section 14 (33–39)

THE SOUL AS AGENT

II. 3. 33. *kartā śāstrārthavattvāt*

(*The soul is*) *an agent, because of Scripture having a meaning.*
kartā: agent; *śāstrārthavattvāt:* because the Scripture has a meaning.

Scriptural injunctions like 'He is to sacrifice' 'He is to give' will have meaning only if the soul is an agent. If the soul were not an agent, these injunctions would become pointless. R. sets forth the opponent's view that the soul is non-active and only *prakṛti* acts. See *Kaṭha U.* II. 18; B.G. III. 27, XIV. 19, XIII. 20. R. refutes this view by declaring that the soul is an agent, not the *guṇas*. The very term *śāstra* is derived from *śas*, to command, and commanding means impelling to action. *śāsanāc ca śāstram, śāsanaṁ ca pravartanam, śāstrasya ca pravartakatvaṁ bodha-janana-dvāreṇa. Pūrva Mīmāṁsā sūtra* III. 7. 18 declares that the fruit of the injunction belongs to the agent. The texts quoted in support of the opponent's view mean that the activity of the soul is due not to its own nature but to its connection with the *guṇas*. See B.G. XIII. 21; XVIII. 16. Śrīnivāsa quotes 'Only doing works here, let one desire to live a hundred years'. (*Iśa U.* 2.) 'One desiring heaven should perform sacrifices.' (*Taittirīya Saṁhitā* II. 5. 5.) 'One desiring salvation should worship *Brahman*. Let one worship calmly.' (C.U. III. 14. 1.)

Ś. and Bhāskara hold that the soul's state of being an agent is not natural but is due to limiting adjuncts.

II. 3. 34. *vihāropadeśāt*

And on account of the teaching of its moving about.
vihāra: moving about; *upadeśāt:* on account of the teaching.

The texts 'The immortal one goes wherever he likes' (B.U. IV. 3. 12); 'He moves about, according to his pleasure, within his own body' (B.U. II. 1. 18), are considered here to be teaching the moving about of the soul.

All commentators agree on this *sūtra*. Only R. takes this and the next *sūtra* as one by adding a *ca: upādānāt vihāropadeśāc ca.*

II. 3. 35. *upādānāt*

On account of (*its*) *taking* (*the organs*).
upādānāt: on account of taking.

B.U. II. 1. 18 says that the soul in the state of dream takes the organs with it. This shows that the soul is an agent.

II. 3. 36. *vyapadeśāc ca kriyāyāṁ na cen nirdeśa-viparyayaḥ*

(*The soul is an agent*) *also because it is designated as such with regard to*

action; if it were not such, the designation (would have been) of a different character.
vyapadeśāt: because of the designation; *ca:* also; *kriyāyām:* with reference to action; *na cet:* if it were not so; *nirdeśa-viparyayaḥ:* the designation (would have been) of a different character.

If the objection is raised that agency belongs to intelligence or *buddhi* from the texts 'Intelligence performs sacrifices and it also performs all acts' (T.U. II. 5), it is said in reply that intelligence refers to the soul as agent. See B.U. II. 1. 17, where intelligence is said to be the instrument through which the self acts.

Buddhi is the instrument of action according to R. As the word used is *vijñānam* and not *vijñānena,* it refers to the soul as agent.

II. 3. 37. *upalabdhivad aniyamaḥ*

The absence of restriction is as in the case of perception.
upalabdhivat: as in the case of perception; *aniyamaḥ:* there is no restriction.

If it is argued that if the soul is the agent apart from *buddhi,* it would, being independent, bring about what is pleasant and useful and not the opposite, the *sūtra* states in reply that there is no such restriction. As the soul perceives what is agreeable and disagreeable, so it can bring about what is pleasant and unpleasant. If it be said that in the act of perception there are causes of perception, that does not invalidate the view that the perceiver is the soul. In action also, the soul is not absolutely free since it depends on differences of place, time and efficient causes but the agent does not cease to be agent because he requires assistance. A cook remains the agent in the action of cooking, though he requires fuel, water and so on.

R., Śrīkaṇṭha, Baladeva interpret the *sūtra* differently. If *prakṛti* were the agent and not the soul, then there would be non-restriction of actions as in the case of perception. Just as it is shown that, if the soul be all-pervading, no definite perception will be possible, so also if *prakṛti* be the agent, no definite activity will be possible; for if *prakṛti* be all-pervading and common to all, all activities would produce results in the case of all souls or produce no results in the case of any soul. For if each soul is held to be omnipresent, they are all of them in equal proximity to all parts of *prakṛti.* We cannot say that the distribution of results will depend on different internal organs for the omnipresent souls cannot be exclusively connected with any particular internal organ.

II. 3. 38. *śakti viparyayāt*

On account of the reversal of power.
śakti: power; *viparyayāt:* on account of reversal.

If intellect or *buddhi,* which is an instrument, becomes the agent and ceases to function as an instrument, then we will have to devise something else as an instrument. The dispute concerns only terms for we need an agent different from the instrument.

R. points out that, if the internal organ were the agent, it would also be the enjoyer. Then there would no longer be any proof for the existence of the self but the texts teach that the person, the soul exists on account of the fact of enjoyment. *puruṣo'sti bhoktṛ-bhāvāt. Sāṁkhya Kārikā* 17.

II. 3. 39. *samādhyabhāvāc ca*

And on account of the impossibility of deep concentration.

samādhi: deep concentration; *abhāvāt:* on account of impossibility; *ca:* and.

We are asked to realise the Self: B.U. II. 4. 5; C.U. VIII. 7. 1; M.U. II. 2. 6. If the soul were not the agent, it would be incapable of activities like 'hearing, reflecting and meditating' which lead to *samādhi* or self-realisation. Then there would be no liberation for the soul. It is therefore clear that the soul alone is the agent and not the intellect.

R. points out that in the final state of meditation called *samādhi*, the meditator realises his difference from *prakṛti* of which the internal organ is a modification. So the self is different from the intellect.

Section 15 (40)

THE SOUL IS AN AGENT WHEN CONNECTED WITH THE ADJUNCTS

II. 3. 40. *yathā ca takṣobhayathā*

And like a carpenter, in both ways.

yathā: like; *ca:* and; *takṣā:* carpenter; *ubhayathā:* in both ways.

The soul's agency is established in the previous *sūtras*. The question is raised whether the agency represents the real nature of the Self or is only a superimposition. The *Nyāya* school holds that it is its real nature. The *Upaniṣads* declare that the Self is non-attached. B.U. IV. 3. 7, 15; *Kaṭha U.* I. 3. 4. The reconciliation is effected by the example of the carpenter. The soul is an agent when connected with the instruments of action, *buddhi*, etc., and ceases to be so when dissociated from them even as a carpenter works so long as he wields his instruments and rests when he lays them aside. The Self is active in waking- and dream-states and is blissful when it ceases to be an agent as in deep sleep. The Self's true nature is inactive but it becomes active when it is connected with its *upādhis* or adjuncts.

R. holds that activity is an essential attribute of the soul but from this it does not follow that the soul is always actually active. A carpenter, for example, though furnished with the requisite instruments, may either work or not work as he chooses. If the internal organ, on the contrary, were essentially active, it would be acting constantly since as a non-sentient being it could not be influenced by particular reasons for action, such as the desire for enjoyment.

Nimbārka holds that the soul acts or does not act according to its own wish. Śrīnivāsa adds that acting or refraining from action is not possible on the part of *buddhi* which is an instrument like the axe, by reason of its non-sentience. On account of the constancy of its proximity to a sentient being and the absence of any desire on its part, being non-sentient, we will have either perpetual activity or perpetual non-activity.

Baladeva points out that the carpenter is an individual agent when he acts through his instruments and a direct agent when he is handling the instruments. So also the soul is an indirect agent through its sense-organs and a direct agent in the act of controlling these sense-organs.

Section 16 (41–42)

THE SOUL'S DEPENDENCE ON THE LORD

II. 3. 41. *parāt tu tac-chruteḥ*

But that (*agency of the soul*) *is* (*derived*) *from the Supreme Lord so Scripture* (*teaches*).

parāt: from the Supreme Lord; *tu:* but; *tat:* that (agency); *śruteḥ:* Scripture (teaches).

The texts considered are K.U. III. 8. 'This one, truly, indeed causes him whom he wishes to lead up from these worlds to perform good actions. This one, indeed, also causes him whom he wishes to lead downward, to perform bad actions.' *Śatapatha Brāhmaṇa* XIV. 6. 7. 30. 'He who dwelling within the self pulls the self within', *ya ātmani tiṣṭhann ātmānam antaro yamayatīti.*

The soul in the state of *saṁsāra* when it appears as agent and enjoyer is brought about through the permission of the Lord who is the Highest Self, the supervisor of all actions, the witness residing in all beings, the cause of all intelligence. We must assume therefore that final release is effected through knowledge caused by the grace of the Lord.[1]

R. supports the view by quotations from the B.G. XV. 15; XVIII. 61.

Nimbārka uses *Taittirīya Āraṇyaka* III. 11. 1. 2 to support the

[1] *avidyāvasthāyām kārya-karaṇa-saṁghāto'vivekadarśino jīvasyāvidyātimirāndhasya sataḥ parasmād ātmanaḥ karmādhyakṣāt sarvabhūtādivāsāt sākṣiṇaś cetayitur īśvarāt tad-anujñayā kartṛtva-bhoktṛtva-lakṣaṇasya saṁsārasya siddhis tad-anugraha-hetukenaiva ca vijñānena mokṣa-siddhir bhavitum arhati. Ś.*

view that the individual soul is not an agent independently. His agency is subject to the control of the Supreme Lord.

II. 3. 42. *kṛta-prayatnāpekṣas tu vihita-pratiṣiddhāvaiyyarthādibhyaḥ*

But (the Lord's making the soul act) is dependent on the efforts made (by it); only thus will the injunctions and prohibitions, etc., be meaningful. *kṛta-prayatna-apekṣaḥ:* is dependent on the efforts made; *tu:* but; *vihita-pratiṣiddha-avaiyyarthādibhyaḥ:* on account of the meaningfulness of injunctions, prohibitions, etc.

This *sūtra* refutes the objection that the Lord must be cruel and whimsical since he makes some do good actions and others evil actions. The Lord directs the soul taking into account previous good and bad deeds. The Lord is a mere occasional cause, in allotting to the souls unequal results. The analogy of rain is used. The rain constitutes the common occasional cause for shrubs, bushes, corn, etc., which belong to different species and spring each from its particular seed, for the inequality of sap, flowers, fruits and leaves results neither when the rain is absent nor when the special seeds are absent; so the Lord arranges favourable or unfavourable conditions for the souls taking into account their previous efforts. Since *saṁsāra* is beginningless and endless, the objection of infinite regress cannot be raised.

R. cites B.G. X. 8, 10, 11; XVI. 8–19.

While in II. 1. 33, it is shown that the Lord is not partial as a *creator*, here it is shown that he is not partial as an *instigator*. So the Lord cannot be accused of cruelty or partiality. Only thus will injunctions and prohibitions have a meaning. This does not take away from the independence of the Lord, even as a king who rewards or punishes his subjects according to their deeds does not lose his independence.

Section 17 (43–53)

THE RELATION OF THE INDIVIDUAL SOUL TO *BRAHMAN*

II. 3. 43. *aṁśo nānā-vyapadeśād anyathā cāpi dāśakitavāditvam adhīyata eke*

(The soul is) a part (of the Lord) on account of the declaration of difference and otherwise also; for in some (rescensions of the Vedas) (it) is spoken of as being (of the nature of) slaves, fishermen, etc. *aṁśaḥ:* part; *nānā-vyapadeśāt:* on account of the declaration of difference; *anyathā:* otherwise; *ca:* and; *api:* also; *dāśa-kitavāditvam:* being of the nature of slaves, fishermen, etc.

In the previous section, it has been said that the Lord controls the soul. Here the question is raised about the relation of the individual soul to *Brahman*. Is the relation between the two one of master and servant or fire and its sparks? This *sūtra* suggests that the soul is a part of *Brahman* as the spark is a part of fire. As *Brahman* does not consist of parts, the soul can only be an imagined part, 'a part as it were'. We do not view the Lord as identical with the soul because of the declaration of difference. See C.U. VIII. 7; B.U. IV. 4. 22. There are also passages which teach the non-difference of the Lord and the soul. Ś.U. IV. 3; *Taittirīya Āraṇyaka* III. 12. 7. There is a certain passage of the *Atharva Veda* which asserts that '*Brahman* are the fishermen, *Brahman* the slaves, *Brahman* these gamblers, etc.' '*brahmadāśā brahmadāsā brahmaiveme kitavāḥ*.' Since there are statements of difference and non-difference, the soul is said to be a part of the Lord.

R. holds that the souls are in reality parts of *Brahman* and not merely in appearance as Ś. suggests by the phrase '*aṁśa iva*'. He refutes the other views of absolute difference, absolute non-difference and imaginary difference due to limiting adjuncts.

Nimbārka and Śrīnivāsa argue that the individual soul is neither absolutely different from the Highest Person nor absolutely non-different from him but is a part of the Highest Self. Part does not mean a portion that can be cut off for that would contradict texts like 'without part'. Ś.U. VI. 19. The individual soul is by nature different from the Supreme Person predicated to be the whole and yet non-different from him as its existence and activity are under the control of the whole.

Śrīkaṇṭha says, if it is declared of the class of intelligent beings that it is an *aṁśa* or fragment of *Brahman*, as a particular mode of what is qualified, being of the same nature as inseparable attributes like light, etc., it may be true of the class of non-intelligent beings as well.

II. 3. 45. *api ca smaryate*

And it is also stated in smṛti.

api: also; *ca:* and; *smaryate:* is stated in the *smṛti*.

The text here is B.G. XV. 7. 'A fragment of my own self (*mamaivāṁśaḥ*), having become a living soul, eternal, in the world of life, draws to itself the senses of which the mind is the sixth, that rest in nature.'

R. omits the *ca*.

II. 3. 46. *prakāśādivan naivaṁ paraḥ*

The Highest Lord is not (affected by pleasure and pain) like this (the individual soul), even as light, etc. (are not affected by the shape of the things they touch).

prakāśādivat: like light, etc.; *na:* is not; *evam:* like this; *paraḥ:* the Highest.

O

The objection that, if the soul is a part of *Brahman*, the imperfections of the soul affect *Brahman* also is answered in this *sūtra*. As the all-pervading sun looks straight or bent when it comes into contact with particular objects or as the ether enclosed in a jar seems to move when the jar is moved or as the sun appears to shake when the water in which it is reflected shakes but in reality none of these undergoes these changes, so also the Supreme is not affected by pleasure and pain which are experienced by the individual soul which is a product of ignorance and is limited by adjuncts of *buddhi*, etc.

R. makes out that the individual soul is a *viśeṣaṇa* of the Highest Self, standing to it in the relation of part to whole. The Highest Self is not of the same nature as the individual soul. As the luminous body is of a nature different from that of its light, so the Highest Self differs from the individual soul which is a part of it. As the attribute and the substratum are not identical, the soul and *Brahman* are not the same.

Śrīkaṇṭha develops here his distinctive *viśiṣṭādvaita*.

Baladeva begins here a new section dealing with the queston of the Lord's incarnations. Supreme (incarnations are) not so, (i.e. parts of the Lord as the individual souls are) as in the case of light. Though incarnations and individual souls are both parts of the Lord, the word *aṁśa* has a different meaning when applied to the incarnations. They represent the entire Lord.

II. 3. 47. *smaranti ca*

And the smṛtis state.

smaranti: the *smṛtis* state*: ca:* and.

The texts M.U. III. 1. 1; *Kaṭha U.* II. 5. 11 state the difference. 'It is not stained by the fruits of actions any more than a lotus leaf by water.' *na lipyate phalaiś cāpi padma-patram ivāmbhasā.* M.B. XII. 13754.

R. and Śrīkaṇṭha quote other texts to show that the soul is an attribute of the Lord.

Baladeva uses other texts to show that incarnations are not parts of the Lord in the same sense in which the individual souls are.

II. 3. 48. *anujñā-parihārau deha-sambandhāj jyotirādivat*

Injunctions and prohibitions (are possible) on account of the connection (of the soul) with the body, as in the case of light, etc.

anujñā-parihārau: injunctions and prohibitions; *deha-sambandhāt:* on account of the connection with the body; *jyotir-ādivat:* like light, etc.

Permissions and prohibitions are possible, because the Self, though one, is connected with various bodies. The connection, however, originates in the erroneous notion that the Self is the aggregate of the body and so on. When the error is removed and knowledge obtained, there are no obligations. Fundamentally all obligation is an erroneous imagination existing in the case of him only who does not see that his Self is no more connected with a body than the ether is with jars and the like. The illustration of light is given to show that, though light is one only, we shun the light which shines on unholy places and not that which falls on pure ground. Some things consisting of earth are desired like diamonds and beryls; others like dead bodies are shunned.

While Ś. develops his doctrine of *adhyāsa*, Bhāskara speaks of his doctrine of *upādhi*.

R. holds that though all souls are essentially of the same nature as parts of *Brahman*, permissions and exclusions are possible for the reason that each individual soul is joined to some particular body, pure or impure.

Baladeva continues his view of the distinction between incarnations and ordinary individuals. While the individual soul, though a part of the Lord, is connected with ignorance and a body and is as such under the control of the Lord for its activity and inactivity, incarnation, though a part of the Lord, is not under his control. The eye or the power of vision though a part of the sun depends on the permission and presence of the sun for its activity or otherwise, while a ray of the sun, though a part of the sun, is identical with it and does not depend on the permission of the sun.

II. 3. 49. *asantateś cāvyatikaraḥ*

And on account of the non-extension (of the individual soul beyond its own body) there is no confusion (of the results of actions).
asantateḥ: non-extension (beyond its own body); *ca*: and; *avyatikaraḥ*: no confusion (of results of actions).

If it is argued that on account of the unity of the Self, there would result a confusion of the results of actions, since everyone would get the results of actions of everyone else, it is said in reply that the individual soul is connected only with a particular body, mind, etc. Since the individual souls are thus different from each other there is no possibility of confusion.

R. understands *avyatikaraḥ* to mean absence of confusion.

There is no mixing up of the accumulated merit and demerit of various souls since they are distinct, are of atomic size and reside in separate bodies. R. suggests that the other views of the soul being *Brahman* deluded or *Brahman* affected by a limiting adjunct are incapable of explaining how the experiences of the different selves are not mixed up.[1]

Nimbārka says that the individual souls are parts of the all-pervasive being and are themselves all-pervasive by reason of the attribute of knowledge, yet they, being atomic in size, are not all-pervasive and so there is no confusion among their actions.

[1] *bhrānta-brahma-jīva-vāde copahita-brahma-jīva-vāde ca jīvaparayor jīvānāṁ ca bhogavyatikarādayaḥ sarve doṣāḥ santi.*

Baladeva argues that the soul is atomic and not full and perfect like an incarnation and so is different from him.

Śrīkaṇṭha reads *avyatirekaḥ* for *avyatikaraḥ*. Though the souls are distinct, their experiences are similar. The experiences, though similar, are not mixed up.

II. 3. 50. *ābhāsa eva ca*

And (the individual soul is) only a reflection (of the Supreme Lord).
ābhāsaḥ: a reflection; *eva:* only; *ca:* and.

The individual soul is a mere reflection of the Highest Self analogous to the reflection of the sun in the water. It is neither directly the Highest Self nor a different thing. Even when one reflected image of the sun trembles, another reflected image does not on that account tremble also, so when one soul is connected with actions and results of actions, another soul is not on that account connected likewise. There is therefore no confusion of actions and results.

Ś. here criticises the *Sāṁkhya* and the *Vaiśeṣika* theories of the self.

This *sūtra* is taken by the *Advaita Vedāntins* as a statement of *pratibimba-vāda*, that the individual soul is but the reflection of the Self in *buddhi* as distinct from the *avaccheda-vāda* or the view that the soul is the Highest Self in so far as it is limited by its adjuncts.

Bhāskara reads *vā* in place of *ca* and criticises Ś.'s view.

R. interprets *ābhāsa* as *hetvābhāsa*, a fallacious argument, and makes out that the view that the soul is *Brahman* in so far as it is limited by non-real adjuncts is an erroneous argument. R. points out that the obscuration of the light of that which is nothing but light means destruction of that light. *prakāśaika-svarūpasya prakāśa-tirodhānam prakāśa-nāśa eva.* If difference is due to *upādhis*, which are the products of *avidyā*, then the spheres of experience are bound to be mixed up as the thing with which all the limiting adjuncts connect themselves is one only: *avidyā-parikalpitopādhi-bhede hi sarvopādhibhir-upahita-svarūpasyaikatvābhyupagamād bhoga-vyatikaras tad-avastha eva.*

Śrīkaṇṭha follows R. in criticising the reflection theory.

Nimbārka and Śrīnivāsa read *ābhāsāḥ* and make out that the arguments of *Sāṁkhya* and *Vaiśeṣika* are fallacious.

Baladeva makes out that the equation of the individual soul with the incarnation is fallacious since it involves the fallacy of undistributed middle. Simply because soul and incarnation are both parts of the Lord we cannot equate the two.

II. 3. 51. *adṛṣṭāniyamāt*

On account of the unseen principle being non-restrictive.
adṛṣṭa: the unseen principle; *aniyamāt:* on account of being non-restrictive.

Adṛṣṭa is the unseen principle of the nature ot religious merit or demerit. According to the *Sāṁkhya* system it inheres not in the self but in *pradhāna*. As the latter is the same for all souls, it cannot determine the enjoyment of pleasure and pain for each individual self. According to the *Vaiśeṣika*, the unseen principle is created by the conjunction of the soul with the mind and there is no reason why any particular *adṛṣṭa* should belong to any particular soul. So confusion of results is inescapable.

R. holds that the attempt to explain different spheres of experience as traceable to beginningless *adṛṣṭas* which are the cause of the limiting adjuncts is futile as the *adṛṣṭas* have for their substrate *Brahman* itself and there is no reason for their definite allotment to particular souls and so there can be no definite separation of spheres of experience. The limiting adjuncts as well as the *adṛṣtas* cannot by their connection with *Brahman* split up *Brahman* itself which is one in reality.

Baladeva begins a new section here stating the mutual differences among the individual souls.

II. 3. 52. *abhisandhyādiṣv api caivam*

And it is so even with regard to resolves, etc.
abhisandhyādiṣu: in regard to resolves, etc.; *api:* even; *ca:* and; *evam:* it is so.

The same objection applies to resolves, etc., for these are formed by the conjunction of the soul and the mind.

Baladeva says that the individual souls are different even with regard to their resolves and the rest.

II. 3. 53. *pradeśād iti cen nāntar-bhāvāt*

If it be said that (the distinction of experiences results) from (the difference of) place, (we say) not so, on account (of the self) being within all (bodies).
pradeśāt: from (difference of) place; *iti cet:* if it be said; *na:* not so; *antar-bhāvāt:* on account of the Self being in all bodies.

If it be said, as the *Nyāya* does, that though each soul is all-pervading, yet if we take its connection with the mind to take place in that part of it which is limited by its body, then a confusion will not result, this is not tenable for since every soul is all-pervading and therefore permeates all bodies, there is nothing to determine that a particular body belongs to a particular soul. Again, there cannot be more than one all-pervading entity. If there were, they would limit each other and so cease to be all-pervading or infinite. There is only one Self and not many. The plurality of selves is a product of ignorance. It is not a reality.

R. takes up the *prima facie* view, that though *Brahman* is one only and cannot be split up by the several limiting adjuncts with which it is connected, still the separation of the spheres of every enjoyment is not impossible since the places of *Brahman* which are connected with the *upādhis* are distinct. R. answers this objection by saying that as the *upādhis* move here and there and so all places enter into connection with all *upādhis*, the mixing up of spheres of enjoyment cannot be avoided. Even if *upādhis* were connected with different places, the pain connected with some particular place would affect the whole of *Brahman* which is one only.

Nimbārka and Śrīnivāsa commenting on this *sūtra* hold that the individual soul is a part of *Brahman*, atomic in size, knowledge by nature, and is possessed of the attributes of being an agent, a knower and so on and is different in every body.

For Baladeva, *adṛṣṭa* or the unseen principle is the cause of the differences among the souls.

Section 1 (1–4)

THE ORIGIN OF THE SENSE-ORGANS

II. 4. 1. *tathā prāṇāḥ*

Likewise the vital breaths.
tathā: likewise; *prāṇāḥ:* the vital breaths.

While many scriptural passages (C.U. VI. 2. 3; T.U. II. 1) speak of the origin of things, it is mentioned in some texts that the vital breaths are not produced. *Śatapatha Brāhmaṇa* VI. 1. 1. 1 states that the vital breaths existed before the origin of things. There are other passages where we read of the origin of vital breaths: B.U. II. 1. 20; M.U. II. 1. 3 and 8; *Praśna U.* VI. 4. There is thus uncertainty. The *sūtra* holds that the vital breaths spring from *Brahman*. In support of it are many texts: B.U. II. 1. 20; M.U. II. 1. 3. So the vital breaths are created. The word 'likewise' refers not to the immediately preceding topic of the last part, i.e: the plurality of souls, but to the creation of *ākāśa*, etc., spoken of earlier. In *Pūrva Mīmāṁsā* III. 4. 32 the word *'tadvat'*, 'in the same manner', refers not to the immediately preceding sections but to an earlier one, III. 4. 28.

Śrīkaṇṭha takes this *sūtra* as setting down the *prima facie* view that (as the individual soul is eternal) so are the vital breaths.

II. 4. 2. *gauṇyasambhavāt*

On account of the impossibility (*of explaining the origination*) *in a secondary sense.*
gauṇī: secondary sense; *asambhavāt:* on account of impossibility.

To take the texts in a secondary sense would lead to the abandonment of the general assertion, 'By the knowledge of one, everything else is known': M.U. I. 1. 3. The reference to the existence of the vital breaths before creation in *Śatapatha Brāhmaṇa* is in regard to *Hiraṇya-garbha* who is not resolved in the partial dissolution of the world, though all other effects are resolved. In complete dissolution, even *Hiraṇya-garbha* is resolved.

R. takes this and the next *sūtra* as one and makes out that the plural number in the text is secondary because of impossibility, i.e. prior to creation *Brahman* alone exists.

Śrīkaṇṭha follows R., takes this and the next *sūtra* as forming one and holds that it answers the *prima facie* view.

II. 4. 3. *tat prāk śruteś ca*

And on account of that (*word which indicates origin*) *being mentioned first* (*in connection with the vital breaths*).
tat: that; *prāk:* first; *śruteḥ:* being mentioned; *ca:* and.

M.U. 1. 3 says: 'from him are born vital breaths, mind and all the organs, ether, air, water, fire and earth'. The word 'born' occurs at the very beginning; if it is interpreted in the primary sense with respect to ether, etc., it should be so interpreted with regard to vital breath, mind and organs mentioned earlier.

II. 4. 4. *tat-pūrvakatvād vācaḥ*

Because the organ of speech is preceded by that (*i.e. fire and the other elements*).

tat-pūrvakatvāt: because of being preceded by that; *vācaḥ:* of the organ of speech.

C.U. VI. 5. 4 shows that the organs are the products of the elements, which, in their turn, arise from *Brahman*. So they also are the products of *Brahman*.

R. holds that *prāṇa* stands not for the sense-organs but for *Brahman*. For him the *sūtra* is 'Because of speech [names of objects] being preceded by that [the existence of the objects]'. Names of objects presuppose the existence of objects. But prior to creation there were no objects and so no speech or organs of speech.

Śrīkaṇṭha and Baladeva follow R.'s interpretation.

Section 2 (5–6)

THE NUMBER OF THE ORGANS

II. 4. 5. *saptagater viśeṣitatvāc ca*

(*The organs are*) *seven* (*in number*) *because it is so known* (*from the Scriptures*).

sapta: seven; *gateḥ:* because it is so known. *viśeṣitatvāt:* on account of the specification; *ca:* and.

There are texts which declare that there are seven organs: 'The seven life-breaths spring from it' (M.U. II. 1. 8) and the specification in the text 'Seven indeed are life-breaths in the head'. (*Taittirīya Saṁhitā* V. 1. 7. 1.) There are other texts which mention eight (B.U. III. 2. 1), ten (*Taittirīya Saṁhitā* V. 3. 2. 3), eleven (B.U. III. 9. 4), twelve (B.U. II. 4. 11), thirteen (*Praśna U.* IV. 8). The opponent argues that the number is seven and the statements of other numbers refer to difference of modifications. R. states the *pūrva-pakṣa* as mentioning seven organs only, the others being organs only in a metaphorical sense since they assist the soul.

II. 4. 6. *hastādayas tu sthite'to naivam*

But the hands, etc. (*are also mentioned as sense-organs in scriptural texts*). *This being so, it is not like this* (*i.e. they are not merely seven in number*).

hastādayaḥ: hands, etc.; *tu:* but; *sthite:* being so; *ataḥ:* therefore; *na:* not; *evam:* like this.

'But' refutes the view of the previous *sūtra*. The number is said to be eleven consisting of the five organs of knowledge, the five organs of action and the inner organ. *Manas* or mind, *buddhi* or understanding, *ahaṁ-kāra* or self-sense and *citta* or consciousness are all modifications of the internal organ. *etat sarvam mana eva*. All this is mind only. They are not separate organs and do not raise the number beyond eleven.

R. says that the organs are not seven only but eleven since the hands and the rest also contribute towards the experience and fruition of that which abides in the body (i.e. the soul) and have their separate functions, such as seizing and so on. While these are to be added to the seven organs, *buddhi*, etc., need not be added since they are only different names of mind when it is functioning in different ways. The number eleven is confirmed by scriptural texts. B.U. II. 4. 11; B.G. XIII. 5.

Sthite in R. means 'because of abiding [in the body and assisting the soul]'.

Section 3 (7)

THE ORGANS ARE MINUTE IN SIZE

II. 4. 7. *aṇavaś ca*

And (they are) minute.

aṇavaḥ: minute; *ca:* and.

The organs are minute, subtle and so are not seen. If they were all-pervading, then the texts which speak of going out of the body, etc., would become self-contradictory. Again, since we do not perceive through the senses what is happening throughout the universe, which would be the case if they were all-pervading, they are said to be subtle and limited in size. R. mentions B.U. I. 5. 13, 'These are all alike, all infinite', and argues that infinity refers to the abundance of activities of the life-breath which is to be meditated on.

Section 4 (8)

THE CHIEF VITAL BREATH IS PRODUCED FROM *BRAHMAN*

II. 4. 8. *śreṣṭhaś ca*

And the chief (vital breath).

śreṣṭhaḥ: the chief (vital breath); *ca:* and.

The text considered is C.U. V. 1. 1. 'The vital breath is, indeed, the oldest and the best.' It is the chief because we will not be able to live without it. (B.U. VI. 1. 13.) *Ṛg Veda* X. 129. 2 says: 'By its own law it was moving without air.' This suggests the doubt that before creation there was the vital breath. That doubt is removed by this *sūtra*. As the words 'was moving' are qualified by 'without air', they do not indicate that the vital breath existed before creation. M.U. II. 1. 3 says 'From this [the Self] is produced the vital breath'.

R. points out that the words 'the one was moving without air' do not refer to the vital breath of living creatures but intimate the existence of the Highest *Brahman*, alone by itself.

Section 5 (9–12)

THE CHIEF VITAL BREATH IS DIFFERENT FROM AIR AND THE SENSE FUNCTIONS

II. 4. 9. *na vāyukriye pṛthag-upadeśāt*

(*The chief vital breath*) *is neither air nor function* (*of the organs*) *on account of its being mentioned separately.*

na: not; *vāyu-kriye:* air or function; *pṛthak:* separately; *upadeśāt:* on account of being mentioned.

The objection is raised that there is no separate principle called *prāṇa* or vital breath. It is just air which exists in the mouth as well as outside. There are texts which make out that *prāṇa* is *vāyu*. Ś. refers to the other view that 'the five breaths, *prāṇa*, are the common function of the other instruments'. The reference is to the *Sāṁkhya Sūtra* II. 31; *sāmānya-karaṇa-vṛttiḥ*. While Ś. understands by *karaṇa* the eleven organs, the *Sāṁkhya* commentator gives another interpretation. *sādhāraṇī karaṇasya antaḥ-karaṇa-trayasya vṛttiḥ pariṇāma-bheda iti.*

The *sūtra* points out that *prāṇa* is neither air nor function as many scriptural texts distinguish *prāṇa* from air and function. See M.U. II. 1. 3; if it is said that as eleven birds shut up in one cage may, although each makes a separate effort, move the cage by the combination of their efforts, even so the functions which abide in one body may, although each has its own special function, by the combination of these functions produce one common function called *prāṇa*, this argument is untenable for we see that the birds by their combined efforts move the cage but we do not see that the different functions in the body produce the function of vital breath. The functions of the organs are not of the same character; they are of a distinct nature from that of the vital breath. So it is different from all functions and air.

II. 4. 10. *cakṣurādivat tu tat-saha-śiṣṭyādibhyaḥ*

But (the life-breath is subordinate to the soul) like the eye, etc., on account of its being taught with them and other reasons.
cakṣurādivat: like eyes, etc.; *tu:* but; *tat-saha-śiṣṭyādibhyaḥ:* on account of its being taught with them and other reasons.

In the *Upaniṣads* C.U. I. 2. 7; B.U. I. 5. 21, the vital breath is mentioned along with the sense-organs. They are grouped together since they are all subordinate to the soul. The other reasons mentioned in the *sūtra* are that they are made up of parts, are non-conscious, etc. The vital breath is under the control of the individual soul and is serviceable to it like the eyes.

II. 4. 11. *akaraṇatvāc ca na doṣas tathā hi darśayati*

And on account of its not being an instrument, the objection is not (valid); for thus (Scripture) shows.
akaraṇatvāt: on account of not being an instrument; *ca:* and; *na:* not; *doṣaḥ:* fault or objection; *tathā hi:* because thus; *darśayati:* (*śruti*) shows.

If the vital breath is an instrument of the soul like the eye and other organs, then there must be some special form of activity by which it assists the soul but no such activity is perceived. To this objection, the present *sūtra* gives an answer. It is not an instrument or organ like the eye, for which a separate sense-object is necessary; yet it has a function in the body, viz. the maintenance of the body, *śarīra-rakṣā*. See B.U. IV. 3. 12, I. 3. 18, 19; *Praśna U.* II. 3.

R. quotes C.U. V. 1. 7ff. where, on the successive departure of speech and so on, the body and the other organs maintain their strength, while on the departure of the vital breath the body and all the organs become weak and powerless. So the vital breath serves the purpose of the individual soul.

II. 4. 12. *pañcavṛttir manovad vyapadiśyate*

It is taught as having a fivefold function like the mind.
pañcavṛttiḥ: (having) fivefold function; *manovat:* like the mind; *vyapadiśyate:* is taught.

It has five functions, *prāṇa, apāna, vyāna, udāna, samāna:* breathing in, breathing out, holding in so as to aid works requiring strength, the ascending when the soul passes out of the body, and the function which carries the nutriment through all the limbs of the body.

R. mentions B.U. I. 5. 3, for the five functions of the air.

Section 6 (13)

THE MINUTENESS OF THE VITAL BREATH

II. 4. 13. *aṇuś ca*

And (*it is*) *minute* (*or atomic*).
aṇuḥ: minute; *ca:* and.

It is minute, limited and subtle like the senses. If the objection is raised that in B.U. I. 3. 22, it is said to be all-pervading, the answer is given that the reference there is to *Hiraṇya-garbha,* the cosmic soul. So far as the individual soul is concerned, it is limited.

Śrīnivāsa mentions *Praśna U.* II. 6.

Section 7 (14–16)

II. 4. 14. *jyotirādy adhiṣṭhānaṁ tu tad-āmananāt*

But the guidance by fire, etc., on account of the declaration of that.
jyotir-ādi-adhiṣṭhānam: guidance (or control) by fire and the rest; *tu:* but; *tat-āmananāt:* on account of the declaration of that.

The question is raised about the dependence or independence of the vital breath and the other organs. They are said to be controlled by gods like fire, etc. See *Aitareya Āraṇyaka* II. 4. 2. 4. Fire, having become speech, entered the mouth, *agnir vāg bhūtvā mukham prāviśat.* They cannot move of themselves and are dependent on presiding deities. See also C.U. IV. 18. 3; B.U. I. 3. 12.

R. and Śrīkaṇṭha read this and the next *sūtra* as one and argue that the fire god and the rest as well as the individual soul rule over the sense-organs but their rule depends on the mind and will of the Lord.

R. quotes B.U. II. 1. 18, III. 7. 8. 9; T.U. II. 8 and argues that the sense-organs together with their guiding divinities and the individual soul depend in all their doings on the thought of the Highest Person. *indriyāṇāṁ sābhimāni-devatānāṁ jīvātmanaś ca sva-kāryeṣu parama-puruṣa-mananāyattatva-śāstrāt.*

Baladeva makes out that the Lord is the primary initiator of the sense-organs while the fire god and the rest as well as the individual soul are secondary initiators.

II. 4. 15. *prāṇavatā śabdāt*

(*It is not so since the breaths are connected*) *with the possessor of the vital breath* (*viz. the individual soul as we know*) *from the Scripture.*
prāṇavatā: one possessing the breaths (the organs); *śabdāt:* from the Scripture.

The gods are not the enjoyers. The soul is the enjoyer in the body.

The Scriptures declare that the relation between the soul and the organs is that of master and servant. See C.U. VIII. 12. 4. Though there are many gods in the body each presiding over a particular organ, there is only one enjoyer. Otherwise we will not be able to account for the memory of the past. *Ratnaprabhā* says, *kiñca yo'ham rūpam adrākṣaṁ sa evāhaṁ śṛṇomīti pratisandhānād ekaś śārīra eva bhoktā na bahavo devāḥ.*

II. 4. 16. *tasya ca nityatvāt*

And on account of the permanence of that (i.e. the embodied soul).
tasya: of that; *ca:* and; *nityatvāt:* on account of permanence.

The soul abides permanently in the body as the experiencer of pleasure and pain and the results of good and evil actions. It is not reasonable to suggest that in the body which is the result of the soul's actions, others like gods enjoy. See B.U. 1. 5. 20 where it is said that evil does not approach the gods. The soul is the enjoyer. See B.U. IV. 4. 2.

R. says that as the quality inhering in all things, of being ruled by the Highest Self, is eternal, it follows that the rule of the soul and the divinities over the organs depends on the will of the Highest Self. See T.U. II. 6. 'Having created it, into it, indeed, he entered.' The Highest Person has entered into all things to be their ruler. See also B.G. X. 42.

Baladeva makes out that the relationship between the Highest Lord and the divinities is eternal, so the divinities rule the sense-organs through the mere will of the Lord.

Section 8 (17–19)

THE ORGANS ARE INDEPENDENT PRINCIPLES AND NOT MODIFICATIONS OF THE CHIEF BREATH

II. 4. 17. *ta indriyāṇi tad-vyapadeśād anyatra śreṣṭhāt*

They (the breaths) are senses on account of their being so designated except the chief.
te: they; *indriyāṇi:* organs; *tad-vyapadeśāt:* on account of being so designated; *anyatra:* except; *śreṣṭhāt:* the chief.

The opponent quotes B.U. I. 5. 21 and argues that the different organs are modes of the vital breath. The *sūtra* says that they are independent since they are separately mentioned. M.U. II. 1. 3. The life-breath is not generally treated as a sense-organ. This difference of designation is appropriate only if there is a difference of being. If there were unity of being, it would be contradictory that the life principle should sometimes be designated as sense-organ and sometimes not. So the other life-breaths are different in being from the chief vital breath.

R. quotes B.G. XIII. 5 and argues that the chief vital breath is not designated as an organ.

Śrīnivāsa points out that B. U.I. 5. 21, 'Let us all assume his form', means that the activities of the sense-organs are under the control of the vital breath and so are said to be vital breaths; even as C.U. III. 14. 1, 'All this is, verily, *Brahman*', means that all this is under the control of the Supreme.

II. 4. 18. *bheda śruteḥ*

On account of scriptural texts regarding difference.
bheda: difference; *śruteḥ:* on account of scriptural texts.

In B.U. I. 3. 2 and I. 5. 3 the organs are treated in one section and the vital breath in another. This shows that they do not belong to the same class. The organs are independent principles and not modes of the vital breath.

R. and Nimbārka treat this and the next *sūtra* as one.

R. says that M.U. II. 1. 3 mentions the vital breath separately from the organs and so it is not one of the organs. We also observe that it is different from the organs of sight, etc. In the state of deep sleep, the activity of breath is noticed while that of sight, etc., is not. While the organs serve as instruments of cognition and action, the work of breath serves to maintain the body and the organs. Since the subsistence of the organs depends on breath, the organs themselves are said to be forms of breath. See B.U. I. 5. 21. When it is said that they become its form it means that they become its body, and that their activity depends on it.

II. 4. 19. *vailakṣaṇyāc ca*

And on account of characteristic differences.
vailakṣaṇyāt: on account of characteristic differences; *ca:* and.

Ś. points out certain differences. The organs do not function in deep sleep while the vital breath does. The organs get tired but not the vital breath. The loss of organs does not affect life but the passing out of the vital breath ends in the death of the body. The passage that the organs assumed the form of the vital breath means that the organs depend on the vital breath even as the servants on the master. The vital breath is the leader of the organs.

Section 9 (20–22)

THE EVOLUTION OF NAMES AND FORMS IS THE WORK OF THE SUPREME LORD, AND NOT OF THE INDIVIDUAL SOUL

II. 4. 20. *saṁjñā-mūrti-kḷptis tu trivṛt-kurvata upadeśāt*

But the fashioning of name and shape (is the function) of him who renders tripartite, on account of the teaching.

saṁjñā-mūrti-kḷptiḥ: the fashioning of name and shape; *tu:* but; *trivṛt-kurvataḥ:* of him who renders tripartite; *upadeśāt:* on account of the teaching.

The question is raised whether the individual soul or the Supreme Lord fashions names and shapes after the three elements have been made by the Lord. C.U. VI. 2 refers to the making of the elements. C.U. VI. 3. 2 says: 'That Divinity thought: well, let me enter into these three divinities by means of this living self and let me then develop names and forms.' So the doubt arises whether the shaping of the gross world after the elements have been made belongs to the individual soul or the Supreme Lord. This *sūtra* makes out that the individual soul has not the power to make the gross world. The next passage, VI. 3. 3, declares that the Supreme Lord alone fashions names and shapes and produces the gross elements and this world. Even when a potter produces pots the Lord is the inner director. He resides in everything and directs the whole creation.

R. makes out that the rendering tripartite cannot belong to *Brahmā* (*Hiraṇya-garbha*) who abides within the *Brahma-egg* for the egg itself is produced from fire, water and earth after these elements have been made tripartite. Manu says *tasminn aṇḍe bhavad brahma sarva-loka-pitāmahaḥ* (119). In that egg originated *Brahmā*, the grandfather of all the worlds. The living self in the passage denotes the Highest *Brahman* as having the soul for its body. *jīva-śarīrakaṁ paraṁ brahmaiva jīva-śabdenābhidhīyate.* So the work of differentiating names and shapes belongs to the Highest *Brahman* which has for its body, *Hiraṇya-garbha*, who represents the soul in its aggregate form.

For Nimbārka and Śrīnivāsa, the Supreme *Brahman* alone who renders tripartite is designated as the creator of names and shapes and the individual soul is incapable of creating them.

II. 4. 21. *māṁsādi bhaumaṁ yathā-śabdam itarayoś ca*

Flesh and the rest are of an earthly nature in accordance with the scriptural text, and of the other too.

māṁsādi: flesh and the rest; *bhaumam:* (are) of an earthly nature; *yathā-śabdam:* according to the Scripture; *itarayoḥ:* of the other (two); *ca:* too, also.

Earth when assimilated by man becomes flesh. See C.U. VI. 5. 1. We have to understand the effects of the other two elements also according to the Scriptures. Water produces blood, vital breath, etc., and fire, bone, marrow and the organ of speech.

R. makes out that the earth when eaten is disposed of in three ways, faeces, flesh and mind; water when drunk becomes urine, blood and breath; fire becomes bones, marrow and speech.

II. 4. 22. *vaiśeṣyāt tu tad-vādaś tad-vādaḥ*

But on account of distinctiveness there is that designation, that designation.

vaiśeṣyāt: on account of distinctiveness; *tu:* but; *tad-vādaḥ:* that designation; *tad-vādaḥ:* that designation.

If all the gross elements contain the three fine elements, why do we have special names for earth, water and fire? The answer is given that as the fine elements are not found in equal proportion in each of the gross elements, they are named after that fine element which is found in a preponderant degree in their composition. The repetition at the end is to indicate the conclusion of a chapter.

Section 1 (1–7)

THE SOUL WHEN PASSING OUT OF THE BODY AT THE TIME OF DEATH IS ENVELOPED BY SUBTLE MATERIAL ELEMENTS

III. 1. 1. *tad-antara-pratipattau raṁhati saṁpariṣvaktaḥ, praśna-nirūpaṇābhyām*

(*The soul*) *goes* (*out of the body*) *enveloped* (*by subtle material elements*) *with a view to obtaining a different* (*body*); (*so is it known*) *from the question and explanation* (*in the Scripture*).

tad-antara-pratipattau: with a view to obtaining a different body; *raṁhati:* goes; *saṁpariṣvaktaḥ:* enveloped (by subtle material elements); *praśna-nirūpaṇābhyām:* from the question and the explanatory answer.

The first part of this chapter explains the significance of the different texts, removes doubts and attempts to produce a sense of dispassion for the world by disclosing its imperfections. The second part tries to produce a yearning for *Brahman* by a discussion of his attributes. The third part describes the different types of meditation, their points of agreement and difference. The fourth part considers the question whether the highest end of man is derived from knowledge or action or both.

The soul, on departing from the body, carries with it subtle material elements. In C.U. V. 3. 3ff., water is called person, as the soul departs enveloped by water. Though the material elements are available everywhere, the seeds for a future body are not easily available. Again, the adjuncts of the individual soul such as the organs, etc. (B.U. IV. 4. 2), cannot accompany the soul unless there is a material basis which carries the impressions left by previous lives, *pūrva-prajña janmāntarīya-saṁskāraḥ*. Ānandagiri. If the scriptural text (B.U. IV. 4. 3) is cited as declaring that like a caterpillar the soul does not abandon the old body before it makes an approach to another body, it is said in reply that the example of the caterpillar is used to suggest not the non-abandonment of the old body but the lengthening out of the creative effort whose object is to obtain a new body which new body is presented by the *karman* of the soul. Ś. repudiates the views of the *Sāṁkhya*, the *Bauddha*, the *Vaiśeṣika* and the *Jaina* thinkers.

III. 1. 2. *tryātmakatvāt tu bhūyastvāt*

But on account of (water) consisting of three (elements) (the soul goes enveloped by all these elements and not merely water though water alone is mentioned) on account of its preponderance.
tryātmakatvāt: on account of (water) consisting of three elements; *tu:* but; *bhūyastvāt:* on account of preponderance.

The answer is here given to the objection that the soul goes enveloped by water only and not the subtle parts of all elements. In water are found the other two elements, fire and earth. Water is specifically mentioned on account of its preponderance and not because it is the only element. 'Water' implies the subtle parts of all the elements which constitute the seed of the body.

R. quotes C.U. VI. 3. 4 to indicate the tripartite character of all the elements. See also B.S. II. 4. 19–21.

Bhāskara reads *ātmakāt tu* but the interpretation is the same.

III. 1. 3. *prāṇa-gateś ca*

And on account of the going of the vital breaths.
prāṇa-gateḥ: on account of the going of the life-breaths; *ca:* and.

B.U. IV. 4. 2 mentions that when the vital breath departs all organs depart. When they leave they must have a material base. So it is inferred that water and the other elements follow the soul and these form a basis for the organs. For the life-breaths cannot either move or abide anywhere without such a base. *na hi nirāśrayāḥ prāṇāḥ kvacid gacchanti tiṣṭhanti vā*. Ś.

R. quotes B.G. XV. 7–8.

III. 1. 4. *agnyādi-gatiśruter iti cen na bhāktatvāt*

If it be said (that the life-breaths and organs do not accompany the soul) on account of the scriptural statements as to entering into fire, etc. (we say

that it is) not so on account of the metaphorical nature (of those statements).
agnyādi-gatiḥ: entering into fire, etc.; *śruteḥ:* from the Scriptures; *iti cet:* if it be said; *na:* not so; *bhāktatvāt:* on account of metaphorical nature.

B.U. III. 2. 13 says that at the time of death the organs are resolved into their presiding deities. How then can they accompany the soul? The answer is given in the *sūtra* that there are many texts which declare that they accompany the soul. B.U. IV. 4. 2. The texts cited should be interpreted in a secondary sense even as the passage (B.U. III. 12. 13.) 'His body hairs to the medicinal herbs, his hairs on the head to the trees' is to be interpreted in a secondary sense for it is not found that the body hairs and the rest of a dead man dissolve into the medicinal herbs, etc.

III. 1. 5. *prathame 'śravaṇād iti cen na tā eva hy upapatteḥ*

If it be said on account of non-mention (of water) in the first (fire), (we reply) it alone, on account of fitness.
prathame: in the first (of the offerings); *aśravaṇāt:* on account of non-mention; *iti cet:* if it be said; *na:* not so; *tāḥ:* that; *eva:* only; *hi:* because; *upapatteḥ:* on account of fitness.

If it be objected that in C.U. V. 4. 2, *śraddhā* is mentioned and not water, it is said in answer that *śraddhā* means water.

Otherwise the answer to the question will not be relevant. Cp. Ānandagiri: *upasaṁhārālocanāyām api śraddhā-śabda-tvam apām evety āha tv iti.* To take *śraddhā* as water is the only coherent interpretation. Cp. *Taittirīya Saṁhitā* I. 6. 8. 1. *Śraddhā*, indeed, is water, as it produces in the person a will for holy works. *āpo hāsmai śraddhāṁ san-namante puṇyāya karmaṇe.* Again, water, when forming the seed of the body, becomes thin and subtle and thus resembles faith. A man who is as strong as a lion is sometimes called a lion. *Śraddhā* may be applied to water since water is intimately connected with religious works which depend on faith even as the word 'platform' is applied to men on the platform.

III. 1. 6. *aśrutatvād iti cen neṣṭādikāriṇāṁ pratīteḥ*

If it be said on account of the non-mention (of water) in the Scripture (the souls also do not depart enveloped by water), (we say) not so because it is understood (from the Scriptures) that the souls who perform sacrifices, etc., (alone go to heaven).
aśrutatvāt: on account of non-mention in the *śruti; iti cet:* if it be said; *na:* not so; *iṣṭādikāriṇām:* the performers of sacrifices, etc.; *pratīteḥ:* being understood.

In C.U. V. 3. 3, there is mention of water only but no reference to the soul. How can we infer that the soul departs enveloped by water and is born again as man? C.U. V. 10. 3–4 state that those who perform sacrifices, etc., go to heaven enveloped by water which is supplied by the materials like curds and the rest which are offered as oblations in sacrifices. These assume a subtle form called *apūrva* and attach themselves to the sacrificer. Ś. says *tāḥ śraddhā-pūrvaka-karma-samavāyinyaḥ āhutimayya āpopūrva-rūpās satyas tān iṣṭādi-kāriṇo jīvān pariveṣṭyāmum lokam phaladānāya nayanti.*

R. refers to those who, while devoid of the knowledge of *Brahman,* practise useful works, reach the heavenly world and become there of the nature of the moon, *soma-rājānaḥ.* When the results of their good works are exhausted, they return again and enter on a new state, *puṇya-karmāvasāne ca punar āgatya garbhaṁ prāpnuvanti.* R. See C.U. V. 10. It is the soul which moves enveloped by water and the other subtle elements.

III. 1. 7. *bhāktaṁ vā'nātmavittvāt tathā hi darśayati*

Or (*the soul's being the food of the gods is*) *metaphorical on account of their not knowing the Self; for thus Scripture shows.*

bhāktam: in a metaphorical or secondary sense; *vā:* or; *anātmavittvāt:* on account of not knowing the Self; *tathā:* thus; *hi:* for; *darśayati:* (*śruti* or Scripture) shows.

C.U. V. 10. 4 says: 'That is the food of the gods. That the gods eat.' See also B.U. VI. 2. 16. How then can the souls enjoy the fruit of their deeds? The *sūtra* says that these statements are not to be taken in a literal sense. The gods, it is said, do not eat or drink. C.U. III. 6. 1. To say that the gods 'eat' means that they rejoice with the performers of sacrifices. Since they do not know the Self they perform the sacrifices which the gods enjoy. See B.U. I. 4. 10. The conclusion is that the soul goes into other spheres enveloped by the subtle elements for experiencing the results of its past deeds.

R. quotes B.G. VII. 23 and says that while those who know the Self attain to *Brahman,* those who do not know are means for enjoyment by the gods.

Bhāskara reads *ca* for *vā.*

Section 2 (8–11)

WHEN THE SOULS DESCEND TO THE EARTH FOR A NEW EMBODIMENT A RESIDUAL *KARMA* CLINGS TO THEM AND DETERMINES THE NATURE OF THE NEW BIRTH

III. 1. 8. *kṛtātyaye' nuśayavān dṛṣṭa-smṛtibhyāṁ yathetam anevaṁ ca*

On the exhaustion of the works (*the soul descends*) *with a remainder according to śruti and smṛti along the path* (*it*) *went by* (*from here*) *and differently too.*

kṛtātyaye: on the exhaustion of works; *anuśayavān:* with a remainder or residual *karma; dṛṣṭa-smṛtibhyām:* (as is known) from the *śruti* and the *smṛti; yathaḥ itam:* as it went (from here); *anevam:* differently; *ca:* and.

The objector quotes C.U. V. 10. 5 and suggests that all the *karma* is exhausted and there is no residual *karma* left. Besides, it is reasonable to think that *karma* earned in one life as man is exhausted in the next as god. The *sūtra* refutes this suggestion and points out that only that *karma* which gave the soul birth in heaven as god is worked out and the remaining *karma* brings it back to earth. Otherwise, it is difficult to explain the happiness or misery of a newborn child. Nor is it possible to work out in one life the entire *karma* of the previous life. The soul is born with residual *karma*. It descends by the same path by which it ascended and with a difference too. See C.U. V. 10. 5; V. 10. 3; V. 10. 6.

R. quotes *Gautama Dharma Sūtra* (XI. 29) which refers to a remnant with which souls are born again, after enjoying after death the results of their works. *varṇāsramāś ca sva-karma-niṣṭhāḥ pretya-karma-phalamanubhūya tataḥ śeṣeṇa viśiṣta-deśa-jāti-kula-rūpāyuḥ śruta-vitta-vṛtta-sukha-medhaso janma pratipadyante.* R. also refers to *Āpastamba Dharma Sūtra* II. 1. 2, 3.

Bhāskara leaves out '*ca*'.

Baladeva breaks the *sūtra* into two, beginning with *kṛtātyaye* and *yathetam*, respectively.

III. 1. 9. *caraṇād iti cen nopalakṣaṇārtheti kārṣṇājiniḥ*

If it be said that on account of conduct (the assumption of a residual karma is not necessary), (we say that) it is not so (for the word conduct is used) to denote indirectly (the residual karma). So (thinks) Kārṣṇājini. *caraṇāt:* on account of conduct; *iti cet:* if it be said; *na:* not so; *upa-lakṣaṇārtha:* to denote indirectly; *iti:* thus; *kārṣṇājiniḥ:* (the sage) *Kārṣṇājini* (thinks).

If it be said that conduct and not residual *karma* determines the new birth (and the two are different: see B.U. IV. 4. 5), the *sūtra* denies this view. The word conduct is used in the sense of residual *karma.*

R. reads *tad* before *upalakṣaṇārthe.* He says that mere conduct does not lead to the experiences of pleasure and pain; pleasure and pain are the results of works in the limited sense. *kevalācārāt sukha-duḥkha-prāpty asambhavāt; sukha-duḥkhe hi puṇya-pāpa-rūpa-karma-phale.*

III. 1. 10. *ānarthakyam iti cen na tad-apekṣatvāt*

If it be said that purposelessness (of conduct would result therefrom), (we say) it is not so on account of the dependence (of work) on that (conduct). *ānarthakyam:* purposelessness; *iti cet:* if it be said; *na:* not so; *tad-apekṣatvāt:* on account of dependence on that.

Good conduct determines *karma* and is therefore not purposeless. The *Vedas* do not purify one who is devoid of good conduct. *ācārahīnaṁ na punanti vedāḥ. Vasiṣṭha Smṛti* VI. 3. As work is the cause of new births, we need not assume that conduct is the cause. If a man is able to run away by means of his feet, he will surely not creep on his knees. *na hi padbhyāṁ palāyituṁ pārayamāṇo jānubhyāṁ raṁhitum arhati*. Ś.

III. 1. 11. *sukṛta-duṣkṛte eveti tu bādariḥ*

But (conduct means) only good and evil works, thus Bādari thinks.
sukṛta-duṣkṛte: good and evil works; *eva:* only; *iti:* thus; *tu:* but; *bādariḥ: Bādari* (thinks).

This *sūtra* makes out that there is no real difference between conduct or *caraṇa* and *karma*. So residual *karma* is the determining cause of a new birth on earth.

Bhāskara omits *iti* in the *sūtra*.

Section 3 (12–21)

THE FUTURE OF THOSE SOULS WHOSE WORKS DO NOT ENTITLE THEM TO GO TO THE LUNAR WORLD

III. 1. 12. *aniṣṭādikāriṇām api ca śrutam*

Even of those also who do not perform sacrifices (the ascent to the moon) is stated by Scripture.
aniṣṭādikāriṇām: of those who do not perform sacrifices; *api:* even; *ca:* also; *śrutam:* is stated by Scripture.

The opponent holds that even those who do not perform sacrifices go to heaven though they may not enjoy there like the performers of sacrifices, because they too require the fifth oblation for a new birth and the Scripture declares that 'those who depart from this world they all, in truth, go to the moon'. K.U. I. 2.

This, for R., implies that all whether they do good works or evil works go to the moon. Śrīnivāsa means by *aniṣṭa*, forbidden deeds; and the word *ādi* means the giving up of what is enjoined.

III. 1. 13. *samyamane tv anubhūyetareṣām ārohāvarohau tad-gati-darśanāt*

But of others (i.e. those who have not performed sacrifices) after having experienced the fruits of their actions in the abode of Yama, ascent and descent take place, as such a course is declared (by the Scripture).
samyamane: in the abode of *Yama*; *tu:* but; *anubhūya:* having experienced; *itareṣām:* of others; *ārohāvarohau:* ascent and descent (take place); *tad-gati-darśanāt:* since such a course is declared (in the Scripture).

saṁyamanaṁ yamālayam. Ś. The abode of *Yama* is said to be the gathering place of men, *sangamanaṁ janānām. Ṛg Veda* X. 14. 1.

This *sūtra* negatives the suggestion made in the previous *sūtra.* Evildoers do not go to heaven; they go to the world of *Yama* where they experience the results of their actions and then descend again to earth. *Kaṭha U.* I. 2. 6. The ascent to the moon is only for the enjoyment of the results of good works and not for any other purpose. So evil-doers do not go there.

Nimbārka and Śrīnivāsa take this *sūtra* as the continuation of the *prima facie* view, the *pūrva-pakṣa.* Even those who do not perform sacrifices after having experienced the results of their actions in the abode of *Yama* ascend to the world of moon and re-descend. While Nimbārka takes this and the next three *sūtras* as stating the *prima facie* view, others hold that they state the correct conclusion.

Śrīkaṇṭha adopts Ś.'s interpretation.

III. 1. 14. *smaranti ca*

The smṛtis also declare (*this*).
smaranti: smṛtis declare; *ca:* also.

That evil works are requited in *Yama's* world is declared by *Manu, Vyāsa,* etc.

R. quotes *Viṣṇu Purāṇa: sarve caite vaśaṁ yānti yamasya bhagavan kila.* III. 7. 5. 'And all these pass under the control of *Yama.*'

III. 1. 15. *api ca sapta*

Moreover there are seven (*hells*).
api ca: moreover; *sapta:* seven.

There are seven hells mentioned in the *Purāṇas* to which the evil-doers go to experience the results of their evil deeds.

R. and Nimbārka omit *ca* in the *sūtra.*

III. 1. 16. *tatrāpi ca tad-vyāpārād avirodhaḥ*

And on account of this activity there also, (*there is*) *no contradiction.*
tatra: there; *api:* also; *ca:* and; *tat-vyāpārāt:* on account of his activity; *avirodhaḥ:* (there is) no contradiction.

To the objection that in the different hells, different persons like *Citragupta* are in control, the answer is given that the different hells and their controllers are directed by *Yama.*

III. 1. 17. *vidyā-karmaṇor iti tu prakṛtatvāt*

But (*the reference is to the two roads*) *of knowledge and work, thus* (*we understand*) *on account of their being the subject under discussion.*
vidyā-karmaṇoḥ: of knowledge and work; *iti:* thus; *tu:* but; *prakṛtatvāt:* on account of their being the subject under discussion.

C.U. V. 10. 8 says that those who do not go along the ways of knowledge which take us to the path of the gods and of works which take us to the path of the fathers go to a third place, where they are born and die and so that place is not full. The evildoers who form a separate group go to this third place. The *Kauṣītaki* text that all go to the sphere of the moon refers only to those who have performed good deeds and not to evil-doers.

Nimbārka and Śrīnivāsa take this *sūtra* as stating the correct conclusion.

III. 1. 18. *na tṛtīye tathopalabdheḥ*

Not in the case of the third place, (for) so it is seen.
na: not; *tṛtīye:* in the case of the third place; *tathā:* so; *upalabdheḥ:* it being seen.

If it be said that all must go to the moon for the purpose of obtaining a new body, to complete the five oblations that cause the new birth, the *sūtra* says that this specification does not apply in the case of evil-doers, who are born irrespective of the oblations.

III. 1. 19. *smaryate'pi ca loke*

And (it is), moreover, declared by smṛti in ordinary life.
smaryate: (it is) declared by *smṛti; api:* moreover; *ca:* and; *loke:* in the world, in ordinary life.

Cases of birth without the completion of the five oblations are recorded. The bodies of some specially meritorious persons like Draupadī, Dṛṣṭadyumna, Sītā, are formed independently of the fifth oblation (i.e. sexual union). Such are cases of immaculate conception.

III. 1. 20. *darśanāc ca*

Also on account of observation.
darśanāt: on account of observation; *ca:* and.

The rule about five oblations is not universal; for of the four forms of life viviparous, oviparous, life springing from moisture and plant life, the last two are born without any mating and there is not the fifth oblation in their case.

III. 1. 21. *tṛtīya-śabdāvarodhaḥ saṁśokajasya*

The third term (plant life) includes that which springs from moisture.
tṛtīya-śabda-avarodhaḥ: inclusion in the third term; *saṁśokajasya:* of that which springs from moisture.

C.U. VI. 3. 1 speaks only of three modes of origin, *aṇḍajam, jīvajam, udbhijjam.* How then can it be maintained that there are four forms of life? The answer is that that which springs from moisture is included in plant life, since they both germinate, one from the earth and the other from water, etc.

It is clear that the evil-doers do not go to the moon.

Section 4 (22)

THE SOUL DESCENDING FROM THE MOON THROUGH THE ETHER, ETC., DOES NOT BECOME IDENTICAL WITH THEM BUT ATTAINS SIMILARITY OF NATURE

III. 1. 22. *sābhāvyāpattir upapatteḥ*

(*The soul when descending from the moon*) *attains similarity of nature with them* (*i.e. ether, air and the rest*) (*that alone*) *being reasonable.*
sābhāvya-āpattiḥ: attainment of a similarity of nature with them; *upapatteḥ:* being reasonable.

C.U. V. 10. 5 says that the souls return through the ether, air and the rest. The question is raised whether they attain identity of nature or likeness or similarity of nature. Not the former; a thing cannot become another of a different nature. All that the passage means is that the souls attain similarity of nature. If the souls become identified with ether, they could no longer descend through air, etc.

R. and Nimbārka read *svābhāvya* for *sābhāvya*.

Section 5 (23)

THE ENTIRE DESCENT OCCUPIES A SHORT TIME

III. 1. 23. *nāticireṇa viśeṣāt*

(*The soul passes through the stages of descent*) *in a not very long time; on account of the special statement.*
na: not; *aticireṇa:* in a very long time; *viśeṣāt:* on account of the special statement.

The descent through different stages takes place quickly. See C.U. V. 10. 6.

Śrīnivāsa says that there is no point in the soul's remaining in a state of likeness to ether, etc., for a long time.

Section 6 (24–27)

WHEN THE SOULS ENTER INTO PLANTS AND THE REST THEY ARE ONLY IN CONTACT WITH THEM BUT DO NOT PARTICIPATE IN THEIR LIFE

III. 1. 24. *anyādhiṣṭhiteṣu pūrvavad abhilāpāt*

(*The descending souls enter*) *into* (*plants, etc.*), *occupied by other* (*souls*) *as in the previous cases, on account of* (*scriptural*) *declaration.*

anya-adhiṣṭhiteṣu: in what is occupied by another; *pūrvavat:* as in the previous cases; *abhilāpāt:* on account of (scriptural) declaration.

If it be said that C.U. V. 10. 6 states 'they are born here as rice and barley, etc.' and so the word 'born' should be taken literally, the *sūtra* says that the word 'born' implies mere connection with rice and barley which are animated by other souls. They enter these plants, etc., independently of their *karma* and while there they do not experience the results of their actions. The next passage, V. 10. 7, says that 'those whose conduct here has been good will quickly attain a good birth, but those whose conduct here has been evil, will quickly attain an evil birth' which makes it clear that the souls dwell, as it were, in plants, etc., till they get the opportunity for a new birth. If we take the passage to mean that the souls are born in plants, then when they are cooked and eaten, the souls will have to leave them. The state of plant existence may be a place for experience but not for those souls which descend from the moon with an unrequited remainder of works.

III. 1. 25. *aśuddham iti cen na śabdāt*

If it be said that (sacrificial work is) impure, (we say it is) not so, on account of scriptural authority.

aśuddham: impure; *iti cet:* if it be said; *na:* not so; *śabdāt:* on account of scriptural authority.

If it be said that scriptural works are impure because they involve injury to animals and so souls who have committed such evil deeds may be born as herbs, etc., the *sūtra* refutes this view on the ground that Scripture is our authority for determining what is right and what is wrong. If it be said that the Scripture also states that we should not hurt any creature, it is said in answer that it is a general rule and other scriptural injunctions give the exceptions. So the souls descending from the moon are not born in plants but are only enclosed in them.

śāstra-hetutvād dharmādharma-vijñānasya. Ś. The same line of conduct may be right in one set of circumstances and wrong in another. *yasmin deśe kāle nimitte ca yodharmo'nuṣṭhīyate sa eva deśa-kāla-nimittāntareṣv adharmo bhavati.* So Ś. asks us to accept the *śāstras* as our sole guide. *tena na śāstrādṛte dharmādharma-viṣayaṁ vijñānaṁ kasyacid asti.*

R. makes out that an action which is the means of supreme exaltation is not of the nature of violence, even if it involves some little pain; it rather is of beneficial nature. *atiśayitābhyudaya-sādhana-bhūto vyāpāro'lpa-duḥkho'pi na hiṁsā pratyuta rakṣaṇam eva.* R. Whether the infliction of pain is right or wrong depends on the motive. An act which is healing though it may cause transitory pain, men of insight declare to be preservative and beneficial. *cikitsakaṁ ca tādātvikālpa-duḥkha-kāriṇam api rakṣakam eva vadanti pūjayanti ca tajjñāḥ.* R. See also *Taittirīya Brāhmaṇa* III. 7. 7. 14.

Thus the commentators allow exceptional circumstances in which we may inflict pain; only the motive should be the welfare of the being who suffers pain. The spirit should be one of love or negatively *vaira-tyāga,* renunciation of hatred.

III. 1. 26. *reṭaḥ-sig-yogo'tha*

After that the connection with him who performs the act of generation.
retaḥ-sik-yogo: connection with him who performs the act of generation; *atha:* then, after that.

C.U. V. 10. 6 says that the soul becomes one with him. It means the soul gets connected with him. This also shows that the soul's becoming plants, etc., is mere connection with them and not actual birth.

III. 1. 27. *yoneḥ śarīram*

From the womb the (new) body.
yoneḥ: from the womb; *śarīram:* body.

Till now it was only conjunction with successive stages but now through its connection with a person, the soul enters the woman, there acquires a new body fit for experiencing the results of the past residual *karma.*

The commentators are at pains to show that connection with plants and animals is metaphorical and real rebirth is as human beings.

Section 1 (1–6)

THE SOUL IN THE DREAM STATE

III. 2. 1. *sandhye sṛṣṭir āha hi*

In the intermediate state (between waking and deep sleep) (there is a real) creation because (the Scripture) says so.
sandhye: in the intermediate state (between waking and deep sleep, i.e. the dream state); *sṛṣṭiḥ:* creation; *āha:* (Scripture) says so; *hi:* because.

The opponent's view is stated that the dream state is just as real as the waking state. B.U. IV. 3. 9 says there is a third intermediate state, the state of dreams, *sandhyaṁ tṛtīyaṁ svapna-sthānam.* Here the two states of waking and deep sleep join. B.U. IV. 3. 10 says: 'He creates tanks, lotus-pools and rivers. He, indeed, is the agent [maker or creator].' Besides, we do not feel any difference between the experience of the waking state and that of the dream state. A meal taken in dream has the effect of giving satisfaction as one taken in the waking state. Therefore the creation in the dream state is real and the creator is the Lord himself. Ś.

R. raises the doubt whether the creation is accomplished by the individual soul or by the Lord. The opponent states that the creator is the dreaming soul.

For R., Nimbārka and Śrīnivāsa the problem is whether the dream creation is due to the individual soul or the Lord, while for Ś. and Bhāskara it is whether the dream creation is real or unreal.

Baladeva holds that this *sūtra* does not express a *prima facie* view but the correct conclusion that the creation in the dream state is due to the Lord and not to the individual soul.

III. 2. 2. *nirmātāraṁ caike putrādayaś ca*

And some (*schools state the self to be*) *the shaper; sons and so on* (*being the objects of desire which he shapes*).

nirmātāram: shaper, creator; *ca:* and; *eke:* some; *putrādayaḥ:* sons and so on; *ca:* and.

The creation even in dreams is by the Lord himself as *Kaṭha U.* II. 2. 8 says: 'That person who is awake in those that sleep, shaping desire after desire, that, indeed, is the pure. That is *Brahman*.' So as in the case of the waking state, even in dreams the Lord is the creator. So the world of dreams is real like the empirical world. *tathya-rūpaiva sandhye sṛṣṭiḥ*. Ś.

For R., this *sūtra* states the *pūrva-pakṣa* that the individual soul is the shaper of dream objects.

For Baladeva this *sūtra* states the correct conclusion that the Lord is the maker of dream objects.

III. 2. 3. *māyāmātraṁ tu kārtsnyenānabhivyakta-svarūpatvāt*

But (*the dream world*) *is mere appearance on account of its nature not being manifest with the totality* (*of attributes of the waking state*).

māyāmātram: mere appearance; *tu:* but; *kārtsnyena:* with the totality; *anabhivyakta-svarūpatvāt:* on account of its nature not being manifest.

For *kārtsnyena*, some read *sākalyena*.

Ś. argues that the dream world does not agree with the waking world in respect of time, place, cause and non-contradiction and so it is not real like the waking world. *na hi paramārtha-vastu-viṣayāṇi deśa-kāla-nimittāny abādhaś ca svapne sambhāvyante.*

Dream states are not bound by the rules of space time, cause and non-contradiction. We cannot find space for chariots and the like in the limited confines of the body. The dreamer sees things at long distances. He cannot go out and return in a moment. B.U. (II. 1. 18) says that 'the dreamer moves about in his own body as he pleases'. So ideas of going out of the body, etc., are a mere deception. Conditions of time are not observed. Lying asleep at night he dreams that it is day. Besides, how can he without materials make chariots and the like? Within the dream itself there is self-contradiction. A chariot becomes a man and man a tree. Objects appear to exist in dreams as silver does in a mother-of-pearl. What we see in dreams is only an appearance. *māyā-mātraṁ svapna-darśanam*. Ś. says that the individual soul creates in dreams and not the Lord.

It is obvious from Ś.'s insistence on the difference between dream states and the waking world that the latter is not an appearance.

Bhāskara criticises the interpretation usually ascribed to Ś. by pointing out that those who hold that objects in the waking state too are *māyā* like the dream states, misinterpret the author of the *sūtra* and delude people. *ye punar jāgaritāvasthā'pi māyāmātram ity āghoṣayanti te sūtra-kārābhiprāyam nāśayantaḥ śrotriyajanam mohayanti*. Bhāskara obviously rebukes those who cannot see the distinction between waking and dream states and reduce the former to the latter.

Bhāskara holds that dream objects are *māyā* as they are created by the mysterious will of the Lord and their nature is not fully manifest, since they are not objects of perception as gross material objects are. All this proves that the dream objects are created by the Lord alone and not by the individual soul.

For R., the things appearing in dreams are absolute *māyā* in the sense that they are wonderful. *māyā-śabdo hy āścaryavācī*. He quotes Vālmiki's *Rāmāyaṇa* I. 27, *janakasya kule jātā devamāyeva nirmitā*. She was born in the family of Janaka appearing like the wonderful power of the divine Being in bodily shape. When it is said 'there are no chariots', etc., it means that they are not perceived by any other person except the dreaming one. They belong to the private world of the individual and not to the public world. The Supreme Person creates these objects to be perceived by the individual though they endure for a short time only. *atha rathān ratha-yogān pathaḥ sṛjate svapnadṛg-anubhāvyatayā tat-kāla-mātrāvasānān sṛjata ity āścarya-rūpatvam evāha*. The creation of these dream objects is possible only for the Supreme Person who can immediately realise all his wishes but not for the individual soul.

III. 2. 4. *sūcakaś ca hi śruter ācakṣate ca tad-vidaḥ*

For (though the dream is an illusion) yet it is indicative (of the future) according to śruti; those who are versed in that (the reading of dreams) also declare it.

sūcakaḥ: indication of the future; *ca:* yet; *hi:* for; *śruteḥ:* (we find) in the *śruti*; *ācakṣate:* declare; *ca:* also; *tad-vidaḥ:* those who are versed in that (in the reading of dreams).

Though the dreams themselves are illusory, their indications about the future may be real, even as the appearance of silver in mother-of-pearl is false and yet produces joy in us. See C.U. V. 2. 8. Ś.

elaborates his view in regard to the metaphysical, the empirical and the apparent reality, if such a term be permitted. The world is not real in the same sense as the world consisting of ether and so on is real. The empirical world which is not to be confused with the dream world is not absolutely real. For in one sense the entire expanse of things is mere appearance. The world consisting of ether, etc., remains fixed and distinct up to the moment that the soul cognises that *Brahman* is the self of all. The world of dreams, on the other hand, is daily sublated by the waking state. That the latter is mere appearance has to be understood with a distinction.

pratipāditaṁ hi, tad-ananyatvam ārambhaṇa-śabdādibhyaḥ (II. 1. 14), *ity atra samastasya prapañcasya māyā-mātratvam. prāk tu brahmātma-darśanāt viyadādi-prapañco vyavasthita-rūpo bhavati, sandhyāśrayas tu prapañcaḥ prati-dinaṁ bādhyata ity ato vaiśeṣikam idam sandhya-sya māyā-mātratvam uditam.* Ś.

Bhāskara says that it is unreasonable to suppose that what is created by the Intelligent Being can be subject to pleasure and pain. So the dream objects cannot be due to the Lord, though he is the cause here, too, as he is the controller of all. *na hi prajñājasya sukha-duḥkha-yogyatā'vakalpate parasyāpi hetu-kartṛtvaṁ niyantṛtvāt. nirmātāram iti cāviruddhaṁ jīva-parayor abhedāt.*

For R., this *sūtra* is the sixth. Since dreams are indicative of future good or ill, they cannot be due to the individual soul for he would create for himself only such dreams as would indicate good fortune. So the creation which takes place in dreams is the work of the Lord only.

Though Ś. does not deny altogether that the Supreme Self, as the controller of the soul at all times and in all states, is also active in the dream states, yet he affirms that the dream objects are created by the individual soul itself and not the Supreme Soul. His view thus differs from that of R. and Nimbārka.

Baladeva begins a new section here ending with the next *sūtra* and declares that the dream objects are real.

III. 2. 5. *parābhidhyānāt tu tirohitaṁ tato hy asya bandha-viparyayau*

But by meditation on the Highest, that which is hidden (*viz. the similarity of the Lord and the soul becomes manifest*), *for from him* (*the Lord*) *are its* (*the soul's*) *bondage and freedom.*

parābhidhyānāt: from meditation on the Highest Self; *tu:* but; *tirohitam:* that which is hidden (by ignorance); *tataḥ:* from him (the Lord); *hi:* for; *asya:* of the soul; *bandha-viparyayau:* bondage and its opposite, i.e. freedom.

If it be said that the individual soul is a part of the Supreme Self and so shares its power of knowledge and rulership, even as a spark and fire have alike the power of burning and should therefore be able to create at will like the Lord, this *sūtra* says that this rulership is covered by ignorance and becomes manifest only when, through meditation on the Supreme, ignorance is destroyed. See Ś.U. I. 11. So long as the soul is subject to ignorance it cannot create anything real. Besides, bondage and freedom of the individual arise from the Lord. Ś.

R. says that the nature of the individual soul is hidden owing to the wish of the Highest. *parābhidhyānāt parama-puruṣa-saṁkalpād asya jīvasya svābhāvikaṁ rūpam tirohitam.* T.U. II. 7. 1; II. 8. 1.

Nimbārka holds that the qualities of the soul remain hidden through the wish of the Supreme Lord in accordance with the deeds of the soul. See Ś.U. VI. 16.

Baladeva's explanation is different. If it be said that the dreams must be unreal, since the dream objects are sublated in the waking state, the answer is that the dream objects are withdrawn by the wish of the Lord alone. There is nothing unnatural in the Lord's creating and withdrawing the dream objects even as he can cause the bondage and release of the soul. The dream objects are not unreal simply because they are sublated.

III. 2. 6. *deha-yogād vā so'pi*

Or that (the concealment of the soul's powers) also (results) from its connection with the body.

deha-yogāt: from its connection with the body; *vā:* or; *saḥ:* that; *api:* also.

Though the soul is not different from the Lord, its powers remain hidden, because of the limiting adjuncts such as connection with the body. Ś.

R. says that the obscuration of the soul's true nature results from the soul's connection with the body or its connection with the power of matter in a subtle state. In the state of creation the soul is connected with a body; in the state of dissolution, *pralaya,* it is connected with subtle matter which does not admit of differentiation by means of name and shape. So as its true nature is not manifest the soul is unable to create dream objects like chariots, etc. The dream objects are specially created by the Supreme Person and are meant by him to be the reward or punishment for deeds of minor importance. They, therefore, last for the time of the dream only and are perceived by that one soul only.

Srīnivāsa says that the Lord takes into consideration the deeds of the soul and connects the soul with *prakṛti* in its effected and causal states. The dream states are created by the Lord and not by the individual soul.

Baladeva takes this as a separate section concerned with showing that the waking consciousness, too, is due to the Lord.

Section 2 (7–8)

THE SOUL IN DREAMLESS SLEEP

III. 2. 7. *tad-abhāvo nāḍīṣu tac-chruter ātmani ca*

The absence of that (i.e. of dreams, i.e. dreamless sleep) takes place in the nāḍīs and in the self; according to Scripture.
tat-abhāvaḥ: the absence of that; *nāḍīṣu:* in the nerves; *ātmani:* in the self; *ca:* and; *tat-śruteḥ:* as it is known from the *śruti* or Scripture.

The self in sleep is said variously to reside in the arteries (*nāḍis*) pericardium (*purītat*) and in *Brahman*. The question is whether these are mutually exclusive or not. The former view is urged on the ground that the statements have all one purpose, viz. the description of the self in deep sleep. When this purpose is served by one statement, the others should be excluded. Where rice and barley are prescribed for one purpose, only one of them is to be used and not both.

In the setting out of this position, with reference to a single purpose, in the disjunctive reading, in the illustration of rice and barley, there is considerable similarity between Ś. and Śrīkaṇṭha.

The *sūtra* holds that the places enumerated are not alternatives but stand in mutual relation and refer to one place only. If we allow option between arteries (C.U. VIII. 6. 3; B.U. II. 1. 19) and the self (B.U. II. 1. 17) the *Vedic* authority is compromised for the acceptance of one authority will mean the denial of the other. If there are two statements to the effect 'he sleeps in the palace', 'he sleeps on a couch', we have to combine the two and say 'he sleeps on a couch in the palace'. Similarly here we should mean that the soul goes through the nerves to the region of the heart and there rests in *Brahman*. If it is asked as to why in deep sleep the soul does not experience the relation of supporter and that which is supported, *ādhārādheya-bheda*, it is possible that the individual soul concerned with ignorance is lost in *Brahman*. 'When a person sleeps . . . he has reached pure being. He has gone to his own' (C.U. VI. 8. 1). K.U. (IV. 20) suggests that he becomes one with the Self. So Self is the soul's place of rest in deep sleep, *ātmaiva suṣupti-sthānam*.

R. says that the arteries and the pericardium answer to a palace and a couch within the palace while *Brahman* is the bed, as it were. So *Brahman* alone is the immediate resting place of the sleeping soul. For a man sleeping on a bed is at the same time sleeping on a couch and in the house.

Section 3 (9)

THE SAME SOUL RETURNS FROM DEEP SLEEP

III. 2. 9. *sa eva tu karmānusmṛti-śabda-vidhibhyaḥ*

But the same soul (returns from Brahman of the deep sleep) on account of work, remembrance, scriptural authority and injunction.

sa eva: the same soul; *tu:* but; *karma-anusmṛti-śabda-vidhibhyaḥ:* on account of work, remembrance, scriptural authority and injunction.

A doubt is raised that we cannot be sure that the same soul returns from *Brahman* of the deep sleep, even as we cannot be sure that the same drop of water comes back after it is once merged in water. The *sūtra* answers this doubt. The same soul comes back for (i) it takes up the work on return from sleep which was left unfinished before falling into sleep; (ii) there is continuity of experience before and after sleep and there is remembrance of past events, *ātmānusmaraṇa* that he is the same as he was before; (iii) there is scriptural authority also. See C.U. VI. 9. 3 (4). If the person who rises after sleep is different from the person who goes to sleep, then injunctions with regard to work or knowledge would be meaningless. If a person attains oneness with *Brahman* by falling into sleep, then sleep will be one with liberation and scriptural instruction to attain liberation would be pointless. The analogy of a drop of water and the ocean is not correct, since the drop merges in the ocean without any adjuncts whereas the soul merges in *Brahman* with adjuncts. The same soul rises again from *Brahman*, with its work and ignorance as these are not lost in *Brahman* completely. The individuality of each soul continues through the states of sleep and waking; in the former it is like the seed; in the latter like the fully developed plant.

R. quotes C.U. VIII. 2. 1; VIII. 12. 3; VII. 25. 2; VII. 26. 2 which imply the distinctiveness of the released soul. The soul in *saṁsāra* puts off his instruments of knowledge and action in deep sleep, repairs to the place of complete rest and having refreshed himself there rises to a new enjoyment of action.

Nimbārka takes *karmānusmṛti* as one, remembrance of work, while Śrīnivāsa takes it as two, as work and remembrance, and thus follows Ś. and others.

Section 4 (10)

THE NATURE OF SWOON

III. 2. 10. *mugdhe'rdha-sampattiḥ pariśeṣāt*

In the swooning person, there is half-attainment, this being the remaining.

mugdhe: in a swooning person; *ardha-sampattiḥ:* half-attainment; *pariśeṣāt:* this being the remaining (hypothesis).

The doubt is raised whether the state of swoon is not to be affiliated to one of the four states, waking, dream, sleep and death, as a fifth state is not known from Scripture. The person in swoon is not conscious of objects as a waking person. We cannot say that on account of concentration on one object he is unaware of other objects. For the swooning person is not conscious of anything. He who is concentrating on an object keeps his body straight while he who is in swoon falls prostrate on the ground. He is not dreaming for he is altogether unconscious. He is not dead for he continues to breathe and feel warm. He rises again to conscious life. He is not in deep sleep when one is peaceful, breathing at regular intervals. The man in a swoon breathes irregularly; his body trembles; his face has a frightful expression. His eyes are staring wide open. A sleeping person may be roused to waking consciousness by a gentle stroke with the hand, the person in a swoon not even by a blow with a club. The state of swoon has some qualities in common with sleep and some with death. It belongs to death in so far as it is the door to death. It is not considered to be a separate fifth state as it is compounded of several states.

For R., swoon is a half-way approach to death. *maraṇāyārdha-sampattir mūrchā.*

For Nimbārka, swoon is half-attainment of death.

Section 5 (11–21)

THE NATURE OF THE SUPREME *BRAHMAN*

III. 2. 11. *na sthānato'pi parasyobhaya-liṅgaṁ sarvatra hi*

Not on account of (difference of) place also, twofold characteristics can belong to the Highest for everywhere (Scripture teaches it to be without any difference).

na: not; *sthānataḥ:* from (difference of) place; *api:* also; *parasya:* of the Supreme (*Brahman*); *ubhaya-liṅgaṁ:* twofold characteristics; *sarvatra:* everywhere; *hi:* for.

For Ś., this *sūtra* declares that the twofold characteristic of the presence of qualities, *sa-viśeṣatva,* and absence of qualities, *nir-viśeṣatva,* cannot belong to the Highest *Brahman* for all passages which aim at setting forth the nature of *Brahman* declare it to be devoid of all distinctive qualities.

In the texts we find passages referring to the qualified *Brahman* (C.U. III. 14. 2) and unqualified *Brahman* (B.U. III. 8. 8). The *sūtra* says that both these cannot be predicated of one and the same reality which cannot have two contradictory natures at the same time as it is opposed to experience. The mere connection of a thing with another cannot change its nature even as the redness of a flower reflected in a crystal does not change the nature of the crystal which is colourless. The imputation of redness is due to ignorance and is not real. A thing cannot change its real nature which means its destruction. So of the two aspects of *Brahman* we have to accept that which is non-determinate as its true nature (*Kaṭha U.* I. 3. 15). It is described as *a-śabdam, a-sparśam, a-rūpam, a-vyayam.* The other description of *Brahman* is only for the sake of *upāsanā* or worship and it is not its real nature.

Bhāskara argues that though *Brahman* has two forms, *nirākāra* and *sākāra,* without form and with form, he is to be meditated on in his formless aspect, for he retains this nature even when he happens to have a connection with the world and the rest.

R. makes this section consist of *sūtras* 11 to 25. In the previous *sūtras,* the different states of the soul are described and the objection is raised, since *Brahman* is the *antaryāmin* of *jīva, Brahman* also will be contaminated by the faults attaching to the *jīva* in its different states. This section shows that *Brahman* is free from faults.

R. holds that the *sūtra* makes out that *Brahman* is everywhere described as having a twofold character 'Not on account of place even [is there any imperfection] in the Highest; for everywhere [it is described] as having twofold characteristics'. The *prima facie* view for R. is, though *Brahman* is the cause of the world and a treasure-house of all auspicious qualities yet it is affected by imperfection since it is connected with matter, bodies and their parts. The answer is stated in this *sūtra* that *Brahman* has a twofold nature, freedom from imperfections and possession of all auspicious qualities. C.U. VIII. 1. 5; *Viṣṇu Purāṇa* VI. 5. 84–5, I. 22. 51.

Nimbārka accepts R.'s interpretation. Kesava Kāṣmīrin follows the same view.

While Ś. contends that *Brahman* cannot be qualified by the limiting adjuncts which do not change its real nature but only conceal it for the finite being, R. and Nimbārka hold that the two-fold nature, viz. negative freedom from all imperfections and the positive possession of all auspicious qualities, applies to *Brahman.*

Vallabha thinks that *sūtras* 11–13 constitute one section, 14–18 another and 19–22 a third.

Baladeva urges that though the Lord manifests himself in various places, he himself undergoes no change, by reason of his mysterious power.

III. 2. 12. *na bhedād iti cen na pratyekam atad-vacanāt*

If it be said (*that it is*) *not so on account of difference* (*taught in the Scripture*), (*we reply*) *not so, because with respect to each* (*such form*) *the Scripture declares the opposite of that.*

na: not so; *bhedāt:* on account of difference (being taught in the

Scripture); *iti cet:* if it be said; *na:* not so; *pratyekam:* with respect to each; *a-tad-vacanāt:* because of the declaration of the opposite of that.

If the Scripture declares *Brahman* to have different forms (see B.U. III. 18. 1; *Praśna* U. 2. VI. 1; C.U. V. 3; B.U. I. 3. 22; C.U. V. 11. 2), every such form is denied of *Brahman* in other texts. See B.U. II. 5. 1. There is only one non-differenced *Brahman.* With regard to various forms the *śruti* explains that the forms are not true and there is only one formless principle. See B.U. II. 5. 1.

R. omits *na* at the beginning and reads: 'If it be said "on account of difference" [we say it is] not so, because with reference to each the text says what is not that.' If it be said that the individual soul has the same twofold attribute, freedom from evil, etc. (C.U. VIII. 7), and yet is affected with imperfections owing to the fact that it is connected with bodies, etc., so the inner ruler may be inferred to be affected by imperfections since it undergoes a variety of conditions on account of its connection with different bodies, the *sūtra* sets aside this objection on the ground that the texts declare the inner ruler to be immortal and denies of him any imperfections due to his connection with the bodies which he voluntarily enters in order to rule them. The perfect nature of the individual soul is obscured as long as it is connected with a body. See III. 2. 5. If it is objected that even the Highest Self, when it enters voluntarily into bodies, cannot escape connection with the imperfections which depend on the essential nature of those bodies, it is said in reply that even non-sentient things are not essentially or intrinsically bad. They cause pain or pleasure to men according to the nature of their past deeds. If the effects of things depended only on their own nature, they would be productive for all beings either of pleasure or of pain. This is not observed to be the case. So to the individual soul subject to *karman,* connection with different things is the source of imperfection and suffering in agreement with the nature of its deeds; with reference to the Highest *Brahman* which is subject to itself only, the same connection is the source of playful activity, in so far as it guides and rules these things in various ways. *parasya tu brahmaṇaḥ svādhīnasya sa eva sambandhas tat-tad-vicitra-niyamana-rūpa-līlā-rasāyaiva syāt.* R.

Nimbārka and Śrīnivāsa adopt R.'s interpretation. Śrīnivāsa says that the imperfections pertain to the individual soul, which, though endowed with the attributes of freedom from evil and the rest, has yet its real nature obscured through the will of the Highest, in accordance with its past *karma*; but the imperfections do not pertain to the Highest who has his real nature ever manifest. There are texts establishing the imperfections of the individual soul in waking state (C.U. V. 10. 7), but none referring to the imperfections of the Highest. In the dream state, in sleep, death, etc., the soul is said to be imperfect. *Aitareya Āraṇyaka* III. 2. 4; C.U. VIII. 3. 2.

Bhāskara continues the topic of the worship of the formless *Brahman.*

Baladeva reads the *sūtra* with a *na* at the beginning and argues that Scripture points out that the Supreme is one, with regard to each of his manifestations.

III. 2. 13. *api caivam eke*

Some also (*teach*) *thus.*

api ca: also; *evam:* thus; *eke:* some.

Ś. means by this *sūtra* that some *śākhās* or rescensions of the *Vedas* teach that the manifoldness is not true for they condemn those who see difference. *Kaṭha U.* I. 4. 11; B.U. IV. 4. 19. Wherever *bheda* or difference is mentioned and *Brahman* is said to be possessed of different forms, the difference is mentioned for the sake of worship and ultimately difference is denied. *na bhinnākāra-yogo brahmaṇaḥ śāstrīya iti śakyate vaktum, bhedasyopāsanārthatvād abhede tātparyam.*

Bhāskara holds that Scripture teaches the essential non-difference of *Brahman.*

R. takes this *sūtra* to state the objection. The connection with one and the same body is for the individual soul a source of disadvantage while for the Highest *Brahman* it is an accession of glory in so far as it manifests him as a Lord and ruler. M.U. III. 1. 1. C.U. VI. 3. 2 says: 'Having entered by means of that *jīva* self, I will differentiate names and forms.' This means that the differentiation of names and forms depends on the entering into the elements of the *jīva* whose self is *Brahman.* As the individual self has definite shapes, *Brahman* also falls within the sphere of beings to whom injunctions and prohibitions are addressed.

Baladeva quotes from M.U. 7 to show that the Lord is one though appearing as many.

III. 2. 14. *arūpavad eva hi tat-pradhānatvāt*

For (Brahman) *is merely devoid of form, on account of this being the main purport of Scripture.*

arūpavat: formless; *eva:* only; *hi:* for; *tat-pradhānatvāt:* on account of this being the main purport.

Since some texts represent *Brahman* as having a form and others as without form, how can we assert that *Brahman* is without form? The *sūtra* gives the answer. *Brahman* is formless. For if it had form the texts which teach it as being without form would become purportless. Those which deal with *Brahman* as having form are meant for meditation; *upāsanā-vidhi-pradhānāni.*

Bhāskara has an additional *sūtra* here which reads: *asthūlam aṇanv ahrasvam, adīrgham, aśabdam, asparśam, arūpam, avyayam,* (*Brahman* is) non-gross, non-fine, non-short, non-long, without sound, without touch, without form, immutable. *Brahman* without form is to be worshipped, according to Bhāskara.

R. points out that though *Brahman* enters into bodies, human and divine, it is itself without form and is therefore not subject to *Karman*, which, in the case of the individual soul, is due to its embodiedness. C.U. VIII. 14. 1 teaches that though *Brahman* enters into all beings, it is not affected by name and form, though it brings about name and form. If it is asked how *Brahman* who is the inner ruler of beings in so far as he has them for his body, can be said to be without form, the answer is that while the individual soul participates in the pleasures and pains to which the body gives rise, *Brahman* does not share the pleasures and pains. Scriptural injunctions apply only to those who are under the power of *Karman*.

Nimbārka makes out that *Brahman* is formless, i.e. he is not an enjoyer since he is only the principal agent with regard to the creation of names and forms but he is not the enjoyer of names and forms to be created by himself and is therefore without form and untouched by imperfection.

Baladeva begins a new section here, with four *sūtras* about the form of *Brahman*. He holds that *Brahman* is formless in the sense that he has no form but is form itself, since the body of *Brahman* is identical with *Brahman* himself.

III. 2. 15. *prakāśavac cāvaiyarthāt*

And as light (*assumes forms by its contact with objects having forms, so does Brahman*) *because* (*the texts ascribing form to Brahman*) *are not without meaning*.

prakāśavat: like light; *ca:* and; *avaiyarthāt:* because of not being meaningless.

Bhāskara substitutes *vā* for *ca*.

Passages which attribute form to *Brahman* are not without a purpose. The worship of *Brahman* with form helps us to attain *brahma-loka*. All parts of the *Veda* are equally authoritative and should be assumed to have a meaning. *na hi veda-vākyānāṁ kasyacid arthavattvam kasyacid anarthavatvam iti yuktam*. The forms, however, are not absolutely real.

R. explains that light (intelligence) constitutes the essential nature of *Brahman*. *Brahman* possesses twofold characteristics for otherwise the texts declaring *Brahman* to be free from imperfection, all-knowing, the cause of the world and so on would become meaningless.

R. and Nimbārka interpret this *sūtra* as *Brahman* consists of light. They cite *Vājasaneyi Saṁhitā* XXXI; *Taittirīya Āraṇyaka* III. 13. 1; Ś.U. III. 8; B.G. VIII. 9.

Baladeva points out that as the Sun who is pure light is conceived as having a definite form for the purpose of meditation, so the Lord, though pure light of knowledge and bliss, is conceived to have a form for the purpose of meditation.

III. 2. 16. *āha ca tanmātram*

And (the Scripture) declares (Brahman to consist of) that (intelligence) only.

āha: declares; *ca:* and; *tat-mātram:* that only.

Ś. quotes B.U. IV. 5. 13 and holds that *Brahman* is mere intelligence, *caitanyam eva tu nirantaram asya svarūpam.* Ś.

R. interprets this *sūtra* to mean that the text says 'so much only' that *Brahman* has light for its essential nature. This does not negative the other attributes of *Brahman,* as omniscience, being the cause of the world, etc.

Śrīkaṇṭha follows R.'s view.

Nimbārka says that when a text states that only, its meaning only, then it is not meaningless.

Baladeva reaffirms his view that the form which the Lord possesses is not different from him but is his very essence.

III. 2. 17. *darśayati cātho api smaryate*

(This Scripture) also shows and thus (it is) also stated in the smṛtis.

Ś. argues that the non-differenced *Brahman* is mentioned in scriptural texts: B.U. II. 3. 6; *Kena U.* I. 4; T.U. II. 9. Ś. relates how Bāhva, questioned about *Brahman* by Vāṣkalin, explained it to him by silence. 'He said to him, learn *Brahman,* O friend' and became silent. Then on a second and a third question he replied, 'I am teaching you, indeed, but you do not understand. Silent is the self.' *brūmaḥ khalu tvaṁ tu na vijānāsi, upaśānto'yam ātmā.* See B.G. XIII. 12, also III. 25. Ś. quotes a *smṛti* text where Nārāyaṇa instructs Nārada: 'The cause, O Nārada, of your seeing me endowed with the qualities of all beings is the *māyā* created by me, do not cognise me as being such [in reality].'

māyā hy eṣā mayā sṛṣṭā yan māṁ paśyasi nārada
sarva-bhūta-guṇair-yuktaṁ naivam māṁ jñātum arhasi.

Bhāskara uses Ś.U. VI. 13 and B.G. VIII. 9 to show that *Brahman* is self-manifest by nature.

R. supports his view that *Brahman* is the abode of all auspicious qualities and free from imperfections by a number of texts: Ś.U. VI. 7–9, 19; M.U. I. 1. 9; T.U. II. 8 and 9; B.G. X. 3, 42, IX. 10, XV. 17; *Viṣṇu Purāṇa* V. 1. 46–8.

Nimbārka and Śrīnivāsa use C.U. VIII. 7. 1, 3; Ś.U. IV. 19; B.G. XV. 18 in addition to others mentioned by Ś. and R.

Baladeva quotes from *Gopāla-pūrva-tāpanī U.* and *Brahma-saṁhitā* to show that the body of the Lord is identical with the Lord himself.

III. 2. 18. *ata eva copamā sūryakādivat*

For this very reason also (there are applied to Brahman) comparisons such as the images of the sun and the like.

ata eva: for this very reason; *ca:* also; *upamā:* comparisons; *sūrya-kādivat:* like the images of the sun and the like.

Ś. points out that the different forms of *Brahman* who is free from all differentiation are comparable to the images of the sun reflected in the water and the like. He gives two passages in support of this view. As the one luminous sun when entering into relation to many different waters is himself rendered multiform by his limiting adjuncts, so also the one divine unborn self: *yathā hy ayaṁ jyotir ātmā vivasvān apo bhinnāḥ bahudhaiko'nugacchan, upādhinā kriyate bheda-rūpo devaḥ kṣetreṣv evam ajo ayam ātmā.* Again: 'The one Self of all beings separately abides in all the individual beings; hence it appears as one and many at the same time, just as the one moon is multiplied by its reflections in the water.'

eka eva tu bhūtātmā bhūte bhūte vyavasthitaḥ
ekadhā bahudhā caiva dṛśyate jala-candravat.

Yājñavalkya Smṛti III. 143. 4.

R. uses these comparisons to point out that *Brahman* does not share the imperfections due to the places with which he is connected even as the sun reflected in water, mirrors, etc., is not affected by the inpurities of the latter. He quotes *Yājñavalkya Smṛti*: As the one ether is rendered manifold by jars and the like or as the one sun becomes manifold in several sheets of water, thus the one Self is rendered manifold by being in many places.

ākāśam ekaṁ hi yathā ghaṭādiṣu pṛthag bhavet
tathātmaiko hy anekastho jalādhāreṣv ivāṁśumān.

III. 144.

Baladeva begins a new section here to show that the worshipper, the individual soul, is different from the object worshipped, the Lord. As the sun (*bimba*) is different from the image (*prati-bimba*) so the Lord is different from the soul.

III. 2. 9. *ambuvad agrahaṇāt tu na tathātvam*

But there is no similarity (of the things compared), since (in the case of Brahman) there is not apprehension of any (separate substance like water).

ambuvat: like water; *agrahaṇāt:* on account of non-apprehension; *tu:* but; *na:* no; *tāthātmyam:* similarity.

In the case of the sun and the other luminous bodies, there is a separate material substance occupying a different place, viz. water. So the light of the sun is reflected. The Self, on the other hand, is not a material being. It is present everywhere and there is nothing different from it. So there is no similarity between the two.

R. says that the imperfections caused by water and mirrors do not attach themselves to the sun or a face because the sun and the face do not really abide in the water and the mirror.

Nimbārka and Śrīnivāsa argue that the example cited is not to the point. The sentient and the non-sentient beings are not apprehended, as in the case of water, to be remote from *Brahman*. There is no parallelism between the Supreme Person and the reflected sun.

Śrīnivāsa quotes B.U. III. 7. 3, 4; *Śatapatha Brāhmaṇa* XIV. 6. 7. 30; *Kaṭha U.* V. 8, VI. 1 and also B.G. XVIII. 61, VII. 7.

III. 2. 20. *vṛddhi-hrāsa-bhāktvam antar-bhāvād ubhaya-sāmañjasyād evam*

Since the Highest Brahman is inside (of the limiting manifestations) it participates in their increase and decrease; owing to the appropriateness of the two cases, it is thus (the comparison is not defective).

vṛddhi-hrāsa-bhāktvam: participation in the increase and decrease; *antarbhāvāt:* on account of its being inside; *ubhaya-sāmañjasyāt:* on account of the similarity in the two cases; *evam:* thus.

Whenever two things are compared, they are so only with reference to some particular point they have in common. Entire equality of the two can never be demonstrated; indeed if it could be demonstrated, there would be an end of that particular relation which gives rise to the comparison. The feature on which the comparison rests is participation in increase and decrease. The image of the sun dilates when the surface of the water expands and contracts when the water shrinks. It trembles when the water is agitated; it divides itself when the water is divided. It thus participates in all the attributes and conditions of water while the real sun remains all the time the same. So also Ś. says that the unchanging *Brahman* participates, as it were, in the attributes and states of the body and the other limiting adjuncts within which it abides. So there is some similarity in the comparison.

R. and Śrīkaṇṭha take this and the next *sūtra* as one. R. takes together the two comparisons of the ether which becomes manifold through jars and so on and the sun which becomes multiplied through the sheets of water in which it is reflected. Like them the Highest Self while abiding within variously shaped things remains unaffected by their imperfections.

Nimbārka and Śrīnivāsa hold that the Supreme dwells in objects as their inner controller and does not participate in their increase and decrease.

III. 2. 21. *darśanāc ca*

And on account of the declaration (of Scripture).

darśanāt: on account of scriptural declaration; *ca:* and.

The texts considered here are B.U. II. 5. 18; C.U. VI. 3. 2 which declare that *Brahman* enters within the body.

Nimbārka points out that when a comparison is made and we say he is a lionlike boy, we do not mean that he has all the qualities of a lion; we mean only that he is as brave as a lion.

Section 6 (22, 24–30)

THE CLAUSE 'NOT THIS, NOT THIS' NEGATIVES THE TWO FORMS OF *BRAHMAN* AND NOT *BRAHMAN* ITSELF

III. 2. 22. *prakṛtaitāvattvaṁ hi pratiṣedhati tato bravīti ca bhūyaḥ*

What has been mentioned up to this (*the clause not this, not this*), (*denies*) *and* (*the śruti*) *says something more than that.*

prakṛta-etāvattvam: what has been mentioned up to this; *pratiṣedhati:* denies; *tataḥ:* than that; *bhūyaḥ:* something more; *bravīti:* says; *ca:* and.

The two forms of *Brahman*, limited and unlimited, *sat:* defined and *tyat:* undefined (B.U. II. 3. 1) are denied by the words 'not this, not this'. The words '*satyasya satyam*', the Truth of truth, indicate that *Brahman* alone is the reality that exists and is the substratum of the world. We experience the world and its reality to perception is not denied; only its transcendental reality is not accepted. The cosmic plurality is not absolutely real.

Bhāskara does not begin a new section here but continues the topic of meditation on *Brahman* in his aspect of non-difference, as pure being and consciousness. He holds that the first 'not this' denies the corporeal and the non-corporeal forms; the second 'not this' denies his *vāsanā-maya* form as the individual soul. The text designates the pure non-differenced form of *Brahman* but does not indicate the non-existence of the world.

R. does not take this *sūtra* as the beginning of a new section. He holds that it continues the discussion started in *sūtra* 11. He asks whether the clause 'not this, not this' denies of *Brahman* all the previously mentioned *prakāras*, so that it can only be called *sanmātra*. The *sūtra* makes out that *Brahman's* nature cannot be confined to the attributes stated.

Śrīnivāsa says that *Brahman* is not limited by the corporeal and incorporeal forms. *Brahman* is higher than these. He quotes *Kaṭha U.* V. 13, Ṡ.U. 'the eternal among the eternal, the conscious among the conscious'.

Vallabha says that, according to *śruti*, the qualities of ordinary things are not to be found in *Brahman*. But *Brahman* has qualities like bliss, etc.

III. 2. 24. *api ca saṁrādhane pratyakṣānumānābhyām*

And (*Brahman is apprehended*) *in perfect meditation also, according to perception* (*śruti*) *and inference* (*smṛti*).

api: also; *ca:* and; *saṁrādhane:* in perfect meditation; *pratyakṣa-anumānābhyām:* from perception and inference.

Brahman, though not apprehended by the senses, is realised in the state of meditation. *Kaṭha U.* II. 4. 1; M.U. III. 1. 8. By *saṁrādhana* is meant the presentation before the mind (of *Brahman*) which is effected through meditation and devotion, *bhakti-dhyāna-praṇidhānāt anuṣṭhānam.* Ś. He also quotes from *smṛti.*

yam vinidrā jitaśvāsās santuṣṭās saṁyatendriyāḥ
jyotiḥ paśyanti yunjānās tasmai yogātmane namaḥ.

He who is seen as light by the *yogins* meditating on him, sleeplessly with controlled breaths, with contented minds, with subdued senses, reverence to him. M.B. XII. 1642. Again,

yoginas taṁ prapaśyanti bhagavantaṁ sanātanam.

The *yogins* see him the August, the Eternal One.

R. quotes *Kaṭha U.* 2. 23; M.U. III. 1. 9; B.G. XI. 53–4.

Vallabha says that the objector is a fool to argue that *Brahman* is not perceived for in contemplation *Brahman* is perceived. *Brahman* is possessed of form and full of infinite qualities and is not non-manifest.

Baladeva takes this *sūtra* as an independent section.

Only in Ś. is *ca* found after *api.*

The Absolute, though it is not perceived by the senses or known by inference, is apprehended in devotion according to *śruti* and *smṛti.*

The ultimate datum is consciousness which is above reason. Western thought stresses reason as the capacity by which ultimate reality can be known and expressed in a clear, intelligible form. Conceptual thought which posits the object over against the subject becomes the dominant feature. While the stress is on dualism in Western thought non-dualism is the prominent feature in Eastern philosophy.

III. 2. 25. *prakāśādivac cāvaiśeṣyaṁ prakāśaś ca karmaṇy abhyāsāt*

And as in the case of light and the like, there is the non-distinction (of the two Selves), the light (being divided) by its activity; on account of repeated declarations (in the Scripture).

prakāśādivat: as in the case of light and the like; *ca:* and; *avaiśeṣyam:* non-distinction; *prakāṣaḥ:* the light (of *Brahman*); *ca:* and; *karmaṇi:* in activity; *abhyāsāt:* on account of repeated declarations (in the Scripture).

If it is said that *Brahman* as the object of meditation and the individual as the meditator are different, the reply is that *Brahman* is manifested as different on account of the adjuncts of activity. In reality the two are one as the texts declare, 'that art thou, I am *Brahman*'.

Ś. is at pains to make out that the difference is due to association with unreal adjuncts. Ānandagiri says: *ātma-prakāśa-śabdito'jñāna-tat-kārye karmaṇi upādhau sa-viśeṣaḥ.*

Bhāskara holds that there is non-distinction between *Brahman* and the individual soul which is effected from the repetition (of meditation) with regard to the object to be worshipped or from repetition with regard to the act of meditation.

R. makes out that light is intuited as constituting *Brahman's* essential nature by repetition of the practice of meditation. For R., *Brahman* has all material and immaterial objects for its distinguishing modes.

Śrīkaṇṭha says that there is no difference between their attaining knowledge, bliss and the rest like the Supreme and attaining lordship and so on like him.

Nimbārka makes out that the direct intuition of *Brahman* results from the incessant practice of the *sādhanas* consisting in perfect meditation.

Śrīnivāsa tells us that though *Brahman* is accessible to all he manifests himself to those alone who are desirous of salvation and meditate on him incessantly.

Baladeva breaks this *sūtra* into two, *prakāśādivac ca vaiśeṣyāt* and *prakāśaś ca karmaṇy-abhyāsāt.*

In the former *sūtra,* he adds a *na* and says that the Lord has not two states, subtle and gross like fire. His manifestation depends on the love of the devotee. The manifestation is brought about through repeated meditation. Mere love is not enough; repeated acts of meditation are also necessary.

III. 2. 26. *ato'nantena tathā hi liṅgam*

Therefore (the individual soul enters into unity) with the infinite (i.e. the Highest Self); for thus (is the scriptural) indication.
ataḥ: therefore; *anantena:* with the infinite; *tathā:* thus; *hi:* for; *liṅgam:* (the Scripture is) indication.

The individual soul is able to attain unity with the Highest Self because the ignorance which is destroyed by knowledge is unreal. See M.U. III. 2. 9; B.U. IV. 4. 6. If the individuality of the soul were real, then it cannot be destroyed and unity with the Highest Self is not possible.

R. makes out that *Brahman* is distinguished by an infinite number of auspicious qualities. So, for him, *Brahman* possesses twofold characteristics. R completes a section here.

Śrīkaṇṭha follows R.'s interpretation.

Nimbārka holds that the individual soul attains similarity with the Infinite, when it intuits the Highest. See M.U. III. 1. 3.

Baladeva points out that the direct vision of the Lord is possible through the grace of the Infinite. The Supreme, though invisible, makes himself visible to his devotees, through his power or grace.

III. 2. 27. *ubhaya-vyapadeśāt tu ahi-kuṇḍalavat*

But on account of the twofold teaching, (the relation of the Highest Self to the individual soul is to be viewed) as that between a serpent and its coils.

ubhaya-vyapadeśāt: on account of twofold teaching; *tu:* but; *ahi-kuṇḍalavat:* as that between a serpent and its coils.

There are texts which suggest a difference between the individual soul and the Highest *Brahman*: M.U. III. 1. 1, see also III. 2. 8; B.U. III. 7. 15. There are passages like C.U. VI. 8. 7: 'That art thou'; B.U. I. 4. 10: 'I am *Brahman*'; III. 4. 1: 'This is thy Self who is within all'; III. 7. 15: 'He is thy self, the ruler within, the immortal.' This means that, prior to liberation, the difference between the two is real, though it is one of identity after liberation. The relation is one of difference and non-difference as that between a serpent and its coils. As a serpent it is one; but if we look at the coils, hood, etc., there is difference. Similarly there is both difference and non-difference between the individual soul and the Highest Self. This is the *prima facie* view for Ś.

Bhāskara: The snake is one as a whole, yet is different as having different postures, coil, erect hood and so on. Similarly, *Brahman* is one but is different as soul, matter and so on.

R. argues that it has been shown that the entire non-sentient universe is the outward form of *Brahman*. The question is raised about the way in which the world constitutes the outward form of *Brahman*. Is the relation like that of the serpent and its coils? Or is it like that of light and the luminous body? Or does the soul form a distinguishing attribute and so a part, *aṁśa*, of *Brahman*? The first alternative is stated here that the non-sentient things are special forms or arrangements of *Brahman* as the coils are of a coiled up snake, *saṁsthāna-viśeṣa*, as the coil is of the serpent. Śrīkaṇṭha follows R.'s view.

For Nimbārka, the universe consisting of the corporeal and the incorporeal abides in its own cause, i.e. *Brahman*, in a relation of difference-non-difference on account of the twofold teaching like the case of the serpent and the coils.

Śrīnivāsa holds that *Brahman* is the one non-different material and efficient cause of the world. The coil is the effect dependent on the serpent which is the cause. The universe is the effect of *Brahman*. See *Ṛg Veda* I. 164. 20; M.U. III. 1. 1; Ś.U. IV. 6, I. 6; C.U. III. 14. 1, VI. 8. 6, VII. 26. 1.

Vallabha says that the *śruti* speaks of *Param-ātman* as both without and with qualities. Even as a serpent assumes a crooked or straight form, so *Brahman* assumes all contradictory forms.

Baladeva begins a new section here devoted to the discussion of the identity of the Lord and his attributes. The Lord is essentially intelligence and bliss and yet possesses them as his attributes, even as the serpent is nothing but the coil, yet possesses it as its attribute.

III. 2. 28. *prakāśāśrayavad vā tejastvāt*

Or else like that of light to its substratum, both being luminous.
prakāśa-āśrayavat: like light and its substratum; *vā:* or; *tejastvāt:* on account of being luminous.

Both being luminous, Ś. says that they are non-different; on account of their varying extensity they are spoken of as different. Even so is the relation between the individual soul and *Brahman;* the former is limited while the latter is all-pervading. This is also the *prima facie* view.

For R., the two are different but at the same time they are identical since they both are luminous. In the same way, the non-sentient world constitutes the form of *Brahman*. This is also the *prima facie* view which criticises the preceding *prima facie* view by pointing out that if the non-sentient would be a state of *Brahman*, as the coil is of the snake, then it will become identical with him seeing that the coil is only the snake. The correct view is that the soul is related to *Brahman* as the ray is to the sun, i.e. is his form and is different from him.

Śrīkaṇṭha follows R.

For Nimbārka, there is no absolute non-difference between the two.

Baladeva argues that even as the sun is essentially light and is the substratum of light, so *Brahman* is essentially knowledge and also the substratum of knowledge.

II. 2. 29. *pūrvavad vā*

Or (*the relation of the two is to be conceived*) *in the manner stated previously.*
pūrvavat: as stated previously; *vā*; or.

This *sūtra* for Ś. refutes the view of difference-non-difference and establishes what is given in *sūtra* 25, that the non-difference is the reality and difference is unreal. For if the difference were real, it could never cease to be. If separateness were real there could be no liberation.

R. points out that non-sentient matter stands to *Brahman* in the same relation as the individual soul does. It is an attribute incapable of being realised apart from *Brahman* and hence is a part, *aṁśa*, of the latter. Those texts which refer to the two as different should be taken in their primary sense, that the distinguishing attribute and that to which the attribute belongs are essentially different.

III. 2. 30. *pratiṣedhāc ca*

And on account of the denial.
pratiṣedhāt: on account of the denial; *ca:* and.

Passages like 'there is no other witness but he' (B.U. III. 7. 23), 'not this, not this' (B.U. II. 3. 6), show that there is no other reality than *Brahman*. Ś.

For R., the relation of the two can only be that of distinguishing attribute and the thing distinguished. *Brahman* distinguished by sentient and non-sentient beings in their subtle state is the cause; distinguished by the same beings in their gross state is the effect. The effect is non-different from the cause and by the knowledge of the causal *Brahman* the effect is known. *Brahman* is free from defects and is the abode of all auspicious qualities.

Nimbārka says that *Brahman* does not possess any imperfection. See *Kaṭha U.*

Srīnivāsa quotes *Kaṭha U.* V. 10. 11.

Section 7 (31–37)

BRAHMAN IS ONE WITHOUT A SECOND

III. 2. 31. *param ataḥ setūn-māna-sambandha-bheda-vyapadeśebhyaḥ*

Beyond this (Brahman there is something further) on account of the designations of bridge, measure, connection and separation.

param: beyond; *ataḥ:* this; *setu-unmāna-sambandha-bheda-vyapadeśāt:* on account of the designations of bridge, measure, connection and separation.

Ś. points out that the objection is raised that on account of texts mentioning bridge which separates things other than itself, 'Now the Self is the bridge, the [separating] boundary for keeping these worlds apart' (C.U. VIII. 4. 1), the self has size and is limited. C.U. III. 18. 2 says *Brahman* has four feet; whatever is limited is limited by some other object. Again, B.U. IV. 3. 21 says that 'the person in the embrace of the intelligent self knows nothing without or within'. This shows that there is something other than *Brahman*. All these suggest that *Brahman* is not one without a second. It has something different, *anya-tattvam.*

For R., the *sūtra* states the *pūrva-pakṣa* that there is a being higher even than the Highest *Brahman*, the supreme cause material as well as operative of the entire world.

Baladeva makes out that the bliss of the Lord is the highest. It is higher than the worldly bliss on account of the designation of bridge, measure, connection and difference. The bliss of *Brahman* is the support of the entire world. C.U. VIII. 4. 1; T.U. II. 4. Human bliss compares to the bliss of the Lord as one to infinity. B.U. IV. 3. 22.

III. 2. 32. *sāmānyāt tu*

But (Brahman is called a bridge) on account of similarity.

sāmānyāt: on account of similarity; *tu:* but.

For Ś., there is nothing different from *Brahman.* It is called a bridge not because there is something beyond it but because like a bridge which keeps back water and marks the boundary of adjacent fields, *Brahman* maintains the world and its boundaries. When C.U. VIII. 4. 2 says 'having passed the bridge', it means 'having attained *Brahman* fully even as we say he has passed in grammar, when we mean that he has mastered it fully'. *yathā vyākaraṇaṁ tīrṇa iti prāpta ucyate nātikrāntas tad-vat.*

For R., *Brahman* is said to be a bridge in so far as it binds to itself (*setu* being derived from *si*: to bind) the whole aggregate of sentient and non-sentient things without any confusion. Again, passing beyond means reaching, as we say he has passed beyond the *Vedānta* meaning that he has mastered it: *taratiś ca prāpti-vacano yathā vedāntaṁ taratīti.*

For Nimbārka, *Brahman* is similar to a bridge in a certain respect for he keeps the worlds apart. C.U. VIII. 4. 1.

For Baladeva, the word 'bliss' is applied to human bliss on account of similarity even as the term 'jar' is applied to all jars irrespective of their individual differences.

III. 2. 33. *buddhyarthaḥ pādavat*

(*The statement that Brahman has size is*) *for the sake of* (*easy*) *comprehension: just like* (*four*) *feet.*

buddhyarthaḥ: for the sake of comprehension; *pādavat:* like feet.

Since it is difficult to comprehend *Brahman,* infinite and all-pervading, for the sake of easy comprehension and meditation *Brahman* is imagined to have size, etc. C.U. III. 18. This is Ś.'s view.

R. quotes C.U. III. 12. 6 and holds that for the purpose of thought, meditation, the Supreme is said to have measure, etc.

III. 2. 34. *sthāna-viśeṣāt prakāśādivat*

(*The statements in regard to connection and difference*) *are due to difference of place; as in the case of light, etc.*

sthāna-viṣesāt: on account of difference of place; *prakāśādivat:* as in the case of light, etc.

Ś. says that differences are made with reference to limiting adjuncts. They do not indicate any difference in the nature of *Brahman.* Light inside the room is distinguished from the light outside, though all light is one. The sense of difference is produced by the connection of the Self with different adjuncts; when these adjuncts are removed, union is effected.

Bhāskara does not mention this *sūtra.*

Śrīnivāsa says that if the objection is raised that the Unlimited can never become limited even for purposes of meditation, the *sūtra* says that though *Brahman* is unlimited, he becomes limited on account of the speciality of place.

Baladeva starts a new section here, showing that the Lord has a variety of manifestations. The Lord, though one, manifests himself in different forms to his devotees in accordance with their different devotions. Those who worship him as the Master see him as the Majestic; those who worship him as the Beloved, see him as the Sweet.

III. 2. 35. *upapatteś ca*

And from reasoning.

upapatteḥ: from reasoning; *ca:* and.

The difference between the soul and *Brahman* is for Ś. not real but is due to ignorance. See C.U. VI. 8. 1 where the connection of the soul with *Brahman* is said to be of essential nature. See also C.U. III. 12. 7ff.

R. quotes the text M.U. II. 2. 5, *amṛtasyaiṣa setuḥ*, he is the bridge of the Immortal, and says that it does not mean a distinction between that which causes to reach and the object reached. The Highest Self is the means as well as the end. See *Kaṭha U.* I. 2. 23.

Baladeva quotes the text: 'as you meditate, so you become', and holds that the devotees realised the Lord differently in accordance with the different modes of worshipping him.

III. 2. 36. *tathānya-pratiṣedhāt*

Similarly, on account of the denial of other (existences).

tathā: similarly; *anya-pratiṣedhāt:* on account of the denial of other (existences).

Ś. says that many texts deny the existence of anything other than *Brahman.* C.U. VII. 25. 1 and 2; M.U. II. 2. 11; B.U. II. 4. 6, IV. 4. 19, II. 5. 19; Ś.U. III. 9.

R. holds that there is nothing higher than the Highest and interprets the text *tato yad uttara-taram* in accordance with the previous verses that that which is the Highest is without form, etc. Again, in M.U. III. 2. 8, the text, 'the knower freed from name and shape, attains to the divine Person higher than the high', the high here means the aggregate soul, *samaṣṭi-puruṣa*, and the higher refers to the Supreme Person with all his transcendent qualities, who is superior to the aggregate soul.

Śrīkaṇṭha begins a new section here dealing with the question whether there is anything equal to the Lord, as the doubt whether there is anything superior to the Lord has been disposed of in the previous section. This section says that there is none equal to the Lord.

Baladeva makes this an independent section proving that the Lord is the Highest for if he were not, there could be no love and devotion for him.

III. 2. 37. *anena sarva-gatatvam āyāma-śabdādibhyaḥ*

By this, the all-pervadingness (of Brahman is established) in accordance with the statements about (Brahman's) extent.

anena: by this; *sarva-gatatvam:* all-pervadingness; *āyāma-śabdādibhyaḥ:* in accordance with (scriptural) statements about (*Brahman's*) extent.

For Ś., texts describing *Brahman* as bank, etc., are not to be taken literally, for then *Brahman* would be limited. Texts denying plurality should be accepted as valid. There are texts which declare the all-pervadingness of *Brahman*: C.U. VIII. 1. 3; *Śatapatha Brāhmaṇa* X. 6. 3. 2; B.G. II. 24.

R. quotes Ś.U. III. 9; M.U. I. 1. 6; and *Mahānārāyaṇa U.* XI. 6. 'Whatever is seen or heard in this world, is pervaded inside and outside by *Nārāyaṇa*.'

yacca kiñcij jagaty asmin dṛśyate śrūyate'pi vā
antar bahiś ca tat sarvaṁ vyāpya nārāyaṇaḥ sthitaḥ.

Śrīkaṇṭha points out that the Lord *Śiva* pervades the entire universe through *Nārāyaṇa*, the material cause who is but a part of himself. So it is known that the Lord himself is all-pervasive.

Nimbārka argues that the all-pervadingness is established on account of the scriptural texts about expansion and so on. While Nimbārka points out that there is nothing higher than *Brahman*, Ś. and Bhāskara take the *sūtra* as establishing that there is nothing besides *Brahman*.

Baladeva makes this an independent section. If it be objected that the Lord is not all-pervasive, but of an intermediate size, i.e. of the size of the body or form in which he appears before his devotees, it is said that even the intermediate form of the Lord is all-pervasive for Scripture declares so.

Section 8 (38–41)

THE REWARD OF WORKS IS ALLOTTED BY THE LORD

III. 2. 38. *phalam ata upapatteḥ*

From him the fruit, for that is reasonable.

phalam: fruit (of action); *ataḥ:* from him; *upapatteḥ:* for that is reasonable.

The question is whether the fruits of actions spring from the actions themselves or from the Lord. Actions which pass away as soon as they are performed have no power of bringing about results at some future time since nothing can spring from nothing. Nor can it be argued that an action passes away only after having produced some result according to its nature and the agent will at some future time enjoy the fruit of that action. The fruit of an action is the fruit only at the time of its enjoyment by the doer. We cannot say that the fruit will spring from some supersensuous principle, *apūrva*, which itself is said to be a direct result of the deed. For *apūrva* is of a non-intelligent nature and cannot act unless moved by some intelligent being. Nor is there any proof for the existence of *apūrva*. The fact that the deeds are actually requited is accounted for by the action of the Lord.

R. makes out that the meditating devotee receives the reward of meditation, i.e. release, which consists in attaining to the Highest Person, only from that Highest Person, for action which is non-intelligent and transitory is incapable of bringing about a result connected with a future time.

For Nimbārka, the Highest Person is the giver of fruits.

III. 2. 39. *śrutatvāc ca*

And because the Scripture so teaches.

śrutatvāt: because the Scripture so teaches; *ca:* and.

Ś. quotes B.U. IV. 4. 20.

R. quotes in addition T.U. II. 7.

III. 2. 40. *dharmaṁ jaiminir ata eva*

Jaimini (thinks) that for the same reasons, religious merit (is what brings about the fruits of actions).

dharmam: religious merit; *jaiminiḥ:* (the sage) Jaimini; *ata eva:* for the same reasons.

Jaimini holds a different view. Scripture says, 'He who is desirous of the heavenly world is to sacrifice', *svarga-kāmo yajeta*. If such injunctions are to be meaningful, the sacrifice itself must bring about the result but a deed cannot effect a result at some future time, unless before passing away, it gives birth to some unseen result. This *apūrva* may be an imperceptible after-state of the deed or an imperceptible antecedent state of the result. We need not think that the Lord effects the results of all actions, for one uniform cause cannot account for a variety of effects. Again, the Lord will be charged with partiality and cruelty; besides, if the deed itself did not bring about its own fruit, it would be useless to perform it at all. For all these reasons the result springs from the deed only, whether meritorious or non-meritorious.

According to the *Pūrva Mīmāṁsā*, the results of sacrifices, etc., are due neither to a Supreme Deity, which it does not admit, nor to the particular deities to whom the offerings are made, but to the unseen potency generated by the very performance of the sacrifices, etc. *Pūrva Mīmāṁsā Sūtra:* II. 1. 5. This *pūrva-pakṣa* is refuted in the next *sūtra*.

III. 2. 41. *pūrvaṁ tu bādarāyaṇo hetu-vyapadeśāt*

Bādarāyaṇa, however, thinks the former (*i.e. the Lord*) (*to be the cause of the fruits of action*) *since he is designated as the cause* (*of the actions themselves*).
pūrvam: the former; *tu:* but; *bādarāyaṇaḥ:* (the sage) Bādarāyaṇa; *hetu-vyapadeśāt:* on account of his being declared to be the cause (of the actions even).
tu: but, refutes Jaimini's view.

According to Bādarāyaṇa, *Brahman* is the dispenser of rewards. The scriptural text declares that *Brahman* is the cause, and not *karma* either by itself or through some other mysterious factor called *apūrva*. According to Ś., the reference is directly to *Brahman* as the dispenser. He quotes a passage from the K.U. III. 8: 'This one, indeed, causes him whom he wishes to lead up from these worlds to perform good actions. This one, indeed, also causes him whom he wishes to lead downward, to perform bad actions.' See also B.G. VII. 21–22. Since the Lord has regard to the merit and demerit of the souls, the objection that a uniform cause is incapable of producing various effects does not stand.

R. considers texts which ascribe potency to the various deities and proves the identity of these deities with *Brahman* by means of the *antaryāmi Brāhmaṇa*.

Śrīkaṇṭha assumes from the start the identity of the deities with the Supreme Lord. *parameśvarātmakatayā vāyvādīnām.*

According to Śuka, *Nārāyaṇa* grants fruits to the individual souls in keeping with their past actions. *nārāyaṇāt tat-tat-jīvānāṁ tat-tat-pūrvānuguṇyena phalaṁ bhavatīti niścetavyam.*

Section 1 (1–4)

THE DIFFERENT MEDITATIONS ARE ONE

III. 3. 1. *sarva-vedānta-pratyayaṁ codanādy aviśeṣāt*

(The forms of meditation) described in all the Vedānta texts (are not different) on account of the non-difference of injunction and so on.
sarva-vedānta-pratyayam: described in all the *Vedānta* texts; *codanādy-aviśeṣāt:* on account of non-difference as regards injunction and so on.

This part describes how the individual can by meditation on *Brahman* obtain final release. In different branches of Vedic learning the same meditations are described with slight or major modifications. But there is unity on the nature of *Brahman* and the relation to it of the human soul. In the present part attempts are made to remove the contradictions in the sacred texts and achieve reconciliation of the different *Vedānta* texts on this matter.

The meditation on *prāṇa* is described in one way in B.U. VI. 1. 1 and in a different way in C.U. V. 1. 1. They are non-different because of the similarity as regards injunction, connection, name and form. There is non-difference even as regards the fruit or the result of meditation. This is true not only of *prāṇa-vidyā* but *dahara-vidyā, Vaiśvānara-upāsanā, Śāṇḍilya-vidyā,* etc. Ś. believes that all these *vidyās* are concerned with *Saguṇa Brahman* and not *Nirguṇa Brahman.* Some of them lead to the attainment of results on earth while others lead on gradually to salvation, by way of producing knowledge.

Baladeva interprets the *sūtra* as stating the settled conclusion *anta-pratyayam* of all the *Vedas.* All the *Vedas* seek to teach *Brahman,* since all of them enjoin meditation on *Brahman.*

III. 3. 2. *bhedān neti cen naikasyām api*

If it be said (that the meditations are) not (one) on account of difference (in minor points) (we reply) not so, since even in one and the same (vidyā there might be minor differences).
bhedāt: on account of difference; *na:* not; *iti cet:* if it be said; *na:* not so; *ekasyām api:* even in the same (*vidyā*).

In spite of secondary differences, it is reasonable to assume that the meditations of the same class are one and not different. Ś. and Bhāskara hold that differences in details are permissible even in the case of one and the same *vidyā.* If the two *vidyās* agree in essential points, differences in details do not make them separate *vidyās.*

Baladeva says that if the objection is raised that *Brahman* is designated differently in different *Upaniṣads*—in one he is said to be knowledge and bliss, B.U. III. 9. 28; in another omniscient and all-knowing, M.U.I.1.9—the reply is that even in the same *Upaniṣad*, *Brahman* is designated as knowledge, bliss as well as omniscient. So all branches speak of the same *Brahman*.

III. 3. 3. *svādhyāyasya tathātvena hi samācāre'dhikārāc ca savavac ca tan-niyamaḥ*

(The rite of carrying fire on the head is connected) with the study of the Veda because (it is described) as such in the samācāra; (this also follows) from its being a qualification (for the students of the Atharva Veda) as is the case with the (seven) oblations.

svādhyāyasya: of the study of the *Vedas*; *tathātvena:* as being such; *hi:* because; *samācāre:* in *samācāra* (a book of that name); *adhikārāt:* on account of the qualification (for the students of the *Atharva Veda*); *ca:* and; *savavat:* like that of the (seven) oblations; *ca:* and; *tan-niyamaḥ:* that rule.

If the objection is raised that in the M.U. which deals with the knowledge of *Brahman*, the carrying of the fire on the head is mentioned, so this *vidyā* of the *Atharvaṇikas* is different from all others, the *sūtra* according to Ś. refutes the objection by holding that the rite of carrying fire on the head is not an attribute of the *vidyā* but of the study of the *Vedas* of the *Atharvaṇikas*. *Samācāra* is a book which deals with Vedic observances.

Bhāskara reads *salila-vac ca* in place of *sava-vac ca*. Interpretation is the same.

R. contends that the ceremony is not a part of the *vidyā*; it is a peculiarity of the study of the *Veda*.

Baladeva breaks the *sūtra* into two independent parts.

svādhyāyasya . . . adhikārāc ca (3).

sava-vac ca tan-niyama (4).

(3) means: For the injunction of the study of the *Veda* being such, (i.e. of a general import) and because of the eligibility (of all) to the sacred duties (mentioned in the *Veda*), (the entire *Veda* must be studied). The followers of one branch are eligible for the duties enjoined by all the branches. *Brahman* may be realised by all the religious practices taught in all the *Vedas*. (4) means that while the libations are open to the followers of the *Atharva Veda* only and cannot be offered by the followers of the other *Vedas*, the worship of *Brahman* is universal and may be performed by all.

III. 3. 4. *darśayati ca*

(Scripture) also declares thus.

darśayati: declares; *ca:* also.

Kaṭha U. I. 2. 15 refers to 'that which all the *Vedas* declare'.

Ś. says that it is the *Nirguṇa Brahman* which is the purport of all *Vedānta* texts: All *vidyās* relating to it are one. So also the meditation on *Saguṇa Brahman* as *Vaiśvānara* who is represented as extending from heaven to earth (see also C.U. V. 18. 1) is one, and not many. The unity of all meditations is indicated here.

Section 2 (5)

PARTICULARS OF IDENTICAL *VIDYĀS* MENTIONED IN DIFFERENT *ŚĀKHĀS* OR BRANCHES SHOULD BE COMBINED IN ONE MEDITATION

III. 3. 5. *upasaṁhāro'rthābhedād vidhiśeṣavat samāne ca*

In the case of (*a meditation*) *common* (*to several śākhās or branches*) *a combination* (*of particulars mentioned in each is to be made*) *since there is no difference of essential matter, even as in the case of what is subsidiary to the main sacrifice.*

upasaṁhāraḥ: combination; *arthābhedāt:* since there is no difference in the object of meditation; *vidhi-śeṣavat:* as in the case of the subsidiary rites to the main sacrifice; *samāne:* common; *ca:* and.

The object of meditation is one only comprehending all the attributes mentioned in the different texts.

The meditations are identical and their meaning is the same and so their special features are to be combined even as the subsidiary rites are combined in the performance of sacrifices like *agni-hotra* and the like.

Baladeva begins a new section here and asks whether *Brahman* described as *Kṛṣṇa, Rāma* and *Nṛsiṁha* to denote sweetness, heroism, terrific character is one or different and answers that all the attributes are to be combined.

Section 3 (6–8)

SOME *VIDYĀS* ARE REALLY SEPARATE, THOUGH APPARENTLY IDENTICAL

III. 3. 6. *anyathātvaṁ śabdād iti cen nāviśeṣāt*

If it be said that (*the udgītha vidyā of the* B.U. I. 3. 7 *and that of the* C.U. I. 2. 7) *are separate on account of* (*the difference of*) *texts,* (*we say*), *not so, on account of the non-difference* (*as regards essentials*).

anyathātvam: separateness; *śabdāt:* on account of (difference of) texts; *iti cet:* if it be said; *na:* not so; *aviśeṣāt:* on account of non-difference (as regards essentials).

The opponent states that the *vidyās* are one because in spite of differences of texts, there is unity in essentials. Both texts state that the *devas* and the *asuras* are fighting; both at first glorify speech and the other vital airs in their relation to the *udgītha* and then find fault with them and pass on to the chief vital air; both relate that through the strength of the latter, the *asuras* are scattered as a ball of earth is scattered when hitting a solid stone. So it is argued that the two texts constitute one *vidyā* only.

Baladeva does not begin a new section here but continues the topic of the coalescence of the different attributes of the Lord.

III. 3. 7. *na vā prakaraṇa-bhedāt parovarīyastvādivat*

Or rather there is no (unity of the vidyās) owing to the difference of subject matter, even as (the meditation on the udgītha) the highest and greatest (is different).

na vā: rather not; *prakaraṇa-bhedāt:* owing to the difference of subject matter; *parovarīyastvādivat:* even as (the meditation on the *udgītha* as) the highest and greatest (is different from the meditation on the *udgītha* as abiding in the eye, etc.).

The two *vidyās* are different on account of differences in subject matter. In C.U. I. 1. 1 only a part of the *udgītha*, the syllable *aum*, is meditated upon as the *prāṇa*; in B.U. I. 3. 2, the whole *udgītha* hymn is meditated on as *prāṇa*. So the two *vidyās* cannot be one. The case is similar to the meditation on *udgītha* enjoined in the passage, 'This is, indeed, the highest and greatest *udgītha*' (C.U. I. 9. 2), which is different from the one enjoined in C.U. I. 6, where the *udgītha* is meditated on as abiding in the eye and the sun.

R. agrees that the meditations are separate since they have different objects of meditation.

Nimbārka follows R.'s interpretation.

Baladeva begins a new section here, with two *sūtras*. While in the previous section all the attributes are said to be combined while meditating on the Lord, here it is pointed out that this is the case only with the *svaniṣṭha* devotees, but in the case of *ekāntin* devotees there is no such combination. He interprets *prakaraṇa* to mean *prakṛṣṭa karaṇam*, excellent act (of devotion). For Baladeva, the *sūtra* reads: or (there is) no combination of attributes (in the case of the *ekāntins*) on account of the difference of devotion (i.e. because the devotion of the *ekāntins*) is one-pointed, while that of the *svaniṣṭha* is universal as in the case of being higher than the high, (i.e. just as the *ekāntin* worshipper of the golden Person in the sun does not combine the qualities of being higher than the high and so on).

III. 3. 8. *saṁjñātaś cet tad uktam asti tu tad api*

If it be said (that they are one) on account of name (being the same) it has already been said (answered) but even that (identity of name in different vidyās) exists.

saṁjñātaḥ: on account of name (being same); *cet:* if it be said; *tat:* it;

uktam: has already been said; *asti:* exists; *tu:* but; *tat:* that; *api:* even.

We have already said that identity of name does not mean unity of the *vidyās*.

Terms like *agnihotra, udgītha* are given to many different acts, says R.

Baladeva holds that even while the same name is given, the attributes of the one need not be combined in the other.

Section 4 (9)

AUM IS COMMON TO ALL THE *VEDAS*

III. 3. 9. *vyāpteś ca samañjasam*

And because (aum) extends (to all the Vedas), to specialise it (by the term udgītha) is appropriate.

vyāpteḥ: owing to extension (to all the *Vedas*); *ca:* and; *samañjasam:* is appropriate.

In C.U. I. 1. 1 the *auṁkāra* and the *udgītha* stand in the relation of one specifying the other. They stand in the relation of *sāmānādhikaraṇya*, abiding in a common substratum.

According to R., the object of meditation is constituted by the *praṇava*; this is termed the *udgītha*, viewed under the form of *prāṇa* in the C.U. In the B.U. the term *udgītha* denotes the whole *udgītha* and the object of meditation is he who produces the *udgītha*, i.e. the *udgātṛi*, viewed under the form of *prāṇa*. So the two *vidyās* are separate.

Śrīkaṇṭha holds that the *udgītha* qualifies *auṁkāra* and so the *auṁkāra* is the object to be meditated on.

Baladeva asks whether the qualities of infancy, etc., are to be included in the meditation on the Supreme and answers that they are to be included as they are not inconsistent with the all-pervadingness of the Supreme.

Section 5 (10)

THE UNITY OF THE *PRĀṆA-VIDYĀS*

III. 3. 10. *sarvābhedād anyatreme*

Since (the vidyās) are non-different everywhere, those (qualities which are found in some are to be inserted) in the other places (also).

sarvābhedāt: on account of non-difference everywhere; *anyatra:* in the other places; *ime:* these qualities (are to be inserted).

Prāṇa is mentioned in C.U. VI; B.U. VI. 1 not only as the eldest and the best but also as the richest and so on. In the text of the K.U.

only the former are mentioned. The question is whether the other attributes are to be imported into it also. The *prima facie* view is against such importation for each meditation is enjoined in a particular form and for each a special result is prescribed. So a mixing up of the meditations should be avoided. The answer is that, as the meditations relate to one entity, *prāṇa,* the qualities mentioned in one context are likely to occur to our minds even in another and so are included in the significance of the particular form of meditation presented.

Śrīkaṇṭha agrees with this view.

Baladeva has a different interpretation and takes the *sūtra* as dealing with the acts of the Lord which are eternal on account of the non-difference of all, viz. the Lord and his companions and they manifest themselves elsewhere. The acts of the Lord which he performs through *cit-śakti* are eternal, while those which he performs through matter are non-eternal.

Section 6 (11–13)

IN ALL MEDITATIONS ON *BRAHMAN*, ESSENTIAL AND UNALTERABLE QUALITIES LIKE BLISS AND KNOWLEDGE ARE TO BE INCLUDED EVERYWHERE BUT NOT OTHERS

III. 3. 11. *ānandādayaḥ pradhānasya*

Bliss and other qualities as belonging to the subject of the qualities (*have to be attributed to Brahman everywhere*).
ānandādayaḥ: bliss and other qualities; *pradhānasya:* of the subject, (i.e. *Brahman*).

The question is raised whether in each place where *Brahman* is mentioned, we have to understand only the qualities mentioned there or all the qualities, the answer is, since *Brahman* to which the qualities belong is one and non-different, the qualities should also be the same.

Nimbārka says that as the substratum of the qualities, *Brahman* is the same, the attributes are to be inserted in all the meditations of the Highest.

III. 3. 12. *priyaśirastvādyaprāpti upacayāpacayau hi bhede*

(*Such qualities as*) *joy being its head and so on have no force* (*for other passages*)*; for increase and decrease* (*are possible only*) *if there is difference* (*and not in Brahman in which there is non-difference*).
priyaśirastvādi: (qualities like) joy being its head, etc.; *aprāptiḥ:* are not to be taken everywhere; *upacaryāpacayau:* increase and decrease; *hi:* because; *bhede:* (are possible) in difference.

Attributes like joy, satisfaction, great satisfaction, bliss are qualities with lower and higher degrees. These degrees are possible only where there is plurality and *Brahman* is devoid of plurality. They are attributed to the Highest *Brahman* merely as a means of fixing one's mind on it and not because they are themselves objects of contemplation. These qualities belong to the *Saguṇa Brahman* only and not to the Highest *Brahman* above all qualifications. This is the view of Ś.

R. holds that these qualities are not those of *Brahman* but are elements in a figurative representation of *Brahman* under the form of an animal body.

III. 3. 13. *itare tu artha-sāmānyāt*

But other (*attributes are valid for all passages relative to Brahman*) *on account of identity of purport.*
itare: other (attributes); *tu:* but; *artha-sāmānyāt:* on account of identity of purport.

Attributes like bliss, knowledge, all-pervadingness which describe the nature of *Brahman* are to be combined since their purport is one and indivisible *Brahman.*

R. and Śrīkaṇṭha interpret *artha-sāmānyāt* differently. 'On account of their equality with the object itself.' The qualities of bliss and the rest determine the very nature of the thing (*Brahman*) and are therefore similar to the thing itself and so are included in all meditations just like the thing itself.

Baladeva argues that the meditation on *Brahman* as possessed of the attributes of all-pervadingness and the rest mentioned in T.U. leads to the attainment of *Brahman,* even as the meditation on him as possessed of other attributes mentioned in other texts.

Section 7 (14–15)

THE HIGHEST SELF IS HIGHER THAN EVERYTHING ELSE

III. 3. 14. *ādhyānāya prayojanābhāvāt*

(*The passage Kaṭha U. I.* 3. 10 *gives information*) *for the purpose of meditation since there is no use* (*of the knowledge of the objects being higher than the senses and so on*).
ādhyānāya: for the purpose of meditation; *prayojanābhāvāt:* since there is no use.

Kaṭha U. says that beyond the senses are the objects, beyond the objects is the mind; beyond the mind is the understanding; and beyond the understanding is the great self; beyond the great self is the unmanifest; beyond the unmanifest is the spirit; beyond the spirit there is nothing. The question is raised whether the aim of the passage is to say that each of the things successively enumerated is higher than the preceding one or only that spirit is higher than all of them. While the opponent splits up the sentence into many and holds that the aim of the passage is to indicate the superiority of one thing over its preceding, the *sūtra* holds that the purport of the passage is that the spirit is higher than everything for it has a purpose, viz. to accomplish final release. See *Kaṭha U.*I. 3. 15: 'one is freed from the mouth of death'.

R. refers to the text T.U. II. 5 which represents *Brahman* as having joy for its head and so on and holds that it is intended for the purpose of meditation. This interpretation is followed by Nimbārka.

Śrīkaṇṭha begins a new section here of four *sūtras* which deals with the question whether the self consisting of food and the rest (T.U. II. 2ff.) is to be meditated on constantly as the self consisting of bliss *is*. The answer is '[they are not to be meditated on constantly] on account of the absence of purpose [for such meditation]'. Meditation on the self consisting of food and the rest has a purpose only so long as the self consisting of bliss is not reached. When it is reached the others become meaningless. So such meditations are not to be practised perpetually.

Śrīkaṇṭha establishes the non-difference of *cit-śakti* from *Brahman.*

III. 3. 15. *ātma-śabdāc ca*

And on account of the word Self.

ātma-śabdāt: on account of the word Self; *ca:* and.

The subject of discussion is called the *Self. Kaṭha U.* I. 3. 12. The enumeration is not useless since it helps to turn the mind, which is outgoing gradually towards the Self.

R. says that since the Self cannot really possess a head, wings and tail, its having joy for its head, etc., can only be meant figuratively, for the sake of easy comprehension.

Nimbārka follows R.

Śrīkaṇṭha continues the topic whether the selves consisting of food, vital breath, etc., are to be meditated on perpetually or not and gives another reason why they are not to be so meditated. The form 'self' applied to each of the selves of food, etc., denotes the presiding deities. *Brahman* alone is to be meditated on and no other deity.

Section 8 (16–17)

THE SELF SPOKEN OF IN *AITAREYA ĀRAṆYAKA* II. 4. 1. 1 IS THE HIGHEST SELF

III. 3. 16. *ātma-gṛhītir itaravad uttarāt*

The Highest Self is meant (*in the Aitareya Āraṇyaka* II. 4. 1. 1) *as in other texts* (*dealing with creation*) *on account of the subsequent qualification.*

ātma-gṛhīti: the Supreme Self is meant; *itaravat:* as in other texts (dealing with creation); *uttarāt:* on account of the subsequent qualification.

The text considered is: 'The Self, verily, was all this; one only in the beginning. Nothing else whatsoever winked. He thought, "let me now create the worlds".' The question is whether the Self refers to the Supreme Self or *Hiraṇya-garbha.* It refers to the Supreme Self as in other texts T.U. II. 1. 'He thought.' The thinking Self is the Supreme.

R. thinks that the reference is to the Self of bliss because of the passage: 'He desired, may I be many.'

Śrīkaṇṭha continues the topic whether the selves consisting of food and so on are to be meditated on or not and says that only the Supreme *Brahman* is to be meditated on and not other selves.

III. 3. 17. *anvayād iti cet syād avadhāraṇāt*

If it be said that on account of the context (*the Highest Self is not meant*) (*we say that*) *it is so on account of the statement* (*that the Self alone existed at the beginning*).

anvayāt: on account of the context; *iti cet:* if it be said; *syāt:* it might be so; *avadhāraṇāt:* on account of the statement.

The Highest Self is meant and not *Hiraṇya-garbha.* Ś. explains this position with reference to other texts. B.U. IV. 3. 7.

R. takes *sūtras* 11–17 as one section.

R. holds that the Self is connected with things which are not self, because the Highest Self is, as it were, viewed in them.

Śrīkaṇṭha concludes the discussion of the question whether the selves consisting of food and the rest are to be meditated on or not with the view that there must be meditation on the Self consisting of bliss alone, on account of definite statement.

Section 9 (18)

WATER AS THE DRESS OF *PRĀṆA*

III. 3. 18. *kāryākhyānād apūrvam*

Since (*the rinsing of the mouth with water*) *is a restatement of an act*

(already enjoined by smṛti) what has not been so enjoined elsewhere (is here intended).
kāryākhyānāt: on account of being a restatement of an act; *apūrvam:* what has not been so enjoined elsewhere.

In C.U. V. 2. 2 and B.U. VI. 1. 14 we find a reference to the rinsing of the mouth with water before and after a meal. The question is whether the *śruti* enjoins both or only the latter. The answer is stated in the *sūtra*. Since the act of rinsing is enjoined on everyone by the *smṛti*, the latter act of meditation on the water as the dress of *prāṇa* is alone enjoined by the *śruti*.

R. and Nimbārka agree with this view.

Baladeva takes this *sūtra* as an independent section dealing with the designation of the Lord as Father. He means by *apūrva*, similar to what precedes (*pūrva*). The attributes of fatherhood and the like are similar to the preceding ones, bliss and so on.

Section 10 (19)

VIDYĀS IN THE SAME *ŚĀKHA* WHICH ARE IDENTICAL OR SIMILAR HAVE TO BE COMBINED FOR THEY ARE ONE

III. 3. 19. *samāna evam cābhedāt*

In the same (śākhā) also it is thus, (there is unity of vidyā) on account of non-difference (of the object of meditation).
samāne: in the same also; *evam:* it is thus; *ca:* also; *abhedāt:* on account of non-difference (of the object of meditation).

Passages in different texts of the same *śākhā* form one *vidyā* as the object of meditation is the same in them. Śāṇḍilya-vidyā is the same in *Agni-rahasya, Śatapatha Brāhmaṇa* X. 6. 3. 1.

Baladeva takes this *sūtra* as dealing with the problem whether the Lord is to be meditated on as a pure soul or as possessed of a body. The answer is 'Even [in the meditation on the form of the Lord] the sentiment is the same [*samāna*], on account of the non-difference [of the Lord's different limbs such as eyes and so on with his very Self]'. Even as a golden image is gold throughout and by looking at different parts of the image, viz. the eyes and so on, one does not get different ideas but only one idea, viz. that of gold, so the different parts of the Lord are identical with the Lord himself and so they do not give rise to different ideas but to one idea of the Lord. Therefore the meditation on the Lord as having a form does, indeed, lead to release. *evam api cakṣurādīnāṁ vailakṣaṇyena bhāne'pi samānaika-rasaḥ sa eva hiraṇya-pratimādivat bhagavān voḍhyaḥ.*

Section 11 (20–22)

THE NAMES GIVEN IN B.U. V. 5. 1–2 CANNOT BE COMBINED AS THEY ARE TWO SEPARATE *VIDYĀS*

III. 3. 20. *sambandhād evam anyatrāpi*

In other cases also, on account of the connection (i.e. the object of meditation is the same Brahman, we have to combine particulars) like this (i.e. as in the Śāṇḍilya-vidyā).

sambandhāt: on account of the connection; *evam:* like this; *anyatra:* in other cases; *api:* also.

In B.U. V. 5. 1–2 it is said: 'The person who is there in that orb and the person who is here in the right eye, these two rest on each other.' On the analogy of the *Śāṇḍilya-vidyā*, these two require to be combined.

R. says that the text mentions two secret names of *Brahman*, *aham* and *ahar* (B.U. V. 5. 3 and 4), and so the opponent argues that both these names are to be comprehended in each of the two meditations.

Baladeva begins a new section here dealing with the worship of the *āveśāvatāras* or God-possessed souls like Nārada and so on. The question is whether they are to be meditated on as possessed of the attributes of the Lord himself. The *prima facie* view holds that they are to be meditated on as possessed of the attributes of the Lord.

III. 3. 21. *na vā viśeṣāt*

Rather not, on account of difference (of abode).

na vā: rather not; *viśeṣāt:* on account of difference (of abode).

Though the *vidyā* is one, still owing to difference in abodes the object of meditation becomes different, according to Ś.

R. says that as *Brahman* is to be meditated on in two different abodes the meditations are separate. On the other hand in both forms of *Śāṇḍilya-vidyā*, *Brahman* is to be meditated on as abiding within the heart.

Baladeva reads *aviśeṣāt* for *viśeṣāt*. God-possessed souls are not to be worshipped as possessed of all God-like attributes, on account of their non-difference from other souls. God-possessed souls are like other individuals and they are to be highly venerated but not worshipped like the Lord himself.

III. 3. 22. *darśayati ca*

(The Scripture) also declares (that).

darśayati: declares; *ca:* also.

The Scripture distinctly states that the attributes are to be kept separate and not combined. It compares the two persons which are distinct. Ś mentions C.U. I. 8. 5.

Śrīkaṇṭha takes this as a new section dealing with *maṇḍala-vidyā* (C.U. I. 6. 6 and the *Māhā-nārāyaṇa U.*) and concludes that the two *vidyās* are identical since Scripture shows their identity.

Baladeva gives an additional reason why the God-possessed souls are not to be meditated on as possessed of the attributes of the Lord himself. Scripture (C.U. VII. 1. 1) shows this. Nārada, a god-possessed soul, approaches Sanat-kumāra with a view to learning about the Supreme Self from him. This shows that god-possessed souls are not perfect like the Lord. They cannot be worshipped as possessed of his attributes.

Section 12 (23)

ATTRIBUTES OF *BRAHMAN* MENTIONED IN *RĀṆĀYANĪYA KHILA* FORM AN INDEPENDENT *VIDYĀ*

III. 3. 23. *sambhṛti dyu-vyāptyapi cātaḥ*

For the same reason, the supporting (of the universe) and the pervading of the sky (attributed to Brahman) also (are not to be included in other meditations of Brahman).

saṁbhṛti: supporting (the universe); *dyu-vyāptiḥ:* the pervading of the sky; *api:* also; *ca:* and; *ataḥ:* for the same reason (as in the previous *sūtra*).

The text considered is '*brahma jyeṣṭhā vīryā sambhṛtāni brahmāgre jyeṣṭhaṁ divam ātatāni*'. '*Brahman* is the best among the powers which are held together. The pre-existent *Brahman* in the beginning pervaded the whole sky.' These two qualities are not to be included in other places treating of *brahma-vidyā* on account of difference of abode. These qualities and those mentioned in other *vidyās* like the *Śāṇḍilya-vidyā* are of such a nature as to exclude each other. The mere fact that certain *vidyās* relate to *Brahman* does not constitute their unity. *Brahman*, though one, is meditated on in manifold ways, on account of its different aspects. *ekam api brahma vibhūti-bhedair anekair anekadhopāsyata iti sthitiḥ*. Ś. So the meditation referred to in this *sūtra* is an independent *vidyā* standing by itself.

Baladeva says that the attributes of holding together and pervading the sky are not to be combined in the meditation on God-possessed souls because they are not equal to the Lord.

Section 13 (24)

THE TWO *VIDYĀS* ARE TO BE HELD APART

III. 3. 24. *puruṣa-vidyāyām iva cetareṣām anāmnānāt*

And (since the qualities) as (mentioned in the puruṣa-vidyā of C.U.*) are not mentioned in that of the others, (the two are not one.)*

puruṣa-vidyāyām iva: as in the *puruṣa-vidyā* (of the C.U.); *ca:* and; *itareṣām:* of the others; *anāmnānāt:* on account of non-mention.

The question relates to the two *vidyās* (C.U. III. 16. 1; *Taittirīya Āraṇyaka* X 64) which compare the sacrifice with life, *puruṣa-yajña*. The details and the purpose in the two are different and the similarities are unimportant. So the *puruṣa-vidyā* of the C.U. cannot be combined with that in the *Taittirīya* text.

R. reads: '*puruṣa-vidyāyām api*' while Ś. reads: '*puruṣa-vidyāyām iva*', though both reach the same conclusion.

Baladeva concludes his discussion of the worship of God-possessed souls. Since they are not equal to the Lord, they are not to be worshipped as possessed of his attributes.

Section 14 (25)

CERTAIN PASSAGES RELATING TO SACRIFICES AT THE BEGINNING OF SOME *UPANIṢADS* DO NOT FORM PART OF *BRAHMA-VIDYĀ*

III. 3. 25. *vedhādy artha-bhedāt*

(Certain mantras relating to) piercing, etc., (are not part of the brahma-vidyā) since they have a different meaning.

vedhādi: piercing and so on; *artha-bhedāt:* because of difference of meaning.

Certain passages met with in the beginning of some *Upaniṣads* do not belong to the main teaching of the *Upaniṣads*, viz. *brahma-vidyā*, since they are obviously connected with sacrificial acts; their textual collation does not make them parts of *brahma-vidyā*.

Baladeva takes this as a separate section dealing with the question whether one should meditate on the Lord not only as possessing the sweet and the majestic attributes like bliss and omnipotence but also of destructive and fearful attributes such as piercing and so on. He answers that we should not: 'One who is desirous of release should not meditate on the Lord as possessed of the attributes of piercing and so on, on account of the difference of result [of such a meditation] which does not lead to release as the meditation on the Lord as sweet and majestic does.'

Section 15 (26)

THE STATEMENT THAT THE GOOD AND EVIL DEEDS OF A PERSON WHO HAS ATTAINED KNOWLEDGE GO TO HIS FRIENDS AND ENEMIES RESPECTIVELY, IS VALID FOR ALL TEXTS WHICH SPEAK OF THE DISCARDING OF GOOD AND EVIL DEEDS BY SUCH A PERSON

III. 3. 26. *hānau tūpāyana-śabda-śeṣatvāt kuśāc chandaḥ stuty-upagānavat tad uktam*

Where the discarding (*of good and evil*) *is mentioned* (*the obtaining of this good and evil by others has to be included*) *on account of this word 'receiving' being supplementary* (*to the statement about discarding*) *as in the case of Kuśas, the metres, the praise and the recitation. This has been stated* (*in the Pūrva Mīmāṁsā*).

hānau: where (only) the discarding (of good and evil is mentioned); *tu:* but; *upāyana-śabda-śeṣatvāt:* on account of the word 'receiving' being supplementary (to the word discarding); *kuśa-chandaḥ-stuti-upagānavat:* as in the case of *Kuśas* (which are used for keeping count of hymns, metres, praise and recitation); *tat:* that; *uktam:* has been stated (in the *Pūrva Mīmāṁsā*).

Jaimini says that while some texts mention only *Kuśas* and others state that they should be made of *udumbara*, tree, the first will have to be completed in the light of the other. (*Pūrva Mīmāṁsā* X. 8–15.) So also if one text mentions the discarding of good and evil by a person attaining knowledge (C.U. VIII. 13; see also M.U. III. 1. 3), and another says that good and evil are obtained by his friends and enemies respectively (K.U. I. 4), the two have to be taken together.

Ś. discusses another possible interpretation from the word *dhu* to tremble, shake and not discard. This would mean that good and evil still cling to a person who attains knowledge though their effects are retarded owing to the knowledge. Ś. argues against this view as the subsequent discussion in K.U. shows that others receive this good and evil which is not possible unless the person who attains knowledge has discarded them.

Baladeva raises a different question here whether the meditation on the Lord is obligatory or optional for freed souls. He reads *āchanda* for *chanda* meaning option. For him the *sūtra* means: 'But on the destruction [of bondage, the released souls are under no obligation to practise meditation because they have obtained] nearness [*upāyana* to the Lord] and because scriptural texts are supplementary [to this, i.e. are meant for leading the soul to this stage, viz. release], just as the singing of hymns with *Kuśa* [in hand] is optional [*āchanda* for a student who has finished his daily duties], it is declared [by Scripture].' The aim of all texts is to teach men meditation so that they may attain salvation. When the end is reached, when men are freed and approach the Lord, it is no longer necessary for them to go on with meditation.

Section 16 (27–28)

ONE SHAKES OFF GOOD AND EVIL DEEDS, NOT ON THE ROAD TO *BRAHMA-LOKA* BUT AT THE MOMENT OF THE SOUL'S DEPARTURE FROM THE BODY

III. 3. 27. *sāmparāye tartavyābhāvāt tathā hy anye*

At the (time of) departure, (he frees himself from the effects of his works), there being nothing to be reached (by him on the way to brahma-loka through these works); for thus others (declare).
sāmparāye: at the time of departure; *tartavya-abhāvāt:* there being nothing to be reached; *tathā:* thus; *hi:* for; *anye:* others.

K.U. (I. 4) says: 'He comes to the river *vijarā* (the Ageless) . . . there he shakes off his good deeds and evil deeds.' The discarding takes place, according to the opponent, on the way to *brahma-loka* and not at the time of death. The *sūtra* says that the man of realisation gets rid of the results of his deeds at the time of death. The man possessing knowledge is about to reach *Brahman* and there is nothing to be reached by him on the way through his good and evil works. This is affirmed by other passages also. C.U. VIII. 13. 1; VI. 14. 2.

R. says that there are no further pleasures and pains to be enjoyed as the result of good and evil deeds, different from the obtaining of *Brahman*, which is the fruit of knowledge.

Śrīkaṇṭha takes 27, 28, 29 as the statement of the *prima facie* view.

Baladeva interprets the word *sāmparāya* as 'love of the Lord'. *Samparāya* means one in whom all the truths meet, *samparayati tattvāni yasmin.* Love of *samparāya* is *sāmparāya.* So Baladeva interprets the *sūtra*: When the love of the Lord (has arisen) (it is no longer obligatory for one to practise meditation) on account of there being nothing to be crossed (there is no bondage any more) for thus others declare.

III. 3. 28. *chandata ubhayāvirodhāt*

According to his liking (he gets rid of good and evil while living) since there is no contradiction between the two.
chandataḥ: according to his liking; *ubhaya-avirodhāt:* on account of non-contradiction between the two.

When the body is left behind, man can no longer accomplish according to his liking, that effort which consists in self-restraint and pursuit of knowledge and which is the cause of the obliteration of all his good and evil deeds. So obliteration cannot take place, and we must assume that the requisite effort is made and the result earned at an earlier moment. A disembodied soul cannot undergo the discipline for attaining knowledge, which only an embodied being can do according to its liking. So if the works of a knower persist after the fall of the body, it will not be possible for him to get rid of them seeing that there is no possibility for acquiring further knowledge. If knowledge be the cause of the destruction of works, the moment one acquires knowledge, the works must decay. This view agrees with all the texts.

The attainment of *brahma-loka* is not possible so long as there is a body but there is no such difficulty about shaking off of good and evil results. This view avoids a contradiction. It makes knowledge the direct cause of the destruction of works and does not contradict Scripture.

R. explains K.U. I. 4 which seems to go against the view that the soul leaves all its works at the time of leaving the body. '[The different parts of the text are to be arranged] at will, on account of the non-contradiction of both [reason and Scripture].' We must put 'he then discards good and evil deeds' before the other, 'having attained the path of the gods, he comes to the world of fire'.

Śrīkaṇṭha is of the view that the *sūtra* states the opponent's view.

Baladeva begins a new section dealing with two ways of meditating on the Lord. We may meditate on him as the sweet or the majestic as both lead to salvation through the will of the Lord since there is no conflict between the two. The word 'no' is taken from III. 3. 22.

Section 17 (29–30)

HE WHOSE KNOWLEDGE IS LIMITED TO THE MANIFESTED ABSOLUTE GOES ON THE PATH OF THE GODS WHILE THE SOUL OF HIM WHO KNOWS THE UNMANIFESTED *BRAHMAN* BECOMES ONE WITH IT WITHOUT GOING TO ANY OTHER PLACE

III. 3. 29. *gater arthavattvam ubhayathā'nyathā hi virodhaḥ*

A meaning has to be given to the going (on the path of the gods) in a twofold manner; for otherwise (there would result) a contradiction.

gateḥ: of the journey (of the soul along the path of the gods) *arthavattvam:* meaningfulness; *ubhayathā:* in a twofold manner; *anyathā:* otherwise; *hi:* for; *virodhaḥ:* a contradiction.

Ś. says that the journey along the path of the gods is true only of the worshippers of *Saguṇa Brahman*; it has no meaning for the devotees of *Nirguṇa Brahman* whose ignorance is destroyed by knowledge. If the journey applies to him also, texts like M.U. III. 1. 3 where the knower 'shaking off good and evil and free from stain' is said to 'obtain supreme equality with the Highest' become meaningless. How can one who has become *Brahman* go to another place?

For R., this *sūtra* states the *prima facie* view. Only on the view that a part of the good and evil works is left behind at the time of the soul's departure from the body and another part later on, a meaning can be found for the scriptural declaration of the soul proceeding on the path of the gods. For otherwise there would be a contradiction. For if all the works perished at the time of the soul's departure from the body, the subtle body would also perish and there can be no going on the part of the self. So it cannot be that at the time of the soul's departure from the body, all works should perish without any remainder.

Nimbārka follows R.'s interpretation.

Śrīkaṇṭha reverses the order of the *sūtras* 29 and 30, makes 30 the *prima facie* view and 29 the correct conclusion. There is meaning for the journey on two ways only if the soul discards a part of its *karma* at the time of its departure from the body and the rest after crossing the river *vijarā*, for otherwise there is contradiction. If all the *karmas* of the soul are destroyed completely at the time of its departure from the body it will become freed immediately and it would not be necessary for it to travel along the path of the gods, attain *Brahman* and then be freed. Thus there will be contradiction between passages which speak of travelling along the path of the gods to attain *Brahman* and release. Again, if the soul becomes freed as soon as it leaves the body, the texts which designate that the soul attains its real form on approaching *Brahman* will also be contradicted. To avoid these twofold contradictions, we must say that all the *karmas* of the soul do not decay completely as soon as it leaves the body. Though the *vidyā* of the soul leads it to travel along the path of the gods, yet as actual release is not attained until one directly approaches *Brahman*, some part of *karma* still clings to the soul until it crosses the sphere of matter and actually attains the Lord.

Baladeva observes that both the paths, meditation on God as the sweet and meditation on God as the majestic, lead to the Lord.

III. 3. 30. *upapannas tal-lakṣaṇārthopalabdher lokavat*

(The twofold view adopted above) is reasonable for we observe a purpose characterised thereby (i.e. a purpose for going); as in the world.

upapannaḥ: is reasonable; *tat-lakṣaṇārtha-upalabdheḥ:* for a purpose characterised thereby is observed; *lokavat:* as in the world.

The texts mention certain results which can be obtained by the worshipper, only by going to different places, such as mounting the couch and holding conversation with *Brahmā*. But a journey is meaningless for one whose ignorance is destroyed. This is seen in the world. To reach a village we have to go by the path which leads to it; to get rid of one's illness no such journey is required. *yathā loke grāma-prāptau deśāntara-prāpaṇaḥ panthā apekṣyate nārogya-prāptau.* Ś.

R. holds that there is the complete decay of all works at the time of the soul's separation from the body, on account of finding things which are marks of that (the soul's connection with the body) as in the world. A pond dug for the purpose of irrigation continues to exist and may be used for other purposes such as supplying drinking water, even when its original purpose has been served, so the subtle body continues to exist for serving a purpose, viz. attainment of *Brahman*, though its original purpose, viz. the undergoing of *karma*, is absent.

Bhāskara says that in the K.U. (I. 5–6) we find that the soul enters into conversation with *Kārya-Brahmā* and this is not possible unless it travels through the path of light and so on. This shows that it is accompanied by the subtle body since in ordinary experience we find that only those who are endowed with sense-organs can enter into conversation. The subtle body disappears only when the soul attains the Supreme *Brahman* through the *Kārya-Brahmā*.

Baladeva asks which of the two paths of meditation, God the Sweet or God the Majestic, is the higher. The devotee who meditates on the Lord as the sweet wins his favour.

What is the stage when the accumulated merit and demerit of an enlightened person leave him? Is it at death or later? The *prima facie* view is that there is no object in its continuance after death, as there is no further use for *karma*. When the death of the body occurs, *karma* ceases for the enlightened person. Ś., Bhāskara, R., Nimbārka and Vijñāna-bhikṣu accept this position. R., Śrīkaṇṭha and Nimbārka believe that even the enlightened one has to proceed along the path of light, *arcirādi-mārga*, before attaining *Brahman*. The gross body being destroyed at death and there being no *karma* left to form a subtle body, how can there be departure along a path? Śrīkaṇṭha argues that the cessation of *karma* should be understood to take place in two instalments, at death and at a later stage on the crossing of the river *virajā*. As long as departure along a path is admitted the continuance of bondage is also admitted. Only with the final attainment of *Brahman* the intellect expands and the self manifests its full stature. Prior to that the intellect is in a state of contraction (*saṁkucita*) which is the characteristic of souls in *saṁsāra*. *Saṁsāra* does not exist in the absence of *karma*. Till the river *Virajā* is crossed, we must admit residual *karma*. Beyond the river is the abode of final release.

R. and Nimbārka do not accept this position. They think that, though *karma* ceases, a subtle body may yet continue by the potency of the meditation on *Brahman*. Though the subtle body may require *karma* for its creation, it may be kept on independently of it, even as a tank dug for irrigation purposes may continue to exist (when that purpose has been otherwise fulfilled) and serve as a source of drinking water.

While Ś. and Vijñāna-bhikṣu deny departure in the case of the enlightened one, Bhāskara upholds the doctrine of departure. He believes that the destruction of good and evil deeds is essential to departure on the path of light. If bad deeds are not destroyed, there will be no upward departure at all; if good deeds are not destroyed the departure will be followed by return to the world of *saṁsāra* and this is inconsistent with enlightenment.

Section 18 (31–32)

III. 3. 31. *aniyamaḥ sarvāsām avirodhaḥ śabdānumānābhyām*

There is no restriction (as to the going on the path of the gods as it applies) to all (vidyās of the Saguṇa Brahman). There is no contradiction as is seen from the śruti and the smṛti.

aniyamaḥ: (there is) no restriction; *sarvāsām:* (the path applies) to all; *avirodhaḥ:* (there is) no contradiction; *śabda-anumānābhyām:* (as is evident) from the *śruti* and the *smṛti.*

Ś. argues that going on the path of the gods is connected equally with all those *vidyās* which have prosperity for their aim. Scripture declares that not only those who know the *pañcāgni-vidyā* (C.U. V. 10. 1) but also those who understand other *vidyās* and those who in the forest follow faith and austerities proceed on the path of the gods. See also B.G. VIII. 26.

R. holds that all those who meditate on *Brahman*, irrespective of the distinction between *saguṇa* and *nirguṇa*, proceed after death on the path of the gods. R. reads *sarveṣām,* all worshippers, and not *sarvāsām,* all *saguṇa-vidyās.* This is *sūtra* 32 in R.

Baladeva reads *avirodhāt* for *avirodhaḥ.* 'There is no rule [that meditation, prayers, singing the name of the Lord and the rest are to be performed conjointly always as a means to salvation, since any one of them may singly lead to salvation] because there is no contradiction of all [texts] on account of verbal testimony and inference.'

III. 3. 32. *yāvad-adhikāram avasthitir ādhikārikāṇām*

Of those who have an office to fulfil, there is subsistence (of the body) as long as the office lasts.

yāvat-adhikāram: so long as the office lasts; *avasthitiḥ:* subsistence (corporeal existence); *ādhikārikāṇām:* of those who have an office to fulfil.

Ś. says that the bliss of *Brahman* is enjoyed here and now by virtue of the knowledge of *Brahman* and there is no question of taking it on trust like the attainment of paradise, *svarga*, after death.

This *sūtra* says that ordinarily a person after attaining knowledge is not reborn. But the case is different with those who have a mission to fulfil. Those perfected sages take one or more births until their mission is fulfilled; after which they are not born again. Though they are reborn, they are not subject to ignorance. Their cases are analogous to those of *jīvan-muktas*, who, even after attaining knowledge, continue their corporeal existence so long as their *prārabdha karma* lasts. The divine mission of these people is comparable to the *prārabdha karma*.

Ś. admits that some persons although knowing *Brahman* attained new bodies, *brahmavidām api keṣāṁcid itihāsa-purāṇayor dehāntarotpatti-darśanāt*. Apāntaratamas, Vasiṣṭha, Bhṛgu, Sanat-kumāra, Dakṣa, Nārada assumed new bodies, after attaining knowledge of *Brahman*. Those to whom the Highest Lord has entrusted certain offices, though they possess complete knowledge which is the cause of release, last as long as their office lasts, their works not yet being exhausted. They obtain release only when their office comes to an end. *teṣām apāntaratamaḥprabhṛtīnāṁ veda-pravartanādiṣu loka-sthiti-hetuṣv adhikāreṣu niyuktānām adhikāra-tantratvāt. sthiteḥ yathā'sau bhagavān savitā sahasra-yuga-paryantaṁ jagato'dhikāraṁ caritvā tad-avasāne udayāstamaya-varjitaḥ kaivalyam anubhavati* (see C.U. III. 11. 1). *evam apāntaratamaḥ-prabhṛtayo'pīśvarāḥ parameśvareṇa teṣu teṣvadhikāreṣu niyuktās santaḥ satyapi samyagdarśane kaivalya-hetāv akṣīṇa-karmāṇo yāvad-adhikāram avatiṣṭhante tad-avasāne cāpavṛjyanta ity aviruddham.*

As long as there is *adhikāra*, they are subject to *prārabdha karma.* They however pass, according to their free will, from one body to another, preserving all the time the memory of their identity.

R. points out that in the case of the persons who hold office, the effects of the works which gave rise to the offices continue to exist as long as the office itself does and so they do not after death enter on the path beginning with light.

Section 20 (33)

NEGATIVE DESCRIPTIONS ARE TO BE COMBINED

III. 3. 33. *akṣaradhiyām tv avarodhaḥ sāmānya-tadbhāvābhyām upasadvat tad uktam*

But the (*negative*) *conceptions concerning the Immutable are to be comprehended* (*in all meditations on the Immutable*) *on account of the similarity and of the object being the same as in the case of the upasad (the offerings). This has been said (in the Pūrva Mīmāṁsā III. 3. 9).*

akṣaradhiyām: of the (negative) conceptions of the Immutable; *tu:* but; *avarodhaḥ:* comprehension; *sāmānya-tadbhāvābhyām:* on account of the similarity (of negative descriptions) and the object (the immutable *Brahman*) being the same; *upasadvat:* as in the case of the *upasad* (offering); *tad:* this; *uktam:* has been said.

In B.U. III. 8. 8–9 and M.U. I. 1. 5–6, we have negative descriptions of the Immutable. Are they to be treated as two separate *vidyās* or one *vidyā*? The opponent says that these descriptions do not directly specify the nature of *Brahman* as the positive characterisations as bliss, truth, etc., do; so the denial is valid only for the text in which it occurs and not for others. The *sūtra* refutes this objection according to Ś. and argues that such denials are to be comprehended since the method of teaching *Brahman* through denial is the same and the object of the instruction is also the same, viz. the Immutable *Brahman*. The case is analogous to the *upasad* offerings. Though the *mantras* are found only in the *Sāma Veda* the priests of the *Yajur Veda* also use them.

For R., he who thinks of *Brahman* must think of it as having for its essential nature bliss, knowledge, etc., in so far as distinguished by the absence of grossness and the like. These qualities are no less essential than bliss and must therefore be included in all meditations on *Brahman*.

Section 21 (34)

M.U. III. 1. 1; *KAṬHA U.* 3. 1 FORM ONE *VIDYĀ*

III. 3. 34. *iyad-āmananāt*

On account of the same being described.

iyat: this much, the same; *āmananāt:* on account of being described.

In the two texts, M.U. III. 1. 1; *Kaṭha U.* I. 3. 1, according to Ś., the opponent says that in the former one eats the fruit while the other does not, in the latter both of them enjoy the results of their good actions and therefore the object of meditation is not identical. The *sūtra* contends that they form one *vidyā*, for both describe the same Lord as existing in the form of the individual. The object is to teach about the Supreme *Brahman* and show the identity of the Supreme and the individual. Since the object of meditation is one, the *vidyās* are also one.

According to R., the *sūtra* contains a reply to an objection raised against the conclusion reached in the previous *sūtra*.

Bhāskara reads *īṣat*. In both the texts the Lord and the individual soul are designated as the objects to be known. So they both constitute the same *vidyā*.

Baladeva means by *āmananāt*: on account of scriptural declaration.

Section 22 (35–36)

B.U. III. 4. 1 AND III. 5. 1 CONSTITUTE ONE *VIDYĀ*

III. 3. 35. *antarā bhūta-grāmavat svātmanaḥ*

(There is the same teaching) as the Self is within all, as in the case of the aggregate of the elements.

antarā: as being within all; *bhūta-grāmavat:* as in the case of the aggregate of elements; *svātmanaḥ:* (teaching) of the same self.

To the objection that the two passages B.U. III. 4. 1; III. 5. 1 refer to two separate teachings, and two separate objects, the answer is given that the Supreme Self is the object in both cases since two different selves cannot be simultaneously the innermost of all in the same body, even as none of the elements constituting the body can be the innermost of all in the true sense of the term though, relatively speaking, one element may be said to be inside another. The same Self is taught in both the texts. Ś. gives S.U. VI. 11 as a possible scriptural text intended by the author: 'The one God hidden in all beings . . . the witness, the knower; the only one devoid of qualities.' The object of knowledge is one and therefore the teaching is one.

Baladeva begins a new section here with three *sūtras* dealing with the topic of the identity of the Lord and his city. In the City of the Lord, everything being a manifestation of the Lord is but the Lord himself though they look like material objects to the devotees. He interprets the next *sūtra* as declaring that the Lord is both the dweller and the residence. He is identical with the city and yet dwells within the city. Everything is possible in the case of the Supreme.

Bhāskara holds that, as there are different teachings, the objects taught are also different.

R. argues that the repetition of question and answer serves the purpose of showing that the same *Brahman* is the cause of breathing, etc. (B.U. III. 4. 1), and is beyond all hunger, thirst and so on (B.U. III. 5. 1).

Nimbārka agrees with this view and holds that in C.U. VI. we have the same kind of repetition to demonstrate the attributes of *Brahman*.

III. 3. 36. *anyathā bhedānupapattir iti cen nopadeśāntaravat*

If it be said that otherwise the separation (of the teachings) cannot be accounted for; (we say) not so; (it is) like (the repetition in) another teaching.

anyathā: otherwise; *bhedānupapattiḥ:* the separation cannot be accounted for; *iti cet:* if it be said; *na:* not so; *upadeśāntaravat:* like another teaching.

The reference is to C.U. VI. where there is repetition intended to make the student understand the subject convincingly.

Section 23 (37)

AITAREYA ĀRAṆYAKA II. 2. 4. 6 CONSTITUTES TWO MEDITATIONS

III. 3. 37. *vyatihāro viśiṁṣanti hītaravat*

(There is) reciprocity (of meditations for the Scriptures) prescribe (this) as in other cases.
vyatihāraḥ: reciprocity (of meditations); *viśiṁṣanti:* (the Scriptures) prescribe (or distinguish); *hi:* for; *itaravat:* as in other cases.

The *Aitareya Āraṇyaka* text II. 2. 4. 6 reads: 'What I am that he is; what he is that am I' *tad yo'ham so'sau, yo'sau so'ham.* The question is raised whether the meditation is to be of a reciprocal nature, i.e. identifying the worshipper with the being in the sun and inversely identifying the being in the sun with the worshipper or only in the first suggested way. The answer is given that he is to be meditated in both ways for *Brahman* who has no form can be worshipped even as possessing a form.

Section 24 (38)

B.U. V. 4. 1 and V. 5. 2 TREAT OF ONE TEACHING

III. 3. 38. *saiva hi satyādayaḥ*

The same (satya-vidyā is taught in both places) for (attributes like) satya and others (are found in both places).
sā eva: the same (*satya-vidyā*); *hi:* for; *satyādayaḥ:* (attributes like) *satya*, etc.

The two texts speak of one meditation and the results are the same. Some commentators think that the reference in the *sūtra* is not to passages in B.U. V. 4 and V. 5 but to the C.U. (I. 6. 1, 8; I. 7. 7). Ś. thinks that this is not so for there is nothing in the B.U. text to connect the meditation with sacrificial acts. The subject-matter is different, the teachings are separate and the details of the two should be held apart.

According to R., *sūtras* 35–38 constitute one section only and the subject-matter is the same as that of section 22 above.

Baladeva reads *sā*, the *Parā-śakti* of the Lord alone is truth and the rest. In other words the attributes of the Lord like truth, omniscience, etc., are modifications of the *Parā-śakti* of the Lord. They are real and constitute the essential nature, *svarūpa*, of the Lord. They are not illusory.

Section 25 (39)

C.U. VIII. 1 AND B.U. IV. 4. 22 ARE ONE TEACHING

III. 3. 39. *kāmādītaratra tatra cāyatanādibhyaḥ*

(*Qualities like true*) *desire, etc.* (*mentioned in* C.U. VIII. 1. 1 *are to be inserted*) *in the other and here on account of the abode and so on.*
kāmādi: desire, etc.; *itaratra:* in the other; *tatra:* (those mentioned) in the other; *ca:* and; *āyatanādibhyaḥ:* on account of the abode and so on.

The *sūtra* says that the two passages form one teaching, and the qualities mentioned in each passage are to be combined in the other for many points are common to both. There is the same abode, the same Lord who is the object of meditation and so on. There is, however, one difference. The C.U. passage treats of *Brahman* with qualities and the B.U. passage of *Brahman* without qualities. But then the determinate *Brahman* is one with the indeterminate. This *sūtra* prescribes a combination of qualities for glorifying *Brahman* and not for the purpose of worship, *guṇavatas tu brahmaṇa ekatvād vibhūti pradarśanāyāyaṁ guṇopasaṁhāras sūtrito nopāsanāyeti draṣṭavyam.* Ś.

Śrīkaṇṭha mentions *Mahā-nārāyaṇa U.* X. 7 in addition to the C.U. and B.U. texts.

Baladeva takes the words *sā eva* from the preceding *sūtra* and makes out that the *Parā-śakti* of the Lord creates all objects of desire elsewhere and here for he is all-pervading, *āyatana.*

Section 26 (40–41)

THE QUESTION ABOUT *PRĀṆĀGNIHOTRA*

III. 3. 40. *ādarād alopaḥ*

On account of respect shown there is non-omission.
ādarāt: on account of respect shown; *alopaḥ:* no omission.

The *sūtra* gives the opponent's view that *prāṇāgnihotra*, which enjoins the offering of food to the priests, should be observed even in the days of fasting. There should be no omission of it. See C.U. V. 19. 1; V. 24. 2, 4.

R. takes *sūtras* 39–41 as one section. This one and the next *sūtra* discuss meditations on *Brahman.* To the objection that the qualities of control and truthful wishes cannot be regarded as real, *pāramārthika,* as other passages describe *Brahman* as free from all qualities, this *sūtra* gives the answer which, according to R., is that these qualities are not to be omitted as they are stated with emphasis.

Śrīkaṇṭha takes it as a separate section. He argues that the attributes of physical form, etc., of *Śiva* are true and eternal and not fictitious and impermanent.

For Baladeva, this *sūtra* raises the question that if *Śrī* is identical with the *Parā-śakti* of the Lord, she must be identical with the Lord himself and so cannot be devoted to the Lord, who is her own self and gives the answer: 'On account of her great regard for the Lord there is non-cessation of her devotion to him.' Though one with the Lord *Śrī* cannot but love and be devoted to him who is her very existence even as a branch cannot but love the tree or the ray the moon.

III. 3. 41. *upasthite'tas tad-vacanāt*

When food is served, from that (the offering is to be made) for so the text declares.

upasthite: when food is served; *ataḥ:* from that; *tat-vacanāt:* for so the text declares.

Only on the days when the food is taken, the first portion is to be offered to the *prāṇās* and not on fasting days.

R. holds that even those who are desirous of release may meditate on the Supreme as possessed of qualities. The possession of the qualities forms part of the experience of the released soul itself.

For Śrīkaṇṭha, attainment of equality with *Śiva* is Supreme release.

Section 27 (42)

MEDITATIONS CONNECTED WITH CERTAIN SACRIFICIAL ACTS ARE NOT PARTS OF THE LATTER

III. 3. 42. *tan-nirdhāraṇāniyamas tad-dṛṣṭeḥ pṛthag hy apratibandhaḥ phalam*

(There is) non-restriction of the assertions concerning them (sacrificial acts) because this is seen (in Scripture); a separate result, viz. non-obstruction (of the success of the sacrifice), (belongs to them).

tat-nirdhāraṇa-aniyamaḥ: (there is) non-restriction of the assertions concerning them; *tat-dṛṣṭeḥ:* that is seen; *pṛthak:* separate; *hi:* for; *apratibandhaḥ:* non-obstruction; *phalam:* result.

Certain meditations are mentioned in connection with some sacrifices. The *sūtra* says that these meditations are not a part of the sacrifices. C.U. I. 1. 10; I. 10. 9, make out that there is no insepara-bility between the two. Besides, meditations and sacrifices have separate results. The meditation does not interfere with the result of the sacrifice. The result of the sacrifice may be delayed owing to the interference of the *karma* of the sacrificer but the meditation destroys the effects of that and the results are attained earlier. But the sacrifice does not depend on the meditation for its results. Meditation is not a part of the sacrifice and it is therefore optional.

Nimbārka and Śrīnivāsa use this *sūtra* to show the superiority of meditation to work.

Baladeva takes this as a separate section and raises an altogether different question, whether the Lord is to be meditated on as *Kṛṣṇa* alone and holds there is no such restriction. While the meditation on *Kṛṣṇa* is the direct (unobstructed) means to salvation, the worship of other deities is the indirect means.

Section 28 (43)

MEDITATION ON AIR AND LIFE ARE TO BE HELD APART

III. 3. 43. *pradānavad eva tad uktam*

Even as in the case of the offerings (Vāyu and Prāṇa must be held apart). This has been stated (in the Pūrva Mīmāṁsā Sūtra).

pradānavat: as in the case of the offerings; *eva:* even; *tat:* that; *uktam:* has been stated.

In B.U. I. 5. 21, *Prāṇa* is said to be the best among the organs of the body and *Vāyu* the best among the *devas*. In C.U. IV. 3. 1 and 3, *Vāyu* is said to be the absorber of the *devas* and *Prāṇa* is said to be the general absorber of the organs of the body. Are they to be treated as separate or not? The *sūtra* says they should be treated as separate. The texts represent *Vāyu* and *Prāṇa* as different. Even as the offerings are given separately to *Indra* the ruler, the monarch and the sovereign according to his different functions though he is one God, so also the meditations on *Vāyu* and *Prāṇa* are to be kept separate.

R. takes up C.U. VIII. 1ff. and points out that there is first a meditation on the Highest Self and then separately a meditation on the qualities. The opponent maintains that as the two can be comprised in one meditation, it is not necessary to repeat the meditations. The *sūtra* holds that the meditation has to be repeated for there is a difference between the Supreme in its essential nature and as possessing the qualities. Here the analogy of offerings is cited.

Baladeva treats this *sūtra* as a separate section dealing with the grace of the spiritual preceptor. This is necessary for salvation in addition to the knowledge of the *Vedas*.

Section 29 (44–52)

THE FIRES MENTIONED IN *ŚATAPATHA BRĀHMAṆA* ARE NOT PARTS OF THE SACRIFICIAL ACTS BUT SUBJECTS OF MEDITATION

III. 3. 44. *liṅgabhūyastvāt taddhi balīyas tad api*

On account of the abundance of indicatory marks, (the fires of the mind, speech, etc., mentioned in the Agni-Rahasya section of the B.U. *are not parts of the sacrificial action) for [this the indicatory mark] is stronger (than the general subject-matter). That also (has been stated in the Pūrve Mīmāṁsā Sūtra).*

liṅga-bhūyastvāt: on account of the abundance of the indicatory marks; *tat:* it (indicatory mark); *hi:* for; *balīyaḥ:* is stronger; *tat:* that; *api:* also.

In the *Agni-rahasya* of the *Śatapatha Brāhmaṇa* (X. 5. 3. 3, 12) certain fires named after mind, speech, etc., are mentioned. The question is raised whether they are parts of the sacrifice or are independent meditations. The *sūtra* adopts the latter view for the indicatory marks that they are subjects of meditation and are stronger than the context or general subject-matter. See *Pūrva Mīmāṁsā Sūtra* III. 3. 14, which states: 'If there be combination of direct association, indicatory mark, syntactical connection, general subject matter [context], place and name, then each succeeding one is weaker [than each preceding one] on account of its remoteness from the meaning.'

R. takes this *sūtra* as an independent section dealing with the question whether the *dahara-vidyā* of *Mahā-nārāyaṇa U.* (XI) is the same as that which is mentioned in the previous section of the *U.* (X), and answers that the same object is meditated on in all *brahma-vidyās* on account of the many specific indications that *Nārāyaṇa* is the object to be meditated on in all *brahma-vidyās*.

Śrīkaṇṭha deals with the matter in the same way as R.; only for *Nārāyaṇa* he substitutes *Rudra* accompanied by *Umā* (see *Mahā-nārāyaṇa U.* XIII).

Nimbārka and Śrīnivāsa follow Ś.

Baladeva takes this as a separate section dealing with the grace of the spiritual teacher.

III. 3. 45. *pūrva-vikalpaḥ prakaraṇāt syāt kriyāmānasavat*

(The fire spoken of) is a particular form of the preceding one on account of the subject-matter; it is a part of the sacrifice as in the case of the mānasa cup.

pūrva-vikalpaḥ: a particular form of the preceding one; *prakaraṇāt:*

on account of the subject-matter; *syāt:* should be; *kriyā:* part of the sacrifice; *mānasavat:* as in the case of the *mānasa* cup.

The opponent points out that in the offering to *Prajā-pati* where the earth is regarded as the cup and the sea as the *soma* (*Tāṇḍya Brāhmaṇa* IV. 9; *Taittirīya Saṁhitā* VII. 3. 1) though it is a mental act only, it is treated as a part of the sacrifice, so also these fires, though mental, are parts of the sacrifice and not independent meditations on account of the subject-matter. They are alternative forms of the first-mentioned fire, *vikalpa-viśeṣa* or, as Ānandagiri puts it, *prakāra-bheda.*

R. and Nimbārka adopt the same interpretation.

Baladeva begins a new section here with two *sūtras* dealing with the meditation on the Self as identical with the Supreme.

III. 3. 46. *atideśāc ca*

And on account of the extension (of the attributes of the first to these fires).

atideśāt: on account of the extension; *ca:* and.

The opponent gives another reason in support of this view. As the text attributes the qualities of the actual fire to the others, they are a part of the sacrifice. See *Śatapatha Brāhmaṇa* X. 3. 3. 11.

Baladeva interprets the *sūtra*: 'Also on account of analogies.'

In the *Gopāla-uttara-tāpanī U.* the Lord is compared to a loving father and the devotee to his son. This shows that the individual soul is not identical with the Lord. So meditations like 'I am he' are only modes of devotion and do not indicate any identity between the two.

III. 3. 47. *vidyaiva tu nirdhāraṇāt*

But (the fires) are indeed a meditation, on account of the assertion.

vidyā: meditation; *eva:* indeed; *tu:* but; *nirdhāraṇāt:* on account of the assertion (of the text).

'But' refutes the opponent's position. The fires constitute a meditation, for the text says: 'they are made of knowledge only.' 'By knowledge and meditation they are made for him who thus knows.' *Śatapatha Brāhmaṇa* X. 5. 3. 12.

R. and Nimbārka take this and the next *sūtra* as one.

Baladeva begins a new section here with three *sūtras* showing that devotion based on knowledge alone is the means to salvation.

III. 3. 48. *darśanāc ca*

And because (indicatory marks of that) are seen (in the text).

darśanāt: because (indicatory marks are) seen; *ca:* and.

The indicatory marks are those mentioned in *sūtra* 44.

R. makes out that there is seen in the text a performance consisting of thought only to which the fires stand in a subsidiary relation. From this it follows that the entire performance is an act of meditation. (See *Śatapatha Brāhmaṇa* X. 5. 3. 3.)

While Ś., Bhāskara and Baladeva take this as a separate *sūtra*, R. and Nimbārka take this *sūtra* along with the previous one.

Baladeva makes out that the direct vision of the Lord is attainable through *vidyā* alone.

III. 3. 49. *śrutyādi-balīyastvāc ca na bādhaḥ*

(And the view that the fires constitute an independent meditation) cannot be refuted, owing to the greater force of the śruti.

śrutyādi-balīyastvāt: because of the greater force of *śruti*, etc.; *ca:* and; *na bādhaḥ:* cannot be refuted.

The *Pūrva Mīmāṁsā* tells us that scriptural statement (*śruti*), indicatory mark (*liṅga*) and syntactical connection (*vākya*) are of greater force than subject-matter (*prakaraṇa*) and these three means of proof confirm the view that the fires are independent meditations. The text is 'they are piled up by the mind alone' (*Śatapatha Brāhmaṇa* X. 5. 3. 12); the indicatory mark is found in the passage: 'All beings at all times pile up [those fires] for him who knows thus, even while he sleeps.' (*Ibid.*) The syntactical connection also is found in the text: 'For through knowledge alone these are piled up for one who knows thus.' (*Ibid.*)

Baladeva considers the objection that *karma* or *karma* and *vidyā* are the means to salvation and holds that *vidyā* alone is the cause of salvation as the scriptural texts quoted in support of this view are of greater authority than the *smṛti* texts quoted in support of the objection.

III. 3. 50. *anubandhādibhyaḥ prajñāntara-pṛthaktva-vad dṛṣṭaś ca tad uktam*

From the connection and so on, (the fires constitute a separate meditation), even as other cognitions are separate. And (it is) seen (that in spite of the subject-matter a sacrifice is treated as independent). This has been stated (in the Pūrva Mīmāṁsā Sūtra).

anubandhādibhyaḥ: from the connection and so on; *prajñāntara pṛthaktva-vat:* even as other cognitions are separate; *dṛṣṭaḥ:* (it is) seen; *ca:* and; *tat:* this; *uktam:* has been stated.

The fires form a separate meditation even as *Śāṇḍilya-vidyā*, *Dahara-vidyā*, etc., form separate meditations, though mentioned along with sacrificial acts. It is also seen in the sacrificial portion of the *Vedas*; the sacrifice *Aveṣṭi*, though mentioned along with the *Rājasūya* sacrifice, is treated as an independent sacrifice by Jaimini in the *Pūrva Mīmāṁsā Sūtra* III. 5. 21; see also X. 4. 22.

Baladeva breaks this *sūtra* into two parts: *anubandhādibhyaḥ* and *prajñāntara*, etc. The first is taken by him as a separate section dealing with the worship of holy men: 'On account of injunction and so on.' Scripture expressly enjoins the worship of great and good men. This worship serves as an auxiliary and indirect means to salvation.

With the next part of the *sūtra*, Baladeva begins a new section concerned with showing that the devotees realise and intuit the Lord differently. He reads *dṛṣṭiś ca* for *dṛṣṭaś ca*. 'And like the difference between *prajñā* and other types of knowledge, the perception [of the Lord too differs in the case of different devotees], that has been said.' In B.U. IV. 4. 21, two types of knowledge, *vijñāna* and *prajñā*, are mentioned. The first is intellectual knowledge, the second is intuitional knowledge or direct realisation. There are different types of intuitional knowledge also. Different devotees following different paths have different intuitions or visions of the Lord. See C.U. III. 14. 1.

III. 3. 51. *na sāmānyād apy upalabdher mṛtyuvan na hi lokāpattiḥ*

Not in spite of similarity (can the fires constitute parts of an action), for it is seen (on the ground of scriptural texts that they are independent); as in the case of death; for the world does not become (fire because it resembles a fire in some points).

na: not; *sāmānyāt:* on account of similarity; *api:* in spite of; *upalabdheḥ:* for it is seen; *mṛtyuvat:* as in the case of death; *na hi lokāpattiḥ:* for the world does not become (fire because of certain resemblances).

One thing may resemble another in certain respects; yet the two things are different. Death applies to fire and the being in the sun. *Śatapatha Brāhmaṇa* X. 5. 2. 3; B.U. III. 2. 10. Fire and the being in the sun are not one. Again, C.U. V. 4. 1 says: 'That world is a fire; the sun itself is its fuel.' From this it does not follow that the fuel and the world actually become fire.

R. and Śrīkaṇṭha hold that the transference of the property of one thing to another does not indicate an identity between them.

Baladeva interprets the *sūtra* differently. The objection is raised that if the vision of the Lord be the cause of salvation, then everyone who sees an incarnation of the Lord like *Rāma* must become freed immediately. Baladeva answers: 'Even on account of the common perception [of the Lord as an incarnation, there is no universal release] like death [which is] not [the cause of] salvation but the attainment of [other worlds].' Death does not lead to release but often to other worlds like heaven and the rest. Similarly, all visions of the Lord are not the cause of release. The vision of the Lord on earth as an incarnation leads only to heavenly regions.

III. 3. 52. *pareṇa ca śabdasya tādvidhyam bhūyastvāttvanubandhaḥ*

And from the subsequent (Brāhmaṇa) the fact of the text being such (enjoining a separate meditation) (is known). The connection, however, (of the imaginary fires with the real one is) due to the abundance (of the

attributes of the latter which are imaginatively connected with the meditation).
pareṇa: from the subsequent (*Brāhmaṇa*); *ca:* and; *śabdasya:* of the text; *tādvidhyam:* the fact of being such; *bhūyastvāt:* on account of the abundance; *tu:* but; *anubandhaḥ:* connection.

In a subsequent *Brāhmaṇa*, it is said: 'By knowledge they ascend there where all wishes are attained. Those skilled in works do not go there.' *Śatapatha Brāhmaṇa* X. 5. 2. 23. Here knowledge is praised as superior to work. From this we find that the fires form a meditation. The connection of the fires with the actual fire is not because they form part of the sacrifice but because many of the attributes of the real fire are imaginatively connected with the fire of meditation.

Baladeva takes this *sūtra* as a separate section dealing with the grace of the Lord. The objection is raised that the view that the direct vision of the Lord alone attainable through devotion is the cause of salvation, is inconsistent with M.U. III. 2. 3 where the vision of the Lord is said to depend on the grace of the Lord. The answer is given: 'On account of what follows, the being of that kind of the word is established, [there is] the mention [of grace in the passage], on the other hand, on account of preponderance, [i.e. because the grace of the Lord is the most important factor in the attainment of salvation].' The *Muṇḍaka* text implies that devotion is the cause of the direct vision of the Lord and the latter the cause of emancipation for the grace of the Lord is not arbitrary but is determined by the devotion of men.

Section 30 (53–54)

THE SELF AS SEPARATE FROM THE BODY

III. 3. 53. *eka ātmanaḥ śarīre bhāvāt*

Some (*maintain the non-existence*) *of a* (*separate*) *self on account of the existence* (*of the self*) (*only*) *where there is a body.*
eke: some (maintain the non-existence); *ātmanaḥ:* of self (apart from the body); *śarīre:* when there is a body; *bhāvāt:* on account of existence.

Ś. thinks that this *sūtra* gives the *Cārvāka* or materialist view. The human being is only the body, having consciousness for its quality. Consciousness is produced even as the intoxicating power is produced, when certain materials are put together even though none of them is by itself intoxicating. Consciousness (*caitanya*), though not observed in earth and the other external elements, either separately or in combination yet appears in them when transformed into the shape of a body. Consciousness is seen to exist only when there is a body. It is nowhere experienced apart from the body. For wherever something exists if some other thing exists, and does not exist if that other thing does not exist, we determine the former to be a mere quality of the latter. Light and heat, for example, are qualities of fire. *yaddhi yasmin sati bhavaty asati ca na bhavati tat tad-dharmatve nādhyavasīyate; yathāgnidharmāv auṣṇya-prakāśau.* So the qualities of the self are qualities of the body only. Bhāskara adopts Ś.'s interpretation.

R. does not deal with the question of the materialist view of self but raises the question of the self of the meditating devotee. His *pūrvapakṣa* is stated thus: 'Some [maintain that the soul of the devotee has in meditation only those attributes which belong to it in the embodied state such as *jñātṛtva* and the like] because the self is in the body [at the time of meditation].' R. quotes here C.U. X. 8. 1.

Nimbārka states the objection that the individual soul is to be meditated on in its state of bondage for only such a soul exists in the body.

Baladeva makes this *sūtra* into a separate section dealing with the worship of the Lord in the different parts of the body, the stomach, the heart, the top of the head and so on. For he exists in these places also and grants salvation to the devotee.

III. 3. 54. *vyatirekas tad-bhāvābhāvitvān na tūpalabdhivat*

There is separation (of the self from the body) because its existence does not depend on the existence of that (viz. the body); but there is not (non-separation); as in the case of cognitive consciousness.

vyatirekaḥ: separation; *tadbhāva-abhāvitvāt:* for (consciousness) does not exist even where there is (the body); *na:* not so; *tu:* but; *upalabdhivat:* as in the case of cognitive consciousness.

The answer is given to the objection raised in the previous *sūtra* by pointing out that consciousness does not exist in a body after a person dies. So it is a quality of something different from the body though residing in it. The *Cārvākas* admit that the cogniser is different from the thing cognised. We cognise the body and the cogniser is different from the body. The cogniser is the self and consciousness is a quality of this self. If consciousness were a quality of the elements, it could not cognise the body. It is contradictory that anything should act on itself. Fire is hot but it does not burn itself. That consciousness is permanent follows from the uniformity of its character. Though connected with different states, it recognises itself as a conscious agent. This recognition is expressed in judgments such as 'I saw this'. It is also inferred from the fact of remembrance. Again, cognitive consciousness arises when there are certain auxiliaries such as the lamp and the like and does not arise when they are absent. From this it does not follow that cognitive consciousness is an attribute of the lamp and the like. So also the fact that consciousness takes place when there is a body and does not take place where there is none, does not imply that it is a quality of the body.

Like lamps and so on the body may be used by the self as a mere auxiliary. Besides, body is not a necessary auxiliary of consciousness. In dreams, we have perceptions while the body is inactive. It is obvious that the self is something separate from the body.

Bhāskara adopts a similar interpretation. Consciousness does not always exist when the body does and so it is not a quality of the body.

R. argues that as the realisation of *Brahman* means the realisation of *Brahman* in his real form, so self-realisation means the realisation of the self in its true realised state. His reading of the *sūtra* is: 'But this is not so but different; since it is of the being of that; as in the case of intuition.' When we meditate on the self, we meditate on the self as released. Nimbārka follows this interpretation.

Baladeva starts a new topic here, viz. different kinds of realisations in accordance with different kinds of devotions. The devotees who meditate on the Lord as the sweet realise him as the sweet in the condition of release. He who meditates on him as the majestic realises him as such.

Section 31 (55–56)

MEDITATION CONNECTED WITH SACRIFICIAL ACTS SUCH AS THE *UDGĪTHA* ARE VALID FOR ALL *ŚĀKHĀS*

III. 3. 55. *aṅgāvabaddhās tu na śākhāsu hi prativedam*

But the (*meditations*) *connected with members* (*of sacrificial acts are*) *not* (*restricted*) *to* (*particular*) *śākhās only of each Veda because* (*the same meditation is described in all*).

aṅgāvabaddhāḥ: (meditations) connected with members (of sacrificial acts); *tu:* but; *na:* not; *śākhāsu:* to (particular) *śākhās*; *hi:* because; *prativedam:* in each *Veda.*

The doubt arises because the *udgītha*, etc., are chanted differently in different *śākhās*; they may be considered different. The *sūtra* says that the meditations are one in all the branches.

Baladeva uses this *sūtra* to point out that the Lord is realised differently by different devotees in accordance with the kind of devotion with which they worship him.

III. 3. 56. *mantrādivad vā'virodhaḥ*

Or else, as in the case of mantras and the like, there is no contradiction.

mantrādivat: as in the case of *mantras* and the like; *vā:* or else; *avirodhaḥ:* there is no contradiction.

Even in the case of *mantras*, acts and qualities of acts which are enjoined in one *śākhā* are taken over by other *śākhās* also.

Baladeva concludes the section about different modes of worship by giving another illustration. 'Or as in the case of sacred formulae and the rest, there is no contradiction', i.e. just as some formulae are employed in many ceremonies, some in two, some in one only, so men worship the Lord in several ways or some only in one.

While *bhakti* or devotion to the Lord is indicated as an essential means for the attainment of freedom, for the common man surrender or *prapatti* is easy. Appaya Dīkṣita in his *Naya-mayūkha-mālikā* which summarises the ideas of R.B. says: *bhakti-rūpāṇāṁ daharādi-vidyānāṁ nyāsa-vidyāyāś ca śabdāntareṇāpi bhedo'stīti darśayitum ayaṁ pūrva-pakṣo darśitaḥ.*

This *pūrva-pakṣa* is indicated in order to show that there is difference among the *vidyās, dahara,* etc., resulting from *bhakti* on the one hand and *nyāsa-vidyā* or surrender on the other.

Section 32 (57)

THE *VAIŚVĀNARA* MEDITATION IS ONE WHOLE

III. 3. 57. *bhūmnaḥ kratuvaj jyāyastvaṁ tathā hi darśayati*

Importance (is given to the meditation) on the entire form (of Vaiśvānara) as in the case of sacrifice; for so (Scripture) shows.

bhūmnaḥ: on the entire form; *kratuvat:* as in the case of sacrifice; *jyāyastvam:* importance; *tathā:* so; *hi:* for; *darśayati:* (the *śruti*) shows.

In C.U. V. 12–17, we have references to the meditation on the different parts of the Cosmic Self and also on the whole. V. 18. The question is whether the meditation is on the whole or on parts. The answer is given that it refers to the whole. It discourages meditation on parts as in the passage 'Your head would have fallen off, if you had not come to me'. C.U. V. 12. 2. The object of meditation is the entire Self.

Baladeva takes this as a separate section dealing with the manifoldness of the Lord.

Section 33 (58)

MEDITATIONS WHICH REFER TO ONE SUBJECT BUT ARE DISTINGUISHED BY DIFFERENT QUALITIES ARE TO BE KEPT SEPARATE

III. 3. 58. *nānā śabdādi-bhedāt*

(The meditations are) different on account of the difference of words and the like.

nānā: different; *śabdādi-bhedāt:* on account of difference of words and the like.

The different meditations, *Dahara-vidyā*, *Śāṇḍilya-vidyā*, etc., are to be kept separate. For they use different words. This is difference of acts according to *Pūrva Mīmāṁsā Sūtra* II. 2. 1ff. Though the Lord is the only object of meditation, each passage teaches different qualities of the Lord.

And the like, for R., means repetition: *abhyāsa*; number: *saṁkhyā*; quality: *guṇa*; subject-matter: *prakriyā*; and name: *nāmadheya*.

Baladeva makes out that the meditations are different on account of difference of words and so on. Meditation on *Kṛṣṇa* is different from meditation on *Nṛsiṁha*. Their forms are different and the texts are also different.

Section 34 (59)

AMONG MEDITATIONS RELATING TO *BRAHMAN* ANY ONE COULD BE SELECTED ACCORDING TO ONE'S CHOICE

III. 3. 59. *vikalpo'viśiṣṭa-phalatvāt*

There is option (with respect to the several meditations), because the fruit (of all meditations) is the same.

vikalpaḥ: option; *aviśiṣṭa-phalatvāt:* on account of having the same fruit.

All forms of meditation have the same result. One has to select one form of meditation and remain intent on it, until, through the intuition of the object meditated on, the fruit of the meditation is obtained. To practise more than one meditation at a time will cause distraction of mind and retard one's progress.

R. makes out that the object of meditation in all the *vidyās* is the determinate *Brahman* and the vision of him is the fruit of all meditations. R. on I. 1. 1.

Baladeva shows that meditation on different forms of the Lord such as *Kṛṣṇa*, *Rāma*, etc., are optional since any one of them leads to release. So the devotee should take one form and adhere to it.

The fruits of all meditations are the same.

Section 35 (60)

MEDITATIONS FOR SPECIAL DESIRES MAY OR MAY NOT BE COMBINED ACCORDING TO ONE'S CHOICE

III. 3. 60. *kāmyās tu yathā-kāmaṁ samuccīyeran na vā pūrva-hetv-abhāvāt*

But (meditations) connected with desires, may, according to one's choice, be combined or not, on account of the absence of the former reason.

kāmyāḥ: (meditations) for desires; *tu:* but; *yathā-kāmam:* according to one's desire (choice); *samuccīyeran:* one may combine; *na vā:* or not; *pūrva-hetu-abhāvāt:* on account of the absence of the former reason.

As for the meditations which are practised not for the realisation of *Brahman* but for obtaining particular desires, one can take one or more of these meditations according to one's pleasure.

Section 36 (61–66)

MEDITATIONS CONNECTED WITH MEMBERS OF SACRIFICIAL ACTS MAY OR MAY NOT BE COMBINED ACCORDING TO ONE'S CHOICE

III. 3. 61. *aṅgeṣu yathāśraya-bhāvaḥ*

With regard to meditations connected with members (of sacrificial acts), it is as with their abodes.

aṅgesu: with regard to meditations connected with members (of sacrificial acts); *yathā-āśraya-bhāvaḥ:* it is as with their abodes.

Four *sūtras* 61–64 state the objection. The same rule applies to the members and to the meditations connected with them, viz. that they may be combined. A meditation is subject to what it refers.

Baladeva begins a section here, which continues to the end of the chapter dealing with the topic of the meditation on the various limbs of the Lord, the benevolent eyes, the smiling face, etc.

III. 3. 62. *śiṣṭeś ca*

And on account of the teaching.

śiṣṭeḥ: from the teaching (of the *śruti*); *ca:* and.

The *Vedas* do not make any distinction between the members of the sacrificial acts and the meditations relating to them. C.U. I. 1. 1.

Baladeva reads *śiṣṭaiś ca*: Such a meditation is performed by those who are taught.

III. 3. 63. *samāhārāt*

On account of combination.

C.U. I. 1. 5 says from the seat of the *hotṛ* he rectifies all defective singing of the *udgātṛ*. The meditation on the *praṇava, aum,* belonging to the *Ṛg Veda* is connected with the meditation on the *udgītha* of the *Sāma Veda*. All meditations on members of the sacrificial acts, in whatever *Veda* they may be mentioned, have to be combined.

Baladeva considers the objection that C.U. I. 6. 7 mentions only the lotus-like eyes of the Lord but not his limbs. This *sūtra* points out that there is no discrepancy on account of comprehensiveness. The word '*na*' is to be put in at the beginning.

III. 3. 64. *guṇa-sādhāraṇya-śruteś ca*

And from the śruti declaring the quality (*of the meditation*) *to be common* (*to all the Vedas*).
guṇa-sādhāraṇya-śruteḥ: from the *śruti* declaring the quality (*aum*) as being common (to all the *Vedas*); *ca:* and.

C.U. I. 1. 9 is considered here. The syllable *aum* is common to all the *Vedas* and the meditations in them. As the abode of all meditations is common, so are the meditations which abide in it.

Baladeva reads that every limb of the Lord must be meditated on as possessed of the powers or attributes of the rest, on account of a scriptural text of the commonness of attributes. B.G. XIII. 14 shows that every limb of the Lord can discharge the function of every other limb. So every member must be so meditated on. This is the *pūrvapakṣa*.

III. 3. 65. *na vā tat-sahabhāvāśruteḥ*

(*The meditations on members of the sacrificial acts are*) *rather not* (*to be combined*) *since the śruti does not say that they go together*.
na vā: rather not; *tat-sahabhāva-aśruteḥ:* their going together not being stated in the *śruti*.

The correct conclusion is set forth in this and the next *sūtra*. The meditations are not inseparable from the sacrifice. They may or may not be practised. See III. 3. 42. The meditations may be performed according to one's liking.

Baladeva refutes the *prima facie* view. 'Or not [i.e. every limb of the Lord is to be meditated on as possessed of its peculiar attributes only] because there is no scriptural text [to the effect that it is to be meditated on] as accompanied by [the attributes of the other limbs].'

III. 3. 66. *darśanāc ca*

And because (*Scripture*) *shows it*.
darśanāt: and because (the *śruti*) shows it; *ca:* and.

C.U. IV. 17. 10 distinguishes *Brahman* priests from the rest. It means that all the priests do not know all of them. The meditations therefore may or may not be combined according to one's taste.

Baladeva makes out that every member of the body of the Lord is to be meditated on as endowed with its own attributes, the eyes with sight and the ears with hearing and so on.

Section 1 (1–17)

KNOWLEDGE OF *BRAHMAN* IS INDEPENDENT AND NOT SUBORDINATE TO ACTION

III. 4. 1. *puruṣārtho'taḥ śabdād iti bādarāyaṇaḥ*

From this (*the knowledge of Brahman results*) *the purpose of man on account of scriptural statement, thus* (*says*) *Bādarāyaṇa.*
puruṣārthaḥ: the purpose of man; *ataḥ:* from this; *śabdāt:* from the Scriptures; *iti:* thus; *bādarāyaṇaḥ:* Bādarāyaṇa.

Bādarāyaṇa, basing himself on the texts C.U. VII. 1. 3; M.U. III. 2. 9; T.U. II. 1, argues that the knowledge of *Brahman* leads to liberation and is not a part of sacrificial acts.

R. asks whether the advantage to the meditating devotee accrues from the meditation directly or from works of which the meditations are members and says that Bādarāyaṇa holds the former view.

Baladeva means by *puruṣārtha* not only salvation but all the four ends of men, righteousness, wealth, enjoyment and salvation. The *prima facie* view is that meditation brings about salvation only. The answer is that all the four ends and not merely salvation arise from meditation.

III. 4. 2. *śeṣatvāt puruṣārthavādo yathā'nyeṣv iti jaiminiḥ*

On account of (*the self*) *being in a supplementary relation* (*to action*) (*the statements as to the fruits of the knowledge of the Self*) *are mere praise of the agent even as in other cases, thus says Jaimini.*
śeṣatvāt: on account of being in a supplementary relation (to action); *puruṣa-arthavādaḥ:* are praise of the agent; *yathā:* even as; *anyeṣu:* in other cases; *iti:* thus; *jaiminiḥ:* Jaimini (says).

The knowledge of the self has no independent fruit of its own for it stands in a subordinate relation to sacrificial action. The self as the agent in all action stands in a subordinate relation to action. By knowing that the self will outlive the body, the agent becomes qualified for action, the fruit of which will appear only after death. As the knowledge of the self has no independent position, it cannot have an independent fruit. The passages which state such fruits are to be taken as *arthavādas* or praise. If it is said that the *Upaniṣads* refer to the Self which stands outside the empirical existence and such a Self cannot be subordinate to activity, the opponent points out that the transmigrating self is clearly referred to in passages of B.U. II. 4. 5.

For R., the *sūtra* means that meditations are constituents of sacrificial actions and are of no advantage by themselves.

III. 4. 3. *ācāra darśanāt*

Because we find (from the Scriptures) (certain lines of) conduct.
ācāra: conduct; *darśanāt:* because of finding.

See B.U. III. 1. 1; C.U. V. 11. 5. Both Janaka and Aśvapati were knowers of the Self. If by knowledge of the Self they had attained liberation there was no need for them to perform sacrifices but the texts quoted show that they did perform sacrifices. This proves that liberation is obtained through sacrificial acts alone and not through the knowledge of the Self. If mere knowledge could effect the purpose of man, why should one perform works troublesome in many ways. 'If a man would find honey in the *arka* tree, why should he go to the hill?' *arke cen madhu vindeta kim arthaṁ parvataṁ vrajet?*

Those who know *Brahman*, says R., apply themselves to works chiefly. This shows that knowledge or meditation has no independent value but serves to set forth the true nature of the active self and is subordinate to work.

III. 4. 4. *tac chruteḥ*

That, the Scriptures (declare).
tat: that; *śruteḥ:* the Scriptures (declare).

C.U. I. 1. 10 says: What a man does with knowledge, faith and the *Upaniṣad* is more powerful. This text directly states that knowledge is subordinate to work. *yad eva vidyayā karoti. Vidyā* or knowledge is directly represented as a means of work.

Nimbārka interprets *tasya śruteḥ* and not *tat śruteḥ*.

III. 4. 5. *samanvānambhaṇāt*

On account of the taking hold together.
samanvānambhaṇāt: on account of taking hold together.

B.U. IV. 4. 2 says: 'Then both his knowledge and his work take hold of him.' The two together manifest their fruits. Knowledge therefore is not independent.

III. 4. 6. *tadvato vidhānāt*

And because (the Scriptures) enjoin (work) for such.
tadvataḥ: for such (as know the purport of the *Veda*); *vidhānāt:* because (the Scriptures) enjoin (work).

The Scriptures enjoin work for those who have a knowledge of the *Vedas*, which includes the knowledge of the Self. So knowledge does not produce any result independently. See C.U. VIII. 15.

R. says that according to this *sūtra*, the knowledge of *Brahman* is enjoined with a view to works only; it has no independent result of its own.

III. 4. 7. *niyamāc ca*

And on account of prescribed rules.
niyamāt: on account of prescribed rules; *ca:* and.
Īśa U. I. 2 and *Śatapatha Brāhmaṇa* XII. 4. 1. 1 indicate that knowledge stands in a subordinate relation to work. *Sūtras* 2–7 state the *prima facie* view.

III. 4. 8. *adhikopadeśāt tu bādarāyaṇasyaivam tad-darśanāt*

But on account of (the scriptural) teaching (that the Supreme Self is) additional (to the agent), Bādarāyaṇa's (view is) correct for that is seen (in the Scriptures).
adhika-upadeśāt: on account of the teaching that (the Supreme Self is) additional to; *tu:* but; *bādarāyaṇasya:* Bādarāyaṇa's view; *evam:* such (correct); *tat-darśanāt:* for that is seen.

The *Vedānta* texts teach as the object of knowledge something different from the embodied self. They teach the Supreme free from all empirical attributes. Knowledge of the Supreme does not only not promote action but cuts all action short. See M.U. I. 1. 9; T.U. II. 8; *Kaṭha U.* II. 6. 2; B.U. III. 8. 9; C.U. VI. 2. 3. There are passages which refer to the empirical self. There is, however, no contradiction, as the Self of the Higher Lord is the real nature of the embodied self. *parameśvaram eva hi śarīrasya pāramārthikaṁ svarūpam upādhi-kṛtaṁ tu śarīratvam.* Ś.

R. says that Bādarāyaṇa holds that knowledge has an independent fruit of its own. Its object is the Highest *Brahman* with all its perfections and exalted qualities, which cannot possibly be attributed to the individual self whether in the state of release or bondage. The fruit of the knowledge is eternal life which consists in attaining to him, *parama-puruṣa-prāpti-rūpam amṛtatvam.*

Baladeva interprets the *sūtra* thus: But on account of the teaching (of *vidyā* or knowledge as) more than (*karma* or action).

III. 4. 9. *tulyaṁ tu darśanam*

But the declarations of Scripture support both views.
tulyam: equal; *tu:* but; *darśanam:* declaration of *śruti.*

There are passages which support that knowledge is incompatible with work: B.U. III. 5. 1; IV. 5. 15.

III. 4. 10. *asārvatrikī*

(*The declaration of the Scripture referred to in sūtra* 4) *is non-comprehensive.*
asārvatrikī: non-comprehensive.

The text that knowledge enhances the fruit of the sacrifice does not refer to all knowledge but is connected only with the *udgītha* which is discussed in the section.

III. 4. 11. *vibhāgaḥ śatavat*

(There is) division (of knowledge and work) as in the case of the hundred (divided between two persons).
vibhāgaḥ: division (of knowledge and work); *śatavat:* as in the case of a hundred.

Knowledge and work (B.U. IV. 4. 2) are to be taken in a distributive sense. Knowledge follows one and work another. There is no combination of the two. Besides, the text refers not to an emancipated soul but to one in *saṁsāra*. See B.U. IV. 4. 6.

III. 4. 12. *adhyayana-mātravataḥ*

(The Scriptures enjoin work) on him who has merely read (the Veda).
adhyayana-mātravataḥ: only on him who has merely read (the *Veda*).

Those who have read the *Vedas* and known about works are entitled to perform work. For those who have knowledge of the Self from the *Upaniṣads,* no work is prescribed.

R. says that reading here means nothing more than the apprehensions of the aggregate of syllables called *Veda* without any insight into their meaning.

Nimbārka quotes C.U. V. III. 15. 1. Śrīnivāsa makes a difference between reading the *Vedas* and understanding the *Vedānta.*

III. 4. 13. *nāviśeṣāt*

There being no special mention, (the rule does) not (apply to him who knows).
na: not; *aviśeṣāt:* on account of the absence of any specification or special mention.

Sūtra 7 quotes *Iśa U.* 2. This, however, is a general statement and does not specially mention the knower or *jñāni.* So it is not binding on him.

R. says that there is no special reason to hold that the text refers to works as independent means of a desirable result. It may be understood as referring to works subordinate to knowledge. As the knower of the Self has to practise meditation so long as he lives, he may also have to practise works that are helpful to meditation for the same period.

III. 4. 14. *stutaye'numatir vā*

Or the permission is for the purpose of glorification (of knowledge).
stutaye: for the glorification (of knowledge); *anumatiḥ:* permission; *vā:* or.

The injunction to do work *Iśa U.* 2. may be for the glorification of knowledge. A knower of the Self may work all his life but on account of his knowledge he will not be bound by his works. *yāvaj jīvam karma kurvatyapi puruṣe viduṣi na karmalepāya bhavati vidyā-sāmarthyāt.*

R. says, owing to the power of knowledge, a man although constantly performing works is not stained by them. *vidyā-māhātmyāt sarvadā karma kurvann api na lipyate karmabhiḥ.*

Śrīnivāsa quotes B.G. XVIII. 56; IV. 14.

III. 4. 15. *kāma-kāreṇa caike*

And some according to their choice (have refrained from all work).
kāma-kāreṇa: according to their choice; *ca:* and; *eke:* some.

There is no obligation for the knowers of the Self in regard to work. Some may choose to work in order to set an example to others while others may abstain from work.

Baladeva begins a new section here and substitutes *vā* in place of *ca*. Such is the glory of knowledge that one who has attained knowledge may act just as he likes or abstain from action and yet be free from consequences, good or bad.

Knowledge of *Brahman* and work in the world are not inconsistent with each other.

III. 4. 16. *upamardaṁ ca*

And (Scripture teaches) the destruction (of the qualification for works by knowledge).
upamardaṁ: destruction; *ca:* and.

Knowledge destroys all ignorance with its distinctions of agent, act and result. See B.U. IV. 5. 15. Knowledge of the Self is antagonistic to all work and so cannot be subsidiary to work.

R. mentions that there is a text which declares that the knowledge of *Brahman* destroys work which is the root of all existence. M.U. II. 2. 8. This also contradicts the view that knowledge is subordinate to works.

Śrīnivāsa quotes B.G. IV. 19 and IV. 3. 7.

Baladeva holds that even *prārabdha-karmas* may be destroyed by knowledge.

III. 4. 17. *ūrdhva-retaḥ su ca śabde hi*

And (knowledge belongs) to those who observe chastity, (i.e. to samnyāsins) because (this fourth stage of life is mentioned) in the Scripture.
ūrdhva-retaḥ su: to those who observe chastity; *ca:* and; *śabde:* in the Scripture; *hi:* because.

To these in the stage of *samnyāsa* there is no work prescribed except discrimination. See C.U. II. 23. 1–2; B.U. IV. 4. 22. See also M.U. I. 2. 11 and C.U. V. 10. 1. Anyone can take to this life without being a householder, etc., which shows the independence of knowledge.

Section 2 (18–20)

IN THE STATE OF *SAṀSĀRA*, ONLY KNOWLEDGE IS PRESCRIBED

III. 4. 18. *parāmarśaṁ jaiminir acodanā cāpavadati hi*

Jaimini (*thinks that the passages mentioned in the previous sūtra contain*) *a reference* (*only to samnyāsa*) *and not injunction, for* (*other texts*) *condemn* (*saṁnyāsa*).
parāmarśam: (mere) reference; *jaiminiḥ:* Jaimini; *acodanā:* (there is) no injunction; *ca:* and; *apavadati:* condemn; *hi:* because.

In C.U. II. 23. 1, we do not find words expressive of injunction. In B.U. IV. 4. 22, there is mere statement of fact and no injunction. The text promises steadfastness in *Brahman*. There are other texts which forbid *samnyāsa*: T.U. I. 11; *Taittīriya Brāhmaṇa* VII. 13. 12.

Baladeva means by this *sūtra*: '[There is a favourable] reference [to works in Scripture], according to Jaimini: there is no injunction [with regard to the giving up of works] because [Scripture] condemns [such a giving up of works].'

III. 4. 19. *anuṣṭheyaṁ bādarāyaṇaḥ sāmya-śruteḥ*

Bādarāyaṇa (*thinks that samnyāsa or monastic life*) *is to be accomplished for the text* (*cited*) *applies equally* (*to all the four stages of life*).
anuṣṭheyam: is to be accomplished; *bādarāyaṇaḥ:* Bādarāyaṇa; *sāmya-śruteḥ:* on account of the common scriptural text.

The text cited speaks of sacrifices, etc., in the *gṛhastha* state, i.e. the householder's life, penance in *vānaprastha*, celibacy in *brahmacarya*, and steadfastness in *Brahman* for the *samnyāsa* stage. As the three former are enjoined elsewhere, the last should also be taken as enjoined.

Baladeva holds that a knower of *Brahman* may perform the obligatory duties partially just as he likes, but is not required to perform them exhaustively like ordinary men. Scripture states that such a partial performance by the knower is equal to a full performance by ordinary men.

III. 4. 20. *vidhir vā dhāraṇavat*

Or rather (*there is*) *an injunction as in the case of the carrying* (*of the sacrificial fuel*).
vidhiḥ: injunction; *vā:* or rather; *dhāraṇavat:* as in the case of the carrying (of the sacrificial fuel).

In the passage 'Let him approach carrying the firewood below [the ladle holding the offering, for above he carries it for the gods]', (*Āpastamba Śrauta Sūtra* IX. 11. 8–9), the last clause is interpreted as an injunction by Jaimini, though it is not in the form of an injunction. On account of its newness (*a-pūrvatā*) it is an injunction. In accordance with this view, C.U. II. 23. 1 is an injunction and not a mere reference. There are other texts which directly enjoin *saṁnyāsa*. *Jābāla U*. 4.

Again, the condition of being grounded in *Brahman* is exalted and is said to be enjoined. This state belongs only to the wandering mendicant. Those belonging to the three former stages of life obtain the world of the blessed, while the fourth, the wandering mendicant, enjoys immortality. Immortality does not accrue merely by belonging to a stage of life. It is the result of being grounded in *Brahman*, *brahmasaṁstha*, to the exclusion of all other activity. This state is impossible for those belonging to the three former stages for they suffer loss on account of the non-performance of works enjoined on them. The mendicant, on the other hand, who has discarded all works can suffer no loss on account of non-performance. The duties incumbent on him such as the restraint of the senses, etc., are not opposed to the state of being grounded in *Brahman* but are helpful to it. Many passages declare that for him who is grounded in *Brahman*, there are no works, M.U. III. 2. 6; B.G. V. 17.

Section 3 (21–22)

CERTAIN SCRIPTURAL STATEMENTS AS IN C.U. I. 1. 3 ARE NOT GLORIFICATORY BUT ENJOIN MEDITATION

III. 4. 21. *stuti-mātram upādānāt iti cen nāpūrvatvāt*

If it be said that (*the texts such as the one about the udgītha are*) *mere glorification, on account of their reference* (*to parts of sacrifices*) (*we say that it is*) *not so on account of the newness* (*of what they teach*).

stuti-mātram: mere glorification; *upādānāt:* because of their reference (to parts of sacrificial acts); *iti cet:* if it be said; *na:* not so; *apūrvatvāt:* on account of newness.

The opponent says that C.U. I. 1. 3; I. 6. 1 simply glorify the ladle and so on. The *sūtra* refutes the view and argues that glorification to have a purpose must be in complementary relation to an injunction. The *Chāndogya* passage where *udgītha* is mentioned as the essence of essences is in the *Upaniṣad* and cannot be taken along with the injunctions about the *udgītha* in the ritual part. On account of newness it is an injunction and not mere glorification.

Baladeva uses this *sūtra* to indicate that the view that the knower is at liberty to act at will is not enjoined before but is enjoined in the above texts.

III. 4. 22. *bhāva-śabdāc ca*

And on account of texts expressive of injunction.
bhāva-śabdāt: on account of texts expressive of injunction; *ca:* and.

In C.U. I. 1. 1 'Let one meditate on *aum* of the *udgītha*'. See also C.U. II. 2. 1; *Aitareya Āraṇyaka* II. 1. 6. All these passages enjoin devout meditations.

Section 4 (23–24)

THE STORIES IN THE *UPANIṢADS* ARE NOT MEMBERS OF SACRIFICIAL ACTS BUT GLORIFY THE INJUNCTIONS WITH WHICH THEY ARE CONNECTED

III. 4. 23. *pāriplavārtha iti cen na viśeṣitatvāt*

If it be said (that the stories in the Upaniṣads are) for the purpose of pāriplavas, (we say it is) not so, because (only certain stories) are specified (for the purpose).
pāriplavārthaḥ: for the purpose of *pāriplavas*; *iti cet:* if it be said; *na:* not so; *viśeṣatvāt:* on account of (certain stories) being specified.

In the horse-sacrifice which lasts for a year, the sacrificer and the members of his family are expected to hear at intervals the recital of certain stories which are called *pāriplavas.* They form part of the ritualistic acts. The question is raised whether the stories of the *Upaniṣads* also serve the purpose of the ritualistic acts. The *sūtra* denies that they serve his purpose for the stories meant for this purpose are specified. *Upaniṣad* stories are not mentioned in this category.

Bhāskara takes this and the next *sūtra* as one.

III. 4. 24. *tathā caikavākyatopabandhāt*

This follows also from the connection (of the stories with the meditations) in one whole.
tathā: this (follows); *ca:* and; *eka-vākyatā-upabandhāt:* being connected in one whole.

The story form is used to attract attention. The stories not serving the purpose of *pāriplavas* are intended to introduce the meditations.

Section 5 (25)

THE *SAMNYĀSINS* NEED NOT OBSERVE RITUAL ACTS SINCE KNOWLEDGE SERVES THEIR PURPOSE

III. 4. 25. *ata eva cāgnīndhanādy-anapekṣā*

And for this very reason there is no need of the lighting of the fire and so on.

ata eva: for this very reason; *ca:* and; *agni-indhanādi:* lighting of the fire and so on; *anapekṣā:* (there is) no need.

Since the purpose is effected through knowledge, the lighting of the sacrificial fire, etc., are not necessary.

While Nimbārka holds that knowledge is independent of works only in the case of those who practise *brahmacarya,* Ś. holds that it is so in all cases.

Baladeva also thinks that knowledge is sufficient for salvation.

Section 6 (26–27)

WORKS PRESCRIBED BY SCRIPTURE ARE USEFUL SINCE THEY HELP THE RISE OF KNOWLEDGE

III. 4. 26. *sarvāpekṣā ca yajñādi-śruter aśvavat*

And there is need of all (works) on account of the scriptural statement of sacrifices and the like; as in the case of the horse.

sarvāpekṣā: need of all; *ca:* and; *yajñādi-śruteḥ:* on account of the scriptural statement of sacrifices, etc. (as means to knowledge); *aśvavat:* as in the case of the horse.

This *sūtra* says that works are useful as a means to knowledge and even the Scriptures prescribe them. But they have no part in producing the result of knowledge which is liberation. Liberation comes only from knowledge and not from work. Work purifies the mind and the knowledge of the Self is manifested in a pure mind. So works are useful as an indirect means to knowledge. Ś. quotes: 'Works are the cleansing away of uncleanliness but knowledge is the highest way. When the impurity has been removed by works, then knowledge begins to act.'

kaṣāyapaktiḥ karmāṇi jñānaṁ tu paramā gatiḥ
kaṣāye karmabhiḥ pakve tato jñānaṁ pravartate.

The illustration of the horse is given. The horse on account of its special character is not used for ploughing but is harnessed to chariots. So works are not required by knowledge for bringing about its results but only with a view to its own origination.

Bhāskara points out that *karma* is not the cause of the origin of knowledge but has an essential part in bringing about salvation. He stresses the doctrine of the combination of knowledge and work. 'Just as a horse is fit for carrying a man, but not for drawing a plough, so knowledge combined with work is fit for leading to salvation and not mere knowledge.'

R. makes out that, in the case of householders, knowledge has for its prerequisite all sacrifices and other works of permanent and occasional obligation. He quotes B.U. IV. 4. 22: 'Him the *Brāhmaṇas* seek to know by the study of the *Veda*, by sacrifices, by gifts, by penance, by fasting.' By knowledge we understand in this connection a mental act different in character from the mere cognition of the sense of the texts and more specifically denoted by such terms as *dhyāna* or *upāsanā*, meditation or worship, which is of the nature of remembrance (i.e. representative thought), but intuitive clearness is not inferior to the clearest presentative thought, *pratyakṣa;* which, by constant daily practice, becomes ever more perfect and being duly continued up to death secures final release.

jñānaṁ ca vākyārtha-jñānād arthāntara-bhūtaṁ dhyānopāsanādi-śabda-vācyam viśada-tama-pratyakṣatāpanna-smṛti-rūpaṁ niratiśaya-priyam ahar-ahar abhyāsādheyātiśayam ā prayāṇād anuvartamānam mokṣa-sādhanam iti.

R. and Śrīkaṇṭha interpret 'as in the case of a horse' differently. Just as a horse, though the real means of going, depends on some other assisting factors, such as the saddle, attendants, grooming and the like, so knowledge, though the real means to salvation, depends on the co-operation of works.

III. 4. 27. *śama-damādy-upetaḥ syāt tathāpi tu tad-vidhes tad-aṅgatayā teṣām avaśyānuṣṭheyatvāt*

But even if it be so (that there is no injunction to do work to attain knowledge in B.U. IV. 4. 22), *one must possess calmness, self-control and the like since they are enjoined as helps to knowledge and (on that account) have necessarily to be accomplished.*

śama-damādi-upetaḥ syāt: one must possess calmness, self-control and the like; *tathā api:* even if it be so; *tu:* but; *tad-vidheḥ:* since they are enjoined; *tad-aṅgatayā:* as helps to it (knowledge); *teṣām avaśya anuṣṭheyatvāt:* and therefore they have necessarily to be accomplished.

Even if B.U. IV. 4. 2. 2 does not enjoin work specificially, B.U. IV. 4. 23: 'He who knows it as such, having become calm, self-controlled, withdrawn, patient and collected sees the Self in his own self' is injunctive in character. These qualities are enjoined and have to be accomplished. Self-control, etc., directly help the attainment of knowledge, while work helps it indirectly.

Section 7 (28–31)

RELAXATIONS OF RULES REGARDING FOOD ARE PERMITTED IN CASES OF EXTREME NEED

III. 4. 28. *sarvānnānumatiś ca prāṇātyaye tad-darśanāt*

(Only) in case of danger of life (there is) permission to take all types of food; because the Scripture shows that.

sarva-anna-anumatiḥ: permission to take all types of food; *prāṇātyaye:* in case of danger of life; *tat-darśanāt:* because the Scripture shows that.

The opponent argues from C.U. V. 2. 1, 'For one who knows this, there is nothing whatever that is not food', that it is an injunction since it is not found anywhere else. This *sūtra* refutes the view and holds that it is only a statement of fact. Forbidden food can be taken only when life is in danger as was done by the sage Cākrāyaṇa when his life was in danger. See C.U. I. 10. 1–5.

III. 4. 29. *abādhāc ca*

And because of non-contradiction.

abādhāt: on account of non-contradiction; *ca:* and.

C.U. VII. 26. 2: 'When the food is pure, the mind is pure.'

Baladeva gives a different interpretation: 'On account of non-obstruction.' Although in ordinary cases the taking of improper food obstructs the full manifestation of knowledge, yet when a knower of *Brahman* does so by necessity, it does not obstruct his knowledge.

III. 4. 30. *api ca smaryate*

Moreover the smṛtis say so.

api ca: moreover; *smaryate:* the *smṛtis* say so.

The *smṛtis* say that both those who have knowledge and those who have not can take any food when life is in danger. They hold that it is normally sinful to take certain types of food. See *Manu* X. 10. 4; B.G. V. 10.

III. 4. 31. *śabdaś cāto'kāmakāre*

And hence also a scriptural passage as to non-acting according to one's wish.

śabdaḥ: a scriptural passage; *ca:* and; *ataḥ:* hence; *a-kāmakāre:* not acting according to one's wish.

There are scriptural passages prohibiting one from acting as one pleases. Freedom from all restraint cannot help us to attain knowledge. *Kāthaka Saṁhitā* (XII. 12) says: 'Therefore a *Brāhmaṇa* should not take liquor.' *tasmād brāhmaṇas surāṁ na pibet.*

Section 8 (32–35)

THE DUTIES OF THE *ĀŚRAMAS* ARE TO BE PERFORMED EVEN BY THOSE WHO DO NOT AIM AT KNOWLEDGE

III. 4. 32. *vihitatvāc cāśrama-karmāpi*

And the duties of the āśramas are (incumbent on him) also (who does not desire release); because they are enjoined (on him by the Scriptures).
vihitatvāt: because they are enjoined; *ca:* and; *āśrama-karma:* duties of the stages of life; *api:* also.

If works are a means to knowledge, the question is raised whether works should be performed by one who does not desire knowledge. The *sūtra* answers that these duties of the stages of life are obligatory for all.

Baladeva begins a new section here with two *sūtras*. He says that even when the devotee has come to acquire knowledge, he should continue to perform his duties in order to increase his knowledge.

III. 4. 33. *sahakāritvena ca*

Also because of being helpful (as a means to knowledge).
sahakāritvena: as a means (to knowledge); *ca:* and.

Duties are helpful in producing knowledge, though not its fruit liberation, which is not attainable except through knowledge.

R. says that works give rise to the desire for knowledge.

Nimbārka and Śrīnivāsa quote B.U. IV. 4. 22: 'Him the *Brāhmaṇas* seek to know by sacrifices.' If it be said that the same works cannot serve the purpose of a stage of life and the goal of knowledge, the answer is given on the basis of the *Pūrva Mīmāṁsā Sūtra* (IV. 3. 5). 'But with regard to one and the same thing being both, there is conjunction and separation.'

III. 4. 34. *sarvathāpi ta evobhayaliṅgāt*

In all cases the same duties (have to be performed) on account of the twofold indicatory mark.
sarvathā api: in all cases; *te eva:* the same duties (have to be performed); *ubhaya-liṅgāt:* on account of the twofold indicatory mark.

The question is raised whether the works done as enjoined in the stages of life or those performed as aids to knowledge are of two different kinds. In either case the same duties are performed as is seen from the *śruti* and the *smṛti* texts. See B.U. IV. 4. 22; B.G. VI. 1. The twofold indicatory mark is *śruti* and *smṛti*.

Baladeva begins a new section here with two *sūtras*. The *pariniṣṭha* devotee should first perform his duties of worship and then his ordinary duties.

III. 4. 35. *anabhibhavaṁ ca darśayati*

And Scripture declares that (those performing works) are not overpowered (by passion and the like).
anabhibhavam: not being overpowered; *ca:* and; *darśayati:* the Scripture declares.

Scripture shows that he who is furnished with self-control, etc., is not overpowered by such afflictions as passion and the like. See C.U. VIII. 5. 3. Sacrifices, etc., are works incumbent on the *āśramas* or stages of life and are helpful for knowledge.

Nimbārka quotes *Mahā-nārāyaṇa U.* XXII. 1: 'By means of religious observance one removes one's sin.'

Baladeva says that the *pariniṣṭha* devotee is not overpowered by the fault of the non-performance of the duties incumbent on his own stage of life.

Section 9 (36–39)

THOSE WHO STAND BETWEEN TWO STAGES OF LIFE ARE ALSO ENTITLED TO KNOWLEDGE

III. 4. 36. *antarācāpi tu tad-dṛṣṭeḥ*

But also (persons standing) between (are qualified for knowledge) for that is seen (in Scripture).
antarā: (persons standing) in between (two *āśramas*); *ca:* and; *api tu:* also; *tad-dṛṣṭeḥ:* because that is seen.

The question considered here is whether those who belong to no recognised stage of life (*āśrama*) are fit for *brahma*-knowledge. The answer is in the affirmative though it is better to belong to one *āśrama* rather than none.

A widower, for example, cannot do the duties of an *āśrama*. The *sūtra* says that such people are qualified for knowledge. Scriptures give examples of people like Raikva and Gārgī, who had the knowledge of *Brahman*. C.U. IV. 1; B.U. III. 6 and 8.

III. 4. 37. *api ca smaryate*

Also this is stated in smṛti.
api ca: also; *smaryate:* stated in *smṛti*.

Samvarta and others paid no regard to the duties incumbent on the stages of life and yet attained the highest knowledge.

R. says that men who do not belong to an *āśrama* or a stage of life grow in knowledge through prayer and the like. He quotes *Manu* II. 87: 'Through prayer also a *Brāhmaṇa* may become perfect. Whether he performs other works or not, one who befriends all creatures is called a *Brāhmaṇa*.'

japyenāpi ca saṁsidhyed brāhmaṇo nātra saṁśayaḥ
kuryād anyan na vā kuryān maitro brāhmaṇa ucyate.

III. 4. 38. *viśeṣānugrahaś ca*

And special works favour (knowledge).

viśeṣa-anugrahaḥ: favour due to special work; *ca:* and.

Those who are not householders or are unable due to poverty, etc., to perform the duties of the stages of life can attain knowledge through special works like prayer, fasting, meditation, etc., which are not opposed to the condition of those who do not belong to any stage of life.

R. quotes *Praśna U.* I. 10. He holds that acts which do not exclusively pertain to any *āśrama* conduce to knowledge, *anāśrama-niyatair dharma-viśeṣaiḥ vidyānugrahaḥ.*

Śrīkaṇṭha interprets the *sūtra* to mean that *āśrama-dharma*, the duties prescribed for each stage of life, has a special efficacy in promoting knowledge.

III. 4. 39. *atastvitaraj jyāyo liṅgāc ca*

But better than this is the other (stage of belonging to an āśrama) on account of the indicatory marks.

ātaḥ: than this; *tu:* but; *itarat:* the other; *jyāyaḥ:* better; *liṅgāt:* because of the indicatory marks; *ca:* and.

Though it is possible for one who stands between two *āśramas* to attain knowledge, both the *śruti* and the *smṛti* say that it is better to belong to some *āśrama*. See B.U. IV. 4. 22; IV. 4. 9.

Baladeva concludes that one who does not belong to any stage of life is higher than one who belongs to a stage of life.

Section 10 (40)

THERE IS NO REVERSION TO FORMER STAGES OF ONE WHO HAS TAKEN TO *SAMNYĀSA*

III. 4. 40. *tad-bhūtasya tu nātad-bhāvo jaiminer api niyamātad-rūpābhāvebhyaḥ*

But of him who has become that (entered on a higher āśrama) there is no becoming not that (i.e. reverting to a lower one), according to Jaimini also, on account of restrictions, on account of the absence of the forms of that.

tad-bhūtasya: of him who has become that; *tu:* but; *na:* no; *atad-bhāvaḥ:* becoming not that; *jaimineḥ:* of Jaimini (in this view); *api:* also; *niyama:* on account of restriction; *atad-rūpa-abhāvebhyaḥ:* on account of the absence of the forms of that.

The question is whether one who has taken to *samnyāsa* can go back to the previous stages of life. The *sūtra* says that he cannot for the texts do not speak of reversion. They speak only of ascent to the higher stages of life. There exist no cases of such reversion.

Baladeva says that a *nirapekṣa* devotee does not deviate from his vow and enter worldly life.

Section 11 (41–42)

EXPIATION FOR ONE WHO VIOLATES THE VIEW OF *SAMNYĀSA*

III. 4. 41. *na cādhikārikam api patanānumānāt, tad ayogāt*

And not also (*can the expiation take place*) *mentioned in the chapter treating of qualification, because a lapse is inferred* (*in his case from the smṛti*) *and because of its inefficacy* (*in his case*).

na: not; *ca:* and; *ādhikārikam:* (expiation) mentioned in the chapter dealing with qualification; *api:* even; *patanānumānāt:* because a lapse is inferred; *tad-ayogāt:* because of its inefficacy.

If a *brahma-cārin* for life breaks from inattention the vow of celibacy, is he to perform the expiatory sacrifice mentioned in the text *Āpastamba Dharma Sūtra* I. 9. 26. 8? The opponent says he is not. *Pūrva Mīmāṁsā Sūtra* VI. 8. 22 speaks of *brahma-cārins* in general and not of perpetual ones. *Smṛti* declares that such sins cannot be expiated by him any more than a head cut off from the body can again be tacked on to the body. The *upakurvāṇa* or a *brahma-cārin* for a certain time only (and not for life) may purify himself by the ceremony mentioned.

Nimbārka quotes the *smṛti* passage: 'But the twice-born who, having reached the state of a perpetual religious student bound by chastity deviates therefrom—I do not see any expiation whereby he, the slayer of himself, may be purified.' (*Agni Purāṇa* 165. 23a–24b.)

III. 4. 42. *upapūrvam api tv eke bhāvam, aśanavat, tad uktam*

But some (*consider the lapse*) *a minor one* (*and claim*) *the existence* (*of expiation for naiṣṭhika brahma-cārins also*) *as in the case of eating* (*forbidden food by ordinary brahma-cārins*). *This has been stated* (*in the Pūrva Mīmāṁsā*).

upa-pūrvam: a minor lapse; *api tu:* but; *eke:* some; *bhāvam:* the existence; *aśanavat:* as in the case of eating; *tat:* this; *uktam:* is stated (in *Pūrva Mīmāṁsā*).

Transgression of the vow of chastity is a minor sin. It is not listed among the deadly sins such as violating a teacher's bed and so on. So the expiatory ceremony is claimed to be valid for both sets of *brahma-cārins*, the *naiṣṭhika* and the *upakurvāṇa*. The case is analogous to that of eating forbidden food. The *brahma-cārins* who eat forbidden food may purify themselves by performing a ceremony. The principle guiding the decision is explained in *Pūrva Mīmāṁsā Sūtra* I. 3. 8.

Section 12 (43)

SUCH TRANSGRESSIONS ARE TO BE KEPT OUTSIDE SOCIETY

III. 4. 43. *bahistūbhayathāpi smṛter ācārāc ca*

But in both cases (they are to be kept) outside society, on account of smṛti and custom.

bahiḥ: outside; *tu:* but; *ubhayathā-api:* in both cases; *smṛteḥ:* from the *smṛti*; *ācārāt:* from custom; *ca:* and.

Whether the lapses are to be regarded as major or minor, good people should avoid such transgressors, since *smṛti* and approved custom both condemn them.

Bhāskara and Baladeva omit the word '*api*'.

Section 13 (44–46)

MEDITATIONS CONNECTED WITH MEMBERS OF SACRIFICIAL ACTS ARE TO BE PERFORMED BY THE PRIEST AND NOT THE SACRIFICER

III. 4. 44. *svāminaḥ phala-śruteḥ ity ātreyaḥ*

To the lord (of the sacrifice only the agentship in meditation belongs) because Scripture declares a fruit (for it); thus Ātreya thinks.

svāminaḥ: to the lord (of the sacrifice); *phala-śruteḥ:* from the declaration of fruits in the *śruti*; *iti:* thus; *ātreyaḥ:* Ātreya.

The question is raised as to the agentship of the meditations connected with members of sacrificial acts. Is the sacrificer or the priest the agent? Ātreya holds that the agentship belongs to the sacrificer since the *śruti* declares a special fruit for these meditations.

Nimbārka quotes C.U. I. 1. 10.

III. 4. 45. *ārtvijyam ity auḍulomis tasmai hi parikriyate*

(They are) the work of the priest; this is the view of Auḍulomi since for that he is paid.

ārtvijyam: the work of the priest (*ṛtvik*); *iti:* this; *auḍulomiḥ:* (is the view of) Auḍulomi; *tasmai:* for that; *hi:* because; *parikriyate:* (he) is paid (engaged).

The meditations have to be observed by the priest, since he is paid for his acts. The fruits of his acts are purchased by the sacrificer. This is the view of the sage Auḍulomi.

Śrīnivāsa quotes two authorities. *Pūrva Mīmāṁsā Sūtra* (III. 7. 18) says that the fruit mentioned in the Scripture (accrues) to the instigator. *Śatapatha Brāhmaṇa* (I. 3. 1. 26) reads: 'Whatever blessings, for sooth, the priests pray for, all those accrue to the sacrificer.'

Baladeva gives a different interpretation. Just as an officiating priest sells himself, as it were, to the sacrificer, so the Lord sells himself to the *nirapekṣa* devotees.

III. 4. 46. *śruteś ca*

And because the śruti so declares.
śruteḥ: from the *śruti*; *ca:* and.

Ś. quotes *Śatapatha Brāhmaṇa* I. 3. 1. 26; C.U. I. 7. 8, and holds that Auḍulomi is correct.

R. and Nimbārka omit this *sūtra*.

Section 14 (47–49)

B.U. III. 5. 1 ENJOINS SILENT MEDITATION BESIDES SCHOLARSHIP AND THE CHILDLIKE STATE

III. 4. 47. *sahakāryantara-vidhiḥ pakṣeṇa tṛtīyaṁ tadvato vidhyādivat*

(Silent meditation is) the injunction of another auxiliary (to knowledge) which is a third one (besides the two expressly enjoined) as an alternative (where perfect knowledge has not arisen) to him who is such (i.e. the saṁnyāsin possessing knowledge): as in the case of injunctions and the like.
sahakāryantara-vidhiḥ: injunction of another auxiliary (to knowledge); *pakṣeṇa:* as an alternative; *tṛtīyam:* a third one; *tadvataḥ:* for one who possesses it (knowledge); *vidhyādivat:* as in the case of injunctions and the like.

The question is raised in regard to B.U. III. 5. 1, whether silent meditation is enjoined or not. The opponent holds that it is not, since there is no word indicating an injunction. The text says that he becomes a *muni*, a silent meditator, whereas with regard to learning and the state of a child, it expressly enjoins one should remain endowed with them. Besides, learning includes silent meditation. The *sūtra* refutes this view and states that silent meditation is enjoined as a third requisite besides learning and the state of a child. Silent meditation is not merely learning but continuous devotion to knowledge, *jñānātiśaya-rūpam.* It has therefore the value of an injunction.

Baladeva begins a new section here and continues the topic of *nirapekṣa* devotees. These already possess sacrifice, calmness and control and so in their case meditation is enjoined.

III. 4. 48. *kṛtsna-bhāvāt tu gṛhiṇopasaṁhāraḥ*

On account (of the householder's life) being all, however, there is the conclusion (with the enumeration of the duties) of the householder.
krtsna-bhāvāt: on account (of the householder's life) including all; *tu:* however; *gṛhiṇaḥ:* with the householder; *upasaṁhāraḥ:* the conclusion.

In C.U. VIII. 15. 1 after enumerating the duties of the *brahmacārin* those of the householder are mentioned but there is no mention of *samnyāsa*. This, the *sūtra* says, is only to lay stress on the householder's life and its importance. The householder's life includes more or less the duties of all *āśramas.*

R. says that B.U. III. 5. 1 mentions duties of all *āśramas.*

III. 4. 49. *maunavad itareṣām apy upadeśāt*

On account of there being injunction of the others also, in the same way as of the state of a silent meditator.
maunavat: even as the state of a *muni* (*samnyāsin*)*; itareṣām:* of the others; *api:* even; *upadeśāt:* on account of instruction (injunction).

Even as the Scriptures enjoin the states of *samnyāsa* and the householder's life, they enjoin all the four stages of life either in sequence or alternatively.

Śrīkaṇṭha begins a new section of two *sūtras* here dealing with the topic whether those who practise the vow of *Pāśupata* and do not belong to any particular stage of life are entitled to salvation and answers that they are entitled to salvation. For the *Pāśupata* vow includes calmness, self-control and the rest.

Section 15 (50)

THE CHILDLIKE STATE IS INNOCENCE, FREE FROM ANGER, PASSION, ETC.

III. 4. 50. *anāviṣkurvann anvayāt*

(The childlike state means) not manifesting himself on account of the context.
anāviṣkurvan: not manifesting himself; *anvayāt:* on account of the context.

What is the childlike state? Is it a state of ignorance of right and wrong or of doing what one likes or is it one of freedom from guile and the sense of egoism. It is the latter for the former is detrimental to knowledge. Only such a meaning is appropriate in the context. The state of a child is not wilful behaviour but freedom from pride and arrogance.

Section 16 (51)

KNOWLEDGE CAN ARISE IN THIS LIFE

III. 4. 51. *aihikam apy aprastuta-pratibandhe tad-darśanāt*

In this life also (the fruition of knowledge may take place) if no obstruction is present; on account of this being seen in the Scripture.

aihikam: in this life; *api:* also; *aprastuta-pratibandhe:* if there is no obstruction present; *tat-darśanāt* of this being seen in Scripture.

Knowledge arises in this life when its rise is not obstructed by some other works whose results are reaching maturity. When there is such an obstruction, then knowledge arises in the next life. See *Kaṭha U.* I. 2. 7; B.G. VI. 43; VI. 45.

Bhāskara reads *aihikam aprasutaṁ pratibandhena darśanāt*: (There is the rise of knowledge) in this life (if the works which obstruct it have) not sprung up, through (the presence of such an) obstruction (however there is the rise of knowledge in the next world) because (that) is seen.

R. says that *vidyā* whose result is mere exaltation, *abhyudaya*, takes place in the present life, if there is not present an obstruction in the form of a serious *karma*, *prabala-karmāntara*, in which case knowledge arises later. *Aihikam* refers to worldly prosperity only as distinct from that which aims at final release.

Śrīkaṇṭha speaks of the time of the rise of salvation and not of knowledge. He reads: '[The result of meditation, viz. salvation, arises] in this life [i.e. as soon as the present body ceases] if obstruction be not present, on account of that being seen.' If there be no contrary works, then a knower attains release as soon as he dies. If there be such works he has to be reborn and exhaust them before he can attain release. So even knowers like Vāmadeva are seen to have rebirths.

Baladeva follows R.'s interpretation.

Section 17 (52)

LIBERATION IS OF ONE KIND IN ALL CASES

III. 4. 52. *evam mukti-phalāniyamas tad-avasthāvadhṛteḥ tad-avasthāvadhṛteḥ*

(There is) no rule like this, with respect to liberation, the fruit (of knowledge) on account of the assertions as to that condition, on account of the assertions as to that condition.

evam: like this; *mukti-phala-aniyamaḥ:* no rule with respect to liberation, the fruit; *tat-avasthā-avadhṛteḥ:* on account of the assertions about that condition.

In the previous *sūtra*, it is said that knowledge may result in this life or the next according to the absence or presence of obstructions and the intensity of the means adopted. The question is raised whether there is any rule with regard to liberation which is the fruit of knowledge, whether it can be delayed after knowledge arises. The *sūtra* states that no such rule exists. The nature of final release is the same and there can be no variations of it. See B.U. II. 4. 6, III. 8. 8, III. 9. 26, IV. 4. 25, IV. 5. 15; C.U. VII. 24. 1; M.U. II. 2. 11. Differences are possible with regard to the worship of *Saguṇa Brahman* but not with regard to the knowledge of *Nirguṇa-Brahman.* There cannot be any delay with regard to the attainment of liberation after knowledge has arisen for the knowledge of *Brahman* is liberation.

The repetition is to indicate that the chapter ends here.

Bhāskara means by this *sūtra* that though there is no fixed rule as to whether salvation is to arise in this life or in after-life yet there is no non-fixity in the nature of salvation for salvation is nothing but the nature of the Highest Lord.

Śrīkaṇṭha holds that salvation means attaining similarity with the Lord. As the Lord is the same, salvation is the same though there may be gradations in the meditations.

Section 1 (1–2)

MEDITATION ON THE SELF IS TO BE REPEATED TILL KNOWLEDGE IS ATTAINED

IV. 1. 1. *āvṛttir asakṛd upadeśāt*

Repetition (*of hearing, reflection and meditation on the Self is necessary*) *on account of the instruction* (*which is given*) *more than once.*
āvṛttiḥ: repetition (is required); *asakṛt:* more than once; *upadeśāt:* on account of instruction (by the Scriptures).

B.U. II. 4. 5, IV. 4. 21; C.U. VIII. 7. 1 require us to realise the Self through hearing, reflection and meditation. The question is whether this is to be done only once or repeatedly. The answer is given that it is to be repeated till the knowledge of *Brahman* arises. Where the text requires repeated instruction, repeated performance of the mental acts is directly intimated.

IV. 1. 2. *liṅgāc ca*

And on account of the indicatory mark.
liṅgāt: on account of the indicatory mark; *ca:* and.

Repetition is necessary for if it were not so, Scriptures would not teach the doctrine 'That thou art' repeatedly. With advanced souls a single hearing of the statement may produce knowledge but such souls are very rare. For ordinary people who are attached to the world, repeated meditation is necessary before the last traces of ignorance are removed.

R. means by 'inferential mark' *smṛti*. *Smṛti* also declares that the knowledge which effects release is of the nature of continued repetition. Meditation therefore has to be repeated.

Nimbārka follows R. and quotes B.G. XII. 9.

Section 2 (3)

THE MEDITATOR SHOULD VIEW *BRAHMAN* AS CONSTITUTING HIS OWN SELF

IV. 1. 3. *ātmeti tūpagacchanti grāhayanti ca*

But as the Self (*scriptural texts*) *acknowledge and also make us comprehend* (*the Supreme*).
ātmeti: as the Self; *tu:* but; *upagacchanti:* acknowledge; *grāhayanti:* make us comprehend; *ca:* also.

The Lord is to be contemplated as the Self in the form 'I am *Brahman*', not as another being. See B.U. I. 4. 10; Mā.U. 2. The

Jābālas hold 'Thou indeed I am, O holy divinity, and I indeed thou art, O holy divinity'.
tvaṁ vā aham asmi bhagavo devate, ahaṁ vai tvam asi bhagavo devate.

R. declares that God is to be contemplated as the Self that controls the individual, which is as the body of God.

Śrīnivāsa says that since the Highest Self is the whole of which the individual soul is a part and since the former is the very soul of the latter, which can have no existence or activity independently of him even as the thousand-rayed sun, having independence, existence and activity in contrast to its own rays is their soul and the rays are non-different from it, so the Lord should be known to be non-different from the individual soul.

Śrīkaṇṭha who generally adopts the *śarīra-śarīri-bhāva,* the relation of God to the soul on the analogy of the soul to the body, here gives it up and supports the view that the Lord is to be meditated on as identical with the Self. This is one of the grounds on which Appaya Dīkṣita maintains that Śrīkaṇṭha was at heart a non-dualist.

Section 3 (4)

WHERE SYMBOLS ARE USED FOR CONTEMPLATION, THE MEDITATOR IS NOT TO CONSIDER THE SYMBOLS AS IDENTICAL WITH HIS SELF

IV. 1. 4. *na pratīke na hi saḥ*

(*The meditator is*) *not* (*to see the Self*) *in the symbol, because he is not* (*that*).

na: not; *pratīke:* in the symbol; *na:* is not; *hi:* because; *saḥ:* he.

In a passage like C.U. III. 18. 1, 'Let one meditate on mind as *Brahman*', the mind is not to be identified with the Self. If the mind is cognised as identical with *Brahman,* then it ceases to be a symbol, even as a gold ornament loses its individual character when it is identified with gold. Again, if the meditator is conscious of his identity with *Brahman,* then he ceases to be the individual soul, the meditator. The act of meditation is possible only where distinctions exist and unity has not been reached.

Section 4 (5)

THE SYMBOL IS TO BE VIEWED AS ONE WITH *BRAHMAN* AND NOT *BRAHMAN* AS ONE WITH THE SYMBOL

IV. 1. 5. *brahma-dṛṣṭir utkarṣāt*

(*The symbol is*) *to be viewed as Brahman* (*and not in the opposite way*) *on account of exaltation* (*bestowed on symbols*).

brahma-dṛṣṭiḥ: viewing as *Brahman; utkarṣāt:* on account of the exaltation.

The symbols are to be regarded as *Brahman* and not vice versa. We can make progress only by looking upon an inferior object as symbolic of the superior and not vice versa. Since our objective is to get rid of the idea of diversity and see *Brahman* in everything, we have to meditate on the symbols as *Brahman.*

R. does not take this as a separate section. It only states, for him, a reason for the conclusion reached in the previous *sūtra.*

Baladeva takes this *sūtra* as a separate section dealing with a different topic. Even as the Lord is to be meditated on as the self of the devotee, he is to be meditated on as *Brahman* also, i.e. as possessed of great attributes and powers. Such a meditation is the highest of all.

Section 5 (6)

IN MEDITATIONS ON MEMBERS OF SACRIFICIAL ACTS THE IDEA OF THE DIVINITY IS TO BE IMPOSED ON THE MEMBERS AND NOT VICE VERSA

IV. 1. 6. *ādityādimatayaś cāṅga upapatteḥ*

And the ideas of the sun and so on (are to be imposed) on the subordinate members (of sacrificial acts) because (only in that way would the statement of the Scriptures) be consistent.

ādityādi-matayaḥ: the ideas of the sun and so on; *ca:* and; *aṅge:* in a subordinate member (of the sacrificial act); *upapatteḥ:* because of consistency.

Ś. reads: *aṅgeṣu'* instead of *aṅge.*

In C.U. I. 3. 1 where 'one should meditate on that which shines yonder as the *udgītha*' and II. 2. 1 where 'one should meditate on the *sāman* as fivefold' the members of the sacrificial acts are to be viewed as the sun and so on. By so doing the fruit of the act is enhanced. This is to be done if the statements of the Scriptures that the meditations enhance the fruits of the sacrifice are to be fulfilled.

R. says that only through the propitiation of gods are sacrifices capable of bringing about their results. The *udgītha* and so on are to be viewed under the aspect of the sun and so on.

Baladeva takes this *sūtra* as a separate section dealing with a different topic. 'The ideas of the sun and the rest [as generating from the eyes of the Lord and so on should be imposed] on the limb [of the Lord], on account of appropriateness.'

Section 6 (7–10)

ONE IS TO MEDITATE SEATED

IV. 1. 7. *āsīnaḥ sambhavāt*

Seated (a man is to meditate) on account of the possibility.
āsīnaḥ: seated; *sambhavāt:* on account of possibility.

One is to meditate seated. It is not possible to meditate standing or lying down. In *upāsanā* one has to concentrate one's mind on a single object. This is not possible when one is standing or lying down.

R. says that the needful concentration of mind can be reached in a sitting posture. Standing and walking demand effort. Lying down may induce sleep. The proper posture is sitting on some support so that no effort may be required for holding the body erect.

IV. 1. 8. *dhyānāc ca*

And on account of meditation.
dhyānāt: on account of meditation; *ca:* and.

Ś. says that *upāsanā* and *dhyāna* mean the same thing, concentrating on a single object, with a fixed look and without any movement of the limbs. This is possible only in a sitting posture.

R. says that meditation means thought directed on one object and not disturbed by ideas of other things, *dhyānaṁ hi vijātīya-pratyayāntarāvyavahitam eka-cintanam ity uktam.*

Śrīkaṇṭha defines release as the attainment of supreme self-hood which is free from the state of the bound creature, characterised by love of bodily conditions such as that of *Brāhmaṇa*, etc., which is full of essential unsurpassable bliss, and is of the form of *Śiva*, the self-luminous witness.

nivṛtta-brāhmaṇādi-dehābhimānamaya-paśubhāvasya niratiśaya-svarūpānandamaya-sākṣi-svaprakāśa-śiva-rūpa-parāhaṁbhāvāpattir muktir iti sarva-śruti-tātparyāt.

IV. 1. 9. *acalatvaṁ cāpekṣya*

And with reference to immobility.
acalatvam: immobility; *ca:* and; *apekṣya:* referring to.

Meditation is ascribed to earth in some passages (C.U. VII. 6. 1) on account of its immobility or steadiness. Steadiness is a concomitant of meditation and this is possible only while sitting and not while standing or walking.

IV. 1. 10. *smaranti ca*

The smṛti texts also say (the same).
smaranti: the *smṛti* texts say; *ca:* also.

The reference is to the B.G. VI. 11–12 where the sitting posture is prescribed for meditation and also to the *Yoga Sūtra* on the *āsanas.*

Section 7 (11)

MEDITATION MAY BE CARRIED ON AT ANY TIME, AT ANY PLACE FAVOURABLE TO CONCENTRATION OF MIND

IV. 1. 11. *yatraikāgratā tatrāviśeṣāt*

Where concentration of mind (is possible) there (meditation may be carried on) on account of there being no difference.

yatra: where; *ekāgratā:* concentration of mind; *tatra:* there; *aviśeṣāt:* on account of there being no difference.

One can meditate at any time, in any place and in any direction where he can with ease concentrate his mind. It is true that certain directions are given as in Ś.U. II. 10. These are only suggestions and are not fixed rules.

Section 8 (12)

MEDITATIONS ARE TO BE CONTINUED UNTIL DEATH

IV. 1. 12. *āprāyaṇāt tatrāpi hi dṛṣṭam*

Till death (meditations have to be continued) because (their continuance) even at that moment is seen (in Scripture).

āprāyaṇāt: till death; *tatra:* then; *api:* even; *hi:* because; *dṛṣṭam:* is seen (from the Scriptures).

The meditations are to be continued till death for the *śruti* and the *smṛti* say so. *Śatapatha Brāhmaṇa* (X. 6. 3. 1) says: 'With whatever thought he passes away from this world, *sa yāvat kratuḥ ayam asmāl lokāt praiti.*' See also B.G. VIII. 6. 'Whatever idea you have in mind when you quit the body at death, that idea you will realise.'[1] S. maintains that the meditations which lead to intuition of *Brahman* are not subject to this rule.

R. quotes C.U. VIII. 15. 1: *sa khalv evaṁ vartayan yāvad āyuṣam brahma-lokam abhi-sampadyate.* He who behaves thus throughout his life reaches the *Brahma*-world.

Śrīkaṇṭha explains the word *'rudra'* as one who drives away the sorrows of bondage, *saṁsāra-rugdrāvakaḥ.*

Baladeva interprets *tatrāpi* to mean 'even after death'. The devotee not only practises meditation so long as he lives but even after death, i.e. even when he is freed. He worships the Lord even though he is not required to do so.

[1] *yay yaṁ vāpi smaran bhāvaṁ tyajaty ante kalevaram taṁ tam eva samāpnoti. Nārada U.*

Section 9 (13)

WHEN THE KNOWLEDGE OF *BRAHMAN* IS ATTAINED, THE KNOWER IS NO LONGER AFFECTED BY THE CONSEQUENCES OF HIS PAST OR FUTURE SINFUL DEEDS

IV. 1. 13. *tad-adhigama uttara-pūrvāghayor aśleṣa-vināśau tad-vyapadeśāt*

On the attainment of this (Brahman) (there occur) the non-clinging and the destruction of the later and the earlier sinful deeds, because it is (so) declared (in the Scriptures).

tat-adhigame: on the attainment of this; *uttara-pūrva-aghayoḥ:* of the later and the earlier sinful deeds; *aśleṣa-vināśau:* non-clinging and destruction; *tad-vyapadeśāt:* because it is (so) declared (in the Scriptures).

The question here relates to the state of *jīvan-mukti* or liberation in life. If it is said that one must experience the results of one's deeds committed before the attainment of liberation, the *sūtra* observes that when a person attains knowledge, all his earlier sins are destroyed and later ones do not cling to him. When he attains knowledge, the sense of agency is lost and the effects of deeds do not affect him. See C.U. IV. 14. 3; V. 24. 3, M.U. II. 2. 8. The law of *karma* does not apply to the knowers of *Brahman*. When we attain liberation, the chain of work is broken. We become superior to time.

Section 10 (14)

GOOD DEEDS LIKEWISE DO NOT AFFECT THE KNOWER OF *BRAHMAN*

IV. 1. 14. *itarasyāpy evam asaṁśleṣaḥ pāte tu*

Of the other (i.e. good works) also there is in the same way non-clinging but on the fall (of the body, i.e. death).

itarasya: of the other; *api:* also; *evam:* in the same way; *asaṁśleṣaḥ:* non-clinging; *pāte:* on the fall (at death); *tu:* but.

The knower of *Brahman*, since he is devoid of the sense of agency, goes beyond good and evil: B.U. IV. 4. 22. Since he is not affected by good or evil after illumination and his past sins are destroyed by knowledge, his liberation takes place at death.

R. says that good works which produce results favourable to knowledge and meditation perish only on the death of the body and not during the lifetime of the meditator.

Śrīkaṇṭha follows R.'s interpretation.

Section 11 (15)

THIS CHARACTERISTIC APPLIES ONLY TO WORKS WHICH HAVE NOT BEGUN TO PRODUCE THEIR EFFECTS

IV. 1. 15. *anārabdhakārye eva tu pūrve tad-avadheḥ*

But only those former (works) whose effects have not yet begun (are destroyed by knowledge); because (Scripture states that) death is the limit. *anārabdha-kārye:* works which have not begun to yield results; *eva:* only; *tu:* but; *pūrve:* former works; *tad-avadheḥ:* that (death) being the limit.

When we say that the past works of a knower of *Brahman* are destroyed, we have to make a distinction between two kinds of past works, *sañcita* or accumulated works which have not yet begun to bear fruit and *prārabdha* or those works which have begun to yield results and have produced the body through which a person has attained knowledge. The *sūtra* says that *prārabdha* works have to be worked out. *prārabdha-karmāṇi bhogād eva kṣayah.* So long as the momentum of the works lasts, the knower of *Brahman* has to be in the body. When they are exhausted, the body falls off and the knower attains perfection. His knowledge cannot check these works even as a potter's wheel comes to rest only when its momentum is exhausted. See C.U. VI. 14. 2. If it were not so, then there would be no teachers of knowledge. The knowledge of Self being essentially non-active destroys all works by means of refuting wrong knowledge but wrong knowledge comparable to the appearance of a double moon lasts for some time even after it has been refuted, owing to the impression it has made. Moreover, it is not a matter for dispute at all whether the body of him who knows *Brahman* continues to exist for some time or not. For how can one man contest the fact of another possessing the knowledge of *Brahman*, vouched for by his heart's conviction—and at the same time continuing to enjoy bodily existence. *kathaṁ hy ekasya svahṛdaya-pratyayam brahma-vedanam deha-dhāraṇam cāpareṇa pratikṣeptum śakyate.* Ś.

Knowledge of reality is self-attested. Besides, along with the possession of the knowledge of the Absolute *Brahman*, embodiment, *deha-dhāraṇam*, is possible. It is clear that even according to Ś., knowledge of *Brahman* can coexist with embodied life and participation in the work of the world.[1]

R. says that there is no proof for the existence of an impetus accounting for the continuance of the body's life, other than the Lord's pleasure or displeasure caused by good or evil deeds: *na ca puṇyāpuṇya-karma-janya-bhagavad-prīty-aprīti-vyatirekeṇa śarīra-sthiti-hetu-bhūta-saṁskāra-sadbhāve pramāṇam asti.* R.

[1] *asya jīvan-muktasya deha-dhāraṇaṁ lokasyopakārārtham.* Ś.
The embodiedness of the liberated soul is for the service of the world.

Section 12 (16–17)

OBLIGATORY WORKS ARE EXCEPTED SINCE THEY PROMOTE THE ORIGINATION OF KNOWLEDGE

IV. 1. 16. *agnihotrādi tu tat-kāryāyaiva tad-darśanāt*

But (the results of daily) agnihotra, etc., (are not destroyed by knowledge as they) contribute to the same result (as knowledge) because that is seen (from the Scriptures).
agnihotrādi (daily) *agnihotra*, etc.; *tu:* but; *tat-kāryāya:* contribute to the same result (as knowledge, i.e. liberation); *eva:* only; *tat-darśanāt:* because that is seen (from the Scriptures).

Works are of two kinds, those which yield specific results and those which help to produce knowledge. Obligatory regular works performed before the rise of knowledge are of the latter kind. Since knowledge leads to liberation, the regular works may be said to contribute indirectly to that. So their results persist till death.

While for Ś. works are indirect means to liberation, i.e. produce knowledge which leads to liberation, Bhāskara holds that they are a direct means.

IV. 1. 17. *ato'nyāpi hy ekeṣām ubhayoḥ*

According to some, (there is) also (a class of good works) other than this. (There is agreement) of both (teachers) (as to the result of these works).
ataḥ: from this; *anyā:* different (or other); *api:* also; *hi:* indeed; *ekeṣām:* of some; *ubhayoḥ:* of both.

Besides the obligatory works like the daily *agnihotra* and the like, there are other good works which are performed with a view to certain results. Of these latter works, it is said that 'his friends enter on his good works', *suhṛdas sādhu-kṛtyām upayanti*. Others profit by one's good deeds. Both Jaimini and Bādarāyaṇa are agreed that works undertaken for the fulfilment of some special wish do not contribute to the origination of true knowledge.

R. means by both works of both kinds, either prior or subsequent to the rise of knowledge.

Baladeva begins a new section here of 3 *sūtras* dealing with the case of some *nirapekṣa* devotees. They become free at once without having to wait for the exhaustion of their *prārabdha-karmas*.

Section 13 (18)

SACRIFICIAL WORKS NOT COMBINED WITH KNOWLEDGE OR MEDITATION ALSO HELP IN THE PRODUCTION OF KNOWLEDGE

IV. 1. 18. *yad eva vidyayeti hi*

For (*the statement*) *whatever he does with knowledge* (*indicates this*).
yat eva: whatever; *vidyayā:* with knowledge; *iti:* thus; *hi:* for.

The reference is to C.U. I. 1. 10. What one performs with knowledge, that indeed becomes more powerful, *vīryavattaram.* Works done without knowledge are not useless though works done with knowledge are more powerful.

Ś. holds that all obligatory works performed before the rise of true knowledge, whether with or without knowledge, either in the present state of existence or a former one, by a person desirous of release with a view to release, all such works act according to their several capacities, as means of the extinction of evil desert which obstructs the attainment of *Brahman* and thus become causes of such attainment, subserving the more immediate causes such as the hearing of and reflecting on the sacred texts, faith, meditation, devotion, etc.

Bhāskara omits this *sūtra.*

Śrīnivāsa argues that works of greater strength first begin to produce their own fruits. When this happens, other good or bad deeds of lesser strength performed with a view to attaining certain ends remain without producing their results even as a weak cow is kept off from water, grass and so on by a stronger one. When the knower becomes free immediately after the decay of those works the effects of which have already begun, those works go to his friends and foes respectively.

Baladeva says that even the *prārabdha-karmas* may be destroyed at once through the grace of *vidyā.*

Section 14 (19)

ON THE EXHAUSTION OF WORKS WHICH HAVE BEGUN TO TAKE EFFECT, THE KNOWER OF *BRAHMAN* ATTAINS ONENESS WITH *BRAHMAN*

IV. 1. 19. *bhogena tv itare-kṣapayitvā sampadyate*

But having exhausted by enjoyment the two other (*sets of work*), *he becomes one with Brahman.*
bhogena: by enjoyment; *tu:* but; *itare:* of the other two works;

kṣapayitvā: having exhausted; *sampadyate:* becomes one (with *Brahman*).

When the works good and bad which have begun to bear fruit are exhausted through enjoyment one attains oneness with *Brahman.* See C.U. VI. 14. 2; B.U. IV. 4. 6. Till then, however, the knower of *Brahman* has to be in the relative world as a *jīvan-mukta,* one liberated in life.

When the works whose effects have begun are destroyed, he who knows necessarily enters into the state of perfect isolation, *kaivalyam.*

Śrīnivāsa says that there is salvation, when on the decay of the works—the effects of which have already begun by enjoyment—there is the fall of the body at the completion of enjoyment.

While for Ś. the fruition is restricted to the present existence, since the complete knowledge attained by him destroys the ignorance, *avidyā,* which otherwise would lead to further embodiments, for R. a number of embodied existences may have to be gone through before the effects of the works which have begun to bear fruit are exhausted.

Section 1 (1–2)

AT THE TIME OF DEATH THE FUNCTIONS OF THE ORGANS MERGE IN MIND

IV. 2. 1. *vāṅ manasi-darśanāc chabdāc ca*

Speech (is merged) in mind on account of observation and the scriptural statement.

vāk: speech: *manasi:* in mind; *darśanāt:* on account of observation; *śabdāt:* on account of scriptural statement; *ca:* and.

In the previous section it is shown that by destruction of actions which have not as yet begun to yield results a knower of *Brahman* attains liberation in life, *jīvan-mukti*, and on the exhaustion of *prārabdha-karma*, works which have begun to yield results, he attains *videha-mukti* at death, when he becomes one with *Brahman*. For Ś. the knower of the *Saguṇa Brahman* travels after death by the path of the gods. The steps by which the soul passes out of the body at death are set forth in many texts. C.U. VI. 8. 6 says that speech gets merged in mind and mind in *prāṇa* or life and so on. The question is raised whether it is the organ or the function that is merged and the answer is that it is the function. As mind is not the material cause of the organ, the organs cannot get merged in mind. The function and the organ to which it belongs are treated as one. We notice that a dying man first loses his function of speech though his mind is still functioning.

When a person departs from this life, speech is said to get merged in mind and so on. This merger is not of forms but only of function. Hence that in which the merger takes place need not be the material cause of what is merged. This is the doctrine of *laya* or mergence. This is Ś.'s view, which is followed by Śrīkaṇṭha.

R. understands *laya* to mean not mergence but a 'going forth', a combination or connection. Speech goes with mind and so on.

While Ś. distinguishes between the knower who has the highest knowledge and the knower of the qualified *Brahman*, for R. the knower is of one type only. For R. the combination *saṁpatti* of the sense-organs with *manas* is a *samyoga* or connection and not *laya* or merging.

Nimbārka holds that the organ of speech is connected with mind. With R., Nimbārka holds that the description of the path belongs to all knowers.

Baladeva is of the view that both the organ of speech and its function are connected with the mind.

IV. 2. 2. *ata eva ca sarvāṇy anu*

And for the same reason all (*sense-organs follow*) *after.*
ataḥ eva: for the same reason; *ca:* and; *sarvāṇi:* all (organs); *anu:* after.

All other sense-organs follow, i.e. get merged in mind. See *Praśna U.* III. 9. The functions of all the organs get merged in mind.

Nimbārka and Śrīnivāsa hold that all sense-organs are united with and not merged in mind.

Section 2 (3)

MIND GETS MERGED IN *PRĀṆA* OR LIFE

IV. 2. 3. *tan manaḥ prāṇa uttarāt*

That mind (*is merged*) *in life owing to the subsequent clause.*
tat: that; *manaḥ:* mind; *prāṇe:* in life; *uttarāt:* from the subsequent clause (of the text previously cited).

Here also it is the function that gets merged for we find that mind ceases to function in a dying man, even while his vital force or *prāṇa* is functioning. The organ itself is not merged in life for life does not constitute its causal substance.

R. and Nimbārka hold that mind is united with the vital breath. Śrīkaṇṭha follows Ś. and holds that the function of the mind merges in life.

Section 3 (4–6)

THE FUNCTION OF LIFE GETS MERGED IN THE INDIVIDUAL SOUL

IV. 2. 4. *so'dhyakṣe tad-upagamādibhyaḥ*

That in the ruler on account of (*statements indicating*) *approach and so on.*
saḥ: that; *adhyakṣe:* in the ruler (*jīva,* the individual soul); *tat-upagamādibhyaḥ:* on account of (statements indicating) approach to that and so on.

The texts here considered are B.U. IV. 3. 38, IV. 4. 2; *Praśna U.* VI. 3.

Life into which the different organs are merged has its abode in the individual soul.

R. and Nimbārka hold that the life-principle is connected with the individual soul.

Śrīkaṇṭha reads *adhyakṣeṇa* for *adhyakṣe.*

IV. 2. 5. *bhūteṣu tac-chruteḥ*

In the elements (the soul with the life-principle is merged) as is seen in the Scriptures.

bhūteṣu: in the elements; *tat-śruteḥ:* from the *śruti* texts to that effect.

The soul with the life-principle takes its abode in the fine essence of the gross elements, fire, etc., which constitute the seed of the future body.

The life-principle is said to be united with fire in C.U. VI. 8. 6 but it means the elements together with fire, on account of scriptural declarations to that effect. See B.U. IV. 4. 5.

IV. 2. 6. *naikasmin darśayato hi*

Not in one (element only) (the soul goes) for both (śruti and smṛti) declare this.

na: not; *ekasmin:* in one; *darśayataḥ:* (both) declare so; *hi:* for.

At the time of death, when the soul leaves our body and goes in for another, it, together with the subtle body, resides in the subtle essence of all the gross elements and not in that of fire only for all the elements are required for a future body. See C.U. V. 3. 3; B.U. IV. 4. 5; *Manu* 1. 27.

R. says that fire denotes fire mixed with the other elements. Life-principle and the soul are therefore united with the aggregate of the elements.

Nimbārka quotes *Viṣṇu Purāṇa* (I. 2. 48): 'These [elements] possessed of various powers but separate were unable to produce beings without aggregation, i.e. without coming together entirely.'

Section 4 (7)

THE MODE OF DEPARTURE FROM THE BODY UP TO THE ENTRANCE OF THE SOUL INTO THE *NĀḌIS* IS COMMON TO BOTH THE KNOWER OF *SAGUṆA BRAHMAN* AND THE ORDINARY MAN

IV. 2. 7. *samānā cāsṛty upakramād amṛtatvaṁ cānupoṣya*

And common (is the mode of departure for both the knower of Saguna Brahman and the ignorant) up to the beginning of the way and the immortality (of him who knows) (is relative only), not having burnt (ignorance).

samānā: common; *ca:* and; *ā sṛti upakramāt:* up to the beginning of the way; *amṛtatvam:* immortality; *ca:* and; *anupoṣya:* not having burnt (ignorance).

According to Ś., for the knower of the *Nirguṇa Brahman*, there is no departure at all. The question arises whether the path to *brahma-loka* to which the knower of *Saguṇa Brahman* goes and the world in which the ignorant is reborn are identical or different. The *sūtra* says that both go by the same way till the knower enters the *suṣumnā nāḍī* and the ignorant some other nerve. After that one goes to the path of the gods and the other to have rebirth. Till they enter on their respective ways the mode of departure is the same.

R. quotes B.U. IV. 4. 7 and explains that the immortality which is ascribed to the knower as soon as he shakes off all desires can only mean the destruction of the effects of good and evil works and the reaching of *Brahman* means the intuition of *Brahman* vouchsafed to the meditating devotee. C.U. VIII. 6. 5 speaks of a hundred veins. As the soul of the knower is said to pass out by way of a particular vein, up to the soul's entering the vein, there is no difference between the knower and the non-knower.

Section 5 (8–11)

THE MERGING OF FIRE, ETC., IN THE SUPREME IS NOT ABSOLUTE MERGING

IV. 2. 8. *tad āpīteḥ saṁsāra-vyapadeśāt*

That (subtle body continues) up to the attainment (of Brahman) on account of the declarations of the empirical state (made by Scripture).
tat: that; *ā apīteḥ:* up to the attainment (of *Brahman*); *saṁsāra-vyapadeśāt:* on account of the declarations of the empirical state.

The mergence cannot be absolute for then all would attain liberation. It is the kind of mergence that we experience in deep sleep. Only the functions of the elements are merged and not the elements themselves. The final dissolution does not take place until knowledge is attained. Till then the Scriptures declare that the individual soul is subject to empirical existence, *saṁsāra*: *Kaṭha U.* II. 5. 7. If the merging of death were absolute, then there could be no rebirth. So the elements continue to exist in a seminal condition.

Bhāskara follows Ś.'s interpretation.

R. does not take this as the beginning of a new section. He refers to the immortality spoken of in the previous *sūtra* and holds that it does not imply the separation of the soul from the body for Scripture declares *saṁsāra* as embodiedness up to the reaching of *Brahman*. *tasya tāvad eva ciraṁ yāvan na vimokṣye atha sampatsye.*

IV. 2. 9. *sūkṣmaṁ pramāṇataś ca tathopalabdheḥ*

And that is subtle in size because it is so experienced.
sūkṣmam: subtle; *pramāṇataḥ:* as regards size; *ca:* and; *tathā:* so; *upalabdheḥ:* because it is experienced.

The body in which the soul abides at the time of death is subtle in nature and size. This is understood from the scriptural statements which declare that it goes out along the *nāḍīs*. It is therefore subtle in size. Its transparency explains why it is not obstructed by gross bodies or is not seen when it passes out at death.

R. says that the bondage of the knower is not dissolved for the reason that the subtle body continues to persist. We know this from Scripture, K.U. I. 3ff.

IV. 2. 10. *nopamardenātaḥ*

Therefore (this subtle body) is not (destroyed) by the destruction (of the gross body).

na: not; *upamardena:* by the destruction; *ataḥ:* therefore.

The subtle body is not destroyed by what destroys the gross body, burning, etc.

R. says that immortality is not effected by means of the total destruction of the body.

IV. 2. 11. *asyaiva copapatter eṣa ūṣmā*

And to this (subtle body) alone does this (bodily) warmth belong, because this (only) is possible.

asya: to this; *eva:* alone; *ca:* and; *upapatteḥ:* because of possibility; *eṣaḥ:* this; *ūṣmā:* (bodily) warmth.

The bodily warmth observed in living animals belongs to this subtle body and not to the gross body for the warmth is felt so long as there is life and not after that.

Section 6 (12–14)

THE LIFE-PRINCIPLES OF A KNOWER OF *NIRGUṆA BRAHMAN* DO NOT DEPART FROM THE BODY AT DEATH

IV. 2. 12. *pratiṣedhāt iti cen na śarīrāt*

If it be said that on account of the denial (made by the Scripture) (the life-principles of a knower of Brahman do not depart) (we say that it is) not so, (because Scripture says that the life-principles do not depart) from the embodied soul.

pratiṣedhāt: on account of denial; *iti cet:* if it be said; *na:* not so; *śarīrāt:* from the embodied soul.

B.U. IV. 4. 6 says: 'His *prāṇas* do not depart. Being *Brahman*, he goes to *Brahman*.' From this express denial it follows that the *prāṇas* do not pass out of the body of him who knows *Brahman*. The opponent denies this and argues that the passage does not deny the passage of the *prāṇas* from the body but only from the embodied soul. For if they do not depart from the body there will be no death at all. This is clear from the *Mādhyandina* rescension, where the ablative, 'from him', *tasmāt,* is used.

IV. 2. 13. *spaṣṭo hy ekeṣām*

For (the denial of the departure) is clear (in the texts) of some (schools).
spaṣṭaḥ: clear; *hi:* for; *ekeṣām:* of some (schools).

This *sūtra* refutes the view of the previous *sūtra* by connecting the denial to the body and not the soul. That the *prāṇas* do not depart from the body is clear from B.U. III. 2. 11. The *Mādhyandina* reading 'from him' refers to the body. It is not true that if the *prāṇas* do not depart there will be no death for they do not remain in the body but get merged, which makes life impossible and we say that the person is dead. Again, if the *prāṇas* departed with the soul from the body, then the rebirth of the soul would be inevitable and there would be no liberation. So the *prāṇas* do not depart from the body in the case of the knower of *Brahman.*

R. takes this and the previous *sūtra* as one. The question relates to the departure of the knower, *vidvān tasya,* in B.U. IV. 4. 5, from the body, *śārīrāt,* so that the passage means from the *jīva* or the individual soul the *prāṇas* do not depart. Again, with reference to the instruction given to Ārtabhāga by Yājñavalkya (B.U. III. 2. 10–11) there is nothing to show that *ayam puruṣa* is the sage who knows *Brahman.*

IV. 2. 14. *smaryate ca*

And the smṛti (also) says (so).
smaryate: the *smṛti* says (so); *ca:* and.

M.B. XII. 270. 22 says that he who has become the self of all beings and has a complete intuition of all, at his way the gods themselves are perplexed, seeking for the path of him who has no path.

sarvabhūtātma-bhūtasya samyag-bhūtāni paśyataḥ
devāpi mārge muhyanti hy apadasya padaiṣiṇaḥ.

It follows that he who knows *Brahman* neither moves nor departs.

R. says that there are *smṛti* passages which declare that the sage also when dying departs from the body. The soul of him who knows departs by means of an artery from the head. R. quotes *Yājñavalkya Smṛti* (III. 167): 'Of those, one is situated above which pierces the disc of the sun and passes beyond the world of *Brahmā*; by way of that the soul reaches the highest goal.'

ūrdhvam ekaḥ sthitas teṣāṁ yo bhitvā sūrya-maṇḍalam
brahma-lokam atikramya tena yāti paraṁ gatim.

According to Nimbārka both knowers and non-knowers go out; only they travel by different paths.

Section 7 (15)

THE ORGANS OF THE KNOWER OF *NIRGUṆA BRAHMAN* ARE MERGED IN IT AT DEATH

IV. 2. 15. *tāni pare tathā hy āha*

Those (*elements, etc.*) (*are merged*) *in the Highest Brahman for thus* (*the Scripture*) *says.*
tāni: those; *pare:* in the Supreme *Brahman*; *tathā:* so; *hi:* for; *āha:* (the Scripture) says.

The question is in regard to the knower of *Brahman* who dies. What happens to the sense-organs and the subtle body in which they abide? These get merged in the Supreme *Brahman.* See *Praśna U.* VI. 5. 1. M.U. III. 2. 7, however, gives the account of the end from a relative standpoint according to which the body disintegrates and goes back to its cause, the elements. The former text speaks from a transcendental standpoint according to which the whole aggregate is merged in *Brahman. kṛtsnaṁ kalājātam para-brahma-vid brahmaiva saṁpadyate.* Ś.

R. says that the elements unite themselves with the Highest Self: C.U. VI. 8. 6. The functionings of those elements are to be viewed in such a way as to agree with Scripture. As in the states of deep sleep and *pralaya,* there is, owing to union with the Highest Self, a cessation of all experience of pain and pleasure, so is it in the case under question.

Section 8 (16)

ON THE DEATH OF THE KNOWER OF THE HIGHEST *BRAHMAN* THE ORGANS AND THE ELEMENTS ARE MERGED IN *BRAHMAN* SO AS TO BE NO LONGER DISTINCT FROM IT IN ANY WAY

IV. 2. 16. *avibhāgo vacanāt*

(*There is*) *non-distinction* (*from Brahman, of the parts merged in it*) *according to* (*scriptural*) *statement.*
avibhāgaḥ: non-distinction; *vacanāt:* on account of the (scriptural) statement.

The text here referred to is *Praśna U.* VI. 5. The merging of elements in the case of the knower of *Brahman* is absolute, whereas in the case of an ordinary person it is not so. The elements exist in a subtle condition, causing future rebirth. In the case of the knower of *Brahman,* knowledge destroys ignorance and its effects get merged in *Brahman* absolutely, without any chance of cropping up again.

R. says that the union is non-division, i.e. connection of such a kind that those subtle elements are altogether incapable of being thought and spoken of as separate from *Brahman*.

Section 9 (17)

THE SOUL OF THE KNOWER OF *SAGUṆA BRAHMAN* PASSES INTO THE HEART AND THENCE DEPARTS OUT OF THE BODY THROUGH THE *SUṢUMNĀ NĀḌI*

IV. 2. 17. *tadoko'grajvalanaṁ tat-prakāśita-dvāro vidyā-sāmarthyāt tac-cheṣagaty-anusmṛti-yogāc ca hārdānugṛhītaḥ śatādhikayā*

(*When the soul of the knower of the Saguṇa Brahman is about to depart from the body, there takes place*) *a lighting up of the top of its* (*the soul's*) *abode* (*the heart*). *With the passage* (*for the departure of the soul*) *being illuminated thereby,* (*the soul departs*), *being favoured by him* (*Brahman*) *who resides in the heart, along that nāḍi which is beyond the hundred,* (*i.e. the suṣumnā*), *owing to the power of knowledge and the appropriateness of his constant meditation on the way which is part of that knowledge.*

tat-okaḥ-agrajvalanam: the lighting of the top of its abode; *tat-prakāśita-dvāraḥ:* with the passage illuminated by this light; *vidyā-sāmarthyāt:* owing to the power of knowledge; *tat-śeṣa-gati-anu-smṛti-yogāt:* owing to the appropriateness of constant meditation as the way which is a part of that (knowledge); *ca:* and; *hārdānugṛhītaḥ:* being favoured by him who resides in the heart; *śatādhikayā:* by the one that is beyond the hundred.

The texts considered here are B.U. IV. 4. 1–2. These texts indicate that, at the time of death, the soul together with the organs come to the heart. For both the knower and the ignorant the point of the heart becomes shining and the door of exit is also thereby lighted up, yet the knower departs through the skull only while the others depart from other places. See C.U. VIII. 6. 6.

R. continues in his comment on this *sūtra*, the departure of the knower. The knower wins the favour of the Supreme Person who abides within the heart and is assisted by him.

Section 10 (18–19)

THE DEPARTING SOUL PASSES UP TO THE SUN BY FOLLOWING THE RAYS

IV. 2. 18. *raśmyanusārī*

(*The soul after departing from the body*) *follows the rays.*

raśmi-anusārī: following the rays.

From C.U. VIII. 6. 2. 5, we learn that the soul of the knower of *Saguṇa Brahman*, after departing from the body along the *suṣumnā*, follows the rays of the sun. Whether it departs in day or night, it follows the rays which exist both in day and night.

IV. 2. 19. *niśi neti cen na sambandhasya yāvad-deha-bhāvitvād darśayati ca*

If it be said (*that the soul does*) *not* (*follow the rays*) *in the night,* (*we reply that it is*) *not so because the connection of* (*the nāḍīs and the rays*) *continues as long as the body lasts; and* (*Scripture*) *also declares* (*this*).

niśi: in the night; *na:* not; *iti cet:* if it be said; *na:* not so; *sambandhasya yāvat-deha-bhāvitvāt:* because the connection continues as long as the body lasts; *darśayati:* (Scripture) declares; *ca:* also.

The connection lasts as long as the body lasts. So it is immaterial whether the soul passes out in day or in night. The sun's rays continue even in night though we do not feel their presence owing to the fact that their number is limited in night. The result of knowledge cannot be made to depend on the accident of death by day or by night. Cp. C.U. VIII. 6. 5.

Section 11 (20–21)

THE KNOWER WHO DIES DURING *DAKṢIṆĀYANA* REACHES *BRAHMAN*

IV. 2. 20. *ataś cāyane'pi dakṣiṇe*

And for the same reason (*the departing soul follows the rays*) *during the southern progress of the soul also.*

ataḥ: for the same reason; *ca:* and; *ayane:* during the sun's course; *api:* also; *dakṣiṇe:* southern.

The objection is raised that the soul of the knower of *Brahman* who passes away during the southern course of the sun does not follow the rays to *Brahma-loka* as both *śruti* and *smṛti* say that only one who dies during the northern course of the sun goes there. Besides, it is said that Bhīṣma waited for the northern course of the sun, to leave the body. The *sūtra* says that the result of knowledge does not depend on the accident of passing in the northern or the southern course of the sun. C.U. V. 10. 1 refers to deities and not to the points in the northern course. Bhīṣma wanted only to show that he could die at will and to uphold approved custom. *ācāra-paripālanārtham, pitṛ-prasāda-labdha-svacchanda-mṛtyutākhyāpanārthaṁ ca.* See also B.G. VIII. 23ff.

IV. 2. 21. *yoginaḥ prati ca smaryate smārte caite*

(These details) are stated in the smṛti with reference to the yogins; and both (Sāṁkhya and Yoga) are smṛti only.

yoginaḥ prati: with reference to the *yogins*; *ca:* and; *smaryate:* the *smṛti* declares; *smārte:* belonging to the class of *smṛti*; *ca:* and; *ete:* these two.

The details as to the time mentioned in B.G. VIII. 23. 24 apply only to *yogins* who adopt the *sādhana* of the *Yoga* and the *Sāṁkhya* systems. They are *smṛtis* and not *śrutis*. These limitations do not apply to those who pursue the path of knowledge described in the *śruti* texts.

Nimbārka and Śrīnivāsa hold that there are no fixed rules about the time of departure.

Section 1 (1)

THE PATH CONNECTED WITH DEITIES BEGINNING WITH LIGHT IS THE ONLY WAY TO *BRAHMA-LOKA*

IV. 3. 1. *arcirādinā tat-prathiteḥ*

(On the road) beginning with light (the departed soul proceeds) on account of that being widely known.
arciḥ-ādinā: (on the road) beginning with light; *tat-prathiteḥ:* on account of that being well known.

There are different declarations about the path of the gods, *deva-yāna* to *brahma-loka*. C.U. V. 10. 1; B.U. VI. 2. 15, see also V. 10. 1; K.U. I. 3; M.U. I. 2. 11. The question is whether these texts refer to different paths or different descriptions of the same path. The *sūtra* says that they give different descriptions of the same path. This is well known from the *śruti* C.U. V. 10. 1. Again, the goal attained is the same in all cases.

While Ś. treats this *sūtra* as referring to the knowers of *Saguṇa Brahman*, R., Nimbārka and others treat it as referring to all knowers.

Section 2 (2)

THE DEPARTING SOUL REACHES THE DEITY OF THE YEAR AND THEN OF THE AIR

IV. 3. 2. *vāyum abdād aviśeṣa-viśeṣābhyām*

From the year to air, on account of the absence and presence of specification.
vāyum: (the deity of) the air; *abdāt:* from (the deity of) the year; *aviśeṣa-viśeṣābhyām:* on account of absence and presence of specification.

The passage that the soul goes to air from the year has reference to the C.U. text V. 10. 1. The B.U. text VI. 2. 3 has reference to month. In the one the world of gods is absent, in the other the year is absent. As both texts are authoritative both stages have to be inserted in each and the distinction has to be made that, owing to its connection with the months, the year has the first place (after the months and before the world of the gods) and the world of the gods the second place.

Ś. and Bhāskara do not identify the world of gods with air. For them the order is light, day, bright fortnight, six months of the northern course of the sun, year, world of gods, air, sun and so on.

R. and Śrīkaṇṭha take *aviśeṣa-viśeṣābhyām* as stating the reason why the air is to be placed after the year and before the sun. For them 'the world of gods' denotes air which is the dwelling-place of gods. Scripture specifically says that the soul comes to the air.

Section 3 (3)

AFTER REACHING THE DEITY OF LIGHTNING, THE SOUL REACHES THE WORLD OF *VARUṆA*

IV. 3. 3. *tadito'dhi varuṇaḥ sambandhāt*

After reaching the deity of lightning (the soul reaches) Varuṇa on account of the connection.
tadito'dhi: after (the deity of) lightning; *varuṇaḥ:* (comes) *Varuṇa; sambandhāt:* on account of the connection.

Varuṇa is the god of rain and lightning precedes rain (C.U. VII. 11. 1). After *Varuṇa* come *Indra* and *Prajā-pati.*

In these three *sūtras* the different accounts are reconciled.

Section 4 (4–6)

LIGHT, ETC., MEAN THE DEITIES IDENTIFIED WITH THEM LEADING THE SOUL TO *BRAHMA-LOKA*

IV. 3. 4. *ātivāhikās tal-liṅgāt*

(These are) deities conducting the soul (on the path of the gods) on account of the indicatory marks of that.
ātivāhikāḥ: deities conducting the soul; *tat-liṅgāt:* on account of indicatory marks of that.

The deities are meant and not places of enjoyment. See C.U. IV. 15. 5; V. 10. 1. These are non-human persons, *a-mānava.*

IV. 3. 5. *ubhaya-vyāmohāt tat-siddheḥ*

This is established on the ground that both (the traveller and the path) are bewildered (unconscious).
ubhaya-vyāmohāt: from the bewildered (unconscious) state of both; *tat-siddheḥ:* that is established.

As the organs of the souls are withdrawn into the mind they cannot guide themselves; light, etc., being without intelligence, cannot guide the souls. So intelligent deities guide the soul along the path to *brahma-loka*. Besides, as the organs of the departed souls are withdrawn into the mind they cannot enjoy. Light and the rest cannot be places of enjoyment.

Ś. says that knowers of *Brahman* enjoy bliss, etc. *tathaiva ca viduṣāṁ tuṣṭy-anubhavādi-darśanāt.*

This *sūtra* is found only in Ś. and Baladeva and not in others.

Baladeva explains it thus: 'On account of the untenableness of the two alternatives, light and the rest can neither be landmarks nor persons standing on the path. The only correct alternative is that they are conducting deities.'

IV. 3. 6. *vaidyutenaiva tatas tac chruteḥ*

From thence (the souls are guided) by him only who belongs to the lightning, that being known from the śruti.

vaidyutena: by the superhuman guide who belongs to lightning; *eva:* alone; *tataḥ:* from thence; *tat-śruteḥ:* that being known from the *śruti.*

After they reach the deity identified with lightning they are led by the very superhuman person who takes charge of them from the deity of lightning to *brahma-loka* through the worlds of *Varuṇa, Indra* and *Prajā-pati*. See C.U. IV. 15. 5, V. 10. 1 and B.U. VI. 2. 15. These do not actually guide but favour the souls either by not obstructing or helping them in some way. From all these it is obvious that by light, etc., deities are meant.

Section 5 (7–14)

BY THE PATH OF THE GODS WE REACH *SAGUṆA BRAHMAN*

IV. 3. 7. *kāryaṁ bādarir asya gaty-upapatteḥ*

To the effected Brahman (the souls are led) (so thinks) Bādari on account of the possibility of its being the goal.

kāryam: the effected *Brahman* (relative *Brahman*); *bādariḥ:* Bādari (thinks); *asya:* its; *gati-upapatteḥ:* on account of the possibility of being the goal.

C.U. V. 10. 1 says that we are led to *Brahman*. Is this *Saguṇa Brahman* or *Nirguṇa Brahman*? Bādari is of the view that *Saguṇa Brahman* is meant for it occupies a place to which souls may go while *Nirguṇa Brahman* is all-pervading. With the Highest *Brahman* we cannot connect the ideas of one who goes or the object of going or act of going; for that *Brahman* is present everywhere and is the inner-self of all.

> *na tu parasmin brahmaṇi gantṛtvaṁ gantavyatvaṁ gatir vā'va kalpate, sarvagatatvāt pratyagātmatvāc ca gantṝṇām.* Ś.

R. makes *sūtras* 7–16 into a single section in which the views of Bādari and of Jaimini are represented as two *pūrva-pakṣas* which are set aside and Bādarāyaṇa's opinion is accepted as the *siddhānta*. The question is whether the guardians of the path lead to *Brahman* only those who worship the effected *Brahman*, i.e. *Hiraṇya-garbha*, or those who worship the Highest *Brahman* or those who worship the individual soul as free from *prakṛti* and having *Brahman* for its self. *ye pratyag-ātmānaṁ prakṛti-viyuktam brahmātmakam upāsate.* Bādari maintains that the guardians lead to *Brahman* those who worship the effected *Brahman* because going is possible towards the latter only. No movement can take place towards the Highest *Brahman* which is absolutely complete, all-knowing, present everywhere, the Self of all. We do not move to some other place in order to reach *Brahman*. *Brahman* is something already reached. *na hi pari-pūrṇam, sarvajñam, sarva-gatam, sarvātma-bhūtam, param brahmopāsīnasya tat-prāptaye deśāntara-gatir upapadyate, prāptatvād eva.* For him the effect of true knowledge is only to put an end to that ignorance which has for its object *Brahman*, which, in reality, is eternally reached. *nitya-prāpta-para-brahma-viṣayāvidyā-nivṛtti-mātram eva hi para-vidyā-kāryam.* R.

IV. 3. 8. *viśeṣitatvāc ca*

And on account (of Brahman to which the souls are led) being qualified (in another passage).

viśeṣitatvāt: on account of being qualified; *ca:* and.

B.U. VI. 2. 15 speaks of the worlds of *Brahman*, *brahma-lokān gamayata*. Plurality of worlds is not possible with regard to the Supreme *Brahman*. *Saguṇa Brahman* may abide in different conditions. Even the term 'world' can denote only some place of enjoyment falling within the sphere of effects and possessing the quality of being entered into.

IV. 3. 9. *sāmīpyāt tu tad-vyapadeśaḥ*

But on account of the proximity (to the higher Brahman) there is designation (of the lower Brahman) as that.

sāmīpyāt: on account of proximity; *tu:* but; *tat-vyapadeśaḥ:* (its) designation as that.

When the higher *Brahman* is described as possessing certain effected qualities for the purposes of pious meditation, then it is what we call lower *Brahman*.

R. says that *Hiraṇya-garbha* as the first created being stands near to *Brahman* and may therefore be designated by the same term, *Brahman*. See Ś.U. VI. 18.

Baladeva interprets thus: 'But the designation of that [viz. salvation] is on account of nearness.' That is, the souls are said to go to the world of *Brahmā* and never return (B.U. VI. 2. 15) not because they obtain salvation directly, but because they are very near getting it.

IV. 3. 10. *kāryātyaye tad-adhyakṣeṇa sahātaḥ param abhidhānāt*

On the passing away of the effected world (brahma-loka) (the souls attain) together with the ruler of that world, what is higher than that, (i.e. the Supreme Brahman) on account of scriptural declaration.

kārya-atyaye: on the passing away of the effected world; *tat-adhyakṣeṇa saha:* together with the ruler of that world; *ataḥ param:* higher than that (i.e. the Supreme *Brahman*); *abhidhānāt:* on account of the scriptural declaration.

If the souls travelling by the path of the gods reach only the world of *Hiraṇya-garbha*, how can it be said that they will not return to the world (C.U. IV. 15. 6, VIII. 6. 5; B.U. VI. 2. 15) since there is no permanence apart from the Supreme *Brahman*? The *sūtra* explains that, at the passing away of the *brahma-loka*, the souls, which by that time have attained knowledge along with *Hiraṇya-garbha*, attain the Highest *Brahman*. Ś. holds that what is higher than that is the pure highest place of *Viṣṇu*, *pariśuddhaṁ viṣṇoḥ paraṁ padam*. Ś. thinks that this passage gives *krama-mukti* or release by gradual steps.

R. quotes M.U. III. 2. 6.

IV. 3. 11. *smṛteś ca*

And on account of smṛti.

smṛteḥ: on account of *smṛti*; *ca:* and.

The *smṛti* passage referred to here states: When the dissolution has come and the end of the highest (*Hiraṇya-garbha*) then they all, together with *Brahmā*, with purified minds enter the highest place.

brahmaṇā saha te sarve samprāpte prati-saṁcare
parasyānte kṛtātmānaḥ praviśanti paraṁ padam.

K.P. XII.

IV. 3. 12. *paraṁ jaiminir mukhyatvāt*

To the Highest (Brahman) (the souls are led) Jaimini (thinks) owing to this being the principal sense of the word (Brahman).

param: the Highest (*Brahman*); *Jaiminiḥ:* Jaimini (thinks); *mukhyatvāt:* owing to this being the principal sense of the word (*Brahman*).

The reference is to C.U. IV. 15. 5.

When two meanings are possible, the higher should be preferred. *Brahman* can mean the higher and the lower. The higher should be adopted, according to Jaimini.

R. makes out that *brahma-loka* means the world which is *Brahman* even as *niṣāda-sthapati* means a *sthapati* who is a *niṣāda* and not a *sthapati* of the *niṣādas*.

Śrīkaṇṭha says that (the souls are led to *Śiva*) higher than (*Hiraṇya-garbha*).

IV. 3. 13. *darśanāc ca*

And on account of the declarations of śruti.
darśanāt: on account of the declarations of *śruti; ca:* and.

The texts are C.U. VIII. 6. 6, VIII. 12. 3, VIII. 2. 23; *Kaṭha U.* II. 6. 16. These declare that the soul which passes out of the body through the *suṣumnā nāḍī* reaches immortality, which can only be the attainment of Supreme *Brahman.*

R. and Nimbārka hold that a knower who travels along the path of the gods reaches *Brahman.*

IV. 3. 14. *na ca kārye pratipatty-abhisandhiḥ*

And the desire to enter (*Brahman*) *cannot be* (*with respect*) *to the effected* (*Brahman*).
na: not; *ca:* and; *kārye:* in the effected (*Brahman*); *pratipatti-abhisandhiḥ:* the desire to enter (*Brahman*).

In C.U. VIII. 14. 1 the desire to attain the assembly hall and abode, *sabhāṁ veśma,* cannot be with respect to the effected *Brahman.* It is appropriate only with respect to the Supreme *Brahman.*

According to Ś., *sūtras* 12–14 give the opponent's view. The *Brahman* attained by those who travel by the path of the gods cannot be the Supreme *Brahman* but only the *kārya Brahman* or effected *Brahman.* The Supreme *Brahman* is all-pervading and the inmost self of all. Journey or attainment is possible only where there is a difference, where the attainer is different from the thing attained. To realise the Supreme *Brahman,* all that is necessary is to remove ignorance. In such a realisation there is neither going nor attaining. The reference to a journey to *Brahman* belongs to the sphere of relative knowledge and if it occurs in a chapter dealing with supreme knowledge, it is only for the glorification of the latter. So the view expressed in *sūtras* 7–11 by Bādari is the correct one.

R. points out that what the soul aims at is the condition of the Universal Self which has for its prerequisite the removal of ignorance. See C.U. VIII. 14. 1. The *Brahma*-world which is the thing to be realised is something non-created, *akṛta,* and reaching that would mean freedom from all bondage whatsoever.
sarva-bandha-vinirmokṣa.

Section 6 (15–16)

ONLY THOSE WHO WORSHIP *BRAHMAN* WITHOUT A SYMBOL ATTAIN *BRAHMA-LOKA*

IV. 3. 15. *apratīkālambanān nayatīti bādarāyaṇa ubhayathā'doṣāt, tat-kratuś ca*

Those who do not take their stand on symbols (*the superhuman being*)

leads, thus Bādarāyaṇa thinks; there being no defects in the twofold relation (resulting from this view); and the meditation on that (i.e. Brahman) (is the reason of this twofold relation).
apratīka-ālambanāt: those who do not take their stand on symbols (in their meditations); *nayati:* (the superhuman being) leads; *iti:* thus; *bādarāyaṇaḥ:* Bādarāyaṇa; *ubhayathā:* the twofold relation; *adoṣāt:* there being no defect; *tat-kratuḥ:* (as is) the meditation on that (so does one become); *ca:* and.

The question is raised whether all worshippers of *Saguṇa Brahman* go to *brahma-loka*. The *sūtra* says that only those who do not use any symbol in their meditations go there. This does not contradict III. 3. 31, if we understand by all only those worshippers who do not use any symbol. This view is justified by the scriptural declaration: 'In whatever form they meditate on him, that they become.' In the worship of symbols, the meditations are not fixed on *Brahman*. They are fixed on symbols. So the worshipper does not attain *brahma-loka*. The case of the worshipper of the five fires is different because Scripture declares that he goes to *brahma-loka*. Where there is no such specific declaration we have to hold that only those whose object of meditation is *Brahman* go to *brahma-loka*, and not others.

Bhāskara holds that those who meditate on the effected *Brahman* are led to the effected *Brahman* while those who meditate on the Highest *Brahman* are led to the Highest *Brahman*. There is no contradiction here since even those who meditate on the effected *Brahman* do not return for they attain a gradual release, while those who meditate on the Highest *Brahman* attain immediate release.

According to R., *sūtras* 7–16 form one section, in which the views of Bādari and Jaimini represent two *pūrva-pakṣas*, while Bādarāyaṇa's opinion is adopted as the correct conclusion or *siddhānta*.

R. interprets the *sūtra* differently. 'Those not depending on symbols he leads, thus Bādarāyaṇa [thinks] there being a defect in both cases; and he whose thought is that.' R. reads *doṣāt* for Ś.'s *adoṣāt:* Bādarāyaṇa thinks that all those who do not take their stand on symbols, i.e. who worship the Highest *Brahman*, and those who meditate on the individual self as dissociated from *prakṛti* and having *Brahman* for its self are led to *Brahman*.

Śrīkaṇṭha and Baladeva adopt R.'s reading. According to Śrīkaṇṭha those who meditate on the Highest *Brahman* alone are led to him but not those who meditate on *Hiraṇya-garbha* or on *Nārāyaṇa*.

IV. 3. 16. *viśeṣaṁ ca darśayati*

And Scripture declares a difference (with respect to meditations on symbols).
viśeṣam: difference; *ca:* and; *darśayati:* the Scripture declares.

C.U. VII. 1. 5; VII. 1. 2 point out that different results accrue from different symbols. There can be no such difference for those who meditate on the Highest *Brahman* which is non-different. Those who use symbols cannot go to *brahma-loka* like those who worship the effected *Brahman*.

Śrīkaṇṭha says that the Scripture shows the difference between *Hiraṇya-garbha*, *Nārāyaṇa* and *Śiva*.

Baladeva points out that the conducting divinities lead the devotees to the Lord. Only in the case of the *nirapekṣa* devotees, the Lord himself comes down to fetch them.

Section 1 (1–3)

THE RELEASED SOUL DOES NOT ACQUIRE ANY NEW CHARACTERISTICS BUT ONLY MANIFESTS ITS TRUE NATURE

IV. 4. 1. *sampadyāvirbhāvaḥ svena śabdāt*

(*On the soul's*) *having attained* (*the Highest light*) *there is manifestation* (*of its real nature*) (*as we know*) *from the word 'own'.*
sampadya: having attained; *āvirbhāvaḥ:* manifestation (of its real nature); *svena śabdāt:* from the word 'own'.

See C.U. VIII. 12. 3. Release is not something new. It is pre-existent. The soul manifests its true nature which is covered with ignorance. This is the attainment of release. It is not anything newly acquired.

R. says that if the soul assumes a new body, the specification 'in its own nature' would be without meaning.

While Ś. refers in this *sūtra* to the knower of *parā-vidyā* or higher knowledge, R. refers to the knower or *vidvān* who goes to *Brahman.*

IV. 4. 2. *muktaḥ pratijñānāt*

(*The self which manifests its true nature*) *is released;* (*as is evident*) *from the promise* (*made in the Scripture*).
muktaḥ: is released; *pratijñānāt:* from the promise.

The self is freed from the three states of waking, dream and sleep and abides in its own nature. See C.U. VIII. 9–11. That the self is free is declared in C.U. VIII. 11. 3; VIII. 7. 1.

IV. 4. 3. *ātmā prakaraṇāt*

(*The light into which the soul enters is*) *the Self; on account of the context.*
ātmā: the Supreme Self; *prakaraṇāt:* on account of the context (or subject-matter).

See C.U. VIII. 3. 4, VIII. 7. 1; B.U. IV. 4. 16. These texts deal with the Supreme Self.

R. says that intelligence, bliss and the other essential qualities of the soul which were obscured and contracted by *karman* expand and manifest themselves when the bondage due to *karman* passes away and the soul approaches the highest light.

Section 2 (4)

THE RELEASED SOUL STANDS TO *BRAHMAN* IN THE RELATION OF NON-SEPARATION

IV. 4. 4. *avibhāgena dṛṣṭatvāt*

(*The released soul exists*) *as inseparable* (*from Brahman*) *because that is seen* (*from Scripture*).

avibhāgena: as inseparable; *dṛṣṭatvāt:* for it is seen from Scripture.

The question is raised whether the released soul exists as different from or as identical with *Brahman*. The *sūtra* says that it exists as inseparable from *Brahman*. See C.U. VI. 8. 7; B.U. I. 4. 10, IV. 4. 6. The released soul should be regarded as identical with *Brahman*. Passages which speak of difference between the two should be treated in a secondary sense as expressing unity. See C.U. VI. 8. 7; B.U. I. 4. 10, IV. 3. 23; C.U. VII. 24. 1.

Avibhāga or non-separation means for Ś. identity.

Ś. says that the released soul abides in non-division from the Highest Self for that is seen from the Scripture.

mukta-svarūpa-nirūpaṇa-parāṇi vākyāny avibhāgam eva darśayanti nadī-samudrādi-nidarśanānica.

R. points out that the question is whether the released soul views itself as separate, *pṛthag-bhūta* from *Brahman* or as non-separate, being a mode of *Brahman*. There are passages favouring both views. The released soul, it is said, stands to the Highest Self in the relation of fellowship, equality, equality of attributes. All this implies consciousness of separation. See T.U. II. 1. 1; B.G. X. IV. 2. The *sūtra* says that the released soul is conscious of itself as non-divided from the Highest *Brahman*. This is seen. The souls have for their inner self the Highest Self. They are modes (*prakāras*) of it.

Section 3 (5–7)

THE CHARACTERISTICS OF THE RELEASED SOUL

IV. 4. 5. *brāhmeṇa jaiminir upanyāsādibhyaḥ*

(*The released soul exists*) *as possessed of the nature of Brahman* (*so thinks*) *Jaimini, on account of the reference, etc.*

brāhmeṇa: as possessed of the nature of *Brahman; Jaiminiḥ:* Jaimini; *upanyāsādibhyaḥ:* on account of reference, etc.

Jaimini thinks that the released soul's nature is like that of *Brahman*. It possesses the qualities mentioned in C.U. VIII. 7. 1. 'The self which is free from evil, free from old age, free from death, free from grief, free from hunger and thirst, whose desire is the real, whose thought is the real. For such there is freedom in all worlds.'

teṣām sarveṣu lokeṣu kāma-cāro bhavati. VIII. 1. 6.

The released soul is said to be all-knowing and all-powerful. He is of the nature of *Brahman* as *Īśvara*.

Nimbārka thinks that the individual soul becomes manifest as endowed with the attributes, 'relating to *Brahman*', such as freedom from evil, etc.

IV. 4. 6. *citi tanmātreṇa tad-ātmakatvād ity auḍulomiḥ*

Solely as pure intelligence (the soul manifests itself) as that is its Self; thus Auḍulomi (thinks).

citi-tanmātreṇa: solely as pure intelligence; *tat-ātmakatvāt:* that being its self (or the nature); *iti:* thus; *auḍulomiḥ:* Auḍulomi (thinks).

Bhāskara and Śrīkaṇṭha read *citi-mātreṇa* for *citi-tanmātreṇa.*

Since the soul is of the nature of pure intelligence it exists as such in the released condition. Cp. B.U. IV. 5. 13. Freedom from sin, etc., cannot constitute the nature of the Self. This is the view of Auḍulomi.

IV. 4. 7. *evaṁ apy upanyāsāt pūrva-bhāvād avirodhaṁ bādarāyaṇaḥ*

Even if it be so, on account of the existence of former qualities (admitted) owing to reference and so on, there is absence of contradiction; (so thinks) Bādarāyaṇa.

evam: thus; *api:* even; *upanyāsāt:* on account of reference; *pūrva-bhāvāt:* on account of the existence of former qualities; *avirodham:* absence of contradiction; *bādarāyaṇaḥ:* (so thinks) Bādarāyaṇa.

Though it is admitted that the nature of the Self is constituted by pure intelligence, the possession of qualities like freedom from evil is not rejected from the standpoint of the world of manifestation.

According to Auḍulomi, the only characteristic of the released soul is thought, *caitanya.* Jaimini maintains that it possesses a number of exalted qualities. Bādarāyaṇa favours a combination of these two views.

Ś. feels that Jaimini speaks with reference to the world of manifestation, Auḍulomi with reference to the transcendental standpoint and Bādarāyaṇa reconciles the two.

Śrīnivāsa thinks that having attained the form of the highest light, the individual soul becomes manifest in its own natural form as endowed with the attributes of freedom from evil and so on, in conformity with both sets of scriptural texts.

Section 4 (8–9)

THE SOUL EFFECTS ITS DESIRES BY MERE WILL

IV. 4. 8. *saṁkalpād eva tu tac-chruteḥ*

But through mere will (the released effect their purposes) for the Scriptures say so.

saṁkalpāt: through will; *eva:* only; *tu:* but; *tat-śruteḥ:* for the Scriptures say so.
'tu' is omitted in some versions.

C.U. (VIII. 2. 1) says: 'If he becomes desirous of the world of the fathers by his mere will [thought] fathers arise.' The doubt arises whether will is enough or it requires an operative cause. The *sūtra* says that the will is enough. If any other causes were required the scriptural statement 'by the will only' will be contradicted. The will of the released differs from that of ordinary men. It has the power of producing results without any operative cause.

R. uses C.U. VIII. 12. 3 and holds that mere will is enough and no further effort is necessary.

IV. 4. 9. *ata eva cānanyādhipatiḥ.*

And for this very reason (the released soul is) without a lord.
ata eva: for this very reason; *ca:* and; *ananyādhipatiḥ:* he is without a lord.

C.U. VIII. 1. 6 says that there is freedom for them in all worlds. A released soul is master of himself.

R. says that the released soul realises all its wishes and is therefore not subject to another ruler. To be under a ruler is to be subject to injunction and prohibition and this is opposed to freedom in the realisation of one's wishes.

While Ś. treats this as relating to *aparā-vidyā*, R. treats this section as a continuation of the topic of the state of the released.

Nimbārka quotes C.U. VII. 25. 2.: *sa svarāḍ bhavati*, He becomes a self-ruler.

Section 5 (10–14)

THE RELEASED SOULS ARE EMBODIED OR DISEMBODIED ACCORDING TO THEIR WILL

IV. 4. 10. *abhāvaṁ bādarir āha hy evam*

There is absence (of body and sense-organs for the released), Bādari (thinks); for thus Scripture says.
abhāvam: absence (of body and sense-organs); *bādariḥ:* Bādari; *āha:* (the Scripture) says; *hi:* because; *evam:* thus.

The possession of the will means that the released soul has a mind. Has it also a body and sense-organs? Bādari thinks that it does not have a body and sense-organs for the Scripture says: 'Now he who knows, let me think this, he is the self, the mind is his divine eye. He, verily, seeing these pleasures through his divine eye (*daivena cakṣusā*), the mind rejoices.' C.U. VIII. 12. 5. This shows that he possesses only the mind, and not the body or organs.

R. quotes C.U. VIII. 12. 1 and 3 and says that the released soul is without a body.

Baladeva reads *abhāve* for *abhāvam.*

IV. 4. 11. *bhāvaṁ jaiminir vikalpāmananāt*

There is presence (of body and sense-organs) Jaimini (thinks) because the Scripture declares (the capacity for a released person to assume) diverse forms.

bhāvam: presence (of body and sense-organs); *jaiminiḥ:* Jaimini; *vikalpa-āmananāt:* because the Scripture declares (the capacity to assume) diverse forms.

C.U. VII. 26. 2 says that a released soul can assume many forms. This implies that it possesses, besides the mind, body and sense-organs. This is the view of Jaimini.

R says that the various forms of manifoldness of which the text speaks must be due to the body. The text which speaks of the absence of the body refers to the absence of that body only which is due to *karman.* It is the latter body which is the cause of pleasure and pain.

IV. 4. 12. *dvādaśāhavad ubhaya-vidhaṁ bādarāyaṇo'taḥ*

For this reason Bādarāyaṇa (thinks that the released soul is) of both kinds; as in the case of the twelve days' sacrifice.

dvādaśāhavat: as in the case of the twelve days' sacrifice; *ubhaya-vidham:* of both kinds; *bādarāyaṇaḥ:* Bādarāyaṇa; *ataḥ:* for this reason.

According to Bādarāyaṇa a released soul which has attained *brahma-loka* can exist both ways, with or without a body according to its desire. The same sacrifice extending over twelve days may be viewed either as a *sattra* or as an *adīna* sacrifice. Both alternatives are indicated in Scripture. See *Pūrva Mīmāṁsā Sūtra* II. 3.

IV. 4. 13. *tanvabhāve sandhyavad upapatteḥ*

In the absence of a body (the fulfilment of desires is possible) as in the dream state, since this is reasonable.

tanu-abhāve: in the absence of a body; *sandhyavat:* as in the dream state; *upapatteḥ:* since this is reasonable.

In the dream state which is midway between waking and sleep, objects wished have an existence even while body and senses do not really exist.

R. says that the released soul may undergo experiences of pleasure by means of instruments created by the highest person though the released soul may not himself be creative. As in the state of dream the individual soul has experiences depending on chariots and other implements created by the Lord (B.U. IV. 3. 10); so the released soul may have experience of different worlds created by the Lord engaged in playful sport.

IV. 4. 14. *bhāve jāgradvat*

In the presence (of a body the fulfilment of desires is) as in the waking state.

bhāve: in the presence (of a body or when the body exists); *jāgrat-vat:* as in the waking state.

When the released soul has a body the objects of his wishes may have real existence, as in the waking state.

R. says that the released soul possessing a body created by its own will enjoys its various delights in the same way as a waking man does. In the same way as the Highest Person creates out of himself, for his own delight, the world of the Fathers and so on, so he sometimes creates such worlds for the enjoyment of the released souls. Sometimes the souls by their own will-power create their own worlds, which are, however, included within the sphere of the sport of the Highest Person.

For Ś. and Bhāskara, when there is a body, the objects desired by the freed soul have real existence.

Śrīkaṇṭha considers the objection that, when there is enjoyment in the nature of the perception of the things of this world by released souls, then by their experience of what does not serve the goal of man, the absence of bondage and suffering cannot be secured, and answers that there is no perception of the world by the liberated ones in the form in which it does not serve the goal of man, for it is perceived as of the form of *Brahman*.

Section 6 (15–16)

THE RELEASED SOUL CAN ANIMATE SEVERAL BODIES AT THE SAME TIME

IV. 4. 15. *pradīpavad āveśaṣ tathā hi darśayati*

The entering (of one soul into several bodies) is like (the multiplication of) the flame of a lamp, for so the Scripture declares.

pradīpavat: like the flame of a lamp; *āveśaḥ:* entering (or animating different bodies); *tathā:* so; *hi:* because; *darśayati:* the Scripture declares.

In *sūtra* 11, it is stated that a liberated soul can assume many bodies at the same time for enjoyment. The objection is raised that enjoyment is possible only in the body in which the soul and mind exist while other bodies will be lifeless puppets. Soul and mind cannot be divided and so cannot exist in more than one body. The *sūtra* says that the released soul can animate, on account of its power, all the bodies even as the flame of a lamp can pass over into several flames (lighted at the original flame). C.U. VII. 26. 2 says that the one self can render itself manifold. The released soul can create other bodies with internal organs comparable to the original sense-organ.

For R., the question is, if the soul is of atomic size, how can it connect itself with many bodies? The answer is given in the *sūtra*. Even as a lamp abiding in one place only enters through light proceeding from it into connection with many places, so the soul also, though limited to one place, may through its light-like consciousness enter into several bodies. R. adds that even in this life the soul, though abiding in one part of the body only, viz. the heart, pervades the whole body by means of its consciousness and thus makes it its own. There is, however, this difference. The non-released soul has its intellectual power contracted by the influence of *karman* and is therefore incapable of that expansive pervasion without which it cannot identify itself with other bodies. The released soul whose intellectual power is not contracted, is capable of extending as far as it likes and making many bodies its own. See Ś.U. V. 9. The non-released soul is ruled by *karman*, the released soul by its will.

IV. 4. 16. *svāpyaya sampattyor anyatarāpekṣam āviṣkṛtaṁ hi*

(*What Scripture says of the absence of all specific cognition*) *refers either to deep sleep or absolute union* (*with Brahman*) *for this is made clear* (*by the scriptural texts*).

svāpyaya-sampatyoḥ: of deep sleep and absolute union with *Brahman*; *anyatara-apekṣam:* having in view either of these two; *āviṣkṛtam:* this is made clear (by the scriptural texts); *hi:* for.

B.U. II. 4. 14; IV. 3. 21, 30, 32 deny specific cognition to a released soul. The objection is raised as to how such a released soul can assume several bodies and enjoy. These texts, it is said in reply, refer to the state of deep sleep or that of liberation, in which the soul attains union with the Absolute *Brahman*. We are not discussing these states but only entrance into *brahma-loka* where there is diversity and cognition is possible. *Brahma-loka* is not heaven for return to the mortal world after the exhaustion of the virtue which raised one to the status of a god is possible, while from *brahma-loka* no return to earth is possible.

R. quotes C.U. VI. 15. 1 and B.U. IV. 5. 13 and refers to the states of deep sleep and death in which the soul is unconscious.

Section 7 (17–21)

THE RELEASED SOUL HAS ALL THE LORDLY POWERS EXCEPT THE POWER OF CREATION

IV. 4. 17. *jagad-vyāpāra-varjam prakaraṇād asannihitatvāc ca*

(*The released soul possesses all lordly powers*) *except the power of activities relating to the world* (*such as creation, etc.*), *on account of* (*the lord being*) *the subject-matter* (*of all texts where creation, etc., are described*) *and* (*the released souls*) *not being near* (*to such activities*).

jagad-vyāpāra-varjam: except the power of activities relating to the world; *prakaraṇāt:* on account of the subject-matter; *asannihitatvāt:* not being near; *ca:* and.

According to Ś., the question relates to the worshippers of *Saguṇa Brahman* who attain *brahma-loka* and worldly powers. Are their powers limited or unlimited? The opponent quotes C.U. VII. 25. 2 and T.U. I. 5 and holds that the powers are unlimited. The *sūtra* says that the released souls have all powers except those of creation, preservation and destruction of the world. If the released souls have these powers which are the prerogatives of *Īśvara*, we will have many *Īśvaras* and there may be conflict.

The released souls work under the control of the Supreme, though they do not participate in the work of creation, ruling and dissolution of the world.

Bhāskara refers this and the following *sūtras* to those who attain *brahma-loka*.

R. quotes M.U. III. 1. 3 and states the objection that the released souls have the power of realising all their wishes. The world-control is the privilege of *Īśvara*. See C.U. VI. 2; B.U. I. 4. 11; *Aitareya Āraṇyaka* II. 4. 1. 1; B.U. III. 7. 3.

The *Vṛtti* which R. follows says: 'With the exception of the business of the world, the released soul is equal [to the Highest Self] through light.'[1] The author of the *Dramiḍa-bhāṣya* says: 'Owing to its intimate union with the Divine, the disembodied soul effects all things like the divinity.'[2]

According to Śrīkaṇṭha the contemplation of oneself as *Śiva* continues, even in him who, in the world of *Parama-Śiva*, has attained union with him, after the complete extinction of merit and demerit. He says: 'Wandering about freely in the worlds of the [celestial] rulers from *Sadāśiva* up to *Brahmā*, eating what he chooses, taking on what forms he desires, rid of the desire for human and other bodies, functioning with the three energies [*icchā*, *jñāna* and *kriyā*] uncontracted, he enjoys the splendour of perfect self-consciousness,

[1] *vṛttir api jagad-vyāpāra-varjaṁ samāno jyotiṣeti.* R.B. I. 1. 1.

[2] *drāmiḍa-bhāṣya-kāraś ca devatā-sāyujyād aśarīrasyāpi devatāvat sarvārtha-siddhiḥ syād ity āha.* R.B. I. 1. 1.

immersed in the world which is of one texture with the nature of *Brahman*, the harmony of *Śiva* with *Śakti*, which abounds in supreme bliss, light and power.'[1] T.U. III. 10 speaks of the released Self being both the food and the food-eater, the subject and the object.

IV. 4. 18. *pratyakṣopadeśād iti cen nādhikārika-maṇḍalasthokteḥ*

If it be said (that the released soul attains unlimited power) on account of direct teaching (we say) no, for the Scriptures declare (that the released soul attains him) who, entrusts (the sun and others with their offices) and resides in those spheres.

pratyakṣa-upadeśāt: on account of direct teaching; *iti cet:* if it be said; *na:* not; *ādhikārika-maṇḍalastha-ukteḥ:* for the Scripture declares (that the soul attains him) who entrusts with their offices (the sun, etc.) and resides in those spheres.

The *sūtra* says that the powers of the released souls depend on the Lord who abides in the spheres like the sun, etc., and entrusts the sun, etc., with their offices. The powers of the released souls are not unlimited for they get their powers from the Lord and depend on him.

R. holds that the soul whose knowledge is no longer obstructed by *karman* freely enjoys all the different worlds in which the power of *Brahman* manifests itself.

IV. 4. 19. *vikārāvarti ca tathā hi sthitim āha*

And (there is a form of the Highest Lord) which abides beyond all effected things; for thus far Scripture declares his abiding.

vikāra-āvarti: which abides beyond all effected things; *ca:* and; *tathā:* so; *hi:* because; *sthitim:* existence; *āha:* the Scripture declares.

C.U. III. 12. 6 says: 'All beings are one-fourth of him; the three-fourths, immortal, are in the sky.' The Supreme Lord abides in two forms, the transcendental and the empirical. He who worships the Lord in his empirical aspect does not attain his transcendental form. Since the worshipper is able to comprehend him only partially, he attains only limited powers and not unlimited powers like the Lord himself.

Bhāskara takes the non-qualified *Brahman* to be real and eternal and the qualified *Brahman* to be real and non-eternal while Ś. takes the former alone to be real.

R. says that the released soul while conscious of *Brahman* with its manifestations experiences also the enjoyments lying within the

[1] *sadāśivādīnām adhikāriṇāṁ brahmāntānām maṇḍaleṣu svecchayā sañcaramāṇaḥ kāmānnī kāmarūpī vigalita-manuṣyādi-dehābhimāno 'saṅkucita-śakti-traya-vyāpāraḥ paramānanda-prakāśa-vibhūti-maya-śiva-śakti-sāmarasya-para-brahma-svarūpaikarasaḥ prapañcāvagāhinaṁ pari-pūrṇam ahaṁ-bhāvam prakaṭam anubhavati.*

sphere of change, which abide in the world of *Hiraṇya-garbha* and similar beings. He does not possess the power of creating and controlling the world which are the distinctive attributes of the Highest Lord.

IV. 4. 20. *darśayataś caivaṁ pratyakṣānumāne*

And thus perception and inference show.

darśayataḥ: (the two) show; *ca:* and; *evam:* thus; *pratyakṣa-anumāne:* perception and inference.

The non-abiding of the highest light within effected changes is a well-known circumstance. See M.U. II. 2. 10; B.G. XV. 6.

R. says that the energies connected with the rule of the world are exclusive qualities of the Highest Person. *Śruti* and *smṛti* also declare it. See T.U. II. 8. 1; B.U. III. 9, IV. 4. 22; B.G. IX. 10, X. 42. *Śruti* and *smṛti* declare that the Highest Person is the cause of the bliss that is enjoyed by the released soul. T.U. II. 7; B.G. XIV. 26–7. The exalted qualities of freedom from evil, sin, etc., belong to the soul's essential nature but that the soul is of such a nature depends on the Supreme Person. The equality to the Lord which the released soul may claim does not extend to world creation and control.

Nimbārka and Śrīnivāsa believe that the freed soul, though similar to the Highest *Brahman*, cannot possibly be the lord of all the sentient and the non-sentient beings, their controller, supporter, etc. The lordship is exclusive of the activities relating to the universe.

IV. 4. 21. *bhoga-mātra-sāmya-liṅgāc ca*

And on account of the indications of equality (*of the released soul with the Lord*) *only with respect to enjoyment.*

bhoga-mātra-sāmya-liṅgāt: on account of indications of equality with respect to enjoyment only; *ca:* and.

B.U. I. 5. 20, 23; K.U. I. 7 describe equality only with respect to enjoyment and do not mention anything about creation, etc.

R. asks us to treat the powers of the released soul in accordance with what the texts say. They speak of the Highest Lord only as possessing the power of ruling and controlling the entire world and so this power cannot be attributed to the released soul.

IV. 4. 22. *anāvṛtti-śabdād anāvṛtti-śabdāt*

There is non-return (*for these released souls*), *according to Scripture; non-return according to Scripture.*

anāvṛttiḥ: non-return; *śabdāt:* according to Scripture.

The doubt arises that, if the powers of the released souls are limited, they may return to the mortal world. The *sūtra* dispels the doubt by a reference to scriptural authority. Those who go to *brahma-loka* by the path of the gods do not return from there. C.U. VIII. 5. 3, IV. 15. 6, VIII. 6. 6; B.U. VI. 2. 15.

Those who through perfect knowledge have dispelled all mental darkness and are devoted to the eternally perfect *nirvāṇa* do not return.

samyag-darśana-vidhvasta-tamasāṁ tu nitya-siddha-nirvāṇa-parāyaṇānāṁ siddhaivānāvṛttiḥ.

Those also who rely on the knowledge of the qualified *Brahman* in the end have recourse to that *nirvāṇa* and so it follows that they also do not return.

The repetition of the words is to indicate the completion of the work.

R. says that we know from Scripture that there is a Supreme Person whose nature is absolute bliss and goodness; who is fundamentally antagonistic to all evil; who is the cause of the origination, maintenance and dissolution of the world; who differs in nature from all other beings, who is all-knowing, who, by his mere thought and will, accomplishes all his purposes; who is an ocean of kindness, as it were, for all those who depend on him, who is all-merciful; who is immeasurably raised above all possibility of anyone being equal or superior to him; whose name is the Highest *Brahman.*

yathā nikhila-heya-pratyanīka-kalyāṇaikatāno jagad-janmādi kāraṇam, samasta-vastu-vilakṣaṇaḥ, sarvajñaḥ satya-saṁkalpa-āśrita-vātsalyaika jaladhiḥ, parama-kāruṇiko nirasta-samābhyadhika-sambhāvanaḥ, para-brahmābhidhānaḥ parama-puruṣo'stīti śabdād avagamyate.

And with equal certainty we know from Scripture, that this Supreme Lord when pleased by the faithful worship of his devotees frees them from the influence of *avidyā* which consists of *karman* accumulated in the infinite progress of time and hence hard to overcome; allows them to attain to the supreme bliss which consists in the direct intuition of his own true nature and after that does not turn them back into the suffering of *saṁsāra.*

R. quotes B.G. VIII. 15–16; VII. 17–19 in confirmation of his view.

Śrīkaṇṭha says that the bodies assumed by released souls are the products of pure *mahā-māyā.*

Those versed in metaphysics and religion have been treated with greater respect in India than those proficient in other branches of learning. Ānandagiri commenting on Ś.B.G. IX. 2 writes: *dīpyate hīti, dṛśyate hi vidvad antarebhyo loke pūjātireko brahmavidām iti bhāvaḥ.* This great work B.S. is capable of answering the main problems of the philosophy of religion, though many of its detailed references may be outdated. It deals with the problems of religious experience and scriptural authority, *mokṣa* as union with the Godhead and worship as the confrontation of the human individual and the Divine Reality, the destiny of the individual, ethics and spiritual life. We have inherited a priceless trust which must be fostered until, as the Arabs say, the stars grow old, the sun grows cold and the leaves of the judgement book unfold.

The *Ṛg Veda* has a prayer which is at least four thousand years old:

trātāro devā adhivocatā no
mā no nidrā īśata mota jalpiṇ.

Protectors, Gods, bless us! Let not sleep overtake us nor idle gossip.

VII. 48. 14; see also X. 82. 7.

śivam astu sarvajagataḥ para-hita-niratāḥ bhavantu bhūta-gaṇāḥ
doṣāḥ prayāntu nāśam sarvatra sukhī bhavatu lokaḥ.

Bṛhat-śānti-stotra.

Let there be peace in the whole world. Let everyone exert for the well-being of the other. Let evil disappear. Let everybody be happy everywhere.

SELECTED BIBLIOGRAPHY

George Thibaut: *The Vedānta Sūtras* with the Commentary by *Saṁkarācārya*. Part I. 1890. Part II. 1896.
George Thibaut: *The Vedānta Sūtras with the Commentary of Rāmānuja*. 1904.
Max Müller: *Six Systems of Indian Philosophy*. 1899.
Paul Deussen: *The System of the Vedānta*. E.T. 1912.
Mādhavācarya: *Sarva-darśana-saṁgraha*. E.T. by E. R. Cowell and A. E. Gough. Popular Edition 1914.
Surendranath Dasupta: *A History of Indian Philosophy*. 5 Vols. 1922–55.
Radhakrishnan: *Indian Philosophy*. 2 Vols. 1923 and 1927.
Appaya Dīkṣita: *Śivādvaita-nirṇaya*. Ed. with E.T. by S. S. Sūryanārāyaṇa Śāstrī. 1929.
S. S. Sūryanārāyaṇa Śāstrī: *The Śivādvaita of Śrīkaṇṭha*. 1930.
Swamī Nikhilānanda: *Dṛg-dṛśya-viveka*. E.T. 1931.
S. S. Sūryanārāyaṇa Śāstrī and C. Kunhan Raja: *The Bhāmatī of Vācaspati on Śaṁkara's Brahma-Sūtra-bhāṣya Catus-sūtrī*. 1933.
B. N. Krishnamurti Sarma: *The catus-sūtrī bhāṣya of Sri Madhvācārya*. 1934.
C. Hayavadana Rao: *Śrīkara Bhāṣya*. 1936.
Kokileswar Śāstrī: *An Introduction to Advaita Philosophy: A Realistic Interpretation of Śaṁkara Vedānta*.
S. Subba Rao: *Pūrna-prajña-darśana*. E.T. 1936.
S. S. Sūryanārāyaṇa Śāstrī and Śaileswar Sen: *Vivaraṇa-prameya-saṁgraha of Bhāratī-tīrtha*. E.T. 1941.
Roma Bose: *The Vedānta-pārijāta-Saurabha of Nimbārka and Vedānta Kaustubha*. Vol. I. 1940; Vol. II. 1941; Vol. III. 1943.
Swamī Vireśvarānanda: *Brahma Sūtras*. 2nd Edition. 1948.
S. S. Sūrayanārāyaṇa Śāstrī: *Siddhanta-leśa-saṁgraha*. E.T. 1937.
Radhakrishnan and others: *History of Philosophy: Eastern and Western*. Vol. I. 1952. pp. 272–428.
Tulsi Das: *Rāma-carit-mānas*. E.T. by Rev. A. G. Atkins. 3 Vols. 1955.
T. R. V. Murti: *The Central Conception of Buddhism*. 1955.
The Cultural Heritage of India. Vol. IV. *The Religions*. 1956.
Radhakrishnan and Moore: *A Source Book of Indian Philosophy*. 1957.
Satyavrata Singh: *Vedānta Deśika*. 1958.

GLOSSARY OF SANSKRIT TERMS

akṣaya: exempt from decay, undecaying.
akṣara: imperishable.
akhaṇḍa: entire, whole, the opposite of fragmented.
agocara: inaccessible (to the senses), what is not seen.
aṅguṣṭha-mātra: of the size of a thumb.
aja: unborn, uncreated.
ajara: not subject to old age, undecaying, ever young.
ajā: a she-goat.
ajāti-vāda: the theory of non-origination.
ajñāna: ignorance, spiritual ignorance.
aṇu: fine, minute, atomic.
atathya: untrue, unreal.
atiśaya: eminence, pre-eminence, superiority in quality or quantity.
adṛṣṭa: unseen, invisible.
advaita: non-dual, sole, unique.
adharma: unrighteousness, demerit.
adhikāra: possession of a right or a claim, competence.
adhikārin: he who has *adhikāra* or competence; he who has a right to, is qualified or fit for.
adhiṣṭhāna: basis, substratum.
ananta: endless, boundless, eternal, infinite.
anādi: having no beginning.
anitya: not everlasting, transitory.
anupalabdhi: non-perception, non-recognition.
anubhava: perception, experience, direct apprehension, knowledge derived from personal experience.
anumāna: the act of inferring, inference, one of the means of obtaining true knowledge.
antaryāmin: the indwelling principle.
antaḥ-karaṇa: the internal organ.
aparā-vidyā: lower knowledge, knowledge of the manifested world.
aparokṣa: not invisible, perceptible.
apavarga: completion, freedom of the soul from *saṁsāra*, release, liberation.
apūrva: not having existed before, the remote or unforeseen consequence of an act, an invisible quality of the soul produced by an act, which bears fruit in other worlds.
apāna: downward breathing.
abhaya: absence of fear, peace, safety, security.
abhāva: non-being, negation, absence.
abheda: non-difference.
abhyāsa: practice, repetition.
amūrta: formless, shapeless, unembodied.
artha: wealth, material possessions.

arhat: the worthy, the elect.
amṛta: immortal, imperishable, eternal.
avatāra: descent, appearance or manifestation of a deity on earth.
avidyā: ignorance, spiritual ignorance, the state of existence in which the soul unawakened to reality lives.
asti-kāyas: *Jain* term for existing bodies.
ahaṁ-kāra: self-sense, conception of individuality, egotism.
ahiṁsā: non-injury, non-killing, non-violence, non-hatred, gentleness.
ākāśa: the subtlest of the five elements, the other four being *agni* (fire), *ap* (water), *vāyu* (air), *pṛthivī* (earth), ether, space, sky.
āgama: sacred work handed down and fixed by tradition.
ācārya: a spiritual guide or teacher.
ātman: the universal Self, the inner principle that exists apart from any definable ego; life, breath.
ānanda: bliss.
āyatana: resting place, support, abode.
āśrama: a stage of life, retreat.
indriya: a sense-organ, power of the senses, virile power.
iṣṭa-devatā: a chosen deity, a favourite God.
īśa: master, lord, the supreme spirit.
Īśvara: personal God.
udāna: breathing upwards.
upaniṣad: sitting down near a teacher to listen to his words, secret knowledge, mystery, esoteric doctrine, the philosophical writings which expound the meaning of the *Vedas*: the source of the *Vedānta* philosophy.
upanayana: the act of leading or drawing to one's self, the ceremony in which a teacher initiates the pupil into spiritual life.
ṛta: order, rule, law, truth, righteousness.
ṛṣi: an inspired sage.
ekāgryam: one-pointedness, a state of concentration, close attention.
aiśvarya: sovereignty, supremacy, power, lordship.
aum: object of meditation, a mystic name for the triad of *Brahmā*, *Viṣṇu* and *Śiva*, representing the oneness of the three gods.
karuṇā: compassion.
karman: action, work, deed, rite, result of acts done in the past.
karma-mārga: the path of action.
karmendriya: organs of action.
kavi: thinker, seer, prophet, poet.
kevala-jñāna: absolute knowledge.
kaivalya: isolation, aloneness, absolute.
kriyā: performance, act, action.
kleśa: affliction, distress.
khyāti: knowledge.
gāyatrī: a hymn composed in the *gāyatrī* metre of twenty-four syllables.

guṇa: quality, virtue, merit, excellence.
guru: spiritual preceptor, teacher.
Cārvāka: a materialist philosopher.
citta: the thinking mind.
cin-mātra: pure intelligence.
cetana: conscious being, intelligence.
indriya: sense-organ.
jarā: old age.
jāti: birth, caste.
jīva: the individual soul, the principle of life.
jīvan-mukta: a person who is liberated, and yet lives in the world.
jina: an enlightened, redeemed person.
jñāna: knowledge, wisdom.
jñāna-mārga: the path of knowledge.
jnānendriya: the sense of apprehension.
tapas: religious austerity, penance, bodily mortification, asceticism.
tamas: darkness, gloom, the quality of inertia, one of the three qualities of *prakṛti*.
tarka: reasoning, speculative enquiry.
tṛṣṇā: desire, craving.
tyāga: renunciation, forsaking worldly desires, liberality.
dama: self-restraint.
dayā: sympathy, compassion, pity.
dāna: the act of giving, charity.
darśana: insight, realising of the Ultimate; a viewpoint, a system of philosophy.
duḥkha: sorrow, pain, suffering.
deva: a bright, shining force, deity.
dravya: substance.
dvandva: pairs of opposites.
dveṣa: hatred, repugnance, dislike.
dharma: moral and religious duties; virtue, morality, religion, custom, rule, law.
dhāraṇā: a stage of *Yoga* in which the mind is fixed on one particular object of meditation.
dhyāna: contemplation.
nāstika: atheist, unbeliever.
nāma-rūpa: name and shape, individual being.
nimitta: efficient cause.
niyama: restraint, rules, self-imposed observances.
nitya: perpetual, continual, eternal.
nirguṇa: devoid of qualities.
nir-grantha: without knots, unfettered.
nirvāṇa: release, emancipation, salvation, bliss, serenity.
niṣ-kriya: devoid of activities, inactive.
paramārtha: metaphysical reality, literally *parama:* highest; *artha:* object.

paramārtha-tattva: absolute truth.
param-ātman: the supreme spirit.
Parameśvara: the Supreme Lord.
parā-vidyā: higher knowledge.
pitṛ-loka: the world of the ancestors.
puruṣa: spirit, individual human being, highest personal principle, Supreme Spirit.
punar-mṛtyu: dying again.
punar-janma: rebirth.
prajā-pati: the Lord of Creatures, Creator.
prakṛti: objective nature, the primordial substance from which all objects spring, the principle of objectivity.
pradhāna: primal matter of the *Sāṁkhya* system.
prasāda: grace, kindness, favour, calmness of mind, clearness of speech.
prajñā: wisdom, discernment.
pramāṇa: that by which anything is measured, standard of truth, the means of true knowledge; *pramā-karaṇam;* like perception, inference or a valid cognition as distinct from invalid or illusory cognitions.
pratyag-ātman: the Supreme Self embodied in the individual.
pratyakṣa: sense perception.
pratyāhāra: withdrawal of attention from sense impressions.
pralaya: dissolution, re-absorption, death.
prāṇa: life-breath, a form of life-breath, forward breathing.
pūjā: worship.
prāṇāyāma: breath-control.
prārabdha-karma: the past or stored works which have begun to yield results.
pūrva-pakṣa: the *prima facie* view or argument in any question.
bandha: bondage.
bāhyendriya: senses working outward.
buddhi: understanding, intelligence.
bodhi: enlightenment, spiritual wisdom.
brahman: Ultimate Reality, an all-embracing, unborn, first principle, the self-existent Universal Spirit.
brahmā: one of the three principal gods, the Creator God.
bhakti: devotion, love.
bhakti-mārga: the path of devotion.
bhagavat: the divine spirit, the adorable one.
bheda: difference.
manana: logical reflection.
manas: mind, internal organ.
maraṇa: death.
mārga: path.
māyā: the phenomenal character of the world; the principle used by the Divine in the creation of the world, creative power, phantom, illusion, world appearance.

mīmāṁsā: investigation, examination.
mukta: set free, liberated.
mukti: freedom, release.
muni: sage, seer, one who has taken the vow of silence.
mumukṣutva: *mokṣa-icchā* or desire for release.
mūla-prakṛti: primeval or root matter, also called *pradhāna* in *Sāṁkhya* philosophy.
mṛtyu: death.
mokṣa: release, emancipation, union with the Ultimate.
yoga: yoking, union, mental concentration, discipline by which the individual attains union with the Absolute. The way to enlightenment.
rajas: the quality of activity, one of the three qualities of *prakṛti.*
rāga: attachment, affection.
rūpa: appearance, form, shape.
liṅga: mark, token, sign, phallic symbol.
līlā: play, sport, pastime.
loka: all things visible to the eye, the world.
varṇa: colour, complexion, lustre, beauty.
vāyu: air.
vāhana: vehicle.
vedanā: feeling.
vidyā: knowledge, opposed to *avidyā.*
viśeṣa: particularity.
Viṣṇu: the second person of the Hindu trinity who takes birth on earth from time to time to save mankind, the symbol of the immanence of Godhead.
vedānta: the philosophy based on the *Vedas* and the *Upaniṣads.* There are varieties of the *Vedānta* philosophy, non-dualism, monism, dualism, etc.
śakti: the energy or active power of the deity.
sañcita-karma: accumulated works.
śabda: sound, verbal testimony.
śama: tranquillity, calmness, quietude.
śānti: tranquillity, peace, quiet.
śāstra: order, command, teaching, instruction, sacred book.
śikṣā: learning, study, knowledge, art, skill.
Śiva: the auspicious one, one of the Hindu triad.
śraddhā: faith, belief, trust with reverence.
śramaṇa: a mendicant, an ascetic.
śravaṇa: the act of hearing.
śruti: that which has been heard or communicated from the beginning, sacred knowledge, the *Veda* heard by the sages.
ṣaḍ-āyatana: the abode of the six senses.
saguṇa: possessed of qualities.
samavāya: inherence, getting together.
samāna: equalising breath.

samādhi: the final stage of meditation, the attainment of union with God.
sādhanā: discipline.
suṣupti: deep, dreamless sleep.
sūkṣma śarīra: subtle body.
Sūrya: the sun God.
saṁkalpa: resolve of the mind, will, purpose.
samnyāsa: renunciation, the state of recluse.
samyoga: conjunction.
samvara: restraint.
samvṛti-satya: relative truth.
saṁsāra: the wheel of time, the round of birth, death and rebirth, the cycle of existence.
saṁskāra: impression, disposition; putting together, accomplishment, making sacred, sanctifying ceremonies leading to regeneration.
sattva: the quality of goodness, one of the three qualities of *prakṛti*, true essence, nature.
satya: reality, truth.
syād-vāda: the *Jaina* doctrine that all judgements are conditional and no judgements are absolute.
sva-dharma: one's duty.
sva-bhāva: one's nature.
svayam-bhū: self-existent.
svarga: heaven, paradise.
sāṁkhya: one of the six orthodox systems of Indian philosophy.
sāmīpya: nearness to the deity.
sāyujya: continual association with God.
siddhānta: established conclusion, any canonical textbook on any subject.
sūtra: a thread, a short or aphoristic sentence.
sthūla śarīra: gross body.
smṛti: memory, knowledge, tradition.
Hiraṇya-garbha: womb of God, *Brahmā*.

INDEX

* Indicates Separate Section

GEORGE ALLEN & UNWIN LTD

Head office:
40 Museum Street, London, W.C.1
Telephone: 01-405 8577

Sales, Distribution and Accounts Departments
Park Lane, Hemel Hempstead, Herts.
Telephone: 0442 3244

Athens: 7 Stadiou Street, Athens 125
Barbados: Rockley New Road, St. Lawrence 4
Bombay: 103/5 Fort Street, Bombay 1
Calcutta: 285J Bepin Behari Ganguli Street, Calcutta 12
Dacca: Alico Building, 18 Motijheel, Dacca 2
Hornsby, N.S.W.: Cnr Bridge Road and Jersey Street, 2077
Ibadan: P.O. Box 62
Johannesburg: P.O. Box 23134, Joubert Park
Karachi: Karachi Chambers, McLeod Road, Karachi 2
Lahore: 22 Falettis' Hotel, Egerton Road
Madras: 2/18 Mount Road, Madras 2
Manila: P.O. Box 157, Quezon City, D-502
Mexico: Serapio Rendon 125, Mexico 4, D.F.
Nairobi: P.O. Box 30583
New Delhi: 4/21-22B Asaf Ali Road, New Delhi 1
Ontario, 2330 Midland Avenue, Agincourt
Singapore: 248C-6 Orchard Road, Singapore 9
Tokyo: C.P.O. Box 1728, Tokyo 100-91
Wellington: P.O. Box 1467, Wellington, New Zealand